Lecture Notes in Computer Science 12561

T0207171

More information about this subseries at http://www.springer.com/series/7407

Maribel Fernández (Ed.)

Logic-Based Program Synthesis and Transformation

30th International Symposium, LOPSTR 2020
Bologna, Italy, September 7–9, 2020
Proceedings

 Springer

Editor
Maribel Fernández
King's College London
London, UK

ISSN 0302-9743   ISSN 1611-3349   (electronic)
Lecture Notes in Computer Science
ISBN 978-3-030-68445-7   ISBN 978-3-030-68446-4   (eBook)
https://doi.org/10.1007/978-3-030-68446-4

LNCS Sublibrary: SL1 – Theoretical Computer Science and General Issues

This Springer imprint is published by the registered company Springer Nature Switzerland AG
The registered company address is: Gewerbestrasse 11, 6330 Cham, Switzerland

Preface

This volume contains a selection of the papers presented at LOPSTR 2020, the 30th International Symposium on Logic-Based Program Synthesis and Transformation, held 7–9 September 2020.

The aim of the LOPSTR series is to stimulate and promote international research and collaboration on logic-based program development. Topics of interest cover all aspects of logic-based program development (including in domain-specific languages), all stages of the software life cycle, and issues of both programming-in-the-small and programming-in-the-large, including: synthesis; transformation; specialisation; composition; optimisation; specification; analysis and verification; testing and certification; program and model manipulation; inversion; machine learning for program development; transformational techniques in SE; applications and tools.

LOPSTR 2020 was part of the Bologna Federated Conference on Programming Languages (together with PPDP, WFLP and Microservices), which was organised as a virtual conference. Previous editions of LOPSTR were held in Porto, Namur, Edinburgh, Siena, Canterbury, Madrid, Leuven, Odense, Hagenberg, Coimbra, Valencia, Lyngby, Venice, London, Verona, Uppsala, Madrid, Paphos, London, Venice, Manchester, Leuven, Stockholm, Arnhem, Pisa, Louvain-la-Neuve, Manchester and Frankfurt.

LOPSTR has a reputation for being a lively, friendly forum that allows the presentation and discussion of both finished work and work in progress. Formal proceedings are produced only after the event so that authors can incorporate the feedback from the conference presentation and discussion. This year, 31 papers were submitted from 20 different countries. Seventeen papers were selected for presentation at LOPSTR 2020. In addition the programme included invited talks by Philipp Rümmer (Uppsala University, Sweden), Ekaterina Komendantskaya (Heriot-Watt University, UK), joint speaker with PPDP 2020, and José Meseguer (University of Illinois at Urbana-Champaign, USA), BOPL keynote speaker. The Program Committee accepted one full paper for immediate inclusion in the formal proceedings, and 14 additional papers presented at the symposium were accepted after a revision and another round of reviewing. Each submission was reviewed by at least 3 program committee members or external referees. In addition to the 15 accepted papers, this volume includes two papers contributed by invited speakers:

- Symbolic Computation in Maude: Some Tapas, by José Meseguer
- Reasoning in the Theory of Heap: Satisfiability and Interpolation, by Zafer Esen and Philipp Rümmer

Thanks to Springer's sponsorship, two awards were available this year. After discussion within the program committee, the awards were given to the following papers:

- Resourceful Program Synthesis from Graded Linear Types, by Jack Hughes and Dominic Orchard;

– Generating Functions for Probabilistic Programs, by Lutz Klinkenberg, Kevin Batz, Benjamin Lucien Kaminski, Joost-Pieter Katoen, Joshua Moerman and Tobias Winkler.

I would like to thank all those who contributed to LOPSTR 2020, particularly the invited speakers, authors, program committee members and external reviewers. I am very grateful to the Local Organization Committee in Bologna, chaired by Maurizio Gabbrielli, for providing a great virtual environment for BOPL, and to the Steering Committee, chaired by Alberto Pettorossi, for their support. It was a pleasure to work with the program chairs of the events colocated with LOPSTR 2020 in BOPL. We are grateful to Springer for sponsoring the LOPSTR 2020 awards and to EasyChair for providing support to deal with the submission and reviewing process.

December 2020   Maribel Fernández

Organization

Steering Committee

Fabio Fioravanti   D'Annunzio University of Chieti–Pescara, Italy
Maurizio Gabbrielli   University of Bologna, Italy
John Gallagher   Roskilde University, Denmark
Manuel Hermenegildo   IMDEA, Spain
Pedro López-García   IMDEA, Spain
Fred Mesnard   Université de la Réunion, France
Alberto Pettorossi (Chair)   Università di Roma Tor Vergata, Italy
Peter Stuckey   Monash University, Australia

Local Organization Committee

Roberto Amadini   University of Bologna, Italy
Davide Berardi   University of Bologna, Italy
Francesca del Bonifro   University of Bologna, Italy
Maurizio Gabbrielli   University of Bologna, Italy
   (General Chair)
Saverio Giallorenzo   University of Bologna, Italy
   (Financial Chair)
Andrea Melis   University of Bologna, Italy
Stefano Pio Zingaro   University of Bologna, Italy
   (Publicity Chair)
Marco Prandini (Chair)   University of Bologna, Italy
Gianluigi Zavattaro   University of Bologna, Italy

Programme Committee

Elvira Albert   Complutense University of Madrid, Spain
Mara Alpuente   Universitat Politècnica de València, Spain
Mauricio Ayala-Rincón   University of Brasilia, Brazil
Clara Bertolissi   Aix-Marseille University, France
Emanuele De Angelis   CNR Inst. for Systems Analysis and Computer Science,
    Italy
Maribel Fernández (Chair)   King's College London, UK
Mário Florido   University of Porto, Portugal
Maurizio Gabbrielli   University of Bologna, Italy
Robert Glück   University of Copenhagen, Denmark
Gopal Gupta   University of Texas at Dallas, US
Michael Hanus   University of Kiel, Germany
Delia Kesner   Université de Paris, France

Andy King   University of Kent, UK
Temur Kutsia   Johannes Kepler University of Linz, Austria
Giselle Reis   Carnegie Mellon University in Qatar, Qatar
Masahito Sakai   Nagoya University, Japan
René Thiemann   University of Innsbruck, Austria
Alwen Tiu   The Australian National University, Australia
Germán Vidal   Universitat Politècnica de València, Spain

Additional Reviewers

Sandra Alves   Cynthia Kop
Joaquin Arias   Robbert Krebbers
Pablo Barenbaum   Daniele Nantes-Sobrinho
Kinjal Basu   Antonina Nepeivoda
Aleš Bizjak   Naoki Nishida
Francesca del Bonifro   Gethin Norman
Ralph Bottesch   Vincent van Oostrom
Thomas Ehrhard   Hugo Pacheco
Maria João Frade   Alberto Pettorossi
Samir Genaim   Fernando Sáenz-Pérez
Pablo Gordillo   Farhad Shakerin
Max W. Haslbeck   Sarat Chandra Varanasi
Nao Hirokawa   Daniel Ventura
Joost-Pieter Katoen

Contents

Model Checking and Probabilistic Programming

Program Analysis and Testing

Logics

Rewriting

Symbolic Computation in Maude: Some Tapas

José Meseguer[(✉)]

Department of Computer Science, University of Illinois, Urbana-Champaign, USA
meseguer@illinois.edu

Abstract. Programming in Maude is executable mathematical modeling. Your mathematical model *is* the code you execute. Both deterministic systems, specified equationally as so-called *functional modules* and concurrent ones, specified in rewriting logic as *system modules*, are mathematically modeled and programmed this way. But rewriting logic is also a *logical framework* in which many different logics can be naturally represented. And one would like not only to execute these models, but to *reason* about them at a high level. For this, *symbolic methods* that can automate much of the reasoning are crucial. Many of them are actually supported by Maude itself or by some of its tools. These methods are very general: they apply not just to Maude, but to many other logics, languages and tools. This paper presents some *tapas* about these Maude-based symbolic methods in an informal way to make it easy for many other people to learn about, and benefit from, them.

1 Introduction

1.1 What is Maude?

Maude is a high-performance declarative language whose modules are *theories in rewriting logic*, a simple, yet expressive, *computational logic* to specify and program *concurrent systems* as rewrite theories. A *rewrite theory* is a triple $\mathcal{R} = (\Sigma, E \cup B, R)$ where:

- Σ specifies a *signature* of typed *function symbols*.
- $(\Sigma, E \cup B)$ is an *equational theory* specifying the concurrent system's *states* as elements of the *algebraic data type* (initial algebra) $T_{\Sigma/E \cup B}$ defined by $(\Sigma, E \cup B)$.
- R are *rewrite rules* specifying the system's *local atomic transitions*.
- *Concurrent Computation = Deduction* in $\mathcal{R}$ = *Concurrent Rewriting* in $\mathcal{R}$.

In Maude, a rewrite theory $\mathcal{R}$ named FOO is specified —with mostly self-explanatory syntax—as a so-called *system module* of the form: mod FOO is $(\Sigma, E \cup B, R)$ endm.

© Springer Nature Switzerland AG 2021
M. Fernández (Ed.): LOPSTR 2020, LNCS 12561, pp. 3–36, 2021.
https://doi.org/10.1007/978-3-030-68446-4_1

But, since when $R = \varnothing$, $\mathcal{R} = (\Sigma, E \cup B, R)$ becomes just an *equational theory*, Maude has a *functional sublanguage* of so-called *functional modules*. A functional module BAR is specified as follows: fmod BAR is $(\Sigma, E \cup B)$ endfm, where:

– $B \subseteq \{A, C, U\}$ is any combination of *associativity* (A) and/or *commutativity* (C) and/or *identity* (U) axioms, specified with the corresponding assoc, comm, and id: keywords, and
– the equations E, when used as left-to-right simplification rules, are *convergent*, i.e., Church-Rosser and terminating,[1] modulo the axioms B.

We make the exact same assumptions about B and E for a system module mod FOO is $(\Sigma, E \cup B, R)$ endm. What this intuitively means is that the states of the concurrent system so specified enjoy *structural axioms* B, and can also have *state-updating functions* computable by equational left-to-right simplification with the equations E modulo B.

1.2   Symbolic Computation in Maude

Since all computation in Maude is performed by *logical deduction* in equational logic and/or rewriting logic, talking about *symbolic computation* seems tautological. But it isn't. The point is that the usual computations in a functional or system module involve elements of an algebraic data type $T_{\Sigma/E \cup B}$, which are represented as *ground terms* (terms without variables) in the syntax of Σ. But Maude supports many useful computations involving *terms with variables*. For example, for u and v terms with variables among the $x_1, \ldots, x_n$, solving the so-called $E \cup B$-*unification problem* $u(x_1, \ldots, x_n) =? v(x_1, \ldots, x_n)$ means answering the question of whether the *constraint* $u(x_1, \ldots, x_n) = v(x_1, \ldots, x_n)$ is *satisfiable* in the algebraic data type $T_{\Sigma/E \cup B}$ for some instantiation of the variables $x_1, \ldots, x_n$. So, roughly speaking, problems involving logical variables and their solutions are those I shall describe as symbolic computation problems. Maude, either directly or through Maude-based tools, supports the following symbolic computation features:

1. B-**Unification** (modulo any $B \subseteq \{A, C, U\}$),
2. B-**Generalization** (modulo any $B \subseteq \{A, C, U\}$),
3. E, B-**Variants** of a term t in a *convergent* $(\Sigma, E \cup B)$, which is *finitary* iff $(\Sigma, E \cup B)$ has the *finite variant property* (FVP), in the sense explained in Sect. 4,
4. $E \cup B$-**Unification** for any *convergent* $(\Sigma, E \cup B)$, which is *finitary* iff $(\Sigma, E \cup B)$ is FVP,
5. **Domain-Specific SMT-Solving**, thanks to CVC4 [19] and Yices [74] interfaces,
6. **Theory-Generic SMT-Solving** for FVP theories $(\Sigma, E \cup B)$ under natural requirements about their constructors,

---

[1] Termination can of course be dropped for some applications: the lambda calculus or a deterministic Turing machine can be easily specified as functional modules in Maude.

7. **Symbolic Reachability Analysis** of any system module **mod** ($\Sigma, E \cup B, R$) **endm** with ($\Sigma, E \cup B$) FVP,
8. **B-Homeomorphic Embedding** (modulo any $B \subseteq \{A, C\}$).

In this paper I will focus on features (1), (3)–(4), and (6)–(7) in the above list. For generalization modulo B—which is dual to unification and is also called "anti-unification"—please see [2,4]. Homeomorphic embedding is a very useful relation for termination criteria in various symbolic analyses. It has been generalized for the first time to work in an order-sorted setting and modulo combinations of associativity and commutativity axioms, with new efficient algorithms, in [1]. Both generalization and homeomorphic embedding modulo axioms are crucial components of the variant-based partial evaluation (PE) approach for Maude functional modules presented in [3].

1.3   Tapas and Paper Napkins

To explain the symbolic features (1), (3)–(4), and (6)–(7) requires explaining some basic technical ideas that convey the precise meaning of such features. But this runs the risk of getting us bogged down in technicalities. How shall we proceed? I propose that we use our imagination a little: think of this paper as an informal conversation that you, dear reader, and I are having in a *Tapas Bar*, as we share some pleasant tapas and wash them down with some good *Rioja*. The bar's setting is informal: instead of sitting at a formal table, we sit at a small wooden table where there is a stack of small paper napkins. Tapas are now gradually making their appearance at two levels: each time our waiter brings us the next tapas serving, there are also some *Maude tapas* that I explain to you by scribbling on the paper napkins in the stack. The Maude tapas have to be *small*, since these are cocktail napkins. I have also brought my laptop to run a few examples; but the main action is our conversation, scribbling on paper napkins. Of course, a few technicalities have to be glossed over: I just give you the main intuitions; but I promise to email you some material to fill in those details later. This is what we are going to do here. In this paper, that more precise technical background can be found in Sect. 7 and in the list of references; but let us disregard them for now.

2   First Tapas Serving: Rewriting Modulo Axioms B

I have always claimed and felt that Maude, unlike other programming languages, *can be explained on a paper napkin* to somebody with no prior acquaintance with computing. Here is the example I would write on such a napkin:

```
fmod NATURAL is
sort Nat .
op 0 : -> Nat [ctor] .
op s : Nat -> Nat [ctor] .
op _+_ : Nat Nat -> Nat .
```

```
vars N M : Nat .

eq N + 0 = N .
eq N + s(M) = s(N + M) .
endfm
```

This module, defining natural number addition in Peano notation, does of course fit the general pattern fmod BAR is $(\Sigma, E \cup B)$ endfm, where here the module's name BAR is NATURAL, the typed signature Σ has a single type (called a *sort* in Maude), which we have *chosen* to call Nat, a constant 0 and two function symbols: s and _+_, where the underbars indicate argument positions, and where the ctor attribute is declared for 0 and s as *data constructors* to distinguish them from the *defined function* _+_, which is *defined* by the two equations E. In this case there are no attributes B, although, if we wished, we could have declared _+_ with the assoc and comm keywords as an associative and commutative operator.

How do we compute with this module? By *simplifying* any arithmetic expression to its *result* as a *data value*, i.e., either to 0 or to $s^n(0)$ for some $n \geqslant 1$, using the two equations E to perform *left-to-right* replacement of *equals for equals* in the usual way this is done in algebraic simplification. This process is called *term rewriting*; and the result of thus simplifying an expression is called its *normal form*. Let us see (in another paper napkin) how this process reduces adding 2 plus 2, i.e., the arithmetic expression s(s(0)) + s(s(0)) to 4, i.e., the data value s(s(s(s(0)))). For this, it is useful to add some simple notation to indicate *where* in an expression a simplification is applied. I will use the notation $t[u]$ to indicate that we are focusing on the subexpression u of the expression, or term, t. The process in this notation is as follows:

$$[s(s(0)) + s(s(0))] \to s([s(s(0)) + s(0)]) \to s(s([s(s(0)) + 0])) \to s(s(s(s(0))))$$

where we have applied the second equation in the first two steps, and the first equation in the last step, to corresponding *instances* by some *matching substitution* instantiating the equation's variables to the term or subterm to be simplified. For example, in the second step, the variables N and M have been instantiated by the substitution $\theta = \{N \mapsto s(s(0)), M \mapsto 0\}$, so that the subterm we focus on, $s(s(0)) + s(0)$, becomes an instance of the pattern term $N + s(M)$ in the second equation's lefthand side, and is *replaced* in this step by the corresponding instance of the righthand side $s(N + M)$. We can summarize this (focused) step in the following notation:

$$s(s(0)) + s(0) \equiv (s(N) + M)\theta \to s(N + M)\theta \equiv s(s(s(0)) + 0)$$

where $\equiv$ denotes syntactic equality, and $t\theta$ denotes the result of instantiating a pattern term, i.e., a term with variables t, by a substitution θ.

But Maude's functional modules do support this kind of algebraic simplification *modulo* structural axioms *B*. Let us illustrate this case with a simple example (it fits on another paper napkin) of a data type of sets:

```
fmod SET is
sort Set .
ops mt a b c d e f g : -> Set [ctor] .
op _U_ : Set Set -> Set [ctor assoc comm] .   *** union
vars S S' : Set .

eq S U mt = S [variant] .                 *** identity
eq S U S = S [variant] .                   *** idempotency
eq S U S U S' = S U S' [variant] .         *** idempotency
endfm
```

Its constants are a b c d e f g and the empty set constant mt. There is also a union operator, for which we have *chosen*[2] the syntax _U_, which has been declared associative (*A*) and commutative (*C*) by the assoc and comm attributes. Note that in this module all constants and _U_ are *data constructors*. Set union is *defined* by the three equations (the third one follows from the second: it is added for technical reasons) of mt as identity element for set union, and set idempotency. Disregard for the moment the [variant] attribute in the equations: it will become clear in Sect. 4. Let us see an example of how we compute in this module *modulo AC*.

$$ mt \cup [a \cup c \cup b \cup a \cup b] \rightarrow [mt \cup a \cup b \cup c] \rightarrow a \cup b \cup c $$

where we have used the third equation in the first step, and the first equation in the second step. Note that, because of associativity, we, as well as the Maude parser, can dispense with parentheses. The most interesting step is the first one, which uses the substitution $\theta = \{S \mapsto (a \cup b), S' \mapsto c\}$. This step can be applied because:

$$ (S \cup S \cup S')\theta \equiv (a \cup b) \cup (a \cup b) \cup c =_{AC} a \cup c \cup b \cup a \cup b. $$

Since, thanks to the *AC* axioms, reordering and parentheses do not matter, the crucial point is that the subterm $a \cup c \cup b \cup a \cup b$ *is* an *instance* of the lefthand side pattern $S \cup S \cup S'$ *modulo AC*. For the same reason, the fact that *mt* appears on the *left* of the expression instead than on the right is no obstacle for applying the first equation in the second step modulo *AC*.

It can be easily checked that the equations in **NATURAL**, resp. **SET**, are *convergent*, and therefore the *normal forms* of, for example, $s(s(0)) + s(s(0))$, resp. $mt \cup a \cup c \cup b \cup a \cup b$, namely, $s(s(s(0)))$, resp. $a \cup b \cup c$, are *unique* modulo *B*, regardless of the order in which the equations are applied to the original term. For example, $b \cup c \cup a$ *is* the *same* normal form as $a \cup b \cup c$ modulo *AC*. The Maude command computing a term's normal form is the **reduce** command.

---

[2] In Maude, all syntax for sort and operator names is *user-definable*.

A Little Notation Does Not Hurt Anybody. The process of performing *one step* of *rewriting* a term t (focusing on *some* subterm) using one of the equations in E *modulo* the axioms B to obtain a term t' is called E, B-*rewriting*, and is denoted $t \rightarrow_{E,B} t'$. Likewise, $t \rightarrow^*_{E,B} t'$ denotes performing zero, one or more steps of E, B-rewriting. The special case when $B = \varnothing$ is called E-rewriting, and then we use the notation $t \rightarrow_E t'$ and $t \rightarrow^*_E t'$. The E, B-*normal form* of term t (unique up to B-equality assuming E convergent) is denoted $t!_{E,B}$, resp. $t!_E$ when $B = \varnothing$.

3   Second Tapas Serving: Unification and Narrowing Modulo B

As already mentioned, solving a B-*unification problem* $u(x_1, \ldots, x_n) = ? \ v(x_1, \ldots, x_n)$ means answering the question of whether the *constraint* $u(x_1, \ldots, x_n) = v(x_1, \ldots, x_n)$ is *satisfiable* in the algebraic data type $T_{\Sigma/B}$, where terms are identified modulo the axioms B, such as any combination of A and/or C and/or U axioms. The case $B = \varnothing$ is called *syntactic unification*. It is well-known from the Prolog language, where the analog of the data type T_{Σ} is the so-called *Herbrand model*, which extends T_{Σ} by adding predicate symbols. Maude supports unification modulo B in any module where the axioms B have been declared. Furthermore, this B-unification is *order-sorted*, i.e., it is carried out with variables which can have different *sorts*, where some of them can be *subsorts* of other sorts. In particular, since for the module **NATURAL** we have $B = \varnothing$, we can perform syntactic unification in it with Maude's **unify** command.

Since the syntactic case is well-known, and we will revisit it soon, let us focus instead on the more interesting case of the **SET** module, where we can perform AC-unification. What does this mean? Except for the fact that we are not dealing with the equation making **mt** the identity for _U_, this means that we can solve *multiset equations*, as opposed to solving *set equations* (but, please, be patient: we will also solve set equations in the next serving of tapas). For example, we may wish to solve the multiset equation: $a \cup a \cup b \cup S = a \cup c \cup S'$, that is, seek substitutions θ such that $(a \cup a \cup b \cup S)\theta =_{AC} (a \cup c \cup S')\theta$, i.e., both side instances yield the same multiset. We can do so in Maude by giving the command:

```
Maude> unify in SET : a U a U b U S =? a U c U S' .

Unifier 1
S --> c U #1:Set
S' --> a U b U #1:Set

Unifier 2
S --> c
S' --> a U b
```

where the second solution is the most obvious, and the first solution allows adding to the multiset $a \cup a \cup b \cup c$ obtained by the second solution an extra multiset denoted by the extra variable **#1:Set**.

Maude supports unification modulo *any* possible combinations of A, C, and U axioms in B; also when some axioms in B are declared associative but are *not* commutative. This is noteworthy, since it is well-known that the number of A-unifiers (or AU-unifiers) of a problem can be infinite. For example, if a is a constant and $\_\cdot\_$ is associative, then the equation $a \cdot x = x \cdot a$ has the infinite set of solutions: $\{\{x \mapsto a^n\} \mid n \geqslant 1\}$. When some operators are A or AU only, Maude's implementation of B-unification takes the following pragmatic approach: (i) the unification algorithm is designed to *favor the cases where the number of A or AU-unifiers is known to be finite*; and (ii) in all other cases, it searches for solutions in a complete manner, but *within a bound*, so that: (a) if *all* solutions are found before reaching the bound, it just returns them, but (b) if the bound is reached without the certainty of having found all solutions, *the solutions already found are returned* with a *warning* that the set of solutions may be incomplete. The good news is that, for a good number of applications—for example in the symbolic analysis of various cryptographic protocols involving associativity axioms—such warnings are never encountered, i.e., the corresponding analyses are then, luckily, *complete*.

Narrowing. This is just technical jargon for *symbolic execution*, in the usual sense one would expect: executing a program, not on concrete inputs, but on "symbolic" inputs specified by variables [38, 40]. In our case, a Maude functional module and a term with variables in its syntax. For example, in our **NATURAL** functional module for natural number addition, the symbolic expression $x + y$ *cannot* be evaluated in the standard sense: it is *already* in normal form, since *no equation* in **NATURAL** can be used to further simplify it. However, it *can* be executed *symbolically*. What does this mean? It means answering the following question:

Are there instances of $x + y$ that can be executed in the standard sense? And, if so, can we systematically describe them and their results?

The answer, for any equational theory $(\Sigma, E \cup B)$ where the equations E are *convergent* modulo the axioms B is an emphatic Yes! The method is very simple, and amounts to a *slight generalization* of the already-described E, B-rewriting relation $\rightarrow_{E,B}$ between terms, to the more general E, B-*narrowing* relation $\rightsquigarrow_{E,B}$ between terms. What is this generalization like? Very simple: we replace the process of B-*matching* a subterm u as a substitution instance of the lefthand side t of an equation $t = t'$ by one of B-*unifying* t and u, that is, of solving the equation $t =? u$ modulo B.

In which sense is this a *slight* generalization? In the precise sense that when u is a *ground term*, i.e., it has no variables, then B-unification *coincides* with B-matching. For example, the matching substitution $\theta = \{S \mapsto (a \cup b), S' \mapsto c\}$ by which we showed that $(S \cup S \cup S')\theta =_{AC} a \cup c \cup b \cup a \cup b$ is indeed an AC-*unifier* (not the only one) of the equality $(S \cup S \cup S') =? a \cup c \cup b \cup a \cup b$.

The crucial point, however, is that when the term u to be evaluated *does have variables*, B-unification is *strictly more general* than B-matching and makes *symbolic execution* possible: because we now view the variables of u as *logical variables* in the Prolog sense, which can be *instantiated*. Let us see how $x + y$ can be symbolically executed this way. In **NATURAL** we have two equations $E = \{N+0 = N, \; N+s(M) = s(N+M)\}$. Focusing on the entire term $x+y$ we get two corresponding unification problems $N + 0 =? \; x + y$ and $N + s(M) =? \; x + y$ with respective unifiers $\theta_0 = \{N \mapsto x, \; y \mapsto 0\}$ and $\theta_1 = \{N \mapsto x, M \mapsto y', \; y \mapsto s(y')\}$. Applying these substitutions to the righthand sides of the equations we get the narrowing steps:

$$[x+y] \leadsto_E^{\theta_0} x \qquad and \qquad [x+y] \leadsto_E^{\theta_1} s(x+y')$$

where we have indicated for each step the substitution used: θ_0, resp. θ_1. Narrowing *is never performed on variables*, so the first narrowing step cannot be continued. But the second can, focusing on the subterm $x + y'$, again in two ways, by the substitutions: $\theta_0' = \{N \mapsto x, \; y' \mapsto 0\}$ and $\theta_1' = \{N \mapsto x, M \mapsto y'', \; y' \mapsto s(y'')\}$, yielding narrowing steps:

$$s([x+y']) \leadsto_E^{\theta_0'} s(x) \qquad and \qquad s([x+y']) \leadsto_E^{\theta_1'} s(s(x+y''))$$

And, obviously, since $s(x)$ cannot be unified with any lefthand side, it is only the second term (focusing on $x+y''$) that can be narrowed again, *in exactly the same way*, ad infinitum. We get this way what is called an (infinite) *narrowing tree* rooted at our original term $x+y$. But we could have started with *any* other term in the syntax of **NATURAL**. In the same way, but in this case performing unification modulo AC, the three equations E in the **SET** module define a narrowing relation $\leadsto_{E,AC}$ which performs *symbolic execution of set expressions*. Of course, we also have a reflexive-transitive closure $\leadsto_{E,AC}^*$, which, when annotated with a substitution, $\leadsto_{E,AC}^{\theta \; *}$ makes explicit the *composed or "accumulated" substitution* $\theta = \theta_1 \cdots \theta_n$ for a length-n narrowing sequence.

Note the interesting fact that, although the equations E of a convergent theory, such as **NATURAL** or **SET**, are always *terminating*, the associated narrowing relation $\leadsto_{E,B}$ in general is not. When does it terminate? This is a topic that we can save for the next tapas serving.

4   Third Tapas Serving: Variants, and Unification Modulo $E \cup B$

Let us you, dear reader, **DR**, and I, **JM**, play a little *language game* à la Wittgenstein. **JM**: What is a variant? **DR**: I don't know what you are talking about. **JM**: I mean, what is a variant in the Comon-Delaune [18] sense? **DR**: I don't know: you tell me. **JM**: An answer to a question. **DR**: Which question? **JM**: What are the normal forms that a term t in a Maude functional module evaluates to? **DR**: But the answer to your question is trivial, since we have already seen that, since the module's equations E are assumed convergent modulo its axioms B, up to

B-equality there is just *one answer*, namely, the unique normal form $t!_{E,B}$ of t, which is the answer provided by Maude's **reduce** command. **JM**: Sorry, what I really meant is: What are the normal forms that a term t *symbolically* evaluates to? Or, slightly more broadly: What are the normal forms of the *instances* of t by various *substitutions*? **DR**: Well, that sounds more interesting. Can you give me an example? **JM**: Why, of course! We have just *seen* an example! **DR**: Where? **JM**: In the last *paper napkin* I scribbled for you, where I sketched the *narrowing tree* for $x + y$. **DR**: What do you mean? **JM**: (1) A little reflection shows that, if we have a narrowing sequence: $t \overset{\theta}{\leadsto}{}^{*}_{E,B} u$, and u is normalized, then, by construction, $u =_B (t\theta)!_{E,B}$ and u is therefore a variant *in the exact sense I meant*. (2) But if you inspect the narrowing tree for $x + y$, all the terms in that tree are either of the form: $s^n(x)$, $n \geqslant 0$, or $s^n(x + y'^n)$, $n \geqslant 1$, which are all *in normal form*. So they are all *variants* of $x + y$ in the sense I just meant. **DR**: Ok, now I see your point. This looks interesting. Tell me more. **JM**: Of course, these terms are not *all* the variants of $x + y$. But they *cover* all the variants of $x+y$ as *instances*. For example, the substitution $\theta = \{x \mapsto s(0+x'),\ y \mapsto s(s(z))\}$ yields the variant: $((x + y)\theta)!_E = s(s(s(0 + x') + z))$, which is itself an *instance* of the term $s(s(x+y''))$ in $x + y$'s narrowing tree. Therefore,—because of the so-called *lifting property of narrowing* (references in Sect. 7.2)—we can use a term's t narrowing tree to compute a *complete set of most general variants* of t by just selecting those narrowing paths in such a tree of the form $t \overset{\theta}{\leadsto}{}^{*}_{E,B} u$, where u is normalized. **A little more notation cannot hurt**. For technical reasons, we do not call such a u a variant of t. Instead, we formally define that variant as the *pair* (u, θ). This is because we might have a quite different (u', γ), with u' just a variable renaming of u, obtained by a completely different narrowing path $t \overset{\gamma}{\leadsto}{}^{*}_{E,B} u'$, and where γ itself might *not* be a variable renaming of θ. We shall see examples like this during this tapas serving.

The Finite Variant Property. Here are two closely-related, yet different, questions. Given a Maude functional module, say, **fmod BAR is** $(\Sigma, E \cup B)$ **endfm**, as always with E assumed *convergent* modulo B,

1. When is it the case that any term t in this module has a *finite*, complete set of most general variants—i.e., that, up to B-equality, any other variant of t is a substitution instance of one in this finite set? If this holds, we then say that $(\Sigma, E \cup B)$ has the *finite variant property* (FVP).
2. When does E, B-narrowing *terminate* for any term t in this module?

Since, as we have just seen, a complete set of variants of a term t can be computed by narrowing, *if* E, B-narrowing terminates for all inputs t, *then* $(\Sigma, E \cup B)$ is obviously FVP. But the converse does not hold in general: a term t may have a *finite* set of most general variants and yet have an *infinite* narrowing tree. Why? Because we should do something *smarter* than just generating t's narrowing tree. The problem we can easily face when generating t's narrowing tree is that, after a while, *if* we had looked carefully enough, *we would have seen it all*. That is, seen that any variant to be generated further down the (infinite!) tree is going to be an *instance* of one that we have already seen. But how can we *find that out*, since the tree is *infinite*? By using the *folding variant narrowing strategy* in [27]. This strategy has the useful property that: (1) $(\Sigma, E \cup B)$ is FVP iff (2) folding variant E, B-narrowing *terminates* for any input term t. Folding variant narrowing *computes* the desired finite set of most general variants of a term t when $(\Sigma, E \cup B)$ is FVP; and *in all cases* —i.e., for any convergent $(\Sigma, E \cup B)$—it computes a *complete* set of variants of t, which may of course be *infinite*. For example, NATURAL is *not* FVP. This is obvious from the fact that, for any two $n, k \geqslant 1$, the terms $s^n(x + y'^n)$ and $s^{n+k}(x + y'^n)$ have *disjoint* sets of instances.

But how does folding variant narrowing work? As its name suggests, by *folding*. That is, we do not generate a *tree*, but a *graph* in a breadth first way. But when we generate a new normalized node, we do not just add it to the graph: we first *check* to see if in the graph generated so far we already have another node of which this new one is an *instance* and, if so, we *fold* the new node into that most general instance. If at some depth all new generated nodes must be folded, then we have terminated with a finite graph that contains a set of most general variants of the input term t.

Folding variant narrowing has been implemented in Maude. The set of variants of a term t can be computed with Maude's `get variants` command. Since in general this set can be infinite, the user can provide a bound n to get the first n variants of a term t. But how can we *know* if a given $(\Sigma, E \cup B)$ is FVP? This property is *undecidable* [8]. However, as explained in [12], if $(\Sigma, E \cup B)$ *is* actually FVP, provided that B-unification is finitary,[3] we can find this out very easily in Maude by computing the variants of each term $f(x_1, \ldots, x_n)$ for each function symbol f in Σ. For example, our SET example, which can easily be shown convergent, *is* FVP, since Maude provides the following answer:

```
Maude> get variants in SET : S U S' .

Variant 1
Set: #1:Set U #2:Set
S --> #1:Set
S' --> #2:Set

Variant 2
Set: %1:Set
S --> mt
S' --> %1:Set

Variant 3
Set: %1:Set
S --> %1:Set
```

---

[3] As already mentioned, if B contains axioms of associativity without commutativity, B-unification will not be finitary. The FVP property has been studied for this more general case in [49].

```
S' --> mt

Variant 4
Set: %1:Set
S --> %1:Set
S' --> %1:Set

Variant 5
Set: %1:Set U %2:Set U %3:Set
S --> %1:Set U %2:Set
S' --> %1:Set U %3:Set

Variant 6
Set: %1:Set U %2:Set
S --> %1:Set U %2:Set
S' --> %2:Set

Variant 7
Set: %1:Set U %2:Set
S --> %2:Set
S' --> %1:Set U %2:Set

No more variants.
```

which shows that **SET** is FVP. Note that, in general, a functional module's equational theory $(\Sigma, E \cup B)$ need not be FVP. In reality, what the **get variants** command for a term t provides is a very *space-efficient* way of describing the narrowing tree of a term t, not as a tree, but as a *graph with folding* storing only *normalized nodes*. In comparison with the tree description itself, this space efficiency is enormous in all cases; and in the FVP case it can reduce an *infinite* tree to a *finite* graph. Pragmatically,—particularly in the case of axioms such as AC where the number of unifiers of a unification problem can be huge and therefore the narrowing tree can have large degrees of branching—the difference between a term's narrowing tree and its narrowing graph with folding is one between a hopeless procedure that can be easily overwhelmed at very small tree depths and a practical procedure that can be used in many applications.

Constructor Variants. As we have seen in the **NATURAL** and **SET** modules, Maude supports the distinction between *constructor operators*, which build data and are specified with the **ctor** attribute, e.g., **0** and **s** in **NATURAL**, and the remaining *defined function symbols*, like **_+_** in **NATURAL**. This offers a very natural distinction at the level of variants: we call a variant (u, θ) of a term t a *constructor variant* iff u is a constructor term, that is, a term built using only constructor symbols and variables. Since in the **SET** module all symbols are constructor symbols, the above seven variants of the term **S U S'** are all constructor variants. Instead, in the already-described complete set of variants for the term $x + y$ in **NATURAL**, only the family of terms $\{s^n(x) \mid n \geqslant 0\}$ are constructor variants. This distinction between variants and constructor variants will prove useful in our next tapas serving.

Variant $E \cup B$-Unification. So far, we have only discussed Maude's algorithm for B-unification, with B any combination of A, C, and U axioms. Though very useful, this is also very limited. Assuming, as I will do throughout, that *all sorts are inhabited*, i.e., algebraic data types that do not have empty types/sorts, what B-unification really means is that we can answer satisfiability questions for constraints of the form: $\bigwedge_{1 \leqslant i \leqslant n} u_i = v_i$ in algebraic data types of the form $T_{\Sigma/B}$. But, of course, what we would like to be able to do is to solve the same kind of constraints for *any* Maude functional module, under the assumptions that it is convergent and that its equations are unconditional. That is, to be able to solve the above constraints over algebraic data types of the form $T_{\Sigma/E \cup B}$. In other words, to perform $E \cup B$-unification. For example, we already saw that for $(\Sigma, E \cup AC)$ the equational theory of the SET module, AC-unification, i.e., solving equations in $T_{\Sigma/AC}$ essentially amounted to *multiset unification*—up to a minor quibbling about the empty set that could have been solved adding an extra U axiom. But what we really would like to perform is *set unification*, i.e., to solve constraints of the above form in the data type $T_{\Sigma/E \cup AC}$ of *sets*. Can we do this? The answer is Yes! Because we can *reduce* such a unification problem to one of *computing variants*. Let us see how. All we need to do[4] is to add to our functional module of choice a new sort Pred of predicates with constant true, and a new *equality predicate*. Let us illustrate this idea for the SET module, extended to the module:

```
fmod SET-EQ is protecting SET .
sort Pred .                      *** Predicates sort
op true : -> Pred [ctor] .
op _=?_ : Set Set -> Pred [ctor] .  *** equality predicate
vars S S' : Set .

eq S =? S = true [variant] .     *** equality definition
endfm
```

It is easy to check that this module is also FVP. This is a general fact: the extension of an FVP theory $(\Sigma, E \cup B)$ to a theory $(\Sigma^{=?}, E^{=?} \cup B)$ by adding an equality predicate $\_ =?\_$ is always also FVP. This can be easily checked in this example by computing the variants of the term S =? S'. Recall that, using AC unification, we were able to answer the *multiset unification problem*: a U a U b U S =? a U c U S'. But what we would like to do is to solve the *set unification problem*: a U a U b U S =? a U c U S'. We can do so by computing variants in SET-EQ of the equality term a U a U b U S =? a U c U S'. Maude returns 88 such variants. But the only ones that interest us are those

---

[4] For simplicity, I treat the case of solving a single equation. The case of solving systems of equalities and disequalities can likewise be treated by adding a binary conjunction operator to Pred with identity true.

of the form: $(true, \theta)$, since those θ are the desired unifiers for this set unification problem. There are only 24 variants of the form $(true, \theta)$, which give us our desired family of set unifiers. Here are the first and the last of these:

```
Maude> get variants in SET-EQ : a U a U b U S =? a U c U S' .
...
```

```
Variant 2
Pred: true
S --> c U %1:Set
S' --> b U %1:Set
...
```

```
Variant 88
Pred: true
S --> b U c
S' --> a U b U c
```

But *why* are these the unifiers of our set equation? **Never let a theorem that fits on a paper napkin go to waste!** Because, as explained in Sect. 7.2, for any convergent theory $(\Sigma, E \cup B)$ we have the *Church-Rosser Equivalence*: $t =_{E \cup B} t' \Leftrightarrow t!_{E,B} =_B t'!_{E,B}$. Therefore, a substitution θ solves an equation $u =? v$ in $T_{\Sigma/E \cup B}$ iff $(u\theta)!_{E,B} =_B (v\theta)!_{E,B}$, i.e., iff $((u =? v)\theta)!_{E=?,B} =_B true$. That is, iff θ is an *instance* of some γ in some variant of $u =? v$ of the form $(true, \gamma)$. q.e.d. Note that this proof is much more general than: (i) solving equations for the SET module; (ii) solving equations for any FVP theory $(\Sigma, E \cup B)$; since (iii) it solves them for *any convergent* theory $(\Sigma, E \cup B)$. That is, this method provides a general $E \cup B$-unification procedure for *any* convergent theory $(\Sigma, E \cup B)$, which we call the *variant unification* procedure. However, the case when $(\Sigma, E \cup B)$ is FVP is noteworthy since, if B-unification is *finitary* (the case when any A axiom is also AC), then variant $E \cup B$-unification *is also finitary* and in fact a *satisfiability decision procedure*. That is, we can decide in a finite number of steps whether a constraint of the form $\bigwedge_{1 \leqslant i \leqslant n} u_i = v_i$ is satisfiable in the algebraic data type $T_{\Sigma/E \cup B}$. For the same reason, we can also decide the satisfiability in $T_{\Sigma/E \cup B}$ of any *positive* (no negations) DNF formula of the form: $\bigvee_{1 \leqslant i \leqslant n} \bigwedge_{1 \leqslant i.j \leqslant n_i} u_{i.j} = v_{i.j}$. This suggests the question: What about satisfiability of *any* quantifier free (QF) formula in $T_{\Sigma/E \cup B}$? We will revisit this question in the next tapas serving.

$E \cup B$-unification is so important that, rather than solving a $E \cup B$-unification problem $u =? v$ by computing the variants of the term $u =? v$ in $(\Sigma^{=?}, E^{=?} \cup B)$, which would yield other useless variants, Maude supports it *directly* in $(\Sigma, E \cup B)$, for systems of equations $\bigwedge_{1 \leqslant i \leqslant n} u_i = v_i$, by the **variant unify** command. But since the set of $E \cup B$-unifiers computed this way often contains some unifiers that are less general than some other unifier in the set and are therefore *redundant*, Maude also supports a somewhat more expensive—yet quite practical for reducing the size of many symbolic search problems— command that filters out redundant $E \cup B$-unifiers, namely, the **filtered variant unify** command. For our example, it reduces the number of set unifiers from 24 to 9:

```
Maude> filtered variant unify in SET : a U b U c U S =? a U b U S' .

Unifier 1
S --> %1:Set
S' --> c U %1:Set

Unifier 2
S --> a U #1:Set
S' --> c U #1:Set

Unifier 3
S --> b U #1:Set
S' --> c U #1:Set

Unifier 4
S --> #1:Set
S' --> a U c U #1:Set

Unifier 5
S --> #1:Set
S' --> b U c U #1:Set

Unifier 6
S --> a U b U %1:Set
S' --> c U %1:Set

Unifier 7
S --> a U %1:Set
S' --> b U c U %1:Set

Unifier 8
S --> b U %1:Set
S' --> a U c U %1:Set

Unifier 9
S --> %1:Set
S' --> a U b U c U %1:Set

No more unifiers.
```

5   Fourth Tapas Serving: Variant Satisfiability

In computer science, decision procedures are used to automate reasoning about *data types*. In a conventional language, such data types may include integers, rational numbers, strings of characters, arrays, and so on. There is typically a finite collection of such data types used in a given programming language, which are often well supported by current SMT solvers. A theorem prover to verify programs in a conventional language can make very good use of such decision procedures to automate large portions of a program's proof of correctness. In Maude the situation is quite different. Why? Because in Maude algebraic data types are completely *user-definable*. That is, *any* functional module fmod BAR is $(\Sigma, E \cup B)$ endfm for *any*, finitely specifiable, convergent equational theory $(\Sigma, E \cup B)$ can be specified by a Maude user to define the algebraic data type $T_{\Sigma/E \cup B}$ of his/her choice. And, unlike the case of a conventional language, there is an *infinite* collection of such data types. Of course, for *some* specific Maude data types, for example integers or rationals, existing *domain-specific* decision procedures supported by an SMT solver may be available. But to automate reasoning about *arbitrary* Maude functional modules as much as possible, we need a new kind of SMT solving: what I call *theory-generic* decision procedures, which apply, not to a given data domain, but to an *infinite* class of *user-definable* data types. The generic decision procedure in question is called *variant satisfiability* [56], and is what this tapas serving is about.

The first piece of good news is that, for B any combination of A, C, and U axioms, where any A symbol f must also be C, satisfiability of QF formulas in the data type $T_{\Sigma/B}$ is *decidable* [56]. The million-dollar question is: How can we take advantage of this piece of good news to obtain a much more general *theory-generic* satisfiability decision procedure to help us reason about *any* algebraic data type $T_{\Sigma/E \cup B}$ defined by a Maude functional module fmod BAR is $(\Sigma, E \cup B)$ endfm? Of course, we know *a priori* that the class of algebraic data types $T_{\Sigma/E \cup B}$ for which we can hope to have decidable satisfiability, even if infinite, must have some restrictions: since just for the data type of natural numbers with addition and multiplication, that is, just by adding a multiplication operator _*_ and the equations $N * 0 = 0$, $N * s(M) = N + (N * M)$ to our NATURAL module, Gödel's Incompleteness Theorem rears its head dashing all our decidable satisfiability hopes to the ground. So, one way to both rephrase the original question and advance towards an answer is to ask the more precise question:

Given a Maude functional module fmod BAR is $(\Sigma, E \cup B)$ endfm, is there a *general method* by which we could seek, and find, a sublanguage of QF formulas, say, determined by a subsignature $\Sigma_1 \subseteq \Sigma$ such that satisfiability of QF Σ_1-formulas in $T_{\Sigma/E \cup B}$ is *decidable*?

What is promising about trying to answer this question is its *practical* character: hoping for decidable satisfiability of just *any* algebraic data type is both an act of self-delusion and a mark of ignorance. But hoping for a *subclass* of formulas enjoying decidable satisfiability is an eminently practical idea, which can help automate large parts of a program's proof of correctness effort.

The second piece of good news is that a general method answering the above question does indeed exist. It is based on the idea of a *telescope*, i.e., a chain of convergent theory inclusions of the form:

$$(\Omega, B_\Omega) \subseteq (\Sigma_1, E_1 \cup B_1) \subseteq (\Sigma, E \cup B)$$

such that: (i) Ω is the subsignature of operators that were specified as constructors, with the ctor attribute, in the functional module specifying $(\Sigma, E \cup B)$, (ii)

$B_\Omega \subseteq B$ are the axioms declared for such constructors, (iii) the constructors are true constructors, i.e., for any ground term in the syntax of Σ we have $t!_{E,B} \in T_\Omega$, (iv) any $u \in T_\Omega$ is already in normal form: $u =_{B_\Omega} u!_{E,B}$, and (v) the intermediate theory $(\Sigma_1, E_1 \cup B_1)$ is convergent, has also Ω as its constructors, is FVP, and any A symbol $f \in \Sigma_1$ is also C.

The third and last piece of good news is that, under conditions (i)–(v), satisfiability of QF Σ_1-formulas in $T_{\Sigma/E \cup B}$ is *decidable* [56], which is what we were fishing for; and there is a *theory-generic* satisfiability decision procedure for such formulas, namely, *variant satisfiability* [56]. Of course, at the very least we may have $(\Omega, B_\Omega) = (\Sigma_1, E_1 \cup B_1)$, and in that case just get decidable satisfiability for QF Ω-formulas in $T_{\Sigma/E \cup B}$. But quite often, finding an FVP $(\Sigma_1, E_1 \cup B_1)$ having a strict containment $(\Omega, B_\Omega) \subset (\Sigma_1, E_1 \cup B_1)$ is relatively easy to do. For example, any *selector* functions for the constructors in Ω will automatically be in $(\Sigma_1, E_1 \cup B_1)$ [30].

Eh bien! But how does this theory-generic decision procedure *work*? Recall that solving the problem of the *satisfiability* in the data type $T_{\Sigma/E \cup B}$ of any QF Σ_1-formula φ means to either: (i) effectively exhibiting a *solution*, i.e., a ground substitution ρ such that the ground formula $\varphi\rho$ is *true* in $T_{\Sigma/E \cup B}$ [which by our telescope is the case iff $\varphi\rho$ is *true* in $T_{\Sigma_1/E_1 \cup B_1}$], or (ii) effectively showing that there is no such solution. If this problem is solvable, in one blow, we have also solved the *validity problem* for a QF Σ_1-formula φ in $T_{\Sigma/E \cup B}$. That is, we can either: (i) effectively prove that φ is a *theorem* of $T_{\Sigma/E \cup B}$, or (ii) effectively show a counterexample when it is not: since φ will be a *theorem* of $T_{\Sigma/E \cup B}$ iff $\neg\varphi$ is *unsatisfiable* in $T_{\Sigma/E \cup B}$. We will solve the satisfiability problem for a QF Σ_1-formula φ in $T_{\Sigma/E \cup B}$ by *reducing* it to that of the satisfiability of QF Ω-formulas in T_{Ω/B_Ω}, which we already know how to decide. Since, without loss of generality, we may assume φ in DNF, that is,

$$\varphi \equiv \bigvee_{1 \leqslant i \leqslant n} \left(\bigwedge_{1 \leqslant i.j \leqslant n_i} u_{i.j} = v_{i.j} \wedge \bigwedge_{1 \leqslant i.k \leqslant m_i} w_{i.k} \neq w'_{i.k} \right)$$

it is enough to decide the satisfiability of a Σ_1-*conjunction of literals* $\bigwedge_{1 \leqslant i \leqslant n} u_i = v_i \wedge \bigwedge_{1 \leqslant j \leqslant m} w_j \neq w'_j$. But we already *know* how to decide the satisfiability of the positive part by variant unification. Therefore, the problem reduces to solving the satisfiability of:

$$\bigvee_{\alpha \in Unif_{E_1 \cup B_1}(\bigwedge_{1 \leqslant i \leqslant n} u_i = v_i)} (\bigwedge_{1 \leqslant j \leqslant m} w_j \neq w'_j)\alpha$$

That is, it is enough to decide the satisfiability of a Σ_1-*conjunction of disequalities* $\bigwedge_{1 \leqslant j \leqslant m} w_j \neq w'_j$. But, as sketched out in Footnote 4, we can view such a conjunction of disequalities as a *term* in the FVP theory $(\Sigma_1^{=?}, E_1 \cup B_1)$, which has $(\Omega^{=?}, B_\Omega)$ as its subspecification of constructors [i.e., $\Omega^{=?}$ contains $true$, $\_ \wedge \_$ and $\_ \neq \_$ as added constructors]. But, if we now recall the notion of *constructor variants*, this reduces to the equivalent problem of deciding the satisfiability of the disjunction of conjunctions of Ω-disequalities:

$$\bigvee_{1 \leqslant i \leqslant n} (\bigwedge_{1 \leqslant j \leqslant m} q_j^i \neq r_j^i)$$

in T_{Ω/B_Ω}, where the $\{\bigwedge_{1 \leqslant j \leqslant m} q_j^i \neq r_j^i \mid 1 \leqslant i \leqslant n\}$ are the *constructor variants* of the $\Sigma_1^{=?}$-term: $\bigwedge_{1 \leqslant j \leqslant m} w_j \neq w_j'$. So, we have reduced the problem to one of QF satisfiability in T_{Ω/B_Ω} and we are done!

To be *really done*, we just need to know how satisfiability of a conjunction of Ω-disequalities $\bigwedge_{1 \leqslant j \leqslant m} q_j \neq r_j$ is decided in T_{Ω/B_Ω}. But this is really easy [56]. First of all, we can *reduce* to the case where each variable $x_i : s_i$ in the conjunction ranges over a sort s_i such that $T_{\Omega/B_\Omega, s_i}$ is an *infinite* set: since if any $x_j : s_j$ ranges over a *finite* set $T_{\Omega/B_\Omega, s_j}$, we can replace our conjunction by a disjunction of conjunctions where $x_j : s_j$ has been instantiated in all possible ways by one of the values in the finite set $T_{\Omega/B_\Omega, s_j}$. Under this infinite-sorts assumption, the conjunction $\bigwedge_{1 \leqslant j \leqslant m} q_j \neq r_j$ is satisfiable in T_{Ω/B_Ω} iff $q_j \neq_{B_\Omega} r_j$, $1 \leqslant j \leqslant m$, which is a trivial check in Maude.

Presburger Arithmetic on a Paper Napkin. There are entire book chapters on Presburger arithmetic decision procedures. But to give you a feeling for the general applicability of variant satisfiability, the good news is that by now you *already know everything you need to know* to realize that satisfiability of QF formulas in Presburger arithmetic is *decidable*, and to decide any such QF formula by yourself in Maude. The theory of Presburger arithmetic does indeed fit on a paper napkin, as the functional module:

```
fmod PRESBURGER is protecting TRUTH-VALUE .
sort Nat .
ops 0 1 : -> Nat [ctor] .
op _+_ : Nat Nat -> Nat [ctor assoc comm id: 0] .
op _>_ : Nat Nat -> Bool .
vars N M K : Nat .

eq N + 1 + M > N = true [variant] .
eq N > N + M = false [variant] .
endfm
```

which imports TRUTH-VALUE, with just two constants true, false of sort Bool. Note that in PRESBURGER we have just specified natural number addition as the free commutative monoid generated by 1 with 0 as the identity element. This module is FVP, as one can easily check by computing the three variants of the term $N > M$ for its only defined symbol `_>_`. Furthermore, all its other operators define a subsignature Ω of constructor symbols, so that it has a constructor sub-specification of the form (Ω, ACU). Therefore, satisfiability of QF Ω-formulas in $T_{\Omega/ACU}$ is *decidable*. And so is also the satisfiability of QF formulas in Presburger arithmetic by our theory-generic variant satisfiability procedure. For example, the transitivity law $N > M = \text{true} \wedge M > K = \text{true} \Rightarrow N > K = \text{true}$ is valid, because its negation $N > M = \text{true} \wedge M > K = \text{true} \wedge N > K \neq \text{true}$ is unsatisfiable, since we get a single solution for the variant unification problem:

```
Maude> filtered variant unify in PRESBURGER : N > M =? true /\ M > K =? true .

Unifier 1
N --> 1 + 1 + %1:Nat + %2:Nat + %3:Nat
M --> 1 + %1:Nat + %2:Nat
K --> %2:Nat

No more unifiers.
```

and when we compute the instantiation $(N > K)\theta$ for this unifier θ and reduce it to its normal form we get:

```
Maude> reduce 1 + 1 + %1:Nat + %2:Nat + %3:Nat > %2:Nat .

result Bool: true
```

making the disequality $true \neq true$ unsatisfiable. q.e.d. Of course, since variant satisfiability is a very general *theory-generic* procedure, there is no fair competition possible with a highly optimized *domain-specific* algorithm for Presburger arithmetic. But this is OK for three reasons: (i) as already mentioned, Maude has interfaces to both the CVC4 and Yices SMT solvers, so optimized implementations of Presburger arithmetic are available that way; (ii) variant satisfiability's sweetspot is not in competing with already existing, optimized *domain-specific* decision procedures, but rather in *complementing* such procedures by making SMT solving *extensible* to an infinite class of *user-definable* algebraic data types; and (iii) nevertheless, a variant satisfiability procedure for Presburger arithmetic is not entirely useless: other colleagues and I have used it in various automated deduction applications, and—as we shall see in a moment—it enjoys the non-negligible advantage of having a *seamless integration* with other variant satisfiability decision procedures.

A Decision Procedure for S-Expressions. This might seem like a bad example to pick in order to show the usefulness of variant satisfiability; but it isn't. After all, domain-specific decision procedures for LISP's S-Expressions go back, at least, to the one by the late Derek Oppen [62]; and similar procedures are a dime a dozen in the SMT solving literature. So, why beating a dead horse? Because it isn't dead. The dirty little secret is that all the procedures of this kind I am aware of are *problematic*. Why so? They are problematic in their *corner cases*, namely, in cases when an S-Expression can be *undefined*. For example, according to the LISP 1.5 Programmer's Manual [45], expressions such as car[A] or cdr[A] for A an atom are *undefined*. The problem is that all the S-Expression decision procedures I am aware of are based on either *unsorted* or *many-sorted* first-order logic. But, as my late friend Joseph Goguen and I showed in [58], the problem of *faithfully* specifying data types involving partial functions such as those for the data *selectors* car and cdr in LISP, *cannot be solved* in unsorted or many-sorted first-order logic.[5] But, as we showed in [58], it is *solved* by specifying such data types in *order-sorted* equational logic; or in the even more general *membership equational logic* [53] used by Maude's functional modules. The upshot of all this is that the existing decision procedures are forced to cut some corners: the answers you will get in such corner cases are anybody's guess or, if documented, they will depend on some arbitrary choices about how to make such partial functions *total* in the undefined cases.

So, the horse is not really dead yet. And there is something to be gained by revisiting this venerable topic of decision procedures for S-Expressions as a representative instance of the much more general problem of having *faithful* decision procedures for algebraic data types with *constructors and selectors*. Furthermore, it gives me a good opportunity to introduce you, dear reader, to the expressive power of *order-sorted* specifications in Maude, which is actually crucial for many variant satisfiability procedures.

LISP is of course an *untyped* language. However, what might be called LISP's *ontology of S-Expressions*, which is part of the lore and essential to know what you are doing when programming in LISP, is captured by the following structure of subsorts of the main sort SExp. Since S-Expressions are *parametric* on the type of *Atoms*, which are basic data values, like numbers, Booleans, identifiers, etc., this can be specified in Maude as a *parameterized module* with the TRIV parameter theory, which just has an Elt parameter sort/type that can be instantiated to any chosen sort/type of basic values, i.e., of atoms.

```
fmod S-EXP{A :: TRIV} is protecting TRUTH-VALUE .
sorts List NeList NLExp NLPair SExp .
subsorts NeList < List < SExp .
subsorts A$Elt NLPair < NLExp < SExp .
op nil : -> List [ctor] .
op [_._] : SExp SExp -> SExp [ctor] .
op [_._] : SExp List -> NeList [ctor] .
op [_._] : SExp NLExp -> NLPair [ctor] .
op car_ : NeList -> SExp .     *** left selector
op car_ : NLPair -> SExp .     *** left selector
op cdr_ : NeList -> List .     *** right selector
op cdr_ : NLPair -> NLExp .    *** right selector
ops atom? nelist? list? nlpair? nlexp?  : SExp -> Bool . *** sort preds

var A : A$Elt . var NeL : NeList .  var L : List .
var NLE : NLExp . var NLP : NLPair . var SE : SExp .

eq car[SE . L] = SE [variant] .     eq cdr[SE . L] = L [variant] .
eq car[SE . NLE] = SE [variant] .   eq cdr[SE . NLE] = NLE [variant] .

eq atom?(A) = true [variant] .      eq nelist?(NeL) = true [variant] .
```

---

[5] Unless of course such partial functions are represented as *binary relations*, or the specification itself is *changed* by introducing *coercion functions* in the way Goguen and I showed in [29].

```
eq atom?(NLP) = false [variant] .        eq nelist?(nil) = false [variant] .
eq atom?(L) = false [variant] .          eq nelist?(NLE) = false [variant] .
eq list?(L) = true [variant] .           eq nlpair?(NLP) = true [variant] .
eq list?(NLE) = false [variant] .        eq nlpair?(A) = false [variant] .
eq nlexp?(NLE) = true [variant] .        eq nlpair?(L) = false [variant] .
eq nlexp?(L) = false [variant] .
endfm
```

This is the only example in this paper that may not fit on a cocktail paper napkin: we may have to unfold one, or to ask our waiter for a dinner paper napkin. The main ideas about the ontology carved out by the above subsort structure can be summarized by the following remarks about LISP lore: (1) An SExp is either an Atom (of the parameter sort A$Elt), or nil, or a binary tree having either atoms or nil in its leaves. (2) A List is either nil, or a binary tree whose rightmost leaf is nil. (3) A NeList is a non-nil List. (4) A NLExp is any *non-list* SExp. (5) A NLPair is any non-atom NLExp. Of course, car and cdr select the left, resp. right, subtrees of any S-Expression that is a binary tree. They make no sense otherwise. The sort predicates have lower case names for their respective sorts: they are **true** for elements of that sort, and **false** otherwise. Thanks to order-sortedness, some operators are *overloaded*.

This module is FVP. Termination is trivial, since all the equations decrease term size; confluence follows from the absence of order-sorted critical pairs; full definition of functions can be easily checked by the method in [47]; and FVP itself can be easily checked by computing variants for each of the defined functions. For example, car and cdr have two variants each (for either of their typings), and the list? predicate has three variants. As already pointed out, it would have been impossible to faithfully model LISP S-Expressions in unsorted or many-sorted first-order logic. But there is more behind the module's deceptive simplicity: Even if we had *not* specified the car and cdr selectors that push this data type outside the pale of many-sorted first-order logic, it would still have been impossible to specify predicates like list? or nlexp? as FVP functions in an unsorted or many-sorted way. The reason for this impossibility is that in such settings these predicates would have to *recurse down the binary tree* to *check* whether the rightmost element is either nil or an atom; and this would have pushed those predicate definitions out of the FVP fold. The moral of this story is that order-sorted first-order logic *silently and kindly absorbs into its syntax* a lot of reasoning that would otherwise require quite complex *first-order reasoning*, in the form of deducing implications between unary predicates modeling the non-existent subsorts.

Since the constructors of S-EXP do not satisfy any axioms and no equations apply to constructor terms, we are again under the conditions ensuring decidable satisfiability. That is, we have a variant satisfiability procedure for S-Expressions in a *parametric* way, in the same sense as for similar parametric variant satisfiability procedures for lists, compact lists, multisets, sets, and hereditarily finite sets in [56]. What this means in practice is that if we *instantiate* S-EXP{A :: TRIV} by choosing a sort of atoms in any FVP data type that also satisfies the variant satisfiability conditions, then, any such instantiation (after checking termination of the equations in the instantiation) is also FVP and does also have decidable satisfiability for its QF formulas. For example, we can instantiate the parameter sort `Elt` in `TRIV` to the `Nat` sort in `PRESBURGER` by defining in Maude a *view* and then instantiating `S-EXP{A :: TRIV}` with this view as follows:

```
view Nat from TRIV to PRESBURGER is
sort Elt to Nat .
endv
```

```
fmod NAT-SEXP is
protecting S-EXP{Nat} .
endfm
```

In this instantiated module—whose termination proof is trivial, since all its equations are term-size decreasing—we can decide the validity of both *parametric* theorems like: $NeL = [(car\ NeL)\ .\ (cdr\ NeL)]$, which hold for any instance of the module and could likewise have been defined directly for `S-EXP{A :: TRIV}`, and that of theorems that only make sense for this instantiation, like the implication:

$$atom?(carNLP) = true \quad atom?(cdrNLP) = true \quad (car\ NLP) + (cdr\ NLP) > (car\ NLP) \neq false \vee (cdr\ NLP) = 0$$

Let us prove both of these theorems by showing that their corresponding negations are unsatisfiable. In the first example, the only constructor variant of the disequality $NeL \neq [(car\ NeL)\ .\ (cdr\ NeL)]$ is the clearly unsatisfiable disequality $[SE\ .\ L] \neq [SE\ .\ L]$. q.e.d. In the second example we have to verify that the conjunction

$$atom?(carNLP) = true \quad atom?(cdrNLP) = true \quad (car\ NLP) + (cdr\ NLP) > (car\ NLP) = false \quad (cdr\ NLP) \neq 0$$

is unsatisfiable. But the positive part of this conjunction has the single unifier $\theta = \{NLP \mapsto [N\ .\ 0]\}$; and then the canonical form of $(cdr\ NLP)\theta \neq 0$ is the unsatisfiable disequality $0 \neq 0$. q.e.d.

Something interesting about this example is the *seamless integration* of the two variant satisfiability decision procedures: the one for `PRESBURGER` and that for `S-EXP{A :: TRIV}`. This is in contrast to the usual Nelson-Oppen (NO) combination procedure [60] required to reason in a combination of theories. No such NO-combination procedure is needed at all for variant satisfiability: we just form the appropriate *union* of theories (in this case by instantiating the `S-EXP{A :: TRIV}` with the `Nat` view), and that's it!

6 Dessert: Narrowing-Based Symbolic Reachability Analysis

By now we have had a fairly substantial sampling of tapas: we should not push this too hard. Let me end on a light, yet interesting, note by explaining to you what symbolic reachability analysis in Maude is about, and some cool things you can do with it. It will be our dessert: a little *divertimento*. We have remained all the time within Maude's sublanguage of functional modules. But, of course, Maude's most unique capability is its declarative programming of concurrent systems by means of rewrite theories in system modules of the form mod FOO is $(\Sigma, E \cup B, R)$ endm, where the system's local concurrent transitions are specified by the rules R using the rl keyword, as opposed to the eq keyword used for equations. Such rules need not be terminating, and can be highly non-deterministic. Maude's **rewrite** command can simulate *one* possible execution sequence for such rules in a fair fashion; but there can be many, many more possible executions. For many reasoning purposes, such as, for example, to check that a cryptographic protocol is secure, one can perform *reachability analysis* in Maude to explore *all* states reachable from a given one using Maude's breadth first **search** command.

However, this may not be powerful enough in some cases: for example, if either the set of reachable states or that of initial states is *infinite*. In such cases one can perform *symbolic reachability analysis* using *narrowing* with Maude's **vu-narrow** command. Thanks to our previous Maude tapas this command is now quite easy to explain. Given a symbolic initial state specified by a term $u(x_1, \ldots, x_n)$ describing a, typically infinite, set of initial state instances, what this command does is to build a *narrowing search graph* rooted at $u(x_1, \ldots, x_n)$. But there are three main differences with equational narrowing: (1) now we narrow symbolic expressions, not with equations E, but *with transition rules* in R; (2) for each narrowing step, instead of performing B-unification as before, we now perform $E \cup B$-unification with all the equations in the rewrite theory; and (3) we check if we have *reached* a goal term $v(y_1, \ldots, y_n)$ using $E \cup B$-unification. There are just two restrictions: (i) to be practical, we want to remain *finitely branching*, so we require the equations $E \cup B$ to be FVP to make sure the number of $E \cup B$-unifiers is finite; and (ii) we also assume that the rules in R are *topmost*—i.e., that they rewrite the entire state—, which is easy to achieve in practice by a theory transformation and ensures completeness of the analysis. The command has the form:

```
vu-narrow [n] in FOO :  u(x1,...,xn) =>* v(y1,...,ym) .
```

where n is the number of desired solutions, $u(x_1, \ldots, x_n)$ is the pattern for initial states, and $v(y_1, \ldots, y_n)$ is the pattern describing the set of states that we wish to reach—or to show that we cannot reach, if they are "bad" states. The meaning of this query is then to seek an answer to the following question:

> *Is there an instance of the set of initial states symbolically specified by* $u(x_1, \ldots, x_n)$ *from which we can reach an instance of the set of target states symbolically specified by* $v(y_1, \ldots, y_n)$ *by a sequence of transitions from R in the* FOO *module?* [$u(x_1, \ldots, x_n)$ *and* $v(y_1, \ldots, y_n)$ *can share some variables*]

What Maude's **vu-narrow** command provides is a *complete* method to get answers for such a question: if an answer exists, we are guaranteed—except for the usual memory and time limitations—to find it. The most common examples of this method involve analyzing the reachability properties of some concurrent system. For example, the Maude-NPA tool [26] uses this kind of narrowing-based symbolic reachability analysis (with some additional optimizations), to symbolically analyze security properties of cryptographic protocols. But I wish to present a completely different kind of example, namely, a Logic Programming (LP) interpreter, because it shows that rewriting logic and Maude have good properties not only as a *semantic framework* to naturally specify and program concurrent systems, but also as a *logical framework* [43] in which a logic's inference rules can be naturally represented as *rewrite rules*. In this case, the inference system in question is that of *Horn Logic*; and we get for free an LP interpreter whose core is the following LP module importing the quoted identifiers module QID with sort Qid:

```
fmod LP is protecting QID .
 sorts U UList Query .
 subsorts Qid < U < UList .
 op true : -> UList .          *** true as "nil"
 op _,_ : UList UList -> UList [assoc id: true] .
 op _[_] : Qid UList -> U .   *** term constructor
 op {_} : UList -> Query .
endfm
```

This tiny functional module is all we need to define an interpreter for Logic Programming (LP) [without negation as failure]; i.e., for computing with Horn Logic programs. Terms of sort U provide a universal language for *atomic predicates*. For example, the binary atomic predicate $s(s(0)) > s(0)$ will be here represented as the term '>['s['s['0]],'s['0]]. The sort Query is used for users of the LP interpreter to enter queries. Such queries ask for a witness proving an existential formula of the form:

$$(\exists x_1, \ldots, x_n) \quad B_1 \wedge \ldots \wedge B_k$$

which is here represented by a term {B1,...,Bk} of sort Query. Prolog's depth first search makes it incomplete. But this interpreter will be *complete*, i.e., if an answer to a query exists, it will be found. Let me explain how we execute a Horn Logic program, i.e., a collection of *Horn clauses*, either of the form A, some atomic predicate, or implications of the form: $A_1 \wedge \ldots \wedge A_n \rightarrow A$, with $A_1, \ldots, A_n, A$ atomic predicates. If we think of *true* as the empty conjunction, we can view all such Horn clauses as implications, since A is equivalent to *true* $\rightarrow A$. In LP, and also in proof theory, the conjunction symbol is often represented just by a comma: _,_ and therefore a Horn clause looks either like *true* $\rightarrow A$ or like $A_1, \ldots, A_n \rightarrow A$. But in logic we often take the goal we want to prove as our starting point and apply the inference rules *in reverse* to search for a proof of the goal. Therefore, to compute with a set of Horn clauses, i.e., with an LP program, we will use the clauses *in reverse* as rewrite rules: $A \rightarrow true$ and $A \rightarrow A_1, \ldots, A_n$. This representation would be just fine for us to get an LP interpreter: we could make _,_ associative-commutative with identity *true* and perform symbolic reachability analysis from our goal $B_1, \ldots, B_k$ —which we want to existentially prove by finding a witness using the reversed rewrite rules of type $A \to true$ and $A \to A_1, \ldots, A_n$— by trying to reach the term *true*, and thus a proof. This would *work* and would be complete; but it would be quite *inefficient*, because the interpreter would waste a lot of time performing *redundant* symbolic searches. We can achieve a much more efficient interpreter by introducing two seemingly small optimizations: (1) Make $\_,\_$ just *AU*, instead of *ACU*. This is harmless, since all lefthand sides of the reverse rules are single atoms. So, they can be applied *anywhere*, i.e., the *C* axiom is *unnecessary*. (2) By using the operator $\{\_\}$ in the above LP module, we can further impose a *left to right order* in searching for proofs of each of our atom goals *one at a time*. This will provide great efficiency. This suggests representing a clause in reverse of the form $A \to true$ as the "clause in context" rewrite rule $\{A, L\} \to \{L\}$, taking advantage of the *AU* axioms, with L a variable of sort ULIst. Likewise, we will represent a clause in reverse $A \to A_1, \ldots, A_n$ as the "clause in context" $\{A, L\} \to \{A_1, \ldots, A_n, L\}$. This is just what we will do. For example, the following Horn clauses define the reverse [mirror image] of a binary tree and a *palindrome* predicate on binary trees, where $\_ \wedge \_$ is the binary tree constructor and with the elements on tree leaves quoted identifiers; so Q ranges over quoted identifiers:

- $rev(Q, Q)$
- $rev(T_1, T_4), rev(T_2, T_3) \to rev((T_1 \wedge T_2), (T_3 \wedge T_4))$
- $rev(T, T) \to pal(T)$

Using our "reversed clauses in context" transformation to compute with these clauses in search for a proof of an existential query, we get the rewrite theory in the following Maude system module, where the [narrowing] attribute instructs Maude that the so-marked rules will be used in narrowing search:

```
mod TREE-REVERSE&PALINDROME is protecting LP .
var Q : Qid .  vars T T' T1 T2 T3 T4 : U .  var L : UList .

rl {('rev[Q,Q]),L} => {L}                     [narrowing] .
rl {('rev[('^[T1,T2]),('^[T3,T4])]),L}
    => {('rev[T1,T4]),('rev[T2,T3]),L}        [narrowing] .
rl {('pal[T]),L} => {('rev[T,T]),L}           [narrowing] .
endm
```

Solving queries for this logic program *is just narrowing with the program's rules!* (in this case *modulo AU*). And, thanks to the completeness of narrowing, such query solving is *complete*. For example:

```
Maude> vu-narrow [1] in TREE-REVERSE&PALINDROME :
{'rev[('^[('^['a,'b]),('^['c,'d])]),T]} =>* {true} .


Solution 1
state: {true}
accumulated substitution:
```

```
T --> 'ˆ[('ˆ['d,'c]),('ˆ['b,'a])]

Maude> vu-narrow [2] in TREE-REVERSE&PALINDROME :
{'rev[('ˆ[('ˆ['a,'b]),T']),T]} =>* {true} .

Solution 1
state: {true}
accumulated substitution:
T' --> @1:Qid
T --> 'ˆ[@1:Qid,('ˆ['b,'a])]
variant unifier:

Solution 2
state: {true}
accumulated substitution:
T' --> 'ˆ[@2:Qid,@1:Qid]
T --> 'ˆ[('ˆ[@1:Qid,@2:Qid]),('ˆ['b,'a])]

Maude> vu-narrow [1] in TREE-REVERSE&PALINDROME :
{'pal[('ˆ[('ˆ['a,'b]),('ˆ['c,'d])])]} =>* {true} .

No solution.

Maude> vu-narrow [1] in TREE-REVERSE&PALINDROME :
{'pal[('ˆ[('ˆ['a,'b]),('ˆ['b,'a])])]} =>* {true} .

Solution 1
state: {true}
```

7   Further Reading

These tapas have been a way of introducing you, dear reader, in an informal, high-bandwith way to some symbolic aspects of Maude that you might find useful. As agreed, I have tried to kept technical details to a bare minimum: just sufficient for an intelligent conversation with someone having a CS background to be *meaningful*. Now is the time to explain to you how a few gaps we had to skirt can be filled in. I focus on Maude in Sect. 7.1, and discuss broader mathematical background readings in Sect. 7.2.

7.1   Further Reading on Maude

The most up-to-date Maude journal paper—also emphasizing symbolic aspects— and covering other aspects such as Maude's **strategy language** and Maude's approach to **concurrent object-oriented programming** and various Maude *external objects*—that allow Maude programs to be executed in a distributed manner and interact with external entities—is [20]. The Maude book [14] is dated—since important new features were added later—but is still useful for those parts it covers and its tutorial examples. For teaching formal methods using Maude, Peter Ölvecky's book [61] is an excellent textbook emphasizing distributed system applications. In particular, [20], [14] and [61] provide more precise definitions of **rewriting modulo B** and a wealth of examples of both functional and system modules, including *parameterized* ones such as the S-EXP{A :: TRIV} one we already encountered, and the use of the reduce and rewrite commands. For *executability conditions* and how to check them, for both functional and system modules, see [22,24,32]. References [14] and [61] also provide good explanations and examples to understand the use of Maude's breadth first search command, and how search supports a basic, yet very useful, form of **model checking** verification. They also explain and illustrate well the more sophisticated **LTL temporal logic model checking** also supported directly by Maude.

Something important that did no come up in our conversation over tapas is **reflection**. It did come up subliminally in *theory transformations* like $(\Sigma, E \cup B) \mapsto (\Sigma^{=?}, E^{=?} \cup B)$, or in transforming a Horn theory into a Maude system module. The point about reflection is that any such transformations can be performed *inside Maude*, because Maude's META-LEVEL module supports *metaprogramming*, i.e., writing programs that manipulate other programs. This is not some kind of useful hack, but a piece of mathematics: the efficient exploitation inside Maude of the fact that both rewriting logic and its underlying equational logic are *reflective* [16], i.e., have *universal theories* that can faithfully represent any theories [including themselves] as *data*, as well as faithfully simulating deduction in them. The reason why this may be of interest to you is because—combined with the symbolic features I have explained—reflection makes it very easy to build many *formal tools*, not just for Maude itself, but for many other logics. Of course, in the Maude team we aggressively practice *dogfooding*, so all the Maude formal verification tools have been built this way; but other researchers use Maude in the same way for many other logics and languages. The Maude book [14], and [20], are good sources to learn more about reflection in Maude.

To learn more about how to use **unification, variants, and narrowing-based reachability analysis** in Maude, the best sources at present are the journal paper [20], the conference paper [21], and the Maude 3.1 Manual [15]. I discuss theoretical foundations for these and other topics in Sect. 7.2.

There are many other aspects of Maude and rewriting logic, and many other applications that I could not discuss here. A somewhat dated but still useful survey of rewriting logic, including also references to many applications developed in Maude, is the 2012 paper [54].

7.2   Further Background Reading

I focus here on answering the question: *Where can I learn more about the mathematical foundations of the topics we have discussed over tapas?* This is different from questions about Maude itself, which, hopefully, were answered in Sect. 7.1.

Logics. The three main logics involved are: (i) *equational logic*; (ii) its extension to *first-order logic*; and (iii) *rewriting logic*. Both (ii) and (iii) are parametric on the equational logic chosen. Since Maude functional modules specify algebraic data types, the million-dollar question is: *What is a good logic to specify algebraic data types?* This question is highly non-trivial, due to the presence of partial functions in many data types. Joseph Goguen and I proposed *order-sorted equational logic* in [29], further developed in [53]. I later proposed the extension of order-sorted equational logic to *membership equational logic* in [53], and developed its computational logic aspects and its rewriting techniques jointly with Adel Bouhoula and Jean-Pierre Jouannaud in [9]. Maude's functional modules are based on membership equational logic; but many examples can be specified as order-sorted theories. Any equational logic is just a fragment of a corresponding first-order logic. For order-sorted logic this is explained in detail in, e.g., [69]. For simplicity of exposition, *rewriting logic* was first presented in [52] as having unsorted equational logic as its sublogic. But from the beginning the intention was to base it on order-sorted equational logic; and it was further extended, based on membership equational logic, in [10]. A latest extension allowing quantifier-free formulas in the conditions of conditional rules is presented in [57].

Rewriting Modulo B, and Rewriting in Rewrite Theories. I have not touched upon *conditional* rewriting, which generalizes the unconditional case and is supported by Maude. For the semantics of conditional rewriting modulo B in *convergent* order-sorted equational theories, a quite comprehensive reference is [41]. I have cheated a little by saying that convergent means Church-Rosser and terminating: in the modulo B case the additional requirement of *B-coherence* [37,55] is needed; but this is automatically enforced by the Maude implementation. Furthermore, in the order-sorted case *sort-decreasingness* (see, e.g., [41]), i.e., that the sorts of terms remain the same or go down by rewriting, is also needed for convergence. The key theorem for equational rewriting is that if $(\Sigma, E \cup B)$ is convergent, then we have the *Church-Rosser Equivalence*:

$$u =_{E \cup B} v \quad \Leftrightarrow \quad u!_{E,B} =_B v!_{E,B}$$

A very general formulation of this equivalence for the conditional order-sorted case can be found in [41]. As already mentioned, rewriting in conditional theories in membership equational logics has been studied in [9].

For a rewrite theory, $\mathcal{R} = (\Sigma, E \cup B, R)$, rewriting with transition rules R should happen *modulo $E \cup B$*. But this is of course very hard to implement, since $E \cup B$-equality may even be undecidable. Furthermore, both the equations E and the rules R can be *conditional*. However, under the natural assumption that $(\Sigma, E \cup B)$ is convergent, a simple requirement called *coherence* of R with E modulo B [24,73] ensures that the unmanageable relation $\to_{R/(E \cup B)}$ can be faithfully simulated by the much simpler relations $\to_{R,B}$ and $\to_{E,B}$. This is what the Maude implementation supports, requiring system modules to be coherent.

Unification, Narrowing, Variants, and Variant Unification. *Unification* is technical jargon for solving equations in an algebra. For algebras whose elements are numbers, this goes back to Classical Greece, where many of these problems arose in conjunction with geometrical constructions, e.g., measuring the diagonal of a unit square. It was advanced by the Arabs, who coined the word "Algebra" for this business, and further developed by the Italians, Newton, Galois, Gauss, the Emmy Noether school, and so on. Two fundamental problems about solving equations in numerical domains were settled in the 20th Century: (i) the effective solvability of polynomial equations and inequalities in any real-closed field, and in particular in the reals, thanks to the Tarski-Seidenberg Theorem [67,72] —which actually decides the satisfiability of any first-order formula in this language—, and (ii) the inexistence of a general algorithm to solve polynomial equations in the integers—the so-called *diophantine equations*, after Diophantus—, thanks to Matiyasevich's negative answer to Hilbert's 10th Problem [44]. But with the rise of symbolic logic in the 20th Century, the need naturally arose to *solve equations in term algebras*, i.e., in T_Σ or $T_\Sigma(X)$ for variables X: it amounts to the same if Σ has constants. This problem was solved by Jacques Herbrand in his thesis (see [33], pg. 148). In Computer Science, Herbrand's algorithm was rediscovered independently by Alan Robinson, who called it "unification," as the main workhorse for *resolution*: his breakthrough in automated theorem proving [65]. Since resolution was based on first-order logic *without* equality, the issue of how to "build in" equational theories in resolution provers so as to avoid falling into the Turing tarpits was recognized as a pressing one by Gordon Plotkin [64], who proceeded to give an A-unification algorithm for this purpose in [64]. Independently, Makanin in Russia provided a different A-unification algorithm in [42]. Likewise, Peterson and Stickel gave an AC-unification algorithm in [63]. This raised the general E-unification problem, that is, how to solve equations in the data type $T_{\Sigma/E}$, or equivalently in $T_{\Sigma/E}(X)$, for various E: see [5,6,36] for three surveys. The treatment of E-unification was unsorted. But this is too restrictive for the reasons already mentioned above. Therefore, the need for more general *order-sorted* E-unification algorithms arose naturally and was answered in [59,66,71]. Additional advances were made in [31] and—crucially for the efficiency of Maude's implementation of order-sorted B-unification—in [25].

Narrowing also emerged from efforts to make resolution theorem provers reason efficiently about equality. Specifically, it was introduced by Slagle [70] as an efficient kind of *paramodulation*, and was further elaborated by Lankford as a component of a resolution-with-equality strategy assuming convergent equations [39]. Hullot further advanced the narrowing ideas, proposed his *basic narrowing* strategy, and explored under some restrictions the notion of narrowing modulo axioms B for a convergent theory $(\Sigma, E \cup B)$ in [34]. A more systematic generalization to this case was carried out by J.-P. Jouannaud, C. Kirchner and H. Kirchner in [35], assuming a B-unification algorithm. The generalization to narrowing with convergent order-sorted *conditional* equational theories modulo B has been carried out in [11].

Both Fay [28] and Hullot [34] realized that narrowing could be used to compute E-unifiers of the convergent equations E used as rules in the narrowing. Furthermore, Hullot discussed in [34] how $E \cup B$-unification algorithms could be obtained via narrowing modulo B for $(\Sigma, E \cup B)$ convergent in some cases. Again, a more systematic extension of narrowing-based $E \cup B$-unification was carried out by J.-P. Jouannaud, C. Kirchner and H. Kirchner in [35], and was later extended to $E \cup B$-unification for convergent order-sorted *conditional* equational theories in [11]. However, narrowing-based $E \cup B$-unification suffers from two main drawbacks: (i) since the conditions for termination of narrowing are very restrictive, what narrowing-based $E \cup B$-unification generally provides is only a *semi-algorithm*: if a $E \cup B$-unifier exists, it will be found in a finite number of steps—up to pragmatic time and space limitations; but if it does *not* exist, we may never find out, making $E \cup B$-unifiability undecidable in general by this method; and (ii) since some axioms B can give rise to huge numbers of B-unifiers, these algorithms can suffer serious combinatorial explosions. Here is where variants, discussed next, can make a big difference.

Comon and Delaune proposed the notion of *variant* and studied its properties in [18]. *Folding variant narrowing* and *variant unification* were defined and developed in [27]. Several alternative notions of variant, their relationships, and ways of checking FVP are discussed in [12]. The extension of the properties and methods of variants modulo axioms B when B-unification can have an infinite set of B-unifiers has been initiated in [49]. As already explained in Sect. 4, $E \cup B$-unification with the folding variant narrowing strategy has two key advantages: (i) it terminates with a complete finite set of $E \cup B$-unifiers iff $(\Sigma, R \cup B)$ is FVP, and (ii) its search space and its efficiency are much better than standard narrowing-based $E \cup B$-unification. There are many applications of variants and variant unification to, e.g., cryptographic protocol analysis, e.g., [13,18,26,46], program termination [23], SMT solving, e.g., [56,68], partial evaluation, e.g., [3], program transformation and symbolic model checking, e.g., [7,57], and theorem proving, e.g., [50,69].

Variant Satisfiability. The foundations and many examples can be found in [56]. Decidable QF satisfiability in $T_{\Sigma/B}$ whenever any A symbol $f \in \Sigma$ is also C, generalizes that of $T_{\Sigma/AC}$ in [17]. Variant satisfiability algorithms are studied in [68]. An extension to specifications with predicates, plus variant satisfiability of data types with constructors and selectors can be found in [30]. For variant satisfiability examples with $B = A$ see [48]. For theorem proving applications see [50,69].

Narrowing-Based Reachability Analysis. Narrowing was developed as an automated deduction method for *equational reasoning*. The idea that narrowing based $E \cup B$-unification could be used to perform *symbolic reachability analysis* in a rewrite theory $\mathcal{R} = (\Sigma, E \cup B, R)$ by narrowing symbolic states with *transition rules R modulo $E \cup B$* was proposed in [51], with cryptographic protocol analysis as an application in mind. In fact, the most impressive application of this technique is the Maude-NPA tool for analysis of cryptographic protocols (see [26] for a tutorial, and more recent references in DBLP). The extension of this technique from reachability analysis to symbolic LTL model checking —with a Maude-based tool supporting it—can be found in [7]. Symbolic reachability analysis with very general conditional rules is studied in [57].

Acknowledgements. I thank the BOPL organizers for giving me the opportunity of presenting these ideas as a BOPL joint invited speaker. I chose the talk's topic having in mind the interests of the various BOPL participants and, in spite of the pandemic, found the online discussions very helpful and stimulating. The ideas I have presented are based on joint work with various colleagues. The symbolic aspects of Maude are part of a long and extremely active effort by the members of the Maude Team; they owe much to Steven Eker's high-performance implementation of its features. Folding variant narrowing is joint work with Santiago Escobar and Ralf Sasse. Variant-based satisfiability has been advanced in joint work with Stephen Skeirik and Raúl Gutiérrez. The Maude-NPA has been developed in joint work with Catherine Meadows, Santiago Escobar, and Ph.D. students at Illinois, Valencia, and Oslo. Maude's Symbolic LTL Model Checker is joint work with Kyungmin Bae and Santiago Escobar. Last but not least, the work on generalization, homeomorphic embedding and variant-based partial evaluation of Maude programs is joint research with María Alpuente, Angel Cuenca-Ortega, Santiago Escobar and Julia Sapiña at TU Valencia, and Demis Ballis at the University of Udine. Given the long list, I hope I have not missed anybody, and apologize in advance if that were inadvertently the case. I warmly thank María Alpuente, Francisco Durán, Santiago Escobar, Maribel Fernádez, Salvador Lucas, Narciso Martí-Oliet, Rubén Rubio and Carolyn Talcott for their very helpful suggestions to improve the manuscript. The research reported herein has been partially supported by NRL under contract N00173-17-1-G002.

References

1. Alpuente, M., Cuenca-Ortega, A., Escobar, S., Meseguer, J.: Order-sorted homeomorphic embedding modulo combinations of associativity and/or commutativity axioms. Fundamenta Informaticae **177**, 297–329 (2020)
2. Alpuente, M., Ballis, D., Cuenca-Ortega, A., Escobar, S., Meseguer, J.: $ACUOS^2$: a high-performance system for modular ACU generalization with subtyping and inheritance. In: Calimeri, F., Leone, N., Manna, M. (eds.) JELIA 2019. LNCS (LNAI), vol. 11468, pp. 171–181. Springer, Cham (2019). https://doi.org/10.1007/978-3-030-19570-0_11
3. Alpuente, M., Cuenca-Ortega, A., Escobar, S., Meseguer, J.: A partial evaluation framework for order-sorted equational programs modulo axioms. J. Log. Algebraic Methods Program. **110**, 100501 (2020)
4. Alpuente, M., Escobar, S., Espert, J., Meseguer, J.: A modular order-sorted equational generalization algorithm. Inf. Comput. **235**, 98–136 (2014)
5. Baader, F., Snyder, W.: Unification theory. In: Handbook of Automated Reasoning. Elsevier (1999)
6. Baader, F., Siekmann, J.H.: Unification theory. In: Handbook of Logic in Artificial Intelligence and Logic Programming, vol. 2, pp. 41–126. Oxford University Press (1994)

7. Bae, K., Escobar, S., Meseguer, J.: Abstract logical model checking of infinite-state systems using narrowing. In: Rewriting Techniques and Applications (RTA 2013). LIPIcs, vol. 21, pp. 81–96. Schloss Dagstuhl-Leibniz-Zentrum fuer Informatik (2013)
8. Bouchard, C., Gero, K.A., Lynch, C., Narendran, P.: On forward closure and the finite variant property. In: Fontaine, P., Ringeissen, C., Schmidt, R.A. (eds.) FroCoS 2013. LNCS (LNAI), vol. 8152, pp. 327–342. Springer, Heidelberg (2013). https://doi.org/10.1007/978-3-642-40885-4_23
9. Bouhoula, A., Jouannaud, J.P., Meseguer, J.: Specification and proof in membership equational logic. Theor. Comput. Sci. **236**, 35–132 (2000)
10. Bruni, R., Meseguer, J.: Semantic foundations for generalized rewrite theories. Theor. Comput. Sci. **360**(1–3), 386–414 (2006)
11. Cholewa, A., Escobar, S., Meseguer, J.: Constrained narrowing for conditional equational theories modulo axioms. Sci. Comput. Program. **112**, 24–57 (2015)
12. Cholewa, A., Meseguer, J., Escobar, S.: Variants of variants and the finite variant property. Technical report, CS Department University of Illinois at Urbana-Champaign, February 2014. http://hdl.handle.net/2142/47117
13. Ciobaca., S.: Verification of composition of security protocols with applications to electronic voting. Ph.D. thesis, ENS Cachan (2011)
14. Clavel, M., et al.: All About Maude - A High-Performance Logical Framework. LNCS, vol. 4350. Springer, Heidelberg (2007). https://doi.org/10.1007/978-3-540-71999-1
15. Clavel, M., et al.: Maude Manual (Version 3.1), October 2020. http://maude.cs.uiuc.edu
16. Clavel, M., Meseguer, J., Palomino, M.: Reflection in membership equational logic, many-sorted equational logic, horn logic with equality, and rewriting logic. Theor. Comput. Sci. **373**, 70–91 (2007)
17. Comon, H.: Unification et disunification: Théorie et applications. Ph.D. thesis, Institute National Polytechnique de Grenoble, France (1988)
18. Comon-Lundh, H., Delaune, S.: The finite variant property: how to get rid of some algebraic properties. In: Giesl, J. (ed.) RTA 2005. LNCS, vol. 3467, pp. 294–307. Springer, Heidelberg (2005). https://doi.org/10.1007/978-3-540-32033-3_22
19. CVC4: https://cvc4.github.io
20. Durán, F., et al.: Programming and symbolic computation in Maude. J. Log. Algebr. Meth. Program. **110** (2020). https://doi.org/10.1016/j.jlamp.2019.100497
21. Durán, F., Eker, S., Escobar, S., Martí-Oliet, N., Meseguer, J., Talcott, C.: Associative unification and symbolic reasoning modulo associativity in Maude. In: Rusu, V. (ed.) WRLA 2018. LNCS, vol. 11152, pp. 98–114. Springer, Cham (2018). https://doi.org/10.1007/978-3-319-99840-4_6
22. Durán, F., Lucas, S., Meseguer, J.: MTT: the Maude termination tool (system description). In: Armando, A., Baumgartner, P., Dowek, G. (eds.) IJCAR 2008. LNCS (LNAI), vol. 5195, pp. 313–319. Springer, Heidelberg (2008). https://doi.org/10.1007/978-3-540-71070-7_27
23. Durán, F., Lucas, S., Meseguer, J.: Termination modulo combinations of equational theories. In: Ghilardi, S., Sebastiani, R. (eds.) FroCoS 2009. LNCS (LNAI), vol. 5749, pp. 246–262. Springer, Heidelberg (2009). https://doi.org/10.1007/978-3-642-04222-5_15
24. Durán, F., Meseguer, J.: On the Church-Rosser and coherence properties of conditional order-sorted rewrite theories. J. Algebraic Log. Program. **81**, 816–850 (2012)

25. Eker, S.: Fast sort computations for order-sorted matching and unification. In: Agha, G., Danvy, O., Meseguer, J. (eds.) Formal Modeling: Actors, Open Systems, Biological Systems. LNCS, vol. 7000, pp. 299–314. Springer, Heidelberg (2011). https://doi.org/10.1007/978-3-642-24933-4_15

26. Escobar, S., Meadows, C., Meseguer, J.: Maude-NPA: cryptographic protocol analysis modulo equational properties. In: Aldini, A., Barthe, G., Gorrieri, R. (eds.) FOSAD 2007-2009. LNCS, vol. 5705, pp. 1–50. Springer, Heidelberg (2009). https://doi.org/10.1007/978-3-642-03829-7_1

27. Escobar, S., Sasse, R., Meseguer, J.: Folding variant narrowing and optimal variant termination. J. Algebraic Log. Program. **81**, 898–928 (2012)

28. Fay, M.: First-order unification in an equational theory. In: Proceedings of the Fourth Workshop on Automated Deduction, Austin, Texas, pp. 161–167 (1979)

29. Goguen, J., Meseguer, J.: Order-sorted algebra I: equational deduction for multiple inheritance, overloading, exceptions and partial operations. Theor. Comput. Sci. **105**, 217–273 (1992)

30. Gutiérrez, R., Meseguer, J.: Variant-based decidable satisfiability in initial algebras with predicates. In: Fioravanti, F., Gallagher, J.P. (eds.) LOPSTR 2017. LNCS, vol. 10855, pp. 306–322. Springer, Cham (2018). https://doi.org/10.1007/978-3-319-94460-9_18

31. Hendrix, J., Meseguer, J.: Order-sorted equational unification revisited. Electr. Notes Theor. Comput. Sci. **290**, 37–50 (2012)

32. Hendrix, J., Meseguer, J., Ohsaki, H.: A sufficient completeness checker for linear order-sorted specifications modulo axioms. In: Furbach, U., Shankar, N. (eds.) IJCAR 2006. LNCS (LNAI), vol. 4130, pp. 151–155. Springer, Heidelberg (2006). https://doi.org/10.1007/11814771_14

33. Herbrand, J.: Logical Writings. Reidel (1971)

34. Hullot, J.-M.: Canonical forms and unification. In: Bibel, W., Kowalski, R. (eds.) CADE 1980. LNCS, vol. 87, pp. 318–334. Springer, Heidelberg (1980). https://doi.org/10.1007/3-540-10009-1_25

35. Jouannaud, J.-P., Kirchner, C., Kirchner, H.: Incremental construction of unification algorithms in equational theories. In: Diaz, J. (ed.) ICALP 1983. LNCS, vol. 154, pp. 361–373. Springer, Heidelberg (1983). https://doi.org/10.1007/BFb0036921

36. Jouannaud, J.P., Kirchner, C.: Solving equations in abstract algebras: a rule-based survey of unification. In: Computational Logic - Essays in Honor of Alan Robinson, pp. 257–321. MIT Press (1991)

37. Jouannaud, J.P., Kirchner, H.: Completion of a set of rules modulo a set of equations. SIAM J. Comput. **15**, 1155–1194 (1986)

38. King, J.C.: Symbolic execution and program testing. Commun. ACM **19**(7), 385–394 (1976)

39. Lankford, D.S.: Canonical inference. Technical report ATP-32, Southwestn University (1975)

40. Levi, G., Sirovich, F.: Proving program properties, symbolic evaluation and logical procedural semantics. In: Bečvář, J. (ed.) MFCS 1975. LNCS, vol. 32, pp. 294–301. Springer, Heidelberg (1975). https://doi.org/10.1007/3-540-07389-2_211

41. Lucas, S., Meseguer, J.: Normal forms and normal theories in conditional rewriting. J. Log. Algebr. Meth. Program. **85**(1), 67–97 (2016)

42. Makanin, G.S.: The problem of solvability of equations in a free semigroup. Math. USSR Sbornik **32**(2), 129–198 (1977)

43. Martí-Oliet, N., Meseguer, J.: Rewriting logic as a logical and semantic framework. In: Gabbay, D., Guenthner, F. (eds.) Handbook of Philosophical Logic, 2nd edn, pp. 1–87. Kluwer Academic Publishers (2002). first published as SRI Technical report SRI-CSL-93-05, August 1993

44. Matiyasevich, Y.V.: Hilbert's 10th Problem. MIT Press, Cambridge (1993)

45. McCarthy, J., Abrahams, P., Edwards, D., Hart, T., Levin, M.: LISP 1.5 Programmer's Manual. MIT Press, Cambridge (1985)

46. Meier, S., Schmidt, B., Cremers, C., Basin, D.: The TAMARIN prover for the symbolic analysis of security protocols. In: Sharygina, N., Veith, H. (eds.) CAV 2013. LNCS, vol. 8044, pp. 696–701. Springer, Heidelberg (2013). https://doi.org/10.1007/978-3-642-39799-8_48

47. Meseguer, J.: Order-sorted parameterization and induction. In: Palsberg, J. (ed.) Semantics and Algebraic Specification. LNCS, vol. 5700, pp. 43–80. Springer, Heidelberg (2009). https://doi.org/10.1007/978-3-642-04164-8_4

48. Meseguer, J.: Variant satisfiability of parameterized strings. In: Escobar, S., Martí-Oliet, N. (eds.) WRLA 2020. LNCS, vol. 12328, pp. 96–113. Springer, Cham (2020). https://doi.org/10.1007/978-3-030-63595-4_6

49. Meseguer, J.: Variants in the infinitary unification wonderland. In: Escobar, S., Martí-Oliet, N. (eds.) WRLA 2020. LNCS, vol. 12328, pp. 75–95. Springer, Cham (2020). https://doi.org/10.1007/978-3-030-63595-4_5

50. Meseguer, J., Skeirik, S.: Inductive reasoning with equality predicates, contextual rewriting and variant-based simplification. In: Escobar, S., Martí-Oliet, N. (eds.) WRLA 2020. LNCS, vol. 12328, pp. 114–135. Springer, Cham (2020). https://doi.org/10.1007/978-3-030-63595-4_7

51. Meseguer, J., Thati, P.: Symbolic reachability analysis using narrowing and its application to the verification of cryptographic protocols. J. Higher-Order Symbolic Comput. **20**(1–2), 123–160 (2007)

52. Meseguer, J.: Conditional rewriting logic as a unified model of concurrency. Theor. Comput. Sci. **96**(1), 73–155 (1992)

53. Meseguer, J.: Membership algebra as a logical framework for equational specification. In: Presicce, F.P. (ed.) WADT 1997. LNCS, vol. 1376, pp. 18–61. Springer, Heidelberg (1998). https://doi.org/10.1007/3-540-64299-4_26

54. Meseguer, J.: Twenty years of rewriting logic. J. Algebraic Log. Program. **81**, 721–781 (2012)

55. Meseguer, J.: Strict coherence of conditional rewriting modulo axioms. Theor. Comput. Sci. **672**, 1–35 (2017)

56. Meseguer, J.: Variant-based satisfiability in initial algebras. Sci. Comput. Program. **154**, 3–41 (2018)

57. Meseguer, J.: Generalized rewrite theories, coherence completion and symbolic methods. J. Log. Algebraic Methods Program. (2019)

58. Meseguer, J., Goguen, J.: Order-sorted algebra solves the constructor-selector, multiple representation and coercion problems. Inf. Comput. **103**(1), 114–158 (1993)

59. Meseguer, J., Goguen, J., Smolka, G.: Order-sorted unification. J. Symbolic Comput. **8**, 383–413 (1989)

60. Nelson, G., Oppen, D.C.: Simplification by cooperating decision procedures. ACM Trans. Program. Lang. Syst. **1**(2), 245–257 (1979)

61. Ölveczky, P.C.: Designing Reliable Distributed Systems. UTCS. Springer, London (2017). https://doi.org/10.1007/978-1-4471-6687-0

62. Oppen, D.C.: Complexity, convexity and combinations of theories. Theor. Comput. Sci. **12**, 291–302 (1980)

63. Peterson, G.E., Stickel, M.E.: Complete sets of reductions for some equational theories. J. Assoc. Comput. Mach. **28**(2), 233–264 (1981)
64. Plotkin, G.: Building-in equational theories. Mach. Intell. **7**, 73–90 (1972)
65. Robinson, J.A.: A machine-oriented logic based on the resolution principle. J. Assoc. Comput. Mach. **12**, 23–41 (1965)
66. Schmidt-Schauß, M. (ed.): Computational Aspects of an Order-Sorted Logic with Term Declarations. LNCS, vol. 395. Springer, Heidelberg (1989). https://doi.org/10.1007/BFb0024065
67. Seidenberg, A.: A new decision method for elementary algebra. Ann. Math. **60**, 365–374 (1954)
68. Skeirik, S., Meseguer, J.: Metalevel algorithms for variant satisfiability. J. Log. Algebr. Meth. Program. **96**, 81–110 (2018)
69. Skeirik, S., Stefanescu, A., Meseguer, J.: A constructor-based reachability logic for rewrite theories. Fundam. Inform. **173**(4), 315–382 (2020)
70. Slagle, J.R.: Automated theorem-proving for theories with simplifiers commutativity, and associativity. J. ACM **21**(4), 622–642 (1974)
71. Smolka, G., Nutt, W., Goguen, J., Meseguer, J.: Order-sorted equational computation. In: Nivat, M., Aït-Kaci, H. (eds.) Resolution of Equations in Algebraic Structures, vol. 2, pp. 297–367. Academic Press (1989)
72. Tarski, A.: A Decision Method for Elementary Algebra and Geometry. University of California Press (1951). prepared with the assistance of J.C.C. McKinsey
73. Viry, P.: Equational rules for rewriting logic. Theor. Comput. Sci. **285**, 487–517 (2002)
74. Yices: https://yices.csl.sri.com

Runtime Complexity Analysis
of Logically Constrained Rewriting

Sarah Winkler[1(✉)] and Georg Moser[2]

[1] Free University of Bolzano, Bolzano, Italy
`sarwinkler@unibz.it`
[2] University of Innsbruck, Innsbruck, Austria
`georg.moser@uibk.ac.at`

Abstract. Logically constrained rewrite systems (LCTRSs) are a versatile and efficient rewriting formalism that can be used to model programs from various programming paradigms, as well as simplification systems in compilers and SMT solvers. In this paper, we investigate techniques to analyse the worst-case runtime complexity of LCTRSs. For that, we exploit synergies between previously developed decomposition techniques for standard term rewriting by Avanzini *et al.* in conjunction with alternating time and size bound approximations for integer programs by Brockschmidt *et al.* and adapt these techniques suitably to LCTRSs. Furthermore, we provide novel modularization techniques to exploit loop bounds from recurrence equations which yield sublinear bounds. We have implemented the method in T꜀T to test the viability of our method.

1 Introduction

Rewriting with constraints over background theories is a highly versatile model of computation and tool for analysis. While user-defined data types are modelled by free function symbols, arbitrary decidable theories can be incorporated, such as integer or bit-vector arithmetic, lists, or array theory. Constraints over these theories can be effectively handled by SMT solvers. Different rewrite formalisms capture this idea [11,19,21]. Here we use the recent notion of *logically constrained term rewrite systems* (*LCTRSs* for short), due to Kop et al. [10,20,28,29].

LCTRSs can abstract programs in a variety of paradigms, comprising imperative, functional, and logic languages. They also subsume integer transition systems (ITSs), which constitute a frequently used program abstraction [8,15,19] but do—in contrast to LCTRSs—not support (non-tail) recursion. On the other hand, LCTRSs can also model simplification routines for expressions, which are crucial procedures in compilers or SMT solvers. For all of these application areas, LCTRSs offer a *uniform* toolset to analyse *termination* (or non-termination) [27,33], *reachability* [10], *uniqueness* [41], or *program equivalence* [20].

© Springer Nature Switzerland AG 2021
M. Fernández (Ed.): LOPSTR 2020, LNCS 12561, pp. 37–55, 2021.
https://doi.org/10.1007/978-3-030-68446-4_2

However, techniques for resource analysis of LCTRSs are so far lacking. This is despite the fact that in their application domains (program analysis, simplification systems), execution time is crucial. As a remedy, this paper investigates methods to analyse (worst-case) innermost runtime complexity of logically constrained rewrite systems. To this end, we unify and generalise the complexity framework for standard rewriting by Avanzini and Moser [4] with the approach by Brockschmidt *et al.* to alternate time and size bound analysis for ITSs [8], and moreover propose processors for modularisation and sublinear bounds.

Contributions. We present a novel resource analysis framework for logically constrained rewrite systems (Sect. 4) coached in the modular processor framework of TcT [5]. Precisely,

1. we present the first fully-automated runtime complexity analysis of LTCRSs;
2. we unify the complexity framework for standard (innermost) rewriting by Avanzini and Moser [4] and the alternating time and size bound approximations for ITSs by Brockschmidt *et al.* [8],
3. generalising this, we introduce a novel modularisation processor, the *splitting processor*;
4. we present a novel processor, dubbed *recurrence processor* to derive sublinear bounds based on recurrences as described by the Master Theorem;
5. we illustrate the viability of our method by providing a prototype implementation as a dedicated module tct-lctrs in TcT, and evaluate it on ITS benchmarks.

In the remainder of the section, we highlight potential application areas of LCTRSs to emphasise their versatility. In the next section (Sect. 2) we give a high-level account of our technical achievements, providing a step-by-step explanation how the runtime complexity of a natural representation of mergesort can be optimally analysed in our framework. In this section, we also discuss to what extent our results can be applied to the below given examples. In Sect. 3 we summarise the foundations of LCTRSs, while in Sect. 4 we detail the complexity framework used. Processors carried over from the ITS setting are presented in Sect. 5, and the novel processors are introduced in Sect. 6. Implementational choices and experimental results are summarized in Sect. 7. Finally, in Sect. 8 we conclude. Some proofs were moved to an extended version [42].

Logically Constrained Rewrite Systems. We emphasise motivational examples from three different domains, focusing on imperative and logic programs, as well as compiler optimisations.

Example 1. The following recursive ITS $\mathcal{R}_1$, due to Albert et al. [1], corresponds to an imperative mergesort implementation after computing loop summaries. It is naturally coached into the LCTRS framework, with the theory of integers as background theory.

(1) $\mathsf{init}(x,y,z) \to \mathsf{m}(x,y,z)$ (2) $\mathsf{m}_3(x,y,z) \to \mathsf{merge}(y,z,z)$

(3) $\mathsf{m}_1(x,y,z) \to \mathsf{m}(y,y,z)$ (4) $\mathsf{merge}(x,y,z) \to \mathsf{merge}(x-1,y,z)\ [x \geqslant 1 \wedge y \geqslant 1]$

(5) $\mathsf{m}_0(x,y,z) \to \mathsf{split}(x,y,z)$ (6) $\mathsf{split}(x,y,z) \to \mathsf{split}(x-2,y,z)\ [x \geqslant 2]$

(7) $\mathsf{m}_2(x,y,z) \to \mathsf{m}(z,y,z)$ (8) $\mathsf{merge}(x,y,z) \to \mathsf{merge}(x,y-1,z)\ [x \geqslant 1 \wedge y \geqslant 1]$

(9) $\mathsf{m}(x,y,z) \to \langle \mathsf{m}_0(x,u,v), \mathsf{m}_1(x,u,v), \mathsf{m}_2(x,u,v), \mathsf{m}_3(x,u,v) \rangle$

$$[x \geqslant 2 \wedge u \geqslant 0 \wedge v \geqslant 0 \wedge x+1 \geqslant 2u \wedge 2u \geqslant x \wedge x \geqslant 2v \wedge 2v+1 \geqslant x]$$

Here a rule of the form $\ell \to r\ [c]$ means that an instance of ℓ is replaced by the respective instance of r provided that the instance of c is satisfied.

Similarly, (constraint) logic programs can be nicely suited to LCTRSs.

Example 2. Consider the following simple Prolog program from the benchmarks collected by Mesnard and Neumerkl [31].

```
max_length(Ls,M,Len)  :- max1(Ls,0,M), len(Ls,Len).
         len([H|T],L)  :- len(T,LT), L is LT + 1.          len([],0).
       max1([H|T],N,M) :- H <= N, max1(T,N,M).            max1([],M,M).
       max1([H|T],N,M) :- H > N, max1(T,H,M).
```

Assuming an instantiated list Ls, max_length(Ls,M,Len) is deterministic and returns the maximal list entry and the length of the list. This function becomes representable as the following LCTRS $\mathcal{R}_2$ over the theory of integers and lists:

$$\mathsf{max\_length}(ls,m,l) \to \langle \mathsf{max}(ls,0,m), \mathsf{len}(ls,l) \rangle$$

$$\mathsf{len}(xs,l) \to \mathsf{len}(t,l-1)\ [xs \approx h :: t] \qquad\qquad \mathsf{len}([],0) \to \langle\rangle$$

$$\mathsf{max}(xs,n,m) \to \mathsf{max}(t,n,m)\ [h \leqslant n \wedge xs \approx h :: t] \quad \mathsf{max}([],m,m) \to \langle\rangle$$

$$\mathsf{max}(xs,n,m) \to \mathsf{max}(t,h,m)\ [h > n \wedge xs \approx h :: t]$$

Here, :: denotes the cons operator and $\langle \cdot, \cdot \rangle$, $\langle\rangle$ are additional constructor symbols to collect the recursive calls of a rule. Conceptually LCTRSs appear as a good fit to express *constraint* logic programs as well, making use of the fact that constraints are natively supported.

In order to emphasise that LCTRSs are not confined to static program analysis, we present a final example which is concerned with program optimisation.

Example 3. The Instcombine pass in the LLVM compilation suite performs *peephole optimisations* to simplify expressions in the intermediate representation. The current optimisation set contains over 1000 simplification rules to e.g. replace multiplications by shifts or perform bitwidth changes. About 500 of them have recently been translated into the domain-specific language Alive [30], and subsequently into LCTRSs [41], resulting in rules of the following shape:

$$\mathsf{add}(x,x) \to \mathsf{shift\_left}(x, \#\mathsf{x}1)$$

$$\mathsf{add}(\mathsf{add}(\mathsf{xor}(\mathsf{or}(x,a),y), \#\mathsf{x}1), w) \to \mathsf{sub}(w, \mathsf{and}(x,b))\ [a \approx {\sim}b]$$

$$\mathsf{add}(\mathsf{xor}(x,a),z) \to \mathsf{sub}(a+z,x)\ [\mathsf{isPowerOf2}(a + \#\mathsf{x}1) \wedge \ldots]\,.$$

These rules are expressed over the background theory of bit-vectors. Naturally, as a compiler pass this simplification suite is a performance-critical routine, hence an automated complexity analysis is of great interest.

2   Step by Step to an Optimal Bound

Consider the rewrite system $\mathcal{R}_1$ from Example 1, and a rewrite sequence starting with an instance of $\mathsf{init}(x_0, y_0, z_0)$. Below we sketch the steps to obtain an upper bound on the runtime complexity of $\mathcal{R}_1$, expressed in $|x_0|$, $|y_0|$, and $|z_0|$, where $|\cdot|$ denotes the absolute value.

An automated runtime complexity analysis of mergesort is notoriously diffi-cult: For this example, CoFloCo [16,17] can only derive a quadratic bound, while KoAT [8] (as well as AProVE [22]) even proposes an exponential bound. PUBS [1] can produce an $\mathcal{O}(n \cdot \log(n))$ bound, using a special *level-counting* feature, which however negatively affects its overall success rate. Due to the work presented in this paper, our complexity analyser TcT can automatically prove the optimal $\mathcal{O}(n \cdot \log(n))$ upper bound. This is obtained by the following recipe.

1. We first compute *dependency tuples* of all rules to focus the analysis on recursive calls (see Definition 4). Then a *dependency graph* approximation is computed to estimate computation paths, where the numbers refer to the respective dependency tuples of rules in Example 1:

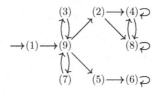

2. Next, we derive bounds on the *size of variables* in left hand sides of rules, in terms of the sizes of the variables in the initial term $\mathsf{init}(x_0, y_0, z_0)$. For example, it is easy to check that for rule (9), $|x|$, $|y|$, and $|z|$ are bounded by $|x_0|$, $|y_0|$, and $|z_0|$, respectively, and all variables in other rules are bounded by $|x_0|$. This is established by the *size bounds processor* (Lemma 3). Formally, we adapt techniques developed for ITSs for that purpose [8].
3. We first derive time bounds for the SCCs $\{2, 4, 8\}$ and $\{6\}$ separately (Lemma 2). Thus, using the size bounds from above and suitable *interpre-tations* [4] (also called polynomial ranking functions [8]) for LCTRSs, one can derive linear runtime bounds $2|x_0| + 1$ and $|x_0|$ for these subproblems, respectively.
4. In order to analyse the SCC $\{3, 7, 9\}$, we first apply *chaining* to combine rule (9) with (3) and (7), respectively (eliminating symbols m_1 and m_2).
5. With respect to the modified rule (9) and the derived subproblem bounds, we exploit the *loop processor* (Lemma 5) to observe that its runtime can thus be overestimated by the following *recurrence* equations.

$$f(|x|, |y|, |z|) = 2 \cdot f(|x|/2, |x|/2, |x|/2) + 3|x| + 1 \quad f(1, |y|, |z|) = 0 \quad (1)$$

Solving the recurrences by the Master Theorem, implies an overall runtime complexity of $\mathcal{O}(|x_0| \cdot \log(|x_0|))$ for $\mathcal{R}_1$, as $|x|$ in rule (9) is bound by $|x_0|$.

Wrt. $\mathcal{R}_2$ from Example 2, we can fully automatically infer an (asymptotic) optimal linear bound on the runtime complexity for the given instantiation. Here, we take an instance of max_length(xs, z, l) as initial term. As for comparison, note that the corresponding logic program cannot be handled by a dedicated variant of AProVE [23] geared towards runtime complexity analysis of logic programs. Only termination can be shown by the most recent version of AProVE [22]. A priori, our approach is restricted to logic programs with instantiation patterns that ensure determinism and avoid failure, but in the conclusion we discuss how to overcome this limitation.

Finally, Example 3 cannot yet be handled, as a successful analysis requires the extension of the proposed framework to *(innermost) derivational complexity* (i.e., the setting of arbitrary starting terms that may contain nested defined symbols). This is subject to future work. However, we conceive the work established in this paper as a solid first step towards the automated analysis of such systems.

3   Logically Constrained Term Rewriting

We assume familiarity with term rewriting [6,37], but briefly recapitulate the notion of logically constrained rewriting [20,28] that our approach is based on. We consider an infinite, sorted set of variables $\mathcal{V}$ and a sorted signature $\mathcal{F} = \mathcal{F}_T \uplus \mathcal{F}_L$ such that $\mathcal{T}(\mathcal{F}, \mathcal{V})$ denotes the set of terms over this disjoint signature. Symbols in $\mathcal{F}_T$ are called *term symbols*, while symbols in $\mathcal{F}_L$ are *theory symbols*. A term in $\mathcal{T}(\mathcal{F}_L, \mathcal{V})$ is a *theory term*. For a non-variable term $t = f(t_1, \ldots, t_n)$, we write root(t) to obtain the top-most symbol f. A *position* p is an integer sequence used to identify subterms, and the subterm of t at position p is denoted $t|_p$. We write $\mathcal{P}os(t)$ for the set of positions in a term t, and given a set of function symbols $\mathcal{F}'$, $\mathcal{P}os_{\mathcal{F}'}(t)$ are those positions $p \in \mathcal{P}os(t)$ such that $t|_p$ is rooted by a symbol in $\mathcal{F}'$. A *substitution* σ is a mapping from variables to terms with finite domain, and $t\sigma$ denotes the application of σ to a term t.

Theory terms $\mathcal{T}(\mathcal{F}_L, \mathcal{V})$ have a fixed semantics: we assume a mapping $\mathcal{I}$ that assigns to every sort ι occurring in $\mathcal{F}_L$ a carrier set $\mathcal{I}(\iota)$. Moreover, we assume that for every element $a \in \mathcal{I}(\iota)$ there is exactly one constant symbol $c_a \in \mathcal{F}_L$, called a *value*. The set of all value symbols is denoted $\mathcal{V}$al. For instance, if the sort of integers occurs in $\mathcal{F}_L$ then $\mathcal{V}$al $\subseteq \mathcal{F}_L$ contains a value c_i for every $i \in \mathbb{Z}$.

Moreover, we assume a fixed interpretation $\mathcal{J}$ that assigns to every theory symbol $f \in \mathcal{F}_L$ a function $f_{\mathcal{J}}$ of appropriate sort, and such that $(c_a)_{\mathcal{J}} = a$ for value symbols c_a, i.e., value symbols are interpreted as the represented element. The interpretation $\mathcal{J}$ naturally extends to theory terms without variables by setting $[f(t_1, \ldots, t_n)]_{\mathcal{J}} = f_{\mathcal{J}}([t_1]_{\mathcal{J}}, \ldots, [t_n]_{\mathcal{J}})$. In particular, we assume a sort bool such that $\mathcal{I}(\text{bool}) = \{\top, \bot\}$ with values $\mathcal{V}$al$_{\text{bool}} = \{\text{true}, \text{false}\}$ such that true$_{\mathcal{J}} = \top$, and false$_{\mathcal{J}} = \bot$. We also assume that $\mathcal{F}_L$ contains equality symbols $\approx_\iota$ for every theory sort ι, and a symbol $\wedge$ interpreted as logical conjunction.

Theory terms of sort bool are called *constraints*, and a *constrained term* is a pair (t, φ) of a term t and a constraint φ. A substitution γ is a *valuation* if its range is a subset of $\mathcal{V}al$. A constraint φ is *valid*, denoted $\models \varphi$, if $[\varphi\gamma]_{\mathcal{J}} = \top$ for all valuations γ, and *satisfiable* if $[\varphi\gamma]_{\mathcal{J}} = \top$ for some valuation γ. We write $\psi \models \varphi$ if all valuations that satisfy ψ also satisfy φ.

Logically Constrained Rewriting. A constrained rewrite rule is a triple $\ell \to r \ [\varphi]$ where $\ell, r \in \mathcal{T}(\mathcal{F}, \mathcal{V})$, $\ell \notin \mathcal{V}$, φ is a constraint, and $\mathsf{root}(\ell) \in \mathcal{F}_T$. If $\varphi = \mathsf{true}$ then the constraint is omitted. For a rule $\rho \colon \ell \to r \ [\varphi]$ we use $lhs(\rho) = \ell$ and $rhs(\rho) = r$ to denote its left- and right-hand sides, respectively. A set of constrained rewrite rules is called a *logically constrained term rewrite system* (*LCTRS* for short). For an LCTRS $\mathcal{R}$, its *defined* symbols $\mathcal{F}_{\mathcal{D}}$ are all root symbols of left-hand sides, that is, $\mathcal{F}_{\mathcal{D}} = \{\mathsf{root}(\ell) \mid \ell \to r \ [\varphi] \in \mathcal{R}\}$. In the remainder we assume that LCTRSs are left-linear, that is, all variables occur at most once in the left-hand side ℓ of a rule $\ell \to r \ [\varphi]$.[1] An LCTRS $\mathcal{R}$ is a *transition system* if all rules in $\mathcal{R}$ are of the form $f(\ell_1, \ldots, \ell_n) \to g(r_1, \ldots, r_m) \ [\varphi]$ such that $f, g \in \mathcal{F}_T$, all $\ell_i \in \mathcal{V}$, and all r_j are in $\mathcal{T}(\mathcal{F}_L, \mathcal{V})$; if moreover the background theory associated with $\mathcal{F}_L$ is the theory of integers then $\mathcal{R}$ is an *integer transition system* (ITS).

The fixed rewrite system $\mathcal{R}_{\mathsf{calc}}$ is the (infinite) set of rules $f(\ell_1, \ldots, \ell_n) \to u$ such that $f \in \mathcal{F}_L \setminus \mathcal{V}al$, $\ell_i \in \mathcal{V}al$ for all $1 \leqslant i \leqslant n$, and $u \in \mathcal{V}al$ is the value symbol of $[f(\ell_1, \ldots, \ell_n)]_{\mathcal{J}}$. A rewrite step using $\mathcal{R}_{\mathsf{calc}}$ is called a *calculation step* and denoted $\to_{\mathsf{calc}}$. A *rule step* $s \to_\rho^\sigma t$ using a rule $\rho \colon \ell \to r \ [\varphi]$ and substitution σ satisfies $s = C[\ell\sigma]$, $t = C[r\sigma]$, and σ respects φ; where a substitution σ is said to *respect* a constraint φ if $\varphi\sigma$ is valid and $\sigma(x) \in \mathcal{V}al$ for all $x \in \mathcal{V}ar(\varphi)$. The substitution in the notation $\to_\rho^\sigma$ is mostly omitted, and a rule step simply denoted $\to_\rho$. For an LCTRS $\mathcal{R}$, we denote the relation $\to_{\mathsf{calc}} \cup \{\to_\rho\}_{\rho \in \mathcal{R}}$ by $\to_{\mathcal{R}}$. The above rewrite step is *innermost*, denoted $s \xrightarrow{\mathsf{i}}_\rho t$, if all proper subterms of $\ell\sigma$ are in normal form with respect to $\to_{\mathcal{R}}$. Given binary relations R and S, we write R/S for $S^* \cdot R \cdot S^*$. For LCTRSs $\mathcal{R}$ and $\mathcal{S}$ we abbreviate $\xrightarrow{\mathsf{i}}_{\mathcal{R}} / \xrightarrow{\mathsf{i}}_{\mathcal{S}}$ by $\xrightarrow{\mathsf{i}}_{\mathcal{R}/\mathcal{S}}$, and $\xrightarrow{\mathsf{i}}_{\mathcal{R}} / \to_{\mathsf{calc}}$ by $\xrightarrow{\mathsf{i}}_{\mathcal{R}/\mathsf{calc}}$.

Example 4 (continued from Example 2). The LCTRS $\mathcal{R}_2$ indicated in Example 2, expressing the predicate `max_length`/3, makes use of the sorts int, list and bool. Furthermore, $\mathcal{F}_L$ consist of symbols :: and [] for lists, $\cdot$, $+$, $-$, $\leqslant$, and $\geqslant$ as well as values n for all $n \in \mathbb{Z}$, with the usual interpretations on $\mathbb{Z}$ and lists of integers. Then $\mathcal{R}$ admits the following rewrite steps:

$$\mathsf{len}([1, 2], 2) \to \mathsf{len}([2], 2 - 1) \to_{\mathsf{calc}} \mathsf{len}([2], 1) \to \mathsf{len}([], 1 - 1) \to_{\mathsf{calc}} \mathsf{len}([], 0)$$

Note that in LCTRS rewriting, calculation steps like the subtractions in Example 4 are explicit in the $\to_{\mathsf{calc}}$ relation, in contrast to ITSs or related formalisms [32], where simplification is implicit. Moreover, innermost rewriting is

---

[1] Non-left-linear rules are rare in practice; and moreover repeated occurrences of a variable x in ℓ can be substituted by a fresh variable x', adding $x \approx x'$ to φ. Though this implies that x can only be substituted by theory terms in rewrite sequences, for innermost evaluation this is not a limitation.

a rather natural restriction for LCTRSs: By the definition of a rule step using some rule ρ, variables in the constraint of ρ need to be substituted by values. Hence non-innermost steps are only possible if nested redexes occur below unconstrained variables. For instance, in a term $f(f(2))$ only the inner f call constitutes a redex for the rule $f(x) \rightarrow x \; [x > 0]$.

Algebras. We assume mappings $|\cdot|_\iota : \mathcal{I}(\iota) \rightarrow \mathbb{N}$ for every sort ι, playing the role of norms to measure size. For instance, one might take the absolute values for integers, the size function for arrays, and the unsigned integer value for bit-vectors. The subscript ι in $|t|_\iota$ is omitted if the sort of t is clear from the context.

We consider well-founded algebras $\mathcal{A}$ over the natural numbers and the Booleans, with interpretation functions $f^{\mathcal{A}}$ for all $f \in \mathcal{F}_T \cup \mathcal{F}_L$, cf. [6,37]. By $t^{\mathcal{A}}$ we denote the interpretation of a term t based on $\mathcal{A}$, and by $[\alpha]_{\mathcal{A}}(t)$ the interpretation of t based on $\mathcal{A}$ and valuation α. In order to bound complexity, we use algebras that incorporate the given complexity measures:

Definition 1. *A* measure interpretation *is given by an algebra $\mathcal{M}$ with carrier $\mathbb{N}$, and measures $|\cdot|_\iota$ for all sorts ι. The interpretation $t^{\mathcal{M}}$ of a term t is $|t|_\iota$ if $t \in \mathcal{V}$ has sort ι, and $f^{\mathcal{M}}(t_1^{\mathcal{M}}, \ldots, t_m^{\mathcal{M}})$ if $t = f(t_1, \ldots, t_m)$. In addition, we demand that $f^{\mathcal{M}}([t_1]_{\mathcal{J}}^{\mathcal{M}}, \ldots, [t_n]_{\mathcal{J}}^{\mathcal{M}}) \geqslant [f(t_1, \ldots, t_n)]_{\mathcal{J}}^{\mathcal{M}}$ for all values $t_1, \ldots, t_n$.*

In the following we suit interpretations (aka ranking functions) to LCTRSs. The ternary relation $>_{[\cdot]}^{\mathcal{M}}$ is defined as $s >_{[\varphi]}^{\mathcal{M}} t$ if and only if $[\alpha]_{\mathcal{M}}(s) > [\alpha]_{\mathcal{M}}(t)$ is satisfied for all valuations α that respect φ. Similarly, $s \geqslant_{[\varphi]}^{\mathcal{M}} t$ if and only if $[\alpha]_{\mathcal{M}}(s) \geqslant [\alpha]_{\mathcal{M}}(t)$ holds for all valuations α that respect φ.

Definition 2. *We call an LCTRS $\mathcal{R}$ weakly compatible with a measure interpretation $\mathcal{M}$ if $\ell \geqslant_{[\varphi]}^{\mathcal{M}} r$ for all $\ell \rightarrow r \; [\varphi] \in \mathcal{R}$, and strictly compatible if $\mathcal{R}$ is weakly compatible and in addition $\ell >_{[\varphi]}^{\mathcal{M}} r$ for some $\ell \rightarrow r \; [\varphi] \in \mathcal{R}$.*

Example 5. Consider the measure interpretation $\mathcal{M}$ such that $\mathsf{m}_3^{\mathcal{M}}(x, y, z) = y$, $\mathsf{merge}^{\mathcal{M}}(x, y, z) = x$, $x +^{\mathcal{M}} y = x +_{\mathbb{N}} y$, $x -^{\mathcal{M}} y = \max(x -_{\mathbb{N}} y, 0)$, $\geqslant^{\mathcal{M}}$ is $\geqslant^{\mathbb{N}}$, and $v^{\mathcal{M}} = \max(v, 0)$ for all $v \in \mathbb{Z}$. The LCTRS $\mathcal{R}'$ consisting of the rules (2), (4), and (8) from Example 1 is strictly compatible with $\mathcal{M}$, since the rules (2) and (8) are weakly decreasing, while (4) is strictly decreasing.

4 Complexity Framework

An LCTRS $\mathcal{R}$ is *terminating* if $\rightarrow_{\mathcal{R}}$ is well-founded. In applications like static analysis, termination of a program is often not enough and more precise resource guarantees are needed. In this section we propose suitable runtime complexity notions for LCTRSs.

Following common notions in complexity analysis [4], the *derivation height* of a term t wrt. a binary relation $\rightarrow$ is defined as follows: $\mathsf{dh}(t_0, \rightarrow) := \sup\{k \mid \exists t_1, \ldots, t_k. \; t_0 \rightarrow \cdots \rightarrow t_k\}$. We assume that an LCTRS $\mathcal{R}$ is associated with a unique *initial state* (t_0, φ_0) such that φ_0 is a constraint and $t_0 = \mathsf{init}(\overline{x})$ is the *initial term*, for a vector of *input variables* $\overline{x} = (x_1, \ldots, x_n)$ and a function symbol init that does not occur on any right-hand side. The intention is that we consider only rewrite sequences starting at $t_0\sigma$, such that σ is a valuation that respects φ_0. Sometimes s_0 will be used as a shorthand for (t_0, φ_0).

For $\overline{u}, \overline{v} \in \mathbb{N}^k$, let $\overline{u} \leqslant_k \overline{v}$ abbreviate $\bigwedge_{i=1}^{k} u_i \leqslant v_i$. Given $\overline{t} = (t_1, \ldots, t_k)$, $|\overline{t}|$ denotes $(|t_1|, \ldots, |t_k|)$, and $\overline{t}\sigma$ denotes $(t_1\sigma, \ldots, t_k\sigma)$ for any substitution σ. For a term t, we write $\overline{Var}(t)$ for a vector containing $Var(t)$ in a fixed order.

Definition 3. *For an LCTRS $\mathcal{R}$ and a constrained term (t, φ) such that $\overline{x} = \overline{Var}(t)$, the (innermost) runtime complexity $\mathsf{rc}_{\mathcal{R}}^{(t,\varphi)} \colon \mathbb{N}^n \to \mathbb{N} \cup \{\omega\}$ is defined as*

$$\mathsf{rc}_{\mathcal{R}}^{(t,\varphi)}(\overline{m}) = \sup \{\mathsf{dh}(t\sigma, \xrightarrow{\mathrm{i}}_{\mathcal{R}/\mathsf{calc}}) \mid |\overline{x}\sigma| \leqslant_n \overline{m} \text{ for some } \sigma \text{ that respects } \varphi\}.$$

Thus, the runtime complexity of an LCTRS is the maximal number of innermost *rule* steps in a rewrite sequence that starts with a size-bounded instance of the initial state (t, φ); calculation steps are not counted. This is common in cost analysis, it also corresponds to the runtime complexity of a program or ITS [8], where the number of transitions are counted but not simplifications of expressions.

Dependency pairs are commonly used in termination and complexity analysis of rewrite systems. For termination of LCTRSs they were already used in earlier work [27]. For complexity analysis, stronger notions were developed for standard rewriting: *dependency tuples* (DTs) [34], *weak* [25], and *grouped* dependency pairs [4]. Since we consider innermost rewriting, we can use an LCTRS variant of dependency tuples. To that end, for every defined symbol f we consider a fresh symbol $f^\sharp$, and for a term $t = f(t_1, \ldots, t_n)$ write $t^\sharp$ to denote $f^\sharp(t_1, \ldots, t_n)$.

Definition 4. *Consider a rule $\rho \colon \ell \to r\ [\varphi]$ such that $\mathcal{P}os_{\mathcal{F}_D}(r)$ is sorted as $p_1, \ldots, p_k$ with respect to a fixed order on positions. Then the* dependency tuple *$\mathsf{DT}(\rho)$ of ρ is the constrained rule $\ell^\sharp \to \langle (r|_{p_1})^\sharp, \ldots, (r|_{p_k})^\sharp \rangle_k\ [\varphi]$. For an LCTRS $\mathcal{R}$, $\mathsf{DT}(\mathcal{R}) = \bigcup_{\rho \in \mathcal{R}} \mathsf{DT}(\rho)$.*

Here $\langle \ldots \rangle_k$ is a fresh tuple symbol for every arity k (but the subscript will be dropped for simplicity).

Definition 5 (Dependency Graph). *Let $\mathcal{R}$ be an LCTRS and $\mathcal{D} \subseteq \mathsf{DT}(\mathcal{R})$. The* dependency graph *(DG) is the directed graph with node set $\mathcal{D}$ and edges from $s^\sharp \to \langle t_1^\sharp, \ldots, t_n^\sharp \rangle\ [\varphi]$ to $u^\sharp \to v\ [\psi]$ if there is some $t_i^\sharp$ such that $t_i^\sharp \sigma \to_{\mathcal{R}}^* u^\sharp \tau$, for some substitutions σ and τ and some i, $1 \leqslant i \leqslant n$.*

The DG is not computable in general, but approximation techniques are well-known [5,22,27,34]. For instance, the graph in Sect. 2 constitutes a dependency graph approximation for the LCTRS from Example 1. Following Noschiniski et al. [34], we assume particular interpretation functions for the tuple operators $\langle \ldots \rangle$. To this end, let a *DT-measure interpretation* $\mathcal{M}$ be a measure interpretation that interprets $\langle t_1, \ldots, t_k \rangle^{\mathcal{M}} = t_1 + \cdots + t_k$, for all $k \geqslant 0$.

Let the set of *bound expressions* UB be inductively defined as follows: (i) $|x|_\iota \in \mathrm{UB}$ for $x \in \mathcal{V}$ of sort ι, (ii) $\mathbb{Z} \subseteq \mathrm{UB}$ and $\omega \in \mathrm{UB}$, (iii) if $p, q \in \mathrm{UB}$ then

$p + q$, pq, and $max(p, q)$ are in UB, and (iv) if $p \in$ UB and $k \in \mathbb{N}$ then k^p, p/k, and $\log_k(p)$ are in UB. Given $p, q \in$ UB, we write $p \leqslant q$ if $[\alpha]_{\mathbb{N}}(p) \leqslant [\alpha]_{\mathbb{N}}(q)$ for all substitutions $\alpha : \mathcal{V} \to \mathbb{N}$. For a bound expression $p \in$ UB and $\overline{m} \in \mathbb{N}^n$ we also write $p(\overline{m})$ to denote the substituted bound expression $p[m_i/x_i]_{1 \leqslant i \leqslant n}$, assuming $\overline{x} \in \mathcal{V}^n$ are the variables in the initial term $t_0 = \text{init}(\overline{x})$.

A triple $P = ((t, \varphi), \mathcal{D}, \mathcal{R})$ of a constrained term (t, φ), a set of DTs $\mathcal{D}$, and an LCTRS $\mathcal{R}$ is called a *(complexity) problem*. Following Brockschmidt et al. [8], we next define time and size bound approximations.

Definition 6. *For a complexity problem* $((t, \varphi), \mathcal{D}, \mathcal{R})$ *with* $\overline{x} = \overline{Var}(t)$, *a function* $T : \mathcal{D} \to$ UB *is a* runtime approximation *if, for all* $\rho \in \mathcal{D}$ *and* $\overline{m} \in \mathbb{N}^n$,

$$T(\rho)(\overline{m}) \geqslant \sup \{\text{dh}(t\sigma, \xrightarrow{i}_{\{\rho\}/\mathcal{D} \cup \mathcal{R}}) \mid |\overline{x}\sigma| \leqslant_n \overline{m} \text{ and } \sigma \text{ respects } \varphi\}.$$

In words, a runtime approximation $T(\rho)$ over-approximates how often a DT $\rho \in \mathcal{D}$ can be used in a rewrite sequence starting from the initial state, expressed in terms of the input variables. For instance, consider Example 1 and let $(1^{\#})$ be the DT corresponding to rule (1). Then the function T such that $T(1^{\#}) = 1$ and $T(\rho)(|x_0|, |y_0|, |z_0|) = |x_0|^2$ for all other DTs $\rho \in \mathcal{D}$ is a valid (though not optimal) runtime approximation.

For a complexity problem $((t, \varphi), \mathcal{D}, \mathcal{R})$, the set of *entry variables* EV is the set of all tuples (ρ, y) such that $\rho \in \mathcal{D}$ and $y \in \mathit{Var}(\mathit{lhs}(\rho))$.

Definition 7. *For a complexity problem* $((t, \varphi), \mathcal{D}, \mathcal{R})$ *with* $\overline{x} = \overline{Var}(t)$, *a function* $S : $ EV $\to$ UB *is a* size approximation *if*

$$S(\rho, y)(\overline{m}) \geqslant \sup \{|y\tau| \mid \exists \sigma, u. \; t\sigma \xrightarrow{i}{}^{*}_{\mathcal{R} \cup \mathcal{D}} \cdot \xrightarrow{i}{}^{\tau}_{\rho} u, \; |\overline{x}\sigma| \leqslant_n \overline{m}\}$$

for $(\rho, y) \in$ EV *such that substitution* σ *respects* φ, *and* $\overline{m} \in \mathbb{N}^n$.

A size approximation over-approximates how large a variable in the left-hand side of a rule in $\mathcal{D}$ can get in a rewrite sequence from the initial state, again expressed in terms of the input variables. A tuple (T, S) is a *bound approximation* for a complexity problem P if T and S are runtime and size approximations for P. We next define a complexity framework in the spirit of Avanzini and Moser [4].

Definition 8. *Given a complexity problem* $P = (s_0, \mathcal{D}, \mathcal{R})$, *a (complexity)* judgement *is a statement* $\vdash P : (T, S)$, *for functions* $T : \mathcal{D} \to$ UB *and* $S : $ EV $\to$ UB. *The judgement is* valid *if* (T, S) *is a bound approximation for* P. *A complexity processor is an inference rule on complexity judgements of the following form:*

$$\frac{\vdash P_1 : (T_1, S_1), \ldots, \vdash P_k : (T_k, S_k)}{\vdash P : (T, S)} \; \text{Proc}$$

and it is sound *if* $\vdash P : (T, S)$ *is valid whenever all* $\vdash P_i : (T_i, S_i)$ *are valid.*

For a problem $P = (s_0, \mathcal{D}, \mathcal{R})$ with initial state $s_0 = (\text{init}(\overline{x}), \varphi)$, a DT $\ell \to r \; [\psi] \in \mathcal{D}$ is *initial* if $\text{root}(\ell) = \text{init}^{\#}$. The *initial processor* for P is given by

$$\frac{}{\vdash P : (T, S_\omega)} \; \text{Initial}$$

where $T(\rho) = 1$ if ρ is initial and $T(\rho) = \omega$ otherwise; and $S_\omega(\rho, x) = \omega$ for all $(\rho, x) \in \mathsf{EV}$. Since $\mathsf{init}^\#$ does not occur on any right-hand side by assumption, the processor Initial is sound. For instance, the DT $\mathsf{init}^\#(x, y, z) \to \mathsf{m}^\#(x, y, z)$ originating from rule (1) in Example 1 is initial. For a problem $P = (s_0, \mathcal{D}, \mathcal{R})$ and an expression $C \in \mathsf{UB}$, we sometimes write $\vdash P\colon ((C)_\Sigma, S)$ to express that there is a runtime approximation T such that $\vdash P\colon (T, S)$ and $C = \sum_{\rho \in \mathcal{D}} T(\rho)$.

The next result states that valid judgements bound the runtime complexity of LCTRSs. It can be proven in a similar way as [4, Theorem 6], using the properties of dependency tuples for innermost rewriting.

Theorem 1. *If an LCTRS $\mathcal{R}$ with initial state (t, φ) admits the valid judgement $\vdash ((t^\#, \varphi), \mathsf{DT}(\mathcal{R}), \mathcal{R} \cup \mathcal{R}_{\mathsf{calc}})\colon (T, S)$ then $\mathrm{rc}_{\mathcal{R}}^{(t,\varphi)} \leqslant \sum_{\rho \in \mathsf{DT}(\mathcal{R})} T(\rho)$ holds.*

5   Processors

This section presents processors that implement the complexity framework from Sect. 4, in particular showing how the respective ITS techniques [8] carry over.

Interpretation Processors. Compatible interpretations are a standard tool in resource analysis, cf. [4,8,34]. We first present a processor using a measure interpretation that orients *all* rules and DTs (cf. [8, Theorem 3.6]). For $p \in \mathsf{UB}$, let $[p]$ denote the bound expression obtained from p by replacing all coefficients in p by their absolute values (such that the resulting expression is weakly monotone).

Lemma 1. *Let $P = ((t_0, \varphi_0), \mathcal{D}, \mathcal{R})$ and $\mathcal{M}$ a DT-measure interpretation with which $\mathcal{R}$ is weakly, and $\mathcal{D}$ is strictly compatible. Then the following processor is sound, where $T'(\rho) = [(t_0)^{\mathcal{M}}]$ for all $\rho \in \mathcal{D}_>$, and $T'(\rho) = T(\rho)$ otherwise:*

$$\frac{\vdash P\colon (T, S)}{\vdash P\colon (T', S)} \quad \text{Interpretation}$$

For instance, for Example 1 one can take the interpretation $\mathcal{M}$ such that $\mathsf{split}^{\mathcal{M}} = 0$ and $f^{\mathcal{M}} = 1$ for all other $f \in \mathcal{F}_T$, and symbols in $\mathcal{F}_L$ are interpreted as in Example 5. $\mathcal{R}_1$ is strictly compatible since all rules are weakly and rule (5) is strictly decreasing. This justifies a runtime approximation setting by $T(5^\#) = 1 = \mathsf{init}^\#(\overline{x})^{\mathcal{M}}$.

Next, we adapt [8, Theorem 3.6] to our setting, by which runtime bounds can be obtained using an interpretation that orients the given LCTRS *partially*. For a dependency graph G and some $\mathcal{D}' \subseteq \mathcal{D}$, let $\mathsf{pre}(\mathcal{D}')$ be the set of all edges (ρ_1, ρ_2) in G, such that $\rho_1 \in \mathcal{D} \setminus \mathcal{D}'$ and $\rho_2 \in \mathcal{D}'$. Moreover, for a DT ρ with $\overline{Var}(lhs(\rho)) = (y_1, \ldots, y_k)$, let $\overline{S}_\rho$ denote $(S(\rho, y_1), \ldots, S(\rho, y_k))$.

Lemma 2. *Suppose $P = (s_0, \mathcal{D}, \mathcal{R})$ is a complexity problem such that $\mathcal{D}' \subseteq \mathcal{D}$ has no initial DTs, $\mathcal{R}$ is weakly, and $\mathcal{D}'$ is strictly compatible with a DT-measure interpretation $\mathcal{M}$. Then the following processor is sound:*

$$\frac{\vdash P\colon (T, S)}{\vdash P\colon (\lambda\rho. \begin{cases} \sum_{(\gamma, \delta) \in \mathsf{pre}(\mathcal{D}')} T(\gamma) \cdot [lhs(\delta)^{\mathcal{M}}](\overline{S}_\delta) & \text{if } \rho \in \mathcal{D}'_> \\ T(\rho) & \text{otherwise} \end{cases}, S)} \quad \text{TimeBounds}$$

where $\mathcal{D}'_>$ is the set of rules $\ell \to r\ [\varphi]$ in $\mathcal{D}'$ such that $\ell >^{\mathcal{M}}_{[\varphi]} r$.

Next, we define a processor to compute size approximations.

Size Bounds. Size approximations were developed for ITSs and tend to be less precise for LCTRSs due to nested terms. However, in many practical examples, a sufficient approximation is feasible. Next, we thus adapt the relevant notions to the LCTRS setting. First, the *local size approximation* overapproximates the size of entry variables in terms of variable sizes in predecessor rules.

Definition 9. *For $\delta, \rho \in \mathcal{D}$ and $(\rho, y) \in \mathrm{EV}$, let $S_{\delta\to\rho} \colon \mathcal{V} \to \mathrm{UB}$ be a local size approximation if*

$$S_{\delta\to\rho}(y)(\overline{m}) \geqslant \sup\{|y\tau| \mid \exists t, \sigma.\ \ell\sigma \to^\sigma_\delta \cdot \to^\tau_\rho t \text{ and } \overline{z}\sigma \leqslant_n \overline{m}\}$$

where $\ell = lhs(\delta)$, $\overline{z} = \overline{Var}(\ell)$, and σ is a valuation.

The intention is that for an entry variable (ρ, y), such that y occurs in the left-hand side of ρ, the expression $S_{\delta\to\rho}(y)$ upper-bounds y in terms of the variables in δ, for the case where ρ is applied after δ. While such an expression is not always computable, it can often be over-approximated. For instance, in Example 1 a local size approximation $S_{(9)\to(2)}(y)$ could be $(|x| + 1)/2$ or $|x|$: the subterm $\mathrm{m}_3^\#(x, u, v)$ on the right-hand side of (9) matches the left-hand side of (2), instantiating the variable y by u, and the side condition of (9) ensures $x + 1 \geqslant 2u$. We next define the *entry variable graph* to track the dependence of entry variables on each other. For $f \in \mathrm{UB}$, let $Var(f)$ be the set of all variables occurring in f.[2]

Definition 10. *An entry variable graph G_{EV} for $(s_0, \mathcal{D}, \mathcal{R})$ with DG G has node set $\mathrm{EV}(\mathcal{D})$, and there is an edge from (δ, z) to (ρ, y) labeled $S_{\delta\to\rho}(y)$ if G has an edge from δ to ρ and $z \in Var(S_{\delta\to\rho}(y))$.*

We illustrate the concept on our running example.

Example 6. Consider again Example 1. We first apply *chaining*, a standard technique in termination an complexity analysis [5, 15], to compress the cycles $(9) - (3) - (9)$ and $(9) - (7) - (9)$ into single-step cycles, such that (9) is replaced by

$$\mathrm{m}(x, y, z) \to \langle \mathrm{m}_0(x, u, v), \mathrm{m}(u, u, v), \mathrm{m}(v, u, v), \mathrm{m}_3(x, u, v)\rangle\ [\psi]$$

$$\psi = x \geqslant 2 \wedge u \geqslant 0 \wedge v \geqslant 0 \wedge x + 1 \geqslant 2u \wedge 2u \geqslant x \wedge x \geqslant 2v \wedge 2v + 1 \geqslant x.$$

Then we obtain the following entry variable graph:

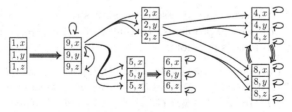

---

[2] For more precision one could restrict to *active* variables, as done in [8].

where a triple arrow $a \Longrightarrow b$ means that there are arrows from (a, x) to (b, x), (a, y) to (b, y), and (a, z) to (b, z). For all $(a, u) \in$ EV, all outgoing edges from (a, u) can be labelled $|u|$, though more precise approximations are possible.

Next, we use the entry variable graph G_{EV} to obtain size bound refinements, following the approach of [8]. To that end, we define two processors S_{triv} and S_{scc} that refine bounds for trivial and non-trivial SCCs in G_{EV}, respectively. Here, an SCC is *trivial* if it consists of a single node without an edge to itself.

Definition 11. *For size bounds S, we define S_{triv} as follows: (i) $S_{triv}(\rho, y) = |y|$ if ρ is initial; (ii)$S_{triv}(\rho, y) = \max\{\alpha(\bar{S}_\delta) \mid (\delta, z) \to^\alpha (\rho, y)$ in $G_{EV}\}$, if (ρ, y) is not in any non-trivial SCC of G_{EV}; (iii) otherwise $S_{triv}(\rho, y) = S(\rho, y)$.*

We distinguish three types of edges in G_{EV}, by partitioning their labels into the three sets $E_=$, E_+, and $E_\times$: for an edge labelled α, (i) $\alpha \in E_=$ if $\alpha = a_\alpha \in \mathbb{N}$ or $\alpha = |x|$ for some $x \in \mathcal{V}$; (ii) $\alpha \in E_+$ if $|x| + a_\alpha \geqslant \alpha$ for some $x \in \mathcal{V}$ and $a_\alpha \in \mathbb{N}$; (iii) $\alpha \in E_\times$ if $c + \sum_{x \in \mathcal{X}} a_x |x| \geqslant \alpha$ for $c, a_x \in \mathbb{N}$ and $\mathcal{X} \subseteq \mathcal{V}$. For an SCC C in G_{EV}, let C_α denote the set of edge labels α of edges in C. For an entry variable graph G_{EV}, let $\mathsf{pre}(\rho, y)$ be the set of all direct predecessors of (ρ, y) in G_{EV}.

Definition 12. *Let (T, S) be a bound approximation and C a non-trivial SCC in G_{EV}. Then S_{scc} is defined as (i) if $C_\alpha \subseteq E_=$ then $S_{scc}(\rho, y) = max\{\alpha \mid \alpha \in C_\alpha\}$, (ii) if $C_\alpha \subseteq E_+$ then let $\alpha_{pre} = max\{S(\rho', z) \mid (\rho', z) \in \mathsf{pre}(\rho, y) \setminus C\}$ and*

$$S_{scc}(\rho, y) = max(\{\alpha_{pre}\} \cup \{a_\alpha \mid \alpha \in C_\alpha\}) + \sum_{\rho \in \mathcal{D}} T(\rho) \cdot max\{a_\alpha \mid \alpha \in C \setminus E_=\}$$

(iii) and $S_{scc}(\rho, y) = S(\rho, y)$ otherwise, for all $\rho \in C$ and $(\rho, y) \in$ EV.

Both S_{triv} and S_{scc} are similar to the bounds developed in [8], though we omitted the case for $E_\times$ for reasons of space. We obtain soundness by similar proofs.

Lemma 3. *The following processors are sound:*

$$\frac{\vdash (s_0, \mathcal{D}, \mathcal{R}): (T, S)}{\vdash (s_0, \mathcal{D}, \mathcal{R}): (T, S_{triv})} \qquad \frac{\vdash (s_0, \mathcal{D}, \mathcal{R}): (T, S)}{\vdash (s_0, \mathcal{D}, \mathcal{R}): (T, S_{scc})} \qquad \text{Size Bounds}$$

6 Processors for Splitting and Loop Summary

In this section we present new processors to decompose a problem into subproblems, as well as to analyse loops based on recurrence relations.

Splitting. We first consider a processor that allows to decompose a problem of a certain shape into two subproblems. To that end, let a subgraph be *forward closed* if it is closed under successors.

Definition 13. *Consider a problem $P = (s_0, \mathcal{D}, \mathcal{R})$ whose DG G exhibits subgraphs G_0 and G_1 with node sets $\mathcal{D}_0$ and $\mathcal{D}_1$, respectively, such that $\mathcal{D} = \mathcal{D}_0 \uplus \mathcal{D}_1$, all initial DTs of P are in $\mathcal{D}_0$, and G_1 is forward closed. Then $(\mathcal{D}_0, \mathcal{D}_1)$ is a splitting for P.*

A splitting thus decomposes a problem according to the scheme illustrated in Fig. 1a. The idea is that we first analyse the subproblems P_0 and P_1 corresponding to $\mathcal{D}_0$ and $\mathcal{D}_1$ separately, considering as initial states for P_1 all possible entry points γ_i. For DTs in $\mathcal{D}_0$ their time bounds in P_0 constitute overall time bounds since G_1 is forward closed; on the other hand, for every $\rho \in \mathcal{D}_1$, we compute time bounds via each entry point γ_i, and obtain an overall time bound by taking the sum over all γ_i. To that end, given γ_i, the time bound for ρ in P_1 is applied to the size bound for γ_i, and multiplied by the time bound for the respective δ_i, which upper-bounds the number of applications of δ_i followed by γ_i.

(a) splitting   (b) recurrence

Fig. 1. Problems of special shapes.

Lemma 4. *If $(s_0, \mathcal{D}, \mathcal{R})$ is a problem with splitting $(\mathcal{D}_0, \mathcal{D}_1)$ such that $\mathsf{pre}(\mathcal{D}_1) = \{(\delta_i, \gamma_i) \mid 1 \leqslant i \leqslant m\}$ and $\gamma_i = (\ell_i \to r_i \ [\varphi_i])$, the following processor is sound:*

$$\frac{\vdash P\colon (T,S) \quad \vdash (s_0, \mathcal{D}_0, \mathcal{R})\colon (T_0, S_0) \quad \bigwedge_{i=1}^{m} \vdash ((\ell_i, \varphi_i), \mathcal{D}_1, \mathcal{R})\colon (T_i, S_i)}{\vdash P\colon \left(\lambda\rho.\begin{cases} T_0(\rho) & \text{if } \rho \in \mathcal{D}_0 \\ \sum_{i=1}^{m} T_0(\delta_i) \cdot T_i(\rho)(\overline{S}_{\gamma_i}) & \text{if } \rho \in \mathcal{D}_1 \end{cases}, S\right)} \text{ Split}$$

Several improvements are conceivable, for instance the conditions of the initial states (ℓ_i, φ_i) could be strengthened using reachability analysis in the DG.

Summarising Self-loops. We next propose a technique for the analysis of (sub)problems whose DG is of the shape shown in Fig. 1b. For vectors $\overline{a}, \overline{b}$, let $\overline{a} >_k \overline{b}$ be a shorthand for the expression $\overline{a} \geqslant_k \overline{b} \wedge (\bigvee_j a_j > b_j)$.

Definition 14. *Let $P = ((f(\overline{x}), \varphi), \mathcal{D}, \mathcal{R})$ with DG G such that $\mathcal{D}$ can be written as $\mathcal{D} = \{\delta\} \uplus \mathcal{D}'$, the graph $G|_{\mathcal{D}'}$ is forward-closed in G, and δ is of the form:*

$$f(\overline{x}) \to \langle f(\overline{r}_1), \dots, f(\overline{r}_p), lhs(\gamma_1), \dots, lhs(\gamma_m) \rangle \ [\psi] \tag{2}$$

for $\{\gamma_1, \dots, \gamma_m\} \subseteq \mathcal{D}'$, such that $\overline{x}, \overline{r}_i \in \mathcal{T}(\mathcal{F}_L, \mathcal{V})^k$ and $\varphi \wedge \psi \models |\overline{x}| >_k |\overline{r}_i|$ for all $1 \leqslant i \leqslant p$. If there is moreover some $\overline{b} \in (\mathbb{N} \cup \{-\infty\})^k$ such that $\varphi \wedge \psi \models |\overline{x}| \geqslant_k \overline{b}$, then P is cyclic with termination condition $\overline{b}$.

Lemma 5. *Let $P = (s_0, \mathcal{D}, \mathcal{R})$ be a cyclic complexity problem with termination condition $\overline{b}$ and a DT δ of the form $((2))$, and let $\gamma_i = (\ell_i \to r_i \ [\varphi_i])$, for all i, $1 \leqslant i \leqslant m$. Then the following processor is sound:*

$$\frac{\vdash P\colon (T,S) \quad \bigwedge_{i=1}^{m} \vdash ((\ell_i, \varphi_i), \mathcal{D}', \mathcal{R})\colon (T_i, S_i)}{\vdash (s_0, \mathcal{D}, \mathcal{R})\colon (F(\overline{x})_\Sigma, S)} \text{ Recurrence}$$

where F is a solution to a recurrence $f(\overline{x}) = f(\overline{r}_1) + \ldots + f(\overline{r}_p) + H(\overline{x})$, $f(\overline{b}) = 0$ for some $H(\overline{x}) \geqslant \sum_{\rho \in \mathcal{D}'} \sum_{i=1}^{m} T_i(\rho)(\overline{S}_{\gamma_i})$.

This processor is key to analyse the main loop in our running example.

Example 7. Consider Example 1 with chaining as applied in Example 6. For the subproblems $P_1 = (\mathsf{m}_0^{\#}(x, u, v), \psi), \mathcal{D}, \mathcal{R})$ and $P_2 = (\mathsf{m}_3^{\#}(x, u, v), \psi), \mathcal{D}, \mathcal{R})$ the judgements $\vdash P_1 \colon ((x+1)_\Sigma, S)$ and $\vdash P_2 \colon (u + v + 1)_\Sigma, S)$ are valid, so we can set $H(x, u, v) = 2|x| + 1 \geqslant x + u + v + 1$ since $u, v \leqslant x/2$. Thus, we solve the recurrence (1) given in Sect. 2. According to one of the cases of the Master Theorem, (1) has a solution in $\mathcal{O}(|x| \cdot \log(|x|))$ which is a complexity approximation according to Lemma 5.

To simplify the presentation, we only considered cycles formed by a single DT, as indicated in Fig. 1b. The result generalizes to longer cycles, but chaining can often reduce these cases to the simpler situation discussed here.

7   Evaluation

To evaluate the viability of the presented framework, we prototyped our approach in the complexity analyser $\mathsf{T_CT}$ [5].

Implementation. We added a new module `tct-lctrs` to the $\mathsf{T_CT}$ tool suite, below we call the resulting tool $\mathsf{T_CT}$-LCTRS.[3] It currently supports the theory of integers, as well as some operations on lists. All processors described in this paper are implemented, using the modular processor framework of $\mathsf{T_CT}$. They are arranged in the following strategy, where the loop indicates exhaustive repetition:

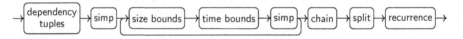

We mention some implementation aspects that seem noteworthy.

– The simp processor combines some straightforward simplification processors: unsatisfiable paths, unreachable rules, and unused arguments are eliminated, and leaves in the DG obtain their time bound from their predecessors.
– Suitable algebras instantiating the interpretation and time bounds processors (Lemmas 1 and 2) are searched for by means of an SMT encoding, as done in the ITS module of $\mathsf{T_CT}$ previously using well-known techniques [7,35].
– Before applying the recurrence processor, $\mathsf{T_CT}$ first applies chaining to obtain loops that involve only a single DT (see Appendix B for details).
– In the recurrence processor (Lemma 5), $\mathsf{T_CT}$ first attempts to solve subproblems corresponding to the functions $h_1, \ldots, h_m$ separately, obtaining bound approximations (T_i, S_i) for all i, $1 \leqslant i \leqslant m$ (see the notation of Lemma 5). Then, it is checked whether a function H corresponding to one of the known recursion patterns satisfies $H(\overline{x}) \geqslant \sum_i \sum_{\rho \in \mathcal{D}'} T_i(\rho)$ using an SMT call.

---

[3] The code is available from https://github.com/bytekid/tct-lctrs.

- The splitting processor (Lemma 4) leaves a lot of choice to the implementation where to split. We currently use it to enable the loop processor, which requires a very particular problem shape.

If a subroutine requires an SMT query, T$_{C}$T interfaces Yices [14] and Z3 [12].

Experiments. We evaluated T$_{C}$T-LCTRS on the ITS benchmarks considered by Brockschmidt *et al.* [8], using a timeout of 60 s. Table 1 compares our implementation with KoAT [8], CoFloCo [16,17], the ITS version of T$_{C}$T [5], and PUBS [1], giving the number of problems for which a bound was derived at all, the number of constant bounds, and the number of bounds that are at most linear, quadratic, and cubic, respectively.

Table 1. Comparison of tools on ITS benchmarks.

	T$_{C}$T-LCTRS	KoAT	CoFloCo	T$_{C}$T-ITS	PUBS
Solved problems	359	404	347	309	285
Constant	119	131	117	118	109
$\leqslant \mathcal{O}(n)$	282	298	270	250	240
$\leqslant \mathcal{O}(n^2)$	345	376	336	300	270
$\leqslant \mathcal{O}(n^3)$	356	383	345	306	278

The new splitting and recurrence processors allow T$_{C}$T-LCTRS to derive sublinear bounds. This is the case for all problems where PUBS derives a (precise) logarithmic bound, such as the examples `divByTwo` and `direct_n_log_n`. (KoAT and CoFloCo do not support sublinear bounds, and hence output linear bounds for these examples.) Moreover, we can precisely analyse subproblems produced by a divide-and-conquer approach like `divide_and_conquer`, where T$_{C}$T (as well as KoAT) produces the tight linear bound, while CoFloCo fails and PUBS gives an exponential bound. Detailed results, including a complete table and T$_{C}$T output, are available on-line.[4]

We moreover tested T$_{C}$T on the set of logic programs collected by Mesnard and Neumerkl [31],[5] restricted to deterministic programs. A list of solved problems is available on-line as well.

8   Conclusion

This paper presented the first complexity framework for LCTRSs. We conclude by relating to earlier work in the area, before indicating leads for future research.

---

[4] See http://cl-informatik.uibk.ac.at/users/swinkler/lctrs_complexity/.
[5] See http://www.complang.tuwien.ac.at/cti/bench/.

Related work. In the last decades there has been significant progress in the area of *fully automated* resource analysis, showing that it can be both practicable and scalable, see e.g. [1–3,18,24,26,32,36,39,40]. In the following, we indicate related work that directly influenced our framework, or employed similar methods.

Our framework differs from earlier work by Avanzini and Moser [4] in three important respects: first, constraints over arbitrary background theories are supported, second, complexity is not expressed in terms of the size of the initial term but in terms of measure functions, and third, sublinear bounds can be derived. While innermost rewriting is a rather natural restriction for LCTRSs, *call by need* strategies could be considered in the future for LCTRSs, too.

LCTRSs generalise ITSs, the complexity analysis of which is subject to a comprehensive line of research [8,34]. Our approach gracefully extends the alternating time and size bound technique by Brockschmidt *et al.* [8], as the ITS case is fully covered. In addition, we can obtain sublinear bounds, and support further modularization. Moreover, LCTRSs offer native support for full recursion.

Sublinear bounds are beyond the scope of this earlier work, but can be inferred by some other tools. Albert *et al.* [1] apply refinements to linear ranking functions and support sufficient criteria for divide-and-conquer patterns. This allows the tool PUBS to recognize logarithmic and $\mathcal{O}(n \log(n))$ bounds for some problems. Chatterjee *et al.* [9] use synthesis ranking functions extended by logarithmic and exponential terms, making use of an insightful adaption of Farkas' and Handelman's lemmas. The approach is able to handle examples such as mergesort. In contrast to our work this amounts to a whole-program analysis. Further, extensibility to a constraint formalism like LCTRS is unclear. Wang *et al.* [38] present an ML-like language with type annotations, also using the Master Theorem to handle divide-and-conquer-like recurrences. To estimate lower bounds for logic programs based on divide-and-conquer, Debray *et al.* [13] consider non-deterministic recurrence relations and propose a technique to obtain a closed-form bound for some cases.

Future work. We see exciting directions for future work both on a theoretical and an application level. Various additional processors can be conceived for our complexity framework, for instance forms of dependency pairs for non-innermost rewriting [25,34], knowledge propagation and narrowing [34].

Simplification systems as, for instance, employed in compiler toolchains (cf. Example 3) or SMT solvers constitute a highly relevant application domain, since these routines operate in performance-critical contexts. In order to tackle such systems, techniques for *derivational* complexity of LCTRSs need to be developed.

On the application level, LCTRSs constitute a natural backend for complexity analysis of constraint logic programs, since constraints can be natively expressed. Our experiments with logic programs did not take backtracking into account, but suitably adapting the transformational frameworks as established by Giesl *et al.* [23] to LCTRSs, this is not a showstopper: There the authors provide an automated complexity and termination analysis of full Prolog programs. In particular, the aforementioned restriction to deterministic programs can be overcome. We thus plan to support CLP as a frontend of our analysis, possibly taking into account *labelling strategies* that control the instantiation of query terms. We furthermore plan to support C programs as a frontend. C programs with integers, as considered in the Termination Competition[6] can be expressed as ITSs. LCTRSs offer more flexibility and can support also strings and floats, as the respective theories are supported by SMT solvers. Just like for the case of CLP, this requires the development of suitable complexity-reflecting transformations. More experiments are planned to evaluate our method on (constrained) logic programs [31] and problems from the software competition.[7]

References

1. Albert, E., Arenas, P., Genaim, S., Puebla, G.: Automatic inference of upper bounds for recurrence relations in cost analysis. In: Alpuente, M., Vidal, G. (eds.) SAS 2008. LNCS, vol. 5079, pp. 221–237. Springer, Heidelberg (2008). https://doi.org/10.1007/978-3-540-69166-2_15

2. Albert, E., Genaim, S., Masud, A.N.: On the inference of resource usage upper and lower bounds. ACM TOCL **14**(3), 22 (2013). https://doi.org/10.1145/2499937.2499943

3. Avanzini, M., Dal Lago, U., Moser, G.: Analysing the complexity of functional programs: higher-order meets first-order. In: Proceedings of the 20th ICFP, pp. 152–164. ACM (2015). https://doi.org/10.1145/2784731.2784753

4. Avanzini, M., Moser, G.: A combination framework for complexity. Inf. Comput. **248**, 22–55 (2016). https://doi.org/10.1016/j.ic.2015.12.007

5. Avanzini, M., Moser, G., Schaper, M.: TcT: Tyrolean complexity tool. In: Chechik, M., Raskin, J.-F. (eds.) TACAS 2016. LNCS, vol. 9636, pp. 407–423. Springer, Heidelberg (2016). https://doi.org/10.1007/978-3-662-49674-9_24

6. Baader, F., Nipkow, T.: Term Rewriting and All That. Cambridge University Press (1998). https://doi.org/10.1017/CBO9781139172752

7. Bagnara, R., Mesnard, F.: Eventual linear ranking functions. In: Proceedings of the 15th PPDP, pp. 229–238 (2013). https://doi.org/10.1145/2505879.2505884

8. Brockschmidt, M., Emmes, F., Falke, S., Fuhs, C., Giesl, J.: Analyzing runtime and size complexity of integer programs. ACM Trans. Program. Lang. Syst. **38**(4), 131–1350 (2016). https://doi.org/10.1145/2866575

9. Chatterjee, K., Fu, H., Goharshady, A.K.: Non-polynomial worst-case analysis of recursive programs. In: Majumdar, R., Kunčak, V. (eds.) CAV 2017. LNCS, vol. 10427, pp. 41–63. Springer, Cham (2017). https://doi.org/10.1007/978-3-319-63390-9_3

10. Ciobâcă, Ş., Lucanu, D.: A coinductive approach to proving reachability properties in logically constrained term rewriting systems. In: Galmiche, D., Schulz, S., Sebastiani, R. (eds.) IJCAR 2018. LNCS (LNAI), vol. 10900, pp. 295–311. Springer, Cham (2018). https://doi.org/10.1007/978-3-319-94205-6_20

11. Clavel, M., et al.: All About Maude - A High-Performance Logical Framework. LNCS, vol. 4350. Springer, Heidelberg (2007). https://doi.org/10.1007/978-3-540-71999-1

---

[6] http://termination-portal.org/.

[7] https://sv-comp.sosy-lab.org/.

12. de Moura, L., Bjørner, N.: Z3: an efficient SMT solver. In: Ramakrishnan, C.R., Rehof, J. (eds.) TACAS 2008. LNCS, vol. 4963, pp. 337–340. Springer, Heidelberg (2008). https://doi.org/10.1007/978-3-540-78800-3_24

13. Debray, S.K., López-García, P., Hermenegildo, M.V., Lin, N.: Lower bound cost estimation for logic programs. In: Proceedings of the 14th ILPS, pp. 291–305 (1997). https://doi.org/10.7551/mitpress/4283.003.0035

14. Dutertre, B.: Yices 2.2. In: Biere, A., Bloem, R. (eds.) CAV 2014. LNCS, vol. 8559, pp. 737–744. Springer, Cham (2014). https://doi.org/10.1007/978-3-319-08867-9_49

15. Falke, S., Kapur, D., Sinz, C.: Termination analysis of C programs using compiler intermediate languages. In: Proceedings of the 22nd RTA, Volume 10 of LIPIcs, pp. 41–50 (2011). https://doi.org/10.4230/LIPIcs.RTA.2011.41

16. Flores-Montoya, A.: Upper and lower amortized cost bounds of programs expressed as cost relations. In: Fitzgerald, J., Heitmeyer, C., Gnesi, S., Philippou, A. (eds.) FM 2016. LNCS, vol. 9995, pp. 254–273. Springer, Cham (2016). https://doi.org/10.1007/978-3-319-48989-6_16

17. Flores-Montoya, A.: Cost analysis of programs based on the refinement of cost relations. Ph.D. thesis, Universität Darmstadt (2017)

18. Frohn, F., Giesl, J.: Complexity analysis for Java with AProVE. In: Polikarpova, N., Schneider, S. (eds.) IFM 2017. LNCS, vol. 10510, pp. 85–101. Springer, Cham (2017). https://doi.org/10.1007/978-3-319-66845-1_6

19. Fuhs, C., Giesl, J., Plücker, M., Schneider-Kamp, P., Falke, S.: Proving termination of integer term rewriting. In: Treinen, R. (ed.) RTA 2009. LNCS, vol. 5595, pp. 32–47. Springer, Heidelberg (2009). https://doi.org/10.1007/978-3-642-02348-4_3

20. Fuhs, C., Kop, C., Nishida, N.: Verifying procedural programs via constrained rewriting induction. ACM TOCL 18(2), 14:1–14:50 (2017). https://doi.org/10.1145/3060143

21. Furuichi, Y., Nishida, N., Sakai, M., Kusakari, K., Sakabe, T.: Approach to procedural program verification based on implicit induction of constrained term rewriting systems. IPSJ Trans. Inf. Syst. 1(2), 100–121 (2008). (in Japanese)

22. Giesl, J., et al.: Analyzing program termination and complexity automatically with AProVE. J. Autom. Reasoning 58(1), 3–31 (2017). https://doi.org/10.1007/s10817-016-9388-y

23. Giesl, J., Ströder, T., Schneider-Kamp, P., Emmes, F., Fuhs, C.: Symbolic evaluation graphs and term rewriting–a general methodology for analyzing logic programs. In: Proceedings of the 14th PPDP, pp. 1–12. ACM Press (2012). https://doi.org/10.1007/978-3-642-38197-3_1

24. Gulwani, S.: SPEED: symbolic complexity bound analysis. In: Bouajjani, A., Maler, O. (eds.) CAV 2009. LNCS, vol. 5643, pp. 51–62. Springer, Heidelberg (2009). https://doi.org/10.1007/978-3-642-02658-4_7

25. Hirokawa, N., Moser, G.: Automated complexity analysis based on the dependency pair method. In: Armando, A., Baumgartner, P., Dowek, G. (eds.) IJCAR 2008. LNCS (LNAI), vol. 5195, pp. 364–379. Springer, Heidelberg (2008). https://doi.org/10.1007/978-3-540-71070-7_32

26. Hoffmann, J., Das, A., Weng, S.-C.: Towards automatic resource bound analysis for OCaml. In: Proceedings of the 44th POPL, pp. 359–373. ACM (2017). https://doi.org/10.1145/3009837

27. Kop, C.: Termination of LCTRSs. In: Proceedings of the 13th WST, pp. 59–63 (2013)

28. Kop, C., Nishida, N.: Term rewriting with logical constraints. In: Fontaine, P., Ringeissen, C., Schmidt, R.A. (eds.) FroCoS 2013. LNCS (LNAI), vol. 8152, pp. 343–358. Springer, Heidelberg (2013). https://doi.org/10.1007/978-3-642-40885-4_24
29. Kop, C., Nishida, N.: Constrained term rewriting tooL. In: Davis, M., Fehnker, A., McIver, A., Voronkov, A. (eds.) LPAR 2015. LNCS, vol. 9450, pp. 549–557. Springer, Heidelberg (2015). https://doi.org/10.1007/978-3-662-48899-7_38
30. Lopes, N., Menendez, D., Nagarakatte, S., Regehr, J.: Practical verification of peephole optimizations with Alive. Commun. ACM **61**(2), 84–91 (2018). https://doi.org/10.1145/3166064
31. Mesnard, F., Neumerkel, U.: Applying static analysis techniques for inferring termination conditions of logic programs. In: Cousot, P. (ed.) SAS 2001. LNCS, vol. 2126, pp. 93–110. Springer, Heidelberg (2001). https://doi.org/10.1007/3-540-47764-0_6
32. Moser, G., Schaper, M.: From Jinja bytecode to term rewriting: a complexity reflecting transformation. Inf. Comput. **261**(Part), 116–143 (2018). https://doi.org/10.1016/j.ic.2018.05.007
33. Nishida, N., Winkler, S.: Loop detection by logically constrained term rewriting. In: Piskac, R., Rümmer, P. (eds.) VSTTE 2018. LNCS, vol. 11294, pp. 309–321. Springer, Cham (2018). https://doi.org/10.1007/978-3-030-03592-1_18
34. Noschinski, L., Emmes, F., Giesl, J.: Analyzing innermost runtime complexity of term rewriting by dependency pairs. J. Autom. Reasoning **51**(1), 27–56 (2013). https://doi.org/10.1007/s10817-013-9277-6
35. Podelski, A., Rybalchenko, A.: A complete method for the synthesis of linear ranking functions. In: Steffen, B., Levi, G. (eds.) VMCAI 2004. LNCS, vol. 2937, pp. 239–251. Springer, Heidelberg (2004). https://doi.org/10.1007/978-3-540-24622-0_20
36. Serrano, A., López-García, P., Hermenegildo, M.: Resource usage analysis of logic programs via abstract interpretation using sized types. TPLP **14**(4–5), 739–754 (2014). https://doi.org/10.1017/S147106841400057X
37. TeReSe: Term rewriting systems. In: Cambridge Tracts in Theoretical Computer Science, vol. 55. Cambridge University Press (2003)
38. Wang, P., Wang, D., Chlipala, A.: TiML: a functional language for practical complexity analysis with invariants. Proc. ACM Program. Lang. **1**(OOPSLA) (2017). https://doi.org/10.1145/3133903
39. Wilhelm, R., et al.: The worst-case execution-time problem - overview of methods and survey of tools. ACM Trans. Prog. Lang. Syst. **7**(3) (2008). https://doi.org/10.1145/1347375.1347389
40. Wilhelm, R., Grund, D.: Computation takes time, but how much? Commun. ACM **57**(2), 94–103 (2014). https://doi.org/10.1145/2500886
41. Winkler, S., Middeldorp, A.: Completion for logically constrained rewriting. In Proceedings of the 3rd FSCD, Volume 108 of LIPIcs, pp. 30:1–30:18 (2018). https://doi.org/10.4230/LIPIcs.FSCD.2018.30
42. Winkler, S., Moser, G.: Runtime complexity analysis of logically constrained rewriting (extended version). http://cl-informatik.uibk.ac.at/users/swinkler/lctrs_complexity/paper.pdf

Confluence and Commutation for Nominal Rewriting Systems with Atom-Variables

Kentaro Kikuchi[1($\boxtimes$)] and Takahito Aoto[2]

[1] RIEC, Tohoku University, Sendai, Japan
`kentaro.kikuchi@riec.tohoku.ac.jp`
[2] Faculty of Engineering, Niigata University, Niigata, Japan
`aoto@ie.niigata-u.ac.jp`

Abstract. Nominal rewriting was introduced as an extension of first-order term rewriting by a binding mechanism based on the nominal approach. Recently, a new format of nominal rewriting has been introduced where rewrite rules are defined with atom-variables rather than atoms. In this paper, we investigate the difference between the new format and the original nominal rewriting, and prove confluence and commutation for some classes of rewriting systems whose rewrite rules have no proper overlaps which are computed using nominal unification with atom-variables. The properties we prove are expected to be used in a form of program transformation that is realised as an equivalence transformation of rewriting systems.

Keywords: Variable binding · Alpha-equivalence · Nominal unification · Nominal rewriting · Atom-variable · Confluence · Commutation

1 Introduction

Confluence is a fundamental property of rewriting systems that guarantees uniqueness of results of computation. *Commutation* is a generalisation of confluence to a property of computation by two rewriting systems. These properties are important in applications of rewriting techniques; for instance, they are essential to correctness of a form of program transformation, called equivalence transformation of rewriting systems [3,10,25]. For first-order term rewriting systems, confluence and commutation have been well studied, and many criteria to ensure them have been developed (e.g. [7,8,12,17,19,23,24]).

Nominal rewriting [4,5] was introduced as an extension of first-order term rewriting by a binding mechanism based on the nominal approach [6,18], where variables that are possibly bound are called *atoms*. A distinctive feature of nominal rewriting is that α-conversion and capture-avoiding substitution are not relegated to the meta-level—they are explicitly dealt with at the object-level. Some basic confluence criteria such as Rosen's criterion [19] (orthogonal systems

© Springer Nature Switzerland AG 2021
M. Fernández (Ed.): LOPSTR 2020, LNCS 12561, pp. 56–73, 2021.
https://doi.org/10.1007/978-3-030-68446-4_3

are confluent), Knuth-Bendix's criterion [12] (terminating systems with joinable critical pairs are confluent) and Huet's criterion [8] (left-linear systems with parallel closed critical pairs are confluent) have been discussed in the case of nominal rewriting [2,4,11,21,22].

Recently, Kutz and Schmidt-Schauß [13] have introduced a somewhat different format of nominal rewriting from the original one. In their systems, rewrite rules are written using *atom-variables* for which atoms are substituted in each rewrite step. The use of atom-variables appears to be problematic, because for keeping binding structures correct, it is necessary to use permutations (or injections) on atoms instead of substitutions. Their systems, however, have a device that makes substitutions for atom-variables injective so that this problem can be avoided.

In the present paper, we treat nominal rewriting with atom-variables in the style of [13], looking into how it differs from nominal rewriting in previous work. We study confluence and commutation for some classes of nominal rewriting systems including those which are difficult to represent by previous approaches.

The main differences between the format of [13] and those in the traditional style are explained as follows:

- First, as mentioned above, rewrite rules are written with atom-variables rather than atoms, and rewriting is performed through substituting atoms for atom-variables where the substitution is not necessarily injective. This is particularly effective when representing rewrite rules with some atoms that are not bound (after being substituted for atom-variables). For example, in traditional nominal rewriting, $a \neq b$ is always supposed in the rewrite rule $\vdash f(a, b) \to a$, while in the format of [13], the same atom can be substituted for A and B in the rewrite rule $\vdash f(A, B) \to A$. (Further examples showing its usefulness can be found in Sect. 1 of [20].) If the substitution should be injective, one can add appropriate freshness constraints on atom-variables in the rewrite rule, which are used in matching process. (Freshness constraints are also extended from those in the traditional style.) In this way, the definition of rewrite relation is given without involving equivariance (as in [4]) or parametrised permutations (as in [21]), and so simpler than those in previous work.
- However, there is a not small price to pay for the above advantages. Since terms with atom-variables are not objects for rewriting to be analysed any more, the language has split into one for rewrite rules and one for objects for rewriting. In [13] and the present paper, the latter is the language of ground nominal terms, i.e. nominal terms with neither (term-)variables nor atom-variables, and those variables are used only for representing rewrite rules[1]. Accordingly, the confluence properties treated in [13] and the present paper

---

[1] In usual papers on rewriting systems with binders such as λ-calculus, meta-variables are used to specify rewrite rules instead of (term-)variables and atom-variables used here. The reason we include those variables in the language to describe rewrite rules is that the set of rewrite rules should keep finite, which is essential when considering some kind of unification procedure to compute overlaps, critical pairs, etc.

are restricted to those on ground nominal terms, and in this sense weaker properties than those discussed in previous work.

Contributions of the Paper. The contributions of the present paper are summarised as follows:

- We prove confluence on ground terms for orthogonal nominal rewriting systems with atom-variables. In Theorem 6.7 of [13], only local confluence is stated for orthogonal systems, and no proof of confluence has been given.
- We prove the commutation property of mutually orthogonal nominal rewriting systems with atom-variables. The commutation property has never been studied in previous work on nominal rewriting.

Although the properties we prove are restricted to those on ground terms, they are enough for application to the form of program transformation mentioned at the beginning of this section.

Organisation of the Paper. The paper is organised as follows. In Sect. 2, we explain basic notions of nominal rewriting systems with atom-variables. In Sect. 3, we study confluence and commutation for some classes of nominal rewriting systems with atom-variables. In Sect. 4, we discuss related work and conclude with suggestions for further work.

2   Nominal Rewriting Systems with Atom-Variables

In this section, we introduce basic notions on nominal rewriting systems with atom-variables [13]. Unlike the original nominal rewriting [4], the framework of [13] uses two different languages: one is for objects for rewriting, called ground nominal terms, and the other is for components of rewrite rules.

2.1   Preliminaries

First, we introduce some notations on nominal terms.

A *nominal signature* Σ is a set of *function symbols* ranged over by $f, g, \ldots$. We fix a countably infinite set $\mathcal{X}$ of *variables* ranged over by $X, Y, \ldots$, a countably infinite set $\mathcal{A}$ of *atoms* ranged over by $a, b, \ldots$, and a countably infinite set $\mathcal{X}_A$ of *atom-variables* ranged over by $A, B, \ldots$. We assume that Σ, $\mathcal{X}$, $\mathcal{A}$ and $\mathcal{X}_A$ are pairwise disjoint. Unless otherwise stated, different meta-variables for objects in Σ, $\mathcal{X}$, $\mathcal{A}$ or $\mathcal{X}_A$ denote different objects.

The domain $dom(\phi)$ of a mapping $\phi : D \to E$ is the set D if $D \neq E$ and $\{d \in D \mid \phi(d) \neq d\}$ if $D = E$. A mapping $\phi : D \to E$ is *finite* if its domain $dom(\phi)$ is a finite set. For finite mappings ϕ and ψ with $dom(\phi) \cap dom(\psi) = \emptyset$, we define the mapping $\phi \cup \psi$ with $dom(\phi \cup \psi) = dom(\phi) \cup dom(\psi)$ by $(\phi \cup \psi)(d) = \phi(d)$ if $d \in dom(\phi)$ and $(\phi \cup \psi)(d) = \psi(d)$ if $d \in dom(\psi)$.

2.2   Ground Nominal Terms

In this subsection, we introduce the set of ground nominal terms, which we call NL_a following [13,20]. (NL_a stands for *N*ominal *L*anguage with *a*toms.)

The set NL_a of *ground nominal terms*, or simply *ground terms*, are generated by the following grammar:

$$t, s ::= a \mid [a]t \mid f\ t \mid \langle t_1, \ldots, t_n \rangle$$

Ground terms of the forms in the right-hand side are called, respectively, atoms, abstractions, function applications and tuples. We assume that function applications bind more strongly than abstractions. We abbreviate $f\ \langle \rangle$ as f, referring to it as a *constant*. An abstraction $[a]t$ is intended to represent t with a bound. The set of *free* atoms occurring in t, denoted by $FA(t)$, is defined as follows: $FA(a) = \{a\}$; $FA([a]t) = FA(t) \setminus \{a\}$; $FA(f\ t) = FA(t)$; $FA(\langle t_1, \ldots, t_n \rangle) = \bigcup_i FA(t_i)$.

Example 1. The nominal signature of the λ-calculus has two function symbols `lam` and `app`. The ground nominal term $\mathtt{app}\langle\mathtt{lam}\langle[a]\mathtt{lam}\langle[b]\mathtt{app}\langle b, a\rangle\rangle\rangle, b\rangle$ represents the λ-term $(\lambda a.\lambda b.ba)b$ in the usual notation. For this ground term t, we have $FA(t) = \{b\}$.   □

A *swapping* is a pair of atoms, written $(a\ b)$. *Permutations* π are bijections on $\mathcal{A}$ such that $dom(\pi)$ is finite. Permutations are represented by lists of swappings applied in the right-to-left order. For example, $((b\ c)(a\ b))(a) = c$, $((b\ c)(a\ b))(b) = a$, $((b\ c)(a\ b))(c) = b$. The permutation action $\pi \cdot t$, which operates on terms extending a permutation on atoms, is defined as follows: $\pi \cdot a = \pi(a)$; $\pi \cdot ([a]t) = [\pi \cdot a](\pi \cdot t)$; $\pi \cdot (f\ t) = f\ \pi \cdot t$; $\pi \cdot \langle t_1, \ldots, t_n \rangle = \langle \pi \cdot t_1, \ldots, \pi \cdot t_n \rangle$.

Positions are finite sequences of positive integers. The empty sequence is denoted by ε. The set of positions in a ground term t, denoted by $Pos(t)$, is defined as follows: $Pos(a) = \{\varepsilon\}$; $Pos([a]t) = Pos(f\ t) = \{1p \mid p \in Pos(t)\} \cup \{\varepsilon\}$; $Pos(\langle t_1, \ldots, t_n \rangle) = \bigcup_i \{ip \mid p \in Pos(t_i)\} \cup \{\varepsilon\}$. The subterm of t at a position $p \in Pos(t)$ is written as $t|_p$.

A *context* is a ground term in which a distinguished constant $\square$ occurs. The ground term obtained from a context C by replacing each $\square$ at positions p_i by ground terms t_i is written as $C[t_1, \ldots, t_n]_{p_1, \ldots, p_n}$ or simply $C[t_1, \ldots, t_n]$.

A pair $a\#t$ of an atom a and a ground term t is called a *freshness constraint*. The rules in Fig. 1 define the validity of freshness constraints. Note that the defined $\vdash_{NL_a} a\#t$ coincides with $a \notin FA(t)$.

The rules in Fig. 2 define the relation $\vdash_{NL_a} t \approx_\alpha s$. This is a congruence relation [4] and coincides with usual α-equivalence (i.e. the relation reached by renamings of bound atoms) [6]. The definition of $\vdash_{NL_a} t \approx_\alpha s$ will be used in some of the proofs afterwards.

The following properties are shown in [4,26].

Proposition 1. *1.* $\vdash_{NL_a} a\#t$ *if and only if* $\vdash_{NL_a} \pi \cdot a\#\pi \cdot t$.
2. $\vdash_{NL_a} t \approx_\alpha s$ *if and only if* $\vdash_{NL_a} \pi \cdot t \approx_\alpha \pi \cdot s$.
3. If $\vdash_{NL_a} a\#t$ *and* $\vdash_{NL_a} t \approx_\alpha s$ *then* $\vdash_{NL_a} a\#s$.

$$\frac{}{\vdash_{NL_a} a\#b} \qquad \frac{\vdash_{NL_a} a\#t}{\vdash_{NL_a} a\#f\,t} \qquad \frac{\vdash_{NL_a} a\#t_1 \quad \cdots \quad \vdash_{NL_a} a\#t_n}{\vdash_{NL_a} a\#\langle t_1,\ldots,t_n\rangle}$$

$$\frac{}{\vdash_{NL_a} a\#[a]t} \qquad \frac{\vdash_{NL_a} a\#t}{\vdash_{NL_a} a\#[b]t}$$

Fig. 1. Rules for freshness constraints on NL_a

$$\frac{}{\vdash_{NL_a} a\approx_\alpha a} \qquad \frac{\vdash_{NL_a} t\approx_\alpha s}{\vdash_{NL_a} f\,t\approx_\alpha f\,s} \qquad \frac{\vdash_{NL_a} t_1\approx_\alpha s_1 \quad \cdots \quad \vdash_{NL_a} t_n\approx_\alpha s_n}{\vdash_{NL_a} \langle t_1,\ldots,t_n\rangle \approx_\alpha \langle s_1,\ldots,s_n\rangle}$$

$$\frac{\vdash_{NL_a} t\approx_\alpha s}{\vdash_{NL_a} [a]t\approx_\alpha [a]s} \qquad \frac{\vdash_{NL_a} (a\ b)\cdot t\approx_\alpha s \quad \vdash_{NL_a} b\#t}{\vdash_{NL_a} [a]t\approx_\alpha [b]s}$$

Fig. 2. Rules for α-equivalence on NL_a

2.3   Nominal Term Expressions

Next, we introduce the set of term expressions used in rewrite rules, which we call NL_{AS} following [13,20]. (NL_{AS} stands for *N*ominal *L*anguage with *A*tom-variables and expre*S*sion variables.)

The set NL_{AS} of *nominal term expressions*, or simply *term expressions*, are generated by the following grammar:

$$e ::= v \mid \pi\cdot X \mid [v]e \mid f\,e \mid \langle e_1,\ldots,e_n\rangle$$
$$\pi ::= \emptyset \mid (v\ v')\cdot\pi$$
$$v ::= \pi\cdot A$$

where π and v are non-terminals for *permutation expressions* and *atom expressions*, respectively. A term expression of the form $\pi\cdot X$ is called a *moderated variable*. Also, an expression of the form $\pi\cdot X$ or $\pi\cdot A$ is called a *suspension*. We abbreviate $\emptyset\cdot X$ and $\emptyset\cdot A$ as X and A, respectively, if there is no ambiguity. We write $Var_{\mathcal{X}}(e)$ for the set of variables occurring in a term expression e, and $Var_{\mathcal{X}_A}(e)$, $Var_{\mathcal{X}_A}(\pi)$ and $Var_{\mathcal{X}_A}(v)$ for the sets of atom-variables occurring in expressions e, π and v, respectively. For a term expression e, we define $Var_{\mathcal{X},\mathcal{X}_A}(e)$ as $Var_{\mathcal{X}}(e)\cup Var_{\mathcal{X}_A}(e)$. A term expression e is *linear* if each variable $X \in Var_{\mathcal{X}}(e)$ occurs only once in e.

The set $Pos(e)$ of positions in a term expression e is defined similarly to that for a ground term (using atom expressions for atoms) with the additional clause that $Pos(\pi\cdot X) = \{\varepsilon\}$. The subexpression of e at a position $p \in Pos(e)$ is written as $e|_p$. If $p \neq \varepsilon$, then $e|_p$ is called a *proper* subexpression. A position $p \in Pos(e)$ is called a *variable position* if $e|_p$ is a moderated variable, and a *non-variable position* otherwise.

A *ground substitution* is a finite mapping that assigns ground terms to variables and atoms to atom-variables. We use σ, δ for ground substitutions. We write

$\sigma_{\mathcal{X}}$ and $\sigma_{\mathcal{X}_A}$ for ground substitutions obtained from σ by restricting the domain to $dom(\sigma) \cap \mathcal{X}$ and $dom(\sigma) \cap \mathcal{X}_A$, respectively. When $Var_{\mathcal{X},\mathcal{X}_A}(e) \subseteq dom(\sigma)$, the application of σ on e is written as $e\sigma$ and called a *ground instance* of e. (Similarly for expressions π and v.) The application of σ does not simply replace the variables X and atom-variables A occurring in e by $\sigma(X)$ and $\sigma(A)$, but, when replacing X and A of suspensions $\pi \cdot X$ and $\pi \cdot A$, induce permutation actions $\pi\sigma \cdot (\sigma(X))$ and $\pi\sigma \cdot (\sigma(A))$ viewing the list $\pi\sigma$ as a permutation. For example, $(((B\ C)(A\ B)) \cdot A)\sigma = ((B\ C)(A\ B))\sigma \cdot (\sigma(A)) = ((b\ c)(a\ b))(a) = c$ for the ground substitution $\sigma = [A := a, B := b, C := c]$. Thus we have $e\sigma \in NL_a$ for every ground instance $e\sigma$.

Lemma 1. *For every permutation expression π and every atom expression v, the following hold.*

1. *For every ground instances $\pi\sigma$ and $\pi\delta$, if $\forall A \in Var_{\mathcal{X}_A}(\pi). \sigma(A) = \delta(A)$ then $\pi\sigma = \pi\delta$ (as lists of swappings).*
2. *For every ground instances $v\sigma$ and $v\delta$, if $\forall A \in Var_{\mathcal{X}_A}(v). \sigma(A) = \delta(A)$ then $v\sigma = v\delta$.*

Proof. By simultaneous induction on the structures of π and v. $\qquad\square$

A pair $v \# e$ of an atom expression v and a term expression e is called a *freshness constraint expression*. A finite set of freshness constraint expressions is called a *freshness context*. For a freshness context ∇, we define $Var_{\mathcal{X},\mathcal{X}_A}(\nabla) = \bigcup_{v \# e \in \nabla}(Var_{\mathcal{X}_A}(v) \cup Var_{\mathcal{X},\mathcal{X}_A}(e))$ and $\nabla\sigma = \{v\sigma \# e\sigma \mid v \# e \in \nabla\}$.

Now we recall nominal unification problems with atom-variables [20].

Definition 1. Let Γ be a finite set of equations of the form $e_1 \approx e_2$ where e_1 and e_2 are term expressions, and let ∇ be a freshness context. Then the pair (Γ, ∇) is called a *variable-atom nominal unification problem* (*VANUP* for short).

Definition 2 (Solution of a VANUP). A ground substitution σ is a *solution* of a VANUP (Γ, ∇) if $\vdash_{NL_a} e_1\sigma \approx_\alpha e_2\sigma$ for every equation $e_1 \approx e_2 \in \Gamma$ and $\vdash_{NL_a} v\sigma \# e\sigma$ for every freshness constraint expression $v \# e \in \nabla$. A VANUP (Γ, ∇) is *solvable* if there exists a solution of (Γ, ∇).

Example 2. Consider the nominal signature for the λ-calculus in Example 1, and let P be the VANUP $(\{\mathtt{lam}\langle[A]\mathtt{app}\langle X, A\rangle\rangle \approx \mathtt{lam}\langle[B]Y\rangle\}, \{A \# X\})$. Then, the ground substitution $[A := a, B := b, X := c, Y := \mathtt{app}\langle c, b\rangle]$ is a solution of P. $\square$

2.4 Nominal Rewriting Systems with Atom-Variables

Next we define nominal rewrite rules and nominal rewriting systems with atom-variables.

Definition 3. A *nominal rewrite rule with atom-variables*, or simply *rewrite rule*, is a triple of a freshness context ∇ and term expressions $l, r \in NL_{AS}$ such that $Var_{\mathcal{X},\mathcal{X}_A}(\nabla) \cup Var_{\mathcal{X},\mathcal{X}_A}(r) \subseteq Var_{\mathcal{X},\mathcal{X}_A}(l)$ and l is not a moderated variable. We write $\nabla \vdash l \to r$ for a rewrite rule, and identify rewrite rules modulo renaming of variables and atom-variables. A rewrite rule $\nabla \vdash l \to r$ is *left-linear* if l is linear.

Definition 4 (Nominal rewriting system with atom-variables). A *nominal rewriting system with atom-variables* (*NRS$_{AS}$* for short) is a finite set of rewrite rules. An *NRS$_{AS}$* is *left-linear* if so are all its rewrite rules.

The following example of an *NRS$_{AS}$* corresponds to Example 8 of [21] written in the style of traditional nominal rewriting. Note that the freshness constraint $A\#B$ is used to mean that distinct atoms should be substituted for the atom-variables A and B.

Example 3. We extend the signature in Example 1 by a function symbol sub. By $\mathsf{sub}\langle[a]t, s\rangle$, we represent an explicit substitution $t\langle a := s\rangle$. Then, an *NRS$_{AS}$* to perform β-reduction is defined by the rule (Beta):

$$\vdash \mathsf{app}\langle \mathsf{lam}\langle[A]X\rangle, Y\rangle \to \mathsf{sub}\langle[A]X, Y\rangle \quad \text{(Beta)}$$

together with an *NRS$_{AS}$* $\mathcal{R}_{\mathsf{sub}}$ to execute substitution:

$$
\begin{aligned}
\vdash \mathsf{sub}\langle[A]\mathsf{app}\langle X,Y\rangle, Z\rangle &\to \mathsf{app}\langle\mathsf{sub}\langle[A]X, Z\rangle, \mathsf{sub}\langle[A]Y, Z\rangle\rangle & \text{(sub}_{\mathsf{app}}) \\
\vdash \mathsf{sub}\langle[A]A, X\rangle &\to X & \text{(sub}_{\mathsf{var}}) \\
A\#B \vdash \mathsf{sub}\langle[A]B, X\rangle &\to B & \text{(sub}_{\mathsf{var}\epsilon}) \\
A\#B, B\#Y \vdash \mathsf{sub}\langle[A]\mathsf{lam}\langle[B]X\rangle, Y\rangle &\to \mathsf{lam}\langle[B]\mathsf{sub}\langle[A]X, Y\rangle\rangle & \text{(sub}_{\mathsf{lam}})
\end{aligned}
$$

In a standard notation, the system $\mathcal{R}_{\mathsf{sub}}$ is represented as follows:

$$
\begin{aligned}
\vdash (XY)\langle A := Z\rangle &\to (X\langle A := Z\rangle)(Y\langle A := Z\rangle) & \text{(sub}_{\mathsf{app}}) \\
\vdash A\langle A := X\rangle &\to X & \text{(sub}_{\mathsf{var}}) \\
A\#B \vdash B\langle A := X\rangle &\to B & \text{(sub}_{\mathsf{var}\epsilon}) \\
A\#B, B\#Y \vdash (\lambda B.X)\langle A := Y\rangle &\to \lambda B.(X\langle A := Y\rangle) & \text{(sub}_{\mathsf{lam}})
\end{aligned}
$$

$\square$

In the sequel, $\vdash_{NL_a}$ is extended to mean to hold for all members of the set in the right-hand side.

Definition 5 (Rewrite relation). Let $R = \nabla \vdash l \to r$ be a rewrite rule. For ground terms $s, t \in NL_a$, the *rewrite relation* is defined by

$$s \to_{\langle R,p,\sigma\rangle} t \overset{\text{def}}{\iff} \vdash_{NL_a} \nabla\sigma, \; s = C[s']_p, \; \vdash_{NL_a} s' \approx_\alpha l\sigma, \; t = C[r\sigma]_p$$

We write $s \overset{p}{\to}_R t$ if there exists σ such that $s \to_{\langle R,p,\sigma\rangle} t$. We write $s \to_R t$ if there exist p and σ such that $s \to_{\langle R,p,\sigma\rangle} t$. For an *NRS$_{AS}$* $\mathcal{R}$, we write $s \to_{\mathcal{R}} t$ if there exists $R \in \mathcal{R}$ such that $s \to_R t$.

The following is an example of rewriting by the *NRS$_{AS}$* in Example 3. It corresponds to Example 10 of [21] using traditional nominal rewriting. We see that a substitution for atom-variables and the additional freshness constraint can provide a mechanism to avoid capture of a free atom (as far as rewriting on ground terms is concerned).

Example 4. Using the rule (Beta) in Example 3, we see that the ground term representing $(\lambda a.\lambda b.ba)b$ rewrites to $(\lambda b.ba)\langle a := b \rangle$, that is, we have

$$\texttt{app}\langle\texttt{lam}\langle[a]\texttt{lam}\langle[b]\texttt{app}\langle b,a\rangle\rangle\rangle, b\rangle \rightarrow_{\langle\text{Beta},\varepsilon,\sigma\rangle} \texttt{sub}\langle[a]\texttt{lam}\langle[b]\texttt{app}\langle b,a\rangle\rangle, b\rangle$$

where σ is the ground substitution $[A := a, X := \texttt{lam}\langle[b]\texttt{app}\langle b,a\rangle\rangle, Y := b]$. The resulting ground term rewrites further to a normal form $\texttt{lam}\langle[c]\texttt{app}\langle c,b\rangle\rangle$ in four steps with rules of the system $\mathcal{R}_{\text{sub}}$. Here we give a detail of the first step with rule (sub$_{\text{lam}}$) to see how capture of a free atom is avoided.

Let $s = \texttt{sub}\langle[a]\texttt{lam}\langle[b]\texttt{app}\langle b,a\rangle\rangle, b\rangle$. Since the rule has a freshness context $\nabla = \{A\#B, B\#Y\}$, to apply (sub$_{\text{lam}}$) to s at the position $p = \varepsilon$, it is necessary to find a ground substitution σ with $\vdash_{NL_a} \nabla\sigma$ and $\vdash_{NL_a} s \approx_\alpha (\texttt{sub}\langle[A]\texttt{lam}\langle[B]X\rangle, Y\rangle)\sigma$. Here one cannot take σ with $\sigma(B) = b$, which together with $\sigma(Y) = b$ from the condition for $\approx_\alpha$ contradicts $\vdash_{NL_a} \nabla\sigma$. So we take, e.g. $\sigma = [A := a, B := c, X := \texttt{app}\langle c,a\rangle, Y := b]$ to satisfy the conditions, and get $(\texttt{lam}\langle[B]\texttt{sub}\langle[A]X, Y\rangle\rangle)\sigma = \texttt{lam}\langle[c]\texttt{sub}\langle[a]\texttt{app}\langle c,a\rangle, b\rangle\rangle$ as the result of rewriting. $\square$

Remark 1. In previous papers on nominal rewriting except for the authors', the rewrite relation is often defined so that α-equivalent terms are allowed on the result of rewriting, like $t \approx_\alpha C[r\sigma]$. However, such a definition makes arguments by induction difficult, since from $s \rightarrow_R t$ one can only say $t \approx_\alpha C[r\sigma]$ for some C and σ, where s is of the form $C[s']$ but t is not necessarily of the form $C[t']$.

The following lemma holds. We give a detailed proof of it in [9]. A closely related property without referring to the position p has been observed in Proposition 4.4 of [13], where no detailed proof of it is given.

Lemma 2. *Let $R = \nabla \vdash l \rightarrow r$ be a rewrite rule, and let s, t be ground terms. If $p \in Pos(s)$ and $s \xrightarrow{p}_R t$ then $\pi \cdot s \xrightarrow{p}_R \pi \cdot t$ for every permutation π.*

2.5   Overlaps and Orthogonality

The notion of overlap is defined using nominal unification with atom-variables.

Definition 6 (Overlap). Let $R_i = \nabla_i \vdash l_i \rightarrow r_i$ ($i = 1, 2$) be rewrite rules. We assume without loss of generality that $Var_{\mathcal{X},\mathcal{X}_A}(l_1) \cap Var_{\mathcal{X},\mathcal{X}_A}(l_2) = \emptyset$. If the variable-atom nominal unification problem $(\{l_1 \approx l_2|_p\}, \nabla_1 \cup \nabla_2)$ is solvable for some non-variable position p of l_2, then we say that R_1 *overlaps* on R_2, and the situation is called an *overlap* of R_1 on R_2. If R_1 and R_2 are identical modulo renaming of variables and atom-variables, and $p = \varepsilon$, then the overlap is said to be *self-rooted*. An overlap that is not self-rooted is said to be *proper*.

Example 5. Let R_1 and R_2 be the rules (Eta) $A\#X \vdash \texttt{lam}\langle[A]\texttt{app}\langle X,A\rangle\rangle \rightarrow X$ and (Beta) $\vdash \texttt{app}\langle\texttt{lam}\langle[B]Y\rangle, Z\rangle \rightarrow \texttt{sub}\langle[B]Y, Z\rangle$, respectively. Then, R_1 overlaps on R_2, since the VANUP $(\{\texttt{lam}\langle[A]\texttt{app}\langle X,A\rangle\rangle \approx \texttt{app}\langle\texttt{lam}\langle[B]Y\rangle, Z\rangle|_{11}(= \texttt{lam}\langle[B]Y\rangle)\}, \{A\#X\})$ is solvable as seen in Example 2. This overlap is proper. $\square$

Example 6. There exists a self-rooted overlap of the rule (Beta) on its renamed variant, since the VANUP $(\{\mathsf{app}\langle\mathsf{lam}\langle[A]X\rangle, Y\rangle \approx \mathsf{app}\langle\mathsf{lam}\langle[B]Z\rangle, W\rangle\}, \emptyset)$ is solvable by taking the ground substitution $[A := a, B := b, X := a, Y := c, Z := b, W := c]$ as a solution.　　　□

In first-order term rewriting, self-rooted overlaps do not matter, and only proper overlaps need to be analysed. However, in the case of nominal rewriting, that is not enough as discussed in [21].

Using the above notion of overlap, we define the notions of orthogonality of an NRS_{AS} and mutual orthogonality of two NRS_{AS}'s.

Definition 7 (Orthogonality). An NRS_{AS} $\mathcal{R}$ is *orthogonal* if it is left-linear and for any rewrite rules $R_1, R_2 \in \mathcal{R}$, there exists no proper overlap of R_1 on R_2.

Definition 8 (Mutual orthogonality). NRS_{AS}'s $\mathcal{R}_1$ and $\mathcal{R}_2$ are *mutually orthogonal* if they are left-linear and for any rewrite rules $R_1 \in \mathcal{R}_1$ and $R_2 \in \mathcal{R}_2$, there exists no overlap of R_1 on R_2, and there exists no overlap of R_2 on R_1.

Unlike in first-order term rewriting, orthogonality is not enough to guarantee a confluence property of an NRS_{AS} as seen in the following example.

Example 7. Consider the NRS_{AS} $\mathcal{R}_{\mathsf{uc\text{-}}\eta}$ with the only rewrite rule (Uncond-eta) $\vdash \mathsf{lam}\langle[A]\mathsf{app}\langle X, A\rangle\rangle \to X$. This system $\mathcal{R}_{\mathsf{uc\text{-}}\eta}$ is orthogonal. However, $\mathsf{lam}\langle[a]\mathsf{app}\langle a, a\rangle\rangle \to_{\mathsf{Uncond\text{-}eta}} a$ and $\mathsf{lam}\langle[a]\mathsf{app}\langle a, a\rangle\rangle \to_{\mathsf{Uncond\text{-}eta}} b$, where the latter holds since $\vdash_{NL_a} \mathsf{lam}\langle[a]\mathsf{app}\langle a, a\rangle\rangle \approx_\alpha \mathsf{lam}\langle[b]\mathsf{app}\langle b, b\rangle\rangle = (\mathsf{lam}\langle[A]\mathsf{app}\langle X, A\rangle\rangle)[A := b, X := b]$.　　　□

3　Confluence and Commutation for Left-Linear Nominal Rewriting Systems with Atom-Variables

In this section, we study confluence and commutation properties of left-linear NRS_{AS}'s. The properties are defined modulo the equivalence relation $\approx_\alpha$ in terms of abstract reduction systems [15]. To do so, we first introduce some notations.

Let $\bowtie$ be a binary relation. We write $\bowtie^=$ for the reflexive closure and $\bowtie^*$ for the reflexive transitive closure. If $\bowtie$ is written using $\to$, then the inverse $\bowtie^{-1}$ is written using $\leftarrow$. In what follows, we write simply $t \approx_\alpha s$ for $\vdash_{NL_a} t \approx_\alpha s$. We use $\circ$ for the composition of two binary relations.

Definition 9. Let $\mathcal{R}$ be an NRS_{AS}.

1. Ground terms s and t are *joinable modulo* $\approx_\alpha$, denoted by $s \downarrow_{\approx_\alpha} t$, iff
   $s \ (\to_{\mathcal{R}}^* \circ \approx_\alpha \circ \leftarrow_{\mathcal{R}}^*) \ t$.
2. $\to_{\mathcal{R}}$ is *confluent modulo* $\approx_\alpha$ iff
   for every ground terms s and t, if $s \ (\leftarrow_{\mathcal{R}}^* \circ \to_{\mathcal{R}}^*) \ t$ then $s \downarrow_{\approx_\alpha} t$.
3. $\to_{\mathcal{R}}$ is *Church-Rosser modulo* $\approx_\alpha$ iff
   for every ground terms s and t, if $s \ (\leftarrow_{\mathcal{R}} \cup \to_{\mathcal{R}} \cup \approx_\alpha)^* \ t$ then $s \downarrow_{\approx_\alpha} t$.

4. $\to_{\mathcal{R}}$ is *strongly compatible with* $\approx_\alpha$ iff
   for every ground terms s and t, if $s\ (\approx_\alpha \circ \to_{\mathcal{R}})\ t$ then $s\ (\to^{\bar{=}}_{\mathcal{R}} \circ \approx_\alpha)\ t$.
5. Let $\mathcal{R}'$ be another NRS_{AS}. $\to_{\mathcal{R}}$ *subcommutes with* $\to_{\mathcal{R}'}$ modulo $\approx_\alpha$ iff for every ground terms s and t, if $s\ (\leftarrow_{\mathcal{R}} \circ \to_{\mathcal{R}'})\ t$ then $s\ (\to^{\bar{=}}_{\mathcal{R}'} \circ \approx_\alpha \circ \leftarrow^{\bar{=}}_{\mathcal{R}})\ t$.
6. Let $\mathcal{R}'$ be another NRS_{AS}. $\to_{\mathcal{R}}$ *commutes with* $\to_{\mathcal{R}'}$ *modulo* $\approx_\alpha$ iff for every ground terms s and t, if $s\ (\leftarrow^*_{\mathcal{R}} \circ \to^*_{\mathcal{R}'})\ t$ then $s\ (\to^*_{\mathcal{R}'} \circ \approx_\alpha \circ \leftarrow^*_{\mathcal{R}})\ t$.

It is known that Church-Rosser modulo an equivalence relation $\sim$ is a stronger property than confluence modulo $\sim$ [15]. In the rest of this section, we aim to show Church-Rosser modulo $\approx_\alpha$ for a class of left-linear NRS_{AS}'s, and commutation modulo $\approx_\alpha$ of two systems in a class of left-linear NRS_{AS}'s.

3.1 Uniformity and α-stability

To our aim mentioned above, we restrict NRS_{AS}'s by some conditions. First we consider the uniformity condition [4]. Intuitively, uniformity means that if an atom a is not free in s and s rewrites to t then a is not free in t. We give an adaptation of the definition of [4] for our setting, which has not been considered in [13].

Definition 10 (Uniformity). A rewrite rule $\nabla \vdash l \to r$ is *uniform* if the following holds: for every atom a and every ground substitution σ such that $Var_{\mathcal{X}, \mathcal{X}_A}(l) \subseteq dom(\sigma)$, if $\vdash_{NL_a} \nabla\sigma$ and $\vdash_{NL_a} a\#l\sigma$ then $\vdash_{NL_a} a\#r\sigma$. A rewriting system is *uniform* if so are all its rewrite rules.

The following properties of uniform rewrite rules are important and will be used in the sequel.

Proposition 2. *Suppose* $s \to_R t$ *for a uniform rewrite rule* R. *Then, for every atom* a, *if* $\vdash_{NL_a} a\#s$ *then* $\vdash_{NL_a} a\#t$.

Proof. By induction on the structure of s (For details, see [9].) $\qquad\square$

Lemma 3. *Let* R *be a uniform rewrite rule. If* $s' \approx_\alpha s \to_{\langle R, p, \sigma\rangle} t$, *then there exist* σ' *and* t' *such that* $s' \to_{\langle R, p, \sigma'\rangle} t' \approx_\alpha t$.

Proof. By induction on the structure of s (For details, see [9].) $\qquad\square$

Next we introduce the notion of α-stability [21]. This notion can be seen as a complement to orthogonality in proving Church-Rosser modulo $\approx_\alpha$.

Definition 11 (α-stability). *A rewrite rule* $R = \nabla \vdash l \to r$ *is α-stable if* $\vdash_{NL_a} s \approx_\alpha s'$, $s \to_{\langle R, \varepsilon, \sigma\rangle} t$ *and* $s' \to_{\langle R, \varepsilon, \sigma'\rangle} t'$ *imply* $\vdash_{NL_a} t \approx_\alpha t'$. *An* NRS_{AS} $\mathcal{R}$ *is α-stable if so are all its rewrite rules.*

3.2   Parallel Reduction

A key notion for proving confluence of left-linear rewriting systems is parallel reduction. Here we define it inductively, using a particular kind of contexts.

Definition 12. The *grammatical contexts*, ranged over by G, are the contexts defined by

$$G ::= a \mid [a]\square \mid f\,\square \mid \langle \square_1, \ldots, \square_n \rangle$$

Let $\mathcal{R}$ be an NRS_{AS}. We define the relation $\twoheadrightarrow_{\mathcal{R}}$ inductively by the following rules:

$$\frac{s_1 \twoheadrightarrow_{\mathcal{R}} t_1 \quad \cdots \quad s_n \twoheadrightarrow_{\mathcal{R}} t_n}{G[s_1, \ldots, s_n] \twoheadrightarrow_{\mathcal{R}} G[t_1, \ldots, t_n]} \text{ (C)} \qquad \frac{s \xrightarrow{\varepsilon}_{\mathcal{R}} t \quad R \in \mathcal{R}}{s \twoheadrightarrow_{\mathcal{R}} t} \text{ (B)}$$

where $n\ (\geq 0)$ depends on the form of G. We write $\sigma \twoheadrightarrow_{\mathcal{R}} \delta$ to denote $\forall X \in dom(\sigma_X).\ X\sigma \twoheadrightarrow_{\mathcal{R}} X\delta$ and $\forall A \in dom(\sigma_{X_A}).\ A\sigma = A\delta$.

Lemma 4. *1.* $s \twoheadrightarrow_{\mathcal{R}} s$.
2. If $s \twoheadrightarrow_{\mathcal{R}} t$ *then* $C[s] \twoheadrightarrow_{\mathcal{R}} C[t]$.
3. If $s \rightarrow_{\langle R,p,\sigma \rangle} t$ *and* $R \in \mathcal{R}$ *then* $s \twoheadrightarrow_{\mathcal{R}} t$.
4. If $s \twoheadrightarrow_{\mathcal{R}} t$ *then* $s \rightarrow^*_{\mathcal{R}} t$.

Proof. 1. By induction on the structure of s.
2. By induction on the context C.
3. By 2 and the rule (B).
4. By induction on the derivation of $s \twoheadrightarrow_{\mathcal{R}} t$. □

Lemma 5. *If* $s \twoheadrightarrow_{\mathcal{R}} t$ *then* $\pi{\cdot}s \twoheadrightarrow_{\mathcal{R}} \pi{\cdot}t$.

Proof. By induction on the derivation of $s \twoheadrightarrow_{\mathcal{R}} t$. If the last applied rule in the derivation is (B), then we use Lemma 2. □

Lemma 6. *If* $\sigma \twoheadrightarrow_{\mathcal{R}} \delta$ *then* $e\sigma \twoheadrightarrow_{\mathcal{R}} e\delta$.

Proof. By induction on the structure of e. If $e = \pi{\cdot}X$, then we use Lemma 5. □

Lemma 7. *Let* $\mathcal{R}$ *be a uniform* NRS_{AS}.

1. If $\vdash_{NL_a} a\#s$ *and* $s \twoheadrightarrow_{\mathcal{R}} t$ *then* $\vdash_{NL_a} a\#t$.
2. If $\vdash_{NL_a} \nabla\sigma$ *and* $\sigma \twoheadrightarrow_{\mathcal{R}} \delta$ *then* $\vdash_{NL_a} \nabla\delta$.

Proof. 1. By Proposition 2 and Lemma 4(4).
2. By 1 and Lemma 6, if $\vdash_{NL_a} v\sigma\#e\sigma$ then $\vdash_{NL_a} v\sigma\#e\delta$. Hence, from $\vdash_{NL_a} \nabla\sigma$, we have $\vdash_{NL_a} \nabla\delta$. □

We define the notions in Definition 9 for $\twoheadrightarrow_{\mathcal{R}}$ as well. Then strong compatibility of $\rightarrow_{\mathcal{R}}$ with $\approx_\alpha$ can be extended to strong compatibility of $\twoheadrightarrow_{\mathcal{R}}$ with $\approx_\alpha$.

Lemma 8 (Strong compatibility with $\approx_\alpha$). *Let $\mathcal{R}$ be a uniform NRS_{AS}. If $s' \approx_\alpha s \twoheadrightarrow_\mathcal{R} t$ then there exists t' such that $s' \twoheadrightarrow_\mathcal{R} t' \approx_\alpha t$.*

Proof. By induction on the derivation of $s \twoheadrightarrow_\mathcal{R} t$. If the last applied rule in the derivation is (B), then the claim follows by Lemma 3. Among the other cases, we treat the case where $G = [a]\square$. Then the last part of the derivation has the form

$$\frac{s_1 \twoheadrightarrow_\mathcal{R} t_1}{[a]s_1 \twoheadrightarrow_\mathcal{R} [a]t_1} \;(\mathsf{C})$$

where $[a]s_1 = s$ and $[a]t_1 = t$. Now we have two cases.

(a) $s' = [a]s_1'$ and $\vdash_{NL_a} [a]s_1' \approx_\alpha [a]s_1$.
   Then $\vdash_{NL_a} s_1' \approx_\alpha s_1$, and so by the induction hypothesis, there exists t_1' such that $s_1' \twoheadrightarrow_\mathcal{R} t_1' \approx_\alpha t_1$. Hence we have $[a]s_1' \twoheadrightarrow_\mathcal{R} [a]t_1' \approx_\alpha [a]t_1$.

(b) $s' = [b]s_1'$ and $\vdash_{NL_a} [b]s_1' \approx_\alpha [a]s_1$.
   Then $\vdash_{NL_a} (b\ a)\cdot s_1' \approx_\alpha s_1$ and $\vdash_{NL_a} a\#s_1'$. So by the induction hypothesis, there exists t_1' such that $(b\ a)\cdot s_1' \twoheadrightarrow_\mathcal{R} t_1' \approx_\alpha t_1$. By taking $\pi = (a\ b)$ in Lemma 5, we have $s_1' \twoheadrightarrow_\mathcal{R} (a\ b)\cdot t_1'$, and by Lemma 7, we have $\vdash_{NL_a} a\#(a\ b)\cdot t_1'$. Hence, we obtain the following derivations, from which the claim follows.

$$\frac{s_1' \twoheadrightarrow_\mathcal{R} (a\ b)\cdot t_1'}{[b]s_1' \twoheadrightarrow_\mathcal{R} [b](a\ b)\cdot t_1'} \;(\mathsf{C}) \quad \text{and} \quad \frac{\vdash_{NL_a} t_1' \approx_\alpha t_1 \quad \vdash_{NL_a} a\#(a\ b)\cdot t_1'}{\vdash_{NL_a} [b](a\ b)\cdot t_1' \approx_\alpha [a]t_1}$$

The cases where $G \neq [a]\square$ are simpler. $\square$

3.3 Proofs of Commutation and Confluence

A key lemma to our theorems of commutation and confluence is Lemma 10. It says that for two mutually orthogonal NRS_{AS}'s $\mathcal{R}_1$ and $\mathcal{R}_2$, if parallel reduction of $\mathcal{R}_1$ takes place from a redex of $\mathcal{R}_2$ then all the reductions are below variable positions of the left-hand side of the rule of $\mathcal{R}_2$. This property is used in the proof of subcommutation lemma (Lemma 11).

First we show an auxiliary lemma to address the separated case of moderated variables.

Lemma 9. *Let $\mathcal{R}$ be a uniform NRS_{AS}. If $\vdash_{NL_a} s \approx_\alpha (\pi\cdot X)\sigma$ and $s \twoheadrightarrow_\mathcal{R} t$ then there exists δ such that $\vdash_{NL_a} t \approx_\alpha (\pi\cdot X)\delta$, $\sigma \twoheadrightarrow_\mathcal{R} \delta$, and $\forall Y \in dom(\sigma_X)\setminus\{X\}$. $Y\sigma = Y\delta$.*

Proof. From $\vdash_{NL_a} s \approx_\alpha (\pi\cdot X)\sigma = \pi\sigma\cdot(X\sigma)$, we have $\vdash_{NL_a} (\pi\sigma)^{-1}\cdot s \approx_\alpha X\sigma$, and from $s \twoheadrightarrow_\mathcal{R} t$, we have $(\pi\sigma)^{-1}\cdot s \twoheadrightarrow_\mathcal{R} (\pi\sigma)^{-1}\cdot t$ by Lemma 5. Hence by Lemma 8, there exists t' such that $X\sigma \twoheadrightarrow_\mathcal{R} t' \approx_\alpha (\pi\sigma)^{-1}\cdot t$. Now we define δ by $X\delta = t'$ and $Y\delta = Y\sigma$ for $Y \in dom(\sigma_X)\setminus\{X\}$ (and $A\delta = A\sigma$ for $A \in dom(\sigma_{X_A})$). Then we have $\sigma \twoheadrightarrow_\mathcal{R} \delta$, and from $X\delta = t' \approx_\alpha (\pi\sigma)^{-1}\cdot t = (\pi\delta)^{-1}\cdot t$, we obtain $t \approx_\alpha \pi\delta\cdot(X\delta) = (\pi\cdot X)\delta$. $\square$

Now we prove the announced lemma. Note that the linearity condition is supposed for variables, but not for atom-variables. We therefore restrict induction to proper subexpressions of the left-hand side of the rule of $\mathcal{R}_2$, rather than all linear expressions, so that the assignment by the ground substitution to each atom-variable is fixed throughout the proof by induction. This is a different point from the proof of Lemma 11 of [11] which uses induction on all linear terms.

Note also that there is not an atom but an atom expression (a suspension on an atom-variable) at each place of binder in a rewrite rule. In the cases 2(a) and 2(b) of the following proof, the atom expression v is instantiated by the ground substitution σ and the ground substitution δ to be constructed, and there we use Lemma 1(2) to show the claim.

Lemma 10. *Let $\mathcal{R}_1$ and $\mathcal{R}_2$ be mutually orthogonal uniform NRS_{AS}'s, and let $\nabla \vdash l \to r \in \mathcal{R}_2$. Suppose that σ is a ground substitution with $Var_{\mathcal{X},\mathcal{X}_A}(l) \subseteq dom(\sigma)$ and $\vdash_{NL_a} \nabla\sigma$. Then, for every proper subexpression l' of l, if $\vdash_{NL_a} s \approx_\alpha l'\sigma$ and $s \twoheadrightarrow_{\mathcal{R}_1} t$ then there exists δ such that $\vdash_{NL_a} t \approx_\alpha l'\delta$, $\sigma \twoheadrightarrow_{\mathcal{R}_1} \delta$, and $\forall X \in dom(\sigma_\mathcal{X}) \setminus Var_\mathcal{X}(l'). X\sigma = X\delta$.*

Proof. By induction on the structure of l'. The case where l' is a moderated variable $\pi \cdot X$ follows from Lemma 9. For the other cases, we first show that the last rule used in the derivation of $s \twoheadrightarrow_{\mathcal{R}_1} t$ cannot be (B). Suppose otherwise. Then by the definition of rewrite relation, we have $\vdash_{NL_a} \hat{\nabla}\hat{\sigma}$ and $\vdash_{NL_a} s \approx_\alpha \hat{l}\hat{\sigma}$ for some $\hat{\nabla} \vdash \hat{l} \to \hat{r} \in \mathcal{R}_1$ and $\hat{\sigma}$, where we assume without loss of generality that $dom(\hat{\sigma}) \cap dom(\sigma) = \emptyset$. However, then the VANUP ($\{\hat{l} \approx l'\}, \hat{\nabla}\cup\nabla$) has a solution $\hat{\sigma} \cup \sigma$, which means that $\hat{\nabla} \vdash \hat{l} \to \hat{r}$ overlaps on $\nabla \vdash l \to r$, contradicting the mutual orthogonality of $\mathcal{R}_1$ and $\mathcal{R}_2$. Hence, the last rule used in the derivation of $s \twoheadrightarrow_{\mathcal{R}_1} t$ must be (C). The rest of the proof is by case analysis according to the form of l'. Here we consider the cases where $l' = \langle l'_1, \ldots, l'_n \rangle$ and $l' = [v]l'_1$.

1. $l' = \langle l'_1, \ldots, l'_n \rangle$. Then the last part of the derivation of $s \twoheadrightarrow_{\mathcal{R}_1} t$ has the form

$$\frac{s_1 \twoheadrightarrow_{\mathcal{R}_1} t_1 \quad \cdots \quad s_n \twoheadrightarrow_{\mathcal{R}_1} t_n}{\langle s_1, \ldots, s_n \rangle \twoheadrightarrow_{\mathcal{R}_1} \langle t_1, \ldots, t_n \rangle} \text{ (C)}$$

and for each $i \in \{1, \ldots, n\}$, $\vdash_{NL_a} s_i \approx_\alpha l'_i\sigma$. By the induction hypothesis, there exist δ_i's such that $\vdash_{NL_a} t_i \approx_\alpha l'_i\delta_i$, $\sigma \twoheadrightarrow_{\mathcal{R}_1} \delta_i$, and $\forall X \notin Var_\mathcal{X}(l'_i)$. $X\sigma = X\delta_i$. Since l' is linear, we can take δ such that if $X \in Var_\mathcal{X}(l'_i)$ then $X\delta = X\delta_i$, and if $X \in dom(\sigma_\mathcal{X}) \setminus Var_\mathcal{X}(l')$ then $X\delta = X\sigma$ (and $A\delta = A\sigma$ for $A \in dom(\sigma_{\mathcal{X}_A})$). It is easy to check that this δ satisfies the required condition.
2. $l' = [v]l'_1$. Since $\vdash_{NL_a} s \approx_\alpha l'\sigma = ([v]l'_1)\sigma = [v\sigma](l'_1\sigma)$, we have two cases. Let $a = v\sigma$.
   (a) $s = [a]s'$. Then $\vdash_{NL_a} s' \approx_\alpha l'_1\sigma$, and the last part of the derivation of $s \twoheadrightarrow_{\mathcal{R}_1} t$ has the form

$$\frac{s' \twoheadrightarrow_{\mathcal{R}_1} t'}{[a]s' \twoheadrightarrow_{\mathcal{R}_1} [a]t'} \text{ (C)}$$

Then by the induction hypothesis, there exists δ such that $\vdash_{NL_a} t' \approx_\alpha l'_1 \delta$, $\sigma \twoheadrightarrow_{\mathcal{R}_1} \delta$, and $\forall X \notin Var_{\mathcal{X}}(l'_1). X\sigma = X\delta$. From $\sigma \twoheadrightarrow_{\mathcal{R}_1} \delta$, we have $\forall A \in dom(\sigma_{\mathcal{X}_A}). A\sigma = A\delta$, and so $v\sigma = v\delta$ by Lemma 1(2). Thus, from $\vdash_{NL_a} t' \approx_\alpha l'_1 \delta$, we have $\vdash_{NL_a} [a]t' \approx_\alpha [a](l'_1 \delta) = [v\sigma](l'_1 \delta) = [v\delta](l'_1 \delta) = ([v]l'_1)\delta$. Hence, the claim follows.

(b) $s = [b]s'$. Then, $\vdash_{NL_a} (b\ a)\cdot s' \approx_\alpha l'_1 \sigma$, $\vdash_{NL_a} a \# s'$ and the last part of the derivation of $s \twoheadrightarrow_{\mathcal{R}_1} t$ has the form

$$\frac{s' \twoheadrightarrow_{\mathcal{R}_1} t'}{[b]s' \twoheadrightarrow_{\mathcal{R}_1} [b]t'} \text{ (C)}$$

From $s' \twoheadrightarrow_{\mathcal{R}_1} t'$, we have $(b\ a)\cdot s' \twoheadrightarrow_{\mathcal{R}_1} (b\ a)\cdot t'$ by Lemma 5. Since $\mathcal{R}_1$ is uniform, we also have $\vdash_{NL_a} a \# t'$ by Lemma 7. Now, by the induction hypothesis for l'_1, there exists δ such that $\vdash_{NL_a} (b\ a)\cdot t' \approx_\alpha l'_1 \delta$, $\sigma \twoheadrightarrow_{\mathcal{R}_1} \delta$, and $\forall X \notin Var_{\mathcal{X}}(l'_1). X\sigma = X\delta$. From $\sigma \twoheadrightarrow_{\mathcal{R}_1} \delta$, we have $\forall A \in dom(\sigma_{\mathcal{X}_A}). A\sigma = A\delta$, and so $v\sigma = v\delta$ by Lemma 1(2). Thus, from $\vdash_{NL_a} (b\ a)\cdot t' \approx_\alpha l'_1 \delta$ and $\vdash_{NL_a} a \# t'$, we have $\vdash_{NL_a} [b]t' \approx_\alpha [a](l'_1 \delta) = [v\sigma](l'_1 \delta) = [v\delta](l'_1 \delta) = ([v]l'_1)\delta$. Hence, the claim follows.

$\square$

Now we show subcommutation modulo $\approx_\alpha$ of mutually orthogonal uniform NRS_{AS}'s.

Lemma 11 (Subcommutation modulo $\approx_\alpha$). *Let $\mathcal{R}$ and $\mathcal{R}'$ be mutually orthogonal uniform NRS_{AS}'s. If $s \twoheadrightarrow_{\mathcal{R}} t$ and $s \twoheadrightarrow_{\mathcal{R}'} t'$ then there exist u and u' such that $t \twoheadrightarrow_{\mathcal{R}'} u$, $t' \twoheadrightarrow_{\mathcal{R}} u'$ and $\vdash_{NL_a} u \approx_\alpha u'$.*

Proof. By induction on the structure of s. We distinguish cases according to the last rules used in the derivations of $s \twoheadrightarrow_{\mathcal{R}} t$ and $s \twoheadrightarrow_{\mathcal{R}} t'$.

1. Both rules are (B). This case contradicts the mutual orthogonality of $\mathcal{R}$ and $\mathcal{R}'$.

2. Both rules are (C). The claim follows from the induction hypothesis.

3. One is (C) and the other is (B). Suppose that $s \twoheadrightarrow_{\mathcal{R}} t$ is derived by (C) and that $s \twoheadrightarrow_{\mathcal{R}'} t'$ is derived by (B). Then there exist $R' = \nabla \vdash l \to r \in \mathcal{R}'$ and σ such that $s \to_{\langle R', \varepsilon, \sigma \rangle} t'$. By the definition of rewrite relation, we have $\vdash_{NL_a} \nabla \sigma$, $\vdash_{NL_a} s \approx_\alpha l\sigma$ and $t' = r\sigma$.
   Here we only consider the case where $s = f\ s_1$. Then the last part of the derivation of $s \twoheadrightarrow_{\mathcal{R}} t$ has the form

$$\frac{s_1 \twoheadrightarrow_{\mathcal{R}} t_1}{f\ s_1 \twoheadrightarrow_{\mathcal{R}} f\ t_1} \text{ (C)}$$

Since $\vdash_{NL_a} s \approx_\alpha l\sigma$, we have $\vdash_{NL_a} f\ s_1 \approx_\alpha l\sigma$. So l is of the form $f\ l_1$ and $\vdash_{NL_a} s_1 \approx_\alpha l_1\sigma$. Hence by Lemma 10 with l_1 as l' (s_1 as s and t_1 as t), there exists δ such that $\vdash_{NL_a} t_1 \approx_\alpha l_1\delta$ and $\sigma \twoheadrightarrow_{\mathcal{R}} \delta$. From the former, we have $\vdash_{NL_a} f\ t_1 \approx_\alpha f\ l_1\delta = l\delta$. From the latter and $\vdash_{NL_a} \nabla \sigma$, we have $\vdash_{NL_a} \nabla \delta$ by Lemma 7(2). Thus $t = f\ t_1 \to_{\langle R', \varepsilon, \delta \rangle} r\delta$, and so $t \twoheadrightarrow_{\mathcal{R}'} r\delta$ by the rule (B). On the other hand, by Lemma 6, we have $t' = r\sigma \twoheadrightarrow_{\mathcal{R}} r\delta$. Hence, we can take $u = u' = r\delta$.

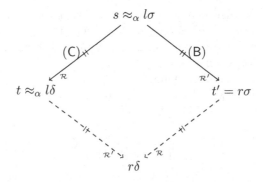

$$\square$$

Actually, the above lemma also holds with the stronger condition $u = u'$. It does not necessarily hold in the case of an orthogonal uniform NRS_{AS} $\mathcal{R} = \mathcal{R}'$ as we see in Lemma 12 below.

Since $\to_{\mathcal{R}} \subseteq \twoheadrightarrow_{\mathcal{R}} \subseteq \to_{\mathcal{R}}^*$ by Lemma 4, we have the following theorem.

Theorem 1 (Commutation modulo $\approx_\alpha$). *Let $\mathcal{R}$ and $\mathcal{R}'$ be mutually orthogonal uniform NRS_{AS}'s. If $s \to_{\mathcal{R}}^* t$ and $s \to_{\mathcal{R}'}^* t'$ then there exist u and u' such that $t \to_{\mathcal{R}'}^* u$, $t' \to_{\mathcal{R}}^* u'$ and $\vdash_{NL_a} u \approx_\alpha u'$.*

This theorem is particularly useful for showing commutation modulo $\approx_\alpha$ of a left-linear uniform NRS_{AS} like the system in Example 3 and a left-linear first-order rewriting system that are mutually orthogonal.

Next we show Church-Rosser modulo $\approx_\alpha$ for orthogonal NRS_{AS}'s. Observing the proof of Lemma 10, we see that the claim also holds for any orthogonal NRS_{AS} $\mathcal{R}_1 = \mathcal{R}_2$ since l' is a proper subexpression of l and there exists no proper overlap in an orthogonal NRS_{AS}.

Lemma 12. *Let $\mathcal{R}$ be an orthogonal uniform NRS_{AS} that is α-stable. Then, if $s \twoheadrightarrow_{\mathcal{R}} t$ and $s \twoheadrightarrow_{\mathcal{R}} t'$ then there exist u and u' such that $t \twoheadrightarrow_{\mathcal{R}} u$, $t' \twoheadrightarrow_{\mathcal{R}} u'$ and $\vdash_{NL_a} u \approx_\alpha u'$.*

Proof. We proceed in a similar way to the proof of Lemma 11 except that in the case where both rules are (B), they may be by the same rewrite rule. In that case, we use the α-stability of $\mathcal{R}$. $\qquad\square$

Theorem 2 (Church-Rosser modulo $\approx_\alpha$). *Let $\mathcal{R}$ be an orthogonal uniform NRS_{AS} that is α-stable. Then, $\to_{\mathcal{R}}$ is Church-Rosser modulo $\approx_\alpha$.*

Proof. By Lemma 8, $\twoheadrightarrow_{\mathcal{R}}$ is strongly compatible with $\approx_\alpha$, and by Lemma 12, $\twoheadrightarrow_{\mathcal{R}}$ subcommutes with $\twoheadrightarrow_{\mathcal{R}}$ modulo $\approx_\alpha$. Hence by the results in [15] (see also Corollary 2.6.5 of [16]), $\twoheadrightarrow_{\mathcal{R}}$ is Church-Rosser modulo $\approx_\alpha$. Since $\to_{\mathcal{R}} \subseteq \twoheadrightarrow_{\mathcal{R}} \subseteq \to_{\mathcal{R}}^*$ by Lemma 4, it follows that $\to_{\mathcal{R}}$ is Church-Rosser modulo $\approx_\alpha$. $\qquad\square$

Example 8. The NRS_{AS} $\mathcal{R}_{sub}$ in Example 3 is orthogonal, uniform and α-stable. Hence by Theorem 2, we see that $\to_{\mathcal{R}_{sub}}$ is Church-Rosser modulo $\approx_\alpha$. $\qquad\square$

Example 9. Consider the NRS_{AS} $\mathcal{R}_{\mathsf{pnfcom}}$ with the following rewrite rules:

$$
\begin{aligned}
A\#Y \vdash\ &\mathsf{and}\langle\mathsf{forall}\langle[A]X\rangle, Y\rangle \rightarrow \mathsf{forall}\langle[A]\mathsf{and}\langle X, Y\rangle\rangle &(\forall_1)\\
A\#X \vdash\ &\mathsf{and}\langle X, \mathsf{forall}\langle[A]Y\rangle\rangle \rightarrow \mathsf{forall}\langle[A]\mathsf{and}\langle X, Y\rangle\rangle &(\forall_2)\\
A\#B \vdash\ &\mathsf{forall}\langle[A]\mathsf{forall}\langle[B]X\rangle\rangle \rightarrow \mathsf{forall}\langle[B]\mathsf{forall}\langle[A]X\rangle\rangle &(\mathsf{COM}_\forall)
\end{aligned}
$$

Then $\mathcal{R}_{\mathsf{pnfcom}}$ has proper overlaps, and hence it is not orthogonal. So we cannot apply Theorem 2. However, it can be shown that $\rightarrow_{\mathcal{R}_{\mathsf{pnfcom}}}$ is Church-Rosser modulo $\approx_\alpha$ (cf. Example 34 of [22]). □

4   Conclusion and Related Work

We have presented proofs of commutation modulo $\approx_\alpha$ of mutually orthogonal uniform NRS_{AS}'s and Church-Rosser modulo $\approx_\alpha$ for orthogonal uniform NRS_{AS}'s that are α-stable. In NRS_{AS}'s, the same atom can be substituted for different atom-variables in a rewrite rule, so in this respect our results on Church-Rosser modulo $\approx_\alpha$ for orthogonal systems generalise previous work on orthogonal systems in traditional nominal rewriting. The results in this paper are about the rewrite relations on ground terms, but they are enough for application to correctness of a form of program transformation. (Commutation of mutually orthogonal systems is used, e.g. in the proof of Lemma 4.3(3) of [10].)

Currently, we are working on implementation of a confluence checking tool that verifies sufficient conditions for confluence and commutation in this paper. To verify non-existence of overlaps in NRS_{AS}'s, it should use some procedure for deciding variable-atom nominal unification problems. Since our previous tool [1] implements an equivariant unification procedure which uses atom-variables and permutation-variables, it is expected to help us to implement such a procedure.

The difference between confluence on ground nominal terms like in this paper and confluence in previous work on traditional nominal rewriting corresponds to the difference between confluence of some concrete calculus and meta-confluence of that calculus with meta-variables (see, e.g. [14]). The traditional nominal rewriting system corresponding to $\mathcal{R}_{\mathsf{pnfcom}}$ in Example 9 above is an example of a system for which confluence on ground terms holds but confluence on general terms does not (cf. Examples 12 and 34 of [22]).

As a rewriting mechanism with matching and overlaps without involving permutations, closed rewriting has been considered [2,4]. However, closed rewriting is incompatible with rewrite rules with free atoms like the rule ($\mathsf{sub}_{\mathsf{var}\epsilon}$) in Example 3. In fact, according to Lemma 5.3 of [2], no rewrite step is induced by such rewrite rules.

Acknowledgements. We are grateful to the anonymous referees for valuable comments. The first author thanks Makoto Hamana for useful discussions. This work was partly supported by JSPS KAKENHI Grant Numbers JP17K00005, JP18K11158, JP19K11891 and JP20H04164.

References

1. Aoto, T., Kikuchi, K.: Nominal confluence tool. In: Olivetti, N., Tiwari, A. (eds.) IJCAR 2016. LNCS (LNAI), vol. 9706, pp. 173–182. Springer, Cham (2016). https://doi.org/10.1007/978-3-319-40229-1_12
2. Ayala-Rincón, M., Fernández, M., Gabbay, M.J., Rocha-Oliveira, A.C.: Checking overlaps of nominal rewriting rules. Electron. Notes Theoret. Comput. Sci. **323**, 39–56 (2016)
3. Chiba, Y., Aoto, T., Toyama, Y.: Program transformation by templates based on term rewriting. In: Proceedings of the 7th PPDP, pp. 59–69. ACM (2005)
4. Fernández, M., Gabbay, M.J.: Nominal rewriting. Inf. Comput. **205**, 917–965 (2007)
5. Fernández, M., Gabbay, M.J., Mackie, I.: Nominal rewriting systems. In: Proceedings of the 6th PPDP, pp. 108–119. ACM (2004)
6. Gabbay, M.J., Pitts, A.M.: A new approach to abstract syntax with variable binding. Formal Aspects Comput. **13**, 341–363 (2002)
7. Gramlich, B.: Confluence without termination via parallel critical pairs. In: Kirchner, H. (ed.) CAAP 1996. LNCS, vol. 1059, pp. 211–225. Springer, Heidelberg (1996). https://doi.org/10.1007/3-540-61064-2_39
8. Huet, G.: Confluent reductions: abstract properties and applications to term rewriting systems. J. ACM **27**(4), 797–821 (1980)
9. Kikuchi, K., Aoto, T.: Omitted proofs. https://www.riec.tohoku.ac.jp/~kxe/cr-nrsas/appendix.pdf
10. Kikuchi, K., Aoto, T., Sasano, I.: Inductive theorem proving in non-terminating rewriting systems and its application to program transformation. In: Proceedings of the 21st PPDP, pp. 13:1–13:14. ACM (2019)
11. Kikuchi, K., Aoto, T., Toyama, Y.: Parallel closure theorem for left-linear nominal rewriting systems. In: Dixon, C., Finger, M. (eds.) FroCoS 2017. LNCS (LNAI), vol. 10483, pp. 115–131. Springer, Cham (2017). https://doi.org/10.1007/978-3-319-66167-4_7
12. Knuth, D.E., Bendix, P.B.: Simple word problems in universal algebras. In: Leech, J. (ed.) Computational Problems in Abstract Algebra, pp. 263–297. Pergamon Press (1970)
13. Kutz, Y., Schmidt-Schauß, M.: Rewriting with generalized nominal unification. Math. Struct. Comput. Sci. **30**, 710–735 (2020)
14. de Moura, F.L.C., Kesner, D., Ayala-Rincón, M.: Metaconfluence of calculi with explicit substitutions at a distance. In: Proceedings of the 34th FSTTCS. LIPIcs, vol. 29, pp. 391–402 (2014)
15. Ohlebusch, E.: Church-Rosser theorems for abstract reduction modulo an equivalence relation. In: Nipkow, T. (ed.) RTA 1998. LNCS, vol. 1379, pp. 17–31. Springer, Heidelberg (1998). https://doi.org/10.1007/BFb0052358
16. Ohlebusch, E.: Advanced Topics in Term Rewriting. Springer, New York (2002). https://doi.org/10.1007/978-1-4757-3661-8
17. Okui, S.: Simultaneous critical pairs and Church-Rosser property. In: Nipkow, T. (ed.) RTA 1998. LNCS, vol. 1379, pp. 2–16. Springer, Heidelberg (1998). https://doi.org/10.1007/BFb0052357
18. Pitts, A.M.: Nominal logic, a first order theory of names and binding. Inf. Comput. **186**, 165–193 (2003)
19. Rosen, B.: Tree-manipulating systems and Church-Rosser theorems. J. ACM **20**(1), 160–187 (1973)

20. Schmidt-Schauß, M., Sabel, D., Kutz, Y.D.K.: Nominal unification with atom-variables. J. Symb. Comput. **90**, 42–64 (2019)
21. Suzuki, T., Kikuchi, K., Aoto, T., Toyama, Y.: Confluence of orthogonal nominal rewriting systems revisited. In: Proceedings of the 26th RTA. LIPIcs, vol. 36, pp. 301–317 (2015)
22. Suzuki, T., Kikuchi, K., Aoto, T., Toyama, Y.: Critical pair analysis in nominal rewriting. In: Proceedings of the 7th SCSS. EPiC, vol. 39, pp. 156–168. EasyChair (2016)
23. Toyama, Y.: On the Church-Rosser property of term rewriting systems. Technical Report 17672, NTT ECL (1981). (in Japanese)
24. Toyama, Y.: Commutativity of term rewriting systems. In: Fuchi, K., Kott, L. (eds.) Programming of Future Generation Computers II, pp. 393–407. North-Holland (1988)
25. Toyama, Y.: How to prove equivalence of term rewriting systems without induction. Theoret. Comput. Sci. **90**(2), 369–390 (1991)
26. Urban, C., Pitts, A.M., Gabbay, M.J.: Nominal unification. Theoret. Comput. Sci. **323**, 473–497 (2004)

Pattern Eliminating Transformations

Horatiu Cirstea, Pierre Lermusiaux, and Pierre-Etienne Moreau[⊠]

Université de Lorraine, CNRS, Inria, LORIA, 54000 Nancy, France
{Horatiu.Cirstea,Pierre.Lermusiaux,Pierre-Etienne.Moreau}@loria.fr

Abstract. Program transformation is a common practice in computer science, and its many applications can have a range of different objectives. For example, a program written in an original high level language could be either translated into machine code for execution purposes, or towards a language suitable for formal verification. Such compilations are split into several so-called passes which generally aim at eliminating certain constructions of the original language to get a program in some intermediate languages and finally generate the target code. Rewriting is a widely established formalism to describe the mechanism and the logic behind such transformations. In a typed context, the underlying type system can be used to give syntactic guarantees on the shape of the results obtained after each pass, but this approach could lead to an accumulation of auxiliary types that should be considered. We propose in this paper a less intrusive approach based on simply annotating the function symbols with the (anti-)patterns the corresponding transformations are supposed to eliminate. We show how this approach allows one to statically check that the rewrite system implementing the transformation is consistent with the annotations and thus, that it eliminates the respective patterns.

Keywords: Rewriting · Pattern-matching · Pattern semantics

1 Introduction

Rewriting is a well established formalism widely used in both computer science and mathematics. It has been used, for example, in semantics in order to describe the meaning of programming languages [28], but also in automated reasoning when describing, by inference rules, a logic, a theorem prover [22], or a constraint solver [21]. Rewriting has turned out to be particularly well adapted to describe program semantics [31] and program transformations [7,27]. There are several languages and tools implementing the notions of pattern matching and rewriting rules ranging from functional languages, featuring relatively simple patterns and fixed rewriting strategies, to rule based languages like Maude [11], Stratego [34], or Tom [5], providing equational matching and flexible strategies; they have been all used as underlying languages for more or less sophisticated compilers.

This work is partially supported by the project ANR-16-CE25-0007 FORMEDICIS.

M. Fernández (Ed.): LOPSTR 2020, LNCS 12561, pp. 74–92, 2021.
https://doi.org/10.1007/978-3-030-68446-4_4

In the context of compilation, the complete transformation is usually performed in multiple phases, also called passes, in order to eventually obtain a program in a different target language. Most of these passes concern transformations between some intermediate languages and often aim at eliminating certain constructions of the original language. These transformations could eliminate just some symbols, like in desugaring passes for example, or more elaborate constructions, like in code optimization passes.

The correction of the transformations could be guaranteed using runtime assertions, but static guarantees are certainly preferable. When using typed languages, we can already rely on the typing system to provide such static guarantees: the type of the transformation function implicitly expresses its expected result. The differences between the source and the target language generally concern only a small number of symbols, making the definition of the latter quite tedious. For example, in a desugaring pass, the target language would contain the same symbols as the source one but the syntactic sugar symbols.

Formalisms such as the one introduced for NanoPass [23] have proposed a method to eliminate a lot of the overhead induced by the definition of the intermediate languages by specifying only the symbols eliminated from the source language and generating automatically the corresponding intermediate language.

Consider, for instance, expressions build out of integers, strings and lists:

$$Expr = int(Int) \qquad\qquad List = nil$$
$$\quad\ |\ str(String) \qquad\qquad\quad\ |\ cons(Expr, List)$$
$$\quad\ |\ lst(List)$$

If we want to define a transformation encoding integers by strings then, the target language in NanoPass would be $Expr^{-int}$, *i.e.* expressions build out of strings and lists. Note that in this case the tool removes the symbol *int* from *Expr* and replaces accordingly *Expr* with the new type in the type of *cons*.

This kind of approaches reach their limitations when the transformation of the source language goes beyond the removal of some symbols. For example, if we want to define a transformation which flattens the list expressions and ensures thus that there is no nested list, the following target type should be considered:

$$Expr = lit(Literal) \quad Literal = int(Int) \qquad List = nil$$
$$\quad\ |\ lst(List) \qquad\qquad\quad |\ str(String) \qquad\qquad |\ cons(Literal, List)$$

Functional approaches to transformation [30] can rely on fine grained type systems, combining overloading, subtyping and polymorphism, through the use of variants [14], to define the transformation and provide such guarantees. While effective, this requires to design such adjusted types in a case by case basis.

We propose in this paper a formalism where function symbols are simply annotated with the patterns that should be eliminated by the corresponding transformation and a mechanism to statically verify that the rewriting system implementing the function does eliminate these patterns. The method is minimally intrusive: for the above example, we should just annotate the flattening function symbol with the pattern $cons(lst(l_1), l_2)$ and the checker verifies that the underlying rewriting system is consistent with the annotation, or exhibits the problematic rule(s) and issue(s) if it is not. The method applies to constructor based term rewriting systems, which correspond to functional programs defined by pattern matching, programs which are commonly used when defining transformations. When the system is complete and terminating, which is usually the case when defining a function, our method verifies that the corresponding normal forms contain no subterms matched by the specified patterns.

First, we introduce the basic notions used in the paper. In Sect. 3 we define the notion of pattern-free terms and their ground semantics, and we characterize semantics preserving rewriting system. Section 4 describes a method for automatically checking pattern-free properties and shows how this method can be used to verify semantics preservation and consequently, the absence of specific patterns from the result of the corresponding transformations. We finally present some related work and conclude. The proofs are available in [9].

2   Preliminary Notions

We define in this section the basic notions and notations used in this paper; more details can be found in [4,33].

A *many-sorted signature* $\Sigma = (\mathcal{S}, \mathcal{F})$, consists of a set of sorts $\mathcal{S}$ and a set of symbols $\mathcal{F}$. The set of symbols is partitioned into two disjoint sets $\mathcal{F} = \mathcal{D} \uplus \mathcal{C}$; $\mathcal{D}$ is the set of *defined symbols* and $\mathcal{C}$ the set of *constructors*. A symbol f with *domain* $\mathcal{D}om(f) = s_1 \times \cdots \times s_n \in \mathcal{S}^*$ and *co-domain* $\mathcal{C}o\mathcal{D}om(f) = s \in \mathcal{S}$ is written $f{:}s_1 \times \cdots \times s_n \mapsto s$; we may write f_s to indicate explicitly the co-domain and use $\mathcal{D}om(f)[i]$ to denote the i-th sort, s_i, in the domain. We denote by $\mathcal{C}_s$, resp. $\mathcal{D}_s$, the set of constructors, resp. defined symbols, with co-domain s. Variables are also sorted and we write $x{:}s$ or x_s to indicate that variable x has sort s. The set $\mathcal{X}_s$ denotes a set of variables of sort s and $\mathcal{X} = \bigcup_{s \in \mathcal{S}} \mathcal{X}_s$ is the set of sorted variables.

The set of terms of sort $s \in \mathcal{S}$, denoted $\mathcal{T}_s(\mathcal{F}, \mathcal{X})$ is the smallest set containing $\mathcal{X}_s$ and such that $f(t_1, \ldots, t_n)$ is in $\mathcal{T}_s(\mathcal{F}, \mathcal{X})$ whenever $f{:}s_1 \times \cdots \times s_n \mapsto s$ and $t_i \in \mathcal{T}_{s_i}(\mathcal{F}, \mathcal{X})$, $i \in [1, n]$. We write $t{:}s$ to indicate that the term t is of sort s, *i.e.* when $t \in \mathcal{T}_s(\mathcal{F}, \mathcal{X})$. The set of *sorted terms* is defined as $\mathcal{T}(\mathcal{F}, \mathcal{X}) = \bigcup_{s \in \mathcal{S}} \mathcal{T}_s(\mathcal{F}, \mathcal{X})$. The set of variables occurring in $t \in \mathcal{T}(\mathcal{F}, \mathcal{X})$ is denoted by $\mathcal{V}ar(t)$. If $\mathcal{V}ar(t)$ is empty, t is called a *ground* term. $\mathcal{T}_s(\mathcal{F})$ denotes the set of all ground terms of sort s and $\mathcal{T}(\mathcal{F})$ denotes the set of all ground terms. Terms in $\mathcal{T}(\mathcal{C})$ are called *values*. A *linear* term is a term where every variable occurs at most once. The linear terms in $\mathcal{T}(\mathcal{C}, \mathcal{X})$ are called *constructor patterns* or simply *patterns*.

A *position* of a term t is a sequence of positive integers describing the path from the root of t to the root of the subterm at that position. The empty sequence representing the root position is denoted by ε. $t_{|\omega}$, resp. $t(\omega)$, denotes the subterm of t, resp. the symbol of t, at position ω. $t[s]_\omega$ denotes the term t with the subterm at position ω replaced by s. $\mathcal{P}os(t)$ denotes the set of positions of t.

We call *substitution* any mapping from $\mathcal{X}$ to $\mathcal{T}(\mathcal{F}, \mathcal{X})$ which is the identity except over a finite set of variables called its domain. A substitution σ extends as expected to an endomorphism σ' of $\mathcal{T}(\mathcal{F}, \mathcal{X})$. To simplify the notations, we do not make the distinction between σ and σ'. Sorted substitutions are such that if $x{:}s$ then $\sigma(x) \in \mathcal{T}_s(\mathcal{F}, \mathcal{X})$. Note that for any such sorted substitution σ, $t{:}s$ iff $\sigma(t){:}s$. In what follows we will only consider such sorted substitutions.

Given two terms t, u of some sort s, we say that t *matches* u (denoted $t \prec\!\!\!\prec u$) if it exists a substitution σ such that $u = \sigma(t)$. When t is linear, we can give an inductive definition to the pattern matching relation:

$$x \prec\!\!\!\prec u \qquad\qquad x \in \mathcal{X}_s$$
$$f(t_1, \ldots, t_n) \prec\!\!\!\prec f(u_1, \ldots, u_n) \text{ iff } \wedge_{i=1}^n t_i \prec\!\!\!\prec u_i, \text{ for } f \in \mathcal{F}$$

In this paper we only consider matchings of the form $p \prec\!\!\!\prec v$ with p a constructor pattern and v a value.

Starting from the observation that a pattern can be interpreted as the set of its instances, the notion of *ground semantics* was introduced in [10] as the set of all ground constructor instances of a pattern $p \in \mathcal{T}_s(\mathcal{C}, \mathcal{X})$: $[\![p]\!] = \{\sigma(p) \mid \sigma(p) \in \mathcal{T}_s(\mathcal{C})\}$. It was shown in [10] that, given a pattern p and a value v, $v \in [\![p]\!]$ iff $p \prec\!\!\!\prec v$. $\perp$ denotes the pattern whose semantics is empty, *i.e.* matching no term.

A *constructor rewrite rule* (over Σ) is a pair of terms $\varphi(l_1, \ldots, l_n) \to r \in \mathcal{T}_s(\mathcal{F}, \mathcal{X}) \times \mathcal{T}_s(\mathcal{F}, \mathcal{X})$ with $s \in \mathcal{S}$, $\varphi \in \mathcal{D}$, $l_1, \ldots, l_n \in \mathcal{T}(\mathcal{C}, \mathcal{X})$ and such that $\varphi(l_1, \ldots, l_n)$ is linear and $Var(r) \subseteq Var(l)$. A *constructor based term rewriting system* (CBTRS) is a set of constructor rewrite rules $\mathcal{R}$ inducing a *rewriting relation* over $\mathcal{T}(\mathcal{F})$, denoted by $\longrightarrow_{\mathcal{R}}$ and such that $t \longrightarrow_{\mathcal{R}} t'$ iff there exist $l \to r \in \mathcal{R}$, $\omega \in Pos(t)$ and a substitution σ such that $t_{|\omega} = \sigma(l)$ and $t' = t[\sigma(r)]_\omega$. The reflexive and transitive closure of $\longrightarrow_{\mathcal{R}}$ is denoted by $\longrightarrow\!\!\!\!\rightarrow_{\mathcal{R}}$.

3   Pattern-Free Terms and Corresponding Semantics

We want to ensure that the normal form of a term, if it exists, does not contain a specific constructor and more generally that no subterm of this normal form matches a given pattern. The sort of the term provides some information on the shape of the normal forms since the precise language of the values of a given sort is implicitly given by the signature. But normal forms often satisfy stronger constraints that also depend on the underlying CBTRS.

To guarantee these constraints we annotate all defined symbols with the patterns that are supposed to be absent when reducing a term headed by the respective symbol and we check that the CBTRS defining the corresponding functions are consistent with these annotations.

We focus first on the notion of pattern-free term and on the corresponding ground semantics, and explain in the next sections how one can check pattern-freeness and verify the consistency of the symbol annotations with a CBTRS.

3.1   Pattern-Free Terms

We consider that every defined symbol $f^{-p} \in \mathcal{D}$ is now annotated with a pattern $p \in \mathcal{T}_\perp(\mathcal{C}, \mathcal{X}) = \mathcal{T}(\mathcal{C}, \mathcal{X}) \cup \{\perp\}$ and we use this notation to define *pattern-free* terms. Intuitively, any value obtained by reducing a ground term of the form $f^{-p}(t_1, \ldots, t_n)$ contains no subterms matched by p. Given the example from the introduction, we can consider two function symbols, $flattenE^{-p} : Expr \mapsto Expr$ and $flattenL^{-p} : List \mapsto List$, with $p = cons(lst(l1), l2)$, to indicate that the normal forms of any term headed by one of these symbols contain no nested lists. The annotation of the function symbol for the concatenation, $concat^{-\perp} : List \times List \mapsto List$, indicates that no particular shape is expected for the reducts of the corresponding terms.

Definition 3.1 (Pattern-free terms). *Given p, a constructor pattern or $\perp$,*

- *a value $v \in \mathcal{T}(\mathcal{C})$ is p-free iff $\forall \omega \in \mathcal{P}os(v), p \not\ll v_{|\omega}$;*
- *a term $u \in \mathcal{T}(\mathcal{C}, \mathcal{X})$ is p-free iff $\forall \sigma$ such that $\sigma(u) \in \mathcal{T}(\mathcal{C})$, $\sigma(u)$ is p-free;*
- *a term $t \in \mathcal{T}(\mathcal{F}, \mathcal{X})$ is p-free iff $\forall \omega \in \mathcal{P}os(t)$ such that $t(\omega) = f_s^{-q} \in \mathcal{D}$, $t[v]_\omega$ is p-free for all q-free value $v \in \mathcal{T}_s(\mathcal{C})$.*

A value is p-free if and only if p matches no subterm of the value. For terms containing no defined symbols, verifying a pattern-free property comes to verifying the property for all the ground instances of the term. Finally, a general term is p-free if and only if replacing (all) the subterms headed by a defined symbol f_s^{-q} by any q-free value of the same sort s results in a p-free term. Intuitively, this corresponds to considering an over-approximation of the set of potential normal forms of an annotated term. While pattern-free properties can be checked for any value by exploring all its subterms, this is not possible for a general term since the property has to be verified by a potentially infinite number of values. We present in Sect. 4 a decision procedure for this problem.

3.2   Generalized Ground Semantics

The notion of ground semantics presented in Sect. 2 and, in particular, the approach proposed in [10] to compute differences (and thus intersections) of such semantics, can be used to compare the shape of two constructor patterns p, q (at the root position). More precisely, when $[\![p]\!] \cap [\![q]\!] = \emptyset$ we have that $\forall \sigma, \sigma(q) \notin [\![p]\!]$ and therefore, we can establish that $\forall \sigma, p \not\ll \sigma(q)$. We can thus compare the semantics of a given pattern p with the semantics of each of the subterms of a constructor pattern t in order to check that t is p-free.

Example 3.1. Consider the signature Σ with $\mathcal{S} = \{s_1, s_2, s_3\}$ and $\mathcal{F} = \mathcal{C} = \{c_1 : s_2 \times s_1 \mapsto s_1, c_2 : s_3 \mapsto s_1, c_3 : s_1 \mapsto s_2, c_4 : s_3 \mapsto s_2, c_5 : s_3 \mapsto s_3, c_6 : \mapsto s_3\}$.

We can compute $[\![c_1(c_4(c_6), y_{s_1})]\!] \cap [\![c_1(x_{s_2}, c_2(c_6))]\!] = [\![c_1(c_4(c_6), c_2(c_6))]\!]$ and thus neither $c_1(c_4(c_6), y_{s_1})$ is $c_1(x, c_2(c_6))$-free nor $c_1(x_{s_2}, c_2(c_6))$ is $c_1(c_4(c_6), y)$-free. Similarly, we can check that $[\![c_3(c_2(z_{s_3}))]\!] \cap [\![c_4(z_{s_3})]\!] = \emptyset$ and that $[\![c_2(z_{s_3})]\!] \cap [\![c_4(z_{s_3})]\!] = \emptyset$ and, as a term of sort s_3 can only contain constructors c_5 and c_6, we can deduce that $c_3(c_2(z_{s_3}))$ is $c_4(z)$-free.

We want to establish a general method to verify pattern-free properties for any term and we propose an approach which relies on the notion of ground semantics extended in order to take into account all terms in $\mathcal{T}(\mathcal{F}, \mathcal{X})$:

Definition 3.2 (Generalized ground semantics). *Given a term* $u \in T(\mathcal{C}, \mathcal{X})$, *and a term* $t \in T(\mathcal{F}, \mathcal{X})$,

- $\llbracket u \rrbracket = \{\sigma(u) \mid \forall \sigma, \sigma(u) \in T(\mathcal{C})\}$;
- $\llbracket t \rrbracket = \bigcup_{\omega \in \mathcal{P}os(t), t(\omega) = f_s^{-p} \in \mathcal{D}} \bigcup_{v \in \mathcal{T}_s(\mathcal{C})\ p\text{-free}} \llbracket t\,[v]_\omega \rrbracket$

Note that the ground semantics of a variable x_s is the set of all possible ground patterns of the corresponding sort: $\llbracket x_s \rrbracket = \mathcal{T}_s(\mathcal{C})$, and for non-variable constructor patterns, since they are linear, we can use a recursive definition: $\llbracket c(p_1, \ldots, p_n) \rrbracket = \{c(v_1, \ldots, v_n) \mid (v_1, \ldots, v_n) \in \llbracket p_1 \rrbracket \times \cdots \times \llbracket p_n \rrbracket\}$ for all $c \in \mathcal{C}$.

Moreover, by definition we have $\llbracket f_s^{-p}(t_1, \ldots, t_n) \rrbracket = \{v \in \mathcal{T}_s(\mathcal{C}) \mid v\ p\text{-free}\}$. The generalized ground semantics of a term rooted by a defined symbol represents an over-approximation of all the possible values obtained by reducing the term with respect to a CBTRS preserving the pattern-free properties.

Pattern-freeness can be checked by exploring the semantics of the term:

Proposition 3.1. *Let* $t \in T(\mathcal{F}, \mathcal{X}), p \in T_\perp(\mathcal{C}, \mathcal{X})$, t *is* p-*free iff* $\forall v \in \llbracket t \rrbracket, v$ *is* p-*free.*

For convenience, we consider also annotated variables whose semantics is that of any term headed by a defined symbol with the same co-domain as the sort of the variable:

$$\llbracket x_s^{-p} \rrbracket = \{v \in \mathcal{T}_s(\mathcal{C}) \mid v\ p\text{-free}\}$$

Thus, $\llbracket f_s^{-p}(t_1, \ldots, t_n) \rrbracket = \llbracket x_s^{-p} \rrbracket$ for all $f_s^{-p} \in \mathcal{D}_s$. Note that $x_s^{-\perp}$ has the same semantics as x_s, and we sometimes use x_s to denote $x_s^{-\perp}$. We denote by $\mathcal{X}^a$ the set of annotated variables.

Given a linear term $t \in T(\mathcal{F}, \mathcal{X})$, we can systematically construct its *symbolic equivalent* $\tilde{t} \in T(\mathcal{C}, \mathcal{X}^a)$ by replacing all the subterms of t headed by a defined symbol f_s^{-p} by a fresh variable x_s^{-p} of the corresponding sort and annotated by the same pattern:

Proposition 3.2. $\forall t \in T(\mathcal{F}, \mathcal{X}), \llbracket t \rrbracket = \llbracket \tilde{t} \rrbracket$.

Example 3.2. We consider the signature from Example 3.1 enriched with the defined symbols $\mathcal{D} = \{f^{-p_1} : s_1 \mapsto s_1, g^{-p_2} : s_2 \mapsto s_2\}$ with $p_1 = c_1(c_4(z), y)$ and $p_2 = c_4(z)$. The symbolic equivalent of the term $r_1 = c_1(g^{-p_2}(x), f^{-p_1}(y))$ is the term $\tilde{r}_1 = c_1(x_{s_2}^{-p_2}, y_{s_1}^{-p_1})$.

We can thus restrict in what follows to patterns using annotated variables and we consider *extended patterns* built out of this kind of patterns:

$$p, q := x \mid c(q_1, \ldots, q_n) \mid p_1 + p_2 \mid p_1 \setminus p_2 \mid p_1 \times p_2 \mid \perp$$

with $x \in \mathcal{X}_s^a, c : s_1 \times \cdots \times s_n \mapsto s \in \mathcal{C}, p, q, p_1, p_2 : s$ and $q_i : s_i, i \in [1, n]$. Extended patterns can share variables but not below a constructor symbol. This corresponds to the fact that p_1 and p_2, in $p_1 + p_2$ (resp. $p_1 \setminus p_2, p_1 \times p_2$), represent independent alternatives *w.r.t.* matching and thus, that their variables are unrelated. For example, the patterns $c_3(c_2(x)) + c_4(x)$ and $c_3(c_2(x)) + c_4(y)$ both represent all values rooted by c_3 followed by c_2, or rooted by c_4.

The pattern matching relation can be extended to take into account disjunctions, conjunctions and complements of patterns:

$$p_1 + p_2 \prec\!\!\!\prec v \text{ iff } p_1 \prec\!\!\!\prec v \ \lor \ p_2 \prec\!\!\!\prec v \qquad p_1 \times p_2 \prec\!\!\!\prec v \text{ iff } p_1 \prec\!\!\!\prec v \ \land \ p_2 \prec\!\!\!\prec v$$
$$p_1 \setminus p_2 \prec\!\!\!\prec v \text{ iff } p_1 \prec\!\!\!\prec v \ \land \ p_2 \not\prec\!\!\!\prec v \qquad \bot \not\prec\!\!\!\prec v$$

Intuitively, a pattern $p_1 + p_2$ matches any term matched by one of its components while a pattern $p_1 \times p_2$ matches any term matched by both its components. The relative complement of p_2 w.r.t. p_1, $p_1 \setminus p_2$, matches all terms matched by p_1 except for those matched by p_2. $\bot$ matches no term. $\times$ has a higher priority than $\setminus$ which has a higher priority than $+$.

The notion of ground semantics extends to such patterns by considering the above recursive definition for patterns headed by constructor symbols and

$$[\![p_1 + p_2]\!] = [\![p_1]\!] \cup [\![p_2]\!] \qquad [\![p_1 \setminus p_2]\!] = [\![p_1]\!] \setminus [\![p_2]\!]$$
$$[\![p_1 \times p_2]\!] = [\![p_1]\!] \cap [\![p_2]\!] \qquad [\![\bot]\!] = \emptyset$$

We still have that given an extended pattern p and a value v, $v \in [\![p]\!]$ iff $p \prec\!\!\!\prec v$ [10].

If an extended pattern contains no $\bot$ it is called *pure*, and if it contains no $\times$ and no $\setminus$ it is called *additive*. A term of $\mathcal{T}(\mathcal{C}, \mathcal{X}^a)$, it is called *symbolic*. We call *regular* patterns that contain only variables of the form $x^{-\bot}$ and *quasi-additive* patterns that contain no $\times$ and only contain $\setminus$ with the pattern on the left being a variable and the pattern on the right being a regular additive pattern.

We can remark that p_1 and p_2 in Example 3.2 are regular patterns, that $x_{s_2}^{-p_1} \setminus p_2$ is a quasi-additive pattern, and that $\tilde{r}_1$ is a symbolic pattern (indeed, the symbolic equivalent of any term is a symbolic pattern).

3.3 Semantics Preserving CBTRS

Generalized ground semantics rely on the symbol annotations and assume thus a specific shape for the normal forms of reducible terms. This assumption should be checked by verifying that the CBTRSs defining the annotated symbols are consistent with these annotations, *i.e.* check that the semantics is preserved by reduction.

Definition 3.3. *A rewrite rule $l \rightarrow r$ is semantics preserving iff $[\![r]\!] \subseteq [\![l]\!]$. A CBTRS is semantics preserving iff all its rewrite rules are.*

Semantics preservation carries over to the induced rewriting relation:

Proposition 3.3. *Given a semantics preserving CBTRS $\mathcal{R}$ we have*

$$\forall t, v \in \mathcal{T}(\mathcal{F}), \ if \ t \longrightarrow_{\mathcal{R}} v, \ then \ [\![v]\!] \subseteq [\![t]\!].$$

As an immediate consequence we obtain the pattern-free preservation:

Corollary 3.1. *Given a semantics preserving CBTRS $\mathcal{R}$ we have*

$$\forall t, v \in \mathcal{T}(\mathcal{F}), p \in \mathcal{T}(\mathcal{C}, \mathcal{X}), \text{ if } t \text{ is p-free and } t \longrightarrow_{\mathcal{R}} v, \text{ then } v \text{ is p-free.}$$

Note that the rules of a CBTRS are of the form $f^{-p}(l_1, \ldots, l_n) \rightarrow r$ and thus, as an immediate consequence of Definition 3.2, the semantics of the left-hand side of the rewrite rule is the set of all p-free values. Therefore, according to Proposition 3.1, such a rule is semantics preserving if and only if its right-hand side r is p-free. We will see in the next section how pattern-freeness and thus, semantics preservation, can be statically checked.

Example 3.3. We consider the signature from Example 3.2 and the CBTRS:

$$\begin{aligned}
f^{-p_1}(c_1(x, y)) &\rightarrow c_1(g^{-p_2}(x), f^{-p_1}(y)) & g^{-p_2}(c_4(z)) &\rightarrow c_3(c_2(z)) \\
f^{-p_1}(c_2(z)) &\rightarrow c_2(z) & g^{-p_2}(c_3(y)) &\rightarrow c_3(f^{-p_1}(y))
\end{aligned}$$

We have seen in Example 3.1 that $c_3(c_2(x))$ is p_2-free and we can thus conclude that the rule $g(c_4(z)) \rightarrow c_3(c_2(z))$ is semantics preserving. In order to verify in a systematic way the corresponding pattern-free properties of all right-hand sides and conclude that the CBTRS is semantics preserving, we introduce in the next section a method to statically check pattern-freeness.

4   Deep Semantics for Pattern-Free Properties

The ground semantics was used in [10] as a means to represent a potentially infinite number of instances of a term in a finite manner and can be employed to check that a pattern matches (or not) a term by computing the intersection between their semantics. For pattern-freeness, we should check not only that the term is not matched by the pattern but also that none of its subterms is matched by this pattern. We would thus need a notion of ground semantics closed by the subterm relation.

We introduce next an extended notion of ground semantics satisfying the above requirements, show how it can be expressed in terms of ground semantics, and provide a method for checking the emptiness of the intersection of such semantics and thus, assert pattern-free properties.

4.1   Deep Semantics

The notion of *deep semantics* is introduced to provide more comprehensive information on the shape of the (sub)terms compared to the ground semantics which describes essentially the shape of the term at the root position.

Definition 4.1 (Deep semantics). *Let t be an extended pattern, its deep semantics $\{\!\{t\}\!\}$ is defined as follows:*

$$\{\!\{t\}\!\} = \{u_{|\omega} \mid u \in [\![t]\!], \omega \in \mathcal{P}os\,(u)\}$$

Note first that, similarly to the case of generalized ground semantics, it is obvious that we can always exhibit a symbolic pattern equivalent in terms of deep semantics to a given term, $i.e.$ $\forall t \in \mathcal{T}(\mathcal{F}, \mathcal{X}), \{\!| t |\!\} = \{\!| \hat{t} |\!\}$; consequently, we can focus on the computation of the deep semantics of extended patterns. Following this observation and as an immediate consequence of the definition we have a necessary and sufficient condition with regards to pattern-free properties:

Proposition 4.1 (Pattern-free vs Deep Semantics). *Let $p \in \mathcal{T}(\mathcal{C}, \mathcal{X}), t \in \mathcal{T}(\mathcal{F}, \mathcal{X})$, t is p-free iff $\{\!| \hat{t} |\!\} \cap [\![p]\!] = \emptyset$.*

To check the emptiness of the above intersection we express the deep semantics of a term as a union of ground semantics and then check for each of them that the intersection with the semantics of the considered pattern is empty.

First, since the deep semantics is based on the generalized ground semantics, we can easily establish a similar recursive definition for constructor patterns:

Proposition 4.2. *For any constructor symbol $c \in \mathcal{C}$ and extended patterns $t_1, \ldots, t_n$, such that $\mathcal{D}om(c) = s_1 \times \cdots \times s_n$ and $t_1 : s_1, \ldots, t_n : s_n$, we have:*

- *If $\forall i \in [1, n], [\![t_i]\!] \neq \emptyset$, then $\{\!| c(t_1, \ldots, t_n) |\!\} = [\![c(t_1, \ldots, t_n)]\!] \cup \left(\bigcup_{i=1}^{n} \{\!| t_i |\!\} \right)$;*
- *If $\exists i \in [1, n], [\![t_i]\!] = \emptyset$, then $\{\!| c(t_1, \ldots, t_n) |\!\} = \emptyset$.*

If we apply the above equation for the non-empty case recursively we eventually have to compute the deep semantics of annotated variables. For this, we use the algorithm introduced in Fig. 1: given an annotated variable x_s^{-p}, getReachable$(s, p, \emptyset, \bot)$ computes a set of pairs $\{(s_1', p_1'), \ldots, (s_n', p_n')\}$ such that $\{\!| x_s^{-p} |\!\} = [\![x_{s_1'}^{-p} \setminus p_1']\!] \cup \cdots \cup [\![x_{s_n'}^{-p} \setminus p_n']\!]$.

Intuitively, the algorithm uses the definition of the deep semantics of a variable $\{\!| x_s^{-p} |\!\} = \{ u_{|\omega} \mid u \in [\![x_s^{-p}]\!], \omega \in \mathcal{P}os(u) \}$ and the observation that the ground semantics of an annotated variable can be also defined as:

$$[\![x_s^{-p}]\!] = \bigcup_{c \in \mathcal{C}_s} [\![c(x_{s_1}^{-p}, \ldots, x_{s_i}^{-p}) \setminus p]\!] \tag{1}$$

By distributing the complement pattern p on the subterms, the algorithm builds a set $Q_c(p)$ of tuples $q = (q_1, \ldots, q_n)$ of patterns, with each q_i being either $\bot$ or a subterm of p, such that

$$[\![c(x_{s_1}^{-p}, \ldots, x_{s_n}^{-p}) \setminus p]\!] = \bigcup_{q \in Q_c(p)} [\![c(x_{s_1}^{-p} \setminus q_1, \ldots, x_{s_n}^{-p} \setminus q_n)]\!] \tag{2}$$

We have thus

$$\{x_s^{-p}\} = \{u_{|\omega} \mid u \in [\![x_s^{-p}]\!], \omega \in \mathcal{P}os\,(u)\}$$

$$= \left\{u_{|\omega} \mid u \in \bigcup_{c\in\mathcal{C}_s}\bigcup_{q\in Q_c(p)} [\![c(x_{s_1}^{-p}\setminus q_1,\ldots,x_{s_n}^{-p}\setminus q_n)]\!], \omega \in \mathcal{P}os\,(u)\right\}$$

$$= \bigcup_{c\in\mathcal{C}_s}\bigcup_{q\in Q_c(p)}\{u_{|\omega} \mid u \in [\![c(x_{s_1}^{-p}\setminus q_1,\ldots,x_{s_n}^{-p}\setminus q_n)]\!], \omega \in \mathcal{P}os\,(u)\}$$

$$= \bigcup_{c\in\mathcal{C}_s}\bigcup_{q\in Q_c(p)}\{c(x_{s_1}^{-p}\setminus q_1,\ldots,x_{s_n}^{-p}\setminus q_n)\} \quad \text{(def. of deep semantics)} \qquad (3)$$

$$= \bigcup_{c\in\mathcal{C}_s}\bigcup_{q\in Q'_c(p)} [\![c(x_{s_1}^{-p}\setminus q_1,\ldots,x_{s_n}^{-p}\setminus q_n)]\!] \cup \bigcup_{c\in\mathcal{C}_s}\bigcup_{q\in Q'_c(p)}\bigcup_{i=1}^{n}\{x_{s_i}^{-p}\setminus q_i\}$$

$$= \qquad [\![x_s^{-p}]\!] \qquad\qquad \cup \bigcup_{c\in\mathcal{C}_s}\bigcup_{q\in Q'_c(p)}\bigcup_{i=1}^{n}\{x_{s_i}^{-p}\setminus q_i\}$$

with $Q'_c(p)\subseteq Q_c(p)$ s.t. $\forall q=(q_1,\ldots,q_n)\in Q'_c(p), [\![x_{s_i}^{-p}\setminus q_i]\!]\neq\emptyset, i\in[1,n]$.

Note that x_s^{-p} is the same as $x_s^{-p}\setminus\bot$ and thus, in order to express the deep semantics of annotated variables as a union of ground semantics the algorithm computes a fixpoint for the equation

$$\{x_s^{-p}\setminus r\} = [\![x_s^{-p}\setminus r]\!] \cup \bigcup_{c\in\mathcal{C}_s}\bigcup_{q\in Q'_c(r+p)}\bigcup_{i=1}^{n}\{x_{s_i}^{-p}\setminus q_i\}$$

Proposition 4.3 (Correctness). *Given $s\in\mathcal{S}, p\in\mathcal{T}_\bot(\mathcal{C},\mathcal{X})$ and $r:s$ a sum of constructor patterns, getReachable$(s,p,\emptyset,r)$ terminates and if we have $R = $ getReachable$(s,p,\emptyset,r)$, then*

$$\{x_s^{-p}\setminus r\} = \bigcup_{(s',p')\in R} [\![x_{s'}^{-p}\setminus p']\!]$$

Moreover, we have $\{x_s^{-p}\setminus r\} = \emptyset$ iff $R = \emptyset$.

Example 4.1. We consider the symbolic patterns from Example 3.2 and express their deep semantics as explained above. According to Proposition 4.2, we have $\{\tilde{r}_1\} = \{c_1(x_{s_2}^{-p_2}, y_{s_1}^{-p_1})\} = [\![c_1(x_{s_2}^{-p_2}, y_{s_1}^{-p_1})]\!] \cup \{x_{s_2}^{-p_2}\} \cup \{y_{s_1}^{-p_1}\}$ and we should expand $\{x_{s_2}^{-p_2}\}$ and $\{y_{s_1}^{-p_1}\}$.

To expand $\{y_{s_1}^{-p_1}\}$ the sets $Q_c(p_1)$ are computed for each $c\in\mathcal{C}_{s_1} = \{c_1,c_2\}$. First, following Eq. (1), $[\![y_{s_1}^{-p_1}]\!] = [\![c_1(x_{s_2}^{-p_1}, y_{s_1}^{-p_1})\setminus c_1(c_4(z_{s_3}^{-\bot}), y_{s_1}^{-\bot})]\!]\cup [\![c_2(z_{s_3}^{-p_1})\setminus c_1(c_4(z_{s_3}^{-\bot}), y_{s_1}^{-\bot})]\!]$ and we can easily see that the complement relation in terms of ground semantics corresponds to set differences of cartesian products: $[\![c_1(x_{s_2}^{-p_1}, y_{s_1}^{-p_1})\setminus c_1(c_4(z_{s_3}^{-\bot}), y_{s_1}^{-\bot})]\!] = [\![c_1(x_{s_2}^{-p_1}\setminus c_4(z_{s_3}^{-\bot}), y_{s_1}^{-p_1})]\!] \cup [\![c_1(x_{s_2}^{-p_1}, y_{s_1}^{-p_1}\setminus y_{s_1}^{-\bot})]\!]$. We get thus, $[\![y_{s_1}^{-p_1}]\!] = [\![c_1(x_{s_2}^{-p_1}\setminus c_4(z_{s_3}^{-\bot}), y_{s_1}^{-p_1})]\!] \cup [\![c_1(x_{s_2}^{-p_1}, y_{s_1}^{-p_1}\setminus y_{s_1}^{-\bot})]\!] \cup [\![c_2(z_{s_3}^{-p_1})]\!]$. Hence, following Eq. (2), $Q_{c_1}(p_1) = \{(c_4(z_{s_3}^{-\bot}),\bot),(\bot,y_{s_1})\} = \{(p_2,\bot),(\bot,y_{s_1})\}$ and $Q_{c_2}(p_1) = \{(\bot)\}$. Moreover, $[\![c_1(x_{s_2}^{-p_1}\setminus p_2, y_{s_1}^{-p_1})]\!]$ and $[\![c_2(z_{s_3}^{-p_1})]\!]$ are not empty (since $c_1(c_3(c_2(c_6)), c_2(c_6))$ and $c_2(c_6)$ belong respectively to each of them) while $[\![c_1(x_{s_2}^{-p_1}, y_{s_1}^{-p_1}\setminus y_{s_1}^{-\bot})]\!]$ is clearly empty. Thus,

$$\{y_{s_1}^{-p_1}\} = [\![y_{s_1}^{-p_1}]\!] \cup \{x_{s_2}^{-p_1}\setminus p_2\} \cup \{y_{s_1}^{-p_1}\} \cup \{z_{s_3}^{-p_1}\}.$$

Function getReachable(s, p, S, r)

Data:
s: current sort,
p: pattern annotation,
S: set of couples (s', p') reached (initially $\emptyset$),
r: induced sum of constructor patterns

Result: set of couples (s', p') reachable from $x_s^{-p} \setminus r$

if $p : s$ **then** $r \longleftarrow r + p$
if $[\![x_s \setminus r]\!] = \emptyset$ **then return** $\emptyset$
if $\exists (s, r') \in S, [\![r']\!] = [\![r]\!]$ **then return** S
$R \longleftarrow S \cup \{(s, r)\}$
$reachable \longleftarrow False$
for $c \in \mathcal{C}_s$ **do**

$\quad Q_c \longleftarrow \{(\overbrace{\perp, \ldots, \perp}^{m})\}$ with $m = arity(c)$
$\quad$**for** $i = 1$ **to** n **with** $r = \sum\limits_{i=1}^{n} r_i$ **do**
$\quad\quad$**if** $r_i(\epsilon) = c$ **then**
$\quad\quad\quad tQ_c \longleftarrow \emptyset$
$\quad\quad\quad$**for** $(q_1, \ldots, q_m) \in Q_c, k \in [1, m]$ **do**
$\quad\quad\quad\quad tQc \longleftarrow \{(q_1, \ldots, q_k + r_{i|k}, \ldots, q_m)\} \cup tQc$
$\quad\quad\quad Q_c \longleftarrow tQc$
$\quad$**for** $(q_1, \ldots, q_m) \in Q_c$ **do**
$\quad\quad subRs \longleftarrow [\,]$
$\quad\quad$**for** $i = 1$ **to** m **do**
$\quad\quad\quad subR \longleftarrow$ getReachable$(\mathcal{D}om\,(c)\,[i], p, R, q_i)$
$\quad\quad\quad$**if** $subR \neq \emptyset$ **then** $subRs \longleftarrow subR : subRs$
$\quad\quad$**if** $|subRs| = m$ **then**
$\quad\quad\quad reachable \longleftarrow True$
$\quad\quad\quad$**for** $subR \in subRs$ **do** $R \longleftarrow R \cup subR$
if $reachable$ **then return** R **else return** $\emptyset$

Fig. 1. Compute the deep semantics of quasi-additive patterns as a union of ground semantics. The boolean *reachable* indicates if we can exhibit at least one p-free value headed by one of the constructors of s. The set Q_c corresponds to $Q_c(p)$ in Eq. 2 with $p = r$ and is built by accumulation of the pattern complements from r for the arguments of a pattern headed by c. Given a tuple $q \in Q_c$, $subRs$ is a list (built with :) which stores the recursive results of getReachable over each element of q.

The getReachable algorithm continues the expansions until a fixpoint is reached. More precisely, we get $\{y_{s_1}^{-p_1}\} = [\![y_{s_1}^{-p_1}]\!] \cup [\![z_{s_3}^{-p_1}]\!] \cup [\![x_{s_2}^{-p_1} \setminus p_2]\!]$ and $\{x_{s_2}^{-p_2}\} = [\![x_{s_2}^{-p_2}]\!] \cup [\![y_{s_1}^{-p_2}]\!] \cup [\![z_{s_3}^{-p_2}]\!]$, and therefore, the deep semantics of $\tilde{r}_1 = c_1(x_{s_2}^{-p_2}, y_{s_1}^{-p_1})$ is the union of $[\![c_1(x_{s_2}^{-p_2}, y_{s_1}^{-p_1})]\!]$, $[\![y_{s_1}^{-p_1}]\!]$, $[\![z_{s_3}^{-p_1}]\!]$, $[\![x_{s_2}^{-p_1} \setminus p_2]\!]$, $[\![x_{s_2}^{-p_2}]\!]$, $[\![y_{s_1}^{-p_2}]\!]$ and $[\![z_{s_3}^{-p_2}]\!]$.

Propositions 4.2 and 4.3 guarantee that the deep semantics of any symbolic pattern and thus, of any term, can actually be expressed as the union of ground semantics of quasi-additive patterns. We introduce in the next section a method to automatically verify that the corresponding intersections with the semantics of a given pattern p are empty and check thus that a term is p-free.

4.2   Establishing Pattern-Free Properties

Compared to the approach proposed in [10], we have to provide a method that also takes into account the specific behaviour of annotated variables. On the other hand, in order to establish pattern-free properties, we only need to check that the intersection of the semantics of a symbolic pattern t with the semantics of the given constructor pattern p is empty: thus, we want a TRS that reduces a pattern of the form $t \times p$ to $\bot$ if and only if its ground semantics is empty.

To this end, we introduce the TRS $\mathcal{R}_p$ presented in Fig. 2. The rules generally correspond to their counterparts from set theory where constructor patterns correspond to cartesian products and the other extended patterns to the obvious corresponding set operations.

Remove empty sets:

(A1) $\qquad\qquad\qquad\qquad\quad \bot + \overline{v} \Rightarrow \overline{v}$

(A2) $\qquad\qquad\qquad\qquad\quad \overline{v} + \bot \Rightarrow \overline{v}$

Distribute sets:

(E1) $\qquad\quad \delta(\overline{v_1}, \ldots, \bot, \ldots, \overline{v_n}) \Rightarrow \bot$

(E2) $\qquad\qquad\qquad\qquad\quad \bot \times \overline{v} \Rightarrow \bot$

(E3) $\qquad\qquad\qquad\qquad\quad \overline{v} \times \bot \Rightarrow \bot$

(S1) $\quad \delta(\overline{v_1}, \ldots, \overline{v_i} + \overline{w_i}, \ldots, \overline{v_n}) \Rightarrow \delta(\overline{v_1}, \ldots, \overline{v_i}, \ldots, \overline{v_n}) + \delta(\overline{v_1}, \ldots, \overline{w_i}, \ldots, \overline{v_n})$

(S2) $\qquad\qquad (\overline{w_1} + \overline{w_2}) \times \overline{v} \Rightarrow (\overline{w_1} \times \overline{v}) + (\overline{w_2} \times \overline{v})$

(S3) $\qquad\qquad \overline{w} \times (\overline{v_1} + \overline{v_2}) \Rightarrow (\overline{w} \times \overline{v_1}) + (\overline{w} \times \overline{v_2})$

Simplify complements:

(M1) $\qquad\qquad\qquad\qquad \overline{v} \setminus \overline{x_s}^{-\bot} \Rightarrow \bot$

(M2) $\qquad\qquad\qquad\qquad\quad \overline{v} \setminus \bot \Rightarrow \overline{v}$

(M3) $\qquad\qquad (\overline{v_1} + \overline{v_2}) \setminus \overline{w} \Rightarrow (\overline{v_1} \setminus \overline{w}) + (\overline{v_2} \setminus \overline{w})$

(M5) $\qquad\qquad\qquad\qquad\quad \bot \setminus \overline{v} \Rightarrow \bot$

(M6) $\qquad \alpha(\overline{v_1}, \ldots, \overline{v_n}) \setminus (\overline{v} + \overline{w}) \Rightarrow (\alpha(\overline{v_1}, \ldots, \overline{v_n}) \setminus \overline{v}) \setminus \overline{w}$

(M7) $\quad \alpha(\overline{v_1}, \ldots, \overline{v_n}) \setminus \alpha(\overline{t_1}, \ldots, \overline{t_n}) \Rightarrow \alpha(\overline{v_1} \setminus \overline{t_1}, \ldots, \overline{v_n}) + \cdots + \alpha(\overline{v_1}, \ldots, \overline{v_n} \setminus \overline{t_n})$

(M8) $\quad \alpha(\overline{v_1}, \ldots, \overline{v_n}) \setminus \beta(\overline{w_1}, \ldots, \overline{w_m}) \Rightarrow \alpha(\overline{v_1}, \ldots, \overline{v_n}) \qquad\qquad with\ \alpha \neq \beta$

Simplify conjunctions:

(T1) $\qquad\qquad\qquad\qquad \overline{v} \times \overline{x_s}^{-\bot} \Rightarrow \overline{v}$

(T2) $\qquad\qquad\qquad\qquad \overline{x_s}^{-\bot} \times \overline{v} \Rightarrow \overline{v}$

(T3) $\quad \alpha(\overline{v_1}, \ldots, \overline{v_n}) \times \alpha(\overline{w_1}, \ldots, \overline{w_n}) \Rightarrow \alpha(\overline{v_1} \times \overline{w_1}, \ldots, \overline{v_n} \times \overline{w_n})$

(T4) $\quad \alpha(\overline{v_1}, \ldots, \overline{v_n}) \times \beta(\overline{w_1}, \ldots, \overline{w_m}) \Rightarrow \bot \qquad\qquad\qquad with\ \alpha \neq \beta$

Simplify p-free:

(P1) $\qquad\quad \overline{x_s}^{-\overline{p}} \times \alpha(\overline{v_1}, \ldots, \overline{v_n}) \Rightarrow \sum\limits_{c \in \mathcal{C}_s} c(z_{1_{s_1}}^{-p}, \ldots, z_{m_{s_m}}^{-p}) \times (\alpha(\overline{v_1}, \ldots, \overline{v_n}) \setminus \overline{p})$

$\qquad\qquad\qquad\qquad\qquad\qquad\qquad\qquad\qquad\qquad\quad with\ m = arity(c)$

(P2) $\quad \alpha(\overline{v_1}, \ldots, \overline{v_n}) \times (\overline{x_s}^{-\overline{p}} \setminus \overline{t}) \Rightarrow (\alpha(\overline{v_1}, \ldots, \overline{v_n}) \times \overline{x_s}^{-\overline{p}}) \setminus \overline{t} \quad if\ \{\!\!\{ \overline{x_s}^{-\overline{p}} \setminus \overline{t} \}\!\!\} \neq \emptyset$

(P3) $\qquad\qquad \overline{x_s}^{-\overline{q}} \times (\overline{x_s}^{-\overline{p}} \setminus \overline{t}) \Rightarrow (\overline{x_s}^{-\overline{q}} \times \overline{x_s}^{-\overline{p}}) \setminus \overline{t} \qquad if\ \{\!\!\{ \overline{x_s}^{-\overline{p}} \setminus \overline{t} \}\!\!\} \neq \emptyset$

(P4) $\qquad\qquad (\overline{x_s}^{-\overline{p}} \setminus \overline{t}) \times \overline{v} \Rightarrow (\overline{x_s}^{-\overline{p}} \times \overline{v}) \setminus \overline{t} \qquad\quad if\ \{\!\!\{ \overline{x_s}^{-\overline{p}} \setminus \overline{t} \}\!\!\} \neq \emptyset$

(P5) $\qquad\qquad (\overline{x_s}^{-\overline{p}} \setminus \overline{t}) \setminus \overline{u} \Rightarrow \overline{x_s}^{-\overline{p}} \setminus (\overline{t} + \overline{u}) \qquad\quad if\ \{\!\!\{ \overline{x_s}^{-\overline{p}} \setminus \overline{t} \}\!\!\} \neq \emptyset$

(P6) $\qquad\qquad\qquad\qquad \overline{x_s}^{-\overline{p}} \setminus \overline{t} \Rightarrow \bot \qquad\qquad\qquad\quad if\ \{\!\!\{ \overline{x_s}^{-\overline{p}} \setminus \overline{t} \}\!\!\} = \emptyset$

Fig. 2. $\mathcal{R}_p$: reduce pattern of the form $t \times p$; $\overline{v}, \overline{v_1}, \ldots, \overline{v_n}, \overline{w}, \overline{w_1}, \ldots, \overline{w_n}$ range over quasi-additive patterns, $\overline{u}, \overline{t}$ range over pure regular additive patterns, $\overline{t_1}, \ldots, \overline{t_n}$ range over pure symbolic patterns, $\overline{p}, \overline{q}$ range over constructor patterns, $\overline{x}$ ranges over pattern variables. α, β expand to all the symbols in $\mathcal{C}$, δ expands to all symbols in $\mathcal{C}^{n>0}$.

The rules A1, A2, resp. E2, E3, describe the behaviour of the conjunction, resp. the disjunction, *w.r.t.* $\perp$. Rule E1 indicates that the semantics of a pattern containing a subterm with an empty ground semantics is itself empty, while rule S1 corresponds to the distributivity of conjunction over cartesian products. Similarly, rules S2 and S3 express the distributivity of conjunction over disjunction.

The semantics of a variable of a given sort is the set of all ground constructor patterns of the respective sort. Thus, the difference between the ground semantics of any pattern and the ground semantics of a variable of the same sort is the empty set (rule M1). The rules M2–M6 correspond to set operation laws for complements. Rule M7 corresponds to the set difference of cartesian products; the case when the head symbol is a constant c corresponds to the rule $c \setminus c \Rightarrow \perp$. Rule M8 corresponds to the special case where complemented sets are disjoint.

The rules T1 and T2 indicate that the intersection with the set of all terms has no effect, rule T3 corresponds to distribution laws for the joint intersection, while T4 corresponds to the disjointed case.

We have seen that the ground semantics of an annotated variable is obtained by considering, for each constructor of the appropriate sort, the set of all terms having this symbol at the root position complemented by the pattern in the annotation and taking the union of all these sets. $\mathcal{R}_p$ uses this property in the rule P1 to expand annotated variables allowing thus for the triggering of the other rules for conjunction. Note that z_i are fresh variables generated automatically. The rules P2–P4 express the respective behaviour of conjunction over complements $(A \cap (B \setminus C) = (A \setminus C) \cap B = (A \cap B) \setminus C)$.

Finally, we can observe that, thanks to the algorithm introduced in Fig. 1, we can determine if $\{\!\!\{ \overline{x}_s^{-\overline{p}} \setminus \overline{v} \}\!\!\} = \emptyset$. Moreover, by definition, $\{\!\!\{ t \}\!\!\} = \emptyset$ if and only if $[\![t]\!] = \emptyset$. Therefore, the TRS is finalized by the rule P6 which eliminates (when possible) annotated variables. In order to apply P6 exhaustively, $\mathcal{R}_p$ also needs a rule to perform some $\setminus$-factorization around variables, resulting in the rule P5.

Proposition 4.4 (Semantics preservation). *For any extended patterns p, q, if $p \longrightarrow_{\mathcal{R}_p} q$ then $[\![p]\!] = [\![q]\!]$.*

We have seen that the algorithm in Fig. 1 always terminates and that it can be used to decide the conditions in the TRS $\mathcal{R}_p$ (Proposition 4.3). Based on this, we can prove the convergence of the TRS $\mathcal{R}_p$. While we cannot provide a simple description of the normal forms obtained by reduction of a general extended pattern, $\mathcal{R}_p$ can be used to establish the emptiness of a given intersection:

Proposition 4.5. *The rewriting system $\mathcal{R}_p$ is confluent and terminating. Given a quasi-additive pattern t and a constructor pattern p, we have $t \times p \longrightarrow_{\mathcal{R}_p} \perp$ if and only if $[\![t \times p]\!] = \emptyset$.*

4.3   Establishing Semantics Preserving Properties

The approach proposed in the previous section allows the systematic verification of pattern-free properties for any term in $t \in \mathcal{T}(\mathcal{F}, \mathcal{X})$ such that $\tilde{t}$ is linear. It is easy to see that if we denote by $L(t)$ the term obtain by replacing all the variables in the term t by fresh ones then, $[\![t]\!] \subseteq [\![L(t)]\!]$. We can thus linearize, if necessary, the right-hand sides of the rules of a CBTRS and subsequently check that it is semantics preserving.

Example 4.2. We apply the approach to check that the CBTRS in Example 3.3 is semantics preserving. For this we need to prove that $c_1(g^{-p_2}(x_{s_2}), f^{-p_1}(y_{s_1}))$ and $c_2(z_{s_3})$ are p_1-free, and that $c_3(c_2(z_{s_3}))$ and $c_3(f^{-p_1}(y_{s_1}))$ are p_2-free.

In order to prove that $r_1 = c_1(g^{-p_2}(x_{s_2}), f^{-p_1}(y_{s_1}))$ is p_1-free, we should first compute the deep semantics of $\tilde{r}_1 = c_1(x_{s_2}^{-p_2}, y_{s_1}^{-p_1})$ and we have seen in Example 4.1 how getReachable is used to compute this deep semantics as the union of $[\![c_1(x_{s_2}^{-p_2}, y_{s_1}^{-p_1})]\!]$, $[\![y_{s_1}^{-p_1}]\!]$, $[\![z_{s_3}^{-p_1}]\!]$, $[\![x_{s_2}^{-p_1} \setminus p_2]\!]$, $[\![x_{s_2}^{-p_2}]\!]$, $[\![y_{s_1}^{-p_2}]\!]$ and $[\![z_{s_3}^{-p_2}]\!]$. For all the terms in the union we compute their conjunction with p_1 using $\mathcal{R}_p$ which reduces them all to $\bot$. Hence, by Proposition 4.1, r_1 is p_1-free.

Similarly, we can check that $c_2(z_{s_3})$ is p_1-free, and $c_3(c_2(z_{s_3}))$ and $c_3(f(y_{s_1}))$ are p_2-free. Thus, the CBTRS is semantics preserving. It is easy to check that it is also terminating and consequently, the normal form of any term $f(t)$, $t \in \mathcal{T}_{s_1}(\mathcal{F})$, is p_1-free and the normal form of any term $g(u)$, $u \in \mathcal{T}_{s_2}(\mathcal{F})$, is p_2-free.

We can now come back to the initial flattening example presented in the introduction. We consider a signature consisting of the sorts and constructors already presented in the introduction to which we add the defined symbols $\mathcal{D} = \{flattenE^{-p} : Expr \mapsto Expr, flattenL^{-p} : List \mapsto List, concat^{-\bot} : List \times List \mapsto List\}$. with $p = cons(lst(l_1), l_2)$, to indicate that the corresponding functions defined by the following CBTRS aim at eliminating this pattern:

$$
\begin{cases}
flattenE^{-p}(str(s)) & \to str(s) \\
flattenE^{-p}(lst(l)) & \to lst(flattenL^{-p}(l)) \\
flattenL^{-p}(nil) & \to nil \\
flattenL^{-p}(cons(str(s), l)) & \to cons(str(s), flattenL^{-p}(l)) \\
flattenL^{-p}(cons(lst(l_1), l_2)) & \to flattenL^{-p}(concat^{-\bot}(l_1, l_2)) \\
concat^{-\bot}(cons(e, l_1), l_2) & \to cons(e, concat^{-\bot}(l_1, l_2)) \\
concat^{-\bot}(nil, l) & \to l
\end{cases}
$$

Thanks to the method introduced in the previous section we can check that the right-hand sides of the first 5 rules are p-free and hence, as explained in Sect. 3.3, that the CBTRS is semantics preserving. This CBTRS is clearly terminating and complete and thus, we can guarantee that the normal forms of terms headed by $flattenE$ or $flattenL$ are p-free values.

The method has been implemented in Haskell[1]. The implementation takes as input a file defining the signature and the CBTRS to be checked and returns the (potentially empty) set of non pattern-free preserving rules (*i.e.* rules that do not satisfy the pattern-free requirements implied by the signature). For each

---

[1] The source code can be downloaded from http://github.com/plermusiaux/pfree_check and the online version is available at http://htmlpreview.github.io/? https://github.com/plermusiaux/pfree_check/blob/webnix/out/index.html.

such rule we provide a set of terms whose ground semantics is included in the deep semantics of the right-hand side of the rule and that do not satisfy the pattern-free property required by the left-hand side.

The complexity of the method for checking the pattern-freeness *w.r.t.* to a given pattern p is exponential on the depth of p with a growth rate proportional to the (maximum) arity of the symbols present in p. Benchmarks performed on the implementation optimized to minimize repetitive computations showed that, when considering terms and patterns of depth 5 with symbols of arity 6, checking the pattern-freeness of a single term takes $\sim$ 200 ms, and checking the semantics preservation of a CBTRS of 25 rules takes $\sim$3 s (on an Intel Core i5-8250U). In practice, the size of the pattern annotations is generally lower that the ones we experimented with and we consider that despite the exponential complexity the concrete performances are reasonable for a static analysis technique.

5 Related Work

While the work presented in this paper introduces an original approach to express and ensure a particular category of syntactical guarantees associated to program transformation, a number of different approaches presenting methods to obtain some guarantees for similar classes of functions exist in the literature.

Tree Automata Completion. Tree automata completion consists in techniques used to compute an approximation of the set of terms reachable by a rewriting relation [15]. Such techniques could, therefore, be applied to solve similar problems to the one presented in this paper. The application of this approach is nevertheless usually conditioned by the termination of both the TRS and the set of equational approximations used [16,32]. Thus, while providing sometimes a more precise characterization of the approximations of the normal forms, these techniques are constrained, in terms of termination, by some syntactical conditions. As we can see in the following table, when testing 5 of our base case scenarios with two popular implementations, Timbuk3 [15] seems less powerful than our approach, while Timbuk4 [19] can check more systems but less efficiently:

	pfree check	Timbuk 3.2	Timbuk 4
flatten1	✓ 21 μs	✗ ∞	✓ 685 ms
flatten2	✗ 31 μs	✗ ∞	✓ 975 ms
flatten3	✓ 36 μs	✓ 1.6 ms	✓ 1,4 s
negativeNF	✓ 395 μs	✓ 3.2 ms	✓ 104 s
skolemization	✓ 45 μs	✗ 1,5 s	✓ 1,6 s

For Timbuk3, the over-approximation strategies were to broad to check the example presented in the previous section (flatten1). Nonetheless, it was able to check the properties using exact normalization for a rewritten version of the flattening TRS which avoided the nested function calls (flatten3) and for a TRS computing negative normal forms (negativeNF). Timbuk4, recently proposed to use a counter-example based abstraction refinement procedure to control the over-approximation [19], could check all the examples including a version of the flattening TRS which could not be verified with our current approach (flatten2). On the other hand, the computational performance is considerably worse than for our approach. Moreover, for Timbuk3 and Timbuk4, the target CBTRS has to be extended with a function encoding the desired pattern-freeness property in order to check it.

Recursion Schemes. Some formalisms propose to deal with higher order functions through the use of higher order recursion schemes, a form of higher order grammars that are used as generators of (possibly infinite) trees [24]. In such approaches, the verification problems are solved by model checking the recursion schemes generated from the given functional program. Higher order recursion schemes have also been extended to include pattern matching [29] and provide the basis for automatic abstraction refinement. These techniques address in a clever way the control-flow analysis of functional programs while the formalism proposed in our work is more focused on providing syntactic guarantees on the shape of the tree obtained through a pass-like transformation. The use of the annotation system also contributes to a more precise way to express and control the considered over-approximation.

Tree Transducers. Besides term rewriting systems, another popular approach for specifying transformations consists in the use of tree transducers [25]. Transducers have indeed been shown to have a number of appealing properties when applied for strings, even infinite [2], and most notably can provide an interesting approach for model checking certain classes of programs thanks to the decidability of general verification problems [1]. Though the verification problems we tackle here are significantly more strenuous for tree transducers, Kobayashi et al. introduced in [25] a class of higher order tree transducers which can be modeled by recursion schemes and thus, provided a sound and complete algorithm to solve verification problems over that class. We claim that annotated CBTRSs are easier to grasp when specifying pass-like transformations and are less intrusive for expressing the pattern-free properties.

Refinement Types. Formalisms such as refinement types [12] can be seen as an alternative approach for verifying the absence, or presence, of specific patterns. In particular, notions such as constructor subtypes [6] could be used to construct complex type systems whose type checking would provide guarantees similar to the ones provided by our formalism. This would however result in the construction of multiple type systems in order to type check each transformation as was the case in the original inspiration of our work [23].

6 Conclusion and Perspectives

We have proposed a method to statically analyse constructor term rewrite systems and verify the absence of patterns from the corresponding normal forms. We can thus guarantee not only that some constructors are not present in the normal forms but we can also be more specific and verify that more complex constructs cannot be retrieved in the result of the reduction. Such an approach avoids the burden of specifying a specific language to characterize the result of each (intermediate) transformation, as the user is simply requested to indicate the patterns that should be eliminated by the respective transformation.

Different termination analysis techniques [3,18,20] and corresponding tools like AProVE [13,17] and TTT2 [26] can be used for checking the termination of the rewriting systems before applying our method for checking pattern-free properties. On the other hand, the approach applies also for CBTRS which are not complete or not strongly normalising and still guarantees that all the intermediate terms in the reduction are pattern-free; in particular, if the CBTRS is weakly normalising the existing normal forms are pattern-free. It is worth mentioning that the approach extends straightforwardly to sums of constructor patterns of the form $p = p_1 + \cdots + p_n$ in the annotations to indicate simultaneously p_i-freeness $w.r.t.$ all the patterns in the sum.

We believe this formalism opens a lot of opportunities for further developments. In the current version, the verification relies on an over-approximation of the set of reducts and thus, can lead to false negatives. For example, an alternative rule $flattenL(cons(lst(l_1), l_2)) \twoheadrightarrow concat(flattenL(l_1), flattenL(l_2))$ in our flattening CBTRS would be reported as non pattern-preserving. In our experience, such false negatives arise when the annotations for some symbols are not precise enough in specifying the expected behaviour (*e.g.* the annotations for *concat* do not specify that the concatenation of two flatten lists is supposed to be a flatten lists) and, although we conjecture this might indicate some issues in the design of the CBTRS, we work on an alternative approach allowing for a finer-grain analysis. While false negatives could also arise when the right-hand side of a rule has to be linearized, the current implementation already uses an aliasing technique to handle such cases; the technical details have been omitted in the paper due to the space restrictions.

We also intend to extend and use the approach in the context of automatic rewrite rule generation techniques, such as the one introduced in [8], in order to automatize the generation of boilerplate code as in [23].

References

1. Alur, R., Cerný, P.: Streaming transducers for algorithmic verification of single-pass list-processing programs. In: ACM SIGPLAN-SIGACT Symposium on Principles of Programming Languages, POPL 2011, pp. 599–610. ACM (2011). https://doi.org/10.1145/1926385.1926454
2. Alur, R., Filiot, E., Trivedi, A.: Regular transformations of infinite strings. In: IEEE Symposium on Logic in Computer Science, LICS 2012, pp. 65–74. IEEE Computer Society (2012). https://doi.org/10.1109/LICS.2012.18

3. Arts, T., Giesl, J.: Termination of term rewriting using dependency pairs. Theoret. Comput. Sci. **236**(1–2), 133–178 (2000). https://doi.org/10.1016/S0304-3975(99)00207-8
4. Baader, F., Nipkow, T.: Term Rewriting and All That. Cambridge University Press, Cambridge (1998)
5. Balland, E., Brauner, P., Kopetz, R., Moreau, P.-E., Reilles, A.: Tom: piggybacking rewriting on Java. In: Baader, F. (ed.) RTA 2007. LNCS, vol. 4533, pp. 36–47. Springer, Heidelberg (2007). https://doi.org/10.1007/978-3-540-73449-9_5
6. Barthe, G., Frade, M.J.: Constructor subtyping. In: Swierstra, S.D. (ed.) ESOP 1999. LNCS, vol. 1576, pp. 109–127. Springer, Heidelberg (1999). https://doi.org/10.1007/3-540-49099-X_8
7. Bellegarde, F.: Program transformation and rewriting. In: Book, R.V. (ed.) RTA 1991. LNCS, vol. 488, pp. 226–239. Springer, Heidelberg (1991). https://doi.org/10.1007/3-540-53904-2_99
8. Cirstea, H., Lenglet, S., Moreau, P.: A faithful encoding of programmable strategies into term rewriting systems. In: International Conference on Rewriting Techniques and Applications, RTA 2015. LIPIcs, vol. 36, pp. 74–88. Schloss Dagstuhl - Leibniz-Zentrum fuer Informatik (2015). https://doi.org/10.4230/LIPIcs.RTA.2015.74
9. Cirstea, H., Lermusiaux, P., Moreau, P.E.: Pattern eliminating transformations, October 2020. https://hal.inria.fr/hal-02476012. Long version
10. Cirstea, H., Moreau, P.: Generic encodings of constructor rewriting systems. In: International Symposium on Principles and Practice of Programming Languages, PPDP 2019, pp. 8:1–8:12. ACM (2019). https://doi.org/10.1145/3354166.3354173
11. Clavel, M., et al.: The Maude 2.0 system. In: Nieuwenhuis, R. (ed.) RTA 2003. LNCS, vol. 2706, pp. 76–87. Springer, Heidelberg (2003). https://doi.org/10.1007/3-540-44881-0_7
12. Freeman, T.S., Pfenning, F.: Refinement types for ML. In: ACM SIGPLAN'91 Conference on Programming Language Design and Implementation (PLDI), pp. 268–277. ACM (1991). https://doi.org/10.1145/113445.113468
13. Fuhs, C., Giesl, J., Parting, M., Schneider-Kamp, P., Swiderski, S.: Proving termination by dependency pairs and inductive theorem proving. J. Autom. Reasoning **47**(2), 133–160 (2011). https://doi.org/10.1007/s10817-010-9215-9
14. Garrigue, J.: Programming with polymorphic variants. In: ACM Workshop on ML (1998)
15. Genet, T.: Towards static analysis of functional programs using tree automata completion. In: Escobar, S. (ed.) WRLA 2014. LNCS, vol. 8663, pp. 147–161. Springer, Cham (2014). https://doi.org/10.1007/978-3-319-12904-4_8
16. Genet, T.: Termination criteria for tree automata completion. J. Log. Algebr. Methods Program. **85**(1), 3–33 (2016). https://doi.org/10.1016/j.jlamp.2015.05.003
17. Giesl, J., Schneider-Kamp, P., Thiemann, R.: AProVE 1.2: automatic termination proofs in the dependency pair framework. In: Furbach, U., Shankar, N. (eds.) IJCAR 2006. LNCS (LNAI), vol. 4130, pp. 281–286. Springer, Heidelberg (2006). https://doi.org/10.1007/11814771_24
18. Giesl, J., Thiemann, R., Schneider-Kamp, P., Falke, S.: Mechanizing and improving dependency pairs. J. Autom. Reasoning **37**(3), 155–203 (2006). https://doi.org/10.1007/s10817-006-9057-7
19. Haudebourg, T., Genet, T., Jensen, T.P.: Regular language type inference with term rewriting. ACM on Program. Lang. **4**(ICFP), 112:1–112:29 (2020). https://doi.org/10.1145/3408994
20. Hirokawa, N., Middeldorp, A.: Automating the dependency pair method. Inf. Comput. **199**(1–2), 172–199 (2005). https://doi.org/10.1016/j.ic.2004.10.004

21. Jouannaud, J., Kirchner, C.: Solving equations in abstract algebras: a rule-based survey of unification. In: Computational Logic - Essays in Honor of Alan Robinson, pp. 257–321. The MIT Press (1991)

22. Jouannaud, J., Kirchner, H.: Completion of a set of rules modulo a set of equations. SIAM J. Comput. **15**(4), 1155–1194 (1986). https://doi.org/10.1137/0215084

23. Keep, A.W., Dybvig, R.K.: A nanopass framework for commercial compiler development. In: ACM SIGPLAN International Conference on Functional Programming, ICFP 2013. pp. 343–350. ACM (2013). https://doi.org/10.1145/2500365.2500618

24. Kobayashi, N.: Types and higher-order recursion schemes for verification of higher-order programs. In: ACM SIGPLAN-SIGACT Symposium on Principles of Programming Languages, POPL 20099, pp. 416–428. ACM (2009). https://doi.org/10.1145/1480881.1480933

25. Kobayashi, N., Tabuchi, N., Unno, H.: Higher-order multi-parameter tree transducers and recursion schemes for program verification. In: ACM SIGPLAN-SIGACT Symposium on Principles of Programming Languages, POPL 2010, pp. 495–508. ACM (2010). https://doi.org/10.1145/1706299.1706355

26. Korp, M., Sternagel, C., Zankl, H., Middeldorp, A.: Tyrolean termination tool 2. In: Treinen, R. (ed.) RTA 2009. LNCS, vol. 5595, pp. 295–304. Springer, Heidelberg (2009). https://doi.org/10.1007/978-3-642-02348-4_21

27. Lacey, D., de Moor, O.: Imperative program transformation by rewriting. In: Wilhelm, R. (ed.) CC 2001. LNCS, vol. 2027, pp. 52–68. Springer, Heidelberg (2001). https://doi.org/10.1007/3-540-45306-7_5

28. Meseguer, J., Braga, C.: Modular rewriting semantics of programming languages. In: Rattray, C., Maharaj, S., Shankland, C. (eds.) AMAST 2004. LNCS, vol. 3116, pp. 364–378. Springer, Heidelberg (2004). https://doi.org/10.1007/978-3-540-27815-3_29

29. Ong, C.L., Ramsay, S.J.: Verifying higher-order functional programs with pattern-matching algebraic data types. In: ACM SIGPLAN-SIGACT Symposium on Principles of Programming Languages, POPL 2011, pp. 587–598. ACM (2011). https://doi.org/10.1145/1926385.1926453

30. Pottier, F.: Visitors unchained. ACM Program. Lang. **1**(ICFP), 28:1–28:28 (2017). https://doi.org/10.1145/3110272

31. Rosu, G., Serbanuta, T.: An overview of the K semantic framework. J. Log. Algebr. Program. **79**(6), 397–434 (2010). https://doi.org/10.1016/j.jlap.2010.03.012

32. Takai, T.: A verification technique using term rewriting systems and abstract interpretation. In: van Oostrom, V. (ed.) RTA 2004. LNCS, vol. 3091, pp. 119–133. Springer, Heidelberg (2004). https://doi.org/10.1007/978-3-540-25979-4_9

33. Bezem, M., Klop, J.W., de Vrijer, R. (eds.) Term Rewriting Systems. Cambridge University Press, Cambridge (2003)

34. Visser, E.: Strategic pattern matching. In: Narendran, P., Rusinowitch, M. (eds.) RTA 1999. LNCS, vol. 1631, pp. 30–44. Springer, Heidelberg (1999). https://doi.org/10.1007/3-540-48685-2_3

Unification

Nominal Unification with Letrec and Environment-Variables

Manfred Schmidt-Schauß[(✉)] and Yunus Kutz

Goethe-University, Frankfurt, Germany
{schauss,kutz}@ki.cs.uni-frankfurt.de

Abstract. Unification algorithms of nominal expressions with letrec and atom- and expression-variables are already described in the literature. However, only explicit environments could be treated in nominal unification and the use of abstract environments was restricted to nominal matching. This severely restricts the use of algorithms in applications. The following two restrictions permit a step forward and strongly improve the coverage of the application cases: expression- and environment-variables are restricted to occur at most once in the input equations. A terminating and complete nominal unification algorithm is described that computes complete sets of constrained unifiers. Since the set of ground instances of a complete set may be empty due to constraints, we also provide a decision algorithm for inputs which do not contain permutation-variables and show that then nominal unifiability is NP-complete. For input without an occurrence-restriction for expression-variables and w.r.t. garbage-free ground expressions, we sketch an adapted unification algorithm that produces a complete set of unifiers in NP time. For the decision problem we conjecture that it is harder in this case. We believe that lifting the linearity restrictions for environment-variables leads to a prohibitively high computational complexity.

Keywords: Nominal unification · Letrec-expressions · Abstract environments · Program transformations · Automated deduction

1 Introduction

The goal of this paper is to extend the expressive power of nominal unification to allow automated reasoning in calculi with let-environments with multiple, and commutative bindings, in particular recursive bindings, but also non-recursive ones and ν-restrictions. Recursive bindings appear for example in functional programming languages such as Haskell [6,12], F# [5] and OCaml [15], and ν-restrictions for example in the pi-calculus [14,18].

Reasoning on program transformations, their correctness and their influence on resource consumption can often be supported by considering overlaps of

The authors are supported by the Deutsche Forschungsgemeinschaft (DFG) under grant SCHM 986/11-1.

M. Fernández (Ed.): LOPSTR 2020, LNCS 12561, pp. 95–112, 2021.
https://doi.org/10.1007/978-3-030-68446-4_5

transformation rules with rules of the operational semantics. In programming languages with binders, first order unification is not powerful enough for this task, and higher-order unification is undecidable or too complex. Nominal unification provides a very good balance between expressiveness and computational properties. Nominal techniques [16,17] support machine-oriented reasoning on the syntactic level for higher-order languages and support alpha-equivalence. An algorithm for (plain) nominal unification was first described in [28], which outputs unique most general unifiers (with constraints). The essential extension to the expressiveness of first order terms are syntactic permutations of atoms (i.e. variable names) and freshness constraints $a\#e$ that can restrict free occurrences of names ($a\#e$ means that a does not occur free in e). Efficient algorithms for nominal unification are given in [1,11], exhibiting a quadratic algorithm. Nominal unification is also used in higher-order logic programming [2] and nominal techniques in automated theorem provers like Nominal Isabelle [26,27]. αCheck [3] was developed for property testing of systems which are specified using nominal logic such as α-Prolog and maybe in a future version of Nominal Isabelle.

The extension of nominal unification to also allow atom-variables was tackled in [2] where an algorithm to produce a specific unifier was provided. This is improved by developing an algorithm to compute unique most general unifiers and showing that the decision problem is NP-complete [24]. A recent investigation of nominal rewriting and confluence checking of nominal rewriting where atom-variables are permitted is [8] which is an extension of [10] which in turn employs the unification algorithm developed in [24]. The particular case of α-stable, orthogonal nominal rewrite rules is investigated and shown to have a confluent rewrite relation. An extension of nominal unification to languages with a recursive let but without atom-variables was worked out in [19], where it was shown that the nominal unification and matching problems are NP-complete. The nominal unification algorithm for letrec was extended to atom-variables in [20,21]. Also, a nominal matching algorithm for letrec with environment-variables, but without atom-variables is proposed in [20,21]. However, adapting the matching algorithm with environment-variables to a unification algorithm was left open as it appeared to require more powerful methods.

A motivating example for this paper is the reduction (and transformation) rule (llet) which is used in the operational semantics of the calculus LR [25], and also in core languages of Haskell [7]. It reads: (llet): (letr env in (letr env' in r)) $\rightarrow$ (letr env, env' in r), which has the restriction that in the right hand side the environment env' must not capture free variables in env, and that the binding variables in env, env' must be distinct. This can be encoded with the extended freshness constraints $LV(env')\#env$, and $LV(env')\#LV(env)$, where $LV(.)$ means the set of binding names in the top-level of a let-environment, and $M_1\#M_2'$ abbreviates $\{e\#M_2 \mid e \in M_1\}$.

The overlap of the subexpression (letr env' in r) with the full left hand side of the same rule is a step in a confluence check of a subset of the rules in LR (see also Example 2). It is computed by applying a nominal unification algorithm, i.e. solving the equation (letr E in S) $\doteq$ letr E_1 in (letr E_2 in S')

with environment-variables E, E_1, E_2, and expression-variables S, S' together with the constraints $LV(E_2)\#E_1, LV(E_2)\#LV(E_1)$. This illustrates that environment-variables and extended freshness constraints are required. Note that environment-variables occur only once in the equation. Naively solving this equation would lead to $E \mapsto E_1, S \mapsto (\texttt{letr } E_2 \texttt{ in } S')$. Unfortunately, this is not the most general unifier, since instances of the two expressions with conflicting names are not covered. A general solution requires permutation variables P, such that the solution includes for example the substitution $E \mapsto P \cdot E_1$. We will show in this paper, how permutation variables that are introduced by the unification algorithm can be tamed by specifying their abstract mapping behavior.

The occurrences of expression- and environment-variables in our examples are linear, which fits the input restrictions of our unification-algorithm. It can also deal with non-linear occurrences of atom-variables as for example in an expression $(\texttt{letr } x = t, env \texttt{ in} \dots x \dots)$. We will sketch a more complex algorithm that also can deal with non-linear occurrences of expression-variables, but non-linear occurrences of environment-variables cannot be handled.

The achievements in this paper are the formulation of a nominal unification and of a decision algorithm for equations and constraints in a higher-order calculus with letrec and atom-, expression-, environment and permutation-variables, where expression- and environment-variables occur linearly in the set of equations (Theorem 1). Theorem 2 on the decision algorithm holds if there are no permutation-variables in the input.

This is a step forward in generalizing nominal unification algorithms to declarative functional programming languages like Haskell. The results are also applicable to (non-recursive) let with multiple commuting bindings and to ν-bindings. The complexity of the decision problem (under the mentioned restrictions) is shown to be NP-complete (see Theorem 2 and Corollary 1).

We also investigate the extension where expression-variables may occur unrestricted, i.e. multiple times. This enforces to restructure the data structure to so-called multi-equations in the unification algorithm, and to adapt in particular the decomposition rules to the data structure. Also, we restrict the semantics to the language of garbage-free ground expressions. A full description of this algorithm would exceed the available space, but we provide a sketch. Fortunately, the complexity of the unification algorithm as a device for producing solutions is nondeterministic polynomial time. However, the decision algorithm could not be adapted in a straightforward way. We are still working on it and conjecture that the complexity of the decision problem for non-linear occurrences of expression-variables and linear occurrences of environment-variables is in NEXPTIME.

The structure of this paper is to first introduce the problem and language (Sect. 2). Section 3 contains a nominal unification algorithm for the extension and Sect. 4 describes the decision algorithm for equations. Section 5 gives a sketchy overview of the extension of the unification algorithm to nonlinear occurrences of expression-variables. Section 6 concludes.

2   Nominal Expressions

We first introduce some notation [24]. Let $\mathcal{F}$ be a set of function symbols $f \in \mathcal{F}$, s.t. each f has a fixed arity $ar(f) \geqslant 0$. Let At be *the set of atoms* ranged over by a, b, c. The ground language NL_a^{letr} is defined by the grammar:

$$e ::= a \mid (f \; e_1 \ldots e_{ar(f)}) \mid \lambda a.e \mid \text{letr } a_1.e_1, \ldots, a_n.e_n \text{ in } e$$

where λ is a binder for atoms, and ($\text{letr} \ldots \text{in} \ldots$) is the recursive let, where a_i are the (binding) atoms in the letrec-environment and where $a_i.e_i$ is called a *binding*. While we are only interested in expressions with environments where the binding atoms are mutually distinct, we also allow other environments, e.g. $\text{letr } a.1, a.1 \text{ in } 1$. However, we will use the constraint system to mark them as invalid. For example, in $t = \text{letr } a.(g \; b \; a), b.(g \; a \; b) \text{ in } (g \; a \; b)$ all occurrences of a, b are bound. Also, the order of bindings in a letr-environment is irrelevant, such that $\text{letr } b.(g \; a \; b), a.(g \; b \; a) \text{ in } (g \; a \; b)$ is the same expression as t.

The basic freshness constraint $a \# e$ is valid if a is not free in e. We write $M \# e$ as an abbreviation of $\{a \# e \mid a \in M\}$. A set of (basic) constraints ∇ is valid if all constraints in ∇ are valid. $LV(Env)$ is the multiset of top let-binders in a letrec-environment Env.

The reason for $LV(Env)$ being a multiset, rather than a set, is that we need to consider invalid environments and constraints, e.g. $a \# a$ and $LV(env) = \{a, a\}$, which may arise during unification and produce a failure.

As a reminder, the α-equivalence relation $\sim$ on NL_a^{letr} is defined as the equivalence closure of renamings of bound atoms. For a better algorithmic treatment of α-equivalence, we will use a decomposition principle for letrec-expressions modulo α, which is improved compared to the method used in [19], since it supports a systematic way of describing the mapping behavior between the bindings with the help of a permutation-variable in the unification algorithm:

Lemma 1. *Let* $e_1 = (\text{letr } a_1.s_1, \ldots, a_n.s_n \text{ in } r)$ *and* $e_2 = (\text{letr } b_1.t_1, \ldots, b_n.t_n \text{ in } r')$ *be* NL_a^{letr}*-expressions, where* a_i *are pairwise distinct,* b_i *are pairwise distinct, but* $\{a_i \mid 1 \leqslant i \leqslant n\} \cap \{b_i \mid 1 \leqslant i \leqslant n\}$ *may be non-empty. Then* $e_1 \sim e_2$ *is equivalent to the following conditions:*

1. *There is a permutation* π *on atoms, such that* $dom(\pi) \subseteq \{a_1, \ldots, a_n\} \cup \{b_1, \ldots, b_n\}$*, and it extends the mapping* $\{b_i \mapsto a_{\rho(i)} \mid i = 1, \ldots, n\}$*, where* ρ *is a permutation on the set* $\{1, \ldots, n\}$*.*
2. $\{a_1, \ldots, a_n\} \# (\text{letr } b_1.t_1, \ldots, b_n.t_n \text{ in } r')$*.*
3. $r \sim \pi(r')$ *and* $s_{\rho(i)} \sim \pi(t_i)$ *for* $i = 1, \ldots, m$ *hold.*

Note also that the permutation π is not necessarily unique, since for $(\text{letr } a.s_1, b.s_2 \text{ in } s_3) \sim (\text{letr } c.s_4, d.s_5 \text{ in } s_6)$ there are two mapping possibilities: The permutation π may map $\{c \mapsto a, d \mapsto b\}$ and it may in addition either map $\{a \mapsto c, b \mapsto d\}$ or $\{a \mapsto d, b \mapsto c\}$. Or π may map $\{c \mapsto b, d \mapsto a\}$ with again two (irrelevant) possibilities for $\pi b, \pi a$. In the case (letr $a.s_1, b.s_2$ in s_3) $\sim$ (letr $b.s_4, c.s_5$ in s_6) with common binding atom b, one possibility is that π maps $\{b \mapsto a, c \mapsto b\}$, and the mapping of a is not used, but since π must be a bijection, it is $\{a \mapsto c\}$. Alpha-equality can be affirmed, if $s_1 \sim \pi s_4, s_2 \sim \pi s_5, s_3 \sim \pi s_6$. These examples show how a decomposition method for exhibiting constraints for α-equality may act, which can be generalized to a decomposition method as a part of a unification algorithm.

Lemma 1 leads to the following decomposition principle for all constructs w.r.t. $\sim$, which is equivalent to the definition of α-equivalence on NL_a^{letr}:

Lemma 2. α-equivalence $\sim$ in NL_a^{letr} is characterized by the following rules:

$$\frac{}{a \sim a} \quad \frac{\forall i : e_i \sim e_i'}{(f\ e_1 \dots e_{ar(f)}) \sim (f\ e_1' \dots e_{ar(f)}')} \quad \frac{e \sim e'}{\lambda a.e \sim \lambda a.e'} \quad \frac{a \# e' \wedge e \sim (a\ b) \cdot e'}{\lambda a.e \sim \lambda b.e'}$$

$$\frac{\textit{The three conditions of Lemma 1 hold.}}{\texttt{letr } a_1.s_1, \dots, a_n.s_n \texttt{ in } r \sim \texttt{letr } b_1.t_1, \dots, b_n.t_n \texttt{ in } r'}$$

Definition 1 (Expression languages). *Let S be a set of expression-variables ranged over by S, T; let A be the set of atom-variables ranged over by A, B; let $\mathcal{E}$ be a set of variables standing for letrec-environments ranged over by E; and let $\mathcal{P}$ be a set of permutation-variables ranged over by P. The grammar of the nominal language NL_{aASPE}^{letr} with atoms, atom-variables, expression-variables, permutation-variables and environment-variables is:*

$$
\begin{aligned}
e &::= W \mid \pi \cdot S \mid (f\ e_1 \dots e_{ar(f)}) \mid \lambda W.e \mid \texttt{letr } env \texttt{ in } e \\
\pi &::= \varnothing \mid (W\ W') \cdot \pi \mid P \cdot \pi \mid P^{-1} \cdot \pi \\
env &::= \varnothing \mid \pi \cdot env \mid (W.e; env) \mid (\pi \cdot E; env) \\
W &::= \pi \cdot a \mid \pi \cdot A
\end{aligned}
$$

where π is a permutation and $\varnothing$ denotes the identity.

One sublanguage is the ground language without variables NL_a^{letr}. For the algorithms we will use sublanguages $NL_{AS}^{letr}, NL_{ASE}^{letr}, NL_{ASPE}^{letr}$, where only the variable sorts mentioned in the index are used in the grammar, and where atoms are not permitted.

Note that this definition permits nested permutation expressions. The expression $((\pi \cdot A)\ (\pi' \cdot A'))$ is a swapping that illustrates the nesting. An expression of the form $\pi \cdot X$ where X is some variable A, S, E is called *suspension*. An environment consists of *binding-components* $W.e$ and environment-variable suspensions $\pi \cdot E$. Both are called *environment-components*. The inverse π^{-1} of a permutation $\pi = w_1 \cdot \ldots \cdot w_n$ is the expression $w_n^{-1} \cdot \ldots \cdot w_1^{-1}$ where $(W_1\ W_2)^{-1} = (W_1\ W_2)$, and $(\pi^{-1})^{-1} = \pi$. We assume that a permutation π applied to an expression s is immediately applied as follows: $\pi \cdot (f\ e_1 \dots e_n) \rightarrow f\ (\pi \cdot e_1) \dots (\pi \cdot e_n)$, $\pi \cdot (\lambda W.e) \rightarrow \lambda \pi \cdot W.\pi \cdot e$, $\pi \cdot (\texttt{letr } env \texttt{ in } e) \rightarrow \texttt{letr } \pi \cdot env \texttt{ in } \pi \cdot e$ and $\pi \cdot (W.e; env) \rightarrow (\pi \cdot W.\pi \cdot e; \pi \cdot env)$.

Let O be a single or a set of syntactic objects. Then $AtVar(O)$ are the atom-variables contained in O, $ExVar(O)$ the expression-variables contained in O and $Var(O) = AtVar(O) \cup ExVar(O)$.

The ground language of each $NL_{ASPE}^{letr} \subset NL_{aASPE}^{letr}$ is NL_a^{letr}. Note that this is a slight abuse of the notion of a ground language. A ground substitution ρ replaces atom-variables with atoms, expression-variables with ground expressions, permutation-variables with ground permutations, and environment-variables with ground environments. After applying a ground substitution ρ, the permutations are ground and can be applied, such that the result is in NL_a^{letr}. In fact every ground substitution ρ is an expression-structure homomorphism from NL_{ASPE}^{letr} into NL_a^{letr}, and from NL_{aASPE}^{letr} into NL_a^{letr}. The language NL_{aASPE}^{letr} serves as an intermediate language during the interpretation of NL_{ASPE}^{letr} expressions in proofs.

Constraints are abstract conditions, formulated for NL_{ASPE}^{letr}-expressions and with semantics in NL_a^{letr}. We will overload the notation, such that it can be used in both languages and in the algorithms.

Definition 2 (Constraints in NL_{ASPE}^{letr})

A freshness constraint has the form $A\#e$, where e is an NL_{ASPE}^{letr}-expression. General constraints extend this by:

- *$\#\{W_1, \ldots, W_n\}$ and $\#LV(env)$, where $\{W_1, \ldots, W_n\}$ is a multiset.*
- *$LV(env)\#e$ and $LV(env)\#E$.*
- *$dom(P) \subseteq LV(env_1) \cup LV(env_2)$*
- *$P \cdot LV(env_2) = LV(env_1)$*
- *$A = \pi \cdot B$, which is an abbreviation of $A\#\lambda\pi \cdot B.A$.*

Let γ be a ground substitution. A constraint $A\#e$ is satisfied by γ if $\gamma(A)$ does not occur free in $e\gamma$. The constraint $\#\{W_1, \ldots, W_n\}$ (for the multiset) is satisfied by γ, if $i \neq j$ implies $W_i\gamma \neq W_j\gamma$. The constraint $LV(env)\#e$ is satisfied by γ if for all $a \in LV(env)\gamma$, $a\#e\gamma$ holds. The constraint $LV(env)\#E$ is satisfied by γ if for all $a \in LV(env)\gamma$, $a\#(\texttt{let } E \texttt{ in } \lambda A.A)\gamma$ holds. Satisfiability of the other constraints is clear from these explanations.

A solution of a set ∇ of (general) constraints is a ground substitution γ, s.t. $\nabla\gamma$ is ground, and all constraints in $\nabla\gamma$ hold in NL_a^{letr}.

Example 1. As an example of the power of the language and of the constraint system we discuss several reduction and transformation rules of the intended applications. In particular we show which constraints are necessary to make the rules correct for every application.

- `letr` E_1 `in letr` E_2 `in` S $\rightarrow$ `letr` E_1, E_2 `in` S (rearranging letrec-environments). To avoid variable capture in the resulting expression, the constraint $LV(E_2)\#E_1$ is sufficient. Syntactic correct instances require also $\#LV(E_1, E_2)$.
- `letr` $A.(\lambda B.S_1), E_1$ `in` $A \rightarrow$ `letr` $A.(\lambda B.S_1), E_1$ `in` $(\lambda B.S_1)$ (a copy-rule for abstractions, also called dereferencing). This requires $\#LV(A.(\lambda B.S_1), E_1)$.

- `letr` $A.(\text{letr } E_2 \text{ in } S_1), E_1 \text{ in } S_2 \rightarrow \text{letr } A.S_1, E_2, E_1 \text{ in } S_2$ (rearranging letrec-environments). The required constraints are $\#LV(A.(\text{let } E_2 \text{ in } S_1), E_1)$, $\#LV(E_2)$, $\#LV(A.S_1, E_2, E_1)$, $LV(E_2)\#(\text{letr } A.S_1, E_1 \text{ in } S_2)$.
- $(\text{letr } E_1, A.S, E_2 \text{ in } S) \rightarrow (\text{letr } E_1 \text{ in } S)$ (a garbage collection rule), where the constraints $\#LV(E_1, A.S, E_2)$ must hold for syntactic correctness, and $LV(A.S, E_2)\#(\text{letr } E_1 \text{ in } S)$ for semantic correctness.

Note that the extension of the algorithm in Sect. 5 assumes a ground language of garbage collected expressions.

3 Nominal Unification with Environments

In this section we construct a unification algorithm for equations and constraints over NL^{letr}_{ASPE} where the intended input is a set of NL^{letr}_{ASE}-equations with expression-variables and environment-variables only occurring linearly.

As data structure we use a set Γ of (symmetric) equations between expressions, freshness constraints ∇, and a substitution θ.

Definition 3. *A set of equations Γ over NL^{letr}_{aASPE} is admissible, if every environment-variable and expression-variable occurs at most once in Γ, i.e. occur linearly in Γ.*

Definition 4. *Let $Q = (\Gamma, \nabla)$ be a unification problem consisting of an admissible set Γ of equations and freshness constraint ∇.*

- *A ground substitution ρ is a solution, if $Q\rho$ is ground, $\nabla\rho$ holds and for all equations $s \doteq t$ in Γ, the relation $s\rho \sim t\rho$ holds.*
- *The pair (Δ, σ) is a nominal unifier if for all ground substitutions ρ s.t. $\Delta\rho$ holds, then $\sigma\circ\rho$ is a solution of Q.*
- *A ground substitution ρ is an instance of the unifier (Δ, σ) of Q, if $\Delta\rho$ is valid and there is some ground substitution γ such that for all $x \in Var(Q)$ of type A, S, P: $(x)\sigma\circ\gamma \sim x\rho$, and for all $E \in Var(Q)$: $(E)\sigma\circ\gamma$ is a permutation of $E\rho$ modulo $\sim$.*
- *A set U of unifiers of Q is complete, if every solution of Q is an instance of some unifier in U.*

The idea of the following decomposition of letrec-expressions is to relate the syntactic components of the two environments by first guessing and then decomposing without losing solutions. For example, $\text{letr } E_1, X_1.S_1 \text{ in } S_2 \doteq \text{letr } Y_1.S'_1, Y_2.S'_2, E_2 \text{ in } S'_3$ has several possibilities for potential solutions: one example is that the instance of E_1 has bindings in common with E_2, and may contain instances of $Y_1.S'_1, Y_2.S'_2$. In a non-deterministic guessing, it is appropriate to first guess, which binding components or environment-variable suspensions of the left- and right-hand side have something in common. For example, $E_1 \text{ } R \text{ } E_2, E_1 \text{ } R \text{ } Y_1.S'_1, X_1.S_1 \text{ } R \text{ } Y_2.S'_2$ is a valid guess. The second part is to apply Lemma 1 and also to specify the introduced permutation-variable.

Definition 5. *[Decomposing letrec.]* *Let* $(\texttt{letr } env_1 \texttt{ in } e_1) \doteq (\texttt{letr } env_2 \texttt{ in } e_2)$ *be the equation to be decomposed, where* env_j *for* $j = 1, 2$ *consists of a list of bindings* $b_{j,i}$ *and environment-variables* $E_{j,i}$. *The decomposition is non-deterministic and proceeds as follows:*

First, guess a relation R *consisting of a set of pairs* (k_1, k_2) *where* k_j *is a environment-component of* env_j *for* $j = 1, 2$, *such that*

1. *Every binding* $b_{1,j}$ *is related to exactly one component of the right hand side.*
2. *Every binding* $b_{2,j}$ *is related to exactly one component of the left hand side.*
3. *Every suspension* $\pi \cdot E$ *is related to at least one component in the other environment.*

Let P *be a fresh permutation-variable and let* $B_1, \ldots, B_l$ *be the binding-components of* env_1 *and* $B'_1, \ldots, B'_{l'}$ *be the binding-components of* env_2.

The resulting equations are:

$$\Gamma_{res} = \{B_i \doteq P \cdot B'_j \mid if\ B_i\ and\ B'_j\ are\ related\ by\ R\} \cup \{e_1 \doteq P \cdot e_2\}$$

The resulting substitution θ_{res} *is constructed as follows: Let* $\pi_{1,1} \cdot E_{1,1}, \ldots,$ $\pi_{1,m'} \cdot E_{1,m'}$ *be the environment-variable suspensions of* env_1 *and* $\pi_{2,1} \cdot E_{2,1}, \ldots, \pi_{2,m} \cdot E_{2,m}$ *of* env_2. *First create fresh environment-variables* $E_{i,j,k,h}$ *which represent the intersection of* $E_{i,j}$ *and* $E_{k,h}$. *There are substitution components for every environment-variable of both environments, s.t.* $\theta_{res} = \theta_{res,1} \cup \theta_{res,2}$. *For the variables on the left hand side the substitution is:*

$$\theta_{res,1} = \left\{ E_{1,j} \mapsto \pi_{1,j}^{-1} \cdot P \cdot (E_{1,j,2,1}, \ldots E_{1,j,2,m}, B_{2,j}) \,\middle|\, \begin{array}{l} B_{2,j}\ are\ the\ bindings \\ related\ to\ E_{1,j}, j \leqslant m' \end{array} \right\}$$

and for the variables of the right hand side:

$$\theta_{res,2} = \left\{ E_{2,j} \mapsto \pi_{2,j}^{-1} \cdot P^{-1} \cdot (E_{1,1,2,j}, \ldots E_{1,m',2,j}, B_{1,j}) \,\middle|\, \begin{array}{l} B_{1,j}\ are\ the\ bindings \\ related\ to\ E_{2,j},\ j \leqslant m \end{array} \right\}$$

The resulting constraints ∇_{res} *are:*

$$\nabla_{res} = \left\{ \begin{array}{l} dom(P) \subseteq LV(env_1) \cup LV(env_2), \\ P \cdot (LV(env_2)) = LV(env_1), \\ LV(env_1) \# \texttt{letr } env_2 \texttt{ in } e_2 \end{array} \right\}$$

The rule removes the equation it decomposes and adds Γ_{res}, ∇_{res} *and* θ_{res}.

Definition 6. *The algorithm* NOMENV1 *is defined by the rules in Fig. 1 on* Γ, ∇, θ *for an admissible* Γ. *The intermediate and final* Γ, ∇, θ *may contain (generated and constrained) permutation-variables. The output is the final pair* (∇, θ) *or a failure if* Γ *is not empty and no rule is applicable.*

(E1) $\dfrac{(\Gamma \cup \{e \doteq e\}, \nabla, \theta)}{(\Gamma, \nabla, \theta)}$ (E2) $\dfrac{(\Gamma \cup \{\pi \cdot S \doteq e\}, \nabla, \theta)}{(\Gamma[S \mapsto \pi^{-1} \cdot e], \nabla[S \mapsto \pi^{-1} \cdot e], \theta \cup \{S \mapsto \pi^{-1} \cdot e\})}$

(E3) $\dfrac{(\Gamma \cup \{\pi_1 \cdot A \doteq \pi_2 \cdot B\}, \nabla, \theta)}{(\Gamma, \nabla \cup \{A = \pi_1^{-1} \cdot \pi_2 \cdot B\}, \theta)}$ (E4) $\dfrac{(\Gamma \cup \{(f\ e_1 \ldots e_{ar(f)}) \doteq (f\ e_1' \ldots e_{ar(f)}')\}, \nabla, \theta)}{(\Gamma \cup \{e_1 \doteq e_1', \ldots, e_{ar(f)} \doteq e_{ar(f)}'\}, \nabla, \theta)}$

(E5) $\dfrac{(\Gamma \cup \{W_1.e_1 \doteq W_2.e_2\}, \nabla, \theta)}{(\Gamma \cup \{W_1 \doteq W_2, e_1 \doteq e_2\}, \nabla, \theta)}$

(E6) $\dfrac{(\Gamma \cup \{\lambda \pi_1 \cdot A_1.e_1 \doteq \lambda \pi_2 \cdot A_2.e_2\}, \nabla, \theta)}{(\Gamma \cup \{((\pi_1 \cdot A_1)\ (\pi_2 \cdot A_2)) \cdot e_1 \doteq e_2\}, \nabla \cup \{(A_1 \# \pi_1^{-1} \cdot (\lambda \pi_2 \cdot A_2.e_2))\}, \theta)}$

(E7) $\dfrac{(\Gamma \cup \{\mathtt{letr}\ env_1\ \mathtt{in}\ e_1 \doteq \mathtt{letr}\ env_2\ \mathtt{in}\ e_2\}, \nabla, \theta)}{(\Gamma \cup \Gamma_{res}, \nabla \cup \nabla_{res}, \theta \circ \theta_{res})}$ guess according to Def. 5

Fig. 1. Rules of the unification algorithm NomEnv1

The set ∇ may contain constraints. Since binders in a letrec must be different, ∇ must also contain constraints which ensure for every environment env that only valid instances are covered, i.e. $\#LV(env)$. For efficiency purposes it is assumed that the abstract representation of permutations uses a sharing structure for components (see e.g. [4]).

Note, that we permit permutation-variables in the input of NomEnv1, but that the decision algorithm in the next section is only correct if the input does not contain permutation-variables and the constraint set is restricted.

Example 2. We illustrate the execution of the algorithm NomEnv1 on an example equation that occurs in unification problems related with a correctness proof of transformations in an extended lambda calculus with letrec, i.e. in the Haskell core-calculus LR [25].

The equation is $\mathtt{letr}\ E_1\ \mathtt{in}\ \mathtt{letr}\ E_2\ \mathtt{in}\ S_1 \doteq \mathtt{letr}\ A.S_2; E_3\ \mathtt{in}\ S_3$. A naive non-general solution would be: $\{E_1 \mapsto A.S_2; E_3, S_3 \mapsto \mathtt{letr}\ E_2\ \mathtt{in}\ S_1\}$ plus constraints for syntactic validity of the represented instances, and for avoiding capture of free variables.

Application of the algorithm NomEnv1D yields:

1. The substitution $\theta = \{E_1 \mapsto P \cdot (A.S_2, E_{13}), E_3 \mapsto P^{-1} \cdot E_{13}, S_3 \mapsto \mathtt{letr}\ P \cdot E_2\ \mathtt{in}\ P \cdot S_1\}$
2. Additional constraints ∇ restricting the permutation P, i.e.

$$\nabla = \left\{ \begin{array}{l} dom(P) \subseteq LV(E_1, E_3, A), \\ P \cdot LV(A, E_3) = LV(E_1), \\ LV(E_1) \# (\mathtt{letr}\ A.S_2; E_3\ \mathtt{in}\ S_3) \end{array} \right\}$$

Based on this most-general unifier we can see what was missing from the naive result above. It did not take possible renamings of binding variables into account and therefore did not cover all possible solutions modulo α-equivalence of the unification problem. The possible renamings are covered in the general solution by the permutation-variable P.

Example 3. We give a further example of the use of nominal unification. We overlap the left hand side, i.e., (letr E_1 in letr E_2 in S), of the first transformation in Example 1 with a (renamed) subexpression of itself, letr E_2 in $S \doteq$ letr E_1' in letr E_2' in S', which results in a solution: $\{E_2 \mapsto P{\cdot}E_1'; S \mapsto P{\cdot}(\text{letr } E_2' \text{ in } S')$. The common instance is letr E_1 in letr $P{\cdot}E_1'$ in letr $P{\cdot}E_2'$ in $P{\cdot}S'$. This reduces in two ways, using the rule as reduction and transformation rule, to letr $E_1, P{\cdot}E_1', P{\cdot}E_2'$ in $P{\cdot}S'$. However, we also have to add the constraint sets for the two sequences that are mentioned Example 1. These are at least: $LV(E_2)\#(\text{letr } E_1 \text{ in } S)$, and $LV(E_2')\#(\text{letr } E_1' \text{ in } S')$. The arguments for showing confluence in the style of Knuth Bendix require a deeper analysis and are left for future work.

Theorem 1. *If Γ is admissible, then the nondeterministic algorithm* NOMENV1 *is terminating, sound and complete; i.e. for every solution the algorithm computes a unifier consisting only of a substitution and a constraint. A single run takes polynomial time (provided the implementation uses sharing). The collection version of the algorithm will generate at most exponentially many unifiers.*

However, the algorithm NOMENV1 does not automatically decide solvability, since it is possible that all computed unifiers have an empty set of instances. We also refrain from providing an algorithm, which decides solvability of the constraint system itself, because the many variable kinds (A,S,E and P-variables) make reasoning on it very difficult. This is (partially) remedied in the next section, where we construct a special (incomplete) variant NOMENV1D for nominal unification, which decides unifiability, if the input does not contain permutation-variables and the input constraints are further restricted. We will show that the algorithm NOMENV1D will find a (small) solution, if there is any solution, and instead of permutation-variables we use the ξ-construct (see below in Definition 8) that replaces (generated) permutation-variables and keeps more information on the mapping behavior of the permutations.

4   A Decision Algorithm

In this section we define a decision algorithm for admissible input without permutation-variables and further restrictions on constraints, complementing the algorithm NOMENV1. We want to keep the description simple and also as close as possible to potential applications. Thus we describe the decision algorithm for the simpler case that in letrec environments at most one environment-variable occurs. The advantage is that this is the variant which is required in most applications, and in addition the rule RemoveE (see Fig. 2) is deterministic.

(RemoveEl)

$$\frac{(\Gamma \cup \left\{ \begin{array}{l} \texttt{letr } W_1.s_1;\ldots;W_k.s_k;E_1 \texttt{ in } s \\ \doteq \texttt{letr } W_1'.s_1';\ldots;W_{k'}'.s_{k'}' \texttt{ in } s' \end{array} \right\}, \nabla, \theta)}{(\Gamma \cup \left\{ \begin{array}{l} \texttt{letr } W_1.s_1;\ldots;W_k.s_k;A_1.S_1;\ldots;A_{k'-k}.S_{k'-k} \texttt{ in } s \\ \doteq \texttt{letr } W_1'.s_1';\ldots;W_{k'}'.s_{k'}' \texttt{ in } s' \end{array} \right\}, \nabla\theta_E, \theta \circ \theta_E)}$$

where $k' \geqslant k$. Let $\theta_E = \{E_1 \mapsto A_1.S_1;\ldots;A_{k'-k}.S_{k'-k}\}$. A_i, S_i are fresh.

(RemoveElr)

$$\frac{(\Gamma \cup \left\{ \begin{array}{l} \texttt{letr } W_1.s_1;\ldots;W_k.s_k;E_1 \texttt{ in } s \\ \doteq \texttt{letr } W_1'.s_1';\ldots;W_{k'}'.s_{k'}';E_1' \texttt{ in } s' \end{array} \right\}, \nabla, \theta)}{(\Gamma \cup \left\{ \begin{array}{l} \texttt{letr } W_1.s_1;\ldots;W_k.s_k;A_1.S_1;\ldots;A_h.S_h \texttt{ in } s \\ \doteq \texttt{letr } W_1'.s_1';\ldots;W_{k'}'.s_{k'}';A_1'.S_1';\ldots;A_{h'}'.S_{h'}' \texttt{ in } s' \end{array} \right\}, \nabla\theta_E, \theta \circ \theta_E)}$$

where $k' \geqslant k$. Let $\theta_E = \{E_1 \mapsto A_1.S_1;\ldots;A_h.S_h, E_1' \mapsto A_1'.S_1';\ldots;A_{h'}'.S_{h'}'\}$
and A_i, S_i, A_i', S_i' are fresh,
and $k' + h' = k + h = k + k' + N_2$; where $N_2 = |AtPos(s_1,\ldots,s_k,s,s_1',\ldots,s_{k'}',s')|$

(RemoveE)   is defined as the union of **RemoveEl**, and **RemoveElr**.
(A symmetric variant of **RemoveEl** is omitted since $\doteq$ is symmetric.)

(DecompLet)

$$\frac{(\Gamma \cup \{\texttt{letr } W_1.e_1,\ldots,W_n.e_n \texttt{ in } r \doteq \texttt{letr } W_1'.e_1',\ldots,W_n'.e_n' \texttt{ in } r'\}, \nabla, \theta)}{(\Gamma \cup \{e_1 \doteq \xi \cdot e_{\rho(1)}',\ldots,e_n \doteq \xi \cdot e_{\rho(n)}', r \doteq \xi \cdot r'\}, \nabla \cup \nabla', \theta)}$$

ρ is a (guessed) permutation on $\{1,\ldots,n\}$, $\xi := \xi((W_{\rho(1)}',\ldots,W_{\rho(k)}'),(W_1,\ldots,W_k))$
$\nabla' := (\{W_i \mid i = 1,\ldots n\}\setminus\{W_i' \mid i = 1,\ldots n\})\#(\texttt{letr } W_1'.e_1',\ldots,W_n'.e_n' \texttt{ in } r')$.

Fig. 2. Extra rules for NomEnv1D

The decidability result also holds in the general case where several environment-variables occur in a single letrec-environment.

Definition 7. *Let Γ be an admissible set of equations. We say Γ is a 1E-problem, if in every letrec-environment in Γ, there is at most one environment-variable.*

A special kind of permutation-variable is introduced by the rule **DecompLet**. These variables are so strongly restricted by constraints, that one can always provide an explicit list of swappings instead.

Hence we introduce an extra notation to avoid explicit permutation-variables. The benefit of this variant is that no new constraint concepts are required and thus it is compatible with [24].

Definition 8. *Let $W_1, W_2, \ldots, W_k, W_1', W_2', \ldots, W_k'$ be W-expressions according to the grammar, where only instantiations are considered that satisfy the constraints $\#\{W_1, W_2, \ldots, W_k\}$, and $\#\{W_1', W_2', \ldots, W_k'\}$. Then we denote with $\xi((W_1, W_2, \ldots, W_k),(W_1', W_2', \ldots, W_k'))$ the permutation instances that obey the following: $W_1 \mapsto W_1', \ldots, W_k \mapsto W_k'$ and the domain of ξ is contained in $\{W_1, \ldots, W_k, W_1', \ldots, W_k'\}$. This does not completely define the permutation, but the omitted parts will have no effect when used in our algorithms, when it is* *applied, due to further freshness constraints. The operations with ξ are the same as for permutations, when applied on the expression level.*

Note that there may be more than one permutation that could be $\xi((W_1, W_2, \ldots, W_k), (W'_1, W'_2, \ldots, W'_k))$ (see the remark after Lemma 1).

Lemma 3. *A representation for one permutation that is $\xi((W_1, W_2, \ldots, W_k), (W'_1, W'_2, \ldots, W'_k))$ as a list of swappings is given by the following recursion scheme: $\pi_0 = \varnothing$; $\pi_i = ((\pi_{i-1} \circ W_i)\ W'_i) \circ \pi_{i-1}$. where $\pi = \pi_k$ is the resulting permutation.*
More precisely, given $\nabla \supseteq \{\#\{W_1, \ldots, W_n\}, \#\{W'_1, \ldots, W'_n\}\}$ – which has to hold due to Definition 8 – every solution of ∇ requires π_i mapping $W_j \mapsto W'_j$ for all $j \leqslant i \leqslant k$.

Note that the plain size of this representation is exponential due to iterated doubling of π_{i-1}. If we use sharing for π_{i-1}, then the representation is of polynomial size.

Definition 9. *The function $AtPos(e)$ is the set of all atom-variable suspensions (W-variables) in e.*

Definition 10. *The (non-deterministic) algorithm* NOMENV1D *is defined for admissible 1E-problems Γ, ∇, which do not contain permutation-variables and the constraints ∇ do not contain P-variables.* NOMENV1D *uses the rules in Fig. 1 on the input Γ_0, ∇_0, with the exception of E7, and in addition the rules* RemoveE *and* DecompLet *in Fig. 2. Let the result be $\Gamma', \nabla', \theta'$. The final test is whether $\Gamma' = \varnothing$, and whether ∇' under θ' is satisfiable using the constraint-test* NOMENV1DCON *below.*
The answer is "yes", if at least one run of the algorithm answers "yes, solvable".

Note that the rules can be applied in any order. All rules are deterministic with the exception of DecompLet, which requires a guess on the permutation of the bindings in a letr-environment.

Note also that the substitution θ is intended to be an instantiation of the input problem. The necessary instantiations of the current Γ, ∇ are done by the rules. However, it is necessary to assume a directed graph implementation of expressions in order to exploit sharing, in particular in the representation of permutations.

Definition 11. *The final constraint-test* NOMENV1DCON *i.e., whether the final constraint ∇', θ' is satisfiable operates on $\nabla'' := \nabla'\theta'$ and then uses the following steps:*

1. Let A_0 be a set of atoms of cardinality $|\Gamma_0|$, where Γ_0 is the original input to the algorithm.
2. Guess for all atom-variables their mapping to atoms in A_0.
3. For all expression-variables and environment-variables, which still occur in ∇'', set their set of free atoms to $\varnothing$.

4. *For all environment-variables E, which still occur in $\nabla'\theta'$, set the set $LV(E)$ to $\varnothing$.*

5. *Check the freshness constraints: This can be done in polynomial time. The algorithm has to respect the sharing by directed graph implementation.*

Note that NOMENV1D is not complete w.r.t. solutions, since by intention, its rules do not cover all solutions. However, it is decision-complete, i.e. sufficient for a decision algorithm, since the algorithm will find a (small) solution if there is one at all.

Example 4. We illustrate NOMENV1D. Let $\Gamma = \{(\texttt{let } E \texttt{ in } A \doteq \texttt{let } E' \texttt{ in } B)\}$ and $\nabla = \{A\#B\}$. The rule RemoveE is not permitted to instantiate E, E' with the empty environment, since there are 2 atom-position which must possibly be bound. The algorithm then instantiates both environment variables with 2 bindings, i.e. $\theta = \{E \mapsto \{A_1.S_1, A_2.S_2\}, E' \mapsto \{B_1.T_1, B_2.T_2\}\}$ with appropriate constraints. Using $\rho = id$ we get $A \doteq \xi \cdot B$ which we can move into the constraints as $A =_{\#} \xi \cdot B$ and $S_i = \xi \cdot T_i$. The final satisfiability check yields true.

Proposition 1. *The rule RemoveE is correct/decision-complete. I.e. if the algorithm NOMENV1D is in the state (Γ, ∇) and the output of RemoveE is (Γ', ∇'), then Γ', ∇' is solvable if and only if the input Γ, ∇ is solvable.*

Lemma 4. *All rules of NOMENV1D are correct and decision-complete, where only DecompLet is non-deterministic.*

Theorem 2. *Given an admissible nominal unification problem Γ, ∇ without permutation-variables such that Γ is $1E$, and the input satisfies the conditions of Definition 10. Then the Algorithm NOMENV1D is a decision algorithm, which runs in NP time, assuming that sharing is used for expressions and permutations.*

Proof. Proposition 1 and Lemma 4 show that the rules are correct and decision-complete. If $\Gamma \neq \varnothing$, then there is an applicable rule. Every application of a rule makes Γ smaller, which can be seen by using the following measure: (i) The number of symbols let, λ, E-variables, binding-dot; (ii) the number of equations in Γ. This holds, since every rule strictly reduces this measure, and since the occurrences of environment- and expression-variables are linear.

The algorithm can be performed in nondeterministic polynomial time, due to this measure, and since sharing ensures polynomial size, and since the evaluation of constraints can be done in polynomial time also for the sharing structure.

From the previous theorems and since a subproblem is already NP-hard [19]:

Corollary 1. *Solvability of admissible nominal unification problem Γ, ∇ without permutation-variables and such that Γ is $1E$ and the input satisfies the conditions of Definition 10 is NP-complete.*

Remark 1. If an application in a Knuth-Bendix-like completion algorithm needs the information that there are no critical pairs, our decision algorithm has the ability to tell us that there is no unifier at all for given term overlap positions. However, if there are unifiers and there is a (possibly trivial) critical pair the analysis of this pair – even checking if it is trivial – requires the extraction of the relevant information from the computed general constraints. An algorithm for further checking and analyzing the constraints is left to future work.

5   Nonlinear Occurrences of Expression-Variables

In this section we sketch the generalization NOMENVNS1E of our nominal unification algorithm NOMENV1 to input problems where expression-variables may occur more than once (i.e., non-linear). In order to focus on simpler descriptions and more practical cases, we use the E1-restriction that all letrec-environments contain at most one environment-variable. An example is the right hand side of the second rule in Example 1.

In addition, we will have a further restriction insofar as we use as semantics only ground expressions that are garbage-free. With this restriction, our algorithmic ideas can be adjusted to non-linear occurrences of expression-variables. The restriction itself is minor with respect to an application to functional programs, since in the application domain garbage does not contribute to the proper actions of programs.

We start by providing a definition of garbage-free expressions. A ground expression e is *garbage-free* if in every subexpression (letr env in s) and for every proper subenvironment env' of env the relation $FV($letr env' in $s) \supset FV($letr env in $s)$ holds. Note that $\supset$ refers to a proper superset.

A nice and useful unification-related property of expressions e in NL_{ASPE}^{letr} with garbage free ground language is that fixpoint equations of the form $\pi \cdot e \doteq e$ can be expressed as a set of freshness constraints: $\{A \# \lambda \pi \cdot A.e \mid A$ occurs in $\pi\}$ as in [20,24]. Information and results on extended alpha-equivalence and garbage-free expressions is in [22], which shows that the graph-structure of letrec-expressions is kept by alpha-equivalence. This implies the claimed representation.

The nominal unification algorithm NOMENVNS1E has as input a set of equations from NL_{ASE}^{letr} where environment-variables occur only linearly. During the algorithm NL_{ASPE}^{letr}-expressions are used. The final result of a single run of the (non-deterministic) algorithm NOMENVNS1E is a solution (i.e. substitution) together with a set of constraint, over NL_{ASPE}^{letr}.

The data structure for NOMENVNS1E are multi-equations [13] instead of equations. We write a multi-equation that equates the expressions $e_1, \ldots, e_n$ as set $\{e_1, \ldots, e_n\}$. Of course, a set of equations is a special set of multi-equations. The final result of a single run of the (non-deterministic) algorithm NOMENVNS1E is a solution together with a set of constraint.

Standard rules for handling multi-equations are:

1. As a standard prerequisite, all expressions must be in a so-called *flat form*: Every deep subexpression e that is not a suspension of a unification variable is lifted to the top of the equations, i.e., $C[e]$ is replaced as $C[S]$ and an extra (multi-)equation $S \doteq e$ is added, where S is fresh. The permitted elements of the multi-equations after the exhaustive flattening operation are of the forms $W \mid \pi \cdot S \mid \lambda W.\pi \cdot S \mid (f\ \pi_1 \cdot S_1 \ldots \pi_n \cdot S_n) \mid$ $(\text{letr } W_1.\pi \cdot S_1, \ldots, W_n.\pi \cdot S_n, \pi_{n+1} \cdot E_1, \ldots, \pi_{n+k} \cdot E_k \text{ in } \pi \cdot S))$.
2. Treat multi-equations as sets, i.e., remove duplicates.
3. Merge: if there are two multi-equations $M_1 = M_1' \cup \{\pi_1 \cdot S\}$ and $M_2 = M_2' \cup \{\pi_2 \cdot S\}$ then replace them by $M_1' \cup \{\pi_1 \cdot S\} \cup \pi_1 \cdot \pi_2^{-1} \cdot M_2'$.
4. Single: if a multi-equation consists of a single expression, then remove it.
5. Solution: A multi-equation that is of the form $\{S, e\}$, where S is not contained in e or in other expressions in Γ and where e is not a suspension of S, can be removed, and $S \mapsto e$ moved to the substitution.
6. A multi-equation that is of the form $\{\pi \cdot S, e_1, e_2, \ldots, e_n\}$ can be changed if necessary into $\{S, \pi^{-1} \cdot e_1, \pi^{-1} \cdot e_2, \ldots, \pi^{-1} \cdot e_n\}$ by applying π^{-1}.
7. Constraint: A multi-equation that contains two suspensions of atom-variables $\pi_1 \cdot A_1, \pi_2 \cdot A_2$ can be made smaller by moving $\pi_1 \cdot A_1 \doteq \pi_2 \cdot A_2$ to the constraints, and removing one of the suspensions.
8. Multi-equations with two occurrences of expression-variable or atom-variable suspensions can be made smaller: $\{\pi_1 \cdot S_1, \pi_2 \cdot X\} \cup M$ for $S_1 \neq S_2$ is changed into $\{\pi_1 \cdot S_1\} \cup M$, and the substitution $S_1 \mapsto \pi_1^{-1} \pi_2 \cdot X$ is applied to M and the rest of Γ.

We will restrict attention to a situation where multisets only contain expressions of the following five forms, where every multiset can contain additional $\pi \cdot S$-expressions: (i) empty, (ii) atom suspension, (iii) application-expression, (iv) lambda-expression, and (v) letrec-expression. The reason is that the following can pairwise not be equated: atom suspension, application-expression, lambda-expression, and letrec-expression. We need only decomposition rules for these types of multi-equations.

- The *decomposition rules* are analogous to the rules for the equation-based algorithm. The general principle to adapt the decomposition rules of the algorithm NomEnv1E to NomEnvNS1E, i.e., to multiset, is as follows:
    If $e_1 \doteq e_2$ is decomposed with a result, then the corresponding rule R for multisets is:
    $\{e_1, e_2\} \cup M$ is replaced by $\{e_2\} \cup M$ and the result of R is added to the corresponding component of the equations or to the constraints and solution.

Fixpoint Rules for handling multi-equations are:

Fixpoints. A multi-equation M that contains two expressions S and $\pi \cdot S$, where π is nontrivial is modified to $M \setminus \{\pi \cdot S\}$, and the constraints $\{A \# \lambda \pi \cdot A.S \mid A$ occurs in $\pi\}$ are added.

Fixpoint-Chains. If there is a chain $S_1 \doteq \pi_2 \cdot S_2 \doteq M_1$, $S_{n-1} \doteq \pi_n \cdot S_n \doteq M_{n-1}, \ldots, S_n \doteq \pi_1 \cdot S_1 \doteq M_n$, then using the derivable equation $S_1 \doteq (\pi_2 \cdot \ldots \cdot \pi_n \cdot \pi_1) \cdot S_1$, let $\pi = (\pi_2 \cdot \ldots \cdot \pi_n \cdot \pi_1)$; then the constraints $\{A \# \lambda \pi \cdot A.S \mid A$ occurs in $\pi\}$ are added. Also, S_1 is removed from the first multi-equation.

Non-unifiability. The following can pairwise not be equated: atom suspension, application-expression, lambda-expression, letrec-expression. There is also a (standard) cycle check as generalized occurs-check.

Soundness and completeness are mainly derived from the arguments for the algorithm NoMENv1E. The *complexity estimation* of the modified algorithm starting with a flattened input is as follows: First we observe that the multi-equation-algorithm does never duplicate or generate expressions in the equation set of one of the three forms: application-expression, lambda-expression, and letrec-expression. Hence the number of occurrences of environment-variables remains linear during the run of the algorithm.

1. The number of letrec-s, lambda-expressions and application-expressions does not increase. These numbers are strictly decreased by decomposition rules.
2. Permutation components can grow exponentially large due to iterated doubling. However, a sharing data structure and clever maintenance leads to a polynomial size increase.

This sums up to a polynomial complexity for a single run, and to a nondeterministic polynomial algorithm for computing unifiers.

Claim: NoMEnvNS1E is sound and complete and runs in NP time.

However, the adaptations of the decision algorithm are not obvious: The reason is that the same expression-variable may occur multiple times and hence there may be interferences.

We **conjecture** that the unification problem corresponding to NoMEnvNS1E is decidable and that there is an exponential upper bound on the maximal number of bindings that have to be generated in the rule adapted from **RemoveE**.

We also **conjecture** that the computational complexity of the more general decision problem without restrictions on the number of occurrences of environment-variables is strictly higher than for the case with linear occurrences of environment-variables.

Example 5. We argue that the current rules and the methods of treatments of decomposition of equations between letrec-expression in the unification algorithm are insufficient if E-variables occur more than once: Let $e_1 = \mathtt{letr}\ a_1.a_2,$ $a_2.a_3, a_3.a_4, a_4.a_5, a_5.a_1$ in 0, and $e_2 = \mathtt{letr}\ a_2.a_3, a_3.a_4, a_4.a_5, a_5.a_6, a_6.a_2$ in 0. Then $e_1 \sim e_2$ and the permutation π with $i \mapsto i - 1$ on the indices can be used. Then the equation $\mathtt{letr}\ a_1.a_2, E, a_5.a_1$ in $0 \doteq \mathtt{letr}\ E, a_5.a_6, a_6.a_2$ in 0 has a solution: $E \mapsto \{a_2.a_3, a_3.a_4, a_4.a_5\}$. Analyzing this example, we see that there are an infinite number of incomparable unifiers.

6   Conclusion and Future Work

Nominal unification of letrec-expressions is extended to also allow abstract environments in letrec-environments, which are encoded as environment-variables. An algorithm for computing a finite set of unifiers is described and proved correct, under linearity constraints for expression- and environment-variables, as well as a decision algorithm if in addition there are no permutation-variables in the input.

A nominal unification algorithm for nonlinear occurrences of expression-variables is also sketched where the semantics are garbage-free ground expressions. The approach and the algorithms have a high potential of improving automated tools for reasoning about program transformations in higher languages with recursive let.

For the generalization to nonlinear occurrences of environment-variables, we did not find a terminating nominal unification algorithm. We conjecture the decision problem to be strictly harder in this case.

Our work provides also the base for an extension of the rewriting mechanisms and confluence checks in [8–10] to further settings, where letrec-expressions, environment-variables and expression-variables are allowed, and where also context-variables as in [23] are permitted.

This would enable the study of the rules of functional (in particular call-by-need) calculi and transformations, by checking the overlaps between them. In fact, several of these rules and transformation have abstract variables for parts of the environment, where usually the occurrences of the environment-variables are linear, yielding a natural field of applications for the work of this paper.

References

1. Calvès, C., Fernández, M.: A polynomial nominal unification algorithm. Theoret. Comput. Sci. **403**(2–3), 285–306 (2008)
2. Cheney, J.: Nominal Logic Programming. Ph.D. thesis, Cornell University, Ithaca, NY, August 2004
3. Cheney, J., Momigliano, A.: α-check: a mechanized metatheory model checker. Theory Pract. Logic Program. **17**(3), 311–352 (2017)
4. A. Gascón, G. Godoy, and M. Schmidt-Schauß. Unification and matching on compressed terms. ACM Trans. Comput. Log. **12**(4):26:1–26:37, 2011
5. Hansen, M.R., Rischel, H.: Functional Programming Using F#. Cambridge (2013)
6. Haskell: Haskell, an advanced, purely functional programming language (2019)
7. Jones, S.P., Santos, A.: Compilation by transformation in the Glasgow Haskell Compiler. In: Hammond, K., Turner, D.N., Sansom, P.M. (eds.) Functional Programming, pp. 184–204. Springer, London (1995). https://doi.org/10.1007/978-1-4471-3573-9_13

8. Kikuchi, K., Aoto., T.: Confluence and commutation for nominal rewriting systems with atom-variables. In: LOPSTR 2020 (2020, to appear)
9. Kutz, Y., Schmidt-Schauß, M.: Rewriting with generalized nominal unification. Frank report 63, Institut für Informatik. Fachbereich Informatik und Mathematik. J. W. Goethe-Universität Frankfurt am Main (2019)
10. Kutz, Y., Schmidt-Schauß, M.: Rewriting with generalized nominal unification. MSCS **30**, 710–735 (2020.) Special issue 6 (Special Issue: Unification)
11. Levy, J., Villaret, M.: An efficient nominal unification algorithm. In: Lynch, C. (ed.) Proceedings of 21st RTA, LIPIcs, vol. 6, pp. 209–226. Schloss Dagstuhl (2010)
12. Marlow, S. (ed.): Haskell 2010 - Language Report (2010)
13. Martelli, A., Montanari, U.: An efficient unification algorithm. ACM Trans. Program. Lang. Syst. **4**(2), 258–282 (1982)
14. Milner, R.: Communicating And Mobile Systems - The Pi-Calculus. Cambridge University Press, Cambridge (1999)
15. Minsky, Y., Madhavapeddy, A., Hickey, J.: Real World OCaml. O'Reilly (2013)
16. Pitts, A.: Nominal techniques. ACM SIGLOG News **3**(1):57–72 (2016)
17. Pitts, A.M.: Nominal Sets: Names and Symmetry in Computer Science. Cambridge University Press, New YorkD (2013)
18. Sangiorgi, D., Walker, D.: on barbed equivalences in π-calculus. In: Larsen, K.G., Nielsen, M. (eds.) CONCUR 2001. LNCS, vol. 2154, pp. 292–304. Springer, Heidelberg (2001). https://doi.org/10.1007/3-540-44685-0_20
19. Schmidt-Schauß, M., Kutsia, T., Levy, J., Villaret, M.: Nominal unification of higher order expressions with recursive let. In: Hermenegildo, M.V., Lopez-Garcia, P. (eds.) LOPSTR 2016. LNCS, vol. 10184, pp. 328–344. Springer, Cham (2017). https://doi.org/10.1007/978-3-319-63139-4_19
20. Schmidt-Schauß, M., Kutsia, T., Levy, J., Villaret, M., Kutz, Y.: Nominal unification of higher order expressions with recursive let. Frank report 62, Institut für Informatik. Fachbereich Informatik und Mathematik. J. W. Goethe-Universität Frankfurt am Main (2019)
21. Schmidt-Schauß, M., Kutsia, T., Levy, J., Villaret, M., Kutz., Y.: Nominal unification of higher order expressions with recursive let (2019, in preparation)
22. Schmidt-Schauß, M., Rau, C., Sabel, D.: Algorithms for Extended Alpha-Equivalence and Complexity. In: van Raamsdonk, F. (ed.) 24th RTA 2013, LIPIcs, vol. 21, pp. 255–270. Schloss Dagstuhl (2013)
23. Schmidt-Schauß, M., Sabel, D.: Nominal unification with atom and context variables. In: Kirchner, H. (ed.) Proceedings of 3rd FSCD 2018, LIPIcs, vol. 108, pp. 28:1–28:20. Schloss Dagstuhl (2018)
24. Schmidt-Schauß, M., Sabel, D., Kutz, Y.: Nominal unification with atom-variables. J. Symb. Comput. **90**, 42–64 (2019)
25. Schmidt-Schauß, M., Schütz, M., Sabel, D.: Safety of Nöcker's strictness analysis. J. Funct. Program. **18**(04), 503–551 (2008)
26. Urban, C.: Nominal techniques in Isabelle/HOL. J. Autom. Reasoning **40**(4), 327–356 (2008)
27. Urban, C., Kaliszyk, C.: General bindings and alpha-equivalence in nominal Isabelle. Log. Methods Comput. Sci. **8**(2), 1–35 (2012)
28. Urban, C., Pitts, A., Gabbay, M.: Nominal unification. In: Baaz, M., Makowsky, J.A. (eds.) CSL 2003. LNCS, vol. 2803, pp. 513–527. Springer, Heidelberg (2003). https://doi.org/10.1007/978-3-540-45220-1_41

Terminating Non-disjoint Combined Unification

Serdar Erbatur[1], Andrew M. Marshall[2], and Christophe Ringeissen[3]([✉])

[1] University of Texas at Dallas, Richardson, USA
[2] University of Mary Washington, Fredericksburg, USA
[3] Université de Lorraine, CNRS, Inria, LORIA, 54000 Nancy, France
Christophe.Ringeissen@loria.fr

Abstract. The equational unification problem, where the underlying equational theory may be given as the union of component equational theories, appears often in practice in many fields such as automated reasoning, logic programming, declarative programming, and the formal analysis of security protocols. In this paper, we investigate the unification problem in the non-disjoint union of equational theories via the combination of hierarchical unification procedures. In this context, a unification algorithm known for a base theory is extended with some additional inference rules to take into account the rest of the theory. We present a simple form of hierarchical unification procedure. The approach is particularly well-suited for any theory where a unification procedure can be obtained in a syntactic way using transformation rules to process the axioms of the theory. Hierarchical unification procedures are exemplified with various theories used in protocol analysis. Next, we look at modularity methods for combining theories already using a hierarchical approach. In addition, we consider a new complexity measure that allows us to obtain terminating (combined) hierarchical unification procedures.

1 Introduction

Unification is a critical tool in many fields such as automated reasoning, logic programming, declarative programming, and the formal analysis of security protocols. For many of these applications we want to consider equational unification, where the problem is defined modulo an equational theory E, such as Associativity-Commutativity. For example, one approach to the analysis of security protocols is based on deductive reasoning, as is done in the following tools [5,6,18,25]. In this approach protocols are usually represented by clauses in first-order logic with equality and equational theories are used to specify the capabilities of an intruder [1]. To support this reasoning approach we need to use E-unification procedures. Since equational unification is undecidable in general, specialized techniques have been developed to solve the problem for particular classes of equational theories, many of high practical interest. For instance, when the equational theory E has the Finite Variant Property (FVP) [11,19], there

© Springer Nature Switzerland AG 2021
M. Fernández (Ed.): LOPSTR 2020, LNCS 12561, pp. 113–130, 2021.
https://doi.org/10.1007/978-3-030-68446-4_6

exists a reduction from E-unification to syntactic unification via the computation of finitely many variants of the unification problem. The class of equational theories with the FVP has attracted a considerable interest since it contains theories that are crucial in protocol analysis [7, 8, 12, 19, 26].

Another ubiquitous scenario is given by an equational theory E involved in a union of theories $F \cup E$. To solve this case, it is quite natural to proceed in a modular way by reusing the unification algorithms available for F and for E. There are terminating and complete combination procedures for signature-disjoint unions of theories [3, 29]. However, the non-disjoint case remains a challenging problem. One approach to the non-disjoint combination problem that has been successful in some cases is the hierarchical approach [14]. In this approach, $F \cup E$-unification can be considered as a conservative extension of E-unification. Then, a new inference system related to F, say U_F, can be combined with an E-unification algorithm to obtain an $F \cup E$ unification algorithm. While this hierarchical approach won't work for every $F \cup E$ it can be a very useful tool when applicable. However, up to now it could be complex to know if a combination $F \cup E$ could be solved via the hierarchical approach. For example, there is no general method for obtaining the inference system U_F, and the resulting hierarchical unification procedure may not terminate.

In this paper, we consider "syntactic" theories $F \cup E$ where U_F can be defined as a system of mutation rules, and we present new terminating instances of the hierarchical unification procedure. When an equational theory fulfills the syntacticness property [22, 28], there exists a rule-based unification procedure in the same vein as the one known for syntactic unification, which is called a mutation-based unification procedure. Unfortunately, being syntactic is not a sufficient condition to ensure the termination of this mutation-based unification procedure. However, terminating mutation-based unification procedures are known for some particular theories such as one-side distributivity [24, 30], distributive exponentiation theories [15], shallow theories [10] and theories closed by paramodulation [23]. All the theories investigated here using the hierarchical approach are both *syntactic* and finitary: each of them is actually a syntactic theory for which a (finitary) unification algorithm is shown. On the one hand, we study theories which are both collapse-free and finitary, that is, finitary theories defined by axioms between non-variable terms. These theories are known to be syntactic [22]. On the other hand, we also examine forward-closed theories that are known to be both syntactic and finitary, just like theories closed by paramodulation [23]. The forward-closed theories we are interested in are actually examples of theories having the Finite Variant Property.

The contributions of the paper consist of several improvements to the hierarchical combination method [13, 14] including: simplifying the method, clarifying the theories for which the approach is applicable, and reducing some of the restrictions. Furthermore, we develop several new results including general reduction procedures for certain types of theories, and modular termination results. More specifically:

- We better define theories for which a hierarchical approach is applicable, constructor-based theories, and simplify the hierarchical unification procedure denoted here by $H_E(U_F)$, where U_F is an additional rule-based procedure to be combined with an E-unification algorithm (Sect. 3).
- We define the requirements for the U_F rule-based procedure, and develop new general rule-based procedures for subterm collapse-free and forward-closed theories (Sect. 3).
- Using the hierarchical approach, we develop new modularity results for the unification problem in unions of constructor-sharing theories. We define a new complexity measure to show terminating combinations of hierarchical unification algorithms. This allows us to obtain new (combined) unification algorithms for a wider variety of theories (Sect. 4).
- We show how the combination of hierarchical unification algorithms can be applied to unions of constructor-sharing forward-closed theories (Sect. 4).

The rest of the paper is organized as follows. Section 2 provides the background material. Section 2.3 contains an introduction to forward-closed theories. Section 3 introduces the notion of hierarchical unification and presents examples of theories admitting a hierarchical unification algorithm. Section 4 focuses on the combination of hierarchical unification algorithms. Finally, Sect. 5 contains the conclusions and future work.

2 Preliminaries

We use the standard notation of equational unification [4] and term rewriting systems [2]. Given a first-order signature Σ and a (countable) set of variables V, the set of Σ-terms over variables V is denoted by $T(\Sigma, V)$. The set of variables in a term t is denoted by $Var(t)$. A term t is $ground$ if $Var(t) = \emptyset$. A term is $linear$ if all its variables occur only once. For any position p in a term t (including the root position ϵ), $t(p)$ is the symbol at position p, $t|_p$ is the subterm of t at position p, and $t[u]_p$ is the term t in which $t|_p$ is replaced by u. A substitution is an endomorphism of $T(\Sigma, V)$ with only finitely many variables not mapped to themselves. A substitution is denoted by $\sigma = \{x_1 \mapsto t_1, \ldots, x_m \mapsto t_m\}$, where the domain of σ is $Dom(\sigma) = \{x_1, \ldots, x_m\}$. Application of a substitution σ to t is written $t\sigma$.

2.1 Equational Theories

Given a set E of Σ-axioms (i.e., pairs of Σ-terms, denoted by $l = r$), the $equational$ $theory$ $=_E$ is the congruence closure of E under the law of substitutivity (by a slight abuse of terminology, E is often called an equational theory). Equivalently, $=_E$ can be defined as the reflexive transitive closure $\leftrightarrow^*_E$ of an equational step $\leftrightarrow_E$ defined as follows: $s \leftrightarrow_E t$ if there exist a position p of s, $l = r$ (or $r = l$) in E, and substitution σ such that $s|_p = l\sigma$ and $t = s[r\sigma]_p$. An axiom $l = r$ is $regular$ if $Var(l) = Var(r)$. An axiom $l = r$ is $linear$ (resp., $collapse\text{-}free$) if l and

r are linear (resp. non-variable terms). An equational theory is *regular* (resp., linear/collapse-free) if all its axioms are regular (resp., linear/collapse-free). A theory E is *subterm collapse-free* if and only if for all terms t it is not the case that $t =_E u$ where u is a strict subterm of t. A theory E is *syntactic* if it has finite *resolvent presentation* S, defined as a finite set of axioms S such that each equality $t =_E u$ has an equational proof $t \leftrightarrow_S^* u$ with at most one equational step $\leftrightarrow_S$ applied at the root position. One can easily check that $C = \{x * y = y * x\}$ (Commutativity) and $AC = \{x * (y * z) = (x * y) * z, \ x * y = y * x\}$ (Associativity-Commutativity) are regular, collapse-free, and linear. Moreover, C and AC are syntactic [22]. A Σ-equation is a pair of Σ-terms denoted by $s =^? t$ or simply $s = t$ when it is clear from the context that we do not refer to an axiom. A *flat Σ-equation* is either an equation between variables or a *non-variable flat Σ-equation* of the form $x_0 = f(x_1, \ldots, x_n)$ where $x_0, x_1, \ldots, x_n$ are variables and f is a function symbol in Σ. An *E-unification problem* is a set of Σ-equations, $G = \{s_1 =^? t_1, \ldots, s_n =^? t_n\}$, or equivalently a conjunction of Σ-equations. The set of variables in G is denoted by $Var(G)$. A solution to G, called an *E-unifier*, is a substitution σ such that $s_i \sigma =_E t_i \sigma$ for all $1 \leq i \leq n$, written $E \models G\sigma$. A substitution σ is *more general modulo E* than θ on a set of variables V, denoted as $\sigma \leq_E^V \theta$, if there is a substitution τ such that $x\sigma\tau =_E x\theta$ for all $x \in V$. A *Complete Set of E-Unifiers* of G, denoted by $CSU_E(G)$, is a set of substitutions such that each $\sigma \in CSU_E(G)$ is an *E*-unifier of G, and for each *E*-unifier θ of G, there exists $\sigma \in CSU_E(G)$ such that $\sigma \leq_E^{Var(G)} \theta$. An *E-unification algorithm* is an algorithm that computes a finite $CSU_E(G)$ for all *E*-unification problems G. An inference rule $G \vdash G'$ for *E*-unification is *sound* if each *E*-unifier of G' is an *E*-unifier of G; and *complete* if for each *E*-unifier σ of G, there exists an *E*-unifier σ' of G' such that $\sigma' \leq_E^{Var(G)} \sigma$. An inference system for *E*-unification is *sound* if all its inference rules are sound; and *complete* if for each *E*-unification problem G on which an inference applies and each *E*-unifier σ of G, there exist an *E*-unification problem G' inferred from G and an *E*-unifier σ' of G' such that $\sigma' \leq_E^{Var(G)} \sigma$. A set of equations $G = \{x_1 =^? t_1, \ldots, x_n =^? t_n\}$ is said to be in *tree solved form* if each x_i is a variable occurring once in G. Given an idempotent substitution $\sigma = \{x_1 \mapsto t_1, \ldots, x_n \mapsto t_n\}$ (such that $\sigma\sigma = \sigma$), $\hat{\sigma}$ denotes the corresponding tree solved form. A set of equations is said to be in *dag solved form* if they can be arranged as a list $x_1 =^? t_1, \ldots, x_n =^? t_n$ where (a) each left-hand side x_i is a distinct variable, and (b) $\forall 1 \leq i \leq j \leq n$: x_i does not occur in t_j. A set of equations $\{x_1 =^? t_1, \ldots, x_n =^? t_n\}$ is a *cycle* if for any $i \in [1, n-1], x_{i+1} \in Var(t_i), x_1 \in Var(t_n)$, and there exists $j \in [1, n]$ such that t_j is not a variable. Given two disjoint signatures Σ_0 and Σ_1 and any $i = 1, 0$, Σ_i-terms (including the variables) and Σ_i-equations (including the equations between variables) are called Σ_i-*pure*. A term t is called a Σ_i-*rooted* term if its root symbol is in Σ_i. An *alien* subterm of a Σ_i-rooted term t is a Σ_j-rooted subterm s $(i \neq j)$ such that all superterms of s are Σ_i-rooted. We define *general E-unification* as the unification problem in the equational theory obtained by extending E with arbitrary free function symbols.

Given a Σ_0-theory E, a theory $F \cup E$ is a *conservative extension* of E if $=_{F \cup E}$ and $=_E$ coincide on Σ_0-terms. When $F \cup E$ is a conservative extension of E, E-unification is said to be *complete for solving the Σ_0-fragment of $F \cup E$-unification* if for any Σ_0-pure $F \cup E$-unification problem G, any $CSU_E(G)$ is a $CSU_{F \cup E}(G)$. If F and E have disjoint signatures, E-unification is known to be complete for solving the Σ_0-fragment of $F \cup E$-unification.

2.2 Equational Term Rewrite Systems

Given a signature Σ, an *equational term rewrite system* (TRS) (R, E) over Σ is defined by a Σ-theory E and a finite set R of oriented Σ-axioms called rewrite rules and of the form $l \rightarrow r$ such that l, r are Σ-terms, l is not a variable and $Var(r) \subseteq Var(l)$. A term s *rewrites* to a term t w.r.t (R, E), denoted by $s \rightarrow_{R,E} t$, if there exist a position p of s, $l \rightarrow r \in R$, and substitution σ such that $s_{|p} =_E l\sigma$ and $t = s[r\sigma]_p$. The term $s_{|p}$ is called a redex. Given a TRS (R, E), $\longleftrightarrow_{R \cup E}$ denotes the symmetric relation $\leftarrow_{R,E} \cup \rightarrow_{R,E} \cup =_E$. A TRS (R, E) is *Church-Rosser modulo E* if $\longleftrightarrow^*_{R \cup E}$ is included in $\rightarrow^*_{R,E} \circ =_E \circ \leftarrow^*_{R,E}$. When $=_E \circ \rightarrow_{R,E} \circ =_E$ is terminating, the following properties are equivalent [20]:

1. (R, E) is Church-Rosser modulo E,
2. for any terms t, t', $t \longleftrightarrow^*_{R \cup E} t'$ if and only if $t\!\downarrow =_E t'\!\downarrow$, where $t\!\downarrow$ (resp., $t'\!\downarrow$) denotes any normal form of t (resp., t') w.r.t (R, E).

A TRS (R, E) is *E-convergent* if $=_E \circ \rightarrow_{R,E} \circ =_E$ is terminating and (R, E) is Church-Rosser modulo E. Let Σ_0 be the subsignature of Σ that consists of function symbols occurring in the axioms of E. An E-convergent TRS (R, E) is said to be *E-constructed* if $\Sigma_0 \cap \{l(\epsilon) \mid l \rightarrow r \in R\} = \emptyset$.

An E-convergent TRS (R, E) is said to be *subterm E-convergent* if for any $l \rightarrow r \in R$, r is either a strict subterm of l or a constant. When (R, E) is clear from the context, a normal form w.r.t (R, E) is said to be *normalized*. A substitution σ is *normalized* if, for every variable x in the domain of σ, $x\sigma$ is normalized. An instance $l\sigma \rightarrow r\sigma$ of a rule $l \rightarrow r \in R$ is a *right-reduced instance* if $\sigma_{|Var(r)}$ is normalized. A term t is an *innermost redex* if no subterm of t is a redex. An E-convergent TRS (R, E) is *IRR* if every innermost redex is R, E-reducible by a right-reduced instance of a rule in R. An E-convergent TRS (R, E) is *IR1* if every innermost redex is R, E-reducible to a normal form in one step.

To simplify the notation, we often use tuples of terms, say $\bar{u} = (u_1, \ldots, u_n)$, $\bar{v} = (v_1, \ldots, v_n)$. Applying a substitution σ to $\bar{u}$ is the tuple $\bar{u}\sigma = (u_1\sigma, \ldots, u_n\sigma)$. The tuples $\bar{u}$ and $\bar{v}$ are said to be *E-equal*, denoted by $\bar{u} =_E \bar{v}$, if $u_1 =_E v_1, \ldots, u_n =_E v_n$. Similarly, $\bar{u} \rightarrow^*_R \bar{v}$ if $u_1 \rightarrow^*_R v_1, \ldots, u_n \rightarrow^*_R v_n$, $\bar{u}$ is normalized if $u_1, \ldots, u_n$ are normalized, and $\bar{u} =^? \bar{v}$ is $u_1 =^? v_1 \wedge \cdots \wedge u_n =^? v_n$.

2.3 Forward Closure

In this section, we introduce the notion of finite forward closure, following the definition given in [21]. Consider the rule:

ForwardOverlap $g \rightarrow d[l'], \quad l \rightarrow r \vdash (g \rightarrow d[r])\sigma$

where $g \rightarrow d[l'], l \rightarrow r \in R$, l' is not a variable and $\sigma \in CSU_E(l' =^? l)$.

For this inference rule, the notion of redundancy is defined with respect to an ordering on terms. We assume the existence of a simplification ordering $>$ such that $>$ is E-compatible, meaning that $s' =_E s > t =_E t'$ implies $s' > t'$, and $l > r$ for any $l \rightarrow r \in R$. **ForwardOverlap** is said to be *redundant* in (R, E) if for each g' such that $g' =_E g\sigma$, g' is R, E-reducible by a right-reduced instance $s\mu \rightarrow t\mu$ of R and either $s\mu < g\sigma$ or $(s\mu =_E g\sigma$ and $t\mu < d[l']\sigma)$.

Let $\mathcal{I}$ be an inference system generating rewrite rules and whose inferences are possibly redundant, like for instance $\mathcal{I} = \{$**ForwardOverlap**$\}$. Given an equational TRS (R, E), the saturation of (R, E) with respect to $\mathcal{I}$ is inductively defined as follows:

- $S_{\mathcal{I}}^0(R) = R$,
- $S_{\mathcal{I}}^{k+1}(R) = S_{\mathcal{I}}^k(R) \cup \{\rho\}$ where the rule ρ is obtained by applying an inference i in $\mathcal{I}$ using $(S_{\mathcal{I}}^k(R), E)$ as equational TRS and such that i is not redundant in $(S_{\mathcal{I}}^k(R), E)$.

Let $S_{\mathcal{I}}(R) = \bigcup_{k \geq 0} S_{\mathcal{I}}^k(R)$. When $S_{\mathcal{I}}(R)$ is finite, $S_{\mathcal{I}}(R)$ is called a finite $\mathcal{I}$-*saturation* of (R, E). An equational TRS (R, E) is $\mathcal{I}$-*saturated* if $S_{\mathcal{I}}(R) = R$. An equational TRS has a finite *forward closure* if it has a finite $\mathcal{I}$-saturation for $\mathcal{I} = \{$**ForwardOverlap**$\}$. An equational TRS is *forward-closed* if it is $\mathcal{I}$-saturated for $\mathcal{I} = \{$**ForwardOverlap**$\}$.

Example 1. Any subterm E-convergent TRS has a finite forward closure. Subterm convergent TRSs are often used in the verification of security protocols [1], e.g., $\{dec(enc(x, y), y) \rightarrow x\}$ and $\{fst(pair(x, y)) \rightarrow x, \; snd(pair(x, y)) \rightarrow y\}$. The equational TRSs $\{dec(enc(x, k), k * y) \rightarrow x\}$ and $\{rm(x * k, k) \rightarrow x\}$ are subterm E-convergent for $E = AC(*) = \{x * (y * z) = (x * y) * z, x * y = y * x\}$.

Forward closure can be connected to the notion of Finite Variant Property (FVP, for short) introduced in [11]. Given an E-convergent TRS (R, E), an (R, E)-*variant* of a term t is a pair $((t\theta)\downarrow, \theta)$ where θ is a normalized substitution whose domain is included in $Var(t)$. (R, E) has the FVP if for any term t there exists a finite set V of (R, E)-variants of t such that any (R, E)-variant of t is componentwise E-equal to an instance of some element in V. If (R, E) has the FVP, then any $R \cup E$-unification problem G reduces to E-unification problems via the computation of finitely many variants of G (viewed as a term with additional symbols). This computation can be performed using folding variant narrowing [12,19]. In [7], it was shown that for any TRS R, R has the FVP iff it has a finite forward closure. A similar equivalence holds for E-constructed TRSs:

Lemma 1. *Assume (R, E) is any E-constructed TRS and E is any regular and collapse-free equational theory such that E-unification is finitary. Then, (R, E) has a finite forward closure iff (R, E) has the FVP.*

Proof. We rely on some results that have been shown in [21] for an inference system $\mathcal{I}$ including **ForwardOverlap** plus an additional **Parallel** rule whose premises are $s \rightarrow t$, $l \rightarrow r \in R$, $v = u[l'] \in E$ such that l' is a non-variable strict subterm of u which is E-unifiable with l. The following statements are proved in [21]:

- (R, E) is *IR1* iff (R, E) is $\mathcal{I}$-saturated.
- If (R, E) is *IR1* and E-unification is finitary, then (R, E) has the FVP.
- If (R, E) has the FVP, then (R, E) has a finite $\mathcal{I}$-saturation.

When (R, E) is E-constructed and E is a regular and collapse-free equational theory, **Parallel** does not apply since a Σ_0-rooted term l' is not E-unifiable with a $\Sigma \backslash \Sigma_0$-rooted term l. Thus, $\mathcal{I}$-saturation reduces to forward closure, $\mathcal{I}$-satured means forward-closed, and the above statements can be reworded accordingly. To conclude the proof, notice that if R' is a finite forward closure of (R, E), then (R', E) is forward-closed and both (R', E) and (R, E) have the FVP. □

In this paper, (R, E) is assumed to be E-constructed and so the signature of (R, E) necessarily includes a non-empty set of function symbols that do not occur in the axioms of E. Thus, this means that we actually need general E-unification, i.e., E-unification with free function symbols, instead of E-unification. Fortunately, when E is regular and collapse-free, E-unification is finitary if and only if general E-unification is finitary. This equivalence is a consequence of a classical disjoint combination method for regular and collapse-free theories [31] that allows us to build a general E-unification algorithm as a combination of the syntactic unification algorithm and an E-unification algorithm.

From now on, the equational theory E is always assumed to be regular and collapse-free when (R, E) is E-constructed.

3   Hierarchical Unification

Consider now a union of theories $R \cup E$ where E is regular and collapse-free and (R, E) is assumed to be E-constructed. Thanks to this assumption, R and E are "sufficiently separated" and thus we can envision the problem of building an $R \cup E$-unification algorithm as a combination of two unification procedures: a mutation-based unification procedure processing some $R \cup E$-equalities, and an E-unification algorithm. The approach we will use for this problem is the *hierarchical* approach. Informally, the approach works as follows:

- The set of equations is processed to separate the terms over the shared signature, Σ_0, from terms over the non-shared one, $\Sigma \backslash \Sigma_0$.
- The mutation-based procedure is then used to simplify the $\Sigma \backslash \Sigma_0$-equations.
- The remaining equations over the shared signature Σ_0 are solved using the E-unification algorithm.
- The process can repeat. If the process terminates in a solved form then the problem is solvable and a unifier is produced.

A hierarchical unification procedure is parameterized by an E-unification algorithm and a mutation-based reduction procedure U. It applies some additional rules given in Fig. 1: **Coalesce**, **Split**, **Flatten**, and **VA** are used to separate the terms, U is used to simplify the $\Sigma \backslash \Sigma_0$-equations, and finally, **Solve** calls the E-unification algorithm.

Coalesce $\{x = y\} \cup G \vdash \{x = y\} \cup (G\{x \mapsto y\})$
where x and y are distinct variables occurring both in G.

Split $\{f(\bar{v}) = t\} \cup G \vdash \{x = f(\bar{v}), x = t\} \cup G$
where $f \in \Sigma \backslash \Sigma_0$, t is a non-variable term and x is a fresh variable.

Flatten $\{v = f(\dots, u, \dots)\} \cup G \vdash \{v = f(\dots, x, \dots), x = u\} \cup G$
where $f \in \Sigma \backslash \Sigma_0$, v is a variable, u is a non-variable term, and x is a fresh variable.

VA $\{s = t[u]\} \cup G \vdash \{s = t[x], x = u\} \cup G$
where t is Σ_0-rooted, u is an alien subterm of t, and x is a fresh variable.

Solve $G \cup G_0 \vdash \bigvee_{\sigma_0 \in CSU_E(G_0)} G \cup \hat{\sigma}_0$
where G is a set of $\Sigma \backslash \Sigma_0$-equations, G_0 is a set of Σ_0-equations, G_0 is E-unifiable and not in tree solved form, $\hat{\sigma}_0$ is the tree solved form associated with σ_0, and w.l.o.g for any $x \in Dom(\sigma_0)$, $x\sigma_0 \in Var(G_0)$ if $x\sigma_0$ is a variable.

Fig. 1. H_E rules

Definition 1 (Hierarchical unification procedure). *Assume a Σ_0-theory E for which an E-unification algorithm is known, a Σ-theory $F \cup E$ for which E-unification is complete for solving the Σ_0-fragment of $F \cup E$-unification, and an inference system U such that: U transforms only non-variable flat $\Sigma \backslash \Sigma_0$-equations; U is sound and complete for $F \cup E$-unification; and U is parameterized by some finite set S of $F \cup E$-equalities for which the soundness of each inference $\vdash_U$ follows from at most one equality in S. Under these assumptions, $H_E(U)$ is the inference system defined as the repeated application of some inference from H_E (cf. Fig. 1) or U, using the following order of priority: Coalesce, Split, Flatten, VA, U, Solve. An $F \cup E$-unification problem is separate, also called in separate form, if it is a normal form w.r.t $H_E \backslash \{Solve\}$. $H_E(U)$ is said to be a hierarchical unification procedure if the normal forms w.r.t $H_E(U)$ are either the separate dag solved forms or problems that are not $F \cup E$-unifiable.*

Note that U is not just a set of inference rules but also a strategy for applying those rules, for instance to avoid non-termination [15]. From now on, an inference system $H_E(U)$ always denotes a hierarchical unification procedure.

Proposition 1. *Let (R, E) be any E-constructed TRS such that an inference system U following Definition 1 is known for the equational theory $R \cup E$, in addition to an existing E-unification algorithm. Then E, $R \cup E$ and U satisfy the assumptions of Definition 1, and a hierarchical unification procedure $H_E(U)$*

provides a sound and complete $R \cup E$-unification procedure, and in particular an $R \cup E$-unification algorithm when $H_E(U)$ is also terminating.

Proof. If (R, E) is E-constructed, then E-unification is complete for solving the Σ_0-fragment of $R \cup E$-unification, and so all the assumptions are satisfied to define $H_E(U)$. By construction, $H_E(U)$ is sound and complete. Since the $R \cup E$-unifiable normal forms w.r.t $H_E(U)$ are assumed to be the separate dag solved forms, collecting all the separate dag solved forms reached by $H_E(U)$ suffices to get a complete set of $R \cup E$-unifiers.   □

3.1 Subterm Collapse-Free Theories

Hierarchical unification algorithms are known for particular subterm collapse-free theories of particular interest for protocol analysis.

Proposition 2 [15,30]. *Let E be the empty Σ_0-theory where Σ_0 only consists of a binary function symbol $*$, $R_{\mathcal{D}} = \{h(x * y) \rightarrow h(x) * h(y)\}$ and $R_{\mathcal{D}1} = \{f(x * y, z) \rightarrow f(x, z) * f(y, z)\}$. The equational TRSs $(R_{\mathcal{D}}, E)$ and $(R_{\mathcal{D}1}, E)$ are E-constructed. Moreover, $R_{\mathcal{D}} \cup E$ (resp., $R_{\mathcal{D}1} \cup E$) is a subterm collapse-free theory admitting a unification algorithm of the form $H_E(U_{\mathcal{D}})$ (resp., $H_E(U_{\mathcal{D}1})$).*

Proof. Subterm collapse-freeness follows from the fact that both theories are *non-size-reducing*. The inference system $U_{\mathcal{D}1}$ can be derived following the approach developed in [15] and based on the one initiated in [30] for one-side distributivity. The same approach can be applied for $R_{\mathcal{D}}$ to get $U_{\mathcal{D}}$.   □

Proposition 3 [15]. *Let $AC = AC(\circledast)$, $R_{\mathcal{E}} = \{exp(exp(x, y), z) \rightarrow exp(x, y \circledast z), exp(x * y, z) \rightarrow exp(x, z) * exp(y, z)\}$ and $R_{\mathcal{F}} = \{enc(enc(x, y), z) \rightarrow enc(x, y \circledast z)\}$. The equational TRSs $(R_{\mathcal{E}}, AC)$ and $(R_{\mathcal{F}}, AC)$ are AC-constructed. Moreover, $\mathcal{E}_{AC} = R_{\mathcal{E}} \cup AC$ (resp., $\mathcal{F}_{AC} = R_{\mathcal{F}} \cup AC$) is a subterm collapse-free theory admitting a unification algorithm of the form $H_{AC}(U_{\mathcal{E}})$ (resp., $H_{AC}(U_{\mathcal{F}})$).*

Proof. In [15] it is shown that both $\mathcal{E}_{AC}$ and $\mathcal{F}_{AC}$ are subterm collapse-free theories. Also in [15] a mutation-based inference system, say $U_{\mathcal{E}}$ (resp., $U_{\mathcal{F}}$), is developed for $\mathcal{E}_{AC}$ (resp., $\mathcal{F}_{AC}$): it reduces the $\Sigma \backslash \Sigma_0$-equations into solved forms after which a solving step applies AC-unification on Σ_0-equations. It is shown in [15] that the solving step needs only be applied once. Hence, the $\mathcal{E}_{AC}$-unification algorithm (resp., $\mathcal{F}_{AC}$-unification algorithm) given in [15] provides a unification algorithm of the form $H_{AC}(U_{\mathcal{E}})$ (resp., $H_{AC}(U_{\mathcal{F}})$).   □

3.2 Forward-Closed E-Constructed TRSs

For any forward-closed E-constructed TRS (R, E) such that E is regular and collapse-free, an $R \cup E$-unification algorithm of the form $H_E(U)$ can be obtained by defining some inference system U, based on the *Basic Syntactic Mutation* approach initiated for the class of theories closed by paramodulation [23], and already applied in [13] to a particular class of forward-closed equational TRSs.

Let BSM_R be the inference system given in Fig. 2. One can notice that each inference rule in BSM_R generates some boxed terms. This particular annotation of terms, detailed in [13,23], allows us to control the rules application, disregarding needless inferences on boxed terms, in such a way that BSM_R is terminating.

Imit $\bigcup_i \{x = f(\bar{v}_i)\} \cup G \vdash \{x = \boxed{f(\bar{y})}\} \cup \bigcup_i \{\bar{y} = \bar{v}_i\} \cup G$
where $f \in \Sigma \backslash \Sigma_0$, $i > 1$, $\bar{y}$ are fresh variables and there are no more equations $x = f(\dots)$ in G.

MutConflict$_R$ $\{x = f(\bar{v})\} \cup G \vdash \{x = \boxed{t}, \boxed{\bar{s}} = \bar{v}\} \cup G$
where $f \in \Sigma \backslash \Sigma_0$, $f(\bar{s}) \to t$ is a fresh instance of a rule in R, $f(\bar{v})$ is unboxed, and there is another equation $x = u$ in G with a non-variable term u or $x = f(\bar{v})$ occurs in a cycle.

ImitCycle $\{x = f(\bar{v})\} \cup G \vdash \{x = \boxed{f(\bar{y})}, \bar{y} = \bar{v}\} \cup G$
where $f \in \Sigma \backslash \Sigma_0$, $f(\bar{v})$ is unboxed, $\bar{y}$ are fresh variables and $x = f(\bar{v})$ occurs in a cycle.

Fig. 2. BSM_R rules

An $R \cup E$-unification algorithm combining BSM_R and an E-unification algorithm has been developed in [13] for the case of any forward-closed convergent TRS R such that the left-hand sides of R are linear and contain no symbols of E. In this paper, we extend [13] to any forward-closed E-constructed TRS (R, E), without any further restriction on R.

The soundness and completeness of BSM_R is shown by the following lemma.

Lemma 2. *Let (R, E) be any forward-closed E-constructed TRS over the signature Σ. For each equality $u =_{R \cup E} v$ such that u is $\Sigma \backslash \Sigma_0$-rooted and v is normalized, one of the following is true:*

1. $u = f(\bar{u})$, $v = f(\bar{v})$ and $\bar{u} =_{R \cup E} \bar{v}$.
2. $u = f(\bar{u})$, there exist $f(\bar{s}) \to t \in R$ and a normalized substitution σ such that $\bar{u} =_{R \cup E} \bar{s}\sigma$, $v =_E t\sigma$ and $\bar{s}\sigma, t\sigma$ are normalized.

Proof. Let us analyze the possible rewrite proofs $\to^*_{R,E}$ of $u =_{R \cup E} v$.

First, if there is no step at the root position, then we get $u = f(\bar{u}) \to^*_{R,E} f(\bar{u}') =_E v$ where $\bar{u} \to^*_{R,E} \bar{u}'$ and $\bar{u}'$ are normalized. Since f is a free symbol for E, we have that $v = f(\bar{v})$ and $\bar{u}' =_E \bar{v}$. Hence, $\bar{u} =_{R \cup E} \bar{v}$ since $\bar{u} =_{R \cup E} \bar{u}'$.

Second, if there is one step at the root position, then we have

$$u = f(\bar{u}) \to^*_{R,E} f(\bar{u}') = f(\bar{s})\sigma \to_{R,E,\epsilon} t\sigma =_E v$$

where $f(\bar{s}) \to t \in R$, $\bar{u} \to^*_{R,E} \bar{u}'$, $\bar{u}'$ are normalized, $\bar{u}' =_E \bar{s}\sigma$, and so $\sigma, \bar{s}\sigma$ are normalized. Since $t\sigma =_E v$ and v is normalized, $t\sigma$ is also normalized. □

A unification procedure of the form $H_E(BSM_R)$ corresponds to the BSC unification procedure given in [13] except that **Solve** is applied in BSC before BSM_R rules. However, the termination proof stated for BSC in [13] also holds when **Solve** is applied after the BSM_R rules.

Lemma 3. *Assume E is any regular and collapse-free theory such that an E-unification algorithm is known. Let (R, E) be a forward-closed E-constructed TRS and BSM_R the inference system given in Fig. 2. Then $H_E(BSM_R)$ is an $R \cup E$-unification algorithm.*

Example 2. Consider $R = \{h(x) \rightarrow a \times x\}$, $R' = \{f(x, y) \rightarrow a'(y) \times x\}$ and $E = \{x \times (y * z) = (x \times y) * (x \times z)\}$. The theory E corresponds to left-distributivity and an E-unification algorithm is given in [30]. Since (R, E) and (R', E) are forward-closed and E-constructed, $H_E(BSM_R)$ and $H_E(BSM_{R'})$ are unification algorithms for $R \cup E$ and $R' \cup E$, respectively. Notice that $h(x * y) =_{R \cup E} h(x) * h(y)$ and $f(x * y, z) =_{R' \cup E} f(x, z) * f(y, z)$.

Example 3. Consider $R = \{\pi_1(x.y) \rightarrow x, \pi_2(x.y) \rightarrow y, dec(enc(x, y), y) \rightarrow x\}$ and $E = \{enc(x.y, z) = enc(x, z).enc(y, z)\}$. An E-unification algorithm can be obtained following the approach developed in [15,30] and can be used in a hierarchical unification procedure of the form $H_E(BSM_R)$. Since (R, E) is forward-closed and E-constructed, $H_E(BSM_R)$ is an $R \cup E$-unification algorithm.

4 Combined Hierarchical Unification

We are now interested in combining hierarchical unification algorithms known for E-constructed TRSs. Given two E-constructed TRSs, say (R_1, E) and (R_2, E), the problem is to study the possible construction of a (combined) hierarchical unification algorithm for $(R_1 \cup R_2, E)$ using the two hierarchical unification algorithms known for (R_1, E) and (R_2, E). We investigate this combination problem for the two classes of E-constructed TRSs introduced in Sect. 3. First, we consider a class of E-constructed TRSs (R, E) such that $R \cup E$ is subterm collapse-free. Second, we study the class of forward-closed E-constructed TRSs (R, E) such that E is regular and collapse-free.

4.1 Combining Subterm Collapse-Free Theories

Let us first consider a technical lemma which is useful to get a hierarchical unification procedure.

Lemma 4. *Let (R_1, E) and (R_2, E) be two E-constructed TRSs over the signatures Σ_1 and Σ_2, respectively, such that $\Sigma_1 \cap \Sigma_2 = \Sigma_0$ for the signature Σ_0 of E, and for $i = 1, 2$, $R_i \cup E$ admits a sound and complete unification procedure of the form $H_E(U_i)$. Assume that $R_1 \cup R_2 \cup E$ is subterm collapse-free, and for any $\Sigma_1 \backslash \Sigma_0$-rooted term t_1 and any $\Sigma_2 \backslash \Sigma_0$-rooted term t_2, t_1 cannot be equal to t_2 modulo $R_1 \cup R_2 \cup E$. Then, $H_E(U_1 \cup U_2)$ is a sound and complete $R_1 \cup R_2 \cup E$-unification procedure.*

Proof. According to the assumptions, $U_1 \cup U_2$ is sound and complete for $R_1 \cup R_2 \cup E$-unification and any normal form w.r.t $H_E(U_1 \cup U_2)$ is $R_1 \cup R_2 \cup E$-unifiable iff it is in dag solved form. So, Proposition 1 applies.   □

We study below a possible way to satisfy the assumptions of Lemma 4.

Definition 2 (Layer-preservingness). *Let (R, E) be an E-constructed TRS over the signature Σ, for which Σ_0 denotes the signature of E. A Σ-term t is said to be E-capped if there exist a constant-free Σ_0-term u and a substitution σ such that $t = u\sigma$, $Dom(\sigma) = Var(u)$ and $Ran(\sigma)$ is a set of $\Sigma \backslash \Sigma_0$-rooted terms. The TRS (R, E) is said to be layer-preserving if $R \cup E$ is subterm collapse-free and any normal form of any $\Sigma \backslash \Sigma_0$-rooted term is E-capped.*

Remark 1. An easy way to get layer-preservingness of (R, E) is to assume that $R \cup E$ is subterm collapse-free and the right hand-sides of rules in R are $\Sigma \backslash \Sigma_0$-rooted. In that case the term u in Definition 2 is simply a variable. Layer-preservingness generalizes this assumption used in [14].

The property of being E-constructed and layer-preserving is modular.

Lemma 5. *Assume E is a subterm collapse-free Σ_0-theory, for $i = 1, 2$, (R_i, E) is an E-constructed layer-preserving TRS over the signature Σ_i, and $\Sigma_1 \cap \Sigma_2 = \Sigma_0$. If $=_E \circ \to_{R_1 \cup R_2} \circ =_E$ is terminating, then $(R_1 \cup R_2, E)$ is an E-constructed layer-preserving TRS, and for any $\Sigma_1 \backslash \Sigma_0$-rooted term t_1 and any $\Sigma_2 \backslash \Sigma_0$-rooted term t_2, t_1 cannot be equal to t_2 modulo $R_1 \cup R_2 \cup E$.*

Proof. To show that $(R_1 \cup R_2, E)$ is layer-preserving, we have to prove that $R_1 \cup R_2 \cup E$ remains subterm collapse-free. The modularity of subterm collapse-freeness has been shown in [14] when the right-hand sides of R_i are $\Sigma_i \backslash \Sigma_0$-rooted, for $i = 1, 2$. Actually, a similar proof by contradiction can be performed in the case (R_i, E) is layer-preserving, for $i = 1, 2$. Let us consider the *height of layers* of a term t, inductively defined as follows:

- $ht(t) = 0$ if t is a variable,
- $ht(t) = 1$ if t is a non-variable pure term,
- $ht(t) = 1 + \max\{ht(u) \mid u$ is an alien subterm of $t\}$ if t is not pure.

Assume there exists a term t and a non-empty position p such that $t =_{R_1 \cup E_2 \cup E} t|_p$. If the path from ϵ to p contains only symbols from one theory, say $R_i \cup E$, this would lead to a contradiction with the subterm collapse-freeness of $R_i \cup E$. Consider now that the path from ϵ to p contains both a $\Sigma_1 \backslash \Sigma_0$-symbol and a $\Sigma_2 \backslash \Sigma_0$-symbol. Let $u = t|_p$ and let t' and u' be the respective normal forms of t and u w.r.t $(R_1 \cup R_2, E)$. Since $t' =_E u'$ and E is necessarily regular collapse-free, we have that t' and u' have the same height of layers. By the layer-preserving assumption, t and t' have the same height of layers, as well as u and u'. Thus t and u have the same height of layers, which leads to a contradiction due to the considered path from ϵ to p.

Assume there exist some $\Sigma_1 \backslash \Sigma_0$-rooted term t_1 and some $\Sigma_2 \backslash \Sigma_0$-rooted term t_2 such that $t_1 =_{R_1 \cup R_2 \cup E} t_2$. Then, $t_1' =_E t_2'$ where t_1' and t_2' are the respective normal forms of t_1 and t_2 w.r.t $(R_1 \cup R_2, E)$. The layer-preserving assumption implies that t_i' must still contain a symbol in $\Sigma_i \backslash \Sigma_0$ for $i = 1, 2$. Since E is necessarily regular and collapse-free, it is thus impossible to have $t_1' =_E t_2'$. $\square$

Remark 2. To satisfy the condition $=_E \circ \rightarrow_{R_1 \cup R_2} \circ =_E$ is terminating, it suffices to exhibit an E-compatible reduction ordering $>$ such that $l > r$ for any $l \rightarrow r \in R_1 \cup R_2$. In that case, $>$ is defined on terms built over $\Sigma_1 \cup \Sigma_2$.

By Lemma 5, the two assumptions of Lemma 4 can be satisfied, and this leads to a hierarchical unification procedure for the combined TRS. In the following, we consider a notion of decreasingness in order to study the termination of this unification procedure.

Definition 3 (Decreasingness). *Consider a complexity measure defined as a mapping C from separate forms to natural numbers. An $H_E(U)$ inference system is said to be C-decreasing if for any separate form $G \cup G_0$ we have that (1) for any G' such that $G \cup G_0 \vdash_U G' \cup G_0$, the separate form of $G' \cup G_0$ does not increase C; (2) for any G'_0 such that $G \cup G_0 \vdash_{Solve} G \cup G'_0$, then either the separate form of $G \cup G'_0$ is in normal form w.r.t $H_E(U)$, or it decreases C.*

Consequently, $H_E(U)$ is terminating if there exists some C such that $H_E(U)$ is C-decreasing.

Theorem 1. *Assume E is a subterm collapse-free theory such that an E-unification algorithm is known, and C is a complexity measure defined on separate forms. Let (R_1, E) and (R_2, E) be two E-constructed TRSs sharing only symbols in E such that, for $i = 1, 2$, (R_i, E) is layer-preserving, and $R_i \cup E$ admits a C-decreasing unification algorithm of the form $H_E(U_i)$. If $=_E \circ \rightarrow_{R_1 \cup R_2} \circ =_E$ is terminating, then $(R_1 \cup R_2, E)$ is an E-constructed TRS such that $(R_1 \cup R_2, E)$ is layer-preserving, and $R_1 \cup R_2 \cup E$ admits a C-decreasing unification algorithm of the form $H_E(U_1 \cup U_2)$.*

Proof. $(R_1 \cup R_2, E)$ is layer-preserving by Lemma 5. In addition, a $\Sigma_1 \backslash \Sigma_0$-rooted term cannot be equal to a $\Sigma_2 \backslash \Sigma_0$-rooted term modulo $R_1 \cup R_2 \cup E$. Applying Lemma 4, $H_E(U_1 \cup U_2)$ provides a sound and complete $R_1 \cup R_2 \cup E$-unification procedure. Moreover, $H_E(U_1 \cup U_2)$ is C-decreasing and so it is terminating.   □

Example 4. Consider the theories $\mathcal{E}_{AC}$ and $\mathcal{F}_{AC}$ introduced in Proposition 3 and the corresponding hierarchical unification algorithms $H_{AC}(U_\mathcal{E})$ and $H_{AC}(U_\mathcal{F})$ where the mutation rules defining $U_\mathcal{E}$ and $U_\mathcal{F}$ can be found in [15]. Let SVC be the complexity measure defined as follows: given an $R \cup E$-unification problem in separate form $G \cup G_0$, $SVC(G \cup G_0)$ is the number of equivalence classes of variables shared by G and G_0 that are variables abstracting $\Sigma \backslash \Sigma_0$-rooted terms.

Let us now check that the unification algorithms $H_{AC}(U_\mathcal{E})$ and $H_{AC}(U_\mathcal{F})$ are both SVC-decreasing. On the one hand, it is routine to verify that any (mutation) rule in $U_\mathcal{E}$ (resp., $U_\mathcal{F}$) does not lead, via a further possible application of **VA**, to new shared variables which are abstracting $\Sigma \backslash \Sigma_0$-rooted terms. Hence, the rules in $U_\mathcal{E}$ (resp., $U_\mathcal{F}$) cannot increase SVC. On the other hand, **Solve** leads to either a normal form w.r.t $H_{AC}(U_\mathcal{E})$ (resp., $H_{AC}(U_\mathcal{F})$), or it generates some equality $x =^? y$ between variables x and y for which there are $\Sigma \backslash \Sigma_0$-equations $x =^? s$ and $y =^? t$ in G. In the last case, the respective equivalence classes of x and y are merged into a single one by applying **Solve** and so,

Solve strictly decreases SVC. By Theorem 1, we get that $\mathcal{E}_{AC} \cup \mathcal{F}_{AC}$ admits a SVC-decreasing unification algorithm of the form $H_{AC}(U_{\mathcal{E}} \cup U_{\mathcal{F}})$. Notice this means that we can use the termination strategy used in the individual $H_{AC}(U_{\mathcal{E}})$ and $H_{AC}(U_{\mathcal{F}})$ algorithms to obtain a termination strategy for the hierarchical combined algorithm, $H_{AC}(U_{\mathcal{E}} \cup U_{\mathcal{F}})$. We suspect that this complexity measure, SVC, could be useful for proving termination in other theories.

To conclude this section, let us mention the problem of combining two copies of the same E-constructed layer-preserving TRS, provided that only the symbols in E are possibly shared. In that very particular case, layer-preservingness is sufficient and there is no need to find a decreasing complexity measure.

Theorem 2. *Consider (R, E) is an E-constructed layer-preserving TRS over the signature Σ such that $R \cup E$ admits a unification algorithm of the form $H_E(U)$. Let (R', E) be a copy of (R, E) obtained by renaming the $\Sigma \backslash \Sigma_0$-symbols. Then, $(R \cup R', E)$ is an E-constructed layer-preserving TRS such that $R \cup R' \cup E$ admits a unification algorithm of the form $H_E(U \cup U')$, where U' is obtained from U by applying the same renaming as the one defining (R', E).*

Proof. Consider the morphism ι replacing each symbol $f' \in \Sigma' \backslash \Sigma_0$ by the corresponding function symbol $f \in \Sigma \backslash \Sigma_0$. For any terms s,t, $s =_E \circ \to_{R \cup R'} \circ =_E t$ implies $\iota(s) =_E \circ \to_R \circ =_E \iota(t)$. Thus, $=_E \circ \to_R \circ =_E$ is terminating implies $=_E \circ \to_{R \cup R'} \circ =_E$ is terminating. By Lemmas 5 and 4, $(R \cup R', E)$ is an E-constructed layer-preserving TRS and $H_E(U \cup U')$ is a sound and complete $R \cup R' \cup E$-unification procedure. For each inference $P \vdash_{H_E(U \cup U')} Q$, there exists an inference $\iota(P) \vdash_{H_E(U)} \iota(Q)$. Thus, the termination w.r.t $H_E(U)$ implies the termination w.r.t $H_E(U \cup U')$. □

Example 5. Consider the two E-constructed layer-preserving TRSs $(R_{\mathcal{D}}, E)$ and $(R_{\mathcal{D}1}, E)$ defined in Proposition 2, and their copies $R'_{\mathcal{D}} = \{h'(x * y) \to h'(x) * h'(y)\}$ and $R'_{\mathcal{D}1} = \{f'(x * y, z) \to f'(x, z) * f'(y, z)\}$. The theories $R_{\mathcal{D}} \cup E$ and $R_{\mathcal{D}1} \cup E$ admit unification algorithms of the form $H_E(U_{\mathcal{D}})$ and $H_E(U_{\mathcal{D}1})$, respectively. By Theorem 2, $R_{\mathcal{D}} \cup R'_{\mathcal{D}} \cup E$ and $R_{\mathcal{D}1} \cup R'_{\mathcal{D}1} \cup E$ admit unification algorithms of the form $H_E(U_{\mathcal{D}} \cup U'_{\mathcal{D}})$ and $H_E(U_{\mathcal{D}1} \cup U'_{\mathcal{D}1})$, respectively.

4.2 Combining Forward-Closed E-Constructed TRSs

The union of two forward-closed E-constructed TRSs remains a forward-closed E constructed TRS. Thus, a hierarchical unification algorithm can be constructed in a modular way in unions of forward-closed E-constructed TRSs.

Theorem 3. *Assume E is a regular and collapse-free theory such that an E-unification algorithm is known. Let (R_1, E) and (R_2, E) be two forward-closed E-constructed TRSs sharing only symbols in E. Then $R_1 \cup R_2 \cup E$ admits a unification algorithm of the form $H_E(BSM_{R_1} \cup BSM_{R_2})$.*

Proof. $(R_1 \cup R_2, E)$ is a forward-closed E-constructed TRS, and so by Lemma 3, $R_1 \cup R_2 \cup E$ admits a unification algorithm of the form $H_E(BSM_{R_1 \cup R_2})$, which coincides with $H_E(BSM_{R_1} \cup BSM_{R_2})$. □

In the following, we investigate the case where E already admits a hierarchical unification algorithm of the form $H_{E'}(U')$ for a subtheory E' of E, like in Example 3 where E has a hierarchical unification algorithm of the form $H_{E'}(U')$ for $E' = \emptyset$. In that case, we can consider the following compositionality lemma:

Lemma 6. *Let (R, E) be an E-constructed TRS such that $R \cup E$ admits a unification algorithm of the form $H_E(U)$, and E admits a unification algorithm of the form $H_{E'}(U')$, where E' is a subtheory of E. Then $R \cup E$ also admits a unification algorithm of the form $H_{E'}(U \cup U')$.*

Proof. Consider $\Sigma' = \Sigma_0$ and E is a Σ'-theory of the form $E = F' \cup E'$. Assume $R \cup E$ (resp., $F' \cup E'$) has a unification algorithm of the form $H_E(U)$ (resp., $H_{E'}(U')$), where U (resp., U') is sound, complete, and parameterized by some finite set S (resp., S') of $R \cup E$-equalities (resp., $F' \cup E'$-equalities) such that the soundness of each inference $\vdash_U$ (resp., $\vdash_{U'}$) follows from at most one equality in S (resp., S').

Since E-unification is complete for solving the Σ'-fragment of $R \cup E$-unification, U' is also sound and complete for $R \cup F' \cup E'$. Hence, the inference system $U \cup U'$ is sound and complete. Moreover, $S \cup S'$ is a finite set of $R \cup F' \cup E'$-equalities such that the soundness of each inference $\vdash_{U \cup U'}$ follows from at most one equality in $S \cup S'$.

Since E-unification is complete for solving the Σ'-fragment of $R \cup E$-unification and E'-unification is complete for solving the Σ_0'-fragment of E-unification, we have that E' is also complete for solving the Σ_0'-fragment of $R \cup F' \cup E'$-unification.

Consequently, E', $R \cup F' \cup E'$ and $U \cup U'$ satisfy all the assumptions of Definition 1, and so $H_{E'}(U \cup U')$ is well-defined. Since $H_{E'}(U \cup U')$ corresponds to an "unfolding" of $H_E(U)$, it is terminating, sound and complete, just like $H_E(U)$. Thus, $H_{E'}(U \cup U')$ is a unification algorithm for $R \cup E = R \cup F' \cup E'$. $\square$

Example 6. (Example 3 continued) $R \cup E$ admits a unification algorithm of the form $H_\emptyset(BSM_R \cup U')$ where $H_\emptyset(U')$ is a hierarchical E-unification algorithm.

Example 7. Let us consider a theory used in practice to model a group messaging protocol [9]. For this protocol, the theory modeling the intruder can be defined [27] as a combination $R_{ENC} \cup K$ where $K = \{keyexch(x, pk(x'), y, pk(y')) = keyexch(x', pk(x), y', pk(y))\}$ and (R_{ENC}, K) is the forward-closed K-constructed TRS where

$$R_{ENC} = \left\{ \begin{array}{r} adec(aenc(m, pk(sk)), sk) \rightarrow m \\ getmsg(sign(m, sk)) \rightarrow m \\ checksign(sign(m, sk), m, pk(sk)) \rightarrow ok \\ sdec(senc(m, k), k) \rightarrow m \end{array} \right\}$$

K is a theory closed by paramodulation and so K-unification is finitary [23]. By Lemma 3, $R_{ENC} \cup K$ has a hierarchical unification algorithm of the form $H_K(BSM_{R_{ENC}})$. The mutation-based unification algorithm known for theories closed by paramodulation [23] can be reworded as a hierarchical unification algorithm, of the form $H_\emptyset(U_K)$ for K. By Lemma 6, $H_\emptyset(BSM_{R_{ENC}} \cup U_K)$ is another $R_{ENC} \cup K$-unification algorithm.

Applying Lemma 6, we can easily obtain a hierarchical unification algorithm for a forward-closed E-constructed TRS combined with a regular and collapse-free E-constructed TRS.

Lemma 7. *Assume E is a regular and collapse-free theory such that an E-unification algorithm is known. Let (R_1, E) and (R_2, E) be two E-constructed TRSs sharing only symbols in E such that (R_1, E) is forward-closed, and $R_2 \cup E$ is a regular and collapse-free theory E_2 admitting a unification algorithm of the form $H_E(U_2)$. Then (R_1, E_2) is a forward-closed E_2-constructed TRS and $R_1 \cup E_2$ admits a unification algorithm of the form $H_E(BSM_{R_1} \cup U_2)$.*

Proof. (R_1, E_2) is forward-closed because (R_1, E) is forward-closed and the equational theory $=_E$ coincides with $=_{E_2}$ on Σ_1-terms. By Lemma 3, $R_1 \cup E_2$ admits a unification algorithm of the form $H_{E_2}(BSM_{R_1})$. According to Lemma 6, $R_1 \cup E_2$ also admits a unification algorithm of the form $H_E(BSM_{R_1} \cup U_2)$. $\square$

Example 8. Let $(R, AC(\circledast))$ be a forward-closed $AC(\circledast)$-constructed TRS such that $\circledast$ is the only function symbol shared by $R \cup AC(\circledast)$ and $\mathcal{E}_{AC}$ (resp., $\mathcal{F}_{AC}$). By Lemma 7, $R \cup \mathcal{E}_{AC}$ (resp., $R \cup \mathcal{F}_{AC}$) admits a unification algorithm of the form $H_{AC}(BSM_R \cup U_\mathcal{E})$ (resp., $H_{AC}(BSM_R \cup U_\mathcal{F})$). According to Example 4, $\mathcal{E}_{AC} \cup \mathcal{F}_{AC}$ admits a unification algorithm of the form $H_{AC}(U_\mathcal{E} \cup U_\mathcal{F})$. Then, by Lemma 7, $R \cup \mathcal{E}_{AC} \cup \mathcal{F}_{AC}$ admits a unification algorithm of the form $H_{AC}(BSM_R \cup U_\mathcal{E} \cup U_\mathcal{F})$.

5   Conclusion

We have introduced a hierarchical unification framework as a generic tool to construct unification procedures for (combined) equational theories defined by E-constructed TRSs. We have presented new combination results for the simplest case of subterm collapse-free theories, and a natural follow-up would be to study the case of regular and collapse-free theories. A challenging future work is to investigate the general case of arbitrary theories.

Hierarchical unification allows us to handle syntactic theories $R \cup E$ while the E-unification algorithm can be arbitrary. According to this observation, we plan to study a weakening of syntacticness, in order to allow theories $R \cup E$ that are just *syntactic modulo E*.

We have also begun the implementation of the above hierarchical combination procedure. To begin with, we are using $E = AC$ as the background theory. However, we will explore expanding this to additional equational theories. In the short term, we plan to experiment the use of our variant-free hierarchical unification procedures (e.g., the ones introduced in Examples 3 and 7) as an alternative to variant-based unification procedures in modern protocol verification tools [6, 18, 25]. In the long term, we want to promote the use of non-disjoint combination procedures [16] and mutation-based procedures [17] in protocol verification tools, targeting unification problems as well as some decision problems related to the knowledge of an intruder, such as intruder deduction (a reachability problem) and indistinguishability (an equivalence problem) [1,8]. The goal is to improve automation of verification methods when theories share for instance AC symbols.

References

1. Abadi, M., Cortier, V.: Deciding knowledge in security protocols under equational theories. Theoret. Comput. Sci. **367**(1–2), 2–32 (2006)
2. Baader, F., Nipkow, T.: Term Rewriting and All That. Cambridge University Press, New York (1998)
3. Baader, F., Schulz, K.U.: Unification in the union of disjoint equational theories: combining decision procedures. J. Symbol. Comput. **21**(2), 211–243 (1996)
4. Baader, F., Snyder, W.: Unification theory. In: Robinson, J.A., Voronkov, A. (eds.) Handbook of Automated Reasoning, pp. 445–532. Elsevier and MIT Press (2001)
5. Basin, D., Mödersheim, S., Viganò, L.: An on-the-fly model-checker for security protocol analysis. In: Snekkenes, E., Gollmann, D. (eds.) ESORICS 2003. LNCS, vol. 2808, pp. 253–270. Springer, Heidelberg (2003). https://doi.org/10.1007/978-3-540-39650-5_15
6. Blanchet, B.: Modeling and verifying security protocols with the Applied Pi calculus and ProVerif. Found. Trends Priv. Secur. **1**(1–2), 1–135 (2016)
7. Bouchard, C., Gero, K.A., Lynch, C., Narendran, P.: On forward closure and the finite variant property. In: Fontaine, P., Ringeissen, C., Schmidt, R.A. (eds.) FroCoS 2013. LNCS (LNAI), vol. 8152, pp. 327–342. Springer, Heidelberg (2013). https://doi.org/10.1007/978-3-642-40885-4_23
8. Ciobâcă, S., Delaune, S., Kremer, S.: Computing knowledge in security protocols under convergent equational theories. J. Autom. Reasoning **48**(2), 219–262 (2012)
9. Cohn-Gordon, K., Cremers, C., Garratt, L., Millican, J., Milner, K.: On ends-to-ends encryption: asynchronous group messaging with strong security guarantees. In: Lie, D., Mannan, M., Backes, M., Wang, X. (eds.) Proceedings of the 2018 ACM SIGSAC Conference on Computer and Communications Security, CCS 2018, Toronto, ON, Canada, 15–19 October 2018, pp. 1802–1819. ACM (2018)
10. Comon, H., Haberstrau, M., Jouannaud, J.-P.: Syntacticness, cycle-syntacticness, and shallow theories. Inf. Comput. **111**(1), 154–191 (1994)
11. Comon-Lundh, H., Delaune, S.: The finite variant property: how to get rid of some algebraic properties. In: Giesl, J. (ed.) RTA 2005. LNCS, vol. 3467, pp. 294–307. Springer, Heidelberg (2005). https://doi.org/10.1007/978-3-540-32033-3_22
12. Durán, F., Eker, S., Escobar, S., Martí-Oliet, N., Meseguer, J., Talcott, C.: Built-in variant generation and unification, and their applications in Maude 2.7. In: Olivetti, N., Tiwari, A. (eds.) IJCAR 2016. LNCS (LNAI), vol. 9706, pp. 183–192. Springer, Cham (2016). https://doi.org/10.1007/978-3-319-40229-1_13
13. Eeralla, A.K., Erbatur, S., Marshall, A.M., Ringeissen, C.: Rule-based unification in combined theories and the finite variant property. In: Martín-Vide, C., Okhotin, A., Shapira, D. (eds.) LATA 2019. LNCS, vol. 11417, pp. 356–367. Springer, Cham (2019). https://doi.org/10.1007/978-3-030-13435-8_26

14. Erbatur, S., Kapur, D., Marshall, A.M., Narendran, P., Ringeissen, C.: Hierarchical combination. In: Bonacina, M.P. (ed.) CADE 2013. LNCS (LNAI), vol. 7898, pp. 249–266. Springer, Heidelberg (2013). https://doi.org/10.1007/978-3-642-38574-2_17
15. Erbatur, S., Marshall, A.M., Kapur, D., Narendran, P.: Unification over distributive exponentiation (sub)theories. J. Automata Lang. Comb. (JALC) **16**(2–4), 109–140 (2011)
16. Erbatur, S., Marshall, A.M., Ringeissen, C.: Notions of knowledge in combinations of theories sharing constructors. In: de Moura, L. (ed.) CADE 2017. LNCS (LNAI), vol. 10395, pp. 60–76. Springer, Cham (2017). https://doi.org/10.1007/978-3-319-63046-5_5
17. Erbatur, S., Marshall, A.M., Ringeissen, C.: Computing knowledge in equational extensions of subterm convergent theories. Math. Struct. Comput. Sci. **30**(6), 683–709 (2020)
18. Escobar, S., Meadows, C., Meseguer, J.: Maude-NPA: cryptographic protocol analysis modulo equational properties. In: Aldini, A., Barthe, G., Gorrieri, R. (eds.) FOSAD 2007-2009. LNCS, vol. 5705, pp. 1–50. Springer, Heidelberg (2009). https://doi.org/10.1007/978-3-642-03829-7_1
19. Escobar, S., Sasse, R., Meseguer, J.: Folding variant narrowing and optimal variant termination. J. Log. Algebr. Program. **81**(7–8), 898–928 (2012)
20. Jouannaud, J.-P., Kirchner, H.: Completion of a set of rules modulo a set of equations. SIAM J. Comput. **15**(4), 1155–1194 (1986)
21. Kim, D., Lynch, C., Narendran, P.: Reviving basic narrowing modulo. In: Herzig, A., Popescu, A. (eds.) FroCoS 2019. LNCS (LNAI), vol. 11715, pp. 313–329. Springer, Cham (2019). https://doi.org/10.1007/978-3-030-29007-8_18
22. Kirchner, C., Klay, F.: Syntactic theories and unification. In: Logic in Computer Science. LICS 1990, Proceedings, Fifth Annual IEEE Symposium on Logic in Computer Science, pp. 270–277, June 1990
23. Lynch, C., Morawska, B.: Basic syntactic mutation. In: Voronkov, A. (ed.) CADE 2002. LNCS (LNAI), vol. 2392, pp. 471–485. Springer, Heidelberg (2002). https://doi.org/10.1007/3-540-45620-1_37
24. Marshall, A.M., Meadows, C. Narendran, P.: On unification modulo one-sided distributivity: Algorithms, variants and asymmetry. Log. Methods Comput. Sci. **11**(2) (2015). https://doi.org/10.2168/LMCS-11(2:11)2015
25. Meier, S., Schmidt, B., Cremers, C., Basin, D.: The TAMARIN prover for the symbolic analysis of security protocols. In: Sharygina, N., Veith, H. (eds.) CAV 2013. LNCS, vol. 8044, pp. 696–701. Springer, Heidelberg (2013). https://doi.org/10.1007/978-3-642-39799-8_48
26. Meseguer, J.: Variant-based satisfiability in initial algebras. Sci. Comput. Program. **154**, 3–41 (2018)
27. Nguyen, K.: Formal verification of a messaging protocol, work done under the supervision of Vincent Cheval and Véronique Cortier
28. Nipkow, T.: Proof transformations for equational theories. In: Logic in Computer Science. LICS 1990, Proceedings, Fifth Annual IEEE Symposium on Logic in Computer Science, pp. 278–288, June 1990
29. Schmidt-Schauß, M.: Unification in a combination of arbitrary disjoint equational theories. J. Symbol. Comput. **8**, 51–99 (1989)
30. Tidén, E., Arnborg, S.: Unification problems with one-sided distributivity. J. Symbol. Comput. **3**(1/2), 183–202 (1987)
31. Yelick, K.A.: Unification in combinations of collapse-free regular theories. J. Symbol. Comput. **3**(1–2), 153–181 (1987)

Types

slepice: Towards a Verified Implementation of Type Theory in Type Theory

František Farka$^{(\boxtimes)}$ (ID)

IMDEA Software Institute, Madrid, Spain
frantisek.farka@imdea.org

Abstract. Dependent types have proven a useful technique for development of verified software. Despite the existence of many systems based in dependent type theory, mostly interactive theorem provers but also programming languages, there is no system that would itself be implemented using dependent types. Recently, a new approach to type inference and term synthesis for type theory with dependent types emerged that separates the process into an analysis phase that is carried out in type theory, and a search phase that is carried out in a logic programming engine.

We describe an architecture of type inference and term synthesis engine for a language with dependent types that is based on the new approach and that is feasible to implement using a dependently typed language. We demonstrate the architecture by describing slepice, its particular implementation.

Keywords: Dependent types · Type inference · Horn clause logic · Term synthesis · Proof-relevant resolution

1 Introduction

Dependent type theory has gained its place as foundations for construction of software verification tools in the form of interactive theorem provers and, more recently, in a form of programming languages with dependent types. Yet, current systems that are based in dependent type theory are not themselves implemented using such technology; to give an example, Coq [4] is implemented in OCaml, Agda [15] and Idris [5] in Haskell. At the same time, the need for formally verified tools has been advocated, *e.g.* by the CompCert project [14]. Such a tool allows to guarantee that there are no compilation-introduced bugs, which is only desirable given that processing languages with dependent types is a complex task.

A canonical example of type theory with dependent types is LF [13]. LF possesses decidable type checking, the metatheory is well-understood, and is strong enough to serve as a basis for a programming language [16]. Urban *et al.* [21] developed a formalisation of the metatheory of LF that provides an implementation of type checking via code generation. However, even this detailed

© Springer Nature Switzerland AG 2021
M. Fernández (Ed.): LOPSTR 2020, LNCS 12561, pp. 133–150, 2021.
https://doi.org/10.1007/978-3-030-68446-4_7

development is carried out in Isabelle/HOL rather than in a constructive type theory and, as a consequence, the authors study only quasi-decidability of the typing judgement.

For any implementation that is to be of a practical use type checking alone is not sufficient. The amount of type annotations and the number of proof obligations becomes unmanageable very quickly. Some amount of automation is necessary, namely type inference to reconstruct omitted type annotations, and term synthesis to infer omitted proofs. In what follows we use *refinement* to refer to type inference and term synthesis at once. A detailed account of issues connected with type inference in LF (as implemented in Beluga system [17]) was given by Pientka [16]. Providing such an implementation in constructive type theory is non-trivial since the problem is in general undecidable [7]. Similar issues arise with term synthesis, that accounts for proof automation.

Further, languages that are used in practice are based in stronger type theory than LF. Abel *et al.* [1] recently formalised a proof of decidability of equality in type theory in Agda. The type theory they consider is an idealised version of Agda itself and the proof can, in principle, be used to extract an implementation of an algorithm for deciding equality in Agda. However, their formalisation depends on inductive-recursive definitions to specify logic-relation that is necessary to proceed by induction and to show that the required assumptions are structurally smaller when proving the main result. Such approach is far from vanilla type theory.

A common objection against the need of having a verified implementation of the refinement engine builds upon Appel's approach [3] to proof-carrying code—only a kernel that handles type checking is verified while any refinement is handled by a non-verified code. Final type checking by the verified kernel ensures that refinement provides well-formed code. While the approach keeps implementation of such a tool tractable it also has several drawbacks. Among other things, it leads to duplication of code as some functionality is implemented twice, first time in the kernel and second time in the non-verified code. These issues were discussed in a greater detail by Guidi *et al.* [12]. But more importantly, this leads to a practice when such compiler is the *de facto* specification of the language—there is no formal specification of the language and even if there were the refinement is not verified to adhere to it. Only the kernel is.

Recently, Farka *et al.* [9] proposed a new, two-stage approach to refinement. In this approach, a refinement problem consist of a signature S and a term M with metavariables that stand for omitted types and terms (proof obligations). The signature S is translated to a logic program P using *refinement calculus* and the term M to a goal G while synthesising a type A of M. Then, proof-relevant resolution is employed and the goal G is resolved by the program P while computing an answer substitution θ and a proof term e. The answer substitution θ provides solution to the refinement problem, that is as a refined term θM and its type θA. The computed proof term e is interpreted as a derivation $\mathcal{D} = (e, \cdot)_{\theta A}^{\mathrm{der}}$ of well-formedness judgement $S; \cdot \vdash \theta M : \theta A$, that is well-formedness of the solution to the refinement problem. Verification of well-formedness of the refined

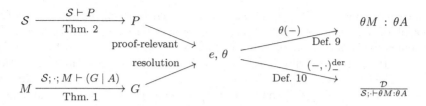

Fig. 1. Refinement by proof-relevant resolution

term then proceeds by straightforward induction on the derivation of the well-formedness judgement. A schematic diagram is listed in Fig. 1. In this paper, we describe an architecture of a refinement engine that is based on the approach, and its particular implementation `slepice`.

First, a refinement problem is parsed resulting in a pair of inductive objects, abstract syntax representations of a signature and a term. Then, a translation of the signature and the term into a logic program and a goal is formulated as a decidability of the refinement calculus; the calculus is decidable in the sense that either a program and a goal can be constructed or the term is ill-typed. The proof is constructive and proceeds by induction on the structure of the abstract syntax representation of the term. The proof is used to either obtain a program and a goal, if these exists, or to reject ill-typed terms.

The reason that the translation can proceed by simple induction is that all parts that either require a complicated argument, like decidability of equality, or that are in general undecidable, like terms to be substituted for metavariables, are postponed in a form of goals. A resolution engine is used to resolve the goal with the generated program. Guidi *et al.* [12] investigate a similar approach with λ-Prolog that is solely based in resolution and argue that resolution is suitable to provide an implementation of type checker and elaborator that is comparable to the state-of-art tools. However, their approach does not give a verified implementation. Unlike Guidi *et al.*, we employ proof-relevant resolution. Proof-relevant resolution provides a proof-term that captures a successful resolution of the generated goal. We state a property that the refined term that is obtained from an interpretation of the proof term is well-formed. The proof proceeds by induction on well-formedness derivation that is obtained from the proof-term as well. Proof of the property constitutes a procedure that obtains the refined term.

Finally, formal specification of LF and the refinement calculus gives a basis for the implementation. Data definitions as well as definitions of well-formedness judgements in the type theory are obtained from the formal specification. One can see the refinement as a rudimentary form of elaboration. The refinement calculus then constitutes a formal semantics of the surface language. Further, the generated logic program has in fact two parts; there is a fixed part that is the same for each generated logic program and that constitutes inference rules of the type theory, and there is the part that is given by a particular signature. The static part is directly obtained from the specification as well.

In this paper, we give an account of a system that implements a proof of concept of a refinement engine using the architecture we just described. The implementation can be found online[1]. We use existing tools to instantiate different parts of the described architecture to obtain a verified implementation of type theory in type theory. Namely, we use the Ott tool [18] to specify the grammar, the typing judgement, and the refinement calculus. Ott is also used to generate a parser of the source language from the grammar. We use Coq to formally state decidability of the refinement calculus and the interpretation. We use ELPI [8] to mimic proof-relevant resolution. We discuss a particular way to do this and why it is possible in Sect. 5. Finally, we need to admit that our implementation falls somewhat short of the ideal architecture that is fully hosted by a dependently typed language. The Coq theorem prover does not execute the code directly but uses extraction to OCaml. The definitions and parser generated by Ott are not generated as Coq code but as OCaml code. The ELPI code is interfaced via OCaml as well. To our defence, the amount of handwritten OCaml code necessary is fairly small and deals exclusively with interfacing of the components and interaction with the user.

Contributions. The contributions of this paper are twofold; we

- describe an architecture for an elaboration and type inference engine of a dependently typed language that allows self-hosting, and
- we report on an implementation that uses such architecture and hence manifests feasibility of the approach.

2   Specification

In this section, we describe LF [13] that is extended with term- and type-level metavariables, the well-typed fragment of the extended language, and the target logic. The strong point of our approach is that the description is carried out as a formal specification and that definitions in a theorem prover (Coq in our case) and in executable code (OCaml in our case) are generated from the specification. This approach forces a correspondence between formal specification of the language and the implementation. We use Ott tool to formalise the specification. Note that, beside any theorem prover or executable code, a human-readable description is obtained from the formal specification as well[2].

We present the extended language of LF using *de Bruijn* indices representation of variables. We use natural numbers for de Bruijn indices in I, we use identifier ι for individual elements of I and we denote successor by $\sigma(-)$. We assume countably infinite disjoint sets $\mathcal{C}$ of *term constants*, and $\mathcal{B}$ of *type constants*. We denote elements of $\mathcal{C}$ by c, c', etc., and elements of $\mathcal{B}$ by α, β, etc.. We assume disjoint countable sets of *term-level metavariables* $?_\mathcal{V}$ and *type-level metavariables* $?_\mathcal{B}$. For technical reasons, we also assume a countable set of metavariables $?_T$ linearly ordered by $\prec$.

---

[1] http://github.com/frantisekfarka/slepice.
[2] *cf.* the generated documentation `doc/slepice.pdf` in the implementation.

```
metavar
I, i ::= {{com de Bruijn indices }}    Definition I : Set := nat.

grammar                                Inductive eTy : Set :=
eTy , eA , eB :: 'eTy_' ::=                (*r extended types *)
         {{ com extended types }}        | ety_tcon (a:tcon)
   | tcon              ::    :: tcon      | ety_pi_intro (eA:eTy) (eB:eTy)
   | Pi eTy1 . eTy2 ::     :: pi_intro    | ety_pi_elim (eA:eTy) (eM:ete)
   | eTy ete           ::    :: pi_elim   | ety_mvar (mA:lvar)
   | ( eTy )           :: S :: paren      | ety_tvar (mT:tvar)
   | lvar              ::    :: mvar     with ete : Set :=
   | tvar              ::    :: tvar        (*r extended terms *)
                                          | ete_con (c:con)
ete , eM , eN :: 'ete_' ::=               | ete_i (i:I)
         {{ com extended terms }}         | ete_pi_intro (eA:eTy) (eM:ete)
   | con               ::    :: con       | ete_pi_elim (eM:ete) (eN:ete)
   | ix                ::    :: ix        | ete_mvar (mA:lvar)
   | \ eTy . ete       ::    :: pi_intro  | ete_tvar (mT:tvar)
   | ete1 ete2         ::    :: pi_elim
   | ( ete )           :: S :: paren
   | lvar              ::    :: mvar
   | tvar              ::    :: tvar
```

Fig. 2. Ott formalisation (on the left) of terms and types and the extracted Coq definition (on the right)

Definition 1 (Extended LF). *The syntax of* extended terms, extended types, *and* extended kinds *as well as* extended signatures *and* extended contexts *is:*

$$
\begin{array}{rcll}
T & \ni & A, B ::= & \mathcal{B} \mid Tt \mid \Pi T.T \mid ?_{\mathcal{B}} \mid ?_{T} & \textit{extended types} \\
t & \ni & M, N ::= & \mathcal{C} \mid I \mid \lambda T.t \mid tt \mid ?_{\mathcal{V}} \mid ?_{T} & \textit{extended terms} \\
K & \ni & L ::= & \mathsf{type} \mid \Pi T.K & \textit{extended kinds} \\
Sgn & \ni & S ::= & \cdot \mid Sgn, \mathcal{C} : T \mid Sgn, \mathcal{B} : K & \textit{extended signatures} \\
Ctx & \ni & \Gamma ::= & \cdot \mid Ctx, T & \textit{extended contexts}
\end{array}
$$

The extended terms include function abstraction $\lambda A.M$ and application MN. The extended types include Π-type elimination AM and formation $\Pi A.B$. We do not include type-level abstraction as it can be safely erased from LF without compromising the expressive power of the calculus [11]. We use parenthesis in the rest of the paper in the usual way. An excerpt of Ott source that formalises extended types and terms as well the generated Coq code is listed in Fig. 2. Note that the formalisation specifies syntax sugar for parenthesis that is not reflected in the Coq definition. In the actual implementation, there are also some decorations that allows us to extract parser and pretty printer. We omit the decorations here for the sake of readability.

We also give syntactic objects of LF proper as a fragment of the extended language. The formalisation is carried out as a subgrammar of the extended language. The actual representation in the generated theorem prover code is by predicates over extended objects.

Definition 2 (LF). *The syntax of* terms, types, *and* kinds *as well as signatures* and contexts *is:*

$$
\begin{aligned}
T &\ni & A, B &::= & \mathcal{B} \mid Tt \mid \Pi T.T & \quad\text{types} \\
t &\ni & M, N &::= & \mathcal{C} \mid I \mid \lambda T.t \mid tt & \quad\text{terms} \\
K &\ni & L &::= & \mathbf{type} \mid \Pi T.K & \quad\text{kinds} \\
Sgn &\ni & S &::= & \cdot \mid Sgn, \mathcal{C} : T \mid Sgn, \mathcal{B} : K & \quad\text{signatures} \\
Ctx &\ni & \Gamma &::= & \cdot \mid Ctx, T & \quad\text{contexts}
\end{aligned}
$$

De Bruijn indices are manipulated by *shifting*; shifting takes a term, type, or kind and an index ι and increments all indices greater than ι by one.

Definition 3. *Term and type shifting, denoted by* $(-)\uparrow^\iota$ *is defined as follows:*

$$
\begin{aligned}
c\uparrow^\iota &\equiv c & \alpha\uparrow^\iota &\equiv \alpha \\
\iota\uparrow^0 &\equiv \sigma\iota & (\lambda A.B)\uparrow^\iota &\equiv \lambda(A\uparrow^\iota).(B\uparrow^{\sigma\iota}) \\
0\uparrow^{\sigma\iota} &\equiv 0 & (AM)\uparrow^\iota &\equiv (A\uparrow^\iota)(M\uparrow^\iota) \\
(\sigma\iota)\uparrow^{\sigma\iota'} &\equiv \sigma(\iota\uparrow^{\iota'}) \\
(\lambda A.M)\uparrow^\iota &\equiv \lambda(A\uparrow^\iota).(M\uparrow^{\sigma\iota}) & \mathbf{type}\uparrow^\iota &\equiv \mathbf{type} \\
(MN)\uparrow^\iota &\equiv (M\uparrow^\iota)(N\uparrow^\iota) & (\lambda A.L)\uparrow^\iota &\equiv \lambda(A\uparrow^\iota).(L\uparrow^{\sigma\iota})
\end{aligned}
$$

Substitution is defined recursively on the structure of objects using index shifting. A substitution of a term M for an arbitrary index ι increases the index when traversing under a binder.

Definition 4. *Term, type, and kind substitution, denoted by* $-[N/\iota]$ *is defined as follows:*

$$
\begin{aligned}
c[N/\iota] &\equiv c & \alpha[N/\iota] &\equiv \alpha \\
\iota[N/\iota'] &\equiv \begin{cases} N & \iota = \iota' \\ \iota & \text{otherwise} \end{cases} & (\lambda A.B)[N/\iota] &\equiv \lambda(A[N/\iota]).(B[N\uparrow^0/\sigma\iota]) \\
& & (AM)[N/\iota] &\equiv (A[N/\iota])(M[N/\iota]) \\
(\lambda A.M)[N/\iota] &\equiv \lambda(A[N/\iota]).(M[N\uparrow^0/\sigma\iota]) \\
(M_1 M_2)[N/\iota] &\equiv (M_1[N/\iota])(M_2[N/\iota]) & \mathbf{type}[N/\iota] &\equiv \mathbf{type} \\
& & (\lambda A.L)[N/\iota] &\equiv \lambda(A[N/\iota]).(L[N\uparrow^0/\sigma\iota])
\end{aligned}
$$

$$\boxed{\mathcal{S}; \Gamma \vdash A : L}$$

$$\frac{\mathcal{S} \vdash \Gamma \qquad \alpha : L \in \mathcal{S}}{\mathcal{S}; \Gamma \vdash \alpha : L} \text{ T-CON} \qquad \frac{\mathcal{S}; \Gamma \vdash A : \textsf{type} \qquad \mathcal{S}; \Gamma, A \vdash B : \textsf{type}}{\mathcal{S}; \Gamma \vdash \Pi A.B : \textsf{type}} \text{ T-}\Pi\text{-INTRO}$$

$$\frac{\mathcal{S}; \Gamma \vdash A : \Pi B_1.L \qquad \mathcal{S}; \Gamma \vdash M : B_2 \qquad \mathcal{S}; \Gamma \vdash B_1 = B_2 : \textsf{type}}{\mathcal{S}; \Gamma \vdash AM : L[M]} \text{ T-}\Pi\text{-ELIM}$$

$$\boxed{\mathcal{S}; \Gamma \vdash M : A}$$

$$\frac{\mathcal{S} \vdash \Gamma \qquad c : A \in \mathcal{S}}{\mathcal{S}; \Gamma \vdash c : A} \text{ CON} \qquad \frac{\mathcal{S} \vdash \Gamma, A}{\mathcal{S}; \Gamma, A \vdash 0 : A{\uparrow}} \text{ ZERO} \qquad \frac{\mathcal{S}; \Gamma \vdash \iota : A}{\mathcal{S}; \Gamma, B \vdash \sigma\iota : A{\uparrow}} \text{ SUCC}$$

$$\frac{\mathcal{S}; \Gamma \vdash A : \textsf{type} \qquad \mathcal{S}; \Gamma, A \vdash M : B}{\mathcal{S}; \Gamma \vdash \lambda A.M : \Pi A.B} \; \Pi\text{-INTRO}$$

$$\frac{\mathcal{S}; \Gamma \vdash M : \Pi A_1.B \qquad \mathcal{S}; \Gamma \vdash N : A_2 \qquad \mathcal{S}; \Gamma \vdash A_1 = A_2 : \textsf{type}}{\mathcal{S}; \Gamma \vdash MN : B[N]} \; \Pi\text{-ELIM}$$

Fig. 3. Well-formedness of terms and types

Since shifting with greater index than 0 and substitution for other indices than 0 is not necessary in the inference rules we introduce the following abbreviations:

$$A{\uparrow} \overset{def}{=} A{\uparrow}^0 \qquad M{\uparrow} \overset{def}{=} M{\uparrow}^0 \qquad A[N] \overset{def}{=} A[N/0] \qquad M[N] \overset{def}{=} M[N/0]$$

Well-formed objects of the internal language are given by means of several judgements; $\vdash \mathcal{S}$ for well-formed signatures, $\mathcal{S} \vdash \Gamma$ for well-formed contexts, $\mathcal{S}; \Gamma \vdash L : \textsf{type}$ for well-formed kinds, $\mathcal{S}; \Gamma \vdash A : L$ for well-formed types of a kind, $\mathcal{S}; \Gamma \vdash M : A$ for well-formed terms of a type, $\mathcal{S}; \Gamma \vdash A = B : L$ for conversion of types, and $\mathcal{S}; \Gamma \vdash M = N : A$ for conversion of terms. In Fig. 3 we define judgements for well formed types and terms. We omit definitions of the remaining judgements as these can be found in the documentation generated from the formal specification.

3 Refinement Calculus

In this section, we set up the refinement calculus. The refinement calculus formalises the semantics of type inference and term synthesis in the extended language. It can be seen as a rudimentary form of elaboration of a surface language into a core language. In our case the surface language is the extended language that allows to omit some type annotations and proof obligations (*i.e.* terms) by introducing metavariables instead. The internal language is the language in Definition 2 that does not contain any metavariables.

The refinement calculus relates objects of the extended language and goals in proof-relevant Horn-clause logic. At the same time, it relates signatures of the language and logic programs. First, we give a syntax of the target logic:

Definition 5. *The syntax of* Atomic formulae, Horn clauses, programs, proof terms, *and* goals *is:*

$$
\begin{array}{llll}
Pc & \ni & c ::= & \kappa_{\text{type}} \mid \kappa_{\mathcal{C}} \mid \kappa_{\mathcal{B}} \mid \kappa_{\mathcal{C}\uparrow} \mid \kappa_{\mathcal{B}\uparrow} \mid \cdots & \textit{proof term constants} \\
Pt & \ni & e ::= & c \mid e\,e & \textit{proof terms} \\
At & \ni & ::= & \top \mid eq_K(K, K, Ctx) \mid eq_T(T, T, K, Ctx) \\
& & & \mid eq_t(t, t, T, Ctx) \mid type(T, K, Ctx) \\
& & & \mid term(t, T, Ctx) \mid T\!\uparrow^I \equiv T \mid T[t/I] \equiv T & \textit{atomic formulae} \\
HC & \ni & ::= & At \leftarrow At \wedge \ldots \wedge At & \textit{Horn clauses} \\
\mathcal{P} & \ni & P ::= & \cdot \mid \mathcal{P}, Pc : HC & \textit{programs} \\
\mathcal{G} & \ni & G ::= & \mathcal{G} \wedge \mathcal{G} \mid At \mid ?_\mathcal{V} : At & \textit{goals}
\end{array}
$$

Proof term constants are distinct names used to identify Horn clauses in programs. Proof terms are applicative terms freely generated from proof term constants. Atoms consist of the trivially satisfied atom $\top$ and atoms that correspond to judgements of the internal language. The judgements in the definition are, in order: equality of kinds, types, and terms and well-formedness of types and terms (recall the discussion of judgements of the internal language on page 6), and relational representation of shifting and substitution. Note that giving atoms in terms of kinds, types, terms and contexts of the internal language is an abuse of notation as these should properly speaking be syntactic reflections of the surface language. We well allow ourselves this imprecision to simplify the notation. Horn clauses, programs and goals are straightforward, we only note that an atom in a goal can be bound to a term-level metavariable. In principle, we could allow binding also to type-level or technical metavariables. However, in this paper we use resolved proof terms to reconstruct only terms of the internal language hence a binding of term-level metavariable suffices.

The presentation we give here is an extension of the original presentation [9]. We handle freshness of variables explicitly. Albeit our solution is simple it suffices for the purposes of our implementation. In a more realistic implementation one would employ a variant of freshness logic (*e.g.* abstract nominal syntax [22]).

We separate logic variables. There are logic variables that correspond to term- and type-level metavariables in $?_\mathcal{V}$ and $?_\mathcal{B}$ respectively and there are logic variables that correspond to technical metavariables $?_\mathcal{T}$ that are introduced as fresh in a derivation of the refinement judgement. From now on, we do not make the distinction between metavariables and the corresponding logic variables and refer to these logic variables as to metavariables in the context of the target logic. We identify metavariables in $?_\mathcal{T}$ with natural numbers in $\mathbb{N}$ and we make use of the linear order on natural numbers. Assumptions in the inference rules are linearly ordered. For the fresh variable we take the least metavariable that

$$\boxed{\mathcal{S}; \Gamma; A \;_{?_T} \vdash_{?'_T} (G \mid L)}$$

$$\frac{a : L \in \mathcal{S}}{\mathcal{S}; \Gamma; a \;_{?_T} \vdash_{?_T} (\top \mid L)} \text{ R-TCON} \qquad \frac{?'_T \# ?''_T ?_T}{\mathcal{S}; \Gamma; ?_A \;_{?'_T} \vdash_{?''_T} (type(?_A, ?_T, \Gamma) \mid ?_T)} \text{ R-T-META}$$

$$\frac{\mathcal{S}; \Gamma; A \;_{?'_T} \vdash_{?''_T} (G_A \mid L_1) \qquad \mathcal{S}; \Gamma, A; B \;_{?''_T} \vdash_{?'''_T} (G_B \mid L_2)}{\mathcal{S}; \Gamma; \Pi A.B \;_{?'_T} \vdash_{?'''_T} (G_A \wedge G_B \wedge eq_K(L_1, \text{type}, \Gamma) \wedge eq_K(L_2, \text{type}, \Gamma) \mid \text{type})} \text{ R-}\Pi\text{-INTRO}$$

$$\frac{\mathcal{S}; \Gamma; A \;_{?'_T} \vdash_{?''_T} (G_A \mid L) \qquad \mathcal{S}; \Gamma; M \;_{?''_T} \vdash_{?'''_T} (G_M \mid B) \qquad ?''_T \# ?'''_T ?_{T_1}, ?_{T_2}}{\mathcal{S}; \Gamma; AM \;_{?'_T} \vdash_{?'''_T} (G_A \wedge G_M \wedge eq_K(L, \Pi B.?_{T_1}, \Gamma) \wedge (?_{T_1}[M] \equiv ?_{T_2}) \mid ?_{T_2})} \text{ R-}\Pi\text{-ELIM}$$

Fig. 4. Refinement of types

$$\boxed{\mathcal{S}; \Gamma; M \;_{?_T} \vdash_{?'_T} (G \mid A)}$$

$$\frac{c : A \in \mathcal{S}}{\mathcal{S}; \Gamma; c \;_{?_T} \vdash_{?_T} (\top \mid A)} \text{ R-CON} \qquad \frac{?'_T \# ?''_T ?_T}{\mathcal{S}; \Gamma; ?_a \;_{?'_T} \vdash_{?''_T} (?_a : term(?_{a'}, ?_T, \Gamma) \mid ?_T)} \text{ R-T-META}$$

$$\frac{?'_T \# ?''_T ?_T}{\mathcal{S}; \Gamma, A; 0 \;_{?'_T} \vdash_{?''_T} (A \uparrow \equiv ?_T \mid ?_T)} \text{ R-ZERO} \qquad \frac{\mathcal{S}; \Gamma; \iota \;_{?'_T} \vdash_{?''_T} (G \mid A) \qquad ?''_T \# ?'''_T ?_T}{\mathcal{S}; \Gamma, B; \sigma\iota \;_{?'_T} \vdash_{?'''_T} (G \wedge (A \uparrow \equiv ?_T) \mid ?_T)} \text{ R-SUCC}$$

$$\frac{\mathcal{S}; \Gamma; A \;_{?'_T} \vdash_{?''_T} (G_A \mid L) \qquad \mathcal{S}; \Gamma, A; M \;_{?''_T} \vdash_{?'''_T} (G_M \mid B)}{\mathcal{S}; \Gamma; \lambda A.M \;_{?'_T} \vdash_{?'''_T} (G_A \wedge G_M \wedge eq_K(L, \text{type}, \Gamma) \mid \Pi A.B)} \text{ R-}\lambda\text{-INTRO}$$

$$\frac{\mathcal{S}; \Gamma; M \;_{?_T} \vdash_{?'_T} (G_M \mid A) \qquad \mathcal{S}; \Gamma; N \;_{?'_T} \vdash_{?''_T} (G_N \mid A_2) \qquad ?''_T \# ?'''_T ?_{T_1}, ?_{T_2}}{\mathcal{S}; \Gamma; MN \;_{?_T} \vdash_{?'''_T} (G_M \wedge G_N \wedge eq_T(A, \Pi A_2.?_{T_1}, \text{type}, \Gamma) \wedge (?_{T_1}[N] \equiv ?_{T_2}) \mid ?_{T_2})} \text{ R-}\lambda\text{-ELIM}$$

Fig. 5. Refinement of terms

is greater than all technical variables on the left. Formally, we state a freshness judgement, $?'_T \# ?''_T ?_T$. The intended meaning of the judgement is that, given a technical variable $?'_T$, a technical variable $?_T$ is fresh and a variable $?''_T$ is the new bound.

Definition 6. *Let* $?_T$, $?'_T$, *and* $?''_T$ *be technical variables. The freshness judgement* $?'_T \# ?''_T ?_T$ *is defined as follows:*

$$\frac{}{\iota \#_{\sigma\iota} \iota}$$

We introduce an abbreviation $?'_T \# ?'''_T ?_{T_1}, ?_{T_2} \overset{def}{=} ?'_T \# ?''_T ?_{T_1} \wedge ?''_T \# ?'''_T ?_{T_2}$ for repeated freshness judgements.

Finally, we give a specification of the refinement judgement. This judgement formalises semantics of type inference in the extended grammar. There are mutually defined judgements $\mathcal{S}; \Gamma; A \;_{?_T} \vdash_{?'_T} (G \mid L)$ for refinement of types, and $\mathcal{S}; \Gamma; M \;_{?_T} \vdash_{?'_T} (G \mid A)$ for refinement of terms. The arguments on the left hand

$$\boxed{\mathcal{S} \ ?_T \vdash_{?'_T} P}$$

$$\frac{\cdot \ ?_T \vdash_{?_T} P_e}{}$$

$$\frac{\mathcal{S} \ ?_T \vdash_{?'_T} P \qquad ?'_T \#_{?''_T} ?_\Gamma, ?_\iota, ?_{\iota'}, ?_{\iota''}}{\mathcal{S}, a : L \ ?_T \vdash_{?''_T} P, \kappa_a : type(a, L, ?_\Gamma) \leftarrow, \kappa_{a\uparrow} : (a\uparrow^{?_\iota} \equiv a) \leftarrow, \kappa_{a[-]} : (a[?_{\iota'}/?_{\iota''}] \equiv a) \leftarrow}$$

$$\frac{\mathcal{S} \ ?_T \vdash_{?'_T} P \qquad ?'_T \#_{?''_T} ?_\Gamma, ?_\iota, ?_{\iota'}, ?_{\iota''}}{\mathcal{S}, c : A \ ?'_T \vdash_{?''_T} P, \kappa_c : term(c, A, ?_\Gamma) \leftarrow, \kappa_{c\uparrow} : (c\uparrow^{?_\iota} \equiv c) \leftarrow, \kappa_{c[-]} : (c[?_{\iota'}/?_{\iota''}] \equiv c) \leftarrow}$$

Fig. 6. Refinement of signatures

side of the dash, that is a signature $\mathcal{S}$, an extended context Γ, an extended type A or an extended term M, and a technical variable $?_T$, are seen as inputs. The arguments on the right hand side, that is a technical variable $?'_T$, a goal G, and an extended kind L or an extended type A are seen as outputs. The judgements are defined in Figs. 4 and 5. We use $A_1 \uparrow \ \equiv \ A_2$ and $A_1[N] \equiv A_2$ to abbreviate atoms $A_1 \uparrow^0 \ \equiv \ A_2$ and $A_1[N/0] \equiv A_2$ respectively and similarly for terms in allusion to abbreviations we introduced for shifting and substitution.

We show decidability of the term and type refinement judgements in the next section and this also justifies our identification of arguments of the judgement as inputs and outputs. A goal that is produced by refinement translation is solved by a logic program. The program is obtained from a signature. We define judgement $\mathcal{S} \ ?_\Gamma \vdash_{?'_\Gamma} P$. A signature $\mathcal{S}$ and a technical variable $?_T$ are seen as inputs and the technical variable $?'_T$ and a program P are seen as outputs. The judgement is defined in Fig. 6. The empty signature is refined into the initial program P_e that captures static inference rules in in Fig. 3. The remaining two rules then extend program with an instance of the inference rules TCON and CON respectively and instantiate shifting and substitution with type and term constants.

We use the formal specification of refinement judgements in Figs. 4, 5, and 6 to obtain definitions in Coq that are used for stating the decidability results. We illustrate the extracted definitions on an excerpt of Coq code in Fig. 7. The data definitions in executable OCaml code are extracted directly from the specification (as opposed to the whole executable code, *including* the data definitions, being extracted from Coq). The reason is we extract a parser of the input language from the specification as well. Coq definitions are then explicitly mapped to extracted OCaml definitions in Coq code extraction.

4   Decidability of Refinement

In this section we prove decidability of the refinement judgements that relate extended types and terms to goals and signatures to programs. The proofs are

```
(* defns Jrefin *)
Inductive r_goaltype
    : esgn -> ectx -> eTy -> tvar -> goal -> eK -> tvar -> Prop :=
    (* defn goaltype *)
 | r_g_Ty_tcon : forall (Sgn:esgn) (eG:ectx) (a:tcon) (t:tvar) (L:eK),
      (boundTCon a   L   Sgn ) ->
      r_goaltype Sgn eG (ety_tcon a) t (goal_at at_true) L t
    ...
with r_goalterm :
    esgn -> ectx -> ete -> tvar -> goal -> eTy -> tvar -> Prop :=
    (* defn goalterm *)
 | r_g_te_con : forall (Sgn:esgn) (eG:ectx) (c:con) (t:tvar) (A:eTy),
    is_Ty_of_eTy A ->
      (boundCon c   A   Sgn ) ->
      r_goalterm Sgn eG (ete_con c) t (goal_at ttat_true) A t
    ...
```

Fig. 7. Coq - Extracted definition of refinement

formalised in Coq theorem prover and serve, after code extraction, as functions that perform the core generation of goals and programs.

The first intermediate result we need to prove in our formalisation is that equality of syntactic objects of the extended language is decidable. The decidability here is to be read in constructive sense, that is either we can produce a derivation of the appropriate equality or such derivation leads to contradiction.

Proposition 1

1. Let A, B be extended types. Then either $A = B$ or $A \neq B$.
2. Let M, N be extended terms. Then either $M = N$ or $M \neq N$.
3. Let L, L' be extended kinds. Then either $L = L'$ or $L \neq L'$.

Proof. Parts 1 and 2 proceed by mutual induction on the type and the term. Part 3 proceeds by induction using part 1.

In order to provide the reader with intuition how are such proposition encoded in Coq, we list statements 1 and 2 of the above proposition. Note that since extended terms and extended types are defined mutually, the statement in Coq is also given mutually in order to allow for structural induction.

```
Lemma eq_eTy_dec : forall A B : eTy, {A = B} + {A <> B}
  with eq_ete_dec : forall M N : ete, {M = N} + {M <> N}.
```

We also need to show that whether a type of a certain kind or a term constant of a certain type is bound in a signature is decidable.

Lemma 1

- *Let S be a signature, and c a term constant. Then either there is a type A such that $c : A \in S$ or, for all A, $c : A \in S$ is impossible.*
- *Let S be a signature, and α a type constant. Then either there is an extended kind L such that $\alpha : L \in S$ or, for all L, $\alpha : L \in S$ is impossible.*

Proof. By induction on signature using decidability of equality of terms and types (Proposition 1).

Now we could state the main theorem that the refinement judgement for terms and types is decidable. However, there is a caveat. The refinement judgements for terms and for types are mutually defined and hence the extracted Coq definitions are mutually defined as well as we demonstrate in Fig. 7. A proof by naive induction fails as Coq cannot establish that recursive calls are structurally smaller. We devise mutually recursive inductive types that we call *structure* of extended types and extended terms and a mapping from extended types and extended terms to the respective structure.

Definition 7. *The syntax of* structure *of extended types and* structure *of extended terms is:*

$$
\begin{array}{llll}
S_T & \ni & s_A ::= & \cdot \mid \Pi S_T.S_T \mid S_T S_t & \text{structure of extended types} \\
S_t & \ni & s_M ::= & \cdot \mid \Pi S_T.S_t \mid S_t S_t & \text{structure of extended terms}
\end{array}
$$

Definition 8. *We define mappings $(-)^s : T \to S_T$ and $(-)^s : t \to S_t$ by*

$$
\begin{array}{ll}
(\alpha)^s = \cdot & (c)^s = \cdot \\
(\Pi A.B)^s = \Pi(A)^s.(B)^s & (\Pi A.M)^s = \Pi(A)^s.(M)^s \\
(AM)^s = (A)^s(M)^s & (MN)^s = (M)^s(N)^s \\
(?_A)^s = \cdot & (?_M)^s = \cdot \\
(?_T)^s = \cdot & (?_T)^s = \cdot
\end{array}
$$

Note that by an abuse of notation we do not distinguish between the names of the mapping from types and the mapping from terms. The more general statement of decidability of refinement is stated using the structure.

Theorem 1 (Decidability of refinement)

- *Let s_M be a structure, S a signature, Γ an extended context, and M an extended term. If $(M)^s = s_M$ then either there is a goal G and an extended type A such that $S; \Gamma; M \vdash (G \mid A)$ or, for any goal G and any type A, $S; \Gamma; M \vdash (G \mid A)$ is impossible.*
- *Let s_A be a structure, S a signature, Γ an extended context, and A an extended type. If $(A)^s = s_A$ then either there is a goal G and a kind L such that $S; \Gamma; A \vdash (G \mid L)$ or, for any goal G and any kind L, $S; \Gamma; A \vdash (\Gamma \mid L)$ is impossible.*

Proof. By mutual induction on structure of the term s_M and structure of the type s_A using Proposition 1 and Lemma 1.

The intended statement of the refinement theorem for terms and types then follows as a corollary.

Corollary 1 (Goal construction)

- *Let S be a signature, Γ an extended context, and M an extended term. Either there is a goal G and an extended type A such that $S; \Gamma; M \vdash (G \mid A)$ or, for any goal G and any type A, $S; \Gamma; M \vdash (G \mid A)$ is impossible.*
- *Let S be a signature, Γ an extended context, and A an extended type. Either there is a goal G and an extended kind L such that $S; \Gamma; A \vdash (G \mid L)$ or, for any goal G and any kind L, $S; \Gamma; A \vdash (G \mid L)$ is impossible.*

Also, we state a decidability result for refinement of signatures that allows us to obtain programs that resolve goals generated from extended types and terms.

Theorem 2 (Refinement of signatures). *Let S be a signature. Either there is a program P such that $S \vdash P$ or, for any P, $S \vdash P$ is impossible.*

Proof. By induction on signature S.

Formalisation of proofs of the above theorems provides a procedures that take terms and types and generate goals and that take signature and generate program. OCaml signatures of the extracted code that correspond to the above theorems are listed in Fig. 8. Signatures Sgn are extracted as the type **sgn**, extended contexts Ctx as **ectx**. Structure of extended types S_T is extracted as **sTy**, extended types T as **eTy**, similarly for terms and kinds. Type level metavariables $?_B$ and term level metavariables $?_V$ are extracted as **lvar** and technical metavariables as **tvar**, goals $\mathcal{G}$ and programs $\mathcal{P}$ as **goal** and **prog** respectively.

```
(** val goalterm_dec_str :
    ste -> sgn -> ectx -> ete -> lvar -> (goal*(eTy*tvar)) sumor **)
(** val goaltype_dec_str :
    sTy -> sgn -> ectx -> eTy -> lvar -> (goal*(eK*tvar)) sumor **)
(** val goalterm_dec :
    sgn -> ectx -> ete -> lvar -> (goal*(eTy*tvar)) sumor **)
(** val goaltype_dec :
    sTy -> sgn -> ectx -> eTy -> lvar -> (goal*(eK*tvar)) sumor **)

(** val progsig_dec : sgn -> lvar -> (prog*tvar) sumor **)
```

Fig. 8. Extracted OCaml translation

5   Proof-Relevant Resolution

In this section we describe our realisation of proof-relevant resolution and interpretation of answer substitutions and computed proof terms. As a resolution engine in our implementation we resort to ELPI [8]. Although ELPI is not proof-relevant resolution engine, it is sufficient for our purposes. In this work we are not interested in finer details of the resolution mechanism (*cf.* [9,10]) and we can obtain sound results by a simple syntactic transformation. In this paper, we omit details of the transformation and focus on interpretation of the computed assignment to type and term level metavariables and on interpretation of computed proof terms. In the following, we assume that the proof relevant resolution for a generated goal G and a program P either computes an answer substitution θ and, for each atomic subgoal, a proof-term e or fails.

First, we extend application of computed substitution to extended types and extended terms in the usual way.

Definition 9. *We define application of a substitution θ by*

$$\theta(\alpha) = \alpha$$
$$\theta(\Pi A.B) = \Pi\theta(A).\theta(B)$$
$$\theta(AM) = \theta(A)\theta(M)$$
$$\theta(?_A) = \theta(?_A)$$
$$\theta(?_T) = ?_T$$

$$\theta(c) = c$$
$$\theta(\iota) = \iota$$
$$\theta(\lambda A.M) = \lambda\theta(A).\theta(M)$$
$$\theta(MN) = \theta(M)\theta(N)$$
$$\theta(?_M) = \theta(?_M)$$
$$\theta(?_T) = ?_T$$

By Definition 5 of syntax of the target logic proof terms are computed for atomic (sub-)goals. We define an interpretation of proof terms that construct a derivation of a well-formedness judgement from such a proof term. We use $S; \Gamma \vdash \mathcal{I}$ to jointly refer to the judgements of LF in the usual way.

Definition 10. *Let S be a signature, and Γ a context such that $S \vdash \Gamma$ and let $S; \Gamma \vdash \mathcal{I}$ be a judgement, and e a proof term. The interpretation of the proof term $(e, \Gamma)_{\mathcal{I}}^{der}$ is defined as follows:*

$$(\kappa_\alpha, \Gamma)_{\alpha:L}^{der} = \frac{S \vdash \Gamma \qquad \alpha : L \in S}{S; \Gamma \vdash \alpha : L} \text{ T-CON}$$

$$(\kappa_{T\text{-}\Pi\text{-}intro}\ e_1\ e_2, \Gamma)_{\Pi A.B:\text{type}}^{der} = \frac{(e_1, \Gamma)_{A:\text{type}}^{der} \qquad (e_2, \Gamma, A)_{B:\text{type}}^{der}}{S; \Gamma \vdash \Pi A.B : \text{type}} \text{ T-}\Pi\text{-INTRO}$$

$$(\kappa_{T\text{-}\Pi\text{-}elim}\ e_1\ e_2\ e_3, \Gamma)_{AM:L[M]}^{der} = \frac{(e_1, \Gamma)_{A:\Pi B_1:L}^{der} \qquad (e_2, \Gamma)_{M:B_2}^{der} \qquad (e_3, \Gamma)_{B_1 = B_2:\text{type}}^{der}}{S; \Gamma \vdash AM : L[M]}$$

$$(\kappa_c, \Gamma)_{c:A}^{der} = \frac{S \vdash \Gamma \qquad c : A \in S}{S; \Gamma \vdash c : A} \text{ CON}$$

$$(\kappa_0, \Gamma)_{0:A\uparrow}^{der} = \frac{S \vdash \Gamma}{S; \Gamma \vdash 0 : A\uparrow} \text{ ZERO}$$

$$(\kappa_\sigma \ e, \Gamma)^{der}_{\sigma\iota:A\uparrow} = \frac{(e, \Gamma)^{der}_{\iota:A}}{\mathcal{S}; \Gamma \vdash \sigma\iota : A\uparrow} \ \text{SUCC}$$

$$(\kappa_{\Pi\text{-intro}} \ e_1 \ e_2, \Gamma)^{der}_{\lambda A.M:\Pi A.B} = \frac{(e_1, \Gamma)^{der}_{A:\text{type}} \quad (e_2, \Gamma, A)^{der}_{M:B}}{\mathcal{S}; \Gamma \vdash \lambda A.M : \Pi A.B} \ \Pi\text{-INTRO}$$

$$(\kappa_{\Pi\text{-elim}} \ e_1 \ e_2 \ e_3, \Gamma)^{der}_{AM:B[M]} = \frac{(e_1, \Gamma)^{der}_{A:\Pi B_1:L} \quad (e_2, \Gamma)^{der}_{M:B_2} \quad (e_3, \Gamma)^{der}_{B_1 = B_2 :\text{type}}}{\mathcal{S}; \Gamma \vdash MN : B[N]}$$

The definition is easiest to understand as a definition of function $(-, -)^{\text{der}}$ that constructs a derivation by pattern matching on its first argument, a proof term. The cases are discriminated by the head symbol of the proof term—each corresponding to one inference rule of the internal language—and there is a subderivation to be computed, the function calls itself recursively on the appropriate subterms of the proof term.

The above definition lists only cases of proof-terms with head symbols that correspond to inference rules in Fig. 3. We omit the remaining cases for well-formedness of contexts and equality judgements for the sake of brevity and since we do not list these rules in the paper. These omitted cases are straightforward and are properly handled in the formalisation.

In Lemma 1, we have already proven that whether a type constant is bound in a signature as a particular kind, that is whether $\alpha : L \in \mathcal{S}$ is decidable. We extend this result to decidability of all judgements involved in Definition 10. Hence we can verify whether proof-relevant resolution produces well-formed types and terms by manifesting a derivation of the well-formedness judgement.

Theorem 3

- Let e be a proof term, $\mathcal{S}$ a signature, Γ a context, M, N terms, and A a type. Then either $(e)^{der}_{M=N:A}$ is well-formed or $(e)^{der}_{M=N:A}$ is impossible.
- Let e be a proof term, $\mathcal{S}$ a signature, Γ a context, A, B types, and L a kind. Then either $(e)^{der}_{A=B:L}$ is well-formed or $(e)^{der}_{A=B:L}$ is impossible.

Proof. – By induction on e using part 2.
- By induction on e using part 1.

Theorem 4. *Let e be a proof term, θ a substitution of metavariables, $\mathcal{S}$ a signature, M an extended term, and A an extended type.*
   Then either $(e)^{der}_{\theta M:\theta A}$ is well-formed or $(e)^{der}_{\theta M:\theta A}$ is impossible.

Proof. By induction using Lemma 1 and Theorem 3.

This theorem concludes our exposition of the interpretation of proof terms that are computed by proof-relevant resolution. When the formalised proof is extracted into OCaml it provides a procedure for verification of solution computed by proof-relevant resolution and hence manifests soundness of the system.

6   Related Work

Type inference and term synthesis as discussed in this paper is mechanically obtained from a specification of a type system in the form of typing judgements. Such approach does not exist in the literature yet. However, the importance of such treatment of type inference and term synthesis can be clearly argued based on the work currently being carried out for languages such as Coq and Agda. The main relevant project is METACOQ [2,19]. The project aims to provide certified metaprogramming facilities for Coq.

Building on METACOQ, Sozeau *et al.* [20] provide a verified implementation of type checker. They as well need to carry out certain amount of type inference. However, the amount is limited by the fact that they work only with a kernel of Coq (in our terms, with the internal language), *i.e.* a limited internal language that has already been elaborated, and by the fact that they assume that the metatheory is sound and hence the language is strongly normalising (and, as a result, typechecking is decidable).

In Agda, there is work being currently done on type-save metaprogramming, albeit it is in less mature state than in Coq. Cockx [6] has introduced type-safe rewriting rules, a type of reflection that is restricted to equality. Due to the restriction, there is no need for type inference and term synthesis. We conjecture that for full-scale metaprogramming it will be necessary as is the case with Coq.

7   Conclusion

Our formalisation of type inference and term synthesis for LF is carried out in Ott, which is used to generate the OCaml code, a parser of the input and Coq definition. We utilise type inference and term synthesis by translation to proof-relevant resolution and formally prove decidability of the translation, give interpretations to the computed proof terms and show their soundness.

Although our implementation is not fully carried out in a dependently typed language, that is Coq in our case, the amount of handwritten OCaml code that is necessary is very small. Such code is necessary only for interfacing different components of the system. The portion of hand-written OCaml code is very small and we believe this makes our approach superior to current implementations of dependently typed languages. We believe that the architecture we just introduced can serve as viable basis both for obtaining reference implementations from formal specifications of a programming languages and, with properly optimised resolution phase, as a basis for a type inference engine.

Acknowledgements. The author is grateful to the anonymous reviewers and to Nikita Zyuzin for their comments.

The author acknowledges support from the Spanish MICINN project BOSCO (PGC2018-102210-B-I00) and the European Research Council project Mathador (ERC2016-COG-724464).

References

1. Abel, A., Öhman, J., Vezzosi, A.: Decidability of conversion for type theory in type theory. PACMPL **2**(POPL), 23:1–23:29 (2018). https://doi.org/10.1145/3158111
2. Anand, A., Boulier, S., Cohen, C., Sozeau, M., Tabareau, N.: Towards certified meta-programming with typed template-coq. In: Avigad, J., Mahboubi, A. (eds.) ITP 2018. LNCS, vol. 10895, pp. 20–39. Springer, Cham (2018). https://doi.org/10.1007/978-3-319-94821-8_2
3. Appel, A.W., Michael, N.G., Stump, A., Virga, R.: A trustworthy proof checker. J. Autom. Reas. **31**(3–4), 231–260 (2003). https://doi.org/10.1023/B:JARS.0000021013.61329.58
4. Bertot, Y., Castéran, P.: Interactive theorem proving and program development - coq'art: the calculus of inductive constructions. In: Texts in Theoretical Computer Science. An EATCS Series. Springer, Heidelberg (2004). https://doi.org/10.1007/978-3-662-07964-5
5. Brady, E.: Idris, a general-purpose dependently typed programming language: design and implementation. J. Funct. Program. **23**(5), 552–593 (2013). https://doi.org/10.1017/S095679681300018X
6. Cockx, J.: type theory unchained: extending agda with user-defined rewrite rules. In: Bezem, M., Mahboubi, A. (eds.) 25th International Conference on Types for Proofs and Programs, TYPES 2019, Oslo, Norway, 11–14 June 2019, LIPIcs 175, Schloss Dagstuhl - Leibniz-Zentrum für Informatik, pp. 2:1–2:27 (2019). https://doi.org/10.4230/LIPIcs.TYPES.2019.2
7. Dowek, G.: The undecidability of typability in the Lambda-Pi-calculus. In: Bezem, M., Groote, J.F. (eds.) TLCA 1993. LNCS, vol. 664, pp. 139–145. Springer, Heidelberg (1993). https://doi.org/10.1007/BFb0037103
8. Dunchev, C., Guidi, F., Sacerdoti Coen, C., Tassi, E.: ELPI: fast, embeddable, λprolog interpreter. In: Davis, M., Fehnker, A., McIver, A., Voronkov, A. (eds.) LPAR 2015. LNCS, vol. 9450, pp. 460–468. Springer, Heidelberg (2015). https://doi.org/10.1007/978-3-662-48899-7_32
9. Farka, F., Komendantskaya, E., Hammond, K.: Proof-relevant horn clauses for dependent type inference and term synthesis. Theory Pract. Log. Program. **18**(3–4), 484–501 (2018). https://doi.org/10.1017/S1471068418000212
10. Fu, P., Komendantskaya, E.: Operational semantics of resolution and productivity in Horn clause logic. Formal Aspects Comput. **29**(3), 453–474 (2016). https://doi.org/10.1007/s00165-016-0403-1
11. Geuvers, H., Barendsen, E.: Some logical and syntactical observations concerning the first-order dependent type system lambda-P. Math. Struct. Comput. Sci. **9**(4), 335–359 (1999)
12. Guidi, F., Coen, C.S., Tassi, E.: Implementing type theory in higher order constraint logic programming. Math. Struct. Comput. Sci. **29**(8), 1125–1150 (2019). https://doi.org/10.1017/S0960129518000427
13. Harper, R., Pfenning, F.: On equivalence and canonical forms in the LF type theory. ACM T. Comp. Log. **6**(1), 61–101 (2005). https://doi.org/10.1145/1042038.1042041
14. Leroy, X., Blazy, S., Kästner, D., Schommer, B., Pister, M., Ferdinand, C.: CompCert - a formally verified optimizing compiler. In: ERTS 2016: Embedded Real Time Software and Systems, 8th European Congress, SEE, Toulouse, France (2016). https://hal.inria.fr/hal-01238879

15. Norell, U.: Towards a practical programming language based on dependent type theory. Ph.D. thesis (2007)
16. Pientka, B.: An insider's look at LF type reconstruction: everything you (n)ever wanted to know. J. Funct. Program. **23**(1), 1–37 (2013). https://doi.org/10.1017/S0956796812000408
17. Pientka, B., Dunfield, J.: Beluga: a framework for programming and reasoning with deductive systems (system description). In: Proceedings of IJCAR 2010, pp. 15–21 (2010). https://doi.org/10.1007/978-3-642-14203-1_2
18. Sewell, P., et al.: Ott: effective tool support for the working semanticist. In: Hinze, R., Ramsey, N. (eds.) Proceedings of the 12th ACM SIGPLAN International Conference on Functional Programming, ICFP 2007, Freiburg, Germany, 1–3 October 2007, pp. 1–12. ACM (2007). https://doi.org/10.1145/1291151.1291155
19. Sozeau, M., et al.: The METACOQ project. J. Autom. Reason. **64**(5), 947–999 (2020). https://doi.org/10.1007/s10817-019-09540-0
20. Sozeau, M., Boulier, S., Forster, Y., Tabareau, N., Winterhalter, T.: Coq Coq correct! verification of type checking and erasure for Coq in Coq. PACMPL **4**(POPL), 8:1–8:28 (2020). https://doi.org/10.1145/3371076
21. Urban, C., Cheney, J., Berghofer, S.: Mechanizing the metatheory of LF. ACM Trans. Comput. Log. **12**(2), 15:1–15:42 (2011). https://doi.org/10.1145/1877714.1877721
22. Urban, C.U., Pitts, A.M., Gabbay, M.: Nominal unification. Theor. Comput. Sci. **323**(1–3), 473–497 (2004). https://doi.org/10.1016/j.tcs.2004.06.016

Resourceful Program Synthesis from Graded Linear Types

Jack Hughes$^{(\boxtimes)}$ (iD) and Dominic Orchard (iD)

School of Computing, University of Kent, Canterbury, UK
{joh6,d.a.orchard}@kent.ac.uk

Abstract. Linear types provide a way to constrain programs by specifying that some values must be used exactly once. Recent work on *graded modal types* augments and refines this notion, enabling fine-grained, quantitative specification of data use in programs. The information provided by graded modal types appears to be useful for type-directed program synthesis, where these additional constraints can be used to prune the search space of candidate programs. We explore one of the major implementation challenges of a synthesis algorithm in this setting: how does the synthesis algorithm efficiently ensure that resource constraints are satisfied throughout program generation? We provide two solutions to this *resource management* problem, adapting Hodas and Miller's input-output model of linear context management to a graded modal linear type theory. We evaluate the performance of both approaches via their implementation as a program synthesis tool for the programming language Granule, which provides linear and graded modal typing.

1 Introduction

Type-directed program synthesis is a long-studied technique rooted in automated theorem proving [29]. A type-directed synthesis algorithm can be constructed as an inversion of type checking, starting from a type and inductively synthesising well-typed subterms, pruning the search space via typing. Via the Curry-Howard correspondence [21], we can view this as proof search in a corresponding logic, where the goal type is a proposition and the synthesised program is its proof. Recent work has extended type-directed synthesis to refinement types [34], cost specifications [27], differential privacy [35], and example-guided synthesis [12,33].

Automated proof search techniques have been previously adapted to linear logics, accounting for resource-sensitive reasoning [7–9,20,31]. By removing the structural rules of contraction and weakening, linear logic allows propositions to be treated as resources that must be used exactly once [17]. Non-linear propositions are captured via the 'exponential' modality !. Linearity introduces a new dimension to proof search and program synthesis: how do we inductively generate terms whilst pruning the search space of those which violate linearity? For example, consider the following inductive *synthesis rule*, mirroring Gentzen's sequent calculus [15], which synthesises a term of type $A \otimes B$:

© The Author(s) 2021
M. Fernández (Ed.): LOPSTR 2020, LNCS 12561, pp. 151–170, 2021.
https://doi.org/10.1007/978-3-030-68446-4_8

$$\frac{\Gamma_1 \vdash A \Rightarrow t_1 \qquad \Gamma_2 \vdash B \Rightarrow t_2}{\Gamma_1, \Gamma_2 \vdash A \otimes B \Rightarrow \langle t_1, t_2 \rangle} \text{ PAIR}$$

Reading the rule *bottom up*: from a context of assumptions Γ_1, Γ_2 we can synthesise the pair $\langle t_1, t_2 \rangle$ from the product type $A \otimes B$ provided that we can inductively synthesise the subterms of the pair, using Γ_1 for the left side and Γ_2 for the right.

But how do we partition a context of free variables Γ into Γ_1 and Γ_2 such that Γ_1 contains only those variables needed by t_1 and Γ_2 only those for t_2? A naïve approach is to try every possible partition of Γ. However, this becomes unmanageable as the number of possible partitions is $2^{|\Gamma|}$, i.e., exponential in the number of assumptions. This issue has been explored in automated theorem proving for linear logic, and is termed the *resource management problem* [7].

To address this, Hodas and Miller described an *input-output context management* scheme for linear logic programming [20], further developed by Cervesato et al. [7]. In this approach, synthesis rules take the form $\Gamma \vdash A \Rightarrow t; \Delta$ with an *input context* Γ and an *output context* Δ which contains all the hypotheses of Γ that were not used in the proof t of A (akin to the notion of *left over* typing for linear type systems [2,36]). This output context is then used as the input context to subsequent subgoals. In the case of $A \otimes B$, synthesis has the form:

$$\frac{\Gamma \vdash A \Rightarrow t_1; \Delta_1 \qquad \Delta_1 \vdash B \Rightarrow t_2; \Delta_2}{\Gamma \vdash A \otimes B \Rightarrow \langle t_1, t_2 \rangle; \Delta_2} \text{ PAIR\_LEFTOVER}$$

The non-determinism of how to divide Γ is resolved by using the entire context as the input for the synthesis of the first subterm t_1 from type A. If this succeeds, the context Δ_1 is returned containing the resources not needed to construct t_1. These remaining resources provide the input context to synthesise t_2 from B, which in turn returns an output context Δ_2 containing the resources not used by the pair $\langle t_1, t_2 \rangle$. We extend this approach, which we term *subtractive resource management*, to *graded modal types* and present its dual: *additive resource management*. In the additive approach, the output context describes what resources were used to synthesise a term, rather than what may still be used.

Graded modal types comprise an indexed family of modal operators whose indices have structure capturing program properties [32]. In the context of linear logic, graded modalities generalise the indexed modality of Bounded Linear Logic [18] $!_r A$ where $r \in \mathbb{N}$ captures the upper bound r on the number of times A is used. Generalising such indices to an arbitrary (pre-ordered) semiring yields a type system which can be instantiated to track various properties via the graded modality, a technique which is increasingly popular [4,13,14,16,24,25,32,36].

Our primary contribution is the extension of the input-output model of resource management for linear program synthesis to graded modal types. Our input and output contexts contain both linear and graded assumptions. Graded assumptions are annotated with a *grade*: an element of a pre-ordered semiring describing the variable's use. For example, grades drawn from $\mathbb{N}$ yield a system akin to BLL which counts the number of times a variable is used, where a graded assumption $x : [A]_2$ means x can be used twice. An example instantiation of our subtractive pair introduction rule is then as follows:

$$\frac{\Gamma, x : [A]_2 \vdash A \Rightarrow x;\ \Gamma, x : [A]_1 \qquad \Gamma, x : [A]_1 \vdash A \Rightarrow x;\ \Gamma, x : [A]_0}{\Gamma, x : [A]_2 \vdash A \otimes A \Rightarrow \langle x, x \rangle;\ \Gamma, x : [A]_0}$$

The initial input context contains graded assumption $x : [A]_2$. The first premise synthesises the term x, returning an output context which contains the assumption x with grade 1, indicating that x has been used once and can be used one more time. The next premise synthesises the second part of the pair as x using its remaining use. In the final output context, x is graded by 0, preventing it from being used to synthesise subsequent terms.

We adapt the input-output model of linear logic synthesis to subtractive and additive approaches in the presence of graded modal types, pruning the search space via the quantitative constraints of grades. We develop a type-directed synthesis tool for Granule, a functional language which combines indexed, linear, and graded modal types [32]. Granule supports various graded modalities, and its type checker leverages the Z3 SMT solver to discharge constraints on grades [30]. As type-based synthesis follows the structure of types, it is necessary to solve equations on grades during synthesis, for which we make use of Granule's SMT integration. Such calls to an external prover are costly, and thus efficiency of resource management is a key concern.

Section 2 introduces our core type theory (a subset of Granule's type system) based on the linear λ-calculus extended with graded modal types, pairs, and sums. Section 3 describes the two core synthesis calculi (subtractive and additive) as augmented inversions of the typing rules, as well as a variant of additive synthesis. Section 4 describes the implementation[1] and gives a quantitative comparison of the synthesis techniques on a suite of benchmark programs. The main finding is that the additive approach is often more efficient than the subtractive, presenting a departure from the literature on linear logic theorem proving which is typically subtractive.

Throughout, we will mostly use *types-and-programs* terminology rather than *propositions-and-proofs*. Through the Curry-Howard correspondence, one can switch smoothly to viewing our approach as proof search in logic.

2   Graded Linear λ-calculus

Our focus is a linear λ-calculus akin to a simply-typed linear functional language with graded modalities, resembling the core languages of Gaboardi et al. [14] and Brunel et al. [4], and a simply-typed subset of Granule [32].

---

[1] https://github.com/granule-project/granule/releases/tag/v0.8.0.0.

Types comprise linear functions, multiplicative conjunction (product types $\otimes$ and unit 1), additive disjunction (sum types $\oplus$), and a *graded modality* $\Box_r$:

$$A, B ::= A \multimap B \mid A \otimes B \mid A \oplus B \mid 1 \mid \Box_r A \qquad \text{(types)}$$

where $\Box_r A$ is an indexed family of type operators where r ranges over the elements of some pre-ordered semiring $(\mathcal{R}, *, 1, +, 0, \sqsubseteq)$ parameterising the calculus (where $*$ and $+$ are monotonic with respect to the pre-order $\sqsubseteq$).

The syntax of terms provides the elimination and introduction forms:

$$t ::= x \mid \lambda x.t \mid t_1\, t_2 \mid [t] \mid \mathbf{let}\,[x] = t_1 \,\mathbf{in}\, t_2 \mid \langle t_1, t_2 \rangle \mid \mathbf{let}\,\langle x_1, x_2 \rangle = t_1 \,\mathbf{in}\, t_2$$
$$\mid () \mid \mathbf{let}\,() = t_1 \,\mathbf{in}\, t_2 \mid \mathbf{inl}\,t \mid \mathbf{inr}\,t \mid \mathbf{case}\,t_1\,\mathbf{of}\,\mathbf{inl}\,x_1 \to t_2 \mid \mathbf{inr}\,x_2 \to t_3 \quad \text{(terms)}$$

We use the syntax $()$ for the inhabitant of multiplicative unit 1. Pattern matching via a **let** is used to eliminate products and unit types; for sum types, **case** is used to distinguish the constructors. The construct $[t]$ introduces a graded modal type $\Box_r A$ by 'promoting' a term t to the graded modality, and $\mathbf{let}\,[x] = t_1\,\mathbf{in}\,t_2$ eliminates a graded modal value t_1, binding a graded variable x in scope of t_2.

Typing judgments are of the form $\Gamma \vdash t : A$, where Γ ranges over contexts:

$$\Gamma ::= \emptyset \mid \Gamma, x : A \mid \Gamma, x : [A]_r \qquad \text{(contexts)}$$

Thus, a context may be empty $\emptyset$, extended with a linear assumption $x : A$ or extended with a graded assumption $x : [A]_r$. For linear assumptions, structural rules of weakening and contraction are disallowed. Graded assumptions may be used non-linearly according to the constraints given by their grade, the semiring element r. Throughout, comma denotes disjoint context concatenation.

Various operations on contexts are used to capture non-linear data flow via grading. Firstly, *context addition* provides an analogue to contraction, combining contexts that have come from typing multiple subterms in a rule. Context addition, written $\Gamma_1 + \Gamma_2$, is undefined if Γ_1 and Γ_2 overlap in their linear assumptions. Otherwise graded assumptions appearing in both contexts are combined via the semiring $+$ of their grades.

Definition 1 (Context addition). *For all* Γ_1, Γ_2 *context addition is defined as follows by ordered cases matching inductively on the structure of* Γ_2:

$$\Gamma_1 + \Gamma_2 = \begin{cases} \Gamma_1 & \Gamma_2 = \emptyset \\ ((\Gamma_1', \Gamma_1'') + \Gamma_2'), x : [A]_{(r+s)} & \Gamma_2 = \Gamma_2', x : [A]_s \wedge \Gamma_1 = \Gamma_1', x : [A]_r, \Gamma_1'' \\ (\Gamma_1 + \Gamma_2'), x : A & \Gamma_2 = \Gamma_2', x : A \wedge x : A \notin \Gamma_1 \end{cases}$$

In the typing of **case** expressions, the *least-upper bound* of the two contexts used to type each branch is used, defined:

Definition 2 (Partial least-upper bounds of contexts). *For all Γ_1, Γ_2:*

$$\Gamma_1 \sqcup \Gamma_2 = \begin{cases} \emptyset & \Gamma_1 = \emptyset & \wedge\ \Gamma_2 = \emptyset \\ (\emptyset \sqcup \Gamma_2'), x : [A]_{0 \sqcup s} & \Gamma_1 = \emptyset & \wedge\ \Gamma_2 = \Gamma_2', x : [A]_s \\ (\Gamma_1' \sqcup (\Gamma_2', \Gamma_2'')), x : A & \Gamma_1 = \Gamma_1', x : A & \wedge\ \Gamma_2 = \Gamma_2', x : A, \Gamma_2'' \\ (\Gamma_1' \sqcup (\Gamma_2', \Gamma_2'')), x : [A]_{r \sqcup s} & \Gamma_1 = \Gamma_1', x : [A]_r \wedge \Gamma_2 = \Gamma_2', x : [A]_s, \Gamma_2'' \end{cases}$$

where $r \sqcup s$ is the least-upper bound of grades r and s if it exists, derived from $\sqsubseteq$.

As an example of the partiality of $\sqcup$, if one branch of a **case** uses a linear variable, then the other branch must also use it to maintain linearity overall, otherwise the upper-bound of the two contexts for these branches is not defined.

$$\frac{}{x : A \vdash x : A}\ \text{Var} \qquad \frac{\Gamma, x : A \vdash t : B}{\Gamma \vdash \lambda x.t : A \multimap B}\ \text{Abs} \qquad \frac{\Gamma_1 \vdash t_1 : A \multimap B \quad \Gamma_2 \vdash t_2 : A}{\Gamma_1 + \Gamma_2 \vdash t_1\, t_2 : B}\ \text{App}$$

$$\frac{\Gamma \vdash t : A}{\Gamma, [\Delta]_0 \vdash t : A}\ \text{Weak} \qquad \frac{\Gamma, x : A \vdash t : B}{\Gamma, x : [A]_1 \vdash t : B}\ \text{Der} \qquad \frac{[\Gamma] \vdash t : A}{r * [\Gamma] \vdash [t] : \Box_r A}\ \text{Pr}$$

$$\frac{\Gamma_1 \vdash t_1 : \Box_r A \quad \Gamma_2, x : [A]_r \vdash t_2 : B}{\Gamma_1 + \Gamma_2 \vdash \text{let } [x] = t_1 \text{ in } t_2 : B}\ \text{Let}\Box \qquad \frac{}{\emptyset \vdash () : 1}\ 1 \qquad \frac{\Gamma_1 \vdash t_1 : 1 \quad \Gamma_2 \vdash t_2 : A}{\Gamma_1 + \Gamma_2 \vdash \text{let } () = t_1 \text{ in } t_2 : A}\ \text{Let1}$$

$$\frac{\Gamma_1 \vdash t_1 : A \quad \Gamma_2 \vdash t_2 : B}{\Gamma_1 + \Gamma_2 \vdash \langle t_1, t_2 \rangle : A \otimes B}\ \text{Pair} \qquad \frac{\Gamma_1 \vdash t_1 : A \otimes B \quad \Gamma_2, x_1 : A, x_2 : B \vdash t_2 : C}{\Gamma_1 + \Gamma_2 \vdash \text{let } \langle x_1, x_2 \rangle = t_1 \text{ in } t_2 : C}\ \text{LetPair}$$

$$\frac{\Gamma, x : [A]_r, \Gamma' \vdash t : B \quad r \sqsubseteq s}{\Gamma, x : [A]_s, \Gamma' \vdash t : B}\ \text{Approx} \qquad \frac{\Gamma \vdash t : A}{\Gamma \vdash \text{inl } t : A \oplus B}\ \text{Inl} \qquad \frac{\Gamma \vdash t : B}{\Gamma \vdash \text{inr } t : A \oplus B}\ \text{Inr}$$

$$\frac{\Gamma_1 \vdash t_1 : A \oplus B \quad \Gamma_2, x_1 : A \vdash t_2 : C \quad \Gamma_3, x_2 : B \vdash t_3 : C}{\Gamma_1 + (\Gamma_2 \sqcup \Gamma_3) \vdash \text{case } t_1 \text{ of inl } x_1 \rightarrow t_2 |\, \text{inr } x_2 \rightarrow t_3 : C}\ \text{Case}$$

Fig. 1. Typing rules of the graded linear λ-calculus

Figure 1 defines the typing rules. Linear variables are typed in a singleton context (Var). Abstraction (Abs) and application (App) follow the rules of the linear λ-calculus. Rules for multiplicative products (pairs) and additive coproducts (sums) are routine, where pair introduction (Pair) adds the contexts used to type the pair's constituent subterms. Pair elimination (LetPair) binds a pair's components to two linear variables in the scope of the body t_2. The Inl and Inr rules handle the typing of constructors for the sum type $A \oplus B$. Elimination of sums (Case) takes the least upper bound (defined above) of the contexts used to type the two branches of the case.

The Weak rule captures weakening of assumptions graded by 0 (where $[\Delta]_0$ denotes a context containing only graded assumptions graded by 0). Dereliction (Der), allows a linear assumption to be converted to a graded assumption with grade 1. Grade approximation is captured by the Approx rule, which allows a grade r to be converted to another grade s, providing that r is *approximated by s*, where the relation $\sqsubseteq$ is the pre-order provided with the semiring. Introduction and elimination of the graded modality is provided by the PR and LET rules respectively. The PR rule propagates the grade r to the assumptions through *scalar multiplication* of Γ by r where every assumption in Γ must already be graded (written $[\Gamma]$ in the rule), defined:

Definition 3 (Scalar context multiplication)

$$r * \emptyset = \emptyset \qquad\qquad r * (\Gamma, x : [A]_s) = (r * \Gamma), x : [A]_{(r*s)}$$

The LET rule eliminates a graded modal value $\Box_r A$ into a graded assumption $x : [A]_r$ with a matching grade in the scope of the **let** body.

We now give three examples of different graded modalities.

Example 1. The natural number semiring with discrete ordering $(\mathbb{N}, *, 1, +, 0, \equiv)$ provides a graded modality that counts exactly how many times non-linear values are used. As a simple example, the S combinator is typed and defined:

$$s : (A \multimap (B \multimap C)) \multimap (A \multimap B) \multimap (\Box_2 A \multimap C)$$
$$s = \lambda x.\lambda y.\lambda z'.\ \textbf{let}\ [z] = z'\ \textbf{in}\ (x\ z)\ (y\ z)$$

The graded modal value z' captures the 'capability' for a value of type A to be used twice. This capability is made available by eliminating $\Box$ (via **let**) to the variable z, which is graded $z : [A]_2$ in the scope of the body.

Example 2. Exact usage analysis is less useful when control-flow is involved, e.g., eliminating sum types where each control-flow branch uses variables differently. The above $\mathbb{N}$-semiring can be imbued with a notion of *approximation* via less-than-equal ordering, providing upper bounds. A more expressive semiring is that of natural number intervals [32], given by pairs $\mathbb{N} \times \mathbb{N}$ written $[r...s]$ here for the lower-bound $r \in \mathbb{N}$ and upper-bound usage $s \in \mathbb{N}$ with $0 = [0...0]$ and $1 = [1...1]$, addition and multiplication defined pointwise, and ordering $[r...s] \sqsubseteq [r'...s'] = r' \leq r \wedge s \leq s'$. Then a coproduct elimination function can be written and typed:

$$\oplus_e : \Box_{[0...1]}(A \multimap C) \multimap \Box_{[0...1]}(B \multimap C) \multimap (A \oplus B) \multimap C$$
$$\oplus_e = \lambda x'.\lambda y'.\lambda z.\textbf{let}\ [x] = x'\ \textbf{in let}\ [y] = y'\ \textbf{in}\ (\textbf{case}\ z\ \textbf{of inl}\ u \to x\ u|\ \textbf{inr}\ v \to y\ v)$$

Linear logic's exponential $!A$ is given by $\Box_{[0...\infty]}A$ with intervals over $\mathbb{N} \cup \{\infty\}$ where ∞ is absorbing for all operations, except multiplying by 0.

Example 3. Graded modalities can capture a form of information-flow security, tracking the flow of labelled data through a program [32], with a lattice-based semiring on $\mathcal{R} = \{\text{Unused} \sqsubseteq \text{Hi} \sqsubseteq \text{Lo}\}$ where $0 = \text{Unused}$, $1 = \text{Hi}$, $+ = \sqcup$ and if $r = \text{Unused}$ or $s = \text{Unused}$ then $r * s = \text{Unused}$ otherwise $r * s = \sqcup$. This allows the following well-typed program, eliminating a pair of Lo and Hi security values, picking the left one to pass to a continuation expecting a Lo input:

$$noLeak : (\Box_{\mathsf{Lo}} A \otimes \Box_{\mathsf{Hi}} A) \multimap (\Box_{\mathsf{Lo}}(A \otimes 1) \multimap B) \multimap B$$

$$noLeak = \lambda z.\lambda u.\mathbf{let} \; \langle x', y' \rangle = z \; \mathbf{in} \; \mathbf{let} \; [x] = x' \; \mathbf{in} \; \mathbf{let} \; [y] = y' \; \mathbf{in} \; u \, [\langle x, () \rangle]$$

Metatheory. The admissibility of substitution is a key result that holds for this language [32], which is leveraged in soundness of the synthesis calculi.

Lemma 1. (Admissibility of substitution). *Let $\Delta \vdash t' : A$, then:*

- *(Linear)* If $\Gamma, x : A, \Gamma' \vdash t : B$ then $\Gamma + \Delta + \Gamma' \vdash [t'/x]t : B$
- *(Graded)* If $\Gamma, x : [A]_r, \Gamma' \vdash t : B$ then $\Gamma + (r * \Delta) + \Gamma' \vdash [t'/x]t : B$

3   The Synthesis Calculi

We present two synthesis calculi with subtractive and additive resource management schemes, extending an input-output approach to graded modal types. The structure of the synthesis calculi mirrors a cut-free sequent calculus, with *left* and *right* rules for each type constructor. Right rules synthesise an introduction form for the goal type. Left rules eliminate (deconstruct) assumptions so that they may be used inductively to synthesise subterms.

3.1   Subtractive Resource Management

Our subtractive approach follows the philosophy of earlier work on linear logic proof search [7,20], structuring synthesis rules around an input context of the available resources and an output context of the remaining resources that can be used to synthesise subsequent subterms. Synthesis rules are read bottom-up, with judgments $\Gamma \vdash A \Rightarrow^- t; \Delta$ meaning from the *goal type* A we can synthesise a term t using assumptions in Γ, with output context Δ. We describe the rules in turn to aid understanding. The appendix [22] collects the rules for reference.

Variable terms can be synthesised from linear or graded assumptions by rules:

$$\frac{}{\Gamma, x : A \vdash A \Rightarrow^- x; \Gamma} \; \text{LinVar}^- \qquad \frac{\exists s. r \sqsupseteq s + 1}{\Gamma, x : [A]_r \vdash A \Rightarrow^- x; \Gamma, x : [A]_s} \; \text{GrVar}^-$$

On the left, a variable x may be synthesised for the goal A if a linear assumption $x : A$ is present in the input context. The input context without x is then returned as the output context, since x has been used. On the right, we can synthesise a variable x for A we have a graded assumption of x matching the type. However, the grading r must permit x to be used once here. Therefore, the premise states that there exists some grade s such that grade r approximates $s + 1$. The grade s represents the use of x in the rest of the synthesised term, and thus $x : [A]_s$ is in the output context. For the natural numbers semiring, this constraint is satisfied by $s = r - 1$ whenever $r \neq 0$, e.g., if $r = 3$ then $s = 2$. For intervals, the role of approximation is more apparent: if $r = [0...3]$ then this rule is satisfied by $s = [0...2]$ where $s + 1 = [0...2] + [1...1] = [1...3] \sqsubseteq [0...3]$. Thus, this premise constraint avoids the need for an additive inverse. In the implementation, the constraint is discharged via an SMT solver, where an unsatisfiable result terminates this branch of synthesis.

In typing, λ-abstraction binds linear variables to introduce linear functions. Synthesis from a linear function type therefore mirrors typing:

$$\frac{\Gamma, x : A \vdash B \Rightarrow^- t; \Delta \quad x \notin |\Delta|}{\Gamma \vdash A \multimap B \Rightarrow^- \lambda x.t; \Delta} \text{ R}\multimap^-$$

Thus, $\lambda x.t$ can be synthesised given that t can be synthesised from B in the context of Γ extended with a fresh linear assumption $x : A$. To ensure that x is used linearly by t we must therefore check that it is not present in Δ.

The left-rule for linear function types then synthesises applications (as in [20]):

$$\frac{\Gamma, x_2 : B \vdash C \Rightarrow^- t_1; \Delta_1 \quad x_2 \notin |\Delta_1| \quad \Delta_1 \vdash A \Rightarrow^- t_2; \Delta_2}{\Gamma, x_1 : A \multimap B \vdash C \Rightarrow^- [(x_1\, t_2)/x_2]t_1; \Delta_2} \text{ L}\multimap^-$$

The rule synthesises a term for type C in a context that contains an assumption $x_1 : A \multimap B$. The first premise synthesises a term t_1 for C under the context extended with a fresh linear assumption $x_2 : B$, i.e., assuming the result of x_1. This produces an output context Δ_1 that must not contain x_2, i.e., x_2 is used by t_1. The remaining assumptions Δ_1 provide the input context to synthesise t_2 of type A: the argument to the function x_1. In the conclusion, the application $x_1\, t_2$ is substituted for x_2 inside t_1, and Δ_2 is the output context.

Note that this rule synthesises the application of a function given by a linear assumption. What if we have a graded assumption of function type? Rather than duplicating every left rule for both linear and graded assumptions, we mirror the dereliction typing rule (converting a linear assumption to graded) as:

$$\frac{\Gamma, x : [A]_s, y : A \vdash B \Rightarrow^- t; \Delta, x : [A]_{s'} \quad y \notin |\Delta| \quad \exists s.\, r \sqsupseteq s + 1}{\Gamma, x : [A]_r \vdash B \Rightarrow^- [x/y]t; \Delta, x : [A]_{s'}} \text{ DER}^-$$

Dereliction captures the ability to reuse a graded assumption being considered in a left rule. A fresh linear assumption y is generated that represents the graded assumption's use in a left rule, and must be used linearly in the subsequent synthesis of t. The output context of this premise then contains x graded by s', which reflects how x was used in the synthesis of t, i.e. if x was not used then $s' = s$. The premise $\exists s.\, r \sqsupseteq s + 1$ constrains the number of times dereliction can be applied so that it does not exceed x's original grade r.

For a graded modal goal type $\Box_r A$, we synthesise a promotion $[t]$ if we can synthesise the 'unpromoted' t from A:

$$\frac{\Gamma \vdash A \Rightarrow^- t; \Delta}{\Gamma \vdash \Box_r A \Rightarrow^- [t]; \Gamma - r * (\Gamma - \Delta)} \; \text{R}\Box^-$$

Recall that typing of a promotion $[t]$ scales all the graded assumptions used to type t by r. Therefore, to compute the output context we must "subtract" r-times the use of the variables in t. However, in the subtractive model Δ tells us what is left, rather than what is used. Thus we first compute the *context subtraction* of Γ and Δ yielding the variables usage information about t:

Definition 4 (Context subtraction). *For all Γ_1, Γ_2 where $\Gamma_2 \subseteq \Gamma_1$:*

$$\Gamma_1 - \Gamma_2 = \begin{cases} \Gamma_1 & \Gamma_2 = \emptyset \\ (\Gamma_1', \Gamma_1'') - \Gamma_2' & \Gamma_2 = \Gamma_2', x : A \quad \wedge \Gamma_1 = \Gamma_1', x : A, \Gamma_1'' \\ ((\Gamma_1', \Gamma_1'') - \Gamma_2'), x : [A]_q & \Gamma_2 = \Gamma_2', x : [A]_s \wedge \Gamma_1 = \Gamma_1', x : [A]_r, \Gamma_1'' \\ & \wedge \exists q . r \sqsupseteq q + s \wedge \forall q' . r \sqsupseteq q' + s \implies q \sqsupseteq q' \end{cases}$$

As in graded variable synthesis, context subtraction existentially quantifies a variable q to express the relationship between grades on the right being "subtracted" from those on the left. The last conjunct states q is the greatest element (wrt. to the pre-order) satisfying this constraint, i.e., for all other $q' \in \mathcal{R}$ satisfying the subtraction constraint then $q \sqsupseteq q'$ e.g., if $r = [2...3]$ and $s = [0...1]$ then $q = [2...2]$ instead of, say, $[0...1]$. This *maximality* condition is important for soundness (that synthesised programs are well-typed).

Thus for $\text{R}\Box^-$, $\Gamma - \Delta$ is multiplied by the goal type grade r to obtain how these variables are used in t after promotion. This is then subtracted from the original input context Γ giving an output context containing the left-over variables and grades. Context multiplication requires that $\Gamma - \Delta$ contains only graded variables, preventing the incorrect use of linear variables from Γ in t.

Synthesis of graded modality elimination, is handled by the $\text{L}\Box^-$ left rule:

$$\frac{\Gamma, x_2 : [A]_r \vdash B \Rightarrow^- t; \Delta, x_2 : [A]_s \qquad 0 \sqsubseteq s}{\Gamma, x_1 : \Box_r A \vdash B \Rightarrow^- \text{let } [x_2] = x_1 \text{ in } t; \Delta} \; \text{L}\Box^-$$

Given an input context comprising Γ and a linear assumption x_1 of graded modal type, we can synthesise an unboxing of x_1 if we can synthesise a term t under Γ extended with a graded assumption $x_2 : [A]_r$. This returns an output context that must contain x_2 graded by s with the constraint that s must approximate 0. This enforces that x_2 has been used as much as required by the grade r.

The right and left rules for products, units, and sums, are then fairly straight-forward following the subtractive resource model:

$$\frac{\Gamma \vdash A \Rightarrow^- t_1; \Delta_1 \qquad \Delta_1 \vdash B \Rightarrow^- t_2; \Delta_2}{\Gamma \vdash A \otimes B \Rightarrow^- \langle t_1, t_2 \rangle; \Delta_2} \; R\otimes^-$$

$$\frac{\Gamma, x_1 : A, x_2 : B \vdash C \Rightarrow^- t_2; \Delta \qquad x_1 \notin |\Delta| \qquad x_2 \notin |\Delta|}{\Gamma, x_3 : A \otimes B \vdash C \Rightarrow^- \textbf{let } \langle x_1, x_2 \rangle = x_3 \textbf{ in } t_2; \Delta} \; L\otimes^-$$

$$\frac{}{\Gamma \vdash 1 \Rightarrow^- (); \Gamma} \; R1^- \qquad \frac{\Gamma \vdash C \Rightarrow^- t; \Delta}{\Gamma, x : 1 \vdash C \Rightarrow^- \textbf{let } () = x \textbf{ in } t; \Delta} \; L1^-$$

$$\frac{\Gamma \vdash A \Rightarrow^- t; \Delta}{\Gamma \vdash A \oplus B \Rightarrow^- \textbf{inl } t; \Delta} \quad \frac{\Gamma \vdash B \Rightarrow^- t; \Delta}{\Gamma \vdash A \oplus B \Rightarrow^- \textbf{inr } t; \Delta} \; R\oplus_2^-$$

$$\frac{\Gamma, x_2 : A \vdash C \Rightarrow^- t_1; \Delta_1 \quad \Gamma, x_3 : B \vdash C \Rightarrow^- t_2; \Delta_2 \quad x_2 \notin |\Delta_1| \quad x_3 \notin |\Delta_2|}{\Gamma, x_1 : A \oplus B \vdash C \Rightarrow^- \textbf{case } x_1 \textbf{ of inl } x_2 \to t_1 \,|\, \textbf{inr } x_3 \to t_2; \Delta_1 \sqcap \Delta_2} \; L\oplus^-$$

The $L\oplus^-$ rule synthesises the left and right branches of a case statement that may use resources differently. The output context therefore takes the *greatest lower bound* ($\sqcap$) of Δ_1 and Δ_2. We elide definition of context $\sqcap$ as it has the same shape as $\sqcup$ for contexts (Definition 2), just replacing $\sqcup$ with $\sqcap$ on grades.

As an example of $\sqcap$, consider the semiring of intervals over natural numbers and two judgements that could be used as premises for the ($L\oplus^-$) rule:

$$\Gamma, y : [A']_{[0\ldots5]}, x_2 : A \vdash C \Rightarrow^- t_1; \, y : [A']_{[2\ldots5]}$$
$$\Gamma, y : [A']_{[0\ldots5]}, x_3 : B \vdash C \Rightarrow^- t_2; \, y : [A']_{[3\ldots4]}$$

where t_1 uses y such that there are 2–5 uses remaining and t_2 uses y such that there are 3–4 uses left. To synthesise **case** x_1 **of inl** $x_2 \to t_1 \,|\, $ **inr** $x_3 \to t_2$ the output context must be pessimistic about what resources are left, thus we take the greatest-lower bound yielding the interval $[2\ldots4]$ here: we know y can be used at least twice and at most 4 times in the rest of the synthesised program.

This completes subtractive synthesis. We conclude with a key result, that synthesised terms are well-typed at the type from which they were synthesised:

Lemma 2. (Subtractive synthesis soundness). *For all Γ and A then:*

$$\Gamma \vdash A \Rightarrow^- t; \Delta \quad \implies \quad \Gamma - \Delta \vdash t : A$$

i.e. t has type A under context $\Gamma - \Delta$, that contains just those linear and graded variables with grades reflecting their use in t. The appendix [22] provides the proof.

3.2   Additive Resource Management

We now propose a dual *additive* resource management approach. Additive synthesis also uses the input-output context approach, but where output contexts describe exactly which assumptions were used to synthesise a term, rather than which assumptions are still available. Additive synthesis rules are read bottom-up, with $\Gamma \vdash A \Rightarrow^+ t; \Delta$ meaning that from the type A we synthesise a term t using exactly the assumptions Δ that originate from the input context Γ.

We unpack the rules, starting with variables:

$$\frac{}{\Gamma, x : A \vdash A \Rightarrow^+ x; \, x : A} \; \text{LinVar}^+ \qquad \frac{}{\Gamma, x : [A]_r \vdash A \Rightarrow^+ x; \, x : [A]_1} \; \text{GrVar}^+$$

For a linear assumption, the output context contains just the variable that was synthesised. For a graded assumption $x : [A]_r$, the output context contains the assumption graded by 1. To synthesise a variable from a graded assumption, we must check that the use is compatible with the grade. The subtractive approach handled this rule (GrVar^-) by a constraint $\exists s. \, r \sqsupseteq s + 1$. Here however, the point at which we check that a graded assumption has been used according to the grade takes place in the $\text{L}\square^+$ rule, where graded assumptions are bound:

$$\frac{\Gamma, x_2 : [A]_r \vdash B \Rightarrow^+ t; \, \Delta \qquad \textit{if } x_2 : [A]_s \in \Delta \textit{ then } s \sqsubseteq r \textit{ else } 0 \sqsubseteq r}{\Gamma, x_1 : \square_r A \vdash B \Rightarrow^+ \textbf{let } [x_2] = x_1 \textbf{ in } t; \, (\Delta \backslash x_2), x_1 : \square_r A} \; \text{L}\square^+$$

Here, t is synthesised under a fresh graded assumption $x_2 : [A]_r$. This produces an output context containing x_2 with some grade s that describes how x_2 is used in t. An additional premise requires that the original grade r approximates either s if x_2 appears in Δ or 0 if it does not, ensuring that x_2 has been used correctly. For the N-semiring with equality as the ordering, this would ensure that a variable has been used exactly the number of times specified by the grade.

Right and left rules for $\multimap$ have a similar shape to the subtractive calculus:

$$\frac{\Gamma, x : A \vdash B \Rightarrow^+ t; \, \Delta, x : A}{\Gamma \vdash A \multimap B \Rightarrow^+ \lambda x.t; \, \Delta} \; \text{R}\multimap^+$$

$$\frac{\Gamma, x_2 : B \vdash C \Rightarrow^+ t_1; \, \Delta_1, x_2 : B \qquad \Gamma \vdash A \Rightarrow^+ t_2; \, \Delta_2}{\Gamma, x_1 : A \multimap B \vdash C \Rightarrow^+ [(x_1 \, t_2)/x_2]t_1; \, (\Delta_1 + \Delta_2), x_1 : A \multimap B} \; \text{L}\multimap^+$$

Synthesising an abstraction ($\text{R}\multimap^+$) requires that $x : A$ is in the output context of the premise, ensuring that linearity is preserved. Likewise for application ($\text{L}\multimap^+$), the output context of the first premise must contain the linearly bound $x_2 : B$ and the final output context must contain the assumption being used in the application $x_1 : A \multimap B$. This output context computes the *context addition* (Definition 1) of both output contexts of the premises $\Delta_1 + \Delta_2$. If Δ_1 describes how assumptions were used in t_1 and Δ_2 respectively for t_2, then the addition of these two contexts describes the usage of assumptions for the entire subprogram.

Recall, context addition ensures that a linear assumption may not appear in both Δ_1 and Δ_2, preventing us from synthesising terms that violate linearity.

As in the subtractive calculus, we avoid duplicating left rules to match graded assumptions by giving a synthesising version of dereliction:

$$\frac{\Gamma, x : [A]_s, y : A \vdash B \Rightarrow^+ t;\ \Delta, y : A}{\Gamma, x : [A]_s \vdash B \Rightarrow^+ [x/y]t;\ \Delta + x : [A]_1} \text{ DER}^+$$

The fresh linear assumption $y : A$ must appear in the output context of the premise, ensuring it is used. The final context therefore adds to Δ an assumption of x graded by 1, accounting for this use of x (temporarily renamed to y).

Synthesis of a promotion is considerably simpler in the additive approach. In subtractive resource management it was necessary to calculate how resources were used in the synthesis of t before then applying the scalar context multiplication by the grade r and subtracting this from the original input Γ. In additive resource management, however, we can simply apply the multiplication directly to the output context Δ to obtain how our assumptions are used in $[t]$:

$$\frac{\Gamma \vdash A \Rightarrow^+ t;\ \Delta}{\Gamma \vdash \Box_r A \Rightarrow^+ [t];\ r * \Delta} \text{ R}\Box^+$$

As in the subtractive approach, the right and left rules for products, units, and sums follow fairly straightforwardly from the resource scheme:

$$\frac{\Gamma \vdash A \Rightarrow^+ t_1;\ \Delta_1 \qquad \Gamma \vdash B \Rightarrow^+ t_2;\ \Delta_2}{\Gamma \vdash A \otimes B \Rightarrow^+ \langle t_1, t_2 \rangle;\ \Delta_1 + \Delta_2} \text{ R}\otimes^+$$

$$\frac{\Gamma, x_1 : A, x_2 : B \vdash C \Rightarrow^+ t_2;\ \Delta, x_1 : A, x_2 : B}{\Gamma, x_3 : A \otimes B \vdash C \Rightarrow^+ \textbf{let } \langle x_1, x_2 \rangle = x_3 \textbf{ in } t_2;\ \Delta, x_3 : A \otimes B} \text{ L}\otimes^+$$

$$\frac{}{\Gamma \vdash 1 \Rightarrow^+ ();\ \emptyset} \text{ R1}^+ \qquad \frac{\Gamma \vdash C \Rightarrow^+ t;\ \Delta}{\Gamma, x : 1 \vdash C \Rightarrow^+ \textbf{let } () = x \textbf{ in } t;\ \Delta, x : 1} \text{ L1}^+$$

$$\frac{\Gamma \vdash A \Rightarrow^+ t;\ \Delta}{\Gamma \vdash A \oplus B \Rightarrow^+ \textbf{inl } t;\ \Delta} \text{ R}\oplus_1^+ \qquad \frac{\Gamma \vdash B \Rightarrow^+ t;\ \Delta}{\Gamma \vdash A \oplus B \Rightarrow^+ \textbf{inr } t;\ \Delta} \text{ R}\oplus_2^+$$

$$\frac{\Gamma, x_2 : A \vdash C \Rightarrow^+ t_1;\ \Delta_1, x_2 : A \qquad \Gamma, x_3 : B \vdash C \Rightarrow^+ t_2;\ \Delta_2, x_3 : B}{\Gamma, x_1 : A \oplus B \vdash C \Rightarrow^+ \textbf{case } x_1 \textbf{ of inl } x_2 \to t_1 \mid \textbf{inr } x_3 \to t_2;\ (\Delta_1 \sqcup \Delta_2), x_1 : A \oplus B} \text{ L}\oplus^+$$

Rule (L$\oplus^+$) takes the least-upper bound of the premise's output contexts (Definition 2).

Lemma 3. (Additive synthesis soundness). *For all Γ and A:*

$$\Gamma \vdash A \Rightarrow^+ t;\ \Delta \quad \Longrightarrow \quad \Delta \vdash t : A$$

The appendix [22] provides the proof.

Additive Pruning. As seen above, the additive approach delays checking whether a variable is used according to its linearity/grade until it is bound. We hypothesise that this can lead additive synthesis to explore many ultimately ill-typed (or *ill-resourced*) paths for too long. Subsequently, we define a "pruning" variant of any additive rules with multiple sequenced premises. For $(R\otimes^+)$ this is:

$$\frac{\Gamma \vdash A \Rightarrow^+ t_1; \Delta_1 \qquad \Gamma - \Delta_1 \vdash B \Rightarrow^+ t_2; \Delta_2}{\Gamma \vdash A \otimes B \Rightarrow^+ \langle t_1, t_2 \rangle; \Delta_1 + \Delta_2} R'\otimes^+$$

Instead of passing Γ to both premises, Γ is the input only for the first premise. This premise outputs context Δ_1 that is subtracted from Γ to give the input context of the second premise. This provides an opportunity to terminate the current branch of synthesis early if $\Gamma - \Delta_1$ does not contain the necessary resources to attempt the second premise. The $(L\multimap^+)$ rule is similarly adjusted.

Lemma 4. (Additive pruning synthesis soundness). *For all Γ and A:*

$$\Gamma \vdash A \Rightarrow^+ t; \Delta \quad \implies \quad \Delta \vdash t : A$$

The appendix [22] provides the proof.

3.3 Focusing

The two calculi provide a foundation for a synthesis algorithm. However, in their current forms, both synthesis calculi are highly non-deterministic: for each rule there are multiple rules which may be applied to synthesise the premise(s).

We apply the idea of *focusing* [3] to derive two *focusing calculi* which are equivalent to the former in expressivity, but with a reduced degree of non-determinism in the rules that may be applied. Focusing is a proof search technique based on the idea that some rules are *invertible*, i.e. whenever the premises of a rule are derivable, the conclusion is also derivable. Rules with this property can be applied eagerly in the synthesis of a term. When we arrive at a goal whose applicable rules are not invertible, we *focus* on either the goal type or a particular assumption by applying a chain of non-invertible rules until we reach a goal to which invertible rules can be applied. The appendix [22] gives focusing versions of the two calculi, which form the basis of our implementation. The proofs for the soundness of these focusing calculi can also be found in the appendix.

4   Evaluation

Prior to evaluation, we made the following hypotheses about the relative performance of the additive versus subtractive approaches:

1. Additive synthesis should make fewer calls to the solver, with lower complexity theorems (fewer quantifiers). Dually, subtractive synthesis makes more calls to the solver with higher complexity theorems (more quantifiers);

2. For complex problems, additive synthesis will explore more paths as it cannot tell whether a variable is not well-resourced until closing a binder; additive pruning and subtractive will explore fewer paths as they can fail sooner.
3. A corollary of the above two: simple examples will likely be faster in additive mode, but more complex examples will be faster in subtractive mode.

Methodology. We implemented our approach as a synthesis tool for Granule, integrated with its core tool. Granule features ML-style polymorphism (rank-0 quantification) but we do not address polymorphism here. Instead, programs are synthesised from type schemes treating universal type variables as logical atoms. We discuss additional details of the implementation at the end of this section.

To evaluate our synthesis tool we developed a suite of benchmarks comprising Granule type schemes for a variety of operations using linear and graded modal types. We divide our benchmarks into several classes of problem:

- **Hilbert**: the Hilbert-style axioms of intuitionistic logic (including SKI combinators), with appropriate $\mathbb{N}$ and $\mathbb{N}$-interval grades where needed (see, e.g., S combinator in Example 1 or coproduct elimination in Example 2).
- **Comp**: various translations of function composition into linear logic: multiplicative, call-by-value and call-by-name using ! [17], I/O using ! [28], and coKleisli composition over $\mathbb{N}$ and arbitrary semirings: e.g. $\forall r, s \in \mathcal{R}$:

$$comp\text{-}coK_{\mathcal{R}} : \Box_r(\Box_s A \multimap B) \multimap (\Box_r B \multimap C) \multimap \Box_{r*s} A \multimap C$$

- **Dist**: distributive laws of various graded modalities over functions, sums, and products [23], e.g., $\forall r \in \mathbb{N}$, or $\forall r \in \mathcal{R}$ in any semiring, or $r = [0...\infty]$:

$$pull_{\oplus} : (\Box_r A \oplus \Box_r B) \multimap \Box_r(A \oplus B) \qquad push_{\multimap} : \Box_r(A \multimap B) \multimap \Box_r A \multimap \Box_r B$$

- **Vec**: map operations on vectors of fixed size encoded as products, e.g.:

$$vmap_5 : \Box_5(A \multimap B) \multimap ((((A \otimes A) \otimes A) \otimes A) \otimes A) \multimap ((((B \otimes B) \otimes B) \otimes B) \otimes B)$$

- **Misc**: includes Example 3 (information-flow security) and functions which must share or split resources between graded modalities, e.g.:

$$share : \Box_4 A \multimap \Box_6 A \multimap \Box_2(((((A \otimes A) \otimes A) \otimes A) \otimes A) \multimap B) \multimap (B \otimes B)$$

The appendix [22] lists the type schemes for these synthesis problems (32 in total). We found that Z3 is highly variable in its solving time, so timing measurements are computed as the mean of 20 trials. We used Z3 version 4.8.8 on a Linux laptop with an Intel i7-8665u @ 4.8 Ghz and 16 Gb of RAM.

Table 1. Results. μT in *ms* to 2 d.p. with standard sample error in brackets

	Problem		Additive μT (ms)	N		Additive (pruning) μT (ms)	N		Subtractive μT (ms)	N
Hilbert	⊗Intro	✓	0.09 (0.00)	0	✓	0.06 (0.01)	0	✓	0.05 (0.00)	0
	⊗Elim	✓	6.23 (0.07)	2	✓	15.05 (0.96)	2	✓	14.27 (0.62)	2
	⊕Intro	✓	0.10 (0.00)	0	✓	0.11 (0.00)	0	✓	0.13 (0.00)	0
	⊕Elim	✓	6.32 (0.22)	2	✓	7.89 (0.26)	2	✓	198.58 (7.01)	15
	SKI	✓	6.38 (0.06)	2	✓	29.39 (0.96)	2	✓	50.59 (5.63)	3
Comp	0/1	✓	32.48 (2.94)	5	✓	41.07 (0.39)	5	×	Timeout	-
	CBN	✓	11.42 (0.35)	3	✓	21.97 (0.60)	3	×	Timeout	-
	CBV	✓	14.57 (0.27)	5	✓	18.60 (0.73)	5	×	Timeout	-
	∘$coK_\mathbb{R}$	✓	21.43 (0.50)	2	✓	25.22 (1.72)	2	×	95.51 (0.94)	8
	∘$coK_\mathbb{N}$	✓	26.04 (1.14)	2	✓	23.70 (1.49)	2	×	101.58 (2.86)	8
	mult	✓	0.14 (0.01)	0	✓	0.13 (0.00)	0	✓	0.15 (0.00)	0
Dist	⊗-!	✓	7.50 (0.21)	2	✓	46.48 (2.68)	2	✓	10482.40 (3.36)	7
	⊕-N	✓	26.43 (0.75)	2	✓	38.33 (2.46)	2	×	15.87 (0.60)	1
	⊗-N	✓	28.18 (0.52)	2	×	35.64 (0.15)	2	×	31.43 (1.21)	2
	⊕-!	✓	11.41 (0.48)	2	✓	13.22 (0.08)	2	✓	165.86 (4.30)	4
	⊗-$\mathcal{R}$	✓	19.35 (0.18)	2	×	23.47 (0.64)	2	×	28.44 (0.80)	2
	⊕-$\mathcal{R}$	✓	20.39 (0.32)	2	✓	23.05 (0.66)	2	×	13.88 (0.16)	1
	⊸-!	✓	10.48 (0.59)	2	✓	12.09 (0.09)	2	✓	344.01 (7.05)	4
	⊸-N	✓	29.22 (1.69)	2	✓	22.02 (0.78)	2	×	64.04 (1.40)	4
	⊸-$\mathcal{R}$	✓	20.20 (0.29)	2	✓	26.75 (0.78)	2	×	54.20 (2.22)	4
Vec	vec5	✓	5.29 (0.14)	1	✓	24.02 (0.81)	1	✓	91.15 (5.07)	6
	vec10	✓	5.46 (0.10)	1	✓	23.74 (3.49)	1	✓	118.95 (1.72)	11
	vec15	✓	9.12 (0.14)	1	✓	23.07 (0.35)	1	✓	181.05 (2.78)	16
	vec20	✓	12.45 (0.05)	1	✓	28.95 (0.10)	1	✓	264.21 (13.54)	21
Misc	split⊕	✓	3.21 (0.05)	1	✓	3.53 (0.10)	1	✓	10715.66 (3.05)	6
	split⊗	✓	9.23 (0.05)	3	✓	43.55 (0.26)	3	×	Timeout	-
	share	✓	268.95 (21.06)	44	✓	112.03 (8.13)	6	✓	190.07 (3.68)	17
	Exm. 3	✓	5.83 (0.14)	2	✓	33.78 (0.79)	2	✓	287.57 (1.56)	3

Results and Analysis. For each synthesis problem, we recorded whether synthesis was successful or not (denoted ✓ or ×), the mean total synthesis time (μT), the mean total time spent by the SMT solver (μSMT), and the number of calls made to the SMT solver (N). Table 1 summarises the results with the fastest case for each benchmark highlighted. For all benchmarks that used the SMT solver, the solver accounted for 91.73%–99.98% of synthesis time, so we report only the mean total synthesis time μT. We set a timeout of 120 s.

Additive vs. Subtractive. As expected, the additive approach generally synthesises programs faster than the subtractive. Our first hypothesis (that the additive approach in general makes fewer calls to the SMT solver) holds for almost all benchmarks, with the subtractive approach often far exceeding the number made by the additive. This is explained by the difference in graded variable synthesis between approaches. In the additive, a constant grade 1 is given for graded assumptions in the output context, whereas in the subtractive, a fresh grade variable is created with a constraint on its usage which is checked immediately. As the total synthesis time is almost entirely spent in the SMT solver (more than 90%), solving constraints is by far the most costly part of synthesis leading to the additive approach synthesising most examples in a shorter amount of time.

Graded variable synthesis in the subtractive case also results in several examples failing to synthesise. In some cases, e.g., the first three *comp* benchmarks, the subtractive approach times-out as synthesis diverges with constraints growing in size due to the maximality condition and absorbing behaviour of $[0...\infty]$ interval. In the case of *coK-R* and *coK-N*, the generated constraints have the form $\forall r.\exists s.r \sqsupseteq s+1$ which is not valid $\forall r \in \mathbb{N}$ (e.g., when $r = 0$), which suggests that the subtractive approach does not work well for polymorphic grades. As further work, we are considering an alternate rule for synthesising promotion with constraints of the form $\exists s.s = s' * r$, i.e., a multiplicative inverse constraint.

In more complex examples we see evidence to support our second hypothesis. The *share* problem requires a lot of graded variable synthesis which is problematic for the additive approach, for the reasons described in the second hypothesis. In contrast, the subtractive approach performs better, with $\mu T = 190.07$ ms as opposed to additive's 268.95 ms. However, additive pruning outperforms both.

Additive Pruning. The pruning variant of additive synthesis (where subtraction takes place in the premises of multiplicative rules) had mixed results compared to the default. In simpler examples, the overhead of pruning (requiring SMT solving) outweighs the benefits obtained from reducing the space. However, in more complex examples which involve synthesising many graded variables (e.g. *share*), pruning is especially powerful, performing better than the subtractive approach. However, additive pruning failed to synthesis two examples which are polymorphic in their grade ($\otimes$-N) and in the semiring/graded-modality ($\otimes$-R).

Overall, the additive approach outperforms the subtractive and is successful at synthesising more examples, including ones polymorphic in grades and even the semiring itself. Given that the literature on linear logic theorem proving is typically subtractive, this is an interesting result. Going forward, a mixed approach between additive and additive pruning may be possible, selecting the algorithm, or even the rules, depending on the class of problem. Exploring this, and further optimisations and improvements, is further work.

Additional Implementation Details. Constraints on resource usage are handled via Granule's existing symbolic engine, which compiles constraints on grades (for various semirings) to the SMT-lib format for Z3 [30]. We use the LogicT monad for backtracking search [26] and the Scrap Your Reprinter library for splicing synthesised code into syntactic "holes", preserving the rest of the program text [10]. The implementation of the rule for additive dereliction (DER^+) requires some care. A naïve implementation of this rule would allow the construction of an infinite chain of dereliction applications, by repeatedly applying the rule to the same graded assumption, as the correct usage of the assumption's grade is only verified after it has been used to synthesise a sub-term. Our solution is to simply disallow immediate consecutive applications of the dereliction rule in additive synthesis, requiring that another rule be applied between multiple applications of the dereliction rule to any assumption. If no other rules can be applied, then the branch of synthesis is terminated.

5 Discussion

Further Related Work. Before Hodas and Miller [20], the problem of resource non-determinism was first identified by Harland and Pym [19]. Their solution delays splitting of contexts at a multiplicative connective. They later explored the implementation details of this approach, proposing a solution where proof search is formulated in terms of constraints on propositions. The logic programming language Lygon [1] implements this approach.

Our approach to synthesis implements a *backward* style of proof search: starting from the goal, recursively search for solutions to subgoals. In contrast to this, *forward* reasoning approaches attempt to reach the goal by building subgoals from previously proved subgoals until the overall goal is proved. Pfenning and Chaudhuri consider forward approaches to proof search in linear logic using the *inverse method* [11] where the issue of resource non-determinism that is typical to backward approaches is absent [8,9].

Non-idempotent intersection types systems have a similar core structure resembling the linear λ-calculus with quantitative aspects akin to grading [6]. It therefore seems likely that the approaches of this paper could be applied in this setting and used, for example, as way to enhance or even improve existing work on the inhabitation problem for non-idempotent intersection types [5]: a synthesised term gives a proof of inhabitation. This is left as further work, including formalising the connection between non-idempotent intersections and grading.

Next Steps and Conclusions. Our synthesis algorithms are now part of the Granule toolchain with IDE support, allowing programmers to insert a "hole" in a term and, after executing a keyboard shortcut, Granule tries to synthesise the type of the hole, pretty-printing generated code and inserting it at the cursor.

There are various extensions which we are actively pursuing, including synthesis for arbitrary user-defined indexed data types (GADTs), polymorphism, and synthesis of recursive functions. We plan to study various optimisations to the approaches considered here, as well as reducing the overhead of starting the SMT solver each time by instead running an "online" SMT solving procedure. We also plan to evaluate the approach on the extended linear logical benchmarks of Olarte et al. [31]. Although our goal is to create a practical program synthesis tool for common programming tasks rather than a general purpose proof search tool, the approach here also has applications to automated theorem proving.

Acknowledgements. Thanks to Benjamin Moon, Harley Eades III, participants at LOPSTR 2020, and the anonymous reviewers for their helpful comments. This work is supported by an EPSRC Doctoral Training Award and EPSRC grant EP/T013516/1 (*Verifying Resource-like Data Use in Programs via Types*).

References

1. Logic programming with linear logic. http://www.cs.rmit.edu.au/lygon/, Accessed 19 June 2020
2. Allais, G.: Typing with leftovers-a mechanization of intuitionistic multiplicative-additive linear logic. In: 23rd International Conference on Types for Proofs and Programs (TYPES 2017). Schloss Dagstuhl-Leibniz-Zentrum fuer Informatik (2018)
3. Andreoli, J.M.: Logic programming with focusing proofs in linear logic. J. Logic Comput. **2**(3), 297–347 (1992). https://doi.org/10.1093/logcom/2.3.297
4. Brunel, A., Gaboardi, M., Mazza, D., Zdancewic, S.: A core quantitative coeffect calculus. In: Shao, Z. (ed.) ESOP 2014. LNCS, vol. 8410, pp. 351–370. Springer, Heidelberg (2014). https://doi.org/10.1007/978-3-642-54833-8_19
5. Bucciarelli, A., Kesner, D., Rocca, S.R.D.: Inhabitation for non-idempotent intersection types. Log. Methods Comput. Sci. **14**(3) (2018). https://doi.org/10.23638/LMCS-14(3:7)2018
6. Bucciarelli, A., Kesner, D., Ventura, D.: Non-idempotent intersection types for the lambda-calculus. Log. J. IGPL **25**(4), 431–464 (2017). https://doi.org/10.1093/jigpal/jzx018
7. Cervesato, I., Hodas, J.S., Pfenning, F.: Efficient resource management for linear logic proof search. Theor. Comput. Sci. **232**(1), 133–163 (2000). https://doi.org/10.1016/S0304-3975(99)00173-5
8. Chaudhuri, K., Pfenning, F.: A focusing inverse method theorem prover for first-order linear logic. In: Nieuwenhuis, R. (ed.) CADE 2005. LNCS (LNAI), vol. 3632, pp. 69–83. Springer, Heidelberg (2005). https://doi.org/10.1007/11532231_6
9. Chaudhuri, K., Pfenning, F.: Focusing the inverse method for linear logic. In: Ong, L. (ed.) CSL 2005. LNCS, vol. 3634, pp. 200–215. Springer, Heidelberg (2005). https://doi.org/10.1007/11538363_15
10. Clarke, H., Liepelt, V.B., Orchard, D.: Scrap your Reprinter (2017). unpublished manuscript
11. Degtyarev, A., Voronkov, A.: Chapter 4 - the inverse method. In: Robinson, A., Voronkov, A. (eds.) Handbook of Automated Reasoning, North-Holland, Amsterdam, pp. 179–272 (2001). https://doi.org/10.1016/B978-044450813-3/50006-0
12. Frankle, J., Osera, P.M., Walker, D., Zdancewic, S.: Example-directed synthesis: a type-theoretic interpretation. ACM SIGPLAN Not. **51**(1), 802–815 (2016)
13. Gaboardi, M., Haeberlen, A., Hsu, J., Narayan, A., Pierce, B.C.: Linear dependent types for differential privacy. SIGPLAN Not. **48**(1), 357–370 (2013). https://doi.org/10.1145/2480359.2429113
14. Gaboardi, M., Katsumata, S., Orchard, D.A., Breuvart, F., Uustalu, T.: Combining effects and coeffects via grading. In: Garrigue, J., Keller, G., Sumii, E. (eds.) Proceedings of the 21st ACM SIGPLAN International Conference on Functional Programming, ICFP 2016, Nara, Japan, 18–22 September 2016, pp. 476–489. ACM (2016). https://doi.org/10.1145/2951913.2951939
15. Gentzen, G.: Untersuchungen über das logische schließen. ii. Mathematische Zeitschrift **39**, 405–431 (1935)

16. Ghica, D.R., Smith, A.I.: Bounded linear types in a resource semiring. In: Shao, Z. (ed.) ESOP 2014. LNCS, vol. 8410, pp. 331–350. Springer, Heidelberg (2014). https://doi.org/10.1007/978-3-642-54833-8_18

17. Girard, J.Y.: Linear logic. Theor. Comput. Sci. **50**(1), 1–101 (1987). https://doi.org/10.1016/0304-3975(87)90045-4

18. Girard, J.Y., Scedrov, A., Scott, P.J.: Bounded linear logic: a modular approach to polynomial-time computability. Theor. Comput. Sci. **97**(1), 1–66 (1992)

19. Harland, J., Pym, D.J.: Resource-distribution via boolean constraints. CoRR cs.LO/0012018 (2000). https://arxiv.org/abs/cs/0012018

20. Hodas, J., Miller, D.: Logic programming in a fragment of intuitionistic linear logic. Inf. Comput. **110**(2), 327–365 (1994). https://doi.org/10.1006/inco.1994.1036

21. Howard, W.A.: The formulae-as-types notion of construction. In: Seldin, J.P., Hindley, J.R. (eds.) To H.B. Curry: Essays on Combinatory Logic, Lambda Calculus and Formalism. Academic Press (1980)

22. Hughes, J., Orchard, D.: Resourceful program synthesis from graded linear types (Appendix) (2020). https://doi.org/10.5281/zenodo.4314644

23. Hughes, J., Vollmer, M., Orchard, D.: Deriving distributive laws for graded linear types (2020), unpublished manuscript

24. Katsumata, S.: Parametric effect monads and semantics of effect systems. In: Jagannathan, S., Sewell, P. (eds.) The 41st Annual ACM SIGPLAN-SIGACT Symposium on Principles of Programming Languages, POPL '14, San Diego, CA, USA, 20–21 January 2014, pp. 633–646. ACM (2014). https://doi.org/10.1145/2535838.2535846

25. Katsumata, S.: A double category theoretic analysis of graded linear exponential comonads. In: Baier, C., Dal Lago, U. (eds.) FoSSaCS 2018. LNCS, vol. 10803, pp. 110–127. Springer, Cham (2018). https://doi.org/10.1007/978-3-319-89366-2_6

26. Kiselyov, O., Shan, C.c., Friedman, D.P., Sabry, A.: Backtracking, interleaving, and terminating monad transformers: (functional pearl). SIGPLAN Not. **40**(9), 192–203 (2005). https://doi.org/10.1145/1090189.1086390

27. Knoth, T., Wang, D., Polikarpova, N., Hoffmann, J.: Resource-Guided Program Synthesis. CoRR abs/1904.07415 (2019). http://arxiv.org/abs/1904.07415

28. Liang, C., Miller, D.: Focusing and polarization in linear, intuitionistic, and classical logics. Theor. Comput. Sci. **410**(46), 4747–4768 (2009)

29. Manna, Z., Waldinger, R.: A deductive approach to program synthesis. ACM Trans. Program. Lang. Syst. (TOPLAS) **2**(1), 90–121 (1980)

30. de Moura, L., Bjørner, N.: Z3: an efficient SMT solver. In: Ramakrishnan, C.R., Rehof, J. (eds.) TACAS 2008. LNCS, vol. 4963, pp. 337–340. Springer, Heidelberg (2008). https://doi.org/10.1007/978-3-540-78800-3_24

31. Olarte, C., de Paiva, V., Pimentel, E., Reis, G.: The ILLTP library for intuitionistic linear logic. In: Ehrhard, T., Fernández, M., de Paiva, V., de Falco, L.T. (eds.) Proceedings Joint International Workshop on Linearity & Trends in Linear Logic and Applications, Linearity-TLLA@FLoC 2018, Oxford, UK, 7–8 July 2018. EPTCS, vol. 292, pp. 118–132 (2018). https://doi.org/10.4204/EPTCS.292.7

32. Orchard, D., Liepelt, V., Eades III, H.E.: Quantitative program reasoning with graded modal types. PACMPL **3**(ICFP), 110:1–110:30 (2019). https://doi.org/10.1145/3341714

33. Osera, P.M., Zdancewic, S.: Type-and-example-directed program synthesis. SIGPLAN Not. **50**(6), 619–630 (2015). https://doi.org/10.1145/2813885.2738007

34. Polikarpova, N., Solar-Lezama, A.: Program synthesis from Polymorphic Refinement Types. CoRR abs/1510.08419 (2015). http://arxiv.org/abs/1510.08419

35. Smith, C., Albarghouthi, A.: Synthesizing differentially private programs. Proc. ACM Program. Lang. **3**(ICFP) (2019). https://doi.org/10.1145/3341698
36. Zalakain, U., Dardha, O.: Pi with leftovers: a mechanisation in Agda. arXiv preprint arXiv:2005.05902 (2020)

Verification

Reasoning in the Theory of Heap: Satisfiability and Interpolation

Zafer Esen and Philipp Rümmer[✉]

Uppsala University, Uppsala, Sweden
philipp.ruemmer@it.uu.se

Abstract. In recent work, we have proposed an SMT-LIB theory of heap tailored to Horn-clause verification. The theory makes it possible to lift verification approaches for heap-allocated data-structures to a language-independent level, and this way factor out the treatment of heap in verification tools. This paper gives an overview of the theory, and presents ongoing research on decision and interpolation procedures.

1 Introduction

Tools for formal program verification are often engineered making use of various existing libraries and frameworks; for instance, compiler front-ends, constraint and SMT solvers, and more recently solvers for Constrained Horn Clauses (CHCs). This way, the effort required to construct verification systems can be reduced significantly, a wider range of languages or applications can be covered, and the quality and performance of the resulting tool is improved. In this paper, we consider the use of Constrained Horn Clauses, which represent an intermediate verification language tailored to the analysis of safety properties, and can be solved by CHC solvers such as Spacer [20] or Eldarica [16]; for an overview see [3,28]. These solvers in turn utilise theorem provers or SMT solvers such as Z3 [23] or Princess [27] to reason about the constraints in CHCs.

A challenging feature of languages, in this context, are heap-allocated data-structures. Such data-structures are today either represented explicitly using the theory of arrays (e.g., [11,19]), or are transformed away with the help of invariants or refinement types (e.g., [4,17,22,26]). In [12], we motivate the alternative approach of introducing heap as a native theory supported by solvers, which turns CHCs into a standardised interchange format for programs with heap data-structures. Figure 1 shows the resulting verification flow: verification tools would take programs, for instance in C or Java, as input, and encode them in a uniform way as CHCs modulo the theory of heap. The encoding keeps heap operations like read, write, or allocation essentially intact, and it is up to CHC and SMT solvers to process those operations further. CHC solvers could, e.g., choose to encode heap as an array, or apply an invariant-based encoding.

In this paper, we present first steps of the development of native decision and interpolation procedures for the theory of heap, covering two main reasoning tasks needed to implement CHC solvers [3,29]. The described procedures are

© Springer Nature Switzerland AG 2021
M. Fernández (Ed.): LOPSTR 2020, LNCS 12561, pp. 173–191, 2021.
https://doi.org/10.1007/978-3-030-68446-4_9

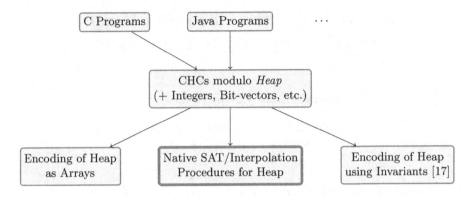

Fig. 1. Program verification using the theory of heap.

intended as a starting point and are currently largely unoptimised. We expect that many optimisations from array solvers (e.g., [7,9,14,30]) can be adapted.

1.1 Encoding Programs Using the Theory of Heap

In Listing 1.1, a C program is given in order to show the intuition behind the encoding, and provide an overview of the theory. The program has a single function insertNode that allocates and initialises a list Node (as defined in line 1), and appends it to the passed list pointed to by p.

One way to encode this program is using CHCs, and to consider the heap as a single shared mutable data-structure. A theory of heap provides *Heap* and *Addr* sorts, so *Heap* and *Addr* terms can be used in the CHCs just like any other term. A diagram illustrating the effect of the CHCs is given in Fig. 2. As an example, the statement at line 4 of Listing 1.1 can be encoded using the topmost constraint on the right-hand side of the diagram, which allocates a Node with uninitialised fields. A CHC can then be constructed using the invariants I_1 and I_2 that encode program state and the constraint C_1 that encodes the transition as $I_1(...) \land C_1 \rightarrow I_2(...)$, where the dots "..." represent the program variables in scope along with the heap term.

A complete CHC encoding of the program from Listing 1.1 is given in Listing 1.2. Lines 1–9 show the heap declaration in SMT-LIB format, where:

- *Heap* and *Addr* are the names of the declared heap and address sorts,
- *Object* at line 4 is the name of the *selected* object sort,
- *Node* and *Object* at line 6 are the declared data-types (ADTs),
- O_Empty is the default *Object* term that is returned on invalid reads.

Specifying a single object sort makes it possible to have a unified sort on the heap, and the flexibility of algebraic data-types (ADTs) simplifies encoding many programming language types. In this case *Object* has two constructors: (i) O_Node creates an *Object* with a *Node* field, (ii) O_Empty creates an *Object* with no fields that is used as the default *Object*. The object sort is said to be

Listing 1.1. A C function that adds a new node to the head of a linked list.

```
1  struct Node { int data; struct Node* next; };
2
3  void insertNode (int d, struct Node* p) {
4    struct Node* n = malloc(sizeof(struct Node));
5    n->data = d; n->next = p->next; p->next = n;
6  }
```

Listing 1.2. Complete encoding of the program from Listing 1.1. The heap declaration is given in SMT-LIB notation, while the clauses and the assertions are given in Prolog notation. ":-" corresponds to a left implication arrow (i.e., "←"), and it is assumed that all variables occurring in the clauses are universally quantified with the correct sort (i.e., $\forall h : Heap. \forall p : Addr. \ldots$).

```
1  (declare-heap
2   Heap                              ; declared Heap sort
3   Addr                              ; declared Address sort
4   Object                            ; chosen Object sort
5   O_Empty                           ; the default Object
6   ((Node 0) (Object 0))             ; ADTs
7   (((Node    (data Int) (next Addr))) ; Class constructors
8    ((O_Node (getNode Node))         ; Object sort constructors
9     (O_Empty))))
10                                     ; invariant declarations
11 (declare-fun I1 (Heap Int Addr)          Bool) ; <h,d,p>
12 (declare-fun I2 (Heap Int Addr Addr)     Bool) ; <h,d,p,n>
13 (declare-fun I3 (Heap Int Addr Addr)     Bool) ; <h,d,p,n>
14 (declare-fun I4 (Heap Int Addr Addr Addr) Bool) ; <h,d,p,n,t>
15 (declare-fun I5 (Heap Int Addr Addr)     Bool) ; <h,d,p,n>
16 (declare-fun I6 (Heap Int Addr)          Bool) ; <h,d,p>
17
18 ; Clauses (given in Prolog notation for readability)
19 I1(h,d,p)     :- h = _nonDet, is_O_Node(read(h,p)).
20 I2(h',d,p,n)  :- I1(h,d,p),
21                  h' = newHeap(alloc(h, O_Node(_nonDet))),
22                  n = newAddr(alloc(h, O_Node(_nonDet))).
23 I3(h',d,p,n)  :- I2(h,d,p,n), h'= write(h,n,
24                      O_Node(Node(d,next(getNode(read(h,n)))))).
25 I4(h,d,p,n,t) :- I3(h,d,p,n), t = next(getNode(read(h,p))).
26 I5(h',d,p,n)  :- I4(h,d,p,n,t), h'= write(h,n,
27                      O_Node(Node(data(getNode(read(h,n))),t))).
28 I6(h',d, p)   :- I5(h,d,p,n), h'= write(h,p,
29                      O_Node(Node(data(getNode(read(h,p))),n))).
30 ; Assertions
31 false :- I2(h,d,p,n),   !is_O_Node(read(h,n)).
32 false :- I3(h,d,p,n),   !is_O_Node(read(h,p)).
33 false :- I4(h,d,p,n,t), !is_O_Node(read(h,n)).
34 false :- I5(h,d,p,n),   !is_O_Node(read(h,p)).
```

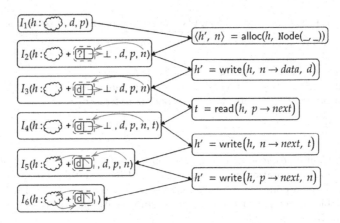

Fig. 2. The boxes on the left-hand side correspond to invariants encoding the state of a program at a certain point. E.g., I_1 is the entry point of insertNode, where the only relevant variables in scope are the arguments of the function, and the heap. The constraints on the right-hand side correspond to executing program statements. Black arrows visualise the execution of the program. h is the *Heap* term representing the heap. A h' term in the constraints is equal to the h term of the next invariant. An underscore represents a term that can have any value (of the correct sort within the context). t is a fresh *Addr* variable. A blue arrow visualises where a pointer is pointing to, and a red-dashed line symbolises an *Object*. (Color figure online)

selected, because it could also be declared outside the heap declaration and only specified here. This is not possible in this example as *Node* has a field with sort *Addr* (line 7), and *Addr* only becomes available with the heap declaration.

Lines 11–16 declare the invariants which are used in the CHCs. The rest of the encoding shows the CHCs in Prolog notation as explained in Fig. 2. The CHC in line 19 corresponds to program entry. The body of the clause at line 19 encodes the assumption that the contents of the heap are unknown at entry, but that there is a pre-condition specifying that p points to a valid location storing a Node object.

The assertions at lines 31–34 check the validity and type safety of heap accesses. These make use of testers that come with ADTs. For instance, the assertions at lines 32 and 34 would fail if it is not asserted at line 19 that p is pointing to a valid location containing a Node.

2   Preliminaries

2.1   The Theory of Heap

Signature. Functions and predicates of the theory are given in Table 1.

nullAddr returns an *Addr* which is unallocated (or invalid) in all heaps.
emptyHeap returns the *Heap* that is unallocated everywhere.

Table 1. Functions and predicates of the theory of heap.

nullAddr : ()	$\rightarrow$ *Addr*
emptyHeap : ()	$\rightarrow$ *Heap*
allocate : *Heap* $\times$ *Object*	$\rightarrow$ *Heap* $\times$ *Addr* (*AllocationResultHeap*)
valid : *Heap* $\times$ *Addr*	$\rightarrow$ *Boolean*
read : *Heap* $\times$ *Addr*	$\rightarrow$ *Object*
write : *Heap* $\times$ *Addr* $\times$ *Object*	$\rightarrow$ *Heap*

Table 2. Interpretation of sorts, functions, and predicates in the theory of heap. The symbol $+\!\!\!+$ denotes concatenation of two sequences.

$$I(\textit{Heap}) = I(\textit{Object})^*$$
$$I(\textit{Addr}) = \mathbb{N}$$

$$I(\mathsf{nullAddr}) = 0$$
$$I(\mathsf{emptyHeap}) = \epsilon$$
$$I(\mathsf{read})(h, a) = \begin{cases} h[a-1] & \text{if } 0 < a \le |h|, \\ defObj & \text{otherwise.} \end{cases}$$
$$I(\mathsf{write})(h, a, o) = \begin{cases} h[a-1 \mapsto o] & \text{if } 0 < a \le |h|, \\ h & \text{otherwise.} \end{cases}$$
$$I(\mathsf{allocate})(h, o) = \langle h +\!\!\!+ [o], |h| + 1 \rangle$$
$$I(\mathsf{valid})(h, a) = 0 < a \le |h|$$

allocate   takes a *Heap* and an *Object*, and returns an *AllocationResultHeap*.
AllocationResultHeap is an ADT representing the pair $\langle \textit{Heap}, \textit{Addr} \rangle$. The returned *Heap* contains the passed *Object* at the returned *Addr*.

valid   is the predicate checking if the passed *Addr* is allocated in the passed *Heap*. If it is allocated then we say that an access is *valid*; it is *invalid* otherwise.

read   returns the *Object* at the passed *Addr* of the passed *Heap* on a valid access. If the access is invalid, then the specified default *Object* is returned instead (line 5 in Listing 1.2).

write, if the access is valid, returns a heap where the passed *Addr* of the passed *Heap* is updated with the passed *Object*, with all other locations unchanged. If the access is invalid, the passed heap is returned without any changes.

Semantics. A many-sorted signature can be defined as the triple $L = \langle S, \Sigma_f, \Sigma_p \rangle$ where S is a set of sorts, Σ_f is a set of function symbols and Σ_p is a set of relation symbols. A structure is a pair $\langle D, I \rangle$ where D is the domain (consisting of disjoint subsets for each sort in S), and I is an interpretation function that associates each $f \in \Sigma_f$ and $p \in \Sigma_p$ to some n-ary function or relation. Arguments of both f and p and the values of f are specified using the sorts in S.

The heap is interpreted as an ordered sequence of zero or more heap objects. The sort *Object* can in principle be any selected sort, but will in most cases be an ADT, and be interpreted as the set of constructor terms of the ADT. Addresses (*Addr*) are interpreted as natural numbers. $h[k]$ denotes the $(k + 1)$–th heap object, where $k \in \mathbb{N}$. Formal definitions are given in Table 2.

2.2   An Interpolating Sequent Calculus for First-Order Logic Modulo Integers

We formulate our decision procedure for heap formulas on top of a simple logic of Presburger arithmetic constraints combined with uninterpreted predicates, introduced in [27] and extended in [5,6] to support Craig interpolation. Since the logic does not support functions, the heap operators (and also ADTs) have to be encoded using relations, with explicit rules for functional consistency; this setting closely models the situation in SMT solvers, where uninterpreted functions are handled by a theory solver implementing congruence closure.

Let x range over an infinite set X of variables, p over a set P of uninterpreted predicates with fixed arity, and α over the set $\mathbb{Z}$ of integers. The syntax of terms and formulae is defined by the following grammar:

$$\phi ::= t = 0 \,\big|\, t \leq 0 \,\big|\, p(t, \ldots, t) \,\big|\, \phi \wedge \phi \,\big|\, \phi \vee \phi \,\big|\, \neg\phi \,\big|\, \forall x.\phi \,\big|\, \exists x.\phi$$
$$t ::= \alpha \,\big|\, x \,\big|\, \alpha t + \cdots + \alpha t$$

The symbol t denotes terms of linear arithmetic. Substitution of a term t for a variable x in ϕ is denoted by $[x/t]\phi$; we assume that variable capture is avoided by renaming bound variables as necessary. For simplicity, we sometimes write $s = t$ as a shorthand of $s - t = 0$, and the inequality $s \leq t$ for $s - t \leq 0$. The abbreviation *true* (*false*) stands for the equality $0 = 0$ ($1 = 0$), and the formula $\phi \rightarrow \psi$ abbreviates $\neg\phi \vee \psi$. Semantic notions such as structures, models, satisfiability, and validity are defined as is common (e.g., [13]), but we assume that evaluation always happens over the universe $\mathbb{Z}$ of integers.

A Sequent Calculus for the Base Logic. For checking whether a formula in the base logic is satisfiable or valid, we work with a simplified version of the calculus presented in [27], a part of which is shown in Table 3. If Γ, Δ are sets of formulae, then $\Gamma \vdash \Delta$ is a *sequent*. A sequent is *valid* if the formula $\bigwedge \Gamma \rightarrow \bigvee \Delta$ is valid. Proofs are trees growing upward, in which each node is labelled with a sequent, and each non-leaf node is related to the node(s) directly above it through an application of a calculus rule. A proof is *closed* if it is finite and all leaves are justified by an instance of a rule without premises. Soundness of the calculus implies that the root of a closed proof is a valid sequent.

In addition to propositional and quantifier rules in Table 3, the calculus in [27] also includes rules for equations and inequalities in Presburger arithmetic; the details of those rules are not relevant for this paper.

Table 3. A selection of the basic calculus rules for propositional and first-order logic. In the rules ∃-LEFT and ∀-RIGHT, x' is a variable that does not occur in the conclusion.

$$\frac{\Gamma, \phi \vdash \Delta \quad \Gamma, \psi \vdash \Delta}{\Gamma, \phi \vee \psi \vdash \Delta} \; \text{V-LEFT} \qquad \frac{\Gamma \vdash \phi, \Delta \quad \Gamma \vdash \psi, \Delta}{\Gamma \vdash \phi \wedge \psi, \Delta} \; \text{∧-RIGHT}$$

$$\frac{\Gamma, \phi, \psi \vdash \Delta}{\Gamma, \phi \wedge \psi \vdash \Delta} \; \text{∧-LEFT} \qquad \frac{\Gamma \vdash \phi, \psi, \Delta}{\Gamma \vdash \phi \vee \psi, \Delta} \; \text{V-RIGHT}$$

$$\frac{\Gamma \vdash \phi, \Delta}{\Gamma, \neg\phi \vdash \Delta} \; \text{¬-LEFT} \qquad \frac{\Gamma, \phi \vdash \Delta}{\Gamma \vdash \neg\phi, \Delta} \; \text{¬-RIGHT}$$

$$\frac{*}{\Gamma, \phi \vdash \phi, \Delta} \; \text{CLOSE}$$

$$\frac{\Gamma, [x/t]\phi, \forall x.\phi \vdash \Delta}{\Gamma, \forall x.\phi \vdash \Delta} \; \text{∀-LEFT} \qquad \frac{\Gamma, [x/x']\phi \vdash \Delta}{\Gamma, \exists x.\phi \vdash \Delta} \; \text{∃-LEFT}$$

$$\frac{\Gamma \vdash [x/t]\phi, \exists x.\phi, \Delta}{\Gamma \vdash \exists x.\phi, \Delta} \; \text{∃-RIGHT} \qquad \frac{\Gamma \vdash [x/x']\phi, \Delta}{\Gamma \vdash \forall x.\phi, \Delta} \; \text{∀-RIGHT}$$

Craig Interpolation in the Base Logic. Given formulas A and B such that $A \wedge B$ is unsatisfiable, Craig interpolation can determine a formula I such that the implications $A \Rightarrow I$ and $B \Rightarrow \neg I$ hold, and non-logical symbols in I occur in both A and B [10]. An interpolating version of our sequent calculus has been presented in [5,6], and is summarised in Table 4. To keep track of the partitions A, B, the calculus operates on labelled formulas $\lfloor \phi \rfloor_L$ (with L for "left") to indicate that ϕ is derived from A, and similarly formulas $\lfloor \phi \rfloor_R$ for ϕ derived from B. If Γ, Δ are finite sets of L/R-labelled formulas, and I is an unlabelled formula, then $\Gamma \vdash \Delta \blacktriangleright I$ is an *interpolating sequent*.

Semantics of interpolating sequents is defined using the projections $\Gamma_L =_{\text{def}} \{\phi \mid \lfloor \phi \rfloor_L \in \Gamma\}$ and $\Gamma_R =_{\text{def}} \{\phi \mid \lfloor \phi \rfloor_R \in \Gamma\}$, which extract the L/R-parts of a set Γ of labelled formulae. A sequent $\Gamma \vdash \Delta \blacktriangleright I$ is *valid* if (i) the sequent $\Gamma_L \vdash I, \Delta_L$ is valid, (ii) the sequent $\Gamma_R, I \vdash \Delta_R$ is valid, and (iii) the variables and uninterpreted predicates in I occur in both $\Gamma_L \cup \Delta_L$ and $\Gamma_R \cup \Delta_R$. As a special case, note that the sequent $\lfloor A \rfloor_L, \lfloor B \rfloor_R \vdash \emptyset \blacktriangleright I$ is valid iff I is an interpolant of $A \wedge B$. Soundness of the calculus guarantees that the root of a closed interpolating proof is a valid interpolating sequent.

To solve an interpolation problem $A \wedge B$, a prover typically first constructs a proof of $A, B \vdash \emptyset$ using the ordinary calculus from Table 3. Once a closed proof has been found, it can be lifted to an interpolating proof: this is done by replacing the root formulas A, B with $\lfloor A \rfloor_L, \lfloor B \rfloor_R$, respectively, and recursively assigning labels to all other formulas as defined by the rules from Table 4. Then, starting from the leaves, intermediate interpolants are computed and propagated back to the root, leading to an interpolating sequent $\lfloor A \rfloor_L, \lfloor B \rfloor_R \vdash \emptyset \blacktriangleright I$.

Table 4. A selection of interpolating rules for propositional and first-order logic. Parameter D stands for either L or R. The quantifier $\exists_{Lt}$ denotes existential quantification over all free variables occurring in t but not in $\Gamma_R \cup \Delta_R$. In $\exists$-LEFT$_D$ and $\forall$-RIGHT$_D$, x' is a fresh variable that does not occur in the conclusion.

$$\frac{\Gamma, \lfloor\phi\rfloor_L \vdash \Delta \blacktriangleright I \qquad \Gamma, \lfloor\psi\rfloor_L \vdash \Delta \blacktriangleright J}{\Gamma, \lfloor\phi \vee \psi\rfloor_L \vdash \Delta \blacktriangleright I \vee J} \ \vee\text{-LEFT}_L$$

$$\frac{\Gamma, \lfloor\phi\rfloor_R \vdash \Delta \blacktriangleright I \qquad \Gamma, \lfloor\psi\rfloor_R \vdash \Delta \blacktriangleright J}{\Gamma, \lfloor\phi \vee \psi\rfloor_R \vdash \Delta \blacktriangleright I \wedge J} \ \vee\text{-LEFT}_R$$

$$\frac{\Gamma, \lfloor\phi\rfloor_D, \lfloor\psi\rfloor_D \vdash \Delta \blacktriangleright I}{\Gamma, \lfloor\phi \wedge \psi\rfloor_D \vdash \Delta \blacktriangleright I} \ \wedge\text{-LEFT}_D \qquad\qquad \frac{\Gamma \vdash \lfloor\phi\rfloor_D, \Delta \blacktriangleright I}{\Gamma, \lfloor\neg\phi\rfloor_D \vdash \Delta \blacktriangleright I} \ \neg\text{-LEFT}_D$$

$$\frac{*}{\Gamma, \lfloor\phi\rfloor_L \vdash \lfloor\phi\rfloor_R, \Delta \blacktriangleright \phi} \ \text{CLOSE}_{LR} \qquad\qquad \frac{*}{\Gamma, \lfloor\phi\rfloor_R \vdash \lfloor\phi\rfloor_R, \Delta \blacktriangleright true} \ \text{CLOSE}_{RR}$$

$$\frac{\Gamma, \lfloor[x/t]\phi\rfloor_R, \lfloor\forall x.\phi\rfloor_R \vdash \Delta \blacktriangleright I}{\Gamma, \lfloor\forall x.\phi\rfloor_R \vdash \Delta \blacktriangleright \exists_{Lt} I} \ \forall\text{-LEFT}_R \qquad \frac{\Gamma, \lfloor[x/x']\phi\rfloor_D \vdash \Delta \blacktriangleright I}{\Gamma, \lfloor\exists x.\phi\rfloor_D \vdash \Delta \blacktriangleright I} \ \exists\text{-LEFT}_D$$

2.3 Reduction for the Theory of Algebraic Data-Types

The heap theory uses ADTs to represent the objects stored on a heap, which means that a decision procedure for heap formulas also has to handle ADTs. For this purpose, in principle any existing algorithm for ADT formulas can be used, e.g., [2,18,25,31]. In this paper, we make use of the reduction approach for ADT formulas defined in [15], which translates a quantifier-free ADT formula to an equisatisfiable formula in the combined theory of equality and uninterpreted functions (EUF) and linear integers (LIA). An EUF+LIA formula can be translated further to a formula in the base logic from the previous section, and this way also Craig interpolants can be computed for ADT formulas.

The details of [15] are not important for the present paper, and we only assume that a function *adtReduction* is available that maps quantifier-free ADT formulas to equisatisfiable formulas in the base language.

3   A Decision Procedure for the Theory of Heap

We now define our calculus and decision procedure for quantifier-free heap formulas. Similarly to the approach chosen in [1,15], the procedure consists of two components: a set of rewriting rules for translating heap formulas to a core language (Sect. 3.2, Table 5), and a set of sequent calculus rules for handling the core language (Sect. 3.3, Table 6).

3.1 The Core Language for Heap Formulas

Our core language for heap constraints is defined on top of first-order logic modulo integers, as introduced in Sect. 2.2. Like in [1,15], in the core language

Table 5. Rewriting rules for translation of flat heap formulas to the core language. The rules only apply in positive positions. In the rules, a is an address variable, h, h' are heap variables, and o, o' are heap object variables.

$$\mathsf{nullAddr} = a \;\;\rightarrowtail\;\; 0 = a$$

$$\mathsf{emptyHeap} = h \;\;\rightarrowtail\;\; heapSize(h, 0)$$

$$\mathsf{allocate}(h, o).\_1 = h' \;\;\rightarrowtail\;\; \begin{aligned} &allocHeap(h, o, h') \wedge \\ &\exists x.(heapSize(h, x - 1) \wedge heapSize(h', x) \wedge read(h', x, o)) \end{aligned}$$

$$\mathsf{allocate}(h, o).\_2 = a \;\;\rightarrowtail\;\; heapSize(h, a - 1)$$

$$\mathsf{read}(h, a) = o \;\;\rightarrowtail\;\; \begin{aligned} &read(h, a, o) \wedge \\ &\exists x.(heapSize(h, x) \wedge ((0 < a \wedge a \leq x) \vee defObj = o))) \end{aligned}$$

$$\mathsf{write}(h, a, o) = h' \;\;\rightarrowtail\;\; \begin{aligned} &write(h, a, o, h') \wedge \\ &\exists x.(heapSize(h, x) \wedge heapSize(h', x) \wedge \\ &\quad (0 \geq a \vee a > x \vee (0 < a \wedge a \leq x \wedge read(h', a, o)))) \end{aligned}$$

$$\mathsf{valid}(h, a) \;\;\rightarrowtail\;\; \exists x.(heapSize(h, x) \wedge 0 < a \wedge a \leq x)$$

$$\neg\mathsf{valid}(h, a) \;\;\rightarrowtail\;\; \exists x.(heapSize(h, x) \wedge (0 \geq a \vee a > x))$$

$$h \neq h' \;\;\rightarrowtail\;\; \begin{pmatrix} \exists x, x', a, o, o'. \\ \left(\begin{aligned} &heapSize(h, x) \wedge heapSize(h', x') \wedge \\ &(x \neq x' \vee \\ &\;\;(x = x' \wedge 0 < a \wedge a \leq x \wedge \\ &\;\;\;\; read(h, a, o) \wedge read(h', a, o') \wedge o \neq o')) \end{aligned} \right) \end{pmatrix}$$

Table 6. Sequent calculus rules for heap formulas in the core language. The rules are only applicable if the equation in the first premise follows from equations between heap variables in Γ; i.e., the compared terms are in the same equivalence class constructed by congruence closure. The dots "..." stand for the matched literals in the conclusion.

$$\frac{\Gamma \vdash h_1 = h_2, \Delta \qquad \Gamma, \ldots, t = t' \vdash \Delta}{\Gamma, heapSize(h_1, t), heapSize(h_2, t') \vdash \Delta} \;\; \text{HEAP-SIZE-FC}$$

$$\frac{\Gamma \vdash h_1 = h_2, \Delta \qquad \Gamma, \ldots \vdash a = a', \Delta \qquad \Gamma, \ldots, a = a', o = o' \vdash \Delta}{\Gamma, read(h_1, a, o), read(h_2, a', o') \vdash \Delta} \;\; \text{READ-FC}$$

$$\frac{\Gamma \vdash h_2 = h_3, \Delta \qquad \Gamma, \ldots, read(h_1, a', o') \vdash a = a', \Delta \qquad \Gamma, \ldots, a = a' \vdash \Delta}{\Gamma, write(h_1, a, o, h_2), read(h_3, a', o') \vdash \Delta} \;\; \text{ROW}^{\downarrow}$$

$$\frac{\Gamma \vdash h_1 = h_3, \Delta \qquad \Gamma, \ldots, read(h_2, a', o') \vdash a = a', \Delta \qquad \Gamma, \ldots, a = a' \vdash \Delta}{\Gamma, write(h_1, a, o, h_2), read(h_3, a', o') \vdash \Delta} \;\; \text{ROW}^{\uparrow}$$

$$\frac{\Gamma \vdash h_2 = h_3, \Delta \qquad \Gamma, \ldots, read(h_1, a', o') \vdash a = a', \Delta \qquad \Gamma, \ldots, a = a' \vdash \Delta}{\Gamma, allocHeap(h_1, o, h_2), heapSize(h_2, a), read(h_3, a', o') \vdash \Delta} \;\; \text{ROA}^{\downarrow}$$

$$\frac{\Gamma \vdash h_1 = h_3, \Delta \qquad \Gamma, \ldots, read(h_2, a', o') \vdash a = a', \Delta \qquad \Gamma, \ldots, a = a' \vdash \Delta}{\Gamma, allocHeap(h_1, o, h_2), heapSize(h_2, a), read(h_3, a', o') \vdash \Delta} \;\; \text{ROA}^{\uparrow}$$

only integer terms are used, and the sorts *Heap* and *Addr* are both replaced with *Int*; in case of *Addr*, the range of values is restricted to non-negative numbers by adding inequalities for all address variables in a formula. The object sort *Object*, and all other ADT sorts, are mapped to integers as in [15].

Our core language provides four predicates specific for heap constraints: *heapSize*(h, n) expresses that heap h contains n allocated locations; predicate *allocHeap*(h, o, h') expresses that allocating a fresh address in heap h, and storing object o at this address, yields the new heap h'; *read*(h, a, o) expresses that reading from address a in heap h yields object o; and *write*(h, a, o, h') expresses that storing object o at address a in heap h yields the new heap h'.

The intended semantics of the four predicates essentially follows the heap semantics in Sect. 2.1, which in particular means that reading from unallocated addresses yields some default value *defObj*, and that writing to unallocated addresses does not change a heap. The null address is, following the standard convention, represented by 0, and the address allocated by *allocHeap*(h, a, o, h') is the next free address in h, and coincides with the size of the heap h'.

In addition to the four heap predicates, the core language also provides the predicates necessary to represent ADTs; the details of this reduction are given in [15], and our calculus is essentially agnostic of the object representation.

3.2   Translation to the Core Language

For sake of presentation, we make several simplifying assumptions when defining the translation of (quantifier-free) heap formulas ϕ to the core language. (i) We assume that ϕ has been brought into a *flat* form upfront. A formula ϕ is flat if function symbols (in particular the functions in Table 1) only occur in equations of the form $g(x_1, \ldots, x_n) = x_0$ (where $x_0, \ldots, x_n$ do not contain functions), and only in positive positions (under an even number of negations). We further assume that (ii) ϕ is in negation normal form, and that (iii) allocate only occurs in the form allocate$(\ldots)._1$ or allocate$(\ldots)._2$, i.e., the result of allocation is directly projected to the new heap or the allocated address. Finally, we assume that (iv) the object domain *Object* is infinite, so that the mapping to *Int* defined in [15] does not introduce any side conditions. The assumptions (i)–(iii) can be established by rewriting the considered heap formula. Flatness can be established at the cost of introducing a linear number of additional variables.

Given a formula ϕ satisfying those assumptions, and containing variables $x_1, \ldots, x_l$ with sorts $\sigma_1, \ldots, \sigma_l$, the translation to a formula $\tilde{\phi}$ in the core language is then defined as follows:

$$\tilde{\phi} \ =_{\text{def}} \ \text{adtReduction}\left(\text{heapRewr}(\phi) \land \bigwedge_{i=1}^{l} In_{\sigma_i}(x_i) \right) \tag{1}$$

In this definition, *heapRewr* is the function defined by the rewriting rules in Table 5, *adtReduction* is the ADT reduction defined in [15], and $In_\sigma(x)$ are domain constraints defined as $In_\sigma(x) = x \geq 0$, if x has sort *Addr*, and $In_\sigma(x) = true$ otherwise. Note that, as a slight abuse of notation, the formulas ϕ and $\tilde{\phi}$

contain the same variables $x_1, \ldots, x_l$, we only interpret the variables in $\tilde{\phi}$ as integer variables.

Example 1. Consider the following formula $\phi = A \wedge B$, which is unsatisfiable in the theory of heap storing integers as heap objects:

$$\underbrace{\mathsf{valid}(h, a) \wedge \mathsf{write}(h, a, 42) = h'}_{A} \wedge \underbrace{\mathsf{read}(h', a) = 43}_{B}$$

The formula contains a write that stores 42 at a valid address of h, so that read from the same address of the updated heap h' must return 42. If the rewriting rules are applied to ϕ using the definition from (1), we obtain the following formula $\tilde{\phi}$ in the core language; *adtReduction* has no effect as there are no ADT functions nor predicates:

$$
a \geq 0 \wedge \exists x.(heapSize(h, x) \wedge 0 < a \wedge a \leq x) \wedge
$$
$$
\begin{pmatrix} write(h, a, 42, h') \wedge \exists x.(heapSize(h, x) \wedge heapSize(h', x) \wedge \\ (0 \geq a \vee a > x \vee (0 < a \wedge a \leq x \wedge read(h', a, 42)))) \end{pmatrix} \wedge \qquad (2)
$$
$$
\big(read(h', a, 43) \wedge \exists x.(heapSize(h', x) \wedge ((0 < a \wedge a \leq x) \vee defObj = 43)))) \big)
$$

3.3   The Sequent Calculus for the Core Language

Table 6 shows the additional calculus rules (beyond the rules discussed in Sect. 2.2) needed to reason about heap formulas in the core language: two rules establishing *functional consistency* of the relations *heapSize* and *read*, two rules capturing the *read-over-write* (row) axiom of heaps, and two rules capturing the *read-over-allocation* (roa) axiom. All of the rules have a first premise that asserts the equality of multiple heap terms; such equalities are handled explicitly since the calculus never rewrites predicate literals.

Functional consistency is not needed for the relations *write* and *allocHeap*, since the read-over-write and read-over-allocation rules are sufficient to reason about the heaps produced by those relations. We do not need rules encoding extensionality of heap either, since the only way to observe heap (dis-)equality is through negated equations $h \neq h'$, which are already transformed away by the last rewriting rule in Table 5.

The ROW$^\downarrow$ and ROW$^\uparrow$ rules can be used to move a *read* literal over a *write* literal, provided that the address a' that is read from is different from the address a written to. The second premise of the rules represents the case that $a \neq a'$, and introduces a new *read* literal; the third premise represents the $a = a'$ case. Interestingly, it is not necessary to check whether the addresses a, a' are valid in the considered heaps, since writing to an invalid address does not mutate a heap.

The rules ROA$^\downarrow$ and ROA$^\uparrow$ describe the same transformation for the combination of a *read* with an *allocHeap* literal.

Example 2. We continue Example 1, and show how to construct a proof tree for (2). For sake of presentation, we first simplify (2) by introducing Skolem symbols for the quantified variables, and contextual simplification, leading to:

$$
\left.
\begin{aligned}
&heapSize(h,n) \wedge heapSize(h',n) \wedge 0 < a \wedge a \le n \wedge \\
&write(h,a,42,h') \wedge read(h',a,42) \wedge
\end{aligned}
\right\} A'
$$

$$
\left.
read(h',a,43) \wedge heapSize(h',n') \wedge ((0 < a \wedge a \le n') \vee defObj = 43)
\right\} B'
$$

We can then prove unsatisfiability of $A' \wedge B'$ by constructing a proof starting with the sequent $A', B' \vdash \emptyset$. The main step in the proof is the application of the rule READ-FC for functional consistency of $read$:

$$
\cfrac{
\cfrac{
\cfrac{*}{\ldots \vdash h' = h'} \quad
\cfrac{*}{\ldots \vdash a = a} \quad
\cfrac{*}{a = a, 42 = 43 \vdash}
}{read(h',a,42), read(h',a,43), \ldots \vdash} \text{READ-FC}
}{A', B' \vdash \emptyset} \wedge\text{-LEFT}^*
\qquad (3)
$$

3.4   Properties of the Calculus

The following theorem observes soundness and completeness of our calculus, when applied to a formula that has been rewritten to the core language. In addition, we can observe that systematic application of the rules terminates (in the sense that no new formulas can be added anymore) because the rules in Table 6 do not introduce new terms, and do not remove atoms, and therefore only finitely many atoms will be generated. This implies that the calculus even represents a decision procedure.

Theorem 1. *Suppose ϕ is a heap formula satisfying the assumptions in Sect. 3.2, and $\tilde{\phi}$ is the corresponding formula in the core language. Then ϕ is unsatisfiable if and only if a closed proof of the sequent $\tilde{\phi} \vdash \emptyset$ exists.*

Proof. "$\Leftarrow$" This is the soundness direction. For a proof by contradiction, assume that ϕ is satisfiable, i.e., there is a variable assignment β satisfying ϕ in the structure defined in Sect. 2.1. There are then bijections $b_{obj} : I(Object) \to \mathbb{Z}$ and $b_{hp} : I(Heap) \to \mathbb{Z}$, and we can construct a solution $(\langle \mathbb{Z}, \tilde{I} \rangle, \tilde{\beta})$ of $\tilde{\phi}$:

$$
\tilde{I}(heapSize) = \{(n, |b_{hp}^{-1}(n)|) \mid n \in \mathbb{Z}\}
$$

$$
\tilde{I}(allocHeap) = \{(n, m, b_{hp}(b_{hp}^{-1}(n) + \!\!\!+\, [b_{obj}^{-1}(m)])) \mid n, m \in \mathbb{Z}\}
$$

$$
\tilde{I}(read) = \{(n, a, b_{obj}(b_{hp}^{-1}(n)[a-1])) \mid n \in \mathbb{Z} \text{ and } a \in \{1, \ldots, |b_{hp}^{-1}(n)|\}\} \cup
$$
$$
\{(n, a, b_{obj}(defObj)) \mid n \in \mathbb{Z} \text{ and } a \notin \{1, \ldots, |b_{hp}^{-1}(n)|\}\}
$$

$$
\tilde{I}(write) = \left\{
\begin{aligned}
&(n, a, o, b_{hp}(b_{hp}^{-1}(n)[a-1 \mapsto b_{obj}^{-1}(o)])) \\
&\quad \mid n, o \in \mathbb{Z} \text{ and } a \in \{1, \ldots, |b_{hp}^{-1}(n)|\}
\end{aligned}
\right\} \cup
$$
$$
\{(n, a, o, n) \mid n, o \in \mathbb{Z} \text{ and } a \notin \{1, \ldots, |b_{hp}^{-1}(n)|\}\}
$$

$$
\tilde{\beta}(x) = b_{obj}(\beta(x)) \text{ if } x : Object
$$

$$
\tilde{\beta}(x) = b_{hp}(\beta(x)) \text{ if } x : Heap
$$

$$
\tilde{\beta}(x) = \beta(x) \text{ if } x : Addr
$$

The translation of other variables and relations is as defined in [15].

By checking the cases in Table 5, we can see that $(\langle \mathbb{Z}, \tilde{I} \rangle, \tilde{\beta})$ is indeed a solution of $\tilde{\phi}$, and that the sequent $\tilde{\phi} \vdash$ is therefore counter-satisfiable. It can also be checked that the rules preserve this counter-model: whenever $(\langle \mathbb{Z}, \tilde{I} \rangle, \tilde{\beta})$ is a counter-model of the conclusion of a rule application, it will also be a counter-model of at least one of the premises. This means that no closed proof can exist.

"$\Rightarrow$" This is the completeness direction. Suppose ϕ is a formula so that no closed proof exists for the sequent $\tilde{\phi} \vdash \emptyset$; we show that ϕ is satisfiable. For this, assume that $\mathcal{P}$ is a proof-attempt for $\tilde{\phi} \vdash \emptyset$ with a branch that cannot be closed; that $\Gamma \vdash \Delta$ is the last sequent on that branch; and that the rules from Table 6 (and the rest of the calculus) have been applied exhaustively on the branch. Since systematic application of the rules terminates, only finitely many atoms with the predicates $P = \{heapSize, read, write, allocHeap\}$ can be generated.

We extract a solution of ϕ from $\Gamma \vdash \Delta$. First consider the sub-sequent $\Gamma' \vdash \Delta$ of $\Gamma \vdash \Delta$ that is obtained by removing the P-atoms from Γ; since the calculus from Sect. 2.2 has been applied exhaustively, a counter-model $(\langle \mathbb{Z}, I' \rangle, \beta')$ of $\Gamma' \vdash \Delta$ exists.

Heap variables h can only occur in equations $h = h'$ or as arguments of P-atoms in Γ. Define an equivalence relation $h \simeq h'$ as the reflexive and transitive closure of equations between heap variables in Γ. We write $[h]$ for the class of variable h, and $R([h]) = \{(\mathrm{val}_{\beta'}(a), \mathrm{val}_{\beta'}(o)) \mid read(h', a, o) \in \Gamma, h' \simeq h\}$ for the reads in Γ from $[h]$. Since the rule READ-FC has been applied exhaustively, $R([h])$ will contain at most one value $\mathrm{val}_{\beta'}(o)$ for each address $\mathrm{val}_{\beta'}(a)$, i.e., the data read is consistent.

Whenever $R([h]) \neq \emptyset$, then Γ also contains an atom $heapSize(h', t)$ for some $h' \simeq h$, since the rules in Table 5 are designed in such a way that every $read$ is accompanied by $heapSize$, and $heapSize$-atoms also exist for the pre- and the post-heap of every $write$ and $allocHeap$. The rule HEAP-SIZE-FC ensures that the elements of $[h]$ are assigned consistent sizes, so that we can set

$$S([h]) = \begin{cases} \mathrm{val}_{\beta'}(t) & \text{if } heapSize(h', t) \in \Gamma \text{ for some } h' \simeq h \\ 0 & \text{otherwise .} \end{cases}$$

As shown in [15], from the counter-model $(\langle \mathbb{Z}, I' \rangle, \beta')$ it is possible to reconstruct ADT terms, and we can define a bijection $b_{\mathrm{obj}} : I(Object) \to \mathbb{Z}$ (where I is the interpretation defined in Sect. 2.1) such that whenever the $Object$-ADT-term t is extracted for $\mathrm{val}_{\beta'}(o)$, for some variable o of sort $Object$ in ϕ, then $b_{\mathrm{obj}}(t) = \mathrm{val}_{\beta'}(o)$. We can then define $H([h]) = [t_1, \ldots, t_{S([h])}]$ as the heap represented by $[h]$, with

$$t_i = \begin{cases} b_{\mathrm{obj}}^{-1}(v) & \text{if there is } (i, v) \in R([h]) \\ defObj & \text{otherwise.} \end{cases}$$

The solution of ϕ is the variable assignment β, defined by

$$
\beta(x) = \begin{cases}
H([x]) & \text{if } x : Heap \\
b_{\text{obj}}^{-1}(\text{val}_{\beta'}(x)) & \text{if } x : Object \\
\beta'(x) & \text{if } x : Addr \\
\beta(x) & \text{(as in [15] for other ADT variables)} .
\end{cases}
$$

To see that β indeed satisfies ϕ, translate β to a structure $(\langle \mathbb{Z}, \tilde{I} \rangle, \tilde{\beta})$ as in "$\Leftarrow$". Because the rules $\text{ROW}^\downarrow, \text{ROW}^\uparrow, \text{ROA}^\downarrow, \text{ROA}^\uparrow$ have been applied exhaustively, this structure is a counter-model of $\Gamma \vdash \Delta$. By checking the rules of the calculus individually, we can further see that whenever $(\langle \mathbb{Z}, \tilde{I} \rangle, \tilde{\beta})$ is a counter-model of one of the premises of a rule application, it is also a counter-model of the conclusion, and therefore a model of $\tilde{\phi}$. Lastly, analysing the rules in Table 5, we can see that then also β has to satisfy ϕ.   □

4   Craig Interpolation in the Theory of Heap

It is well-known that the (standard) quantifier-free theory of arrays does not admit Craig interpolation: in some cases all interpolants for an unsatisfiable, quantifier-free conjunction $A \wedge B$ will need quantifiers [21]. The same observation applies to the theory of heap. For software verification, however, even imperfect interpolation procedures are useful, and the interesting question arises how the interpolating calculus from Sect. 2.2 can be generalised to heap formulas.

For interpolation, the conjuncts of an interpolation problem $A \wedge B$ can be translated to the core language independently, i.e., an interpolant $\tilde{I}$ of the rewritten conjunction $\tilde{A} \wedge \tilde{B}$ is computed. Since $\tilde{I}$ will be an interpolant in the core language as well, it has to be mapped back to a normal heap formula I by replacing the relations from Sect. 3.1 with the original heap functions (Sect. 2.1). Whether this is possible in all cases is a question that require more research.

For interpolation in the core language, interpolating versions of the heap rules (Table 6) are needed. We follow the approach used in [1,5] (which in turn resembles the use of theory lemmas in SMT in general), which we summarise in this section. When translating a proof to an interpolating proof, we replace applications of the heap rules with instantiation of an equivalent theory axiom QAx. Suppose a non-interpolating proof contains a rule application

$$
\cfrac{\begin{array}{ccc} \vdots & & \vdots \\ \Gamma, \Gamma', \Gamma_1 \vdash \Delta_1, \Delta', \Delta & \cdots & \Gamma, \Gamma', \Gamma_n \vdash \Delta_n, \Delta', \Delta \end{array}}{\Gamma, \Gamma' \vdash \Delta', \Delta} \; R
$$

$$\vdots$$

in which Γ', Δ' are the formulas assumed by the rule application, Γ, Δ are side formulas not required or affected by the application, and $\Gamma_1, \Delta_1, \ldots, \Gamma_n, \Delta_n$ are newly introduced formulas in the individual branches.

The (unquantified) theory axiom Ax corresponding to the rule application expresses that the conjunction of the premises has to imply the conclusion;

the quantified theory axiom $QAx =_{def} \forall S. Ax$ in addition contains universal quantifiers for all variables S occurring in Ax.

$$Ax =_{def} \bigwedge_{i=1}^{n} \left(\bigwedge \Gamma_i \rightarrow \bigvee \Delta_i \right) \rightarrow \left(\bigwedge \Gamma' \rightarrow \bigvee \Delta' \right)$$

Ax and QAx are specific to the *application* of R: the axioms for two distinct applications of R will in general be different formulas. QAx is defined in such a way that the effect of R can be simulated by introducing QAx in the antecedent, instantiating it with the right terms, and applying propositional rules.

This construction leads to a proof using only the standard rules from Sect. 2.2, which can be interpolated as discussed earlier. Since QAx is a valid formula not containing any free variables, it can be introduced in a proof at any point, and labelled $\lfloor QAx \rfloor_L$ or $\lfloor QAx \rfloor_R$ on demand.

An immediate consequence of this approach is the possibility of quantifiers occurring in interpolants. This is because the interpolating rules $\forall$-LEFT$_{L/R}$ (Table 4) have to introduce quantifiers $\forall_{Rt}/\exists_{Lt}$ for local symbols in the substituted term t; whether such quantifiers actually occur in the final interpolant depends on the applied heap rules, and on the order of rule application. However, as we have observed in the beginning of the section, quantifiers in heap interpolants are in general unavoidable.

Example 3. We continue Example 2, and show how to extract an interpolant for the conjunction $A \wedge B$. Since A' and B' in Example 2 are simplified versions of the conjuncts $\tilde{A}$ and $\tilde{B}$ in the core language, respectively, interpolation can start from A', B'. The rule application READ-FC can be encoded as the following theory axioms:

$$Ax = (h' = h' \wedge a = a \wedge 42 \neq 43) \rightarrow \neg(read(h', a, 42) \wedge read(h', a, 43))$$
$$\equiv \neg read(h', a, 42) \vee \neg read(h', a, 43)$$
$$QAx \equiv \forall h, a. \, (\neg read(h, a, 42) \vee \neg read(h, a, 43))$$

Replacing the application of READ-FC with the axiom, and adding formula labels, we obtain the following interpolating proof of the conjunction $A' \wedge B'$:

$$
\cfrac{
  \cfrac{
    \cfrac{
      \cfrac{
        \cfrac{*}{\lfloor read(h', a, 42) \rfloor_L \vdash \lfloor read(h', a, 42) \rfloor_R \; \blacktriangleright \tilde{J}} \text{CLOSE}_{LR}
      }{\lfloor read(h', a, 42) \rfloor_L, \lfloor \neg read(h', a, 42) \rfloor_R \vdash \; \blacktriangleright \tilde{J}} \text{$\neg$-LEFT}_R
    }{\begin{array}{c}\lfloor read(h', a, 42) \rfloor_L, \lfloor read(h', a, 43) \rfloor_R, \\ \lfloor \neg read(h', a, 42) \vee \neg read(h', a, 43) \rfloor_R\end{array} \vdash \; \blacktriangleright \tilde{J} \wedge true} \text{$\vee$-LEFT}_R
  }{\lfloor read(h', a, 42) \rfloor_L, \lfloor read(h', a, 43) \rfloor_R, \lfloor QAx \rfloor_R, \ldots \vdash \; \blacktriangleright \tilde{I}} \text{$\forall$-LEFT}_R \times 2
}{\lfloor A' \rfloor_L, \lfloor B' \rfloor_R \vdash \emptyset \; \blacktriangleright \tilde{I}} \text{$\wedge$-LEFT}^*
$$

The interpolant extracted from this proof is $\tilde{I} \equiv read(h', a, 42)$, and stems from the application of the rule CLOSE$_{LR}$ in the left sub-proof. In the right sub-proof (not shown here), only R-labelled formulas are needed, and the sub-interpolant generated by the rule CLOSE$_{RR}$ is *true*. The interpolant $\tilde{I}$ in the core language can be translated back to the heap formula $I = (\text{read}(h', a) = 42)$. Note that this formula is a correct interpolant even though it does not explicitly state that a is a valid address in h'.

The proof could also be rewritten to use the L-labelled axiom $\lfloor QAx \rfloor_L$ instead of $\lfloor QAx \rfloor_R$. As a result, the label of several formulas and rule applications would then change from R to L, and the final interpolant becomes $\text{read}(h', a) \neq 43$.

5   Related Work

Since the theory of heap is quite close to the theory of arrays, we discuss some existing work on array decision and interpolation procedures.

There is a large body of research on array decision procedures for SMT, going back to the 1980s. Stump et al. present a decision procedure for the extensional theory of arrays, including several extensions [30]. Our rules for heap have similarities with this procedure. De Moura et al. define a decision procedure for combinatory array logic [24]. Hoenicke et al. present an algorithm for the theory of arrays where lemmas are created lazily based on weak equivalences [9]. Brummayer et al. present a decision procedure for the extensional theory of arrays that introduces lemmas lazily, guided by congruence closure [7].

Interpolation procedures for arrays have been presented in a number of recent publications, in particular tackling the problem of defining array theories that admit quantifier-free interpolation. Bruttomesso et al. observe that adding a *diff* function to the theory of arrays establishes quantifier-free interpolation, and present an interpolation procedure [8]. Totla et al. present an interpolation procedure for arrays based on complete instantiation [32]. An interpolation procedure based on weak equivalences, extending [9], is given in [14], again ensuring quantifier-free interpolants by adding a *diff* function.

6   Conclusions and Outlook

This paper presents the first decision procedure for the theory of heap, and shows soundness and completeness of the calculus underlying the decision procedure. As an extension of the decision procedure, a procedure to generate interpolants using the standard rules from Sect. 2.2 is presented. The procedures are intended as a starting point, and at this point largely unoptimised: in particular, the decision procedure will likely suffer from too unrestricted applicability of the calculus rules, and no attempts are made to minimise the number of quantifiers that might occur in computed interpolants. To address those shortcomings, we believe that many of the approaches surveyed in the previous section, developed for the theory of arrays, could be adapted to the theory of heap. This is left as future work.

An orthogonal line of research concerns simplification techniques for CHCs modulo the theory of heap. Such techniques can for instance use Abstract Interpretation to derive the validity of heap addresses, or the type of objects at specific addresses. CHCs could also be simplified by eliminating repeated reads from the same address, across multiple clauses, or by adding arguments to predicates in order to partially expand heap arguments. Experience with CHC indicates that such preprocessing can have dramatic effect on the performance of solvers.

Acknowledgements. This work was supported by the Swedish Research Council (VR) under grant 2018-04727, and by the Swedish Foundation for Strategic Research (SSF) under the project WebSec (Ref. RIT17-0011).

References

1. Backeman, P., Rümmer, P., Zeljic, A.: Bit-vector interpolation and quantifier elimination by lazy reduction. In: Bjørner, N., Gurfinkel, A. (eds.) 2018 Formal Methods in Computer Aided Design, FMCAD 2018, Austin, TX, USA, 30 October–2 November 2018, pp. 1–10. IEEE (2018). https://doi.org/10.23919/FMCAD.2018.8603023

2. Barrett, C., Shikanian, I., Tinelli, C.: An abstract decision procedure for a theory of inductive data types. JSAT **3**(1–2), 21–46 (2007)

3. Bjørner, N., Gurfinkel, A., McMillan, K., Rybalchenko, A.: Horn clause solvers for program verification. In: Beklemishev, L.D., Blass, A., Dershowitz, N., Finkbeiner, B., Schulte, W. (eds.) Fields of Logic and Computation II. LNCS, vol. 9300, pp. 24–51. Springer, Cham (2015). https://doi.org/10.1007/978-3-319-23534-9_2

4. Bjørner, N., McMillan, K., Rybalchenko, A.: On solving universally quantified horn clauses. In: Logozzo, F., Fähndrich, M. (eds.) SAS 2013. LNCS, vol. 7935, pp. 105–125. Springer, Heidelberg (2013). https://doi.org/10.1007/978-3-642-38856-9_8

5. Brillout, A., Kroening, D., Rümmer, P., Wahl, T.: Beyond quantifier-free interpolation in extensions of Presburger arithmetic. In: Jhala, R., Schmidt, D. (eds.) VMCAI 2011. LNCS, vol. 6538, pp. 88–102. Springer, Heidelberg (2011). https://doi.org/10.1007/978-3-642-18275-4_8

6. Brillout, A., Kroening, D., Rümmer, P., Wahl, T.: An interpolating sequent calculus for quantifier-free Presburger arithmetic. J. Autom. Reasoning **47**, 341–367 (2011)

7. Brummayer, R., Biere, A.: Lemmas on demand for the extensional theory of arrays. J. Satisfiability Boolean Model. Comput. **6**(1–3), 165–201 (2009). https://doi.org/10.3233/sat190067

8. Bruttomesso, R., Ghilardi, S., Ranise, S.: Quantifier-free interpolation of a theory of arrays. Log. Methods Comput. Sci. **8**(2) (2012). https://doi.org/10.2168/LMCS-8(2:4)2012

9. Christ, J., Hoenicke, J.: Weakly equivalent arrays. In: Rümmer, P., Wintersteiger, C.M. (eds.) Proceedings of the 12th International Workshop on Satisfiability Modulo Theories, SMT 2014, affiliated with the 26th International Conference on Computer Aided Verification (CAV 2014), the 7th International Joint Conference on Automated Reasoning (IJCAR 2014), and the 17th International Conference on Theory and Applications of Satisfiability Testing (SAT 2014), Vienna, Austria, 17–18 July 2014. CEUR Workshop Proceedings, vol. 1163, pp. 39–49. CEUR-WS.org (2014). http://ceur-ws.org/Vol-1163/paper-06.pdf

10. Craig, W.: Linear reasoning. A new form of the Herbrand-Gentzen theorem. J. Symbolic Log. **22**(3), 250–268 (1957)
11. De Angelis, E., Fioravanti, F., Pettorossi, A., Proietti, M.: Program verification using constraint handling rules and array constraint generalizations. Fundam. Inform. **150**(1), 73–117 (2017). https://doi.org/10.3233/FI-2017-1461
12. Esen, Z., Rümmer, P.: Towards an SMT-LIB theory of heap. In: Fribourg, L., Heizmann, M. (eds.) Proceedings 8th International Workshop on Verification and Program Transformation and 7th Workshop on Horn Clauses for Verification and Synthesis, VPT/HCVS@ETAPS 2020 2020, and 7th Workshop on Horn Clauses for Verification and SynthesisDublin, Ireland, 25–26th April 2020. EPTCS, vol. 320 (2020)
13. Fitting, M.C.: First-Order Logic and Automated Theorem Proving. TCS, 2nd edn. Springer, New York (1996). https://doi.org/10.1007/978-1-4612-2360-3
14. Hoenicke, J., Schindler, T.: Efficient interpolation for the theory of arrays. In: Galmiche, D., Schulz, S., Sebastiani, R. (eds.) IJCAR 2018. LNCS (LNAI), vol. 10900, pp. 549–565. Springer, Cham (2018). https://doi.org/10.1007/978-3-319-94205-6_36
15. Hojjat, H., Rümmer, P.: Deciding and interpolating algebraic data types by reduction. In: Jebelean, T., Negru, V., Petcu, D., Zaharie, D., Ida, T., Watt, S.M. (eds.) 19th International Symposium on Symbolic and Numeric Algorithms for Scientific Computing, SYNASC 2017, Timisoara, Romania, 21–24 September 2017, pp. 145–152. IEEE Computer Society (2017). https://doi.org/10.1109/SYNASC.2017.00033
16. Hojjat, H., Rümmer, P.: The ELDARICA horn solver. In: Bjørner, N., Gurfinkel, A. (eds.) 2018 Formal Methods in Computer Aided Design, FMCAD 2018, Austin, TX, USA, 30 October–2 November 2018, pp. 1–7. IEEE (2018). https://doi.org/10.23919/FMCAD.2018.8603013
17. Kahsai, T., Kersten, R., Rümmer, P., Schäf, M.: Quantified heap invariants for object-oriented programs. In: Eiter, T., Sands, D. (eds.) LPAR-21, 21st International Conference on Logic for Programming, Artificial Intelligence and Reasoning, Maun, Botswana, 7–12 May 2017. EPiC Series in Computing, vol. 46, pp. 368–384. EasyChair (2017) https://easychair.org/publications/paper/Pmh
18. Kapur, D., Majumdar, R., Zarba, C.G.: Interpolation for data structures. In: SIGSOFT 2006/FSE-14, pp. 105–116. ACM, New York (2006)
19. Komuravelli, A., Bjørner, N., Gurfinkel, A., McMillan, K.L.: Compositional verification of procedural programs using Horn clauses over integers and arrays. In: Kaivola, R., Wahl, T. (eds.) Formal Methods in Computer-Aided Design, FMCAD 2015, Austin, Texas, USA, 27–30 September 2015, pp. 89–96. IEEE (2015)
20. Komuravelli, A., Gurfinkel, A., Chaki, S., Clarke, E.M.: Automatic abstraction in SMT-based unbounded software model checking. In: Sharygina, N., Veith, H. (eds.) CAV 2013. LNCS, vol. 8044, pp. 846–862. Springer, Heidelberg (2013). https://doi.org/10.1007/978-3-642-39799-8_59
21. McMillan, K.L.: An interpolating theorem prover. In: Jensen, K., Podelski, A. (eds.) TACAS 2004. LNCS, vol. 2988, pp. 16–30. Springer, Heidelberg (2004). https://doi.org/10.1007/978-3-540-24730-2_2
22. Monniaux, D., Gonnord, L.: Cell morphing: from array programs to array-free horn clauses. In: Rival, X. (ed.) SAS 2016. LNCS, vol. 9837, pp. 361–382. Springer, Heidelberg (2016). https://doi.org/10.1007/978-3-662-53413-7_18
23. de Moura, L., Bjørner, N.: Z3: an efficient SMT solver. In: Ramakrishnan, C.R., Rehof, J. (eds.) TACAS 2008. LNCS, vol. 4963, pp. 337–340. Springer, Heidelberg (2008). https://doi.org/10.1007/978-3-540-78800-3_24

24. de Moura, L.M., Bjørner, N.: Generalized, efficient array decision procedures. In: Proceedings of 9th International Conference on Formal Methods in Computer-Aided Design, FMCAD 2009, Austin, Texas, USA, 15–18 November 2009, pp. 45–52. IEEE (2009). https://doi.org/10.1109/FMCAD.2009.5351142

25. Reynolds, A., Blanchette, J.C.: A decision procedure for (co)datatypes in SMT solvers. J. Autom. Reasoning **58**(3), 341–362 (2017). https://doi.org/10.1007/s10817-016-9372-6

26. Rondon, P.M., Kawaguchi, M., Jhala, R.: Liquid types. In: Gupta, R., Amarasinghe, S.P. (eds.) Proceedings of the ACM SIGPLAN 2008 Conference on Programming Language Design and Implementation, Tucson, AZ, USA, 7–13 June 2008, pp. 159–169. ACM (2008). https://doi.org/10.1145/1375581.1375602

27. Rümmer, P.: A constraint sequent calculus for first-order logic with linear integer arithmetic. In: Cervesato, I., Veith, H., Voronkov, A. (eds.) LPAR 2008. LNCS (LNAI), vol. 5330, pp. 274–289. Springer, Heidelberg (2008). https://doi.org/10.1007/978-3-540-89439-1_20

28. Rümmer, P.: Competition report: CHC-COMP-20. In: Fribourg, L., Heizmann, M. (eds.) Proceedings 8th International Workshop on Verification and Program Transformation and 7th Workshop on Horn Clauses for Verification and Synthesis, VPT/HCVS@ETAPS 2020 2020, and 7th Workshop on Horn Clauses for Verification and SynthesisDublin, Ireland, 25–26th April 2020. EPTCS, vol. 320, pp. 197–219 (2020). https://doi.org/10.4204/EPTCS.320.15

29. Rümmer, P., Hojjat, H., Kuncak, V.: Disjunctive interpolants for horn-clause verification. In: Sharygina, N., Veith, H. (eds.) CAV 2013. LNCS, vol. 8044, pp. 347–363. Springer, Heidelberg (2013). https://doi.org/10.1007/978-3-642-39799-8_24

30. Stump, A., Barrett, C.W., Dill, D.L., Levitt, J.R.: A decision procedure for an extensional theory of arrays. In: 16th Annual IEEE Symposium on Logic in Computer Science, Boston, Massachusetts, USA, 16–19 June 2001, Proceedings, pp. 29–37. IEEE Computer Society (2001). https://doi.org/10.1109/LICS.2001.932480

31. Suter, P., Dotta, M., Kuncak, V.: Decision procedures for algebraic data types with abstractions. In: SIGPLAN Not., vol. 45, no. 1, pp. 199–210 (2010)

32. Totla, N., Wies, T.: Complete instantiation-based interpolation. J. Autom. Reasoning **57**(1), 37–65 (2016). https://doi.org/10.1007/s10817-016-9371-7

Algorithm Selection for Dynamic Symbolic Execution: A Preliminary Study

Roberto Amadini[1(✉)], Graeme Gange[3], Peter Schachte[2], Harald Søndergaard[2], and Peter J. Stuckey[3]

[1] University of Bologna, Bologna, Italy
roberto.amadini@unibo.it
[2] University of Melbourne, Parkville, VIC, Australia
[3] Monash University, Clayton, VIC, Australia

Abstract. Given a portfolio of algorithms, the goal of Algorithm Selection (AS) is to select the best algorithm(s) for a new, unseen problem instance. Dynamic Symbolic Execution (DSE) brings together concrete and symbolic execution to maximise the program coverage. DSE uses a constraint solver to solve the path conditions and generate new inputs to explore. In this paper we join these lines of research by introducing a model that combines DSE and AS approaches. The proposed AS/DSE model is a generic and flexible framework enabling the DSE engine to solve the path conditions it collects with a portfolio of different solvers, by exploiting and extending the well-known AS techniques that have been developed over the last decade. In this way, one can increase the coverage and sometimes even *outperform* the aggregate coverage achievable by running simultaneously all the solvers of the portfolio.

Keywords: Software verification · Dynamic symbolic execution · Algorithm selection · Constraint solving · Portfolio solving

1 Introduction

The *Algorithm selection* (AS) problem was formalised by Rice in 1976 [27]. In a nutshell, given a set of algorithms $\mathcal{A}$ and a problem instance i,the aggregate coverage. AS aims to select the best algorithm in $\mathcal{A}$ to solve i according to a given performance metric m [33]. AS approaches are also known as *portfolio* approaches, where "solver" is used as a synonym of algorithm, "portfolio" indicates a subset of solvers of $\mathcal{A}$, and the solver selection is performed on a per-instance basis.

Algorithm selection typically uses machine learning techniques (e.g., decision trees or k-nearest neighbours) and it is not limited to the choice of a single solver: a portfolio approach can first select a number of different solvers, and then schedule their (sequential or parallel) execution [20].

The solver selection is typically performed by extracting a number of *features* from each problem. Features are numerical attributes characterizing a given problem instance (e.g., the number of variables or constraints).

M. Fernández (Ed.): LOPSTR 2020, LNCS 12561, pp. 192–209, 2021.
https://doi.org/10.1007/978-3-030-68446-4_10

Over the last years a large number of effective AS approaches have been proposed in different fields, including SAT solving [24,36], constraint programming (CP) [3,12], answer-set programming (ASP) [11], and planning [35].

Dynamic symbolic execution (DSE) [9,22] also known as concolic execution/testing, or directed automated random testing (DART) is a software verification technique combining the concrete (or dynamic) execution of a program together with its *symbolic execution* [17]. DSE first collects all the constraints involving symbolic variables (the so called *path conditions*) encountered during the dynamic execution at each conditional statement. Then, a constraint solver (or theorem prover) is used to generate alternative execution paths by systematically negating the path conditions. This process is repeated until all the feasible paths are covered, or a resource limit (e.g., a time limit or a maximum number of iterations) is reached.

A possible bottleneck of DSE is the solver used for solving path conditions. Indeed, despite the significant progress made by constraint solvers over the last years, it is still hard for a single, arbitrarily efficient solver to properly encode and solve the great variety of path conditions arising from the DSE of different programs. This is partly due to the complexity of precisely encoding the semantics of modern programming languages. Unfortunately, depending on the shape of the input program, failing to solve even just one path condition could result in a significant loss in terms of code coverage.

In this work we propose the AS/DSE framework, a generic model that aims to get the best of the AS and DSE worlds. The goal is to mitigate the issues of single-solver DSE approaches with a portfolio of different solvers. This can be beneficial in terms of robustness (if a solver fails on a path condition, the overall DSE is not compromised), runtime minimisation and code coverage maximisation.

To our knowledge, the few approaches proposed so far [26] merely run in parallel different DSE engines—each of them running a different solver of the portfolio. Here we take a step forward by proposing a model that can be arbitrarily instantiated depending on the available solvers, the input language, the program to analyse, the execution environment, and so on. In particular, we show that a AS/DSE model may even *outperform* the aggregate coverage achievable by running independently all the solvers of the portfolio.

As a proof-of-concept, we implemented and evaluated two basic portfolio approaches on top of ARATHA [1], a tool for JavaScript DSE enabling the use of both SMT and CP solvers for solving path conditions. Preliminary results are encouraging and show the potential of combining AS with DSE. For each analysed program the coverage achieved by portfolio approaches is never worse than the one achievable with a single solver and, in particular, one of the approaches is able to outperform the coverage reachable by running simultaneously all the solvers of the portfolio.

Paper structure. In Sect. 2 we give the basic notions about AS and DSE. In Sect. 3 we describe the AS/DSE model, while in Sect. 4 we show the results of the preliminary investigation we performed. In Sect. 5 we report the related literature before concluding in Sect. 6.

2 Preliminaries

We start with some background notions related to algorithm selection and dynamic symbolic execution.

2.1 Algorithm Selection

The main ingredients of an AS scenario are: *(i)* the algorithms to be selected, *(ii)* the problem instances on which algorithms are applied, *(iii)* the performance metric used to evaluate an algorithm on a given problem. More formally, an AS scenario is a triple $(\mathcal{I}, \mathcal{A}, m)$ where $\mathcal{I}$ is a set of *instances*, $\mathcal{A}$ is a set (or portfolio) of *algorithms* (or solvers) with $|\mathcal{A}| > 1$, and $m : \mathcal{I} \times \mathcal{A} \rightarrow \mathbb{R}$ is a *performance metric* that w.l.o.g. we can assume to be *minimized*.

An algorithm selector (or portfolio selector) aims to return the best algorithm, according to the performance metric, for a given instance. Formally, given an AS scenario $(\mathcal{I}, \mathcal{A}, m)$, a selector ξ is a total mapping $\xi : \mathcal{I} \rightarrow \mathcal{A}$. The AS problem consists in finding a selector ξ minimizing $\sum_{i \in \mathcal{I}} m(i, \xi(i))$.

Note that m is a *partial* function, i.e., we do not know *a priori* the value of $m(i, A)$ for each possible $i \in \mathcal{I}, A \in \mathcal{A}$ (otherwise the AS problem would be trivial). This means that an AS selector has to *estimate* $m(i, A)$ when it is unknown, and *predict* the best algorithm(s) for i. For each scenario we can define the *virtual best solver* (VBS) baseline, i.e., an "oracle selector" always choosing the algorithm $VBS(i)$ such that $m(i, VBS(i))$ is minimal for each $i \in \mathcal{I}$. Hence, $m(i, VBS(i)) \leq m(i, \xi(i))$ for each selector ξ and $i \in \mathcal{I}, A \in \mathcal{A}$.

The above schema can be however extended by enabling the *scheduling* of $k > 1$ algorithms $[(A_1, t_1) \ldots, (A_k, t_k)]$ for a given problem i, where t_j is the time slot assigned to each A_j for $j = 1, \ldots, k$. Note that, because the instances of $\mathcal{I}$ might be too hard to solve, often a timeout T is used: $m(i, A) \leq T$ for each $i \in \mathcal{I}, A \in \mathcal{A}$. So, if $A_1, \ldots, A_k$ are scheduled for time $t_1, \ldots, t_k$ then $\sum_{j=1}^{k} t_j = T$.

An advantage of scheduling k solvers is that algorithm A_j can use the information computed by $A_{j'}$, with $j' < j$, to improve its performance. For example, consider an optimization problem i where the best objective value v found by solver $A_{j'}$ can be exploited by another solver A_j to narrow its search space (i.e., A_j solves a modified problem i_v where value v is "injected" to i [6]). It is important to note that such a collaborative approach may allow a portfolio solver to *outperform* the VBS, i.e., it might be $m(i_v, A_j) < m(i, VBS(i))$.

Finally, note that AS scenarios usually characterize each instance $i \in \mathcal{I}$ with a corresponding feature vector $\mathcal{F}(i) \in \mathbb{R}^n$, and the selection of the best algorithm A for i is actually performed according to $\mathcal{F}(i)$. For example, if i is a constraint satisfaction problem then $\mathcal{F}(i)$ may include the number of variables or constraints of i. If i is an optimization problem, we may also want to capture numeric information about the objective function of i (e.g., its lower and upper bounds).

There is an extensive literature about selecting the presumably best set of features for a given instance. In particular, the process of refining a feature vector $\mathcal{F}(i) \in \mathbb{R}^n$ by deriving a smaller vector $\mathcal{F}'(i) \in \mathbb{R}^m$ with $m \leq n$ is known as *feature selection*. The purpose of feature selection is to simplify the prediction model, reducing the training and feature extraction costs, and improving the prediction accuracy.

2.2 Dynamic Symbolic Execution

DSE is a combination of *concrete* and *symbolic* execution.

Symbolic execution is a whole-program analysis technique that has its roots in the 1970s [17]. The idea is that, during execution, some variables take on *symbolic values*, maintained as expressions involving unknown input values. A symbolic interpreter explores the possible program paths that concrete executions could take, by reasoning about the conditions under which execution will branch this way or that. More precisely, a *symbolic state* (σ, Γ) is maintained, consisting of a mapping σ that associates variables with expressions, and a *path constraint* Γ. The latter is a conjunction of primitive constraints involving symbolic names for inputs. It effectively determines the set of input values that would take concrete execution along the current execution path; that is, a path is feasible if and only if the corresponding constraints are satisfiable.

The test for satisfiability, and the generation of a witness (a solution) in the affirmative case, is delegated to a constraint solver (or theorem prover). The symbolic state evolves according to simple rules: (1) an assignment x = e updates the symbolic state (σ, Γ) to $(\sigma[x \mapsto \sigma(e)], \Gamma)$, and (2) for a conditional if (e) s1 else s2, two path constraints are generated, namely $\Gamma \wedge \sigma(e)$ and $\Gamma \wedge \neg\sigma(e)$; if $\Gamma \wedge \sigma(e)$ is satisfiable, s1 is symbolically executed under the new path constraint, and similarly for $\Gamma \wedge \neg\sigma(e)$ and s2.

Two significant limitations of symbolic execution are: *(i)* the whole program —including libraries—is often not available to the interpreter; *(ii)* the underlying constraint solver is often not expressive and efficient enough to handle the generated path conditions.

DSE combines symbolic execution with concrete execution, by performing the symbolic execution along with concrete execution of the given program. The motivation for this is to sidestep the two limitations mentioned above. Having the concrete runtime state allows the tool to replace symbolic variables by concrete values when faced by external function calls, and also to simplify difficult constraints. This enables progress of the symbolic execution, albeit at the sacrifice of completeness.

So DSE needs to be *seeded* with concrete values for symbolic variables. It can then perform a sequence of well-chosen concrete/symbolic executions (aimed at maximizing code coverage), by taking a recently generated path constraint, negating one of its conjuncts, asking a constraint solver whether the result is satisfiable, and, if so, to provide a model, which can serve as a new seed.

Consider, for example, the snippet of pseudo-code in Fig. 1. Suppose the initial input is $x \leftarrow 0$. The concrete execution of $f(x)$ will print 'bar', and

```
1: function f(x)
2:     if x < 0 then
3:         print('foo')
4:     else if x ≥ 5 then
5:         print('fee')
6:     else
7:         print('bar')
```

Fig. 1. Pseudo-code example. The set of inputs $\{x \leftarrow -1, x \leftarrow 0, x \leftarrow 5\}$ covers all the lines of function f.

the DSE engine will track the corresponding path conditions: $\neg(x < 0)$ and $\neg(x \geq 5)$. After that, one path condition will be negated, let us say $\neg(x \geq 5)$, and a constraint solver will solve $\neg(x < 0) \wedge x \geq 5$. A computed solution (say, $x = 5$) will be the input of the next concrete execution, that will print 'fee'. This process is repeated until all the feasible paths are covered, or a pre-set resource limit (usually a time limit or a maximum number of iterations) is reached.

DSE can mitigate the aforementioned symbolic execution issues by: *(i)* directly invoking unavailable functions (a complete symbolic interpreter is not required); *(ii)* ignoring or approximating unsupported constraints. This implies that, in general, DSE cannot guarantee full coverage. In most applications, such as test data generation, this is acceptable, provided a "good enough" coverage is achieved in a reasonable time.

3   The **AS/DSE** Model

The purpose of this section is to map out the considerable space for algorithm selection in DSE. We list an array of opportunities for "selection" that may provide avenues to better DSE tools. Presently there is very limited support for this, as existing tools tend to be tightly coupled with specific solvers. In Sect. 4 we report on whatever experiments we have been able to run, based on existing technology.

The AS/DSE model is depicted in Fig. 2. The upper dashed box refers to the "classical" DSE framework. The first step is to annotate the input program $\mathbb{P}$ with $n > 0$ *symbolic variables* $x_1, \ldots, x_n$ of interest, i.e., with meta-variables using symbolic values to represent input values. This can be performed manually or automatically (e.g., by means of *taint analysis* [29]). The result is a symbolic program $\mathbb{P}'$ containing both symbolic and "concrete" (i.e., non-symbolic) variables.

Given initial concrete values $\mathbf{v_0} = (v_{0,1}, \ldots, v_{0,n})$ we first execute $\mathbb{P}'[\mathbf{v_0}]$, i.e., the program $\mathbb{P}'$ where value $v_{0,i}$ is assigned to variable x_i for $i = 1, 2, \ldots, n$. Concurrently, a symbolic engine collects the *path conditions* $\Gamma_0 = (C_1, \ldots, C_m)$ encountered during the concrete execution as explained in Sect. 2. At this stage, for generating the next input, the last path condition C_k not already negated is flipped (notice that the choice of C_k can be generalised to the j-th path condition

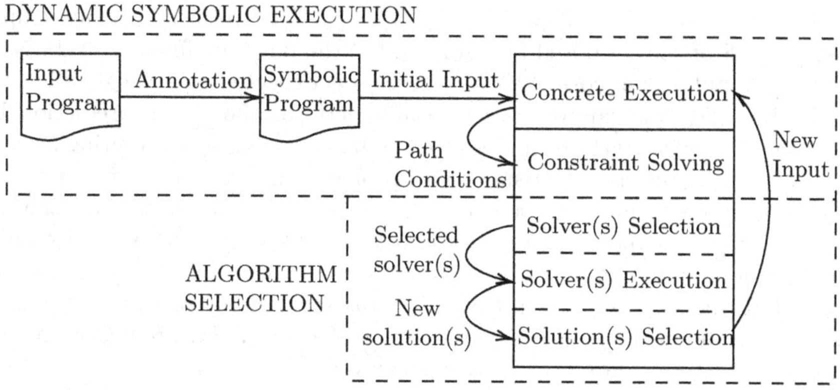

DYNAMIC SYMBOLIC EXECUTION

Fig. 2. The AS/DSE model.

not already negated, with $j \in \{1, \ldots, k\}$). If all the conditions have been already negated, the DSE terminates.

Let $\Gamma'_0 = (C_1, \ldots, C_{k-1}, \neg C_k)$. In the single-solver DSE a solver S is now used to solve $\bigwedge_{C \in \Gamma'_0} C$. If S returns a solution $\mathbf{v_1} = (v_{1,1}, \ldots, v_{1,n})$ then we execute $\mathbb{P}'[\mathbf{v_1}]$ to get new path conditions Γ_1; otherwise, we repeat the procedure by negating the last condition of Γ_0 not already negated until either we find a solution $\mathbf{v_1}$ or all the conditions are negated. By iterating this process until the DSE terminates (or a given threshold is reached, e.g., a timeout or a maximum number of DSE iterations) we get a set of inputs $\{\mathbf{v_1}, \mathbf{v_2}, \ldots\}$ that ideally covers all the execution paths of $\mathbb{P}$.

The AS/DSE model extends the single-solver model by using a portfolio of solvers $\mathcal{S} = \{S_1, \ldots, S_p\}$. In Fig. 2, the lower dashed box shows how AS is plugged into the DSE framework. To solve a given tuple of path conditions Γ with $\mathcal{S}$, we define three different (yet interoperable) phases: (i) the solver selection phase, (ii) the solver execution phase, (iii) the solution selection phase.

3.1 Solver Selection

The first stage is selecting the solver(s) from the portfolio $\mathcal{S}$. We are not aware of portfolio approaches for DSE that actually perform a *discriminating* solver selection, that is, selection on a per-instance basis. The only alternative is to run *all* the solvers of $\mathcal{S}$ (possibly in parallel). This is straightforward and might work if $\mathcal{S}$ is small but it is impractical if $\mathcal{S}$ contains (many) more solvers than available cores (e.g., the literature presents portfolios with more than 20 solvers). Note that we can get different solvers by tuning the parameters of the same solver. Moreover, the synchronisation issues due to the simultaneous execution of too many solvers may significantly slow down the performance, especially when the running solvers have to share information.

Given the growing number of solvers based on different technologies (e.g., SAT/SMT, CP, MIP solvers), it makes sense to have an heterogeneous portfolio together with a proper *solver selection heuristic* $\mathcal{H}_{sel}$ returning a non-empty subset $\mathcal{S}' \subseteq \mathcal{S}$ of the supposed best solver(s) of the portfolio for solving Γ. Note that the computational cost of solver selection is expected to be negligible.

The best portfolio approaches typically perform the solver prediction by extracting a set of *features* from the problem to solve, i.e., by computing a set of numerical attributes characterising that problem. Once features are computed, machine learning techniques can be used to determine the candidate solvers. Clearly, this process needs a proper *feature extractor* (e.g., [2]) and, in case of supervised learning, a dataset of known instances for which we know the performance of all the solvers of $\mathcal{S}$. In this case, *cross-validation* techniques are often used to split the dataset into a training set (used to build a prediction model) and a test set (to validate that prediction model).

In our model, feature extraction can happen at different levels depending on when the solver selection is actually performed. We distinguish between three levels of solver selection: static, dynamic and hybrid.

Static Solver Selection is an "offline" AS procedure where the solvers are selected *eagerly* according to the input program $\mathbb{P}$, or the symbolic program $\mathbb{P}'$, regardless of the path conditions generated while analyzing $\mathbb{P}$.

The advantages of this approach are its simplicity and efficiency: there is no need to modify the internals of the DSE engine, and the solver selection is performed only once per program: we do not need to collect the path conditions to build a training set. Static solver selection is suitable, e.g., when the size of the portfolio $\mathcal{S}$ is much bigger than the number of available cores c: in this case one can select c solvers from $\mathcal{S}$ and run all of them in parallel.

The features extracted for static solver selection depends on the input program $\mathbb{P}$ and/or the symbolic program $\mathbb{P}'$ (depending of whether we want to take into account also the symbolic variables of $\mathbb{P}'$). These features can be language-independent (e.g., the number of loops or symbolic variables) or bound to a specific language (e.g., the number of property accesses for JavaScript objects).

Note that, apart from the "syntactic" features extracted from the source code of the program, we can also have *probing features* derived from its actual execution. For example, we could execute $\mathbb{P}'[\mathbf{v}]$, where $\mathbf{v}$ is a tuple of concrete values, and run the solvers for a short time on the corresponding path conditions to track their behaviour.

Unfortunately, a purely static solver selection lacks flexibility and is unable to exploit *marginal contributions* of different solvers. It risks excluding good solvers from $\mathcal{S}$ only on the basis of the shape of $\mathbb{P}$. However, a solver that behaves poorly on average might well be turn out to be highly effective for smaller classes of specific problems, on which other solvers struggle.

Dynamic Solver Selection refers to the "online" selection of solvers according to the path conditions to be solved. While the static solver selection occurs just once for each program, dynamic solver selection is performed for each collected path condition. Because of its high frequency, it is essential that dynamic selection has a low computational cost.

The features extracted from each path condition Γ are, e.g., statistics over the number and the type of the variables and constraints of Γ. One can also compute probing features by running one or more solvers of S on Γ. For example, one can retrieve the number of failures or the depth of the search tree after running a solver $S \in S$ for a short time (e.g., 2 s).

Dynamic solver selection delivers flexibility and is, potentially, far more effective than static selection. What is less straightforward here is how to extract the features and train the model. The feature extraction has to be integrated into the DSE engine, while for static solver selection it can be performed "externally" without any modification to the DSE engine. Moreover, the training set can be very big because for each program a large number of (often similar) path conditions can be collected: we need some criteria to select "good representatives" among all the path conditions.

Hybrid Solver Selection combines, as the name suggests, static and dynamic selection. We can use static selection as a pre-processing step where, especially when we have a high number of solvers, we can reduce the original portfolio S into a smaller portfolio S'. One may also use static selection to decide a proper *parameter configuration* for solvers that have a high number of parameters to be tuned. Then, dynamic selection is used on S' to select the presumably best solver(s) $S_\Gamma \subseteq S'$ for each collected path conditions Γ. At this stage one can also reuse some of the features extracted in the static selection phase.

Finally, note that one can apply AS not only to select the best solver(s), but also to decide the best *encoding* for a given Γ. For example, assume $S = S_{sat} \cup S_{smt} \cup S_{cp}$ where S_{sat} are SAT solvers, S_{smt} are SMT solvers, and S_{cp} are CP solvers. Instead of directly selecting the best solver(s) in S for Γ, one might think to first choose the best encoding for Γ, i.e., whether it is better to convert Γ into a SAT, a SMT or a CP problem. This actually means performing AS to first choose $S' \in \{S_{sat}, S_{smt}, S_{cp}\}$ and then choose solver(s) $S'' \subseteq S'$. An example of this hierarchical approach is provided by Hurley *et al.* [12] who use it to decide whether or not to encode a given CP problem to SAT before deciding the best solver for that problem.

3.2 Solver Execution

Let $S' = \{S_1, \ldots, S_k\}$ be the selected solver(s) returned by $\mathcal{H}_{sel}$. Because we typically solve hard combinatorial problems (where a solver either solves a problem in a short time or it cannot solve it in a reasonable time) it is often desirable to select $k > 1$ solvers. In this case we have to use a proper *solver execution heuristic* $\mathcal{H}_{exe}$ to schedule the execution of each solver of S'. The $\mathcal{H}_{exe}$ heuristic decides the *running mode* of the selected solvers, e.g.:

- how to run the solvers of S' (sequentially, concurrently or both)
- how much time is allocated to each solver (typically a solving timeout is set)

```
1: if x ≥ 10 then
2:     Stmt₁
3:     if C(x) then
4:         Stmt₂
```

Fig. 3. Example of program where C is unsupported.

- the execution order of each solver
- if and how to exchange information between them (e.g., nogoods or SMT queries)
- the configuration of their parameters
- when to stop *all* the solvers of $\mathcal{S}'$.

Let us focus on the last point, which may appear counter-intuitive. Indeed, it might look more reasonable to just stop as soon as a solver finds a solution. However, waiting until a number $1 < j \leq k$ of solvers terminate can also be beneficial. In this case we sacrifice the runtime minimisation to possibly have $j > 1$ distinct solutions for Γ. Clearly, $\mathcal{H}_{exe}$ can also force the same solver to produce more than one solution.

Having different solutions $\mathbf{v_1}, \ldots, \mathbf{v_j}$ for the same path condition can be advantageous in terms of code coverage maximisation because often solvers are forced to over-approximate the path conditions, owing to unsupported constraints or unknown program functions. Considering $\mathbf{v_1}, \ldots, \mathbf{v_j}$ is somehow an *"educated fuzzing"* where we try distinct yet related inputs potentially leading to different program paths. In other terms, we might try to offset the "incompleteness" of solvers with the diversity of their solutions.

3.3   Solution Selection

Let us suppose that the solver execution phase returns $j > 1$ distinct solutions $\mathbf{v_1}, \ldots, \mathbf{v_j}$. In this case, we use a *solution selection heuristic* $\mathcal{H}_{sol}$ to decide which $\mathbf{v}_i$ will be the input of the next DSE iteration. This phase is important because it enables us to *rank* $\mathbf{v_1}, \ldots, \mathbf{v_j}$ according to a given criteria.

For example, we may give low priority to solutions containing "default" values (e.g., 0 or the empty string) or rank solutions according to their type (note that, especially for weakly-typed languages such as JavaScript or Python, we may not have any information about the actual type of a symbolic variable).

As mentioned, it might be that the conjuncts in Γ get *relaxed*, resulting in new path conditions Γ', because the available solvers are not expressive or efficient enough to cope with the constraints of Γ. In this case, a solution of Γ' is not necessarily a solution of Γ, so having different solutions for Γ' may increase the probability of finding a solution for Γ too (or for other path conditions).

For instance, consider the pseudo-code in Fig. 3 where we assume that x is a symbolic variable and the condition C is not supported by any solver (e.g., it can be an unknown third-party function or a difficult mathematical function). If we start the DSE with $x \leftarrow 0$, then we collect path condition $\neg(x \geq 10)$, we flip it and we solve $x \geq 10$. Let us suppose that we stop as soon as a solver returns a solution, say $x = 10$. If $C(10)$ evaluates to false, then the next collected path conditions are $x \geq 10$ and $\neg C(x)$. Once flipped $\neg C(x)$, solvers should solve $x \geq 10 \wedge C(x)$ but they cannot because they do not support C. A possible way to mitigate this issue is to generate different solutions for $x \geq 10$ and try them to see if we can increase the code coverage (e.g., it might be that $C(11)$ evaluates to true).

Another nice aspect is that we can use the solutions as *nogoods*: if at a given DSE iteration we get solution $\mathbf{v} = (v_1, \ldots, v_n)$, then we can add the constraint $x_1 \neq v_1 \vee \cdots \vee x_n \neq v_n$ to the path conditions of all future DSE iterations in order to narrow the search and avoid exploring already visited paths. As we shall see in Sect. 4, this approach can improve the code coverage in practice.

3.4 Aggregate Coverage

The well-known benefits of AS are the average runtime minimisation and the maximization of the number of problems solved. However, in the context of DSE we have a further advantage. Let $COV_S(\mathbb{P})$ be the set of statements (or lines) in $\mathbb{P}$ covered using the portfolio S. Then, significantly, the coverage $COV_{\{S_1,\ldots,S_p\}}(\mathbb{P})$ can be *greater* than the sum of its parts, that is, we may well have:

$$COV_{\{S_1,\ldots,S_p\}}(\mathbb{P}) \supset COV_{S_1}(\mathbb{P}) \cup \cdots \cup COV_{S_p}(\mathbb{P}).$$

Note that $\bigcup_{S \in \mathcal{S}} COV_S(\mathbb{P})$ is exactly the coverage achievable by running p *independent* DSE analysis, each of which with a different solver $S \in \mathcal{S}$. In the following, we will refer to $\bigcup_{S \in \mathcal{S}} COV_S(\mathbb{P})$ as the *aggregate coverage* for portfolio $\mathcal{S}$ on program $\mathbb{P}$.

Consider the example in Fig. 4a where x is a symbolic variable and both conditions $C_1(x)$ and $C_2(x)$ are feasible. Let us suppose that S_1 can solve $C_1(x)$ but cannot solve $C_2(x)$, while S_2 can solve $C_2(x)$ but not $C_1(x)$; in this case with $\mathcal{S} = \{S_1, S_2\}$ we are able to cover both the statements $Stmt_1$ and $Stmt_2$, while with either S_1 or S_2 we can only cover either $Stmt_1$ or $Stmt_2$ respectively. For this example, a *static* approach running S_1 and S_2 independently is enough to reach the maximum coverage. Even if $COV_{\mathcal{S}}(\mathbb{P}) \supset COV_{S_1}(\mathbb{P}), COV_{S_2}(\mathbb{P})$, we cannot, in this case, improve on the aggregate coverage: $COV_{\mathcal{S}}(\mathbb{P}) = COV_{S_1}(\mathbb{P}) \cup COV_{S_2}(\mathbb{P})$ in the best case scenario.

It is important to understand the difference between aggregate coverage and the *virtual best solver* (VBS) of the portfolio. By definition, the VBS selects the best algorithm according to a given performance metric for every problem instance. For static solver selection we define the performance metric as: "maximize the coverage for a given program, breaking ties with minimum runtime". So, for the example discussed above (Fig. 4a), the VBS is either S_1 or S_2 depending on which one is faster in solving C_1 or C_2 respectively. However, there is no case where the VBS is able to cover *both* the statements $Stmt_1$ and $Stmt_2$. In general, for static solver selection the coverage of the VBS is always less than, or equal to, the aggregate coverage. Conversely, as seen in the example above, a static scheduling (or a parallel execution) of solvers can yield better coverage than the VBS.

1: **if** $C_1(x)$ **then**	1: **if** $C_1(x)$ **then**
2: $Stmt_1$	2: $Stmt_1$
3: **if** $C_2(x)$ **then**	3: **if** $C_2(x)$ **then**
4: $Stmt_2$	4: $Stmt_2$
(a) Non-nested 'if' statements.	(b) Nested 'if' statements.

Fig. 4. If statements.

Figure 4b shows a trickier example where we also assume that $C_1(x) \wedge C_2(x)$ can be solved by S_2 but not by S_1. As above, S_1 can only cover $Stmt_1$ while S_2 cannot solve $C_1(x)$ and thus will not cover neither $Stmt_1$ nor $Stmt_2$. However, unlike the case of Fig. 4a, independently running two different DSE engines using S_1 and S_2 respectively yields an insufficient coverage because none of them is able to reach line 4 and thus $Stmt_2$ will not be covered.

Because $COV_{S_1}(\mathbb{P}) = \{Stmt_1\}$ and $COV_{S_2}(\mathbb{P}) = \emptyset$, the aggregate coverage of S will only cover $Stmt_1$. However, this does not mean that $Stmt_2$ cannot be covered using the solvers of S. Indeed, with a proper *dynamic* solver selection, we would be able to reach first $Stmt_1$ (thanks to S_1, solving $C_1(x)$) and then $Stmt_2$ (thanks to S_2, solving $C_1(x) \wedge C_2(x)$), thus outperforming the aggregate coverage. Clearly this approach is only possible with an *integrated* AS/DSE implementation able to select the solvers on a path condition basis.

Following the standard definition, the VBS for dynamic solver selection is the solver that solves a given path condition in the shortest time. In this case, the coverage achieved with the VBS will never be worse than the aggregate coverage.

4   A Preliminary Evaluation

We have experimented with a portfolio approach to DSE, to the extent that existing DSE tools allow this. We have based experiments on ARATHA [1], a tool for the DSE of JavaScript, because uniquely, ARATHA can use both SMT solvers (viz. Z3 [25] and CVC4 [19]) and CP solvers (viz. G-STRINGS [5]). With this, we have implemented two static approaches, to explore whether portfolio solving turns out to improve on single-solver DSE in practice, and if so, by how much.

The first approach, which we call ARATHA$^+$, runs the DSE with G-STRINGS first, then with Z3 and finally with CVC4 (except that, if execution with a solver reaches 100% coverage, we do not run any subsequent solvers). ARATHA$^+$ does not perform algorithm selection itself, but uses $S = \{$G-STRINGS, Z3, CVC4$\}$ to perform three individual dynamic symbolic executions (one for each solver) and then collate the results. In practice, ARATHA$^+$ will actually compute the aggregate coverage for portfolio S.

The second approach, which we call ARATHA^{++}, is a variant of ARATHA$^+$ where the inputs found by a solver (i.e., the solutions of each path condition) are passed to the next solver to avoid the regeneration of the same inputs. As ARATHA$^+$, ARATHA^{++} does not perform algorithm selection in the strict sense because it uses all the available solvers. ARATHA^{++} is a collaborative approach where at each DSE iteration i with associated path conditions Γ_i, the execution heuristics $\mathcal{H}_{exe}$ is this: "solve $\Gamma_i \cup \Delta$", where Δ is a set of *nogoods* of the form $x_1 \neq v_1 \vee \cdots \vee x_n \neq v_n$ for each input $\mathbf{v} = (v_1, \ldots, v_n)$ computed so far. In practice, ARATHA^{++} tries to outperform the aggregate coverage by relying on the *diversity* of the generated inputs.

We compared ARATHA$^+$ and ARATHA^{++} against the single-solver versions of ARATHA using G-STRINGS, Z3, and CVC4. We evaluated them on the same benchmark of 197 already annotated JavaScript programs, coming from the EXPoSE [21] test suite, used in [1]. As in [1], we set: a solving time-out of $T_{pc} = 10\,$s for each path condition, a maximum number of $N = 1024$ DSE iterations for each program, and an overall DSE timeout of $T_{tot} = 300\,$s (because sometimes reaching N iterations can take too long). For ARATHA$^+$ and ARATHA^{++} we set a timeout of $T_{tot}/3 = 100\,$s for the execution of each individual solver of the portfolio. We ran all the experiments on an Ubuntu 15.10 machine with 16 GB of RAM and 2.60 GHz Intel® i7 CPU. We computed the coverage with the Istanbul tool [14].

Table 1. Evaluation results. Coverage is given in percentages, time in seconds.

Solver	LINE	STMT	TIME	TOUT
VBS_{stmt}	*85.60*	*82.91*	*2.33*	*0*
Z3	74.74	72.10	4.96	2
CVC4	79.44	76.56	**4.27**	2
G-STRINGS	81.54	78.74	6.93	0
ARATHA$^+$	85.73	83.04	10.51	0
ARATHA^{++}	**85.93**	**83.24**	10.13	0

Table 1 shows the results in terms of coverage and solving time: LINE is the average line coverage and STMT the average statement coverage (in percentage), TIME the average DSE time (in seconds) and TOUT the number of times the DSE reached timeout T_{tot}. To provide a baseline, we have added the performance of the "static" virtual best solver VBS_{stmt}, i.e., the fictitious selectors always choosing the solver achieving the maximum statement coverage for any given program. We do not include the VBS maximizing the line coverage because its performance is basically the same of VBS_{stmt}.

As can be seen, the DSEs using a portfolio of solvers is advantageous, both in terms of line and statement coverage. In fact, coverage achieved by ARATHA$^+$ and ARATHA^{++} is slightly better than coverage achieved by VBS_{stmt}. As discussed in Sect. 3.4, this can happen in the absence of a "dominant" solver that can solve all the path conditions of the program.

As could be expected, the average DSE time comes out better for the single-solver approaches and VBS_{stmt}, because of the static, sequential approach used by ARATHA$^+$ and ARATHA^{++}. A proper parallel implementation and/or $\mathcal{H}_{sel}$ heuristic would likely reduce this gap. Note, however, that TIME is not the most critical metric here. At least for the purpose of test data generation, the aim is to find the right balance among three competing objectives: maximizing coverage while minimizing test suite size, all in the shortest possible time.

The interesting thing in Table 1 is that ARATHA^{++} is greater than the sum of its parts, because it can slightly improve the coverage computed by ARATHA$^+$. We can see why by looking at the cross-comparisons of Table 2.

Table 2. Coverage cross-comparisons.

Solver	Z3	CVC4	G-STRINGS	ARATHA$^+$	ARATHA^{++}
Z3	0	19	19	0	0
CVC4	47	0	16	0	0
G-STRINGS	65	31	0	0	0
ARATHA$^+$	67	43	29	0	0
ARATHA^{++}	**68**	**44**	**30**	**1**	0

Table 2 reports the number of times the solver on that row achieves a better statement coverage than the solver on that column (again, we do not report the table for line coverage, which is essentially the same) for each program of the benchmarks. Here we do not include VBS_{stmt} as it makes little sense to make cross-comparisons between real and fictitious solvers.

No single-solver approach improves on ARATHA$^+$ or ARATHA^{++} (this holds for line coverage too), even if the timeout of ARATHA$^+$ and ARATHA^{++} is one third of their timeout. This confirms that the coverage of ARATHA$^+$ is the aggregate coverage for $\mathcal{S} = \{$G-STRINGS, Z3, CVC4$\}$. Note that this might be no longer true if the best coverage $COV_S(\mathbb{P})$ for a program $\mathbb{P}$ was computed by a solver S in more than $T_{tot}/3$ s, because each solver of the portfolio is run for at most $T_{tot}/3$ s.

ARATHA$^+$ and ARATHA^{++} are able to *outperform* the coverage achievable with the best single solver of $\mathcal{S}$ for a given program (i.e., the one reaching the maximum coverage) for 4 and 5 programs respectively thanks to the combination of different solvers (as discussed in Sect. 3.4). Interestingly, in one case ARATHA^{++} also outperforms the coverage of ARATHA$^+$. This happens because Z3 exploits the inputs computed by G-STRINGS and generates a new input that allows ARATHA^{++} to achieve the full coverage.

A snippet of that program is shown in Fig. 5, where x is its only symbolic variable. The DSE with G-STRINGS generates inputs {'', [null], 'hello'}, the one with Z3 produces {false, {'length':39}, 'hello'} while the one with CVC4 computes {'', {'length':true}, 'hello'}. None of these will cause line 4 to be reached, because x.replace('h...o', '') === '' only succeeds when x is equal to 'h...o'.[1] ARATHA expects the function replace to be applied to strings only, and so an invocation x.replace('h...o', '') causes ARATHA to abort DSE for the current execution trace for objects such as [null], {'length':true}, nor {'length':39}. Using ARATHA⁺ does not bring any benefit because the input it yields is just the union of the inputs produced by G-STRINGS, CVC4, and Z3.

If we instead use ARATHA⁺⁺, then Z3 can take advantage of the inputs computed by G-STRINGS and use the "nogoods" $x \neq$ '', $x \neq$ [null], and $x \neq$ 'hello' each time it solves a new path condition. This enables Z3 to produce new inputs '\u0000' and 'h...o'. The latter in particular allows ARATHA⁺⁺ to reach line 4. This witnesses that generating multiple solutions and exchanging information between solvers is an aspect that deserves to be deepened.

```
1        // x is a symbolic variable
2        if (x.length > 0 && x !== 'hello'
3        &&  x.replace('h...o', '') === '') {
4          // Do something...
5        }
```

Fig. 5. Snippet JavaScript program where ARATHA⁺⁺ outperforms ARATHA⁺.

5   Related Work

Algorithm selection started to attract the attention of the SAT community about a decade ago. *SATzilla* [36,37] was one of the first SAT portfolio solvers. Its first version [37] used a ridge regression method to predict the performance of a SAT solver, while a subsequent version [36] improved the previous one with a weighted random forest approach provided with a cost-sensitive loss function for punishing mis-classifications in direct proportion to their performance impact. Another well-known AS approach for SAT problems is *3S* [15] which first executes a static schedule of solvers computed offline and then, at run time, selects via k-Nearest Neighbour a solver to be executed for the remaining time. *CSHC* [24] is a clustering-based approach that combines 3S's static scheduling with an algorithm selector based on cost sensitive hierarchical clustering. SATzilla, 3S, and CHSC won several gold medals in different editions of the SAT competition.

---

[1] In JavaScript, z.replace(x,y) returns a new string where x is replaced by y in z. Note that x may be a regular expression, but for simplicity ARATHA only considers string values for x. In this case, the *first* occurrence of x in y is replaced.

AS was successfully applied in other fields such as constraint programming [3, 12], answer-set programming [11], and planning [35]. For more comprehensive surveys on AS, we refer the reader to [4,13,16,18,33].

The ideas behind dynamic symbolic execution go back to Godefroid, Klarlund and Sen's *DART* project [9]. Since then, advances in solver technology saw DSE tools improve rapidly, in some cases finding large-scale use. For example, Microsoft's *SAGE* [10] DSE tool reportedly detected up to one third of all bugs discovered during the development of Windows 7—bugs that were missed by other testing methods. Other popular DSE tools nowadays are for example [7,8,23,30,32,34].

DSE seems particularly suitable for dynamic languages such as *JavaScript*. The first DSE application to JavaScript programs was the *Kudzu* project [28]. More recently, EXPOSE [21] was proposed to reason about JavaScript string matching via (extended) regular expressions, although in a limited fashion. ARATHA [1] is the first JavaScript DSE tool capable of solving path conditions with different constraint solvers. It was built on top of *Jalangi* 2 [31], a framework for implementing dynamic analyses for JavaScript.

The only previous work we are aware of, combining both AS and DSE is that of Palikareva and Cadar [26], where different solvers are run in parallel, without any actual solver selection or information exchange between solvers. Note that this approach can never outperform the virtual best solver: its best possible implementation would only improve the DSE time of the ARATHA$^+$ and ARATHA^{++} approaches defined in Sect. 4, but it will never achieve the coverage of ARATHA^{++}.

6   Conclusions

We have explored the scope and use of Algorithm Selection (AS) in Dynamic Symbolic Execution (DSE), proposing a generic AS/DSE framework. The framework is independent of the target language to analyse, as well as of the underlying solvers. The idea is to improve the DSE engine by using a portfolio of different solvers. The work is constrained by the fact that current DSE tools have not been built with portfolio solving in mind, but we have been able to conduct preliminary experiments in the context of JavaScript DSE. The results encourage further research in this direction, and we hope to spur sufficient interest to open a bridge between the AS, the DSE, and the constraint solving communities.

There are numerous directions in which this work should be extended. It would be interesting to extend the pool of solvers, benchmarks, and target languages. It would also be worthwhile exploring the use of other (including more sophisticated) coverage metrics.

A main goal is to develop an integrated DSE tool that is able to select a number of solvers from an arbitrarily large portfolio, and to run them in a concurrent and cooperative way (i.e., by enabling the information exchange between solvers). A useful step in this direction would be the definition of a constraint language able to encode the path conditions of a given programming language regardless of the target solver(s) used to solve the path conditions.

References

1. Amadini, R., Andrlon, M., Gange, G., Schachte, P., Søndergaard, H., Stuckey, P.J.: Constraint programming for dynamic symbolic execution of javascript. In: Rousseau, L.-M., Stergiou, K. (eds.) CPAIOR 2019. LNCS, vol. 11494, pp. 1–19. Springer, Cham (2019). https://doi.org/10.1007/978-3-030-19212-9_1
2. Amadini, R., Gabbrielli, M., Mauro, J.: An enhanced features extractor for a portfolio of constraint solvers. In: Proceedings 29th Annual ACM Symposium Applied Computing, pp. 1357–1359. ACM (2014)
3. Amadini, R., Gabbrielli, M., Mauro, J.: SUNNY: a lazy portfolio approach for constraint solving. Theory Pract. Logic Program. **14**(4–5), 509–524 (2014)
4. Amadini, R., Gabbrielli, M., Mauro, J.: Why CP portfolio solvers are (under)utilized? issues and challenges. In: Falaschi, M. (ed.) LOPSTR 2015. LNCS, vol. 9527, pp. 349–364. Springer, Cham (2015). https://doi.org/10.1007/978-3-319-27436-2_21
5. Amadini, R., Gange, G., Stuckey, P.J.: Sweep-based propagation for string constraint solving. In: Proceedings of 32nd AAAI Conference Artificial Intelligence, pp. 6557–6564. AAAI (2018)
6. Amadini, R., Stuckey, P.J.: Sequential time splitting and bounds communication for a portfolio of optimization solvers. In: O'Sullivan, B. (ed.) CP 2014. LNCS, vol. 8656, pp. 108–124. Springer, Cham (2014). https://doi.org/10.1007/978-3-319-10428-7_11
7. Artzi, S., et al.: Finding bugs in web applications using dynamic test generation and explicit-state model checking. IEEE Trans. Softw. Eng. **36**(4), 474–494 (2010)
8. Cadar, C., Dunbar, D., Engler, D.: KLEE: Unassisted and automatic generation of high-coverage tests for complex systems programs. In: Proceedings of 8th USENIX Conference Operating Systems Design and Implementation, OSDI, vol. 8, pp. 209–224 (2008)
9. Godefroid, P., Klarlund, N., Sen, K.: DART: directed automated random testing. In: Proceedings of ACM SIGPLAN Conference Programming Language Design and Implementation (PLDI 2005), pp. 213–223. ACM (2005)
10. Godefroid, P., Levin, M.Y., Molnar, D.: SAGE: whitebox fuzzing for security testing. Commun. ACM **55**(3), 40–44 (2012)
11. Hoos, H., Lindauer, M.T., Schaub, T.: Claspfolio 2: advances in algorithm selection for answer set programming. TPLP **14**(4–5), 569–585 (2014)
12. Hurley, B., Kotthoff, L., Malitsky, Y., O'Sullivan, B.: Proteus: a hierarchical portfolio of solvers and transformations. In: Simonis, H. (ed.) CPAIOR 2014. LNCS, vol. 8451, pp. 301–317. Springer, Cham (2014). https://doi.org/10.1007/978-3-319-07046-9_22
13. Hutter, F., Xu, L., Hoos, H.H., Leyton-Brown, K.: Algorithm runtime prediction: methods and evaluation. Artif. Intell. **206**, 79–111 (2014)
14. Istanbul Team: Istanbul website (2020). https://istanbul.js.org
15. Kadioglu, S., Malitsky, Y., Sabharwal, A., Samulowitz, H., Sellmann, M.: Algorithm selection and scheduling. In: Lee, J. (ed.) CP 2011. LNCS, vol. 6876, pp. 454–469. Springer, Heidelberg (2011). https://doi.org/10.1007/978-3-642-23786-7_35
16. Kerschke, P., Hoos, H.H., Neumann, F., Trautmann, H.: Automated algorithm selection: survey and perspectives. Evol. Comput. **27**(1), 3–45 (2019)
17. King, J.C.: Symbolic execution and program testing. Commun. ACM **19**(7), 385–394 (1976)

18. Kotthoff, L.: Algorithm selection for combinatorial search problems: A survey. AI Mag. **35**(3), 48–60 (2014)
19. Liang, T., Reynolds, A., Tinelli, C., Barrett, C., Deters, M.: A DPLL(T) theory solver for a theory of strings and regular expressions. In: Biere, A., Bloem, R. (eds.) CAV 2014. LNCS, vol. 8559, pp. 646–662. Springer, Cham (2014). https://doi.org/10.1007/978-3-319-08867-9_43
20. Lindauer, M., Bergdoll, R.-D., Hutter, F.: An empirical study of per-instance algorithm scheduling. In: Festa, P., Sellmann, M., Vanschoren, J. (eds.) LION 2016. LNCS, vol. 10079, pp. 253–259. Springer, Cham (2016). https://doi.org/10.1007/978-3-319-50349-3_20
21. Loring, B., Mitchell, D., Kinder, J.: ExpoSE: practical symbolic execution of standalone JavaScript. In: Proceedings of 24th ACM SIGSOFT International SPIN Symposium Model Checking of Software, pp. 196–199. ACM (2017)
22. Majumdar, R., Sen, K.: Hybrid concolic testing. In: Proceedings of 29th International Conference Software Engineering (ICSE 2007), pp. 416–426. IEEE (2007)
23. Majumdar, R., Xu, R.-G.: Reducing test inputs using information partitions. In: Bouajjani, A., Maler, O. (eds.) CAV 2009. LNCS, vol. 5643, pp. 555–569. Springer, Heidelberg (2009). https://doi.org/10.1007/978-3-642-02658-4_41
24. Malitsky, Y., Sabharwal, A., Samulowitz, H., Sellmann, M.: Algorithm portfolios based on cost-sensitive hierarchical clustering. In: Proceedings of 23rd International Joint Conference Artificial Intelligence. IJCAI/AAAI (2013)
25. de Moura, L., Bjørner, N.: Z3: an efficient SMT solver. In: Ramakrishnan, C.R., Rehof, J. (eds.) TACAS 2008. LNCS, vol. 4963, pp. 337–340. Springer, Heidelberg (2008). https://doi.org/10.1007/978-3-540-78800-3_24
26. Palikareva, H., Cadar, C.: Multi-solver support in symbolic execution. In: Sharygina, N., Veith, H. (eds.) CAV 2013. LNCS, vol. 8044, pp. 53–68. Springer, Heidelberg (2013). https://doi.org/10.1007/978-3-642-39799-8_3
27. Rice, J.R.: The algorithm selection problem. Adv. Comput. **15**, 65–118 (1976)
28. Saxena, P., Akhawe, D., Hanna, S., Mao, F., McCamant, S., Song, D.: A symbolic execution framework for JavaScript. In: Proceedings of 2010 IEEE Symposium Security and Privacy, pp. 513–528. IEEE Computer Society (2010)
29. Schwartz, E.J., Avgerinos, T., Brumley, D.: All you ever wanted to know about dynamic taint analysis and forward symbolic execution (but might have been afraid to ask). In: Proceedings of 31st IEEE Symposium on Security and Privacy, pp. 317–331 (2010)
30. Sen, K., Agha, G.: CUTE and jCUTE: concolic unit testing and explicit path model-checking tools. In: Ball, T., Jones, R.B. (eds.) CAV 2006. LNCS, vol. 4144, pp. 419–423. Springer, Heidelberg (2006). https://doi.org/10.1007/11817963_38
31. Sen, K., Kalasapur, S., Brutch, T.G., Gibbs, S.: Jalangi: a selective record-replay and dynamic analysis framework for JavaScript. In: Joint Meeting of the European Software Engineering Conference and the ACM SIGSOFT Symposium Foundations of Software Engineering, pp. 488–498 (2013)
32. Sen, K., Marinov, D., Agha, G.: CUTE: A concolic unit testing engine for C. In: Proceedings of 10th European Software Engineering Conference, pp. 263–272. ACM (2005)
33. Smith-Miles, K.: Cross-disciplinary perspectives on meta-learning for algorithm selection. ACM Comput. Surv. **41**(1), 1–25 (2008)
34. Tillmann, N., de Halleux, J.: Pex–white box test generation for.NET. In: Beckert, B., Hähnle, R. (eds.) TAP 2008. LNCS, vol. 4966, pp. 134–153. Springer, Heidelberg (2008). https://doi.org/10.1007/978-3-540-79124-9_10

35. Valenzano, R.A., Nakhost, H., Müller, M., Schaeffer, J., Sturtevant, N.R.: Arvand-Herd: parallel planning with a portfolio. In: European Conference Artificial Intelligence, Frontiers in Artificial Intelligence and Applications, vol. 242, pp. 786–791. IOS Press (2012)
36. Xu, L., Hutter, F., Hoos, H., Leyton-Brown, K.: Evaluating component solver contributions to portfolio-based algorithm selectors. In: Cimatti, A., Sebastiani, R. (eds.) SAT 2012. LNCS, vol. 7317, pp. 228–241. Springer, Heidelberg (2012). https://doi.org/10.1007/978-3-642-31612-8_18
37. Xu, L., Hutter, F., Hoos, H.H., Leyton-Brown, K.: SATzilla: Portfolio-based algorithm selection for SAT. J. Artif. Intell. Res. 32, 565–606 (2008)

Translation of Interactive Datalog Programs for Microcontrollers to Finite State Machines

Mario Wenzel$^{(\boxtimes)}$ and Stefan Brass

Martin-Luther-Universität Halle-Wittenberg, Institut für Informatik,
Von-Seckendorff-Platz 1, 06099 Halle (Saale), Germany
{mario.wenzel,brass}@informatik.uni-halle.de

Abstract. "Smart" devices have become ubiquitous in modern households and industry. Especially in home-automation, robotics, and sensing tasks, rule-based approaches seem ideal to describe the behavior of the interactive systems. But managing input data and state is hard. With little choice of programming language, most code targeted at microcontrollers is written in imperative C or assembler.

Microlog is a deductive database language with a strong logic foundation based on Datalog extended with a representation of time and calls to external functions that may be used to control sensors and actors.

In this paper we describe a method to precalculate sets of Datalog facts that may be derivable for a point in time. Values that will be known only at runtime are represented as parameters of those "states". During "state transition", a small number of conditions on parameters and input values must be checked. By representing a possibly quite large number of facts as a single state number and a few parameter values, memory and computing time are saved. If no parameters are needed, the result of this compilation is basically a finite state machine.

Keywords: Deductive database · Datalog · Microcontroller · Arduino · Compiler

1 Introduction

With the introduction of cheap programmable microcontrollers, powerful reprogrammable "smart" devices have found their way into our homes and offices. "Smart everything" is not an understatement as we find smart vacuum cleaners, smart light-bulbs, smart coffee machines, smart radios and TVs, smart ovens and microwaves, smart sex-toys, smart toothbrushes, smart washing machines and the like. Alternative open source firmwares are available for quite a few of the mentioned device types. With expanded lifespan and utility from what the vendor originally intended to sell, the aftermarket for flashable devices flourishes. So do the open source communities around those devices.

© Springer Nature Switzerland AG 2021
M. Fernández (Ed.): LOPSTR 2020, LNCS 12561, pp. 210–227, 2021.
https://doi.org/10.1007/978-3-030-68446-4_11

Naturally those cheap programmable devices find their way into hobbyists' workshops as well as school and university courses and curricula [1,12]. However, the programming languages and paradigms that are supported by microcontroller systems such as the Arduino are limited.

We believe that declarative programming can be an interesting option even for such small devices. Declarative languages have many advantages:

- Declarative programs are usually shorter than an equivalent program in a procedural language. This enhances the productivity of the programmers.
- There can be no problems with uninitialized variables or memory leaks.
- The language has a mathematically precise semantics based on logic, which makes programs easier to verify and programming arguably easier to teach.

Our declarative language Microlog is a language that allows us to model both program state and side-effects in a declarative manner [14]. Based on the Datalog variant Dedalus [2], Microlog has strong foundations in logic. Dedalus captures a notion of state, similar to the Statelog language [10], but is embedded in Datalog. Our model of side-effects is similar to action atoms and external atoms from Answer Set Programming [5,7] with deterministic semantics. Rules are usually quite small, have a simple structure, and a well-defined and explicit interface to the rest of the program. This allows us to reason deductively about program and world states. Our goal is to declaratively program microcontrollers and give static safety guarantees for data-driven interactive programs on microcontrollers. The safe use of our limited resources is quite important. The GPIO pins, for example, should only be used in a consistent and deterministic manner. We should be able to guarantee that the microcontroller never runs out of memory.

In this paper, we present a novel compilation technique for Microlog-programs. It precomputes possible "states", which are sets of Datalog-facts that are true at a point in time. This does not work for all Microlog-programs, because one can write programs for which the number of facts keeps growing over time. However, if we cannot prove that the number of facts for a time point is bounded, the program is anyway problematic, especially for small microcontroller systems. If the approach is applicable for a program, the result is often similar to a finite state machine where the IO is done during state transitions.

Our approach mainly targets AVR-based microcontrollers, like the Arduino, with an 8-bit CPU such as the ATmega168:

- There is only 1 KB of SRAM available that is used for both heap and stack data. This means we are limited in operational memory for storing database facts and in algorithm design with regards to function call depth.
- 16 KB of Flash memory can be used to store the program. This might seem a lot in comparison, but this is also used to store additional libraries for peripheral access that are wanted by the user.
- It has an operational speed of 20 MHz, which is a lot compared to the amount of data we have to operate on.

These limitations, along with the difficulty of dynamic memory management, preclude complex approaches where a possible runtime must model non-deterministic choice or have backtracking semantics. From a Microlog program we generate simple C-code and we generically interface with the rest of the system by calling external C-functions (e. g., from libraries).

This approach works for other embedded systems and processors as well. To test the utility of our language we also build programs for LEGO EV3 robots. EV3 units have a "proper" ARM CPU and run Linux. With 64 MB of SRAM, resource management is less of a concern there, and more complex approaches for modelling and planning are also available.[13]

In Sect. 2 we will recapitulate syntax and semantics of the Microlog language. In contrast to our earlier paper [14], we have simplified the IO: All calls of external procedures are now done in the head. In Sect. 3, we do the transition from the standard minimal model to the computation by states. Sect. 4 explains the precomputation of states at compile time, which is the main technical contribution of this paper. Ideas for generating more compact code are discussed in Sect. 5, termination in Sect. 6, and negation very briefly in Sect. 7.

2   Language, State Management, Example Application

Our query language is modeled after the Dedalus$_0$ language [2]. Dedalus$_0$ and our language "Microlog" are based on Datalog. A Datalog program is a finite set of rules of the form $A \leftarrow B_1 \wedge \cdots \wedge B_n$, where the head literal A and the body literals B_i are atomic formulas $p(t_1, \ldots, t_m)$ with a predicate p and terms $t_1, \ldots, t_m$. Terms are constants or variables. We also allow arithmetic comparisons in the rule body (i. e., $=$, $\neq$, $<$, $\leq$, $>$, $\geq$). Furthermore, we need the successor predicate for natural numbers succ, but this is only allowed as last literal in so-called "inductive rules" (see below). Let $\mathcal{I}_B$ be the standard interpretation for the built-in predicates (comparisons and succ), e.g., $\mathcal{I}_B[\![\mathsf{succ}]\!] = \{(i, i+1) \mid i \in \mathbb{N}_0\}$.

Rules must be range-restricted, i.e., all variables that appear anywhere in the rule must appear also in a body literal with a predicate that is not a comparison (the use of succ is specially restricted, see below). This ensures that all variables are bound to a value when the rule is applied.

In order to explicitly model time, Microlog programs have the syntactic restriction that every predicate must have a first argument from the domain of the natural numbers which we refer to as the *timestamp*. Some fact $p(\ldots)$ is true in timestamp n iff $p(n, \ldots)$ is in the minimal model of our program. We refer to the selection of all facts with a certain timestamp as a *state*.

All body literals in a rule body must have as their timestamp the same special variable T, as rules may only rely on facts from a single timestamp (the variable T always refers to "now"). The rule head either shares the same T as its timestamp (as in Dedalus, this is called a *deductive rule*) or it has the timestamp T' and the literal $\mathsf{succ}(T, T')$ is the last literal of the rule body (as in Dedalus, this is called an *inductive rule*).

Deductive rules allow for normal Datalog deduction steps and inductive rules govern how data from facts of one timestamp is reproduced into facts of the following timestamp.

Rules without body are only allowed as initial facts if their timestamp is 0. Syntactically, no other configurations of the timestamp arguments are allowed. The special variables T and T' are not allowed to be used elsewhere in any other part of a rule or bound to other variables, neither is the succ-predicate.

This model can be used to update relations in a stateful fashion. If a fact is not transported from one timestamp to the next, we have a notion of deletion. The notion of state captured by the timestamp is similar to the Statelog language [10]. The facts with some timestamp n can be seen as "happening earlier" than the facts with timestamp m with $n < m$. This is useful to model interactions with the environment. The minimal model for such a logic program may extend into infinity. The evaluating program does not terminate and as an interactive system we do not want it to.

Of course, a Datalog program for a Microcontroller must interface with the libraries for querying input devices and performing actions on output devices. One approach would be to have a fixed set of built-in predicates, but there are quite a lot of library functions and new libraries are being developed, e.g., for new types of input and output devices, or controller boards. A few examples of interface functions are shown in Fig. 1.

```
#define HIGH    0x1
#define LOW     0x0
void digitalWrite(uint8_t pin, uint8_t val);
int  digitalRead(uint8_t pin);
```

Fig. 1. Extract from Arduino.h header file

Our modelling of side-effects in logic programs can be likened to HEX programs with action atoms [7]. The observation of the actions is similar to an external source of computation [5]. External sources of computation in logic programs have been modeled as functional oracles which, in our case, describe the environment during a particular run of a Microlog program.

For each function f that can be called,[1] there is a special predicate call_f with a reserved prefix "call_". The predicate has arguments of the function to be called, arguments for the return values, and of course the standard time argument. E.g., derived facts from the predicate call_digitalWrite(T', Pin, Val) lead to the corresponding calls of the interface function digitalWrite in the following state T'. The set-semantics ensures that duplicate calls are eliminated, i.e., even

---

[1] We actually allow users to define a whole statement block as a special predicate. This allows combining interface functions that always need to be called together, defining multiple return arguments, or just doing arithmetic. To avoid confusion, we only refer to function calls from here on out.

if there are different ways to deduce the fact, only one call is done. The sequence of calls within the same timestamp is undefined. If a specific sequence is required, the calls must be spread out over multiple timestamps.

For each interface function f there is a second predicate ret_f that contains all parameters of the call and a parameter for the return value. For instance, for the function `digitalRead`, there are two predicates:

- call_digitalRead($\mathcal{T}'$, Pin, ?), and
- ret_digitalRead($\mathcal{T}$, Pin, Val).

For the output positions that are not assigned a value in the "call_" predicate but are in the "ret_" we use the special marker ? to achieve a consistent argument list. One could view this as an existentially quantified anonymous variable with the promise that in the corresponding ret_-predicate, there will be some return value.

A call is only ever done in the next state, so that the result value is also only available in the next state. This ensures, e.g., that the occurrence of a call cannot depend on its own result.

Since calls of interface functions usually have side effects and cannot be taken back, it is important to clearly define which calls are actually done. In contrast, the evaluation sequence of literals in a rule body can be chosen by the optimizer. Therefore the special call_f predicate can be used only in rule heads. Correspondingly, the ret_f predicate can only be used in the rule body and is defined by the derived call_f-facts and the environment.

A form of condition-action rules can be seen (amongst other systems for event theory) in Event Calculus [11] and Logic Production Systems [9] with the main difference that Microlog does not allow for negation or disjunction in the rule heads. Also, all actions that are are possible are taken, not just a single one. This removes backtracking and nondeterministic choice from our system. We claim that the embedding into Datalog is powerful enough (e. g., to implement some decision procedure for action prioritization, or planning procedures) and allows us to readily apply well-researched methods and techniques.

We add some syntactic sugar to make it easier to work with the syntactic restrictions. From the rule structure and syntactic restrictions it should be clear when we refer to the sugared version of Microlog:

Unsugared Version	Sugared Version
Deductive Rules: the time argument is left out in the rule head and every subgoal.	
$p(T,X) \leftarrow q(T,X,Y) \land p(T,Y).$	$p(X) \leftarrow q(X,Y) \land p(Y).$
Inductive Rules: the suffix "@next" is added to the rule head and the time argument is left out in the rule head and every subgoal and we leave out the succ predicate.	
$p(T',X) \leftarrow q(T,X,Y) \land p(T,Y) \land \mathsf{succ}(T,T').$ $\quad p(X)@next \leftarrow q(X,Y) \land p(Y).$	
Initial Facts: replacing the time argument 0, the suffix "@0" is added.	
$p(0,5).$	$p(5)@0.$
Static Facts: We leave the body empty. time is a reserved predicate defined by time(0) and $\mathsf{time}(T') \leftarrow \mathsf{time}(T) \land \mathsf{succ}(T,T')$. These two rules are added to every program. They ensure that time will be true for all states.	
$p(T,5) \leftarrow \mathsf{time}(T).$	$p(5).$
IO: We replace the call_-prefix, which can only appear in rule heads, with #. As the ret_-prefix can only appear in rule bodies, we replace that with # as well.	
$\mathsf{call\_f}(T',X,?) \leftarrow p(T,X) \land \mathsf{succ}(T,T').$	$\#f(X,?)@next \leftarrow p(X).$
$p(T,X) \leftarrow \mathsf{ret\_f}(T,5,X).$	$p(X) \leftarrow \#f(5,X).$

Finally, we need also constants from the interface definition. If our Datalog program contains e.g. #HIGH, this corresponds to the constant HIGH in the generated C-code.

With the fixpoint semantics of Datalog and external function calls, we can describe reactive data-driven programs with more complex behavior than, for example, typical home automation rules.

Example 1. We can easily describe a system where the heating not only shuts off in a room with an open window (a common use case for home automation), but also in all (other) rooms connected via open doors (see Fig. 2). The function calls are from a fictitious library that wraps communication to the sensors and actors, #open is a C constant from that library. It is usually the case that control to hardware is provided by some library[2] and the call semantics provide a generic way to interface with them. The static rules of hasWindow and adjacent are the configuration of our program to our specific example home with two connected rooms where the second room has window (also used in Sect. 4). A user, if this program was provided to them, would only need to add those facts to configure it for their home.

3   Computing a Sequence of States

After replacing the abbreviations, a Microlog-program is a set P_M of Datalog-rules (and facts). However, for the deduction, not only these rules are used, but also input facts from the external environment that contain the return values of function calls. Let $\mathcal{E}$ be the set of all such facts for the ret_f-predicates. The semantics of the Microlog program P_M is the mapping from input facts $\mathcal{E}$ to the minimal model $\mathcal{I}_{\min}$ of $P := P_M \cup \mathcal{E}$, i.e., the set of all derivable facts. We can

---

[2] At the time of writing, PlatformIO.org hosts over 7.000 libraries for embedded devices. More than half are available for Arduino.

```
% static example configuration
hasWindow(2).
adjacent(1, 2).
% gathering world state
#readWindow(R, ?)@next   :- hasWindow(R).
#readDoor(A, B, ?)@next :- adjacent(A, B).
% deduce model using transitive closure
windowOpen(R)   :- #readWindow(R, #open).
doorOpen(A, B) :- #readDoor(A, B, #open).
connected(A, B) :- doorOpen(A, B).
connected(B, A) :- doorOpen(A, B).
connected(A, C) :- connected(A, B), connected(B, C), A != C.
% effects
#heatingOff(R)@next :- windowOpen(R).
#heatingOff(O)@next :- windowOpen(R), connected(R, O).
```

Fig. 2. Heating control program in Microlog (actual concrete syntax)

use the standard T_P operator for deriving facts that are immediate consequences of the rules and already known facts:

$$T_P(\mathcal{I}) := \{A\theta \,|\, A \leftarrow B_1 \wedge \cdots \wedge B_m \in P,$$
$$\theta \text{ is a ground substitution for this rule such that}$$
$$\text{for all } i = 1, \ldots, m: \ B_i\theta \in \mathcal{I} \text{ or}$$
$$B_i \text{ has a built-in predicate and } \mathcal{I}_B \models B_i\theta\}.$$

The least fixed point of this operator, $\mathsf{lfp}(T_P)$, is the minimal Herbrand model of P. It can be obtained by iterating the operator, i.e., one starts with $\mathcal{I}_0 := \emptyset$, and then has a series of Herbrand interpretations (sets of facts) $\mathcal{I}_{i+1} := T_P(\mathcal{I}_i)$. The "limit" of this construction yields $\mathcal{I}_{\min} = \mathsf{lfp}(T_P) = \bigcup_{i=0}^{\infty} \mathcal{I}_i$.

We are actually not interested in arbitrary sets $\mathcal{E}$, but only sets satisfying the causality requirement that the ret_f-facts in $\mathcal{E}$ correspond to derived call_f-facts:

Definition 1 (Causal Set of Input Facts). *Let a Microlog-Program P_M be given. A set $\mathcal{E}$ of facts is causal (for P_M) iff*

- *it contains only facts with return predicates (ret_f), and*
- *for each fact $\mathsf{ret\_f}(i, c_1, \ldots, c_n) \in \mathcal{E}$ there is $\mathsf{call\_f}(i, c'_1, \ldots, c'_n) \in \mathsf{lfp}(T_{P_M \cup \mathcal{E}})$ with the same timestamp i and such that for each j, $1 \leq j \leq n$, $c'_j = c_j$ or $c'_j = ?$ (the special marker for return arguments),*
- *and, vice versa, for each fact $\mathsf{call\_f}(i, c'_1, \ldots, c'_n) \in \mathsf{lfp}(T_{P_M \cup \mathcal{E}})$ there is exactly one fact $\mathsf{ret\_f}(i, c_1, \ldots, c_n) \in \mathcal{E}$ that is matching in the above sense.*

It might be a philosophical problem that the input facts seem to be there before the computation starts that can produce the calls that cause them. But in this way, the formal definition is simpler and in the spirit of standard Datalog. By considering only sets $\mathcal{E}$ that satisfy the causality property, we eliminate the unreasonable cases. Because calls are derived in Microlog always for the next point in time, it is not possible that a call depends on its own return value.

However, we will also give the definitions for a computation in the sequence of timestamps, which is a more realistic model of what should happen in practice. Fortunately, both views lead to the same model.

We want to compute a sequence $\mathcal{S}_0, \mathcal{S}_1, \ldots$ of sets of facts, where $\mathcal{S}_i$ contains facts derived at time i. Because the time information is contained in the position i of the set $\mathcal{S}_i$ in the sequence, we can get rid of the time argument in the facts. This is quite similar to getting back from the full Datalog version of a Microlog program to a version that uses the syntactic sugar for hiding the time argument. However, the result is now pure Datalog with special predicates. Since at time i, also facts for the next state are derived, we need the following special predicates:

- For all normal predicates p, we introduce a new predicate next_p, and
- for the call_f predicates, we introduce a predicate ncall_f (calls are always derived for the next state).

Now for literals A, we write $\bar{A}$ for a version without time argument. More precisely, if A is $p(t_0, t_1, \ldots, t_n)$, $\bar{A}$ is

- ncall_f$(t_1, \ldots, t_n)$ if p is of the form call_f,
- next_$p(t_1, \ldots, t_n)$ if p is a normal predicate and t_0 is the special variable $\mathcal{T}'$ for the successor timestamp,
- $p(t_1, \ldots, t_n)$ otherwise.

This removal of the time argument can also be applied to a set of rules $\mathcal{R}$. Let

$$\bar{\mathcal{R}} := \{\bar{A} \leftarrow \bar{B}_1 \wedge \cdots \wedge \bar{B}_{n-1} \mid A \leftarrow B_1 \wedge \cdots \wedge B_n \in \mathcal{R}$$
$$\text{and } B_n \text{ is succ}(\mathcal{T}, \mathcal{T}') \text{ or time}(\mathcal{T}) \} \cup$$
$$\{\bar{A} \leftarrow \bar{B}_1 \wedge \cdots \wedge \bar{B}_n \quad \mid A \leftarrow B_1 \wedge \cdots \wedge B_n \in \mathcal{R}$$
$$\text{and } B_n \text{ is neither succ}(\mathcal{T}, \mathcal{T}') \text{ nor time}(\mathcal{T}) \}.$$

We also need the converse operation, i.e., adding a time argument, for the obtained facts. Let $p(c_1, \ldots, c_n)[i]$ be:

- call_f$(i + 1, c_1, \ldots, c_n)$ if p is of the form ncall_f,
- $q(i + 1, c_1, \ldots, c_n)$ if p is of the form next_q,
- $p(i, c_1, \ldots, c_n)$ otherwise.

This definition is extended to sets of facts: $\mathcal{F}[i] := \{F[i] \mid F \in \mathcal{F}\}$.

Since we need to apply the rules piecewise we need to partition the program P_M into

- P_{init}, all facts with time argument 0,
- P_{always}, consisting of the rules and static facts, which are applicable for any point in time: $P_{always} := P_M - P_{init}$.

Now we can compute the facts in the minimal model in the chronological order, timestamp by timestamp. We do so by using the predicates without time argument, i.e., $\bar{P}_{init}$ and $\bar{P}_{always}$.

- $\mathcal{N}_0 := \bar{P}_{init}$
  The set $\mathcal{N}_i$ contains seed facts for the next state i. Since at time 0, there is no previous state, the initial facts take the role of the seed facts here.
- $\mathcal{E}_0 := \emptyset$
  At time 0, there are no calls, and therefore no external input facts.
- $\mathcal{S}_i := \mathsf{lfp}(\mathsf{T}_{\bar{P}_{always} \cup \mathcal{N}_i \cup \mathcal{E}_i})$
  The "state i", i.e., the facts for time i are obtained iteratively by applying the rules in $\bar{P}_{always}$ to the seed facts $\mathcal{N}_i$, the static facts (also part of $\bar{P}_{always}$) and the input facts $\mathcal{E}_i$ until a fixpoint is reached. The derived facts include also calls and next_p-facts that refer to the next state.
- $\mathcal{N}_i := \{p(c_1, \ldots, c_n) \mid \mathsf{next\_}p(c_1, \ldots, c_n) \in \mathcal{S}_{i-1}\}$.
  This extracts and transforms the seed facts for next point in time i, $i \geq 1$.
- $\mathcal{C}_i := \{\mathsf{call\_}p(c_1, \ldots, c_n) \mid \mathsf{ncall\_}p(c_1, \ldots, c_n) \in \mathcal{S}_{i-1}\}$.
  These are the call facts for next point in time i, $i \geq 1$. One can see these calls as "output" of some kind of state machine (not yet a finite state machine).
- $\mathcal{E}_i := \{\mathsf{ret\_}f(c_1, \ldots, c_n) \mid \mathsf{ret\_}f(i, c_1, \ldots, c_n) \in \mathcal{E}\}$.
  These are the input facts from $\mathcal{E}$ for time $i \geq 1$ (with the time argument removed). They are given by the external environment, but note that causality requires that each fact in $\mathcal{E}_i$ is the result of a call in $\mathcal{C}_i$. Since the calls were computed in the previous state, we can actually execute them to compute $\mathcal{E}_i$.

Theorem 1. *This iterative computation by timepoints yields exactly the minimal model of the given program if we add the time argument:* $\mathcal{I}_{min} = \bigcup_{i=0}^{\infty} \mathcal{S}_i[i]$.

Theorem 2. *If P_M is finite and $\mathcal{E}$ is causal, each state $\mathcal{S}_i$, $i \in \mathbb{N}_0$, is finite.*

This ensures that we can effectively compute each state. Please remember that succ can only be used for switching to the next point in time. It cannot be used for computations within a state.

4   Precomputation of States

Our goal is to precompute the possible states, i.e., sets of derivable facts for a timestamp. Of course, such a precomputation is not always possible, because for some programs the set of facts at a point in time can possibly grow without limits over time. However, for the given small hardware, such programs would be problematic anyway (see also Sect. 6).

Of course, there are a number of values that are only known at runtime (input values). We use special variables to model them:

Definition 2 (Parameter Variable). *Let $V_1, V_2, \ldots$ be a sequence of pairwise distinct variables that do not occur in the given Datalog program (they are reserved). We call these variables "parameter variables".*

The parameter variables correspond to memory locations that are used for storing return values of the function calls (unknown at "compile time").

Definition 3 (Parameterized Fact). *A parameterized fact is a formula of the form $p(t_1, \ldots, t_m)$ where each t_i, $1 \leq i \leq m$, is a constant or a parameter variable.*

Definition 4 (Parameterized State). *A parameterized state is a finite set of parameterized facts.*

Parameters have a global meaning in the state: If two parameterized facts in a state both contain V_1, they will have the same value. This is a difference to normal variables in rules, which have only local scope (limited to a rule).

The initial state is S_0 as in Sect. 3. It does not contain parameters because it does not depend on input.

Definition 5 (Initial State). *The initial state is $S_0 = \mathsf{lfp}(T_{\bar{P}_{always} \cup \bar{P}_{init}})$.*

For instance, the example (see Fig. 2) contains the following rule (after elimination of syntactic sugar and the removal of the time argument as in Sect. 3):

$$\text{ncall\_readWindow}(R, ?) \leftarrow \text{hasWindow}(R).$$

This rule can be applied with the static configuration fact hasWindow(2). All rules depending on input are not yet applicable in the initial state. Therefore, the complete initial state S_0 in the example is:

hasWindow(2).	ncall_readWindow(2, ?).
adjacent(1, 2).	ncall_readDoor(1, 2, ?).

Now let any parameterized state be given (for instance, the initial one). Our goal is to compute the possible successor states. The given state contains a number of (parameterized) ncall_f-facts. For each such ncall_f-fact, there will be a ret_f-fact in the next (with a "fresh" parameter variable instead of the return value indicator "?"). In the example, we have two facts corresponding to the returns of the called functions:

ret_readWindow$(2, V_1)$.	Generated Code: `V1 = readWindow(1);`
ret_readDoor$(1, 2, V_2)$.	`V2 = readDoor(1, 2);`

If parameter variables appear as arguments in derived ncall_f-facts, we need to check at runtime whether the facts are unifiable, to prevent duplicate calls.

In the example, there are no next_p-facts. In general, the computation of the next state starts with the following facts:

Definition 6 (Seed Facts). *Let S be a parameterized state, and let*

- *next_$p_i(t_{i,1}, \ldots, t_{i,k_i})$ for $i = 1, \ldots, m$ be all (parameterized) next_p-facts in S, and*
- *ncall_$f_i(u_{i,1}, \ldots, u_{i,l_i})$ for $i = 1, \ldots, n$ be all (parameterized) ncall_f-facts in S (in some fixed order).*

Then the seed facts seed(S) for the next state are:

- $p_i(t_{i,1}, \ldots, t_{i,k_i})$ for $i = 1, \ldots, m$, and
- $\mathsf{ret\_f}_i(\hat{u}_{i,1}, \ldots, \hat{u}_{i,l_i})$ for $i = 1, \ldots, n$, where $\hat{u}_{i,j}$ is $u_{i,j}$, unless $u_{i,j}$ is ?, in which case $\hat{u}_{i,j}$ is the first currently unused parameter variable (not occurring in any $\mathsf{next\_p}$ or $\mathsf{ncall\_f}$ facts in $\mathcal{S}$, and not substituted already for ? in a previous $\mathsf{ncall\_f}$ fact in $\mathcal{S}$ or an argument to the left in the same fact).

With these "seed" facts (and the static facts), we want to apply again the rules to compute the next state. Now the problem is that for some rules, the values of the parameters do matter. E.g., consider the rule:

$$\mathsf{windowOpen}(R) \leftarrow \mathsf{ret\_readWindow}(R, \#open).$$

So the question is whether the parameter V_1 is equal to the constant $\#open$ or not. Now, when we want to apply the rule, we do a unification between the rule body and existing parameterized facts. In the example, this will bind the parameter V_1 to the constant $\#open$. Since at compile time, we do not know the value of V_1, the result will be a "conditional fact":

$$\mathsf{windowOpen}(2) \leftarrow V_1 = \#open.$$

"Conditional facts" were used by Brass and Dix for characterizing and computing negation semantics [3]. There, the conditions were delayed negative literals.

Definition 7 (Conditional Fact). *A conditional fact is a formula of the form* $p(t_1, \ldots, t_m) \leftarrow \varphi$ *where each* t_i, $i = 1, \ldots, m$, *is a constant or a parameter variable, and* φ *is a consistent conjunction of atomic formulas* $u \,\gamma\, u'$ *with* $\gamma \in \{=, \neq, <, \leq, \geq, >\}$ *and* u *and* u' *are parameters or constants.*

For the unification, we would need only conditions of the form $V = c$ and $V = V'$. However, we permit comparisons as built-in predicates in the rules, and if body literals with such predicates cannot be evaluated at compile time, they also become part of the condition.

Note that "consistent" means here that there is a variable assignment for the parameters such that the formula is true in the standard interpretation of the built-in predicates $\mathcal{I}_B$ with these values of the variables. E.g., $V_1 = 5 \wedge V_1 < 3$ is inconsistent. In the same way, φ_1 and φ_2 are called equivalent, if they have identical truth values in $\mathcal{I}_B$ for all variable assignments (ground substitutions).

Conditional facts with inconsistent conditions would not be useful. The consistency of conjunctions of the above form can be easily checked [4,8]. If one wants additional built-in predicates, one might need a more powerful constraint solver. However, forbidding inconsistent conditions is only an optimization: Without this, states might be obtained that are actually not reachable.

Definition 8 (Rule Application to Conditional Facts). *Let*

$$A \leftarrow B_1 \wedge \cdots \wedge B_m \wedge C_1 \wedge \cdots \wedge C_n$$

be a rule, where the B_i, $i = 1, \ldots, m$, *are normal literals, and the* C_i, $i = 1, \ldots, n$, *are literals with a built-in predicate. Let* $B_i' \leftarrow \varphi_i$, $i = 1, \ldots, m$, *be conditional facts and* θ *be a most general unifier for* $(B_1, \ldots, B_m)$ *and* $(B_1', \ldots, B_m')$ *that does not map parameters to variables of the rule (since the direction of variable-to-variable bindings is arbitrary, this is always possible). Let*

$\Phi := \{\varphi_i \mid i = 1, \ldots, m\} \cup \{C_i\theta \mid i = 1, \ldots, n\} \cup$
$\{V = V\theta \mid V$ *is a parameter variable occuring in some* $B_i', 1 \leq i \leq m\}$.

If Φ *is consistent, then the rule application yields* $A\theta \leftarrow \varphi$, *where* φ *is equivalent to a conjunction of all formulas in* Φ. *Else, the rule application is not possible.*

We permit any formula equivalent to Φ, because we want to eliminate duplicate conditions, as well as trivial conditions such as $V = V$ (when θ is the identity mapping for V), and of course conditions not containing parameter variables (can happen for $C_i\theta$—because of the required consistency, this must be true in the standard interpretation of the built-in predicates). The implementation is free to add or remove implied conditions. This might help to find duplicates. Actually, we want to eliminate not only duplicates, but conditional facts that are "weaker" than another conditional fact:

Definition 9 (Subsumed Conditional Fact). *A conditional fact* $A_1 \leftarrow \varphi_1$ *is subsumed by a conditional fact* $A_2 \leftarrow \varphi_2$ *iff for every ground substitution* θ *(for the parameters that occur in at least one of them) whenever* $\mathcal{I}_B \models \varphi_1\theta$, *also* $A_1\theta = A_2\theta$ *and* $\mathcal{I}_B \models \varphi_2\theta$ *hold.*
   Two conditional facts are called equivalent iff they subsume each other.

In other words: $p(t_1, \ldots, t_n) \leftarrow \varphi_1$ is subsumed by $p(u_1, \ldots, u_n) \leftarrow \varphi_2$ iff φ_1 implies $\varphi_2 \wedge (t_1 = u_1) \wedge \cdots \wedge (t_n = u_n)$.
   Obviously, subsumed conditional facts can be deleted in the fixpoint iteration, because the subsuming conditional fact is more general (in the case of equivalent facts, all except one can be deleted). An example for a quite complex case is: $p(V_1) \leftarrow V_1 \leq V_2 \wedge V_1 \geq V_2$ is subsumed by $p(V_2)$. The first conditional fact is only applicable if $V_1 = V_2$, and then it produces the same fact as the second.
   One possible algorithm is to "normalize" derived conditional facts in the following way. First, expand the condition in the rule body by all easily derived consequences, especially equations. Now, if the condition contains $V_i = c$ with a constant c, eliminate V_i from the head and other conditions by replacing it there by c (note that $V_i = c$ must be kept in the condition, because the conditional fact is applicable only under this condition). In the same way, if the condition contains $V_i = V_j$ with $i < j$, replace V_j everywhere else by V_i. Finally, order the remaining non-trivial conditions in some standard order. Then delete conditional facts with the same head and a superset of the conditions in the body.

Definition 10 (Successor State). *We write* $\check{T}_P$ *for the immediate consequence operator for conditional facts (possibly with elimination of subsumed conditional facts). Let a parameterized state* S *be given. The conditional successor state is*
$S' := \mathsf{lfp}(\check{T}_{\text{seed}(S) \cup \bar{P}_{always}})$.
   From the conditional successor state, we get one successor state for each consistent valuation ν *of the atomic formulas appearing in the conditions. A valuation is consistent if the conjunction of the atomic formulas it assigns* true *and the conjunction of the negations of the formulas it assigns* false *is consistent. Then* $S'|_\nu := \{A \mid A \leftarrow \varphi \in S', \nu \models \varphi\}$ *is the successor state for* ν.

In the example, the conditional successor state is:

ret_readWindow$(2, V_1)$.	windowOpen$(2) \leftarrow V_1 = $#open.
ret_readDoor$(1, 2, V_2)$.	doorOpen$(1, 2) \leftarrow V_2 = $#open.
hasWindow(2).	connected$(1, 2) \leftarrow V_2 = $#open.
adjacent$(1, 2)$.	connected$(2, 1) \leftarrow V_2 = $#open.
ncall_readWindow$(2, ?)$.	ncall_heatingOff$(2) \leftarrow V_1 = $#open.
ncall_readDoor$(1, 2, ?)$.	ncall_heatingOff$(1) \leftarrow V_1 = $#open $\land V_2 = $#open.

Thus, depending on the values of V_1 and V_2, there are four possible states (leaving out the unconditional part, i.e., the left side above).

	$V_1 = $#open		$V_1 \neq $#open	
	$V_2 = $#open	$V_2 \neq $#open	$V_2 = $#open	$V_2 \neq $#open
windowOpen(2)	×	×	−	−
doorOpen$(1, 2)$	×	−	×	−
connected$(1, 2)$	×	−	×	−
connected$(2, 1)$	×	−	×	−
ncall_heatingOff(2)	×	×	−	−
ncall_heatingOff(1)	×	−	−	−
	S_1	S_2	S_3	S_4

However, two states differ in their outside behavior only if they have different ncall_f or next_p-facts. These facts determine the calls that are done (the "output" of the machine), and the information moved into the next state (the state transition). Other facts are only needed during the computation. Thus, we can merge two states S and S' if seed$(S) = $ seed(S'). In the example, S_3 and S_4 have the same behavior as S_0. We do not have to compute their successor states.

In contrast, S_1 and S_2 behave differently, because of the calls to heatingOff. However, since ret_heatingOff does not appear in the rule bodies, this actually does not influence the successor states. So in this simple example, we are already done and have only three states: S_0, S_1, and S_2.

The function calls in these states are (with parameter variables for the result):

S_0	S_1	S_2
readWindow$(2, V_1)$	readWindow$(2, V_1)$	readWindow$(2, V_1)$
readDoor$(1, 2, V_2)$	readDoor$(1, 2, V_2)$	readDoor$(1, 2, V_2)$
	heatingOff(2)	heatingOff(2)
	heatingOff(1)	

In the example, the transition function is independent of the current state:

$V_1 = $#open		$V_1 \neq $#open
$V_2 = $#open	$V_2 \neq $#open	
S_1	S_2	S_0

Note that if V_1 (the sensor of the window) is not #open, the value of V_2 (the sensor at the door) does not matter. If we look at the full set of conditional facts, it does influence the connected-facts, but these are important for the observable

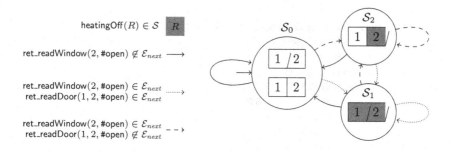

Fig. 3. The finite state machine for the example

outside behavior only if the window is open. The resulting finite state machine is shown in Fig. 3 (gray box means heatingOff in that room).

In general, states can be computed as shown in Fig. 4. The choice of the condition φ_i for the case analysis is important for the size of the generated code. E.g., if in the example, one would first choose $V_2 = $ #open, one would have to duplicate the case analysis for V_1. As a heuristics, we propose to minimize in each step the number of split conditions, i.e., remaining conditions in conditional facts that appear in both cases.

5   Generating Compact Code for Small Microcontrollers

The resulting code shown at the bottom of Fig. 4 is quite naive: While it implements a finite state machine, and has no problems with the small RAM, one will soon reach the limit of the flash memory for the program.

In the example, the state transition is actually independent of the "from" state. Obviously, we should not duplicate the quite large code block for the case analysis to compute the next state. In general, if the seed facts of two states differ only in facts that do not match any body literal, they do not influence the state transition. This is typical for function calls without a return value.

Another possibility to save machine instructions is to compile the same function call only once, and not once per state. For instance, in the example, the calls to the sensor functions happen in each state. So far, the algorithm has used simple sequential numbers to identify the states. However, one could use a bit in the state ID to specify whether some set of function calls must be done.

In effect, one can replace the `switch` over the sequential state numbers by (1) a sequence of `if`-statements that check bits in the current state ID and do some set of function calls, and (2) a much smaller `switch` or `else if`-chain guided by a part of the state ID that selects the code block for state transition (representing each distinct such block only once). Basically, a state is a set of facts. State IDs can be used as an efficient encoding of relevant subsets of facts.

```
(1)  Algorithm compile_to_extended_fsm:
(2)      STATES = {seed(S₀)};
(3)      DONE = ∅;
(4)      print_start();
(5)      while(STATES - DONE ≠ ∅) {
(6)          choose S ∈ STATES - DONE;
(7)          DONE = DONE ∪ {S};
(8)          print_case(S);
(9)          print_calls(S);
(10)         S' := lfp(Ť_{S∪P̄_always});
(11)         gen(S', ∅);
(12)         print_break();
(13)     }
(14)     print_end();
(15)
(16) Procedure gen(S', Φ):
(17)     S_poss := {A | A ← φ ∈ S' and Φ∪{φ} is consistent};
(18)     S_true := {A | A ← φ ∈ S' and Φ ⊢ φ};
(19)     if(S_true = S_poss) {
(20)         STATES = STATES ∪ {seed(S_true)};
(21)         print_trans(seed(S_true));
(22)     } else {
(23)         Choose A ← φ₁ ∧···∧ φₙ ∈ S' and i ∈ {1,...,n} such that
(24)             (1) A ∉ S_true,
(25)             (2) Φ∪{φ₁,...,φₙ} is consistent, and
(26)             (3) Φ ⊬ φᵢ;
(27)         print_if(φᵢ);
(28)         gen(S', Φ∪{φᵢ});
(29)         print_else();
(30)         gen(S', Φ∪{¬φᵢ});
(31)         print_fi();
(32)     }
```

```
/* print_start: */        /* print_if: */        /* print_fi: */
int state = 0;            if(V1 == open) {        }
#include "param_decls.h"    /* print_if: */       /* print_else: */
/* int V1; int V2; */       if(V2 == open) {      }
while(true) {                 /* print_trans: */   else {
  switch(state) {             state = 1;            /* print_trans: */
  /* print_case: */        /* print_else: */        state = 0;
  case 0:                   }                      /* print_fi: */
    /* print_calls: */      else {                 }
    V1 = readWindow(2);       /* print_trans: */   /* print_break: */
    V2 = readDoor(1, 2);       state = 2;          break;
```

Fig. 4. Computation of states with simple code generation result

6   Termination

Of course, there is the question of termination. If no input values are copied to the next state, i.e., no next_p-fact and no ncall_f-fact contains a parameter variable, termination is guaranteed, and we get a classic finite state machine as in the example: First, the number of calls is bounded, because they can contain only constants explicitly occurring in the program. Thus, also the number of parameter variables is bounded (for new parameter variables, the one with the smallest index is chosen that is not currently used). Finally, the number of facts in a state is bounded because there is only a fixed set of predicates and arguments.

However, the method works more generally for some input programs that lead to states with parameters (then the result is not really a finite state machine). While there are simple syntactic criteria to ensure that no input values are moved to the next state, we do not have this yet for the more general case. So one cannot know beforehand whether state generation will terminate. A simple solution is to set a limit for the number of states, or a limit for the number of parameter variables in a state, and stop if that limit is exceeded.

In future work, we will consider additional mechanisms to improve termination. For instance, we do not actually need parameter variables with types that permit only two values (e.g., open and closed), but do a case analysis instead. Functional dependencies for derived predicates [6] can be used to prove that only one of several parameter variables will be moved to the next state.

7   Negation

It is possible to allow also time-stratified negation as in [2] (i.e., negation is stratified when only deductive rules are considered). For the standard Datalog semantics, we would then use the well-founded model instead of the minimal model. For the conditional facts, we would delay also negative body literals as in [3], which can later be evaluated by positive and negative reduction as the other conditions are eliminated by the case analysis.

8   Conclusion

Our Datalog-based language Microlog can be used to manage state and state transitions through IO in a declarative fashion. By compilation into C-Code, we generate sources that are compatible with a vast amount of libraries available in the Arduino ecosystem. However, the approach is not limited to the Arduino microcontroller system.

Some programs can be translated to finite state machines where the state transitions of our logic program are precalculated, as we can deduce all possible behaviors throughout a program run independent of the concrete environment. This is particularly important because we then have a limit for the required memory. In systems with e.g., 1 KB RAM, it is obvious that the correctness of a program depends also on its ability to run with these very limited resources.

The result is a Finite State Machine when the behaviors depend only on values from the environment that do not lie arbitrarily long in the past.

The presented approach for compilation can also handle the more general case, where behaviors do depend on values from environment states long past, but only on a bounded number of those. Then the generated states have data values as parameters. Not all Microlog-programs can be translated in this way. In some cases states are being generated with more and more parameters. But when microcontrollers are embedded in some hardware application, one would expect that the program is provably correct, and does never stop with an "out of memory" error. Often the hardware does not even permit to communicate such a message.

Our compiler already supports program transformation for some classes of Microlog programs, as well as the naive evaluation, and we have developed example programs for Arduino and the LEGO EV3 robotics platform showing the viability of our approach. The compiler and example programs are available at https://dbs.informatik.uni-halle.de/microlog/.

References

1. Agatolio, F., Moro, M.: A workshop to promote Arduino-based robots as wide spectrum learning support tools. In: Merdan, M., Lepuschitz, W., Koppensteiner, G., Balogh, R. (eds.) Robotics in Education. AISC, vol. 457, pp. 113–125. Springer, Cham (2017). https://doi.org/10.1007/978-3-319-42975-5_11
2. Alvaro, P., Marczak, W.R., Conway, N., Hellerstein, J.M., Maier, D., Sears, R.: DEDALUS: Datalog in Time and Space. In: de Moor, O., Gottlob, G., Furche, T., Sellers, A. (eds.) Datalog 2.0 2010. LNCS, vol. 6702, pp. 262–281. Springer, Heidelberg (2011). https://doi.org/10.1007/978-3-642-24206-9_16
3. Brass, S., Dix, J.: A general approach to bottom-up computation of disjunctive semantics. In: Dix, J., Pereira, L.M., Przymusinski, T.C. (eds.) NMELP 1994. Lecture Notes in Computer Science, vol. 927, pp. 127–155. Springer, Heidelberg (1995). https://doi.org/10.1007/BFb0030663
4. Brass, S., Goldberg, C.: Proving the safety of SQL queries. In: Cai, K.Y., Ohnishi, A., Lau, M. (eds.) Proceedings of the 5th International Conference on Quality Software (QSIC 2005), pp. 197–204. IEEE Computer Society (2005)
5. Calimeri, F., Ianni, G.: External sources of computation for answer set solvers. In: Baral, C., Greco, G., Leone, N., Terracina, G. (eds.) LPNMR 2005. LNCS (LNAI), vol. 3662, pp. 105–118. Springer, Heidelberg (2005). https://doi.org/10.1007/11546207_9
6. Engels, C., Behrend, A., Brass, S.: A rule-based approach to analyzing database schema objects with datalog. In: Fioravanti, F., Gallagher, J.P. (eds.) LOPSTR 2017. LNCS, vol. 10855, pp. 20–36. Springer, Cham (2018). https://doi.org/10.1007/978-3-319-94460-9_2
7. Fink, M., Germano, S., Ianni, G., Redl, C., Schüller, P.: ActHEX: implementing HEX programs with action atoms. In: Cabalar, P., Son, T.C. (eds.) LPNMR 2013. LNCS (LNAI), vol. 8148, pp. 317–322. Springer, Heidelberg (2013). https://doi.org/10.1007/978-3-642-40564-8_31
8. Guo, S., Sun, W., Weiss, M.A.: Solving satisfiability and implication problems in database systems. ACM Trans. Database Syst. **21**, 270–293 (1996)

9. Kowalski, R., Sadri, F.: Reactive computing as model generation. New Gener. Comput. **33**(1), 33–67 (2015). https://doi.org/10.1007/s00354-015-0103-z
10. Lausen, G., Ludäscher, B., May, W.: On active deductive databases: the statelog approach. In: Freitag, B., Decker, H., Kifer, M., Voronkov, A. (eds.) Transactions and Change in Logic Databases, pp. 69–106. Springer, Berlin Heidelberg, Berlin, Heidelberg (1998)
11. Mueller, E.T.: Commonsense Reasoning: An Event Calculus Based Approach, 2nd edn. Morgan Kaufmann Publishers Inc., San Francisco (2014)
12. Russell, I., Rosiene, C.P., Gold, A.: A CS course for non-majors based on the Arduino platform. In: Proceedings of the 51st ACM Technical Symposium on Computer Science Education. SIGCSE 2020, p. 1309. Association for Computing Machinery, New York (2020). https://doi.org/10.1145/3328778.3372595
13. Schwarz, S., Wenzel, M.: ev3dev-prolog - prolog API for LEGO EV3. In: Draude, C., Lange, M., Sick, B. (eds.) INFORMATIK 2019: 50 Jahre Gesellschaft für Informatik - Informatik für Gesellschaft (Workshop-Beiträge), 23–26 September 2019, Kassel, Deutschland. LNI, vol. P-295, pp. 385–398. GI (2019). https://doi.org/10.18420/inf2019_ws41
14. Wenzel, M., Brass, S.: Declarative programming for microcontrollers - datalog on Arduino. In: Hofstedt, P., Abreu, S., John, U., Kuchen, H., Seipel, D. (eds.) INAP/WLP/WFLP -2019. LNCS (LNAI), vol. 12057, pp. 119–138. Springer, Cham (2020). https://doi.org/10.1007/978-3-030-46714-2_9

Model Checking and Probabilistic Programming

Generating Functions for Probabilistic Programs

Lutz Klinkenberg[1]([📧]) [ID], Kevin Batz[1] [ID], Benjamin Lucien Kaminski[1,2] [ID],
Joost-Pieter Katoen[1] [ID], Joshua Moerman[1] [ID], and Tobias Winkler[1] [ID]

[1] RWTH Aachen University, 52062 Aachen, Germany
{lutz.klinkenberg,kevin.batz,katoen,joshua,
tobias.winkler}@cs.rwth-aachen.de
[2] University College London, London, UK
b.kaminski@ucl.ac.uk

Abstract. This paper investigates the usage of generating functions (GFs) encoding measures over the program variables for reasoning about discrete probabilistic programs. To that end, we define a denotational GF-transformer semantics for probabilistic while-programs, and show that it instantiates Kozen's seminal distribution transformer semantics. We then study the effective usage of GFs for program analysis. We show that finitely expressible GFs enable checking super-invariants by means of computer algebra tools, and that they can be used to determine termination probabilities. The paper concludes by characterizing a class of—possibly infinite-state—programs whose semantics is a rational GF encoding a discrete phase-type distribution.

Keywords: Probabilistic programs · Quantitative verification · Semantics · Formal power series

1 Introduction

Probabilistic programs are sequential programs for which coin flipping is a first-class citizen. They are used e.g. to represent randomized algorithms, probabilistic graphical models such as Bayesian networks, cognitive models, or security protocols. Although probabilistic programs are typically rather small, their analysis is intricate. For instance, approximating expected values of program variables at program termination is as hard as the universal halting problem [22]. Determining higher moments such as variances is even harder. Deductive program verification techniques based on a quantitative version of weakest preconditions [20,25] enable to reason about the outcomes of probabilistic programs, such as what is the probability that a program variable equals a certain value. Dedicated analysis techniques have been developed to e.g., determine tail bounds [5], decide almost-sure termination [7,26], or to compare programs [1].

This research was funded by the ERC AdG project FRAPPANT (787914) and the DFG RTG 2236 UnRAVeL.

M. Fernández (Ed.): LOPSTR 2020, LNCS 12561, pp. 231–248, 2021.
https://doi.org/10.1007/978-3-030-68446-4_12

This paper aims at exploiting the well-tried potential of *probability generating functions* (PGFs) [19] for analyzing probabilistic programs. In our setting, PGFs are power series representations encoding *discrete* probability mass functions of joint distributions over program variables. PGF representations — in particular if finite—enable a simple extraction of important information from the encoded distributions such as expected values, higher moments, termination probabilities or stochastic independence of program variables.

To enable the usage of PGFs for program analysis, we define a denotational semantics of a simple probabilistic while-language akin to probabilistic GCL [25]. Our semantics is defined in a *forward* manner: given an input distribution over program variables as a PGF, it yields a PGF representing the resulting subdistribution. The "missing" probability mass represents the probability of non-termination. More accurately, our denotational semantics transforms *formal power series* (FPS). Those form a richer class than PGFs, which allows for overapproximations of probability distributions. The meaning of while-loops are given as least fixed points of FPS transformers. It is shown that our semantics is in fact an instantiation of Kozen's seminal distribution-transformer semantics [23].

The semantics provides a sound basis for program analysis using PGFs. Using Park's Lemma, we obtain a simple technique to prove whether a given FPS overapproximates a program's semantics i.e., whether an FPS is a so-called superinvariant. Such upper bounds can be quite useful: for almost-surely terminating programs, such bounds can provide *exact* program semantics, whereas, if the mass of an overapproximation is strictly less than one, the program is *provably non-almost-surely terminating*. This result is illustrated on a non-trivial random walk and on examples illustrating that checking whether an FPS is a superinvariant can be *automated* using computer algebra tools.

In addition, we characterize a class of—possibly infinite-state—programs whose PGF semantics is a rational function. These *homogeneous bounded programs* (HB programs) are characterized by loops in which each unbounded variable has no effect on the loop guard and is in each loop iteration incremented by a quantity independent of its own value. Operationally speaking, HB programs can be considered as finite-state Markov chains with rewards that can grow unboundedly large. It is shown that the rational PGF of any program that is equivalent to an almost-surely terminating HB program represents a multi-variate discrete phase-type distribution [29]. We illustrate this result by obtaining a closed-form characterization for the well-studied infinite-state dueling cowboys example [25,32].

Related Work. This paper presents a denotational semantics of probabilistic programs using PGFs and shows how the PGF representation can be exploited for program analysis. Our PGF semantics is defined in a forward manner: starting from an initial distribution on inputs, it determines the exact probability distribution over the program variables on termination. This fits within the realm of Kozen's denotational semantics [23]. Di Pierro and Wiklicky [10] provided a forward, denotational semantics of a similar programming language using infinite-dimensional

Hilbert spaces to provide a basis for program analysis by means of probabilistic abstract interpretation. Other semantics include backward denotational semantics using weakest preconditions [25] and operational semantics, e.g., using Markov chains [13].

Whereas advanced simulation techniques are the primary analysis technique for modern probabilistic programming languages, our approach using PGFs is exact. Our PGF approach is a forward approach and yields full probability distributions for a given program input. This is similar in spirit as in EfProb [8], a calculus based on a categorical semantics to reason about loop-free programs with discrete, continuous and quantum probability. Wp-reasoning [25] is an alternative analysis technique to prove properties of probabilistic programs. It determines the weakest pre-expectation function—the quantitative analogue of preconditions in classical program verification—in a backward manner for a given post-expectation, the property to be proven. Related program analysis techniques include the usage of couplings to prove program equivalence [1], abstract interpretation [9] and Hoare logics [15].

To the best of our knowledge, PGFs have recent scant attention in the analysis of probabilistic programs. A notable exception is [4] in which generating functions of finite Markov chains are obtained by Padé approximation. Computer algebra systems have been used to transform probabilistic programs [6], and more recently in the automated generation of moment-based loop invariants [2].

Organization of this Paper. After recapping FPSs and PGFs in Sects. 2–3, we define our FPS transformer semantics in Sect. 4, discuss some elementary properties and show it instantiates Kozen's distribution transformer semantics [23]. Section 5 presents our approach for verifying upper bounds to loop invariants and illustrates this by various non-trivial examples. In addition, it characterizes programs that are representable as finite-state Markov chains equipped with rewards and presents the relation to discrete phase-type distributions. Section 6 concludes the paper. The full paper can be found on ArXiv.[1]

2   Formal Power Series

Our goal is to make the potential of probability generating functions available to the formal verification of probabilistic programs. The programs we consider will, without loss of generality, operate on a fixed set of k program variables. The valuations of those variables range over $\mathbb{N}$. A *program state* σ is hence a vector in $\mathbb{N}^k$. We denote the state $(0, \ldots, 0)$ by $\mathbf{0}$.

A prerequisite for understanding probability generating functions are (multivariate) *formal power series—a special way of representing a potentially infinite k-dimensional array*. For $k=1$, this amounts to representing a *sequence*.

---

[1] https://arxiv.org/abs/2007.06327.

Definition 1 (Formal Power Series). *Let* $\mathbf{X} = X_1, \ldots, X_k$ *be a fixed sequence of k distinct formal indeterminates. For a state $\sigma = (\sigma_1, \ldots, \sigma_k) \in \mathbb{N}^k$, let $\mathbf{X}^\sigma$ abbreviate the formal multiplication $X_1^{\sigma_1} \cdots X_k^{\sigma_k}$. The latter object is called a monomial and we denote the set of all monomials over $\mathbf{X}$ by* $\mathrm{Mon}(\mathbf{X})$. *A (multivariate) formal power series (FPS) is a formal sum*

$$ F = \sum_{\sigma \in \mathbb{N}^k} [\sigma]_F \cdot \mathbf{X}^\sigma , \qquad \text{where} \qquad [\cdot]_F : \quad \mathbb{N}^k \to \mathbb{R}_{\geq 0}^\infty , $$

where $\mathbb{R}_{\geq 0}^\infty$ denotes the extended positive real line. We denote the set of all FPSs by FPS. *Let $F, G \in$ FPS. If $[\sigma]_F < \infty$ for all $\sigma \in \mathbb{N}^k$, we denote this fact by $F \ll \infty$. The addition $F + G$ and scaling $r \cdot F$ by a scalar $r \in \mathbb{R}_{\geq 0}^\infty$ is defined coefficient-wise by*

$$ F + G = \sum_{\sigma \in \mathbb{N}^k} \left([\sigma]_F + [\sigma]_G\right) \cdot \mathbf{X}^\sigma \qquad \text{and} \qquad r \cdot F = \sum_{\sigma \in \mathbb{N}^k} r \cdot [\sigma]_F \cdot \mathbf{X}^\sigma . $$

For states $\sigma = (\sigma_1, \ldots, \sigma_k)$ and $\tau = (\tau_1, \ldots, \tau_k)$, we define $\sigma + \tau = (\sigma_1 + \tau_1, \ldots, \sigma_k + \tau_k)$. The multiplication $F \cdot G$ is given as their Cauchy product (or discrete convolution)

$$ F \cdot G = \sum_{\sigma, \tau \in \mathbb{N}^k} [\sigma]_F \cdot [\tau]_G \cdot \mathbf{X}^{\sigma + \tau} . $$

Drawing coefficients from the extended reals enables us to define a *complete lattice* on FPSs in Sect. 4. Our analyses in Sect. 5 will, however, only consider FPSs with $F \ll \infty$.

3   Generating Functions

> A generating function is a device somewhat similar to a bag. Instead of carrying many little objects detachedly, which could be embarrassing, we put them all in a bag, and then we have only one object to carry, the bag.

> — George Pólya [31]

Formal power series pose merely a particular way of encoding an infinite k-dimensional array as yet another infinitary object, but we still carry all objects forming the array (the coefficients of the FPS) detachedly and there seems to be no advantage in this particular encoding. It even seems more bulky. We will now, however, see that this bulky encoding can be turned into a one-object bag carrying all our objects: the *generating function*.

Definition 2 (Generating Functions). *The* generating function *of a formal power series $F = \sum_{\sigma \in \mathbb{N}^k} [\sigma]_F \cdot \mathbf{X}^\sigma \in$ FPS with $F \ll \infty$ is the partial function*

$$ f : \quad [0, 1]^k \dashrightarrow \mathbb{R}_{\geq 0}, \quad (x_1, \ldots, x_k) \mapsto \sum_{\sigma = (\sigma_1, \ldots, \sigma_k) \in \mathbb{N}^k} [\sigma]_F \cdot x_1^{\sigma_1} \cdots x_k^{\sigma_k} . $$

In other words: in order to turn an FPS into its generating function, we merely treat every *formal* indeterminate X_i as an *"actual"* indeterminate x_i, and the formal multiplications and the formal sum also as *"actual"* ones. The generating function f of F is *uniquely determined* by F as we require all coefficients of F to be non-negative, and so the ordering of the summands is irrelevant: For a given point $x \in [0, 1]^k$, the sum defining $f(x)$ either converges *absolutely* to some positive real or diverges absolutely to ∞. In the latter case, f is undefined at x and hence f may indeed be partial.

Since generating functions stem from formal power series, they are infinitely often differentiable at $\mathbf{0} = (0, \ldots, 0)$. Because of that, we can recover F from f as the (multivariate) Taylor expansion of f at $\mathbf{0}$.

Definition 3 (Multivariate Derivatives and Taylor Expansions). *For $\sigma = (\sigma_1, \ldots, \sigma_k) \in \mathbb{N}^k$, we write $f^{(\sigma)}$ for the function f differentiated σ_1 times in x_1, σ_2 times in x_2, and so on. If f is infinitely often differentiable at $\mathbf{0}$, then the Taylor expansion of f at $\mathbf{0}$ is given by*

$$\sum_{\sigma \in \mathbb{N}^k} \frac{f^{(\sigma)}(\mathbf{0})}{\sigma_1! \cdots \sigma_k!} \cdot x_1^{\sigma_1} \cdots x_k^{\sigma_k} \ .$$

If we replace every indeterminate x_i by the *formal* indeterminate X_i in the Taylor expansion of generating function f of F, then we obtain the formal power series F. It is in precisely that sense, that f *generates* F.

Example 1 (Formal Power Series and Generating Functions). Consider the infinite (1-dimensional) sequence $1/2$, $1/4$, $1/8$, $1/16$, ... Its (univariate) FPS—the entity carrying all coefficients detachedly—is given as

$$\frac{1}{2} + \frac{1}{4}X + \frac{1}{8}X^2 + \frac{1}{16}X^3 + \frac{1}{32}X^4 + \frac{1}{64}X^5 + \frac{1}{128}X^6 + \frac{1}{256}X^7 + \ldots \ . \tag{$\dagger$}$$

On the other hand, its generating function—the bag—is given concisely by

$$\frac{1}{2 - x} \ . \tag{$\flat$}$$

Figuratively speaking, ($\dagger$) is itself the infinite sequence $a_n := \frac{1}{2^n}$, whereas ($\flat$) is a bag with the label "infinite sequence $a_n := \frac{1}{2^n}$". The fact that ($\dagger$) generates ($\flat$), follows from the Taylor expansion of $\frac{1}{2-x}$ at 0 being $\frac{1}{2} + \frac{1}{4}x + \frac{1}{8}x^2 + \ldots$. $\triangle$

The potential of generating functions is that manipulations to the functions—i.e. to the concise representations—are in a one-to-one correspondence to the associated manipulations to FPSs [12]. For instance, if $f(x)$ is the generating function of F encoding the sequence $a_1, a_2, a_3, \ldots$, then the function $f(x) \cdot x$ is the generating function of $F \cdot X$ which encodes the sequence $0, a_1, a_2, a_3, \ldots$

As another example for correspondence between operations on FPSs and generating functions, if $f(x)$ and $g(x)$ are the generating functions of F and G, respectively, then $f(x) + g(x)$ is the generating function of $F + G$.

Example 2 (Manipulating Generating Functions). Revisiting Example 1, if we multiply $\frac{1}{2-x}$ by x, we change the label on our bag from "infinite sequence $a_n := \frac{1}{2^n}$" to "a 0 followed by an infinite sequence $a_{n+1} := \frac{1}{2^n}$" and—just by changing the label—the bag will now contain what it says on its label. Indeed, the Taylor expansion of $\frac{x}{2-x}$ at 0 is $0 + \frac{1}{2}x + \frac{1}{4}x^2 + \frac{1}{8}x^3 + \frac{1}{16}x^4 + \dots$ encoding the sequence $0, 1/2, 1/4, 1/8, 1/16, \dots$ △

Due to the close correspondence of FPSs and generating functions [12], we use both concepts interchangeably, as is common in most mathematical literature. We mostly use FPSs for definitions and semantics, and generating functions in calculations and examples.

Probability Generating Functions. We now use formal power series to represent probability distributions.

Definition 4 (Probability Subdistribution). *A probability subdistribution (or simply subdistribution) over $\mathbb{N}^k$ is a function*

$$\mu: \quad \mathbb{N}^k \to [0,1], \quad such\ that \quad |\mu| = \sum_{\sigma \in \mathbb{N}^k} \mu(\sigma) \le 1 .$$

We call $|\mu|$ the mass *of μ. We say that μ is a (full) distribution if $|\mu| = 1$, and a proper subdistribution if $|\mu| < 1$. The set of all subdistributions on $\mathbb{N}^k$ is denoted by $\mathcal{D}_{\le}(\mathbb{N}^k)$ and the set of all full distributions by $\mathcal{D}(\mathbb{N}^k)$.*

We need subdistributions for capturing non-termination. The "missing" probability mass $1 - |\mu|$ precisely models the probability of non-termination.

The generating function of a (sub-)distribution is called a *probability generating function.* Many properties of a distribution μ can be read off from its generating function G_μ in a simple way. We demonstrate how to extract a few common properties in the following example.

Example 3 (Geometric Distribution PGF). Recall Example 1. The presented formal power series encodes a *geometric distribution* μ_{geo} with parameter $1/2$ of a single variable X. The fact that μ_{geo} is a proper probability distribution, for instance, can easily be verified computing $G_{geo}(1) = \frac{1}{2-1} = 1$. The expected value of X is given by $G'_{geo}(1) = \frac{1}{(2-1)^2} = 1$.   △

Extracting Common Properties. Important information about probability distributions is, for instance, the first and higher moments. In general, the kth factorial moment of variable X_i can be extracted from a PGF by computing $\frac{\partial^k G}{\partial X_i^k}(1, \dots, 1)$.[2] This includes the mass $|G|$ as the 0th moment. The marginal distribution of variable X_i can simply be extracted from G by $G(1, \dots, X_i, \dots, 1)$. We also note that PGFs can treat *stochastic independence.* For instance, for a bivariate PGF H we can check for stochastic independence of the variables X and Y by checking whether $H(X,Y) = H(X,1) \cdot H(1,Y)$.

---

[2] In general, one must take the limit $X_i \to 1$ from below.

4   FPS Semantics for pGCL

In this section, we give denotational semantics to probabilistic programs in terms of FPS transformers and establish some elementary properties useful for program analysis. We begin by endowing FPSs and PGFs with an order structure:

Definition 5 (Order on FPS). *For all* $F, G \in$ FPS, *let*

$$F \preceq G \quad \text{iff} \quad \forall \sigma \in \mathbb{N}^k: \quad [\sigma]_G \leq [\sigma]_F .$$

Lemma 1 (Completeness of $\preceq$ on FPS). (FPS, $\preceq$) *is a complete latttice.*

4.1   FPS Transformer Semantics

Recall that we assume programs to range over exactly k variables with valuations in $\mathbb{N}^k$. Our program syntax is similar to Kozen [23] and McIver & Morgan [25].

Definition 6 (Syntax of pGCL [23,25]). *A program P in* probabilistic Guarded Command Language *(pGCL) adheres to the grammar*

$$P ::= \texttt{skip} \mid \texttt{x}_i := E \mid P; P \mid \{P\} \, [p] \, \{P\}$$
$$\mid \texttt{if}(B) \, \{P\} \, \texttt{else} \, \{P\} \mid \texttt{while} \, (B) \, \{P\} ,$$

where $\texttt{x}_i \in \{\texttt{x}_1, \ldots, \texttt{x}_k\}$ *is a program variable, E is an arithmetic expression over program variables, $p \in [0,1]$ is a probability, and B is a predicate (called* guard*) over program variables.*

The FPS semantics of pGCL will be defined in a forward denotational style, where the program variables $\texttt{x}_1, \ldots, \texttt{x}_k$ correspond to the formal indeterminates $X_1, \ldots, X_k$ of FPSs.

For handling assignments, if-conditionals and while-loops, we need some auxiliary functions on FPSs: For an arithmetic expression E over program variables, we denote by $\text{eval}_\sigma(E)$ the evaluation of E in program state σ. For a predicate $B \subseteq \mathbb{N}^k$ and FPS F, we define the *restriction of F to B* by

$$\langle F \rangle_B := \sum_{\sigma \in B} [\sigma]_F \cdot \mathbf{X}^\sigma ,$$

i.e. $\langle F \rangle_B$ is the FPS obtained from F by setting all coefficients $[\sigma]_F$ where $\sigma \notin B$ to 0. Using these prerequisites, our FPS transformer semantics is given as follows:

Definition 7 (FPS Semantics of pGCL). *The semantics* $[\![P]\!]\colon \text{FPS} \to \text{FPS}$ *of a loop-free pGCL program P is given according to the upper part of Table 1.*

The unfolding operator $\Phi_{B,P}$ *for the loop* $\texttt{while} \, (B) \, \{P\}$ *is defined by*

$$\Phi_{B,P}\colon \quad (\text{FPS} \to \text{FPS}) \to (\text{FPS} \to \text{FPS}), \quad \psi \mapsto \lambda F. \, \langle F \rangle_{\neg B} + \psi\Big([\![P]\!](\langle F \rangle_B)\Big).$$

The partial order (FPS, $\preceq$) *extends to a partial order* (FPS $\to$ FPS, $\sqsubseteq$) *on FPS transformers by a point-wise lifting of $\preceq$. The least element of this partial order is the transformer $\mathbf{0} = \lambda F. \, 0$ mapping any FPS F to the zero series. The semantics of* $\texttt{while} \, (B) \, \{P\}$ *is then given by the least fixed point (with respect to $\sqsubseteq$) of its unfolding operator, i.e.* $[\![\texttt{while} \, (B) \, \{P\}]\!] = \text{lfp} \, \Phi_{B,P} .$

Table 1. FPS transformer semantics of pGCL programs.

P	$[\![P]\!](F)$
skip	F
$\mathbf{x}_i := E$	$\sum_{\sigma \in \mathbb{N}^k} \mu_\sigma X_1^{\sigma_1} \cdots X_i^{\mathrm{eval}_\sigma(E)} \cdots X_k^{\sigma_k}$
$\{P_1\} \, [p] \, \{P_2\}$	$p \cdot [\![P_1]\!](F) + (1-p) \cdot [\![P_2]\!](F)$
$\mathbf{if}\,(B)\,\{P_1\}\,\mathbf{else}\,\{P_2\}$	$[\![P_1]\!](\langle F \rangle_B) + [\![P_2]\!](\langle F \rangle_{\neg B})$
$P_1 \,\mathbf{;}\, P_2$	$[\![P_2]\!]\big([\![P_1]\!](F)\big)$
$\mathbf{while}(B)\{P\}$	$(\mathsf{lfp}\ \Phi_{B,P})(F)\,,\quad$ for $$\Phi_{B,P}(\psi) = \lambda F.\ \langle F \rangle_{\neg B} + \psi\Big([\![P]\!](\langle F \rangle_B)\Big)$$

Example 4. Consider the program $P = \{\mathbf{x} := 0\}\,[{}^1\!/{}_2]\,\{\mathbf{x} := 1\} \,\mathbf{;}\, \mathbf{c} := \mathbf{c} + 1$ and the input PGF $G = 1$, which denotes a point mass on state $\sigma = \mathbf{0}$. Using the annotation style shown in the right margin, denoting that $[\![P']\!]\,(G) = G'$, we calculate $[\![P]\!]\,(G)$ as follows:

$$/\!/\!/\ G$$
$$P'$$
$$/\!/\!/\ G'$$

$$/\!/\!/\ 1$$
$$\{\mathbf{x} := 0\}\,[{}^1\!/{}_2]\,\{\mathbf{x} := 1\}\,\mathbf{;}$$
$$/\!/\!/\ \tfrac{1}{2} + \tfrac{X}{2}$$
$$\mathbf{c} := \mathbf{c} + 1$$
$$/\!/\!/\ \tfrac{C}{2} + \tfrac{CX}{2}$$

As for the semantics of $\mathbf{c} := \mathbf{c} + 1$, see Table 2. $\qquad\qquad\triangle$

Before we study how our FPS transformers behave on PGFs in particular, we now first argue that our FPS semantics is well-defined. While evident for loop-free programs, we appeal to the Kleene Fixed Point Theorem for loops [24], which requires ω-continuous functions.

Theorem 1 (ω-continuity of pGCLSemantics). *The semantic functional $[\![\cdot]\!]$ is ω-continuous, i.e. for all programs $P \in$ pGCL and all increasing ω-chains $F_1 \preceq F_2 \preceq \ldots$ in* FPS,

$$[\![P]\!]\left(\sup_{n\in\mathbb{N}} F_n\right) = \sup_{n\in\mathbb{N}}\ [\![P]\!]\,(F_n)\,.$$

Theorem 2 (Well-definedness of FPS Semantics). *The semantics functional* $[\![\cdot]\!]$ *is well-defined, i.e. the semantics of any loop* while $(B)\{P\}$ *exists uniquely and can be written as*

$$[\![\text{while}\,(B)\,\{P\}]\!] = \text{lfp}\ \Phi_{B,P} = \sup_{n\in\mathbb{N}}\ \Phi_{B,P}^n(\mathbf{0})\ .$$

Table 2. Common assignments and their effects on the input PGF $F(X,Y)$.

P	$[\![P]\!](F)$
x := x + k	$X^k \cdot F(X,Y)$
x := k $\cdot$ x	$F(X^k, Y)$
x := x + y	$F(X, XY)$

4.2 Healthiness Conditions of FPS Transformers

In this section we show basic, yet important, properties which follow from [23]. For instance, for any input FPS F, the semantics of a program cannot yield as output an FPS with a mass larger than $|F|$, i.e. *programs cannot create mass.*

Theorem 3 (Mass Conservation). *For every* $P \in$ pGCL *and* $F \in$ FPS, *we have* $\big|[\![P]\!](F)\big| \leq |F|$.

A program P is called *mass conserving* if $\big|[\![P]\!](F)\big| = |F|$ for all $F \in$ FPS. Mass conservation has important implications for FPS transformers acting on PGFs: given as input a PGF, the semantics of a program yields a PGF.

Corollary 1 (PGF Transformers). *For every* $P \in$ pGCL *and* $G \in$ PGF, *we have* $[\![P]\!](G) \in$ PGF.

Restricted to PGF, our semantics hence acts as a subdistribution transformer. Output masses may be smaller than input masses. The probability of non-termination of the programs is captured by the "missing" probability mass.

As observed in [23], semantics of probabilistic programs are fully defined by their effects on point masses, thus rendering probabilistic program semantics linear. In our setting, this generalizes to linearity of our FPS transformers.

Definition 8 (Linearity). *Let* $F, G \in$ FPS *and* $r \in \mathbb{R}_{\geq 0}^\infty$ *be a scalar. The function* $\psi\colon$ FPS $\to$ FPS *is called a* linear transformer *(or simply* linear*), if*

$$\psi(r \cdot F + G) = r \cdot \psi(F) + \psi(G)\ .$$

Theorem 4 (Linearity of pGCL Semantics). *For every program* P *and guard* B, *the functions* $\langle \cdot \rangle_B$ *and* $[\![P]\!]$ *are linear. Moreover, the unfolding operator* $\Phi_{B,P}$ *maps linear transformers onto linear transformers.*

As a final remark, we can unroll while loops:

Lemma 2 (Loop Unrolling). *For any FPS* F,

$$[\![\text{while}\,(B)\,\{P\}]\!](F) = \langle F \rangle_{\neg B} + [\![\text{while}\,(B)\,\{P\}]\!]\big([\![P]\!](\langle F \rangle_B)\big)\ .$$

4.3   Embedding into Kozen's Semantics Framework

Kozen [23] defines a generic way of giving distribution transformer semantics based on an abstract measurable space $(X^n, M^{(n)})$. Our FPS semantics instantiates his generic semantics. The state space we consider is $\mathbb{N}^k$, so that $(\mathbb{N}^k, \mathcal{P}(\mathbb{N}^k))$ is our measurable space.[3] A measure on that space is a countably-additive function $\mu \colon \mathcal{P}(\mathbb{N}^k) \to [0, \infty]$ with $\mu(\emptyset) = 0$. We denote the set of all measures on our space by $\mathcal{M}$. Although, we represent measures by FPSs, the two notions are in bijective correspondence $\tau \colon \mathsf{FPS} \to \mathcal{M}$, given by

$$\tau(F) \;=\; \lambda S. \sum_{\sigma \in S} [\sigma]_F \;.$$

This map preserves the linear structure and the order $\preceq$.

Kozen's syntax [23] is slightly different from pGCL. We compensate for this by a translation function $\mathfrak{T}$, which maps pGCL programs to Kozen's. The following theorem shows that our semantics agrees with Kozen's semantics.[4]

Theorem 5. *The* FPS *semantics of* pGCL *is an instance of Kozen's semantics, i.e. for all* pGCL *programs P, we have*

$$\tau \circ [\![P]\!] = \mathfrak{T}(P) \circ \tau \;.$$

Equivalently, the following diagram commutes:

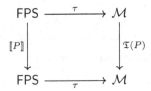

For more details about the connection between FPSs and measures, as well as more information about the actual translation, see Appendix A.3.

5   Analysis of Probabilistic Programs

Our PGF semantics enables the representation of the effect of a pGCL program on a given PGF. As a next step, we investigate to what extent a program analysis can exploit such PGF representations. To that end, we consider the overapproximation with loop invariants (Sect. 5.1) and provide examples showing that checking whether an FPS transformer overapproximates a loop can be checked with computer algebra tools. In addition, we determine a subclass of pGCL programs whose effect on an arbitrary input state is ensured to be a rational PGF encoding a phase-type distribution (Sect. 5.2).

---

[3] We note that we want each point σ to be measurable, which enforces a *discrete* measurable space.

[4] Note that Kozen regards a program P itself as a function $P \colon \mathcal{M} \to \mathcal{M}$.

5.1 Invariant-Style Overapproximation of Loops

In this section, we seek to overapproximate loop semantics, i.e. for a given loop $W = \texttt{while}\,(B)\,\{P\}$, we want to find a (preferably simple) FPS transformer ψ, such that $[\![W]\!] \sqsubseteq \psi$, meaning that for any input G, we have $[\![W]\!]\,(G) \preceq \psi(G)$ (cf. Definition 7). Notably, even if G is a PGF, we do not require $\psi(G)$ to be one. Instead, $\psi(G)$ can have a mass larger than one. This is fine, because it still overapproximates the actual semantics coefficient-wise. Such overapproximations immediately carry over to reading off expected values (cf. Sect. 3), for instance

$$\tfrac{\partial}{\partial X}[\![W]\!]\,(G)\,(\mathbf{1}) \quad \leq \quad \tfrac{\partial}{\partial X}\psi(G)(\mathbf{1})\;.$$

We use invariant-style reasoning for verifying that a *given* ψ overapproximates the semantics of $[\![W]\!]$. For that, we introduce the notion of a *superinvariant* and employ Park's Lemma [30]—well-known in fixed point theory—to obtain a conceptually simple proof rule for verifying overapproximations of while loops.

Theorem 6 (Superinvariants and Loop Overapproximations). *Let $\Phi_{B,P}$ be the unfolding operator of* $\texttt{while}(B)\{P\}$ *(cf. Def. 7) and $\psi\colon$ FPS $\to$ FPS. Then*

$$\Phi_{B,P}(\psi) \sqsubseteq \psi \quad \text{implies} \quad [\![\texttt{while}\,(B)\,\{P\}]\!] \sqsubseteq \psi\;.$$

We call a ψ satisfying $\Phi_{B,P}(\psi) \sqsubseteq \psi$ a *superinvariant*. We are interested in linear superinvariants, as our semantics is also linear (cf. Theorem 4). Furthermore, linearity allows to define ψ solely in terms of its effect on monomials, which makes reasoning considerably simpler:

Corollary 2. *Given $f\colon \mathrm{Mon}\,(\mathbf{X}) \to$ FPS, let the* linear extension $\hat{f}$ *of f be*

$$\hat{f}\colon \quad \mathrm{FPS} \;\to\; \mathrm{FPS}, \quad F \;\mapsto\; \sum_{\sigma \in \mathbb{N}^k} [\sigma]_F\, f(\mathbf{X}^\sigma)\;.$$

Let $\Phi_{B,P}$ be the unfolding operator of $\texttt{while}\,(B)\,\{P\}$*. Then*

$$\forall\, \sigma \in \mathbb{N}^k\colon \quad \Phi_{B,P}(\hat{f})(\mathbf{X}^\sigma) \sqsubseteq \hat{f}(\mathbf{X}^\sigma) \quad \text{implies} \quad [\![\texttt{while}\,(B)\,\{P\}]\!] \sqsubseteq \hat{f}\;.$$

We call an f satisfying the premise of the above corollary a *superinvariantlet*. Notice that superinvariantlets and their extensions agree on monomials, i.e. $f(\mathbf{X}^\sigma) = \hat{f}(\mathbf{X}^\sigma)$. Let us examine a few examples for superinvariantlet-reasoning.

Example 5 (Verifying Precise Semantics). In Program 1.1, in each iteration, a fair coin flip determines the value of x. Subsequently, c is incremented by 1. Consider the following superinvariantlet:

$$f(X^i C^j) \;=\; C^j \cdot \begin{cases} \dfrac{C}{2-C}, & \text{if } i = 1; \\[2mm] X^i, & \text{if } i \neq 1. \end{cases}$$

```
while (x = 1){
   {x := 0} [½] {x := 1};
   c := c + 1
}
```

Program 1.1. Geometric distribution generator.

To verify that f is indeed a superinvariantlet, we have to show that

$$\Phi_{B,P}(\hat{f})(X^iC^j) = \langle X^iC^j \rangle_{x\neq 1} + \hat{f}\left(\llbracket P \rrbracket (\langle X^iC^j \rangle_{x=1})\right)$$

$$\overset{!}{\sqsubseteq} \hat{f}(X^iC^j) .$$

For $i \neq 1$, we get

$$\Phi_{B,P}(\hat{f})(X^iC^j) = \langle X^iC^j \rangle_{x\neq 1} + \hat{f}(\llbracket P \rrbracket (0))$$

$$= X^iC^j = f(X^iC^j) = \hat{f}(X^iC^j) .$$

For $i = 1$, we get

$$\Phi_{B,P}(\hat{f})(X^1C^j) = \hat{f}\left(\tfrac{1}{2}X^0C^{j+1} + \tfrac{1}{2}X^1C^{j+1}\right)$$

$$= \tfrac{1}{2}f\left(X^0C^{j+1}\right) + \tfrac{1}{2}f\left(X^1C^{j+1}\right) \qquad \text{(by linearity of } \hat{f})$$

$$= \tfrac{C^{j+1}}{2-C} = f\left(X^1C^j\right) = \hat{f}\left(X^1C^j\right) . \qquad \text{(by definition of } f)$$

Hence, Corollary 2 yields $\llbracket W \rrbracket (X) \sqsubseteq f(X) = \tfrac{C}{2-C}$.

For this example, we can state even more. As the program is almost surely terminating, and $|f(X^iC^j)| = 1$ for all $(i,j) \in \mathbb{N}^2$, we conclude that $\hat{f}$ is exactly the semantics of W, i.e. $\hat{f} = \llbracket W \rrbracket$. $\triangle$

```
while (x > 0){
   {x := x + 1} [½] {x := x - 1};
   c := c + 1
}
```

Program 1.2. Left-bounded 1-dimensional random walk.

Example 6 (Verifying Proper Overapproximations). Program 1.2 models a one dimensional, left-bounded random walk. Given an input $(i,j) \in \mathbb{N}^2$, this program can only terminate in an even (if i is even) or odd (if i is odd) number of steps. This insight can be encoded into the following superinvariantlet:

$$f(X^0C^j) = C^j \quad \text{and}$$

$$f(X^{i+1}C^j) = C^j \cdot \begin{cases} \frac{C}{1-C^2}, & \text{if } i \text{ is odd;} \\ \frac{1}{1-C^2}, & \text{if } i \text{ is even.} \end{cases}$$

It is straightforward to verify that f is a *proper* superinvariantlet (proper because $\frac{C}{1-C^2} = C + C^3 + C^5 + \ldots$ is *not* a PGF) and hence f *properly* overapproximates the loop semantics. Another superinvariantlet for Program 1.2 is given by

$$h(X^i C^j) \;=\; C^j \cdot \begin{cases} \left(\frac{1-\sqrt{1-C^2}}{C}\right)^i, & \text{if } i \geq 1; \\ 1, & \text{if } i = 0. \end{cases}$$

Given that the program terminates almost-surely [16] and that h is a superinvariantlet yielding only PGFs, it follows that the extension of h is *exactly* the semantics of Program 1.2. An alternative derivation of this formula for the case $h(X)$ can be found, e.g., in [17].

For both f and h, we were able to prove that they are indeed superinvariantlets *semi-automatically*, using the computer algebra library SymPy [27]. The code is included in Appendix B (Program 1.5). △

```
while (x > 0){
    {x := x - 1} [¹/ₓ] {x := x + 1}
}
```

Program 1.3. A non-almost-surely terminating loop.

Example 7 (Proving Non-almost-sure Termination). In Program 1.3, the branching probability of the choice statement depends on the value of a program variable. This notation is just syntactic sugar, as this behavior can be mimicked by loop constructs together with coin flips [3, pp. 115f].

To prove that Program 1.3 does *not* terminate almost-surely, we consider the following superinvariantlet:

$$f(X^i) \;=\; 1 - \frac{1}{e} \cdot \sum_{n=0}^{i-2} \frac{1}{n!}, \qquad \text{where } e = 2.71828\ldots \text{ is Euler's number.}$$

Again, the superinvariantlet property was *verified semi-automatically*, by this we mean that we have constructed functions f and Φ by hand and Mathematica [18] confirmed that $\Phi(f) - f = 0$. Now, consider for instance $f(X^3) = 1 - \frac{1}{e} \cdot \left(\frac{1}{0!} + \frac{1}{1!}\right) = 1 - \frac{2}{e} < 1$. This proves, that the program terminates on X^3 with a probability strictly smaller than 1, witnessing that the program is not almost surely terminating. Note that in general this technique cannot be used for proving almost-sure termination. △

5.2   Rational PGFs

In several of the examples from the previous sections, we considered PGFs which were *rational functions*, that is, fractions of two polynomials. Since those are a particularly simple class of PGFs, it is natural to ask which programs have rational semantics. In this section, we present a semantic characterization of a class of while-loops whose output distribution is a (multivariate) *discrete phase-type* distribution [28,29]. This implies that the resulting PGF of such programs is an effectively computable rational function for any given input state. Let us illustrate this by an example.

```
while (x < 1 and t < 2){
        if (t = 0){
                {x := 1} [a] {t := 1}⨟ c := c + 1
        } else {
                {x := 1} [b] {t := 0}⨟ d := d + 1
        }
}
```

Program 1.4. Dueling cowboys.

Example 8 (Dueling Cowboys). Program 1.4 models two dueling cowboys [25]. The hit chance of the first cowboy is a and the hit chance of the second cowboy is b, where $a, b \in [0, 1]$.[5] The cowboys shoot at each other in turns, as indicated by the variable t, until one of them gets hit (x is set to 1). The variable c counts the number of shots of the first cowboy and d those of the second cowboy.

We observe that Program 1.4 is somewhat independent of the value of c. More specifically, placing the additional statement c := c + 1 either immediately before or after the loop yields two equivalent programs. In our notation, this is expressed as $[\![W]\!](C \cdot H) = C \cdot [\![W]\!](H)$ for all PGFs H. By symmetry, the same applies to variable d. Unfolding the loop once on input 1, yields

$$[\![W]\!](1) = (1 - a)C \cdot [\![W]\!](T) + aCX .$$

A similar equation for $[\![W]\!](T)$ involving $[\![W]\!](1)$ on its right-hand side holds. This way we obtain a system of two linear equations, although the program itself is infinite-state. The linear equation system has a unique solution $[\![W]\!](1)$ in the field of rational functions over the variables C, D, T, and X which is the PGF

$$G := \frac{aCX + (1 - a)bCDTX}{1 - (1 - b)(1 - a)CD} .$$

From G we can easily read off the following: The probability that the first cowboy wins (x = 1 and t = 0) equals $\frac{a}{1-(1-a)(1-b)}$, and the expected total number of shots of the first cowboy is $\frac{\partial}{\partial C}G(1) = \frac{1}{a+b-ab}$. Notice that this quantity equals ∞ if a and b are both zero, i.e. if both cowboys have zero hit chance.

If we write $G_{\mathbf{V}}$ for the PGF obtained by substituting all but the variables in $\mathbf{V}$ with 1, then we moreover see that $G_C \cdot G_D \neq G_{C,D}$. This means that C and D (as random variables) are stochastically dependent.   △

---

[5] These are *not* program variables.

The distribution encoded in the PGF $[\![W]\!](1)$ is a discrete phase-type distribution. Such distributions are defined as follows: A *Markov reward chain* is a Markov chain where each state is augmented with a reward vector in $\mathbb{N}^k$. By definition, a (discrete) distribution on $\mathbb{N}^k$ is of phase-type iff it is the distribution of the total accumulated reward vector until absorption in a Markov reward chain with a single absorbing state and a finite number of transient states. In fact, Program 1.4 can be described as a Markov reward chain with two states (X^0T^0 and X^0T^1) and 2-dimensional reward vectors corresponding to the "counters" (c, d): the reward in state X^0T^0 is $(1, 0)$ and $(0, 1)$ in the other state.

Each pGCL program describes a Markov reward chain [13]. It is not clear which (non-trivial) syntactical restrictions to impose to guarantee for such chains to be finite. In the remainder of this section, we give a characterization of while-loops that are equivalent to finite Markov reward chains. The idea of our criterion is that each variable has to fall into one of the following two categories:

Definition 9 (Homogeneous and Bounded Variables). *Let $P \in$ pGCL be a program, B be a guard and x_i be a program variable. Then:*

- *x_i is called* homogeneous *for P if $[\![P]\!](X_i \cdot G) = X_i \cdot [\![P]\!](G)$ for all $G \in$ PGF.*
- *x_i is called* bounded *by B if the set $\{\sigma_i \mid \sigma \in B\}$ is finite.*

Intuitively, homogeneity of x_i means that it does not matter whether one increments the variable before or after the execution of P. Thus, a homogeneous variable *behaves like an increment-only counter* even if this may not be explicit in the syntax. In Example 8, the variables c and d in Program 1.4 are homogeneous (for both the loop-body and the loop itself). Moreover, x and t are clearly bounded by the loop guard. We can now state our characterization.

Definition 10 (HB Loops). *A loop while (B) $\{P\}$ is called homogeneous-bounded (HB) if for all program states $\sigma \in B$, the PGF $[\![P]\!](\mathbf{X}^\sigma)$ is a polynomial and for all program variables x it either holds that*

- *x is homogeneous for P and the guard B is independent of x, or that*
- *x is bounded by the guard B.*

In an HB loop, all the possible valuations of the bounded variables satisfying B span the *finite* transient state space of a Markov reward chain in which the dimension of the reward vectors equals the number of homogeneous variables. The additional condition that $[\![P]\!](\mathbf{X}^\sigma)$ is a polynomial ensures that there is only a finite amount of terminal (absorbing) states. Thus, we have the following:

Proposition 1. *Let W be a while-loop. Then $[\![W]\!](\mathbf{X}^\sigma)$ is the (rational) PGF of a multivariate discrete phase-type distribution if and only if W is equivalent to an HB loop that almost-surely terminates on input σ.*

To conclude, we remark that there are various simple *syntactic* conditions for HB loops: For example, if P is loop-free, then $[\![P]\!](\mathbf{X}^\sigma)$ is always a polynomial. Similarly, if x only appears in assignments of the form x := x + k, $k \geq 0$, then x is homogeneous. Such updates of variables are e.g. essential in *constant probability programs* [11]. The crucial point is that such conditions are only sufficient but not necessary. Our *semantic* conditions thus capture the essence of phase-type distribution semantics more adequately while still being reasonably simple (albeit—being non-trivial semantic properties—undecidable in general).

6   Conclusion

We have presented a denotational distribution transformer semantics for probabilistic while-programs where the denotations are generating functions (GFs). The main benefit of using GFs lies in representing the entire probability distribution for a given input. Moreover, we have provided a simple invariant-style technique to prove that a given GF overapproximates the program's semantics and identified a class of (possibly infinite-state) programs whose semantics is a rational GF encoding a discrete phase-type distribution. Directions for future work include the (semi-)automated synthesis of invariants and the development of notions on how precise overapproximations by invariants actually are. On that end, a rule for verifying *under*approximations (e.g. à la [14], which provides inductive rules for underapproximating expected values) would be a major step in that direction.

Another direction for future work is to support $\mathbb{Z}$-valued program variables. For expected values, work on verifying signed random variables exists [21]—for PGFs, the situation is less clear. An obvious choice would be to employ formal *Laurent series*, but those only allow for *finitely many* negative indices, thus eluding distributions with both infinite positive and infinite negative support.

Acknowledgements. The authors thank the reviewers for their constructive and helpful comments and Marcel Hark for fruitful discussions.

References

1. Barthe, G., Grégoire, B., Hsu, J., Strub, P.: Coupling proofs are probabilistic product programs. In: POPL, pp. 161–174. ACM (2017)
2. Bartocci, E., Kovács, L., Stankovič, M.: Automatic generation of moment-based invariants for prob-solvable loops. In: Chen, Y.-F., Cheng, C.-H., Esparza, J. (eds.) ATVA 2019. LNCS, vol. 11781, pp. 255–276. Springer, Cham (2019). https://doi.org/10.1007/978-3-030-31784-3_15
3. Batz, K., Kaminski, B.L., Katoen, J., Matheja, C., Noll, T.: Quantitative separation logic: a logic for reasoning about probabilistic pointer programs. In: PACMPL 3 (POPL), pp. 34:1–34:29 (2019)
4. Boreale, M.: Analysis of probabilistic systems via generating functions and Padé approximation. In: Halldórsson, M.M., Iwama, K., Kobayashi, N., Speckmann, B. (eds.) ICALP 2015. LNCS, vol. 9135, pp. 82–94. Springer, Heidelberg (2015). https://doi.org/10.1007/978-3-662-47666-6_7

5. Bouissou, O., Goubault, E., Putot, S., Chakarov, A., Sankaranarayanan, S.: Uncertainty propagation using probabilistic affine forms and concentration of measure inequalities. In: Chechik, M., Raskin, J.-F. (eds.) TACAS 2016. LNCS, vol. 9636, pp. 225–243. Springer, Heidelberg (2016). https://doi.org/10.1007/978-3-662-49674-9_13

6. Carette, J., Shan, C.-C.: Simplifying probabilistic programs using computer algebra. In: Gavanelli, M., Reppy, J. (eds.) PADL 2016. LNCS, vol. 9585, pp. 135–152. Springer, Cham (2016). https://doi.org/10.1007/978-3-319-28228-2_9

7. Chatterjee, K., Fu, H., Novotný, P., Hasheminezhad, R.: Algorithmic analysis of qualitative and quantitative termination problems for affine probabilistic programs. ACM Trans. Program. Lang. Syst. **40**(2), 7:1–7:45 (2018)

8. Cho, K., Jacobs, B.: The EfProb library for probabilistic calculations. In: CALCO. LIPIcs, vol. 72, pp. 25:1–25:8. Schloss Dagstuhl - Leibniz-Zentrum für Informatik (2017)

9. Cousot, P., Monerau, M.: Probabilistic abstract interpretation. In: Seidl, H. (ed.) ESOP 2012. LNCS, vol. 7211, pp. 169–193. Springer, Heidelberg (2012). https://doi.org/10.1007/978-3-642-28869-2_9

10. Di Pierro, A., Wiklicky, H.: Semantics of probabilistic programs: a weak limit approach. In: Shan, C. (ed.) APLAS 2013. LNCS, vol. 8301, pp. 241–256. Springer, Cham (2013). https://doi.org/10.1007/978-3-319-03542-0_18

11. Giesl, J., Giesl, P., Hark, M.: Computing expected runtimes for constant probability programs. In: Fontaine, P. (ed.) CADE 2019. LNCS (LNAI), vol. 11716, pp. 269–286. Springer, Cham (2019). https://doi.org/10.1007/978-3-030-29436-6_16

12. Graham, R., Knuth, D., Patashnik, O.: Concrete Mathematics: A Foundation for Computer Science. Addison-Wesley, Boston (1994)

13. Gretz, F., Katoen, J., McIver, A.: Operational versus weakest pre-expectation semantics for the probabilistic guarded command language. Perform. Eval. **73**, 110–132 (2014)

14. Hark, M., Kaminski, B.L., Giesl, J., Katoen, J.: Aiming low is harder: induction for lower bounds in probabilistic program verification. Proc. ACM Program. Lang. **4**(POPL), 37:1–37:28 (2020)

15. den Hartog, J., de Vink, E.P.: Verifying probabilistic programs using a Hoare like logic. Int. J. Found. Comput. Sci. **13**(3), 315–340 (2002)

16. Hurd, J.: A formal approach to probabilistic termination. In: Carreño, V.A., Muñoz, C.A., Tahar, S. (eds.) TPHOLs 2002. LNCS, vol. 2410, pp. 230–245. Springer, Heidelberg (2002). https://doi.org/10.1007/3-540-45685-6_16

17. Icard, T.: Calibrating generative models: the probabilistic Chomsky-Schützenberger hierarchy. J. Math. Psychol. **95**, 102308 (2020). https://www.sciencedirect.com/journal/journal-of-mathematical-psychology/vol/95/suppl/C

18. Inc., W.R.: Mathematica, Version 12.0, champaign, IL (2019). https://www.wolfram.com/mathematica

19. Johnson, N., Kotz, S., Kemp, A.: Univariate Discrete Distributions. Wiley, Hoboken (1993)

20. Kaminski, B.L.: Advanced weakest precondition calculi for probabilistic programs. Ph.D. thesis, RWTH Aachen University, Germany (2019)

21. Kaminski, B.L., Katoen, J.: A weakest pre-expectation semantics for mixed-sign expectations. In: ACM/IEEE Symposium on Logic in Computer Science. LICS, pp. 1–12. IEEE Computer Society (2017)

22. Kaminski, B.L., Katoen, J.-P., Matheja, C.: On the hardness of analyzing probabilistic programs. Acta Informatica **56**(3), 255–285 (2018). https://doi.org/10.1007/s00236-018-0321-1

23. Kozen, D.: Semantics of probabilistic programs. In: FOCS, pp. 101–114. IEEE Computer Society (1979)
24. Lassez, J.L., Nguyen, V.L., Sonenberg, L.: Fixed point theorems and semantics: a folk tale. Inf. Process. Lett. **14**(3), 112–116 (1982)
25. McIver, A., Morgan, C.: Abstraction, refinement and proof for probabilistic systems. Monogr. Comput. Sci. Springer (2005). https://doi.org/10.1007/b138392
26. McIver, A., Morgan, C., Kaminski, B.L., Katoen, J.: A new proof rule for almost-sure termination. In: PACMPL **2**(POPL), pp. 33:1–33:28 (2018)
27. Meurer, A., et al.: SymPy: symbolic computing in python. PeerJ Comput. Sci. **3**, e103 (2017). https://doi.org/10.7717/peerj-cs.103
28. Navarro, A.C.: Order statistics and multivariate discrete phase-type distributions. Ph.D. thesis, DTU Lyngby (2018)
29. Neuts, M.F.: Matrix-geometric solutions to stochastic models. In: Steckhan, H., Bühler, W., Jäger, K.E., Schneeweiß, C., Schwarze, J. (eds.) DGOR, pp. 425–425. Springer, Heidelberg (1984). https://doi.org/10.1007/978-3-642-69546-9_91
30. Park, D.: Fixpoint induction and proofs of program properties. Mach. Intell. **5**, 59–78 (1969)
31. Pólya, G.: Mathematics and Plausible Reasoning: Induction and Analogy in Mathematics. Princeton University Press, Princeton (1954)
32. Wiklicky, H.: On dynamical probabilities, or: how to learn to shoot straight. In: Lluch Lafuente, A., Proença, J. (eds.) COORDINATION 2016. LNCS, vol. 9686, pp. 262–277. Springer, Cham (2016). https://doi.org/10.1007/978-3-319-39519-7_16

Verification of Multiplayer Stochastic Games via Abstract Dependency Graphs

Søren Enevoldsen, Mathias Claus Jensen, Kim Guldstrand Larsen,
Anders Mariegaard[(✉)], and Jiří Srba

Department of Computer Science, Aalborg University, Selma Lagerlöfs Vej 300,
9220 Aalborg East, Denmark
{senevoldsen,mcje,kgl,am,srba}@cs.aau.dk

Abstract. We design and implement an efficient model checking algorithm for alternating-time temporal logic (ATL) on turn-based multiplayer stochastic games with weighted transitions. This logic allows us to query about the existence of multiplayer strategies that aim to maximize the probability of game runs satisfying resource-bounded next and until logical operators, while requiring that the accumulated weight along the successful runs does not exceed a given upper bound. Our method relies on a recently introduced formalism of abstract dependency graphs (ADG) and we provide an efficient reduction of our model checking problem to finding the minimum fixed-point assignment on an ADG over the domain of unit intervals extended with certain-zero optimization. As the fixed-point computation on ADGs is performed in an on-the-fly manner without the need of a priori generating the whole graph, we achieve a performance that is comparable with state-of-the-art model checker PRISM-games for finding the exact solutions and sometimes an order of magnitude faster for queries that ask about approximate probability bounds. We document this on a series of scalable experiments from the PRISM-games benchmark that we annotate with weight information.

1 Introduction

Advances in model checking over the last decades allow us to verify larger systems using less resources. More recently, addition of quantitative aspects to model checking techniques became an important research topic. In order to model real-world applications, modelling formalisms must reflect both *probabilistic choices* [5] that model the uncertainties in system behaviour and at the same time be able to reason about quantitative aspects such as *cost* [22]. Moreover, in order to take into account the unpredictable environment, we need to verify that the desirable properties hold for all possible environmental behaviours. These aspects are usually modelled as *games*—in our case multiplayer games [39] where the players form coalitions in order to enforce a given property.

In order to reason about the probabilistic, cost and game aspects, we study the model of turn-based multiplayer stochastic games [40] where transitions contain multidimensional cost (weight) vectors, representing different

© Springer Nature Switzerland AG 2021
M. Fernández (Ed.): LOPSTR 2020, LNCS 12561, pp. 249–268, 2021.
https://doi.org/10.1007/978-3-030-68446-4_13

cost quantities. Multidimensional verification is necessary in applications where the system must respect bounds on several dependent quantities simultaneously (see e.g. [12,26,27]), such as consumption of energy and the discrete progression of time. We assume that any play of a game eventually accumulates some weight, which is natural for many models that include quantities such as time and energy, as executing an infinite number of actions without progressing time or consuming energy, is in many cases unrealistic. Our model can be seen as a weight extension of PRISM-games [32], where we consider properties formulated in an extension of alternating-time temporal logic (ATL) [1] that contains operators that specify existence of strategies for player coalitions ensuring cost- and probability bounded next or until properties. Hence we can ask questions like "is the probability that player 1 and 3 can form a coalition such that they enforce that a certain state is reachable within a total cost of c_1 time units and c_2 units of energy, greater than 0.8"?. We can thus reason about strategies that enforce strict bounds on multiple accumulating quantities *simultaneously*. This has many practical applications for systems that e.g. have to complete a number of tasks within a given time-limit, but must at the same time also stay within an energy budget, no matter how the environment behaves.

Our verification approach is based on a novel reduction to the problem of finding fixed points on *abstract dependency graphs* (ADG) [23,25], a recently introduced formalism that extends classical dependency graphs by Liu and Smolka [35]. Dependency graphs allow us to assign Boolean values to nodes in the graph, whereas ADGs assign to nodes values from a more abstract domain. In our case, we use the domain of the unit interval, representing probabilities, extended with a special value called "certain-zero" [20] that allows for an early termination of the on-the-fly computation of the fixed point on the ADG. We formally prove the correctness of our encoding and provide an efficient implementation that allows us to take as input the models described in PRISM-games and perform model checking in an on-the-fly manner. On three different PRISM-games case studies (annotated with the cost information), we demonstrate that our implementation is performance-wise comparable to the state-of-the-art model checker PRISM-games on queries that include exact probability bounds. However, once we lower the probability threshold from the exact probability bound, our on-the-fly algorithm demonstrates the potential of significantly outperforming PRISM-games.

Related Work. Since the introduction of stochastic games in the seminal work by Shapley [39], a number of variations and extensions of the classical formalism have been studied by the verification community. From a theoretical perspective, Condon [18,19] studies the complexity and algorithms for (simple) stochastic two-player games where the objective is to determine the winning probability for a given player. More recently, [4,10] consider controller synthesis for turn-based stochastic two-player games with PCTL winning objectives. Compared to our work, these papers consider controller synthesis instead of model-checking, and do not consider quantitative games and offer no implementation.

For *quantitative* verification of turn-based stochastic multiplayer games, [13] presents the logic rPATL (Probabilistic Alternating-Time Temporal Logic with Rewards) that naturally extends the logic Probabilistic Alternating-Time Temporal Logic [16] (PATL) with reward-operators. PATL is itself a probabilistic extension of ATL. A similar logic is introduced in [36], interpreted on concurrent games. The logic rPATL allows one to state that a *coalition* of players has a strategy such that either the probability of an event happening or an expected reward measure, is within a given threshold. Verifying rPATL properties on stochastic multiplayer games has been implemented in PRISM-games [32]. PRISM-games supports analysis of various types of games, verification of multi-objective properties [14] and has been applied to several case-studies (see e.g. [13,15]). Compared to our approach, PRISM-games does not directly support multidimensional reward-bounded properties and the current implementation offers no on-the-fly verification techniques that we demonstrate can yield a considerable speedup. Recently, a number of papers [6,28,38] have improved *value iteration*, the underlying technique of PRISM-GAMES, to deal with inaccuracies in the computed results stemming from certain termination criteria based on lower bound approximations. The approach has been applied to simple stochastic games [3,31] but has yet to be incorporated into PRISM-GAMES. Although our approach also computes lower bounds, we prove that we always terminate and compute the exact answer, relying on the fact that any formula is weight-constrained and any path of any game eventually accumulates weight. Another approach to computing measures on probabilistic models with multi-dimensional rewards and non-determinism (MDPs) is presented in [27]. A performance comparison is left for the future work.

Lastly, our work is a continuation of the work done in [30], where a special-purpose algorithm is developed for PCTL model-checking on models with multi-dimensional weights.We lift the approach to games by showing how to formally treat the game features in ADGs and we consider a new set of domain values that treat the probabilities symbolically while the weights are encoded explicitly; our novel encoding outperforms the pure symbolic implementation provided in [30] by an order of magnitude. Finally, our approach is more generic as it relies on the notion of ADGs and variations of the logic and/or the model can often be dealt with by minor modifications of the ADG construction, without the need of changing the underlying fixed-point algorithm. A related abstract approach is presented in [7,8], for solving systems of fixed-point equations over (continuous) lattices via a game-theoretic approach. An example application is (lattice-valued) μ-calculus model-checking [8] that deals with systems of fixed-point equations over infinite lattices (e.g. the reals), which in turn can be applied to model-checking probabilistic CTL or probabilistic μ-calculi.

2   Turn-Based Stochastic Games

Before introducing turn-based stochastic games, we present some preliminaries. For any set X, X^n is the set of all n-dimensional vectors with elements from

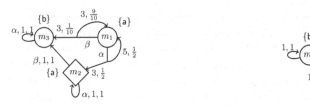

(a) Turn-based stochastic game   (b) Markov reward model

Fig. 1. Two simple models

X and x^n denotes the n-dimensional vector where $x \in X$ is at all coordinates. Thus, $\mathbb{N}^n$ is the set of all n-dimensional vectors of natural numbers and 0^n is the 0-vector. We assume a fixed dimensionality $n > 0$ and any vector is written in boldface e.g. $\mathbf{x} = (x_1, \ldots, x_n)$ and $\mathbf{y} = (y_1, \ldots, y_n)$ are vectors. For any such two vectors, we let $\mathbf{x} \geq \mathbf{y}$ if and only if $x_i \geq y_i$ for all $1 \leq i \leq n$. For any countable non-empty set X, we let $\mathcal{D}(X) = \{\mu \colon X \to [0,1] \mid \sum_{x \in X} \mu(x) = 1\}$ denote the set of probability distribution on X. For any distribution $\mu \in \mathcal{D}(X)$, the *support* of μ is defined as $\mathsf{support}(\mu) = \{x \in X \mid \mu(x) > 0\}$. By $\mathcal{D}_{\mathsf{fin}}(X) \subseteq \mathcal{D}(X)$ we denote the set of all distributions on X with finite support. For any two sets X and Y we denote by $f \colon X \rightharpoonup Y$ that f is a partial function from domain $dom(f) = X$ to range $ran(f) = Y$. For a set X, let X^* be the set of all finite strings over X and for any string $w = a_1 a_2 a_3 \cdots a_n \in X^*$, let $|w| = n$ denote the length of w and for all $1 \leq i \leq |w|$, let $w[i] = a_i$ be the i'th symbol of w. The empty string is denoted by ε.

2.1 Definition of Stochastic Games

We now present turn-based stochastic multiplayer games [39], where the states are partitioned into a number of sets, each set owned by a player of the game. The game begins in a state owned by one of the players and proceeds in turns, by letting the owner of the current state play one of the available actions after which the game then transitions to the next state by a probabilistic choice. Each such transition has an associated cost vector, that can naturally be interpreted as the cost of the transition. Hence, given a *strategy* for each player in the game, any non-determinism is resolved and the induced model is what is known as a Markov reward model with impulse rewards [2,17]. It is a folklore result that deterministic strategies are sufficient (see e.g. [37]). We assume a fixed finite set of atomic propositions AP.

Definition 1. *A Markov reward model (MRM) is a tuple $\mathcal{M} = (M, \rightarrow, \ell)$ where M is a finite set of states, $\rightarrow \colon M \to \mathcal{D}_{\mathsf{fin}}(\mathbb{N}^n \times M)$ is the transition function and $\ell \colon M \to 2^{\mathsf{AP}}$ is the labelling function.*

For any state $m \in M$, the probability of transitioning to another state m' with cost $\mathbf{w}$ is given by $\rightarrow(m)(\mathbf{w}, m')$. A $\mathbf{w}$-successor of a state m is any state m'

such that $\rightarrow(m)(\mathbf{w}, m') > 0$. A path is an infinite sequence of transitions $\pi = (m_1, \mathbf{w_1}, m_2), (m_2, \mathbf{w_2}, m_3) \cdots$ where s_{i+1} is a $\mathbf{w_i}$-successor of s_i for all $i \geq 1$. We let $\mathsf{Paths}(m)$ denote the set of all paths starting in m and for any path $\pi \in \mathsf{Paths}(m)$ we let $\pi[i]$ denote the i'th state of π and by π_n denote the finite prefix of π ending in state $\pi[n]$. We let $\mathcal{W}(\pi)(j) = \sum_{i=1}^{j-1} \mathbf{w_i}$ denote the accumulated cost up until the state $\pi[j]$. Finally, we let $\mathsf{Paths}(M)$ be the set of all paths of M. An example of an MRM can be seen in Fig. 1b.

In order to measure events of any MRM $\mathcal{M} = (M, \rightarrow, \ell)$, we introduce the classical cylinder set construction from [5, Chapter 10]. For any finite sequence $w = (m_1, \mathbf{w_1}, m_2), (m_2, \mathbf{w_2}, m_3) \cdots (m_{n-1}, \mathbf{w_{n-1}}, m_n)$, the cylinder set of w, $C(w)$ is the set of all paths having w as a prefix, i.e., $C(w) = \{\pi \in \mathsf{Paths}(M) \mid \pi_n = w\}$ and the measure associated to the cylinder of w is given by $\mathbb{P}_M(C(w)) = \prod_{i=1}^{n-1} \rightarrow(m_i)(\mathbf{w_i}, m_{i+1})$. We can now define the probability space $(M^\omega, \Sigma, \mathbb{P}_M)$ where Σ is the smallest σ-algebra that contains the cylinder sets of all finite alternating sequences of states and costs.

We now lift MRMs to stochastic games. Let Act be a fixed finite set of actions.

Definition 2. *A turn-based stochastic multiplayer game is a structure* $\mathcal{G} = (\Pi, M, \{M_i\}_{i \in \Pi}, \rightarrow, \ell)$ *where* Π *is a finite set of players,* M *is a finite set of state,* $\{M_i\}_{i \in \Pi}$ *is a partition of* M *such that for any* $i \in \Pi$, M_i *is a finite set of states controlled by player* i, $\rightarrow\colon M \times \mathsf{Act} \rightharpoonup \mathcal{D}_{\mathsf{fin}}(\mathbb{N}^n \times M)$ *is the finite (partial) transition function and* $\ell\colon S \rightarrow 2^{\mathsf{AP}}$ *is a labelling function.*

For any state $m \in M$ we let $\mathsf{Act}(m) = \{\alpha \in \mathsf{Act} \mid (m, \alpha) \in dom(\rightarrow)\}$ denote the set of *enabled* actions in state m and assume any game to be *non-blocking* by requiring all states to have at least one enabled action, i.e $\mathsf{Act}(m) \neq \emptyset$. An α-successor of a state m is any state m' such that the probability of transitioning from m by playing the α action is strictly positive for some cost vector $\mathbf{w} \in \mathbb{N}^n$, i.e. $\rightarrow(m, \alpha)(\mathbf{w}, m') > 0$. We let $\mathsf{succ}(m)_\alpha$ be the set of all α-successors of m. A path is an infinite sequence of transitions $\pi = (m_1, \alpha_1, \mathbf{w_1}, m_2), (m_2, \alpha_2, \mathbf{w_2}, m_3), \cdots$ where m_{i+1} is an α_i-successor of m_i with cost vector $\mathbf{w_i}$ for all $i \geq 1$. For any action $\alpha \in \mathsf{Act}(m)$ we let $\mathbf{k} = \min\{\mathbf{w} \mid \rightarrow(m, \alpha)(\mathbf{w}, m') > 0\}$ be the smallest possible transition cost when playing action α in m and say that α is $\mathbf{k'}$-enabled in m whenever $\mathbf{k'} \geq \mathbf{k}$ with $\mathsf{Act}_{\mathbf{k'}}(m) \subseteq \mathsf{Act}(m)$ being the set of all $\mathbf{k'}$-enabled actions in m. Thus, the set $\mathsf{Act}_{\mathbf{k'}}(m)$ contains the actions available to the player owning state m, if only transitions with a cost at most $\mathbf{k'}$ are permitted. We extend the path notation introduced for MRMs by letting Paths_i^* be the set of all finite paths that end in a state owned by player $i \in \Pi$ and for any such finite path $\pi \in \mathsf{Paths}_i^*$, the last state is given by $\mathsf{last}(\pi)$.

Remark 1. Notice that if $|\Pi| = 1$, the resulting model is a Markov decision process (MDP) [37] with impulse rewards and if furthermore $|\mathsf{Act}| = 1$, the model is an MRM. Hence, turn-based stochastic multiplayer games subsume both MDPs and MRMs.

In the rest of the paper, we restrict the class of games, by assuming that the accumulated cost of any loop of any game is of strictly positive magnitude. Formally, for any state $m \in M$, it is the case that for all paths $\pi \in \mathsf{Paths}(m)$ such that $\pi[j] = m$ for some $j \in \mathbb{N}$ (a loop), we have that $\mathcal{W}(\pi)(j) \neq 0^n$.

Example 1. Figure 1a depicts a simple turn-based stochastic game $\mathcal{G}$ with two players $\Pi = \{\bigcirc, \Diamond\}$. The states depicted as circles, m_1 and m_3 belong to player $\bigcirc$ while the state m_3 belongs to player $\Diamond$. The transition function is depicted by edges labelled by a given enabled action, followed by the cost of the transition and probabilities to successor states. The labelling of each state is given next to the state. In case the probability distribution assigns probability 1 to a single state, there is no branching and we simply label the edge with the action, probability 1 and the associated weight.

Starting from the state m_1, player $\bigcirc$ is in control and may choose either of the actions β and α. For β, there is a small probability, $\frac{1}{10}$, of transitioning to state m_3 whereas for action α, the game transitions to m_2 with probability $\frac{1}{2}$. In m_2, player $\Diamond$ may choose to let the game stay in state m_2 by the self-loop, or decide to transition to m_3.

If the two players are considered opponents and the goal of player $\bigcirc$ is to maximize the probability of reaching a state labelled b (m_3) within a given bound on the accumulated cost of reaching b, the only safe option is to always choose the action β in state m_1 as player $\Diamond$ can force the game to stay in state m_2 if it is ever reached. On the other hand, if the two players work together, player $\Diamond$ always plays the action β in m_2 to ensure that state m_3 is reached.

2.2   Strategies

As indicated by Example 1, any game unfolds by applying concrete *strategies* for each player, specifying which action to play in a given state. We now formally define strategies by first fixing a game $\mathcal{G} = (\Pi, M, \{M_i\}_{i \in \Pi}, \rightarrow, \ell)$. Given a player, $i \in \Pi$, a (history-dependent deterministic) strategy for player i in $\mathcal{G}$ is a function $\sigma : \mathsf{Paths}_i^* \rightarrow \mathsf{Act}$, that associates an action with each finite path ending in a state owned by player i. Thus, a strategy prescribes which action a player should play in a given state, given the full history of the game. For a strategy to be *sound*, only actions enabled in the given state must be played. Formally, a strategy σ for player i is sound if for any finite path $\pi \in \mathsf{Paths}_i^*$ with $\mathsf{last}(\pi) = m_i \in M_i$, it holds that $\sigma(\pi) \in \mathsf{Act}(m_i)$. We let $\mathfrak{S}_i$ denote the set of all sound strategies for player i in $\mathcal{G}$.

Remark 2. If $\sigma(\pi_1) = \sigma(\pi_2)$ for all $\pi_1, \pi_2 \in \mathsf{Paths}_i^*$ with $\mathsf{last}(\pi_1) = \mathsf{last}(\pi_2)$, we say that σ is a *memoryless strategy* for player i, as the action prescribed depends only on the last state of the game.

Strategies naturally extend to sets of players by considering what is commonly known as a *coalition* of players. A *coalition strategy* for any coalition $C \subseteq \Pi$ in $\mathcal{G}$, is a set of sound strategies, $\{\sigma_i\}_{i \in C}$, such that $\sigma_i \in \mathfrak{S}_i$ for all $i \in C$. We let $\mathfrak{S}_C$ denote the set of all coalition strategies for the coalition C, use σ_C to range over elements of $\mathfrak{S}_C$ and let $\overline{C} = \Pi \setminus C$ be the coalition containing the players in the complement of C. Given a state $m \in M$, coalition strategies σ_C and $\sigma_{\overline{C}}$, a unique MRM is induced from $\mathcal{G}$ by resolving the non-deterministic choices as prescribed by σ_C and $\sigma_{\overline{C}}$. We let $\mathbb{P}_{\mathcal{G}}^{\sigma_C, \sigma_{\overline{C}}}$ denote the probability measure on the induced MRM.

Example 2. Consider again the game from Fig. 1a and the memoryless strategies $\sigma_{\bigcirc}^{\alpha}$ and $\sigma_{\Diamond}^{\beta}$, respectively defined for any $\pi_{\bigcirc} \in \mathsf{Paths}_{\bigcirc}^*$ and $\pi_{\Diamond} \in \mathsf{Paths}_{\Diamond}^*$ as $\sigma_{\bigcirc}^{\alpha}(\pi_{\bigcirc}) = \alpha$ and $\sigma_{\Diamond}^{\beta}(\pi_{\Diamond}) = \beta$. The induced MRM is the one depicted in Fig. 1b.

3   Probabilistic Weighted ATL

As a specification language, we employ an extension of Alternating-time Temporal Logic (ATL [1]) to reason about whether or not a given *coalition* of players can together enforce the game to enjoy a given property, regardless of the strategy of the remaining players of the game. Hence, a witness of satisfaction is a coalition-strategy. Our logic is syntactically similar to probabilistic resource-bounded ATL proposed by Nguyen and Rakib [36], but interpreted on turn-based games instead of concurrent games. It is also similar to rPATL [13] employed by PRISM-games, except that we do no support expected reward measures but we allow instead for multi-cost bounded path formulae. We restrict negation to atomic propositions and therefore include conjunction and disjunction explicitly.

Definition 3 (Syntax).   *The set of PWATL formulae is given by the grammar:*

$$\phi ::= a \mid \neg a \mid \phi \wedge \phi \mid \phi \vee \phi \mid \langle\!\langle C \rangle\!\rangle_{\triangleright \lambda}[\psi] \qquad \text{(State Formulae)}$$
$$\psi ::= X_{\leq \mathbf{k}} \phi \mid \phi U_{\leq \mathbf{k}} \phi \qquad \text{(Path Formulae)}$$

where $a \in \mathsf{AP}$, $C \subseteq \Pi$, $\lambda \in [0, 1]$, $\mathbf{k} \in \mathbb{N}^n$ *and* $\triangleright = \{>, \geq\}$.

The set of PWATL state-formulae is denoted by $\mathcal{L}_{\mathsf{ATL}}$. A formula $\langle\!\langle C \rangle\!\rangle_{\triangleright \lambda}[\psi] \in \mathcal{L}_{\mathsf{ATL}}$ is satisfied by a state $m \in M$ of a game $\mathcal{G} = (\Pi, M, \{M_i\}_{i \in \Pi}, \rightarrow, \ell)$, if there exists a coalition strategy σ_C for the players in $C \subseteq \Pi$ such that, no matter which coalition strategy $\sigma_{\overline{C}}$ is assigned to the remaining players in $\overline{C}$, measuring paths that satisfy ψ in the MRM induces from $\mathcal{G}$ by σ_C and $\sigma_{\overline{C}}$, yields a probability p such that $p \triangleright \lambda$.

Definition 4 (Semantics). *For a game* $\mathcal{G} = (\Pi, M, \{M_i\}_{i \in \Pi}, \rightarrow, \ell)$, *state* $m \in M$, *and path* $\pi \in \mathsf{Paths}$, *PWATL satisfiability is defined inductively:*

$$
\begin{aligned}
\mathcal{G}, m &\models \mathsf{a} && \textit{iff} \quad \mathsf{a} \in \ell(m) \\
\mathcal{G}, m &\models \neg\mathsf{a} && \textit{iff} \quad \mathsf{a} \notin \ell(m) \\
\mathcal{G}, m &\models \phi_1 \wedge \phi_2 && \textit{iff} \quad \mathcal{G}, m \models \phi_1 \text{ and } \mathcal{G}, m \models \phi_2 \\
\mathcal{G}, m &\models \phi_1 \vee \phi_2 && \textit{iff} \quad \mathcal{G}, m \models \phi_1 \text{ or } \mathcal{G}, m \models \phi_2 \\
\mathcal{G}, m &\models \langle\!\langle C \rangle\!\rangle_{\rhd\lambda}[\psi] && \textit{iff} \quad \exists \sigma_C \in \mathfrak{S}_C. \forall \sigma_{\overline{C}} \in \mathfrak{S}_{\overline{C}}. \\
& && \qquad \mathbb{P}^{\sigma_C, \sigma_{\overline{C}}}_{\mathcal{G}}(\{\pi \in \mathsf{Paths}(m) \mid \mathcal{G}, \pi \models \psi\}) \rhd \lambda \\
\mathcal{G}, \pi &\models \phi_1 U_{\leq\mathbf{k}}\phi_2 && \textit{iff} \quad \exists j \in \mathbb{N}. \mathcal{G}, \pi[j] \models \phi_2, \mathcal{W}(\pi)(j) \leq \mathbf{k} \\
& && \qquad \text{and } \mathcal{G}, \pi[i] \models \phi_1 \text{ for all } i < j \\
\mathcal{G}, \pi &\models X_{\leq\mathbf{k}}\phi && \textit{iff} \quad \mathcal{G}, \pi[2] \models \phi \text{ and } \mathcal{W}(\pi)(1) \leq \mathbf{k}
\end{aligned}
$$

Example 3. Consider once again the game in Fig. 1a and the formula $\phi = \langle\!\langle C \rangle\!\rangle_{>\frac{1}{2}}[\mathsf{a}\, U_{\leq 8}\mathsf{b}]$ with $C = \{\bigcirc, \diamondsuit\}$ By the memoryless strategies from Example 2,.

$$
\mathbb{P}^{\sigma_C, \emptyset}_{\mathcal{G}}(\{\pi \in \mathsf{Paths}(m_1) \mid \mathcal{G}, \pi \models \mathsf{a}\, U_{\leq 8}\mathsf{b}\}) = \frac{1}{2}
$$

where $\sigma_C = \{\sigma^\alpha_\bigcirc, \sigma^\beta_\diamondsuit\}$. This is easily verified by inspecting the induced MRM in Fig. 1b. Hence, the two memoryless strategies do not prove $\mathcal{G}, m_1 \models \phi$.

To construct a strategy for $\mathcal{G}, m_1 \models \phi$, we modify the player $\bigcirc$ strategy. Instead of always playing action α, the action will depend on the accumulated cost of the game history: for any finite path $\pi_\bigcirc \in \mathsf{Paths}^*_\bigcirc$ of length at least j,

$$
\sigma^*_\bigcirc(\pi_\bigcirc) = \begin{cases} \beta & \text{if } \mathcal{W}(\pi_\bigcirc)(j) \leq 4 \\ \alpha & \text{otherwise} \end{cases}.
$$

4   Model Checking Through Dependency Graphs

In this section we demonstrate how the PWATL model-checking problem for turn-based stochastic multiplayer games can be reduced to computing fixed points on so-called *abstract dependency graphs* [25]. For a model-checking problem $\mathcal{G}, m \models \phi$, the corresponding abstract dependency graph represents the decomposition of the problem into sub-problems (*dependencies*) given by the inductive definition of PWATL semantics.

4.1   Abstract Dependency Graphs

An abstract dependency graph [25] is a (directed) graph consisting of a collection of vertices V, together with a function that to each $v \in V$ assigns a set of vertices being the *dependencies* of v and a function for computing the value of v, given the value of all its dependencies. The vertex values are drawn from a triple $\mathfrak{D} = (D, \sqsubseteq, \bot)$ where $(D, \sqsubseteq)$ is a partial order, $\bot \in D$ the least element of D and $\sqsubseteq$ must satisfy the *ascending chain condition*: for any infinite chain $d^1 \sqsubseteq d^2 \sqsubseteq d^3 \ldots$ of elements $d^i \in \mathfrak{D}$, there exists an integer k such that $d^k = d^{k+j}$ for all $j > 0$. This kind of ordering is referred to in [25] as a Noetherian ordering relation with least element (NOR). For any NOR we assume the elements are finitely representable, meaning that elements can be represented by finite strings.

For the computation of the value of each vertex we consider the application of *monotone* functions to the values of all its dependencies. Formally, for any $n \in \mathbb{N}$, $\mathcal{F}(\mathfrak{D}, n)$ on a NOR $(\mathfrak{D}, \sqsubseteq, \perp)$ is the set of all monotone functions $f : \mathfrak{D}^n \to \mathfrak{D}$ of arity n, where f is monotone if $d_i \sqsubseteq d'_i$ for all i, $1 \le i \le n$, implies $f(d_1, \ldots, d_n) \sqsubseteq f(d'_1, \ldots, d'_n)$ for any $d_1, \ldots, d_n, d'_1, \ldots d'_n \in D$, and we let $\mathcal{F}(\mathfrak{D}) = \bigcup_{n \ge 0} \mathcal{F}(\mathfrak{D}, n)$ be the collection of all such functions. We assume all functions $f \in \mathcal{F}(\mathfrak{D}, n)$ for any $n \in \mathbb{N}$ to be *effectively computable*, meaning that for any $f \in \mathcal{F}(\mathfrak{D}, n)$ and $d_1, \ldots, d_n \in D$, there exists an algorithm that terminates and computes the finite representation of $f(d_1, \ldots, d_n) \in D$.

We are now ready to define abstract dependency graphs.

Definition 5 (Abstract Dependency Graph [25]). *An* abstract dependency graph *(ADG) is a tuple* $G = (V, E, \mathfrak{D}, \mathcal{E})$ *where*

- *V is a finite set of vertices,*
- *$E : V \to V^*$ is an edge function from vertices to sequences of vertices such that $E(v)[i] \ne E(v)[j]$ for every $v \in V$ and every $1 \le i < j \le |E(v)|$, i.e. the co-domain of E contains only strings over V where no symbol appears more than once,*
- *$\mathfrak{D}$ is NOR with finitely representable elements, and*
- *$\mathcal{E}$ is a labelling function $\mathcal{E} : V \to \mathcal{F}(\mathfrak{D})$ such that $\mathcal{E}(v) \in \mathcal{F}(\mathfrak{D}, |E(v)|)$ for each $v \in V$, i.e. each edge $E(v)$ is labelled by an effectively computable monotone function f of arity that corresponds to the length of $E(v)$.*

In the following, we assume a fixed ADG $G = (V, E, \mathfrak{D}, \mathcal{E})$. For each vertex $v \in V$, $E(v)$ is a string containing all the vertices that represent dependencies of v and $\mathcal{E}(v)$ is the function computing the value of v given the values of all the dependencies of v in $E(v)$. An *assignment* is then a function $A : V \to D$, mapping each vertex to an element of the NOR $\mathfrak{D} = (D, \sqsubseteq, \perp)$. We let $\mathfrak{A}$ denote the set of all assignments and lift the ordering from $\mathfrak{D}$ to assignments: for any two assignments $A_1, A_2 \in \mathfrak{A}$, $A_1 \sqsubseteq A_2$ iff $\forall v \in V . A_1(v) \sqsubseteq A_2(v)$. It follows that $(\mathfrak{A}, \sqsubseteq)$ is a NOR, with minimum element $A_\perp$ defined for any $v \in V$ as $A_\perp(v) = \perp$. We define the *minimum fixed-point assignment* $A_{\min}$ for G as the minimum fixed point of the function $F : \mathfrak{A} \to \mathfrak{A}$, defined for any $v \in V$ as $F(A)(v) = \mathcal{E}(v)(A(v_1), A(v_2), \ldots, A(v_k))$ where $E(v) = v_1 v_2 \cdots v_k$. As each $\mathcal{E}(v)$ is monotone, it follows that F is a monotone function. In [25] it is proven, by applying standard reasoning for fixed points of monotonic functions [41], that $A_{\min}$ exists and is computable by repeated application of F on $A_\perp$. We end this section by presenting the result of [25]. For any $A \in \mathfrak{A}^k$ let $F^i(A)$ be the i'th repeated application of F on A, defined for $i = 0$ as $F^i(A) = A$ and $F^i(A) = F(F^{i-1}(A))$ for $i > 0$.

Theorem 1 [25]. *There exists $j \in \mathbb{N}$ such that $F^k(A_\perp) = A_{\min}$ for all $k \ge j$.*

4.2   The Reduction

We fix a game $\mathcal{G} = (\Pi, M, \{M_i\}_{i \in \Pi}, \rightarrow, \ell)$ for the remainder of this section and present the encoding of the problem $\mathcal{G}, m \models \phi$ for some state $m \in M$ and PWATL formula $\phi \in \mathcal{L}_{\mathsf{ATL}}$ by reduction to computing the minimal fixed point of a suitable abstract dependency graph $G = (V, E, \mathfrak{D}, \mathcal{E})$. In general, vertices of the graph are pairs (m, ϕ) where m is a state of $\mathcal{G}$ and $\phi \in \mathcal{L}_{\mathsf{ATL}}$ is a state-formula. These are referred to as *concrete vertices*. As our approach is symbolic, we introduce another type of vertex. For this, we let $\mathcal{L}_{\mathsf{ATL}}^? = \{\langle\!\langle C \rangle\!\rangle_{\triangleright?}[\phi_1 U_{\leq \mathbf{k}} \phi_2] \mid \mathbf{k} \in \mathbb{N}^n, \phi_1, \phi_2 \in \mathcal{L}_{\mathsf{ATL}}\} \cup \{\langle\!\langle C \rangle\!\rangle_{\triangleright?}[X_{\leq \mathbf{k}}\phi] \mid \mathbf{k} \in \mathbb{N}^n, \phi \in \mathcal{L}_{\mathsf{ATL}}\}$ be the set of all symbolic state-formulae. The *symbolic* vertices are then on the form $(m, \phi_?)$, where $\phi_? \in \mathcal{L}_{\mathsf{ATL}}^?$. We proceed by defining the domain $\mathfrak{D}$.

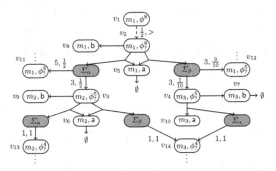

(a) ADG encoding of $\mathcal{G}, m_1 \models \phi$ for $\mathcal{G}$ from Figure 1a and $\phi = \langle\!\langle \bigcirc, \Diamond \rangle\!\rangle_{> \frac{1}{2}}[a \, U_{\leq 8} b]$

	v_1	v_2	v_3	v_4	$v_5 \cdots v_7$	$v_8 \cdots v_{10}$	$A_{\min}(v_{11 \cdots 12})$	$A_{\min}(v_{13 \cdots 14})$
A'	0	0	0	0	0	0	$\frac{1}{10}$	1
$F(A')$	0	$\frac{9}{100}$	1	1	1	$\widetilde{0}$	$\frac{1}{10}$	1
$F^2(A')$	0	$\frac{11}{20}$	1	1	1	$\widetilde{0}$	$\frac{1}{10}$	1
$F^3(A')$	1	$\frac{11}{20}$	1	1	1	$\widetilde{0}$	$\frac{1}{10}$	1

(b) Fixed point computation of ADG in Figure 2a

Fig. 2. Abstract dependency graph encoding example

The domain $\mathfrak{D}$. During the fixed point computation, the value of any node is, in general, a number that represents a lower bound on the probability of satisfaction. However, as we employ the *certain-zero* optimization of [20], we use also a special value $\widetilde{0}$, indicating that the value is 0 and can never change. Hence, 0 is a lower bound whereas $\widetilde{0}$ is an upper bound on the probability of satisfaction. We define the ordering depicted in Fig. 3, where the dotted line represents all numbers between 0 and 1, and where $0 \sqsubseteq \widetilde{0}$ and $p_1 \sqsubseteq p_2$ if $p_1 \leq p_2$ and $p_1, p_2 \in [0, 1]$. Hence, the certain zero value $\widetilde{0}$ and the strictly positive probabilities in $(0, 1]$ are incomparable. Thus, the domain is given by $\mathfrak{D} = ([0, 1] \cup \{\widetilde{0}\}, \sqsubseteq, 0)$. For any concrete vertices

Fig. 3. Ordering $\sqsubseteq$

(m, ϕ), the value assigned is either 0, 1 or $\widetilde{0}$. If the value becomes 1, m satisfies ϕ, thus whenever the root is assigned 1, the algorithm can safely terminate. However, if the value is 0, the current belief is that m does not satisfy ϕ and the algorithm cannot terminate as the value is a lower bound that may change. Once the value becomes $\widetilde{0}$, it is *certain* that m does not satisfy ϕ and the algorithm can terminate. For symbolic vertices $(m, \langle\!\langle C \rangle\!\rangle_{\triangleright?}\psi)$, assigning a probability p to the vertex indicates the existence of a strategy for the coalition C, such that measuring paths from m satisfying ψ, yields a probability at least p, no matter the strategy for the remaining players in $\overline{C}$. Hence, $\mathcal{G}, m \models \langle\!\langle C \rangle\!\rangle_{\triangleright p}\psi$.

Anticipating the definition of the vertex labelling function, we define the operations $\min, \max, +$ and $\cdot$ on elements from the domain $\mathfrak{D}$. If the operands are regular probabilities in $[0,1]$, the operations are defined in the natural way. Otherwise, for the certain zero value $\widetilde{0}$ and for any probability $p \in [0,1]$ we let $\min\{\widetilde{0},p\} = \widetilde{0}$, $\max\{\widetilde{0},p\} = p$, $\widetilde{0} + p = p$ and $\widetilde{0} \cdot p = \widetilde{0}$. Hence, $\widetilde{0}$ behaves like 0 when used in operations with regular probabilities. If both operands are $\widetilde{0}$ we let $\min\{\widetilde{0},\widetilde{0}\} = \widetilde{0}$, $\max\{\widetilde{0},\widetilde{0}\} = \widetilde{0}$, $\widetilde{0} + \widetilde{0} = \widetilde{0}$ and $\widetilde{0} \cdot \widetilde{0} = \widetilde{0}$.

Graph Construction. We define the set of vertices V and for each $v \in V$, the edge function $E(v)$ and labelling function $\mathcal{E}(v)$. The root of the graph is $(m, \phi) \in V$ and the rest of the graph is constructed by induction on ϕ.

For any vertex on the form $v = (m_*, \phi_*)$, where $\phi_* \in \mathcal{L}_{\mathsf{ATL}}$, the following rules define the edge function $E(v)$ and labelling function $\mathcal{E}(v)$.

$[\phi_* = \mathsf{a}]$: The formula has no dependencies and can be verified directly by inspecting the labelling of the state. Hence, $E(v) = \varepsilon$ and if $\mathsf{a} \in \ell(m_*)$ then $\mathcal{E}(v) = 1$, otherwise $\mathcal{E}(v) = \widetilde{0}$.

$[\phi_* = \neg\mathsf{a}]$: We let $E(v) = \varepsilon$, $\mathcal{E}(v) = 1$ if $\mathsf{a} \notin \ell(m_*)$ and $\mathcal{E}(v) = \widetilde{0}$ otherwise.

$[\phi_* = \phi_1 \vee \phi_2]$: We let the vertices $(m_*, \phi_1), (m_*, \phi_2) \in V$ be the dependencies of v, hence $E(v) = (m_*, \phi_1)(m_*, \phi_2)$. As each successor receives a Boolean value, disjunction is naturally defined as the maximum of the values of the two successor vertices and we let $\mathcal{E}(v)(p_1, p_2) = \max\{p_1, p_2\}$.

$[\phi_* = \phi_1 \wedge \phi_2]$: Similar to disjunction we let $(m_*, \phi_1), (m_*, \phi_2) \in V$ be the dependencies of v, i.e, $E(v) = (m_*, \phi_1)(m_*, \phi_2)$ and $\mathcal{E}(v)(p_1, p_2) = \min\{p_1, p_2\}$.

$[\phi_* = \langle\!\langle C \rangle\!\rangle_{\triangleright\lambda}(\phi_1 U_{\leq k}\phi_2)]$: The only dependency of v is the symbolic vertex $v' = (m_*, \langle\!\langle C \rangle\!\rangle_{\triangleright?}[\phi_1 U_{\leq k}\phi_2]) \in V$, i.e. $E(v) = v'$. As the value of v' is the probability p of satisfying the inner path formula, the value of v is 1 if and only if $p \triangleright \lambda$:

$$\mathcal{E}(v)(p) = \begin{cases} 1 & \text{if } p \triangleright \lambda \\ \widetilde{0} & \text{if } p = \widetilde{0} \wedge (\lambda > 0 \vee \triangleright = >) \\ 0 & \text{otherwise} \end{cases}$$

$[\phi_* = \langle\!\langle C \rangle\!\rangle_{\triangleright\lambda}(X_{\leq k}\phi)]$: We let the symbolic vertex $v' = (m_*, \langle\!\langle C \rangle\!\rangle_{\triangleright?}(X_{\leq k}\phi)) \in V$ be the dependency of v, i.e. $E(v) = v'$. The labelling of v is given by:

$$\mathcal{E}(v)(p) = \begin{cases} 1 & \text{if } p \triangleright \lambda \\ \widetilde{0} & \text{if } p = \widetilde{0} \wedge (\lambda > 0 \vee \triangleright = >) \\ 0 & \text{otherwise} \end{cases}$$

For any vertex $v = (m_*, \phi_?)$ with $\phi_? \in \mathcal{L}_{\mathsf{ATL}}^?$, the edge function $E(v)$ and labelling function $\mathcal{E}(v)$ are given by the following rules:

$[\phi_? = \langle\langle C \rangle\rangle_{\triangleright?}(\phi_1 U_{\leq \mathbf{k}} \phi_2)]$: To satisfy the inner path formula $\phi_1 U_{\leq \mathbf{k}} \phi_2$ for any path starting in m_*, either ϕ_2 must be satisfied by m_* or ϕ_1 must be satisfied by m_*. Hence, we let $v_1 = (m_*, \phi_1)$, $v_2 = (m_*, \phi_2)$ with $v_1, v_2 \in V$ be the two immediate dependencies of v. In case ϕ_2 is not satisfied by m_* but ϕ_1 is, the satisfaction of the inner path formula is due to the successors of m_*. Hence, any successor of m_* is also a dependency, if the cost of transitioning to the successor is within the formula bound $\mathbf{k}$. We let $\mathsf{Act}_\mathbf{k}(m_*) = \{\alpha_1, \ldots, \alpha_n\}$ be the $\mathbf{k}$-enabled actions in m_* and for any $\alpha_k \in \mathsf{Act}_\mathbf{k}(m_*)$ let $\mathsf{succ}(m_*)_{\alpha_k} = \{m_1^{\alpha_k}, \ldots, m_{j_{\alpha_k}}^{\alpha_k}\}$ be the set of all α_k-successors of m_* where, for all $1 \leq i \leq j_{\alpha_k}$, $\mathbf{w}_i^{\alpha_k} \leq \mathbf{k}$ is the cost and $p_i^{\alpha_k}$ is the probability of transitioning to $m_i^{\alpha_k}$, respectively.

For each $m_i^{\alpha_k}$ we let $v_i^{\alpha_k} = (m_i^{\alpha_k}, \langle\langle C \rangle\rangle_{\triangleright?}(\phi_1 U_{\leq \mathbf{k} - \mathbf{w}_i^{\alpha_k}} \phi_2)) \in V$ be a dependency of m_*. Hence, the edge function of v is given as

$$E(v) = v_1 v_2 v_1^{\alpha_1} \cdots v_{j_{\alpha_1}}^{\alpha_1} \cdots v_1^{\alpha_n} \cdots v_{j_{\alpha_n}}^{\alpha_n} \ .$$

For defining the labelling $\mathcal{E}(v)(q_1, q_2, q_1^{\alpha_1}, \ldots, q_{j_{\alpha_1}}^{\alpha_1}, \ldots, q_1^{\alpha_n}, \ldots, q_{j_{\alpha_n}}^{\alpha_n})$, we let $q_\Sigma^{\alpha_k} = \sum_{i=1}^{j_{\alpha_k}} p_i^{\alpha_k} \cdot q_i^{\alpha_k}$ be the weighted sum of successor values for any action $\alpha_k \in \mathsf{Act}_\mathbf{k}(m_*)$. The exact labelling function of m_* depends on whether m_* is owned by a player in the coalition or not. If $m_* \in M_i$ for some player $i \in C$ we let

$$\mathcal{E}(v)(q_1, q_2, q_1^{\alpha_1}, \ldots, q_{j_{\alpha_1}}^{\alpha_1}, \ldots, q_1^{\alpha_n}, \ldots, q_{j_{\alpha_n}}^{\alpha_n}) =$$
$$\max\{q_2, \min\{q_1, q_\Sigma^{\alpha_1}\}, \ldots, \min\{q_1, q_\Sigma^{\alpha_n}\}\} \ .$$

Otherwise, if $m_* \notin M_i$ for all players $i \in C$ we let

$$\mathcal{E}(v)(q_1, q_2, q_1^{\alpha_1}, \ldots, q_{j_{\alpha_1}}^{\alpha_1}, \ldots, q_1^{\alpha_n}, \ldots, q_{j_{\alpha_n}}^{\alpha_n}) =$$
$$\max\{q_2, \min\{q_1, q_\Sigma^{\alpha_1}, \ldots, q_\Sigma^{\alpha_n}\}\} \ .$$

$[\phi_? = \langle\langle C \rangle\rangle_{\triangleright?}(X_{\leq \mathbf{k}} \phi)]$: Let $\mathsf{Act}_\mathbf{k}(m_*) = \{\alpha_1, \ldots, \alpha_n\}$ be the set of $\mathbf{k}$-enabled actions in m_* and for any $\alpha_k \in \mathsf{Act}_\mathbf{k}(m_*)$ let $\mathsf{succ}(m_*)_{\alpha_k} = \{m_1^{\alpha_k}, \ldots, m_{j_{\alpha_k}}^{\alpha_k}\}$ be the set of all α_k-successors of m_* where, for all $1 \leq i \leq j_{\alpha_k}$, $\mathbf{w}_i^{\alpha_k} \leq \mathbf{k}$ is the cost and $p_i^{\alpha_k}$ is the probability of transitioning to $m_i^{\alpha_k}$, respectively.

For each $m_i^{\alpha_k}$ we let $v_i^{\alpha_k} = (m_i^{\alpha_k}, \phi) \in V$ be a dependency of m_*. Hence, the edge function of v is given as $E(v) = v_1^{\alpha_1} \cdots v_{j_{\alpha_1}}^{\alpha_1} \cdots v_1^{\alpha_n} \cdots v_{j_{\alpha_n}}^{\alpha_n}$. For defining the labelling $\mathcal{E}(v)(q_1^{\alpha_1}, \ldots, q_{j_{\alpha_1}}^{\alpha_1}, \ldots, q_1^{\alpha_n}, \ldots, q_{j_{\alpha_n}}^{\alpha_n})$, we let $q_\Sigma^\gamma = \sum_{i=1}^{j_{\alpha_k}} p_i^{\alpha_k} \cdot q_i^{\alpha_k}$ be the weighted sum of successor values for any action $\alpha_k \in \mathsf{Act}_\mathbf{k}(m_*)$. The exact labelling function of m_* depends on whether m_* is owned by a player in the coalition or not. If $m_* \in M_i$ for some player $i \in C$ we let

$$\mathcal{E}(v)(q_1^{\alpha_1}, \ldots, q_{j_{\alpha_1}}^{\alpha_1}, \ldots, q_1^{\alpha_n}, \ldots, q_{j_{\alpha_n}}^{\alpha_n}) = \max\{q_\Sigma^{\alpha_1}, \ldots, q_\Sigma^{\alpha_n}\} \ .$$

Otherwise, if $m_* \notin M_i$ for all players $i \in C$ we let

$$\mathcal{E}(v)(q_1^{\alpha_1}, \ldots, q_{j_{\alpha_1}}^{\alpha_1}, \ldots, q_1^{\alpha_n}, \ldots, q_{j_{\alpha_n}}^{\alpha_n}) = \min\{q_\Sigma^{\alpha_1}, \ldots, q_\Sigma^{\alpha_n}\} \ .$$

Monotonicity of the constructed labelling function $\mathcal{E}$ follows from the fact that the functions max, min, sum and product are monotonic functions. By applying the above definitions repeatedly from the root (m, ϕ), we obtain an abstract dependency graph encoding of the problem $\mathcal{G}, m \models \phi$.

Example 4. Consider again the stochastic game depicted in Fig. 1a. For any $k \in \mathbb{N}$ we let $\phi^k = \langle\!\langle \mathsf{O}, \Diamond \rangle\!\rangle_{>\frac{1}{2}}[\mathsf{a}\, U_{\leq k}\mathsf{b}]$ and $\phi_?^k = \langle\!\langle \mathsf{O}, \Diamond \rangle\!\rangle_{>?}[\mathsf{a}\, U_{\leq k}\mathsf{b}]$. We now encode the model-checking problem $\mathcal{G}, m_1 \models \phi^8$ into an abstract dependency graph $G = (V, E, \mathfrak{D}, \mathcal{E})$. A part of the resulting graph is visualised in Fig. 2a. Edges connecting the vertices correspond to the specific monotone functions given by our encoding. The greyed out shapes are not vertices but part of the monotonic function for a symbolic node, responsible for computing a weighted sum of successor values, q_Σ^γ, as prescribed by the encoding. We let $\mathcal{E}(v_i) = \varepsilon$ for $5 \leq i \leq 10$, $\mathcal{E}(v_i) = \tilde{0}$ for $8 \leq i \leq 10$ and $\mathcal{E}(v_i) = 1$ for $5 \leq i \leq 7$. This is visualised by vertices having either no outgoing edge or an edge pointing to the empty set. In general, separate unlabelled edges encode a maximum, while a minimum is computed over each unlabelled edge. For vertex v_2, the edge function is given by $E(v_2) = v_3 v_4 v_5 v_8 v_{11} v_{12}$ and the function computed at v_2 is thus

$$\mathcal{E}(v_2)(q_3, q_4, q_5, q_8, q_{11}, q_{12}) = \max\left\{q_8, \min\{q_5, q_\Sigma^\alpha\}, \min\{q_5, q_\Sigma^\beta\}\right\}$$

where $q_\Sigma^\alpha = \frac{1}{2} \cdot q_{11} + \frac{1}{2} \cdot q_3$ and $q_\Sigma^\beta = \frac{1}{10} \cdot q_4 + \frac{9}{10} \cdot q_{12}$. The dashed edge encodes

$$\mathcal{E}(v_1)(q_2) = \begin{cases} 1 & \text{if } q_2 > \frac{1}{2} \\ \tilde{0} & \text{if } q_2 = \tilde{0} \\ 0 & \text{otherwise} \end{cases} \ .$$

Theorem 2 (Correctness). *Let $\mathcal{G} = (\Pi, M, \{M_i\}_{i \in \Pi}, \to, \ell)$ be a game, $m \in M$ a state and $\phi \in \mathcal{L}_{\mathsf{ATL}}$ a property. For the abstract dependency graph rooted by (m, ϕ) it holds that $\mathcal{G}, m \models \phi$ iff $A_{\min}((m, \phi)) = 1$.*

As our domain $\mathfrak{D}$ does not satisfy the ascending chain condition, we cannot reuse the termination argument from [25]. We instead prove the termination by relying on our assumption that all loops are of strictly positive magnitude.

Theorem 3 (Termination). *There is $k \in \mathbb{N}$ s.t. $F^j(A_\perp) = A_{\min}$ for all $j \geq k$.*

Example 5. Consider the abstract dependency graph in Fig. 2a. For vertices $v_{11}, \ldots, v_{14}$, the minimal fixed point assignment is given by $A_{\min}(v_{11}) = A_{\min}(v_{12}) = \frac{1}{10}$ and $A_{\min}(v_{13}) = A_{\min}(v_{14}) = 1$. Assuming that these assignments have been pre-computed, we now repeatedly apply the fixed point operator to compute the minimal fixed point assignment to the remaining vertices. Hence, we start from an assignment A' such that $A'(v_i) = A_{\min}(v_i)$ for $11 \leq i \leq 14$ and $A'(v_i) = A_\perp(v_i)$ otherwise. The result can be seen in Fig. 2b After 3 iterations, the fixed point has been computed with a value of 1 assigned to v_1, hence by Theorem 2 we can conclude $\mathcal{G}, m_1 \models \langle\!\langle \bigcirc, \Diamond \rangle\!\rangle_{>\frac{1}{2}} [\mathsf{a}\, U_{\leq 8}\mathsf{b}]$.

5   Implementation and Experimental Evaluation

We evaluate our implementation on three different PRISM-games case studies. In *robot coordination* [34] problem two robots must reach a goal by traversing a square grid without crashing into each other; a 3-dimensional weight encodes the energy consumption of both robots and the time elapsed. In *collective decision making for sensor networks* [13] 4 sensors must agree on 3 preferable sites; a 2-dimensional weight encodes total energy consumption and time elapsed. In

experiment	prism	above	$\frac{\text{prism}}{\text{above}}$	exact	$\frac{\text{prism}}{\text{exact}}$	below10	$\frac{\text{prism}}{\text{below10}}$	below20	$\frac{\text{prism}}{\text{below20}}$
R-1-20-5	5.96	3.10	1.92	2.27	2.63	2.21	2.69	2.18	2.73
R-1-20-6	9.54	5.73	1.66	4.39	2.17	4.44	2.15	4.38	2.18
R-1-30-5	14.74	10.50	1.40	10.32	1.43	7.69	1.92	7.87	1.87
R-1-30-6	45.99	25.93	1.77	23.23	1.98	20.71	2.22	20.59	2.23
R-2-20-5	6.38	4.00	1.59	2.84	2.25	2.86	2.23	2.88	2.22
R-2-20-6	9.08	7.67	1.18	5.78	1.57	5.94	1.53	5.87	1.55
R-2-30-5	12.76	11.55	1.10	11.55	1.10	8.75	1.46	9.11	1.40
R-2-30-6	38.11	32.02	1.19	25.56	1.49	25.61	1.49	25.44	1.50
Average	17.82	12.56	1.48	10.74	1.83	9.78	1.96	9.79	1.96
S-1-10	1.03	0.17	6.11	0.11	9.06	0.12	8.54	0.10	10.34
S-1-20	3.32	2.14	1.55	2.07	1.60	0.95	3.48	0.91	3.64
S-2-10	1.00	0.19	5.21	0.10	9.66	0.11	9.15	0.11	9.27
S-2-20	3.74	2.47	1.51	2.37	1.57	1.03	3.62	1.08	3.45
S-3-10	0.98	0.18	5.55	0.11	8.70	0.11	9.19	0.10	9.57
S-3-20	3.95	2.59	1.52	2.30	1.72	1.29	3.05	1.07	3.69
S-4-10	1.22	0.20	6.11	0.10	11.73	0.12	10.16	0.11	11.23
S-4-20	4.84	2.49	1.94	2.47	1.96	2.31	2.10	1.11	4.36
Average	2.51	1.30	3.69	1.20	5.75	0.76	6.16	0.57	6.94
T-29-1697	50.30	55.54	0.91	56.27	0.89	55.75	0.90	53.73	0.94
T-18-1115	73.83	60.40	1.22	64.39	1.15	59.37	1.24	61.59	1.20
T-28-1803	34.43	40.21	0.86	38.53	0.89	36.94	0.93	34.84	0.99
T-29-1871	38.18	45.06	0.85	45.55	0.84	41.84	0.91	39.69	0.96
T-27-1907	38.32	20.17	1.90	17.44	2.20	17.33	2.21	17.89	2.14
T-20-1209	30.21	23.60	1.28	23.81	1.27	22.36	1.35	20.49	1.47
T-23-1565	37.27	28.34	1.32	30.49	1.22	26.96	1.38	26.96	1.38
T-16-828	20.92	27.90	0.75	26.92	0.78	26.33	0.79	25.16	0.83
Average	40.43	37.65	1.14	37.93	1.16	35.86	1.21	35.04	1.24

Fig. 4. R-A-B-C is a 2-robot model with A collaborating robots, cost-bound of B on a grid of size C with queries of the type $\langle\!\langle r1, \ldots, rA \rangle\!\rangle_{\triangleright\lambda}(\neg\text{crash } U_{\leq(\mathbf{B},\mathbf{B},\mathbf{B})} \text{ goal}1)$. S-X-Y is a sensor model with 4 sensors with X collaborating sensors with a cost-bound of Y and the query $\langle\!\langle s1, \ldots, sX \rangle\!\rangle_{\triangleright\lambda}(\text{true } U_{\leq(\mathbf{Y},\mathbf{Y})} \text{ decision\_made})$. T-Q-R is task graph problem and checks whether all tasks can be completed within at most Q time using R energy by the query $\langle\!\langle \text{sched} \rangle\!\rangle_{\triangleright\lambda}(\text{true } U_{\leq(\mathbf{Q},\mathbf{R})} \text{ tasks\_complete})$.

task-graph-scheduling [9,33], a set of tasks must be scheduled on two processors; a 3-dimensional weight encodes energy consumption for each processor and time elapsed. We also compare with a Python implementation for PCTL model-checking from [30] on the PRISM case study *synchronous leader election* [29].

A package to reproduce our results can be found at http://people.cs.aau. dk/~am/LOPSTR2020/. Our open-source implementation is written in C++ without platform specific code. To obviate the need to create our own parser for PRISM models, we modify the export functionality in PRISM-games to construct an explicit transition system that becomes an input to implementation. Furthermore, as PRISM-games do not directly support verification of multidimensional cost-bounded properties, we cannot rely on built-in reward structures and instead introduce variables to capture the accumulated cost. For each model-checking question, we bound the variables by a precision derived from the property, effectively creating a bounded unfolding of the original model, sufficient for verifying the query in question. As the model is bounded by the query precision, it is sufficient to verify in PRISM-games the corresponding unbounded query to solve the original model-checking problem.

experiment	tool	above	$\frac{python}{adg}$	exact	$\frac{python}{adg}$	below10	$\frac{python}{adg}$	below20	$\frac{python}{adg}$
L-4-4-10	python	0.45	11.25	0.48	12.00	0.42	10.50	0.36	12.00
	adg	0.04		0.04		0.04		0.03	
L-5-4-12	python	3.67	14.12	2.97	11.88	3.14	12.56	2.71	16.94
	adg	0.26		0.25		0.25		0.16	
L-4-6-10	python	3.8	15.83	3.64	15.83	3.16	21.07	3.24	21.60
	adg	0.24		0.23		0.15		0.15	
L-6-4-14	python	36.99	25.69	38.32	27.57	35.99	25.89	28.29	31.79
	adg	1.44		1.39		1.39		0.89	
L-5-6-12	python	88.52	42.56	91.2	45.37	86.31	63.93	85.57	62.92
	adg	2.08		2.01		1.35		1.36	
Average	python	26.69	21.89	27.32	22.53	25.80	26.79	24.03	29.05
	adg	0.81		0.78		0.64		0.52	

Fig. 5. L-N-K-W is a leader election model with N processes, K choices and queries of the form $\mathcal{P}_{\rhd\lambda}(\text{true } U_{\leq(\mathbf{w},\mathbf{2w},\mathbf{3w})} \text{ elected})$. Additionally, python denotes the implementation from [30] and adg denotes our implementation.

5.1   Results

Experiments are run on a Ubuntu 14.04 cluster with AMD Opteron 6376 processors. Each experiment has a maximum time-out of two hours and 14GB of virtual memory. Figure 4 displays the experimental data for the PRISM-games comparison. The verified formulae are of the form $\langle\!\langle C \rangle\!\rangle_{\rhd\lambda}(\psi)$ and specified in the caption of the table—the weight dimension being 3 for the robot experiment and 2 for the remaining two. The column labelled with 'prism' shows the time (in seconds) it took PRISM-games to verify a query (as PRISM-games computes the exact solution, the times do not vary for the different variants of the formula). The columns for 'above' ($\lambda = p + 0.000001$), 'exact' ($\lambda = p$), 'below10' ($\lambda = p - \frac{p}{10}$) and 'below20' ($\lambda = p - \frac{p}{5}$) describe the different instantiations of λ used in the queries, where p is the exact probability computed by PRISM-games. Hence, it is always the case that a formula is satisfied for 'exact', 'below10', 'below20' and never for 'above'. The remaining columns, e.g. $\frac{prism}{above}$, show the speedup-ratio. As both tools rely on the explicit engine of PRISM-games for model construction, we report only the time spent on verification, as the model construction time is identical for both tools.

The experiments show that for formulae that query the exact or slightly above probability, our on-the-fly approach achieves verification times comparable or better than those of PRISM-games. Our approach takes slightly more time to derive that a formula does not hold, which is expected for an on-the-fly method. Our running times in general improve as we allow for more slack in the λ bound. The robot experiment achieves on average about twice as fast verification for the 'below10' and 'below20' queries. In the sensor experiment, the certain-zero approach in combination with on-the-fly verification achieves for the 'below20' on average seven times faster verification, sometimes showing an order of magnitude improvement. Regarding the memory consumption, our method uses on average 3.4 times less memory on the robot experiment, 11.0 times less memory on the sensor experiment and 1.5 times less memory on task graphs.

The efficiency of our approach comes from i) early termination including the certain-zero optimization and ii) the local (on-the-fly) construction and exploration of the ADG. In contrast to PRISM-GAMES, we do not calculate the entire fixed point but only what is necessary to answer the model-checking question. Experiments show that we are on average 30%, 50%, and 15% (resp.) times faster for the robot, sensor, and task graph cases (resp.) when terminating early as opposed to computing the entire fixed point.

Figure 5 displays the experimental data for the comparison with the Python PCTL model checker from [30], for the synchronous leader election case-study where the weight dimension is 3. Each row in Fig. 5 describes a leader election instance, run using both the Python implementation (python) and our C++ implementation (adg). The columns labelled $\frac{python}{adg}$ show the speedup relative to the previous column (i.e. the column to left). The C++ implementation is an order of magnitude faster than the Python implementation and tends toward two orders of magnitude as the size of the model increases.

6   Conclusion

We presented an on-the-fly technique for answering whether a turn-based stochastic multiplayer game with weighted transitions satisfies a given alternating-time temporal logic formula with upper-bounds on the accumulated weight in the temporal operators and lower-bounds on the probabilities that a certain path formula is satisfied. Our approach reduces the problem to the computation of minimum fixed point on a recently introduced notion of abstract dependency graphs, using a novel reduction relying on a special abstract domain that includes the certain-zero optimization. We formally prove the correctness of our reduction and provide an efficient C++ implementation. On a series of experiments, we compare the performance of our approach with PRISM-games and show in several instances the advantage of using on-the-fly algorithm compared to the traditional value-iteration method. Our current implementation does not explicitly output winning strategies, however, this information can be recovered from the fixed point computed on the constructed ADG. Other interesting applications of the framework include verifying logics involving both minimal and maximal fixed points, such as the modal μ-calculus [24], efficient analysis of various process algebra such as CCS with quantities (generalizing [21]) and symbolic analysis of timed systems (see e.g. [11]).

References

1. Alur, R., Henzinger, T.A., Kupferman, O.: Alternating-time temporal logic. J. ACM **49**(5), 672–713 (2002). https://doi.org/10.1145/585265.585270
2. Andova, S., Hermanns, H., Katoen, J.: Discrete-time rewards model-checked. In: Formal Modeling and Analysis of Timed Systems: First International Workshop, FORMATS 2003, 6–7 September 2003, Marseille, France. Revised Papers, pp. 88–104 (2003). https://doi.org/10.1007/978-3-540-40903-8_8
3. Ashok, P., Chatterjee, K., Kretínský, J., Weininger, M., Winkler, T.: Approximating values of generalized-reachability stochastic games. In: LICS 2020: 35th Annual ACM/IEEE Symposium on Logic in Computer Science, 8–11 July 2020, Saarbrücken, Germany, pp. 102–115 (2020). https://doi.org/10.1145/3373718.3394761
4. Baier, C., Größer, M., Leucker, M., Bollig, B., Ciesinski, F.: Controller synthesis for probabilistic systems (Extended Abstract). In: Levy, J.-J., Mayr, E.W., Mitchell, J.C. (eds.) TCS 2004. IIFIP, vol. 155, pp. 493–506. Springer, Boston, MA (2004). https://doi.org/10.1007/1-4020-8141-3_38
5. Baier, C., Katoen, J.: Principles of Model Checking. MIT Press, Cambridge (2008)
6. Baier, C., Klein, J., Leuschner, L., Parker, D., Wunderlich, S.: Ensuring the reliability of your model checker: interval iteration for Markov decision processes. In: Majumdar, R., Kunčak, V. (eds.) CAV 2017. LNCS, vol. 10426, pp. 160–180. Springer, Cham (2017). https://doi.org/10.1007/978-3-319-63387-9_8
7. Baldan, P., König, B., Mika-Michalski, C., Padoan, T.: Fixpoint games on continuous lattices. Proc. ACM Program. Lang. **3**(POPL), 26:1–26:29 (2019). https://doi.org/10.1145/3290339
8. Baldan, P., König, B., Padoan, T., Mika-Michalski, C.: Fixpoint games on continuous lattices. CoRR abs/1810.11404 (2018). http://arxiv.org/abs/1810.11404
9. Bouyer, P., Fahrenberg, U., Larsen, K.G., Markey, N.: Quantitative analysis of real-time systems using priced timed automata. Commun. ACM **54**(9), 78–87 (2011). https://doi.org/10.1145/1995376.1995396
10. Brázdil, T., Brozek, V., Forejt, V., Kucera, A.: Stochastic games with branching-time winning objectives. In: 21th IEEE Symposium on Logic in Computer Science (LICS 2006), Proceedings, 12–15 August 2006, Seattle, WA, USA, pp. 349–358 (2006). https://doi.org/10.1109/LICS.2006.48

11. Cassez, F., David, A., Fleury, E., Larsen, K.G., Lime, D.: Efficient on-the-fly algorithms for the analysis of timed games. In: CONCUR 2005 - Concurrency Theory, 16th International Conference, CONCUR 2005, Proceedings, 23–26 August 2005, San Francisco, CA, USA, pp. 66–80 (2005). https://doi.org/10.1007/11539452_9

12. Chatterjee, K., Randour, M., Raskin, J.: Strategy synthesis for multi-dimensional quantitative objectives. Acta Informatica 51(3-4), 129–163 (2014). https://doi.org/10.1007/s00236-013-0182-6

13. Chen, T., Forejt, V., Kwiatkowska, M.Z., Parker, D., Simaitis, A.: Automatic verification of competitive stochastic systems. Formal Meth. Syst. Des. 43(1), 61–92 (2013). https://doi.org/10.1007/s10703-013-0183-7

14. Chen, T., Forejt, V., Kwiatkowska, M., Simaitis, A., Wiltsche, C.: On stochastic games with multiple objectives. In: Chatterjee, K., Sgall, J. (eds.) MFCS 2013. LNCS, vol. 8087, pp. 266–277. Springer, Heidelberg (2013). https://doi.org/10.1007/978-3-642-40313-2_25

15. Chen, T., Kwiatkowska, M., Simaitis, A., Wiltsche, C.: Synthesis for multi-objective stochastic games: an application to autonomous urban driving. In: Joshi, K., Siegle, M., Stoelinga, M., D'Argenio, P.R. (eds.) QEST 2013. LNCS, vol. 8054, pp. 322–337. Springer, Heidelberg (2013). https://doi.org/10.1007/978-3-642-40196-1_28

16. Chen, T., Lu, J.: Probabilistic alternating-time temporal logic and model checking algorithm. In: Fourth International Conference on Fuzzy Systems and Knowledge Discovery, FSKD 2007, Proceedings, 24–27 August 2007, Haikou, Hainan, China, vol. 2, pp. 35–39 (2007). https://doi.org/10.1109/FSKD.2007.458

17. Cloth, L., Katoen, J., Khattri, M., Pulungan, R.: Model checking Markov reward models with impulse rewards. In: 2005 International Conference on Dependable Systems and Networks (DSN 2005), 28 June - 1 July 2005, Yokohama, Japan, Proceedings, pp. 722–731 (2005). https://doi.org/10.1109/DSN.2005.64

18. Condon, A.: On algorithms for simple stochastic games. In: Advances In Computational Complexity Theory, Proceedings of a DIMACS Workshop, 3–7 December 1990, New Jersey, USA, pp. 51–71 (1990). https://doi.org/10.1090/dimacs/013/04

19. Condon, A.: The complexity of stochastic games. Inf. Comput. 96(2), 203–224 (1992). https://doi.org/10.1016/0890-5401(92)90048-K

20. Dalsgaard, A.E., et al.: A distributed fixed-point algorithm for extended dependency graphs. Fundam. Inform. 161(4), 351–381 (2018). https://doi.org/10.3233/FI-2018-1707

21. Dalsgaard, A.E., Enevoldsen, S., Larsen, K.G., Srba, J.: Distributed computation of fixed points on dependency graphs. In: Fränzle, M., Kapur, D., Zhan, N. (eds.) SETTA 2016. LNCS, vol. 9984, pp. 197–212. Springer, Cham (2016). https://doi.org/10.1007/978-3-319-47677-3_13

22. Droste, M., Kuich, W., Vogler, H.: Handbook of Weighted Automata. Springer (2009). https://doi.org/10.1007/978-3-642-01492-5

23. Enevoldsen, S., Larsen, K.G., Mariegaard, A., Srba, J.: Dependency graphs with applications to verification. International Journal on Software Tools for Technology Transfer (STTT) pp. 1–22 (2020). https://doi.org/10.1007/s10009-020-00578-9

24. Enevoldsen, S., Larsen, K.G., Srba, J.: Extended abstract dependency graphs, manuscript Under Submission

25. Enevoldsen, S., Guldstrand Larsen, K., Srba, J.: Abstract dependency graphs and their application to model checking. In: Vojnar, T., Zhang, L. (eds.) TACAS 2019. LNCS, vol. 11427, pp. 316–333. Springer, Cham (2019). https://doi.org/10.1007/978-3-030-17462-0_18

26. Fahrenberg, U., Juhl, L., Larsen, K.G., Srba, J.: Energy games in multiweighted automata. In: Cerone, A., Pihlajasaari, P. (eds.) ICTAC 2011. LNCS, vol. 6916, pp. 95–115. Springer, Heidelberg (2011). https://doi.org/10.1007/978-3-642-23283-1_9

27. Hartmanns, A., Junges, S., Katoen, J., Quatmann, T.: Multi-cost bounded reachability in MDP. In: Tools and Algorithms for the Construction and Analysis of Systems - 24th International Conference, TACAS 2018, Held as Part of the European Joint Conferences on Theory and Practice of Software, ETAPS 2018, Proceedings, 14–20 April 2018, Thessaloniki, Greece, Part II, pp. 320–339 (2018). https://doi.org/10.1007/978-3-319-89963-3_19

28. Hartmanns, A., Kaminski, B.L.: Optimistic value iteration. In: Computer Aided Verification - 32nd International Conference, CAV 2020, Proceedings, Part II, 21–24 July 2020, Los Angeles, CA, USA, pp. 488–511 (2020). https://doi.org/10.1007/978-3-030-53291-8_26

29. Itai, A., Rodeh, M.: Symmetry breaking in distributed networks. Inf. Comput. **88**(1), 60–87 (1990). https://doi.org/10.1016/0890-5401(90)90004-2

30. Jensen, M.C., Mariegaard, A., Larsen, K.G.: Symbolic model checking of weighted PCTL using dependency graphs. In: NASA Formal Methods - 11th International Symposium, NFM 2019, Proceedings, 7–9 May 2019, Houston, TX, USA, pp. 298–315 (2019). https://doi.org/10.1007/978-3-030-20652-9_20

31. Kelmendi, E., Krämer, J., Křetínský, J., Weininger, M.: Value iteration for simple stochastic games: stopping criterion and learning algorithm. In: Chockler, H., Weissenbacher, G. (eds.) CAV 2018. LNCS, vol. 10981, pp. 623–642. Springer, Cham (2018). https://doi.org/10.1007/978-3-319-96145-3_36

32. Kwiatkowska, M., Norman, G., Parker, D., Santos, G.: PRISM-games 3.0: stochastic game verification with concurrency, equilibria and time. In: Lahiri, S.K., Wang, C. (eds.) CAV 2020. LNCS, vol. 12225, pp. 475–487. Springer, Cham (2020). https://doi.org/10.1007/978-3-030-53291-8_25

33. Kwiatkowska, M., Norman, G., Parker, D.: Verification and control of turn-based probabilistic real-time games. In: Alvim, M.S., Chatzikokolakis, K., Olarte, C., Valencia, F. (eds.) The Art of Modelling Computational Systems: A Journey from Logic and Concurrency to Security and Privacy. LNCS, vol. 11760, pp. 379–396. Springer, Cham (2019). https://doi.org/10.1007/978-3-030-31175-9_22

34. Kwiatkowska, M., Norman, G., Parker, D., Santos, G.: Equilibria-based probabilistic model checking for concurrent stochastic games. In: Formal Methods - The Next 30 Years - Third World Congress, FM 2019, Proceedings, 7–11 October 2019, Porto, Portugal, pp. 298–315 (2019). https://doi.org/10.1007/978-3-030-30942-8_19

35. Liu, X., Smolka, S.A.: Simple linear-time algorithms for minimal fixed points (extended abstract). In: Automata, Languages and Programming, 25th International Colloquium, ICALP 1998, Proceedings, 13–17 July 1998, Aalborg, Denmark, pp. 53–66 (1998). https://doi.org/10.1007/BFb0055040

36. Nguyen, H.N., Rakib, A.: A probabilistic logic for resource-bounded multi-agent systems. In: Proceedings of the Twenty-Eighth International Joint Conference on Artificial Intelligence, IJCAI 2019, 10–16 August 2019, Macao, China, pp. 521–527 (2019). https://doi.org/10.24963/ijcai.2019/74

37. Puterman, M.L.: Markov Decision Processes: Discrete Stochastic Dynamic Programming. Wiley Series in Probability and Statistics, Wiley (1994). https://doi.org/10.1002/9780470316887

38. Quatmann, T., Katoen, J.: Sound value iteration. In: Computer Aided Verification - 30th International Conference, CAV 2018, Held as Part of the Federated Logic Conference, FloC 2018, Proceedings, Part I, 14–17 July 2018, Oxford, UK, pp. 643–661 (2018). https://doi.org/10.1007/978-3-319-96145-3_37

39. Shapley, L.S.: Stochastic games. Proc. Nat. Acad. Sci. **39**(10), 1095–1100 (1953). https://doi.org/10.1073/pnas.39.10.1095
40. Svorenová, M., Kwiatkowska, M.: Quantitative verification and strategy synthesis for stochastic games. Eur. J. Control **30**, 15–30 (2016). https://doi.org/10.1016/j.ejcon.2016.04.009
41. Tarski, A., et al.: A lattice-theoretical fixpoint theorem and its applications. Pac. J. Math. **5**(2), 285–309 (1955). https://doi.org/10.2140/pjm.1955.5.285

Program Analysis and Testing

Testing Your (Static Analysis) Truths

Ignacio Casso[1]([✉]) [iD], José F. Morales[1] [iD], P. López-García[1,3] [iD],
and Manuel V. Hermenegildo[1,2] [iD]

[1] IMDEA Software Institute, Madrid, Spain
[2] ETSI Informática, Universidad Politécnica de Madrid (UPM), Madrid, Spain
[3] Spanish Council for Scientific Research (CSIC), Madrid, Spain
{ignacio.decasso,josef.morales,pedro.lopez,manuel.hermenegildo}@imdea.org

Abstract. Static analysis is nowadays an essential component of many software development toolsets. Despite some notorious successes in the validation of compilers, comparatively little work exists on the systematic validation of static analyzers, whose correctness and reliability is critical if they are to be inserted in production environments. Contributing factors may be the intrinsic difficulty of formally verifying code that is quite complex and of finding suitable oracles for testing it. In this paper, we propose a simple, automatic method for testing abstract interpretation-based static analyzers. Broadly, it consists in checking, over a suite of benchmarks, that the properties inferred statically are satisfied dynamically. The main advantage of our approach is its simplicity, which stems directly from framing it within the `Ciao` assertion-based validation framework, and its blended static/dynamic assertion checking approach. We show that in this setting, the analysis can be tested with little effort by combining the following components already present in the framework: the *static analyzer*, the assertion *run-time checking* mechanism, the *random test case generator*, and the *unit-test framework*. Together they compose a tool that can effectively discover and locate errors in the different components of the analysis framework. We apply our approach to test some of `CiaoPP`'s analysis domains over a wide range of programs, successfully finding non-trivial, previously undetected bugs, with a low degree of effort.

Keywords: Static analysis · Run-time checks · Random testing · Assertions · Abstract interpretation · Program analysis · (Constraint) logic programming

1 Introduction and Motivation

Static analysis tools are nowadays a crucial component of the development environments for many programming languages. They are widely used in different

Partially funded by MICINN PID2019-108528RB-C21 *ProCode* and the Madrid P2018/TCS-4339 *BLOQUES-CM* program.

M. Fernández (Ed.): LOPSTR 2020, LNCS 12561, pp. 271–292, 2021.
https://doi.org/10.1007/978-3-030-68446-4_14

steps of the software development cycle, such as code optimization and verification, and they are the subject of significant research interest and practical application. Unfortunately, modern analyzers are often very large and complex software artifacts, and this makes them prone to bugs. This is a limitation to their applicability in real-life production compilers and development environments, where they are typically used in critical tasks like verification or code optimization, that need to rely strongly on the soundness of the analysis results.

However, the validation of static analyzers is a challenging problem, which is not well covered in the literature or by existing tools. Well-established methodologies or even guidelines to this end do not really exist. This is due to the fact that direct application of formal methods is not always straightforward with code that is so complex and large, even without considering the problem of having precise specifications to check against—a clear instance of the classic problem of who checks the checker. In current practice, extensive testing is the most extended and realistic option, but it poses some significant challenges too. Testing separate components of the analyzer misses integration testing, and designing proper oracles for testing the complete tool is really challenging.

Our objective in this paper is to develop a simple, automatic method for testing abstract interpretation-based static analyzers. Although the approach is general, we develop it for concreteness in the context of the Ciao [21] logic programming-based, multiparadigm language. The Ciao programming environment includes an abstract interpretation-based static analyzer, CiaoPP, which faces this very problem. As other "classic" analyzers, this analyzer has evolved for a long time, incorporating a large number of abstract domains, features, and techniques, adding up to over 1/2 million lines of Ciao code. These components have in turn reached over the years different levels of maturity. While the essential parts, such as the fixpoint algorithms and the classic abstract domains, have been used routinely for a long time now and it is unusual to find bugs, other parts are less developed and yet others are prototypes or even proofs of concept. A recent, shallow effort of applying a new testing tool to some parts of the Ciao analyzers as a case study [10] revealed subtle bugs, not only in the less-developed parts of the system, but also in corner cases of the parts that are considered more mature, such as, e.g., in the handling of rarely-used built-ins.

Another feature of Ciao that will be instrumental to our approach is the use of a unified assertion language and framework across its different components [22,23], which together implement its unique blend of static and dynamic assertion checking. These components include: 1) the PLAI *static analyzer* [19,25,40], which expresses the inferred information as Ciao assertions interspersed within the original program; 2) the assertion *runtime-checking framework* [45,46], which instruments the code to ensure that any assertions remaining after static verification are not violated at run time; 3) the *(random) test case* generation framework [10], which generates random test cases satisfying the properties present in an assertion preconditions; 4) the *unit-test framework* [36], which executes those test cases.

In this paper, we propose an algorithm that combines these four basic components in a novel way that allows testing the static analyzer almost for free. Intuitively, it consists in checking, over a suite of benchmarks, that the properties inferred statically are satisfied dynamically. The overall testing process, for each benchmark, can be summarized as follows: first the code is analyzed and the analysis results are expressed by the analyzer as assertions interspersed within the original code. Then these assertions are *switched* into run-time checks, that will ensure that violations of those assertions are reported at run time. Finally, random test cases are generated and executed to exercise those *run-time checks*. If any assertion violation is reported, since these assertions (the analyzer output) must cover all possible concrete executions, it means that the assertion was incorrectly inferred by the analyzer and thus that an error in the analyzer has been found. This process can be easily automated, and if it is repeated for an extensive and varied enough suite of benchmarks, it can be used to effectively validate (even if not fully verify) the analyzer or to discover new bugs. Furthermore, the implementation, when framed within the `Ciao` assertion-based validation framework, is very simple, since, as we will show, only a basic code transformation and a simple driver need to be implemented to obtain a very useful, working system.

The idea of checking at run time the properties or assertions inferred by the analysis for different program points is not new. For example, [49] successfully applied this technique for checking a range of different aliasing analyses. However, these approaches require the development of tailored instrumentation or monitoring, and require significant effort in their design and implementation. We argue that the testing approach is made more applicable, general, and scalable by the use of a unified assertion-based framework for static analysis and dynamic debugging, as the one of `Ciao`. As mentioned before, framing things in such a framework, the approach can be implemented with the already existing components in the system, in a very simple way, so much so that our initial prototype was, in fact, barely 50 lines of code long. We argue also that our approach is particularly useful in a mixed production and research setting like that of `CiaoPP`, in which there is a mature and domain-parametric abstract interpretation framework used routinely, but new, experimental abstract domains and overall improvements are in constant development. Those domains can easily be tested relying only on the existing abstract-interpretation framework, runtime-checking framework, and unified assertion language, provided only that the assertion language is extended to include the properties relevant for the domains.

The rest of the paper is structured as follows. Section 2 gives background knowledge needed to describe the main ideas and contributions of this paper. In particular, we recall some relevant aspects of the `CiaoPP` unified assertion framework. Then, Sect. 3 gives an overview of our approach illustrating it with an example. Section 4 presents our concrete algorithm to combine the different elements of the framework for the task of testing the static analyzer. In Sect. 5 we show some examples and applications of our approach. In Sect. 6 we apply the idea to testing the analysis results for a wide range of `CiaoPP`'s abstract domains and properties. Finally, Section 7 discusses related work and Sect. 8 summarizes our conclusions and plans for future work.

2 Preliminaries

In this section we review in some more detail those aspects of the Ciao model that are relevant to our approach, including the assertion language and the blended static and dynamic assertion checking framework built around it. A more detailed presentation can be found in [4,21,22,24,36,42] and their references.

The Assertion Language. Ciao assertions are linguistic constructs, which allow expressing properties of programs. There are two types of assertions in Ciao that are relevant herein: *predicate* assertions and *program-point* assertions. The first ones are declarations that provide partial specifications of a predicate. They have the following syntax: :- [Status] pred Head : [Calls] => [Success] + [Comp], indicating that if a call to the goal Head satisfies precondition Calls, it must satisfy post-condition Success on success and global computational properties Comp. *Program-point* assertions are reserved literals that appear in clause bodies and describe the constraint store at the corresponding program point. Their syntax is [Status](State). Examples of both types of assertions are provided in the code fragment below:

```
1  :- check pred append(X,Y,Z) : (list(X),list(Y)) => list(Z) + is_det.
2  :- check pred append(X,Y,Z) : (var(X),var(Y),list(Z)) => (list(X),list(Y)) +
       non_det.
3
4  append([],X,X).
5  append([X|Xs],Ys,[X|Zs]) :-
6      append(Xs,Ys,Zs),
7      check((list(Xs),list(Ys),list(Zs))).
```

Assertion fields Calls, Success, Comp and State, are conjunctions of *properties*. Such properties are predicates, typically written in the source language (user-defined or in libraries), and thus runnable, so that they can be used as run-time checks, and which, for our purposes, are typically *native* to CiaoPP, i.e., abstracted and inferred by some domain in CiaoPP. This includes a wide range of properties, from types, modes and variable sharing, to determinism, (non)failure and resource consumption. We refer the reader to [21,24,41] and their references for a full description of the Ciao assertion language.

Assertions are used everywhere in Ciao, from documentation and foreign interface definitions to static analysis and dynamic debugging. Depending on their origin and intended use, they have a different status, the Status field in the syntax described above. Assertion statuses relevant herein include true, which is used for assertions that are output from the analysis (and thus must be safe approximations), or the default status check, which indicates that the validity of the assertion is unknown and it must be checked, statically or dynamically. We will return to this crucial issue below.

Figure 1 depicts the overall architecture of the Ciao unified assertion framework. Hexagons represent tools, and arrows indicate the communication paths among them. The input to the process is the user program, *optionally* including a set of assertions; this set al.ways includes any assertion present for predicates exported by any libraries used (left part of Fig. 1).

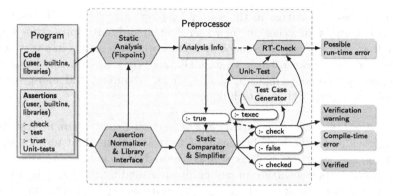

Fig. 1. The Ciao assertion framework (CiaoPP's verification/testing architecture).

Static Analysis. One use of Ciao assertions is as an interface to the static analyzer. As mentioned above, assertions can be used to indicate what we want the analyzer to check (the default check status), or to guide the analysis by feeding it information that it might be unable to infer by itself (trust status). The latter includes as a special case providing information on the entry points to the module being analyzed (i.e., on the calls to the predicates exported by the module –entry status). But more importantly for this paper, assertions are one of the possible output formats in which the analysis results are produced by the static analyzer (assertions with true status). If this type of output is chosen, a new source file for the analyzed program will be created, exactly as the original but with true *program-point* assertions interspersed between every two consecutive literals of each clause, and with one or more true *predicate* assertions for each predicate.

The technical and theoretical details of how this is achieved are omitted for space constraints. For our purposes it is sufficient to say that the CiaoPP analyzer is abstract interpretation-based, and its design consists of a common abstract-interpretation framework (the fixpoint algorithm(s)) parameterized by different, "pluggable" abstract domains. Depending on the domain or combination of domains selected for the analysis, different properties will be inferred and will appear in the emitted true assertions.

Run-time Checking. Static analysis can be used for compile-time checking of assertions (the Static Comparator & Simplifier, in Fig. 1) but the inherent imprecision of the analysis can lead to some assertions, specially those with user-defined properties that are not native to abstract domains, to not be proved or disproved statically (although perhaps they are simplified). In those cases, the remaining unproved (parts of) assertions are written into the output program with *check* status and then this output program can optionally be instrumented with *run-time checks*. These dynamic checks will encode the meaning of the *check* assertions, ensuring that an error is reported at run-time if any of these remaining assertions is violated (the dynamic part of the model). Note that the fact that properties are written in the source language and runnable is essential in this process, and allows checking new user-defined and native properties without having to extend the *run-time checking* framework. This results in a very rich set of properties being checkable in `Ciao`, including types, modes, variable sharing, failure, exceptions, determinism, choice-points, resources, and more, blending smoothly static and dynamic techniques.

Unit Tests, Test Case Generation, and Assertion-Based Testing. Test inputs can be provided by the user, by means of `test` assertions (unit tests), and used to test the test assertion itself as well as, through the *runtime-checking* mechanism, also any other assertion in any predicate called by the test case, that was not eliminated in the static checking. The unit-testing framework in principle requires the user to manually write individual test cases for each assertion to be tested. However, the `Ciao` model also includes mechanisms for generating test cases automatically from the assertion preconditions, using the corresponding property *predicates* as generators. This has been extended recently [10] to a *random* test case generation framework, which automatically generates, using the same technique, *random* test cases that satisfy assertion preconditions. We refer to the combination of this test generation mechanism with the run-time checking of the intervening assertions as *assertion-based testing*, that is, generating and running relevant test cases which exercise the *run-time checks* of the assertions in a program, thus testing if those assertions are correct. This yields similar results to *property-based testing* [11] but in a more integrated way within the overall model. Such automatic generation is supported for native properties, *regular types*, and user-defined properties as long as they are restricted to pure Prolog with arithmetic or mode and sharing constraints. In particular, it is always supported for the *native* properties used by the different analyses in the assertions that they output.

3   Overview of the Approach

After introducing the relevant elements of the Ciao assertion model, we can now sketch the main idea of our approach with a motivating example. Assume we have this simple Prolog program, where the `entry` assertion indicates that the predicate is always called with its second argument instantiated to a list and the third a free variable:

```
1    :- entry prepend(X,Xs,Ys) : (list(Xs), var(Ys)).
2
3    prepend(X,Xs,Ys) :-
4        Ys=[X|Rest],
5        Rest=Xs.
```

Assume that we analyze it with a *simple modes* abstract domain that assigns to each variable in an abstract substitution one the following abstract values: *g* (variable is ground), *v* (variable is free), *ng* (variable is not ground), *nv* (variables is not free), *ngv* (variable is not ground nor free), or *any* (nothing can be said about the variable). Assume also that the analysis is incorrect because it does not consider sharing (aliasing) between variables, so when updating the abstract substitution after the `Rest=Xs` literal, the abstract value for `Ys` is not modified at all. The result of the analysis will be represented, as explained in the previous section, as a new source file with interspersed assertions, as shown in Fig. 2 (lines 3–5, 8, 10, and 12). Note that the correct result, if the analysis considered aliasing, would be that there is no groundness information for `Ys` at the end of the clause (line 12), since there is none for `X` or `Xs` at the beginning either. `Ys` could only be inferred to be *nonvar*, but instead is incorrectly inferred to be *nonground* too (line 10). Normally **unknown/1** properties would not actually appear in the analysis output, but are included for clarity.

```
1    :- entry prepend(X,Xs,Ys) : (list(Xs), var(Ys)).
2
3    :- true pred prepend(X,Xs,Ys)
4        :   (unknown(X), nonvar(Xs), var(Ys))
5        => (unknown(X), nonvar(Xs), nonground(Ys), nonvar(Ys)).
6
7    prepend(X,Xs,Ys) :-
8        true((unknown(X), nonvar(Xs), var(Ys), var(Rest))),
9        Ys=[X|Rest],
10       true((unknown(X), nonvar(Xs), nonground(Ys), nonvar(Ys), var(Rest))),
11       Rest=Xs,
12       true((unknown(X), nonvar(Xs), nonground(Ys), nonvar(Ys), nonvar(Rest))).
```

Fig. 2. An incorrect simple mode analysis.

What we would like at this point, is to be able to check dynamically the validity of the **true** assertions from the analyzer. Thanks to the different aspects of the **Ciao** model presented previously, the only thing needed in order to achieve this is to (**1**) *turn the status of the* **true** *assertions produced by the analyzer into* **check**, as shown in Fig. 3. This would normally not make any sense since these **true** assertions have been proved by the analyzer. But that is exactly what we want to check, i.e., whether the information inferred is incorrect. To do this, (**2**) we run the transformed program (Fig. 3) again through **CiaoPP** (Fig. 1) but *without performing any analysis*. In that case the **check** literals (stemming from the **true** literals of the previous run) will not be simplified in the comparator (since there is no abstract information to compare against) and instead will be converted directly to run-time tests. I.e., the **check(Goal)** literals will be expanded and compiled to code that, every time that this program point is reached, in every execution, will check dynamically if the property (or properties) within the **check** literal (i.e., those in **Goal**) succeed, and an error message will be emitted if they do not. The only missing step to complete the automation of the approach is to (**3**) use the random test case generator to generate a set of test cases for **prepend/3**, and run those test cases. The framework will ensure that instances of the goal **prepend(X,Xs,Ys)** are generated where **Xs** is a list and **Ys** is a free variable, but otherwise **X** and the elements of **Xs** will be instantiated to random terms. In this example, as soon as a test case is

```
1   :- entry prepend(X,Xs,Ys) : (list(Xs), var(Ys)).
2
3   :- check pred prepend(X,Xs,Ys)
4       : (unknown(X), nonvar(Xs), var(Ys))
5       => (unknown(X), nonvar(Xs), nonground(Ys), nonvar(Ys)).
6
7   prepend(X,Xs,Ys) :-
8       check((nonvar(Xs), var(Ys), var(Rest))),
9       Ys=[X|Rest],
10      check((nonvar(Xs), nonground(Ys), nonvar(Ys), var(Rest))),
11      Rest=Xs,
12      check((nonvar(Xs), nonground(Ys), nonvar(Ys), nonvar(Rest))).
```

Fig. 3. The instrumented program.

generated where both X and all elements in Xs are ground, the program will report a runtime-checking error in the check in line 12, letting us know that the third program-point assertion, and thus the analysis, is incorrect.[1]

The same procedure can be followed to debug different analyses with different benchmarks. If the execution of any test case reports a runtime-checking error for one assertion, it will mean that the assertion was not correct and the analyzer computed an incorrect over-approximation of the semantics of the program. Alternatively, if this experiment, which can be automated easily, is run for an extensive suite of benchmarks without errors, we can gain more confidence that our analysis implementation is correct, even if perhaps imprecise (although of course we cannot have actual correctness in general by testing).

4   The Algorithm

In this section we present in more detail the actual algorithm for combining the components of the framework used in order to test the static analyzer.

4.1   Basic Reasoning Behind the Approach

We start by establishing more concretely the basic reasoning behind the approach in terms of abstract interpretation and safe upper and lower approximations. The mathematical notation in this subsection is purely for readability, as a proper formalization is outside the scope of the paper, and in any case arguably not really necessary, thanks to the simplicity of the approach.

---

[1] In the discussion above we have assumed for simplicity that the original program did not already contain check assertions. In that case these need to be treated separately and there are several options, including simply ignoring them for the process or actually turning them into trusts, so that we switch roles and trust the user-provided properties while checking the analyzer-inferred ones. This very interesting issue of when and whether to use the user-provided assertions to be checked during analysis, and its relation to run-time checking is discussed in depth in [18].

An abstract interpretation-based static analysis computes an over-approximation S_P^+ of the collecting semantics S_P of a program P. Such collecting semantics can be broadly defined as a control flow graph for the program decorated at each node with the set of all possible states that could occur at run-time at that program point. Different approximations of this semantics will have smaller or larger sets of possible states at each program point. Let us denote by $S_P' \sqsubseteq_P S_P''$ the relation that establishes that an approximation of S_P, S_P'', is an over-approximation of another, S_P'. The analysis will be correct if indeed $S_P \sqsubseteq_P S_P^+$.

Since S_P is undecidable, this relation cannot be checked in general. However, if we had a good enough under-approximation S_P^- of S_P, it can be tested as $S_P^- \sqsubseteq_P S_P^+$. If it does not hold and $S_P^- \not\sqsubseteq_P S_P^+$, then it would imply that $S_P \not\sqsubseteq_P S_P^+$, and thus, the results of the analysis would be incorrect, i.e., the computed S_P^+ would not actually be an over-approximation of S_P.

An under-approximation of the collecting semantics of P is easy to compute: it suffices with running the program with a subset I^- of the set I of all possible initial states. We denote the resulting under-approximation $S_P^{I^-}$, and note that $S_P = S_P^I$, which would be computable if I is finite and P always terminates. That is the method that we propose for testing the analysis: selecting a large and varied enough I^-, computing $S_P^{I^-}$ and checking that $S_P^{I^-} \sqsubseteq_P S_P^+$.

A direct implementation of this idea is challenging. It would require tailored instrumentation and monitoring to build and deal with a partially constructed collecting semantic under-approximation as a programming structure, which then would need to be compared to the one the analysis handles. However, as we have seen the process can be greatly simplified by reusing some of the components already in the system, following these observations:

- We can work with one initial state i at a time, following this reasoning:
  $S_P^{I^-} \sqsubseteq_P S_P^+ \iff \forall i \in I^-, S_P^{\{i\}} \sqsubseteq_P S_P^+$.
- We can use the random test case generation framework for selecting each initial state i.
- Instead of checking $S_P^{\{i\}} \sqsubseteq_P S_P^+$, we can instrument the code with *run-time checks* to ensure the execution from initial state i does not contradict the analysis at any point. That is, that the state of the program at any program point is contained in the over-approximation of the set of possible states that the analysis inferred and output as Ciao assertions.

4.2   The Algorithm

We now show the concrete algorithm for implementing our proposal, i.e., the driver that combines and inter-operates the different components of the framework to achieve the desired results. The essence of the algorithm (Algorithm 1) is the following: non-deterministically choose a program P and a domain D from a collection of benchmarks and domains, and execute the ANATEST(P, D) procedure until an error is found or a limit is reached. Unless the testing part is ensured to explore the complete execution space, it could in principle be useful to

---

Algorithm 1. Analysis Testing Algorithm (for program P and domain D)

1: **procedure** ANATEST(P, D)
2:     $result \leftarrow$ NONE
3:     $P_{an} \leftarrow$ analyze and annotate P with domain D (incl. program-point assertions).
4:     $P_{check} \leftarrow P_{an}$ where $true$ assertion status is replaced by $check$
5:     $P_{rtcheck} \leftarrow$ instrument P_{check} with $run\text{-}time\ checks$
6:     **repeat**
7:         Choose an exported predicate p and generate a test case $input$
8:         **if** $p(input)$ in P_{check} produces runtime errors **then**
9:             $result \leftarrow$ ERROR($input$)
10:        **else if** maximum number of test executions is reached **then**
11:            $result \leftarrow$ TIMEOUT
12:    **until** $result \neq$ NONE **return** $result$

---

revisit the same (P, D) pair more than once. When the algorithm detects a faulty program-point assertion for some $input$ (ERROR($input$)), it means that the concrete execution reaches a state not captured by the (over-approximation of the) analysis. In such case it is possible to reconstruct (or store together with the test output) additional information to diagnose the problem. E.g., comparing the concrete execution trace (which is logged during testing) with the analysis graph (recoverable from P_{an}, the program annotated with analysis results), domain operations (inspecting the analysis graph), and transfer functions (from predicates that are $native$ to each domain).

4.3 Other Details and Observations

We now discuss some details and observations on the algorithm that may have been left out or oversimplified in the algorithm sketch:

Analysis Crashes. An implicit assumption throughout our discussion so far is that the analysis always terminates without errors, but the results computed may be unsound. Of course, it is also possible that a bug in the analysis produces a crash, or even leads to non-termination. It is also possible that the analysis output is malformed (e.g., there are missing assertions in P_{an}). Those errors are of course also checked and reported by our tool. Non-termination is handled with timeouts and possible warnings (both for analyses and concrete executions).

Benchmark Selection. No prior requirement is imposed on the origin or characteristics of the benchmark suite. It could consist of automatically generated programs, an existing benchmark suite, or just real-life code. Each may have its own advantages and disadvantages (e.g., automatically generated code may test more convoluted or corner cases, but real-life code may find the bugs that actually occur in programs), but in principle, our approach is agnostic in this regard.

Entry Points. There is no restriction regarding the number of entry points or inputs to a program to be analyzed for. It is common in tools related to ours to use as benchmarks programs with a single entry point with no inputs (e.g., just a single void main() function as entry point for C). Our benchmarks are typically Ciao modules, and their entry points to analysis and testing are their exported predicates. In Ciao programs signatures and types (as well as *entry* assertions) are optional. Admissible inputs (i.e., the initial set of possible states for analysis or test case generation) can be specified by writing assertions for the exported predicates, by means of *entry* assertions, or skipped altogether. Note also that if our benchmarks had the restriction mentioned above (in our case, exporting only a main/0 predicate), then test case generation would not be needed for our algorithm.

Test Case Generation. In the absence of *entry* assertions, the test case generation framework [10] has already some mechanisms to generate relevant test cases, instead of random, nonsensical inputs which would exercise few *run-time checks* before failing. However, these generators have limitations, and the assertion-based testing framework is in fact best used with assertions that have descriptive-enough call patterns, or with custom user-defined generators in their absence. To tackle this problem, our tool makes also use of *test* assertions when available in the benchmarks, using also the test cases specified in the benchmarks besides those randomly generated. This can help, e.g., when using a benchmark that works with files and has paths as input, for which relevant test cases would not likely be found with random generation. Note however that the tool would still work without any *entry* or *test* assertions; it would just become less effective.

Error Diagnosis and Debugging. It is important to note that although error diagnosis and debugging is primarily left for the user to manually perform, our tool facilitates the task in some aspects. Firstly, the *assertion-based testing* tool supports shrinking of failed test cases, so we can expect reasonably small variable substitutions in the errors reported. Note however that benchmark reduction, e.g., by delta debugging [51], is currently not supported. Secondly, as sketched in Algorithm 1, the error location and trace reported by the *runtime-checks* instrumentation provide an approximated idea of the point where the analysis went wrong, if not of the reason why. For example, if the *runtime-check* error points to a *program-point* assertion right after a call to a builtin, then we typically know that the analysis erred in the builtin handler.

Multivariance and Path-Sensitivity. As presented, our approach might miss some analysis errors even when the right test cases are used, since we have apparently disregarded multi-variance and path-sensitivity. In fact in CiaoPP the information inferred is fully multi-variant, and separate path information is kept to each variant. However, in order to produce an output that is easy for the programmer to inspect, i.e., that is close to the source program, when outputting the analysis results CiaoPP by default combines the different versions of each predicate (and the associated information) into a single code version and a single combined assertion for each program point and predicate. If this default output is used when implementing our approach, it is indeed entirely possible that the analysis errs at a program point in one path but the algorithm never detects it: this can happen if, for example, in another path leading to the same program point (such that the two paths and their corresponding analysis results are collapsed –lubbed– together at the same program point) the analysis infers a too general value (higher in the domain lattice) at that program point and thus, the error is not detected. However, this potential problem is easily addressed by simply changing the corresponding flag in `CiaoPP` so that the different versions are not collapsed and are instead *materialized* into different predicate instances. This is done in `CiaoPP` by selecting the *versions* transformation prior to emitting the output. In this case multiple versions may be generated for a given predicate, if there are separate paths to it with different abstract information, and the corresponding analysis information will be annotated separately for each abstract path through the program in the program text of the different versions, avoiding the problem mentioned above.

5   Applications and Examples

In this section we discuss interesting use cases and applications of our approach. As observed before, our testing technique can be seen as a sanity or coherence check, and thus it can be targeted to test different components of the system depending on which ones are assumed to be trusted. Some examples follow. A few of them have actually been implemented and we report on them in the following section. We hope to implement the others in our future work.

Debugging Abstract Domains. The first application of our approach, which has been illustrated in the examples, is to test the abstract domains. In general the `Ciao` abstract interpretation engine (the *fixpoint algorithms* and all the surrounding infrastructure of the system, into which the domains are "plugged-in") includes the components of the analyzer we trust most, since they have been used and refined for more than 30 years. Thus, it makes sense to take this as the trusted base and try to find errors in the domains. This situation is realistic and frequent, since `CiaoPP` is at the same time a production and a research tool, and new domains are constantly being developed. In order to test a new domain with the algorithm proposed, two components need to be present. The first one is a translation interface from the abstract values in the domain to `Ciao` properties, which is needed to express the analysis results as assertions. But note that this is actually already a requirement for any abstract domain that intends to make full use of the framework, so it is normally implemented anyway in all domains. The other component is to have builtin checks for those properties to be used by the *run-time checking* framework, if those properties are declared native and not written in the source language and thus already runnable and checkable. This is also a standard requirement on domains to be able to make full use of the framework, so they are typically also implemented with the domain. In particular, all current `Ciao` abstract domains include the functionalities mentioned, and can be tested as is with the proposed approach. We show the results for some of them in the case study described in Sect. 6.

Debugging Trust Assertions and Custom Transfer Functions. One feature of CiaoPP's analyses is that they can be guided by the user, which can feed the analyzer with information that can be assumed to be true at points where otherwise the analysis would lose precision. We have already introduced in Sec. 2 one of these mechanisms, *trust* assertions, but there are others. One is custom abstract transfer functions, similar to those that need to be implemented for abstracting each builtin within each domain, but that the user can provide for any predicate. A particular instance of this mechanism is when the user specifies that one predicate is indistinguishable from or should behave like another with respect to a domain: the *equiv* declaration. Our approach can be used to test these mechanisms too. Both to test that they are applied correctly by the analyzer, if the user-provided information is trusted to be correct, and to test that the user-provided information is correct, if what is trusted is that the information is applied correctly. The latter is in particular very useful, since even a completely sound analyzer can produce unsound results if it assumes some property to be true when it is actually not, and thus there will always be the need to test such properties.

Testing the Abstract Interpretation Engine. Another idea that comes to mind is whether we can test the abstract interpretation engine (the *fixpoint algorithms* and all the surrounding infrastructure of the framework) instead of the domains, by using domains that are simple enough to be used as a trusted base. While the classic algorithms are quite stable, new fixpoints are also added to the system (e.g., recently a modular and incremental fixpoint) which can of course bring new bugs. A first abstract domain that could be useful for this purpose is the *concrete domain* itself (which is actually implemented in CiaoPP as the *pd* – partial deduction– domain). If we give the analysis a singleton set of initial states as entry point, the analyzer should behave as an interpreter for the program starting from that initial state, provided the program terminates. The assertions resulting from this "analysis" will use the =/2 property and be essentially a program which is adorned at each program point with the concrete states(s) that the analyzer infers will be occurring at run time, expressed as conjunctions of substitutions using =/2. Then, when running this program, the *run-time checks* would check that the variables are indeed instantiated to the concrete values inferred. Non-deterministic programs could be equally handled with member/2 ($\in$) instead of =/2 (=). A second domain that could be useful in this context is the *pdb* domain, which can be used to perform *reachability* analysis. The properties appearing in the assertions resulting from this analysis would just be possibly_reachable/0 ($\top$) and not_reachable/0 ($\bot$), which indicates if a program point is definitely unreachable at run-time.[2] The *run-time checks* would

---

[2] Note that this, combined with non-failure analysis [5,15], can also infer definitely_reachable/0, but that is a more complex domain.

just report an error any time a check for the property not_reachable/0 ($\perp$) is invoked at run time. This test would then detect if the analyzer incorrectly marks reachable parts of the program as unreachable.

Testing the Overall Consistency of the Framework. So far we have focused on applications in testing analysis soundness. But doing so has the implicit assumption that there are clear semantics and specifications for the analyzer to follow, and that is not always the case. Sometimes the semantics is underspecified, and then a discrepancy between what the analysis infers and what the program executes is not so much an error but a disparity in the interpretation of such an under-specification. In those cases our tool helps ensure that at least the analysis and run-time semantics are consistent. A relevant example can be found in the case of the abstraction of built-ins within abstract domain implementations. For some of them the specification is not complete (sometimes even the ISO-Prolog standard) and again our tool can at least check for inconsistencies in the interpretations made by the analyses and the run-time system.

In this same line, the tool has helped us find inconsistencies between the understanding of Ciao properties in the analysis and in the *runtime-checks* framework. With many properties this cannot happen (e.g., with pure predicates) because both the analysis and the run-time checking derive the semantics from the actual code defining the property. But for more complex properties the implementations may be different, perhaps developed by different people, with different interpretations of the property semantics. An actual example is the property cardinality/3, which provides upper and lower bounds to the number of solutions that a predicate might produce. It is a property that has not seen a lot of use (determinacy and/or non-failure are the ones used most frequently), and our experimental evaluation exposed that for cardinality/3 the analysis was considering only different solutions while the *runtime-checks* framework counted also repeated ones.

Integration Testing of the Analyzer and Third Parties. Finally, even if every piece of the analyzer is validated separately, our tool can still help in testing how all its parts integrate together to form a functional and sound analyzer, and, even more interestingly, it can also test the correctness of the different integrations with external or third party solvers used by the analyzer (e.g., the PPL library).

6   A More Detailed Case Study

As a case study, in order to validate our approach and confirm its effectiveness, we have studied further the *Debugging Abstract Domains* application of Sect. 5, by applying our prototype more systematically to some of the analyses in CiaoPP.

Setup. The analyses tested all use the standard configuration of the abstract interpretation framework (i.e., the *PLAI* fixpoint, multi-variance on calls, etc.) but differ in the abstract domains used for the analysis. The complete list of abstract domains tested can be seen in the first column of Table 1. The second column indicates the different properties which the domains reason about, such as variable aliasing, variable modes, variable types, (non)failure, or determinism. The domains range in maturity, from stable domains like *shfr* and *eterms*, to mere prototypes like *etermsvar*. The third column of the figure indicates this level of maturity with three different values: *mature, intermediate, experimental*. For more details about the domains we refer to the citations in the fourth column.

Table 1. Domains used for the evaluation of the approach.

Abstract domain	Properties abstracted	Maturity level	References
shfr	Aliasing, modes	Mature	[39]
def	Aliasing, modes	Intermediate	[20]
gr	Aliasing, modes	Intermediate	[6]
eterms	Types	Mature	[48]
etermsvar	Types	Experimental	[48]
nf	Failure	Mature	[5, 15]
det	Determinism	Mature	[33, 34]

The experiment has been run over some selected benchmarks with increasing levels of complexity and language features. We have started with simple, existing CiaoPP benchmarks used for, e.g., demos, statistics and integration testing, for which in principle the analyses tested should be correct. Then we have continued with a large database of anonymized solutions for Prolog assignments in undergraduate courses, which on one hand are not expected to use necessarily the most sophisticated features of the language (although there are always exceptions), but on the other hand are known to exhibit a high degree of creativity in combining language elements in unusual and unpredictable ways, including many that do not make sense at all. The intuition is that these combinations may exercise corner cases of the analyses in a similar (but hopefully somewhat more focused way) than random program generation. Finally, we have applied the experiment to some selected modules of the Ciao code base using more advanced features. Additionally, we have cherry-picked some benchmarks which were expected to reveal some known bugs, either still unfixed or explicitly reintroduced in the system for this experiment, and some using deliberately features not supported by a particular analysis such as, e.g., attributed variables. Some of the benchmarks have been modified by adding *entry* assertions to guide test case generation, and existing test cases from unit tests (i.e., *test* assertions) have been used in modules where using random test cases is ineffective or just plain dangerous (e.g., predicates that have files as input). The experiments were run with Ciao/CiaoPP version 1.19-221.

Results. While we are planning on performing a larger set of experiments, [3] the results so far are promising and have allowed us to draw some interesting conclusions and observations. A good number of bugs and inconsistencies were indeed found using the technique, many of them known but also some new ones. First, our experiment was successful in finding known bugs in previous versions of the analyses, that have now been fixed, and also in revealing known limitations of different analyses for some language features. For example, the fact that some of the aliasing domains do not support rational terms was easily detected, and also that many domains do not support attributed variables. Some new, but still not unexpected bugs were found in one of the most experimental domains (*etermsvar*). Furthermore, also a few new bugs were found even in mature domains. These are typically related to the handling of rarely-used built-ins, which explains why they have gone unnoticed, but they are still bugs and have been (or are being) fixed. In addition, while the testing process was aimed at the domains, it also uncovered some bugs in related components of the Ciao assertion framework and their integration, which have been fixed too. We thus conclude that our approach is indeed effective in revealing and discovering bugs and inconsistencies in the domains and also in the overall framework.

Another overall conclusion from the experiment is that benchmark selection is very important when focusing our approach on testing specific domains. No bugs were found for the most mature domains using standard benchmarks and the undergraduate Prolog assignments. The subtle bugs mentioned before in less-used built-ins were found instead when using benchmarks extracted from Ciao's code base, i.e., in complex, system code. On the other hand, a good number of errors were found in the experimental domain with even the simpler benchmarks. In fact, in this case, the many errors triggered obfuscated sometimes the real (possibly multiple) origin of the problems, but this is to be expected in immature code: consider for example that just the ISO-standard contains a very large set of built-ins and the implementation of an experimental domain typically does not support all of them.

Finally, it is important to point out that we also found out that there are some bugs that are unlikely to be found with benchmarks like the ones used in the tests, because they are bugs that will probably never occur in realistic programs. One example is the simple bug found in [10] for the handler of the builtin =/2 in the *sharing-freeness* domain. The code did not consider that the two arguments could be the same variable, and thus the analysis failed for any program with the literal X=X. Since that literal always succeeds and is redundant in every program, it will likely not appear in any reasonable benchmark and this error would not be detected by our tool. To find bugs of this kind with our approach, randomly generated benchmarks would be needed.

---

[3] We are working on including the technique as part of the Ciao continuous integration infrastructure, and plan to report on a larger number of CiaoPP analyses over a wider range of programs.

7   Related Work

The need for validating program analyzers was discussed by [8], and the topic has motivated interesting research over the past years. On the formal verification side, there have been some pen-and-paper proofs, such as that of the Astree analyzer [12], some automatic and interactive proofs, such as [16,44], and some verification efforts, which include [2,26,31]. Testing efforts for program analyzers include e.g., static analyzers [13,28,49,52], symbolic execution engines [27], refactoring engines [14], compilers [29,30,32,43,47,50], SMT solvers [3], among others. Most of these testing approaches use programs in the target language as test cases and and apply testing techniques like fuzzing (e.g., [3,27,50]) or differential testing [35], (e.g., [3,27–29,50]). In [7] and [38] abstract domain properties are tested, the latter using QuickCheck [11]. Among the different approaches mentioned, the closest to ours are those that cross-check dynamically observed and statically inferred properties [1,13,49,52].

In [49] the actual pointer aliasing in concrete executions is cross-checked with the pointer aliasing inferred by an aliasing analyzer. Compared to us, they require significant tailored instrumentation which cannot be reused for testing other analyses. However, their approach is agnostic to the (C) aliasing analyzer.

Another cross-check is done in [52] for C model checkers and the *reachability* property, but they obtain the assertions dynamically, and check them statically, complementarily to our approach. Unlike us, they again need tailored instrumentation that cannot be reused to test other analyses, and their benchmarks must be deterministic and with no input, the latter limiting the power of the approach as a testing tool. However, their approach is agnostic to the (C) model checker.

In [13] a wide range of static analysis tests are performed over randomly generated programs. Among others, they check dynamically, at the end of the program, one assertion inferred statically, and they perform the sanity check of ensuring that the analyzer behaves as an interpreter when run from a singleton set of initial states.

8   Conclusions and Future Work

We have proposed a simple, automatic method for testing abstract interpretation-based static analyzers based on checking that the properties inferred statically are satisfied dynamically. We have leveraged the Ciao unified assertion language and framework, and have constructed a prototype implementation of our method with little effort by combining components already present in the framework: the static analyzer, the runtime-checker, the random test-case generator, and the unit-tester. We just wrote a very reduced amount of glue code that pilots the combination and interplay of the intervening components. We have applied our prototype to a good number of the abstract interpretation-based analyses in CiaoPP, which represent different levels of code maturity. The results are encouraging and show that our tool can effectively discover and locate, not only old errors in previous versions (that are obviously less interesting since they were fixed in newer versions), but also new, interesting and unexpected, non-trivial, previously undetected bugs.

Our technique can also be applied to testing the correctness of the analyzers for many other types of properties that were not discussed for brevity, such as the *computational* properties inferred by CiaoPP. These include, e.g., determinacy, non-failure, upper and lower bounds on costs and complexity, or accumulated costs and profiling, and the required run-time checking support exists for many of them (see, e.g., [37]). Of course some properties cannot be checked fully (e.g., termination, beyond just checking for timeouts). There are also many other interesting sanity checks enabled by Ciao's integrated and unified assertion language and framework which we have left as future work, such as testing the assertion simplifier, which simplifies programs discarding (parts of) check assertions that have been proven statically. This could be done by analyzing a benchmark without assertions, simplifying the assertions output, and checking that there are no assertions left. We also plan to use the test case generation framework to do differential testing of several program optimizations and transformations over a suite of benchmarks, by just checking that they produce the same outputs for the same randomly generated inputs. A recent paper [9] suggested defining and using distances in abstract domains and between abstract semantics (i.e., between abstract AND-OR trees inferred by the analyzer). We plan to implement an instrumentation that uses such distances to test analysis precision and measure coverage within our approach: if the distance between the dynamic under-approximation and the static over-approximation of the program semantics is small, it means that the analysis was precise and the random inputs had good coverage; otherwise, either the analysis was imprecise, or the test case generation had poor coverage. We plan to investigate heuristics to distinguish both cases. Another interesting avenue for future research is to combine our approach with more directed testing techniques, such as, e.g., concolic testing [17].

References

1. Andreasen, E.S., Møller, A., Nielsen, B.B.: Systematic approaches for increasing soundness and precision of static analyzers. In: Proceedings of the 6th ACM SIG-PLAN International Workshop on State of the Art in Program Analysis, SOAP 2017, pp. 31–36. Association for Computing Machinery, New York (2017). https://doi.org/10.1145/3088515.3088521

2. Blazy, S., Laporte, V., Maroneze, A., Pichardie, D.: Formal verification of a C value analysis based on abstract interpretation. In: Logozzo, F., Fähndrich, M. (eds.) SAS 2013. LNCS, vol. 7935, pp. 324–344. Springer, Heidelberg (2013). https://doi.org/10.1007/978-3-642-38856-9_18

3. Brummayer, R., Biere, A.: Fuzzing and delta-debugging SMT solvers. In: Proceedings of the 7th International Workshop on Satisfiability Modulo Theories, SMT 2009, pp. 1–5. Association for Computing Machinery, New York (2009). https://doi.org/10.1145/1670412.1670413

4. Bueno, F., et al.: On the Role of Semantic Approximations in Validation and Diagnosis of Constraint Logic Programs. In: Proceedings of the 3rd International Workshop on Automated Debugging-AADEBUG 1997, pp. 155–170. University of Linköping Press, Linköping, Sweden, May 1997. ftp://cliplab.org/pub/papers/aadebug_discipldeliv.ps.gz

5. Bueno, F., López-García, P., Hermenegildo, M.: Multivariant non-failure analysis via standard abstract interpretation. In: Kameyama, Y., Stuckey, P.J. (eds.) FLOPS 2004. LNCS, vol. 2998, pp. 100–116. Springer, Heidelberg (2004). https://doi.org/10.1007/978-3-540-24754-8_9

6. Bueno, F., Lopez-Garcia, P., Puebla, G., Hermenegildo, M.V.: A Tutorial on Program Development and Optimization using the Ciao Preprocessor. Technical report. CLIP2/06, Technical University of Madrid (UPM), Facultad de Informática, 28660 Boadilla del Monte, Madrid, Spain, January 2006

7. Bugariu, A., Wüstholz, V., Christakis, M., Müller, P.: Automatically testing implementations of numerical abstract domains. In: Proceedings of the 33rd ACM/IEEE International Conference on Automated Software Engineering, ASE 2018, pp. 768–778. Association for Computing Machinery, New York, NY, USA (2018). https://doi.org/10.1145/3238147.3240464

8. Cadar, C., Donaldson, A.: Analysing the program analyser. In: International Conference on Software Engineering, Visions of 2025 and Beyond Track (ICSE V2025), pp. 765–768 (5 2016)

9. Casso, I., Morales, J.F., López-García, P., Giacobazzi, R., Hermenegildo, M.V.: Computing abstract distances in logic programs. In: Gabbrielli, M. (ed.) LOPSTR 2019. LNCS, vol. 12042, pp. 57–72. Springer, Cham (2020). https://doi.org/10.1007/978-3-030-45260-5_4

10. Casso, I., Morales, J.F., López-García, P., Hermenegildo, M.V.: An integrated approach to assertion-based random testing in prolog. In: Gabbrielli, M. (ed.) LOPSTR 2019. LNCS, vol. 12042, pp. 159–176. Springer, Cham (2020). https://doi.org/10.1007/978-3-030-45260-5_10

11. Claessen, K., Hughes, J.: QuickCheck: a lightweight tool for random testing of Haskell programs. In: Fifth ACM SIGPLAN International Conference on Functional Programming, ICFP 2000, pp. 268–279. ACM (2000)

12. Cousot, P., et al.: The ASTRÉE analyzer. In: Sagiv, M. (ed.) ESOP 2005. LNCS, vol. 3444, pp. 21–30. Springer, Heidelberg (2005). https://doi.org/10.1007/978-3-540-31987-0_3

13. Cuoq, P., et al.: Testing static analyzers with randomly generated programs. In: Goodloe, A.E., Person, S. (eds.) NFM 2012. LNCS, vol. 7226, pp. 120–125. Springer, Heidelberg (2012). https://doi.org/10.1007/978-3-642-28891-3_12

14. Daniel, B., Dig, D., Garcia, K., Marinov, D.: Automated testing of refactoring engines. In: Proceedings of the 6th Joint Meeting of the European Software Engineering Conference and the ACM SIGSOFT Symposium on The Foundations of Software Engineering, ESEC-FSE 2007, pp. 185–194. Association for Computing Machinery, New York (2007). https://doi.org/10.1145/1287624.1287651

15. Debray, S., Lopez-Garcia, P., Hermenegildo, M.V.: Non-failure analysis for logic programs. In: 1997 International Conference on Logic Programming, pp. 48–62. MIT Press, Cambridge, June 1997

16. Dubois, C.: Proving ML type soundness within Coq. In: Aagaard, M., Harrison, J. (eds.) TPHOLs 2000. LNCS, vol. 1869, pp. 126–144. Springer, Heidelberg (2000). https://doi.org/10.1007/3-540-44659-1_9

17. Fortz, S., Mesnard, F., Payet, E., Perrouin, G., Vanhoof, W., Vidal, G.: An SMT-based concolic testing tool for logic programs. In: Nakano, K., Sagonas, K. (eds.) FLOPS 2020. LNCS, vol. 12073, pp. 215–219. Springer, Cham (2020). https://doi.org/10.1007/978-3-030-59025-3_13

18. Garcia-Contreras, I., Morales, J.F., Hermenegildo, M.V.: Multivariant assertion-based guidance in abstract interpretation. In: Mesnard, F., Stuckey, P.J. (eds.) LOPSTR 2018. LNCS, vol. 11408, pp. 184–201. Springer, Cham (2019). https://doi.org/10.1007/978-3-030-13838-7_11

19. Garcia-Contreras, I., Morales, J.F., Hermenegildo, M.V.: Incremental analysis of logic programs with assertions and open predicates. In: Gabbrielli, M. (ed.) LOPSTR 2019. LNCS, vol. 12042, pp. 36–56. Springer, Cham (2020). https://doi.org/10.1007/978-3-030-45260-5_3

20. García de la Banda, M., Hermenegildo, M.V., Bruynooghe, M., Dumortier, V., Simoens, W.: Global analysis of constraint logic programs. ACM Trans. Program. Lang. Syst. 18(5), 564615 (1996)

21. Hermenegildo, M.V., et al.: An overview of ciao and its design philosophy. Theory Pract. Logic Program. 12(12), 219–252 (2012). https://doi.org/10.1017/S1471068411000457. http://arxiv.org/abs/1102.5497

22. Hermenegildo, M.V., Puebla, G., Bueno, F.: Using global analysis, partial specifications, and an extensible assertion language for program validation and debugging. In: Apt, K.R., Marek, V., Truszczynski, M., Warren, D.S. (eds.) The Logic Programming Paradigm: a 25-Year Perspective, pp. 161–192. Springer, Heidelberg (1999). https://doi.org/10.1007/978-3-642-60085-2_7

23. Hermenegildo, M.V., Puebla, G., Bueno, F., López-García, P.: Program development using abstract interpretation (and the ciao system preprocessor). In: Cousot, R. (ed.) SAS 2003. LNCS, vol. 2694, pp. 127–152. Springer, Heidelberg (2003). https://doi.org/10.1007/3-540-44898-5_8

24. Hermenegildo, M.V., Puebla, G., Bueno, F., Lopez-Garcia, P.: Integrated program debugging, verification, and optimization using abstract interpretation (and the ciao system preprocessor). Scie. Comput. Program. 58(1–2), 115–140 (2005). https://doi.org/10.1016/j.scico.2005.02.006

25. Hermenegildo, M.V., Puebla, G., Marriott, K., Stuckey, P.: Incremental analysis of constraint logic programs. ACM Trans. Program. Lang. Syst. 22(2), 187–223 (2000)

26. Jourdan, J.H., Laporte, V., Blazy, S., Leroy, X., Pichardie, D.: A formally-verified c static analyzer. SIGPLAN Not. 50(1), 247–259 (2015). https://doi.org/10.1145/2775051.2676966

27. Kapus, T., Cadar, C.: Automatic testing of symbolic execution engines via program generation and differential testing. In: IEEE/ACM International Conference on Automated Software Engineering (ASE 2017), pp. 590–600, 11 November 2017

28. Klinger, C., Christakis, M., Wüstholz, V.: Differentially testing soundness and precision of program analyzers. In: Proceedings of the 28th ACM SIGSOFT International Symposium on Software Testing and Analysis. p. 239–250. ISSTA 2019, Association for Computing Machinery, New York, NY, USA (2019). DOI: 10.1145/3293882.3330553, https://doi.org/10.1145/3293882.3330553

29. Le, V., Afshari, M., Su, Z.: Compiler validation via equivalence modulo inputs. In: Proceedings of the 35th ACM SIGPLAN Conference on Programming Language Design and Implementation, PLDI 2014, pp. 216–226. Association for Computing Machinery, New York (2014). https://doi.org/10.1145/2594291.2594334

30. Le, V., Sun, C., Su, Z.: Finding deep compiler bugs via guided stochastic program mutation. In: Proceedings of the 2015 ACM SIGPLAN International Conference on Object-Oriented Programming, Systems, Languages, and Applications, pp. 386–399. OOPSLA 2015, Association for Computing Machinery, New York (2015). https://doi.org/10.1145/2814270.2814319

31. Leroy, X.: Formal verification of a realistic compiler. Commun. ACM **52**(7), 107–115 (2009). https://doi.org/10.1145/1538788.1538814

32. Lidbury, C., Lascu, A., Chong, N., Donaldson, A.F.: Many-core compiler fuzzing. In: Proceedings of the 36th ACM SIGPLAN Conference on Programming Language Design and Implementation, PLDI 2015, pp. 65–76. Association for Computing Machinery, New York, NY, USA (2015). https://doi.org/10.1145/2737924.2737986

33. López-García, P., Bueno, F., Hermenegildo, M.: Determinacy analysis for logic programs using mode and type information. In: Etalle, S. (ed.) LOPSTR 2004. LNCS, vol. 3573, pp. 19–35. Springer, Heidelberg (2005). https://doi.org/10.1007/11506676_2

34. Lopez-Garcia, P., Bueno, F., Hermenegildo, M.V.: Automatic inference of determinacy and mutual exclusion for logic programs using mode and type analyses. New Gener. Comput. **28**(2), 117–206 (2010). https://doi.org/10.1007/s00354-008-0085-1

35. McKeeman, W.M.: Differential testing for software. Digit. Tech. J. **10**, 100–107 (1998)

36. Mera, E., Lopez-García, P., Hermenegildo, M.: Integrating software testing and run-time checking in an assertion verification framework. In: Hill, P.M., Warren, D.S. (eds.) ICLP 2009. LNCS, vol. 5649, pp. 281–295. Springer, Heidelberg (2009). https://doi.org/10.1007/978-3-642-02846-5_25

37. Mera, E., Trigo, T., Lopez-García, P., Hermenegildo, M.: Profiling for run-time checking of computational properties and performance debugging in logic programs. In: Rocha, R., Launchbury, J. (eds.) PADL 2011. LNCS, vol. 6539, pp. 38–53. Springer, Heidelberg (2011). https://doi.org/10.1007/978-3-642-18378-2_6

38. Midtgaard, J., Møller, A.: QuickChecking static analysis properties. Softw. Test., Verif. Reliab.**27**(6) (2017). https://doi.org/10.1002/stvr.1640

39. Muthukumar, K., Hermenegildo, M.: Combined determination of sharing and freeness of program variables through abstract interpretation. In: International Conference on Logic Programming (ICLP 1991), pp. 49–63. MIT Press, June 1991

40. Muthukumar, K., Hermenegildo, M.: Compile-time derivation of variable dependency using abstract interpretation. J. Logic Program. **13**(2/3), 315–347 (1992)

41. Puebla, G., Bueno, F., Hermenegildo, M.: An assertion language for constraint logic programs. In: Deransart, P., Hermenegildo, M.V., Małuszynski, J. (eds.) Analysis and Visualization Tools for Constraint Programming. LNCS, vol. 1870, pp. 23–61. Springer, Heidelberg (2000). https://doi.org/10.1007/10722311_2

42. Puebla, G., Bueno, F., Hermenegildo, M.: Combined static and dynamic assertion-based debugging of constraint logic programs. In: Bossi, A. (ed.) LOPSTR 1999. LNCS, vol. 1817, pp. 273–292. Springer, Heidelberg (2000). https://doi.org/10.1007/10720327_16

43. Regehr, J., Chen, Y., Cuoq, P., Eide, E., Ellison, C., Yang, X.: Test-case reduction for C compiler bugs. In: Proceedings of the 33rd ACM SIGPLAN Conference on Programming Language Design and Implementation, pp. 335–346. PLDI '12, Association for Computing Machinery, New York (2012). https://doi.org/10.1145/2254064.2254104

44. Shao, Z., Saha, B., Trifonov, V., Papaspyrou, N.: A type system for certified binaries. SIGPLAN Not. **37**(1), 217–232 (2002). https://doi.org/10.1145/565816. 503293

45. Stulova, N., Morales, J.F., Hermenegildo, M.V.: Practical run-time checking via unobtrusive property caching, theory and practice of logic programming. In: 31st Internationl Conference on Logic Programming (ICLP 2015) Special Issue 15(04–05), pp. 726–741, September 2015. https://doi.org/10.1017/S1471068415000344, http://arxiv.org/abs/1507.05986

46. Stulova, N., Morales, J.F., Hermenegildo, M.V.: Reducing the overhead of assertion run-time checks via static analysis. In: 18th International ACM SIGPLAN Symposium on Principles and Practice of Declarative Programming (PPDP 2016), pp. 90–103. ACM Press, September 2016

47. Sun, C., Le, V., Su, Z.: Finding compiler bugs via live code mutation. In: Proceedings of the 2016 ACM SIGPLAN International Conference on Object-Oriented Programming, Systems, Languages, and Applications, OOPSLA 2016, pp. 849–863. Association for Computing Machinery, New York, NY, USA (2016). https://doi.org/10.1145/2983990.2984038

48. Vaucheret, C., Bueno, F.: More precise yet efficient type inference for logic programs. In: Hermenegildo, M.V., Puebla, G. (eds.) SAS 2002. LNCS, vol. 2477, pp. 102–116. Springer, Heidelberg (2002). https://doi.org/10.1007/3-540-45789-5_10

49. Wu, J., Hu, G., Tang, Y., Yang, J.: Effective dynamic detection of alias analysis errors. In: Proceedings of the 2013 9th Joint Meeting on Foundations of Software Engineering, ESEC/FSE 2013, pp. 279–289. Association for Computing Machinery, New York (2013). https://doi.org/10.1145/2491411.2491439

50. Yang, X., Chen, Y., Eide, E., Regehr, J.: Finding and understanding bugs in C compilers. In: Proceedings of the 32nd ACM SIGPLAN Conference on Programming Language Design and Implementation, PLDI 2011, pp. 283–294. Association for Computing Machinery, New York, NY, USA (2011). https://doi.org/10.1145/1993498.1993532

51. Zeller, A.: Yesterday, my program worked. Today, it does not. Why? SIGSOFT Softw. Eng. Notes **24**(6), 253–267 (1999). https://doi.org/10.1145/318774.318946

52. Zhang, C., Su, T., Yan, Y., Zhang, F., Pu, G., Su, Z.: Finding and understanding bugs in software model checkers. In: Proceedings of the 13th Joint Meeting of the 18th European Software Engineering Conference and the 27th Symposium on the Foundations of Software Engineering, pp. 763–773 (2019). https://doi.org/10.1145/3338906.3338932

Slicing Unconditional Jumps with Unnecessary Control Dependencies

Carlos Galindo⬭, Sergio Pérez$^{(\boxtimes)}$⬭, and Josep Silva⬭

VRAIN, Universitat Politècnica de València, Camí de Vera s/n, 46022 València, Spain
{cargaji,serperu,jsilva}@dsic.upv.es

Abstract. Program slicing is an analysis technique that has a wide range of applications, ranging from compilers to clone detection software, and that has been applied to practically all programming languages. Most program slicing techniques are based on a widely extended program representation, the System Dependence Graph (SDG). However, in the presence of unconditional jumps, there exist some situations where most SDG-based slicing techniques are not as accurate as possible, including more code than strictly necessary. In this paper, we identify one of these scenarios, pointing out the cause of the inaccuracy, and describing the initial solution to the problem proposed in the literature, together with an extension, which solves the problem completely. These solutions modify both the SDG generation and the slicing algorithm. Additionally, we propose an alternative solution, that solves the problem by modifying only the SDG generation, leaving the slicing algorithm untouched.

Keywords: Program analysis · Program slicing · Unconditional jumps

1 Introduction

Program slicing [18,20] is a technique for program analysis and transformation whose main objective is to extract from a program the set of statements that affect a given set of variables in a specific statement, the so-called *slicing criterion*. The programs obtained with program slicing are called *slices*, and they are used in many areas such as debugging [1], program specialization [2], software maintenance [7], code obfuscation [13], etc.

There exist several algorithms and data structures to represent programs that can be used to compute slices, but the most efficient and broadly used data structure is the *system dependence graph* (SDG), introduced by Horwitz et al. [9]. It is computed from the program's source code, and once built, a slicing criterion is chosen and mapped to the graph, that is then traversed with the algorithm proposed in [9] to compute the corresponding slice.

The SDG is the result of assembling a set of graphs that represent information about a program. Figure 1 depicts how the SDG is built using the control-flow

© Springer Nature Switzerland AG 2021
M. Fernández (Ed.): LOPSTR 2020, LNCS 12561, pp. 293–308, 2021.
https://doi.org/10.1007/978-3-030-68446-4_15

graph (CFG) as the starting graph. First, using the CFG of each function definition in the code, two different graphs are built: (i) the control dependence graph (CDG) [6] and (ii) the data dependence graph (DDG) [6,19]. The union of both graphs results in the program dependence graph (PDG) [6,14], which represents all data and control dependencies inside a concrete function. Finally, PDG's function calls, definitions and their parameters are linked with interprocedural arcs, generating the final SDG. The SDG can be traversed from a slicing criterion to produce a slice in linear time with the algorithm proposed in [9].

Fig. 1. Sequence of graphs generated to build the SDG.

As all the aforementioned graphs conforming the SDG represent different relationships of the program, an improvement in the accuracy of these graphs results in a direct impact on the accuracy of the SDG. Throughout the years, the SDG has been augmented with different dependencies, and several techniques have been defined to properly represent complex situations: interprocedural alternatives to compute executable slices [4], extensions of the CFG to represent interprocedural control dependencies [17], object-oriented language representations and slicing [12], or program slicing in concurrent environments [5,10] are some examples of the evolution of the SDG.

For the purpose of this paper, we are interested in the evolution of the unconditional control flow treatment for program slicing. In this specific area, the initial proposal was the one introduced by Ball and Horwitz [3]. In their work, the authors considered a simplified language with scalar variables and constants, assignment statements, jump statements (`goto`, `break`, `halt`, etc.), conditional statements (`if-then`, `if-then-else`), and loops (`while` and `repeat`). Despite the simplicity of the given programming language, the ideas proposed can be applied to any kind of unconditional jumps present in other programming languages. In this paper, we provide examples using the `break` statement in the Java programming language, even though the problem presented and its solution can be applied to any statement that represents an unconditional jump. The following example illustrates the problem identified by Ball and Horwitz after their proposal.

Example 1 (Unconditional jump subsumption [3]). Consider the Java method shown below on the left-hand side:

```
1   public void f() {        1   public void f() {        1   public void f() {
2     while (X) {             2     while (X) {             2     while (X) {
3       if (Y) {              3       if (Y) {              3       if (Y) {
4         if (Z) {            4         if (Z) {            4
5           A;                5                              5
6           break;            6           break;            6
7         }                   7         }                   7
8         B;                  8                              8
9         break;             9         break;              9         break;
10      }                    10      }                     10      }
11      C;                   11      C;                    11      C;
12    }                      12    }                       12    }
13    D;                     13                            13
14  }                        14  }                         14  }
```

| Original program | SDG slice | Minimal slice |

This method contains a `while` statement, from which the execution may exit naturally or through any of the `break` statements. To represent the rest of statements and conditional expressions, uppercase letters are used; and, for simplicity, we can assume that there are no data dependencies between them.

Now consider statement C as the slicing criterion: each input that produces a computation in the original program that reaches C must produce a computation in the slice that also reaches C. Note that C is only executed when X is `true` and Y is `false`.

The code in the centre displays the computed slice by Ball and Horwitz's approach; the code on the right-hand side is the minimal slice. As can be observed, the `break` in line 6 and its surrounding `if` statement (`if (Z)`) have been unnecessarily included in the slice, since the evaluation of Z does not influence the execution of a `break` after being the Y statement evaluated to `true`. Their inclusion would not be specially problematic, if it were not for the condition of the `if` statement (Z), which may include extra data dependencies that are unnecessary in the slice and that may lead to include other unnecessary statements, making the slice even more imprecise.

The rest of the paper is structured as follows: Section 2 illustrates the rationale behind the problem shown in Example 1, detailing how dependencies are generated, identifying when the problem shows up, and describing the solution proposed by Kumar and Horwitz in [11], where the authors introduced changes in two steps of the process shown in Fig. 1. Section 3 proposes an alternative solution that is simpler and does not need to change the slicing algorithm, lowering the time complexity while preserving completeness at all times. Section 4 explains the problem in presence of `switch` statements and how to represent them to solve the problem. Section 5 outlines our implementation of the proposed solution. Finally, Sect. 6 concludes the article outlining the main contributions.

2 Unconditional Jumps and the PPDG

To keep the paper self-contained, we start with the definition of control flow graph.

Definition 1 (Control-flow graph). *Given a program P, the control flow graph of P is a graph (N, A) where N is a set of nodes that contains one node for each statement in the program, and A are arcs that represent the execution flow between the nodes:*

Statement node. Any statement that is not a conditional jump. These nodes have one outgoing edge pointing to the next statement of the program.

Predicate node. Any conditional jump statement, such as `if`, `while`, etc. These nodes have two outgoing edges labelled *true* and *false*, leading to the statements that would be executed regarding the condition evaluation.

The CFG of the `Original program` in Example 1 is shown in Fig. 2 (left), where we can ignore the dashed arcs for now, since they are not part of the CFG. In this graph, all nodes with just one outgoing arc represent statements, while all nodes with two outgoing arcs labeled with *T* or *F* represent predicates. In the graph, unconditional jumps, such as `break` are represented with a node whose outgoing arc leads to the statement that will be executed after the jump. Other representations of unconditional jumps, such as representing them with a single arc connecting the previous statement with the jumps' target are inadequate for program slicing, as we require a mapping from each statement in the source code to a node in each graph.

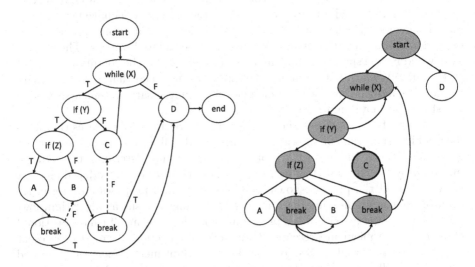

Fig. 2. ACFG (left) and CDG (right) of the code in Example 1.

The control flow graph is the basis to calculate control dependencies in a program and, thus, the control dependence graph.

Definition 2 (Control dependence). *Let G be a CFG. Let X and Y be nodes in G. A node Y post-dominates a node X in G if every directed path from X to* *the End node passes through Y. Node Y is* control dependent *on node X if and only if Y post-dominates one but not all of X's CFG successors.*

Definition 3 (Control dependence graph). *Given a program P and its associated CFG $G_{CFG} = (N, A)$, the* control dependence graph *(CDG) of P is a graph $G_{CDG} = (N, A')$ where $(x, y) \in A'$ if and only if node $y \in N$ is control-dependent on node $x \in N$.*

Unconditional jump statements distort the usual understanding of control dependence, and they invalidate the standard representation of control dependencies in the CDG. Example 2 shows that the standard definition of control dependence is insufficient in presence of unconditional jumps.

Example 2 (Control dependencies induced by unconditional jumps). Consider the following code on the left-hand side and the slicing criterion x in the last line.

```
1   x = 0;
2   while (true) {
3       x++;
4       if (x>10)
5           break;
6   }
7   print(x);
```
                    Original program

```
1   x = 0;
2   while (true) {
3       x++;
4       if (x>10)
5
6   }
7   print(x);
```
                    Wrong slice

The slice of this code is the whole code (everything is needed to reach the slicing criterion). Nevertheless, according to Definition 2, the `break` statement in line 5 does not control any other statement, that is, no statement depends on the `break` statement. Therefore, the (wrong) slice computed with the standard definition of control dependence would be the code on the right. This is an infinite loop that never reaches the slicing criterion. Clearly, the execution of `print(x)` is in some way controlled by the execution of `break` and, thus, unconditional jumps induce some kind of control dependencies that are not captured in Definition 2.

To deal with this problem (i.e. unconditional control flow statements), Ball and Horwitz [3] proposed a modification of the CFG in presence of unconditional control flow statements, which result in a CDG with augmented dependencies. This approach is the most popular one and the one used in most of the subsequent literature [11,15,16]. The main modification applied to the CFG consists in the introduction of a third category of nodes in the definition of the CFG:

Pseudo-predicates. Unconditional jumps (i.e. `break`, `goto`, `return`[1], etc.) are treated like predicates, where the outgoing edge labelled *false* is marked as non-executable—because there is no possible execution where such edge would be possible, according to the definition of the CFG [8]. For unconditional jumps, the *true* edge leads to the statement at the jump destination, and the *false* edge to the statement that would be executed if the jump was skipped.

---

[1] The target of the jump in a `return` statement is the *End* or *Exit* node of the procedure it's in, from which control will be handed back to the previous procedure in the call stack.

The graph obtained from adding the *false* arcs to the pseudo-predicate nodes of a CFG is called the *Augmented CFG* (ACFG). As a consequence of the appearance of pseudo-predicate nodes, in an ACFG every statement between an unconditional jump and its destination is control-dependent on it (see Definition 2), as can be seen in Example 3.

Example 3 (Control dependencies generated by unconditional jumps). Consider again the ACFG in Fig. 2 (left), which represents the code in Example 1. Here, solid arrows represent edges that come out from statements, predicates, and *true* pseudo-predicate branches; and dashed arrows represent the non-executable (*false*) branches of pseudo-predicates. When we transform this ACFG to a CDG, we obtain the CDG in Fig. 2 (right), where the slice with respect to variable C is represented with grey nodes.

Even though Ball and Horwitz solved the exposed problem with the definition of the ACFG, there was still a problem they were not able to solve. This problem is represented in the code of Example 1. It appears when there are two different unconditional jumps with the same jump destination. Due to the *false* pseudo-predicate arcs in the ACFG, all the statements between the first unconditional jump and the second one become directly control-dependent on the first jump, including the second one. Similarly, all the statements located between the second jump and the destination statement become directly control-dependent on the second jump. As a result of the transitive dependence, when any statement between the second jump and the destination statement is required, the inclusion of both unconditional jump statements in the slice is unavoidable. The inclusion of the first jump statement will increase the size of the slice with all its dependencies, leading to an imprecise slice. The solution proposed in [3] is complete, but not as accurate as it was expected to be.

Ball and Horwitz were aware of the aforementioned problem and, some years later, Kumar and Horwitz proposed a solution in [11]. Their solution was based on two main modifications:

1. **A new definition of control dependence in the presence of pseudo-predicates.** *"Node Y is control-dependent on node X if and only if Y post-dominates, in the CFG, one but not all of X's ACFG successors".* The resulting graph was called the pseudo-predicate PDG (PPDG).
2. **A new slicing algorithm.** The new algorithm established some restrictions in the slicing traversal. *"To compute the slice from node S, include S itself and all of its data and control-dependence predecessors in the slice. Then follow backwards all data-dependence edges, and all control-dependence edges whose targets are not pseudo-predicates; add each node reached during this traversal to the slice."*

By the introduction of these novelties, the accuracy of the slice was improved, since it is not possible to add in the slice two pseudo-predicate nodes that jump to the same destination unless one of them is the slicing criterion itself. This approach solved the problem of Example 1, proposed in [3].

3   Alternative Solution: Unnecessary Control Dependencies

In this section, we propose an alternative solution to the unconditional jump problem shown in the previous section. The key idea of our approach is to identify which edges of the CDG are responsible for the inaccurate slices and define a method to avoid building them in the graph generation process.

To properly reason about the accuracy of our approach, we provide a formal definition of slicing criterion and slice.

Definition 4 (Slicing criterion). *Let P be a program. A slicing criterion C of P is a tuple $\langle s, v \rangle$ where s is a statement in P and v is a set of variables that are used or defined in s.*

Definition 5 (CDG slice). *Given a CDG $G = (N, A)$ and a slicing criterion $\langle s, v \rangle$, where $n \in N$ represents s in G, a CDG slice of n is a subgraph $G' = (N', A')$ such that:*

1. *$N' \subseteq N$.*
2. *$\forall n' \in N'$, n is control dependent on n' and n' is needed to execute n the same number of times as in G (the original program).*
3. *$A' = \{(x, y) \in A \mid x, y \in N'\}$.*

The standard slicing algorithm, denoted $slice(G, C)$, collects all nodes that are reachable from the node in G associated with the slicing criterion C traversing backwards the CDG arcs.

We have identified a general situation in which some control dependencies should be omitted. If those control dependencies are removed from the CDG, then the standard slicing algorithm is still complete and precision is kept the same or improved. Consider a CDG G with two unconditional jump statements x and y that jump to the same destination, with an arc (x, y) in G. There exists a CDG G' with the same set of nodes and a set of arcs obtained by deleting all the control arcs in G with y as target, that produces more accurate program slices.

Theorem 1. *Let $G = (N, A)$ be a CDG. Let $x \in N$ be any unconditional jump statement. Let $y \in N$ be an unconditional jump statement without any variable use or definition that jumps to the same destination as x. Let $G' = (N, A')$ where $A' = (A \setminus \{(w, y) \mid w \in N\})$. For all slicing criteria C, $slice(G', C)$ is a CDG slice.*

Proof. We prove the theorem by means of a generic code that captures all possible scenarios that can happen under the conditions of the theorem. We consider two unconditional jump statements, x as the first jump statement and y as the second one. First, x and y cannot be sequential statements because in that case y would be dead code. This forces us to enclose x inside a conditional structure. As y does not define or use any variable, we add the statement s_1 and place an

external conditional structure to also prevent it to be dead code. This generic
code is depicted in Fig. 3 (left). Any statement or groups of them added to this
code before or after x or y would produce a similar topology that would not
affect the proof. The reason is that any statement represented by a set of nodes
has only one successor in the CFG and can never be the source of a control
dependence (see Section 2.3 in [3]).

We graphically illustrate this proof by means of Figs. 3 and 4. Figure 3
represents the ACFG (centre) of the aforementioned code with the ACFG extra
arcs represented with dashed arrows, and its associated CDG (right). Figure 4
represents the same CDG removing two control dependence arcs (dashed arcs).
The figure represents two program slices with respect to two different slicing
criteria: x (left) and s_1 (right).

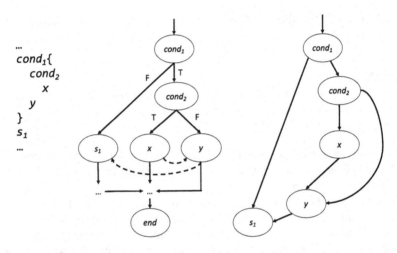

Fig. 3. Piece of code (left), its ACFG (centre) and its associated CDG (right).

We distinguish two possible scenarios according to the slice computed by
$slice(G', n)$:

(i) $y \notin slice(G', n)$ (Fig. 4, left). In this case, node y is not needed to execute n
and, thus, the removal of the arcs that end in y do not affect the computation
of $slice(G', n)$ because they are never traversed. Therefore, all nodes needed
to execute n belong to the slice (condition 2. in Definition 5) and also all
arcs induced by them are kept in the slice (condition 3. in Definition 5).
Hence, $slice(G', n)$ is a CDG slice.

(ii) $y \in slice(G', n)$ (Fig. 4, right). First, according to Definition 4, node y cannot be selected as slicing criterion, as it does not define or use any variables
of the program according to the theorem conditions imposed on y. Then,
because no data dependence exists on y, the only possibility to include y in
$slice(G', n)$ is because some statement between y and the jump destination

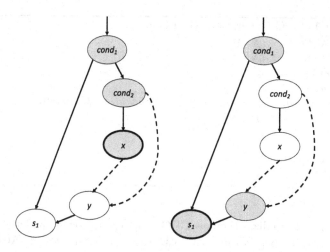

Fig. 4. CDG of our approach and CDG slices w.r.t. x (left) and s_1 (right).

of y is included in the slice (s_1 in our graph in Fig. 4 (right)). Because of that, there is an execution path where y affects the execution of this statement. In the case that $cond_1$ was a loop, y would be control dependent on $cond_1$ itself, including $cond_1$ in $slice(G', n)$ but, in this case, we would obtain the same result because s_1 is also control dependent on $cond_1$ and thus, included in $slice(G', n)$.

We have two possible scenarios to execute n (see the ACFG in Fig. 3 (centre)):

- s_1 is executed. Then, $cond_1$ is *false* and $cond_2$, x, and y are not executed (they can be excluded from $slice(G', n)$).
- Either x or y are executed. As the result of executing x and y is functionally the same (the program execution continues at the destination of y), there is no difference between taking one path of $cond_2$ or another. Therefore, $cond_2$, x and y can be replaced by y without modifying the behaviour of the program; making the control dependency arcs from $cond_2$ and x to y unnecessary.

In the three cases, the removal of the arcs that end in y ensure that the three conditions in Definition 5 hold. Thus, $slice(G', n)$ is a CDG slice.

$\square$

Theorem 1 proves that slices produced with this solutions are complete, as their result is a CDG slice. Additionally, due to the fact that the same nodes, but fewer arcs exist, all slices produced from G' will be equal or smaller than those generated from the original CDG G, thus guaranteeing that our solution is, at least, as correct as the previous solution. Finally, a CDG with fewer arcs means that the input size for the slicing algorithm is smaller, therefore lowering the time required to slice the graph once generated.

Algorithm 1. CDG Generation Algorithm

Input: An ACFG $G = (N, A)$.
Output: A CDG $G' = (N', A_c)$.
1: $A_c = genControlArcs(G)$
2: **for all** $(n_s, n_e) \in A_c$ **do**
3:     **if** $(n_s, n_e \in un_{jumps} \wedge jumpDest(n_s) == jumpDest(n_e))$ **then**
4:         $A_c = A_c \setminus (x, n_e) \,\forall\, x \in N$
5:     **end if**
6: **end for**
7: $N' = N \setminus \{End\}$
8: $G' = (N', A_c)$

Algorithm 1 formalizes the new CDG generation process, which removes the unnecessary arcs. To perform that task, the algorithm uses an ACFG as the starting point. The algorithm uses the following functions and sets:

- $genControlArcs\backslash 1$. It inputs an ACFG and outputs all control arcs that can be obtained according to Definition 2.
- un_{jumps}. This is a set with all nodes that represent an unconditional jump.
- $jumpDest\backslash 1$. This function inputs a CDG node n that represents an unconditional jump statement and outputs the destination of the jump.

Algorithm 1 first generates all control dependencies in the ACFG. Then, each control dependency $n \rightarrow n'$ is inspected to determine whether both n and n' are unconditional jumps with the same destination. If this is the case, then all control arcs that target node n' are removed. This forms the set A'. Finally, N' is calculated by removing the *End* node from N and the CDG $G' = (N', A')$ is obtained.

With this generation process, the CDG produced is more accurate than the one produced by Ball and Horwitz. For instance, the CDG associated to the *Original program* in Example 1 is shown in Fig. 5. The CDG slice associated to the slicing criterion C is shown in grey, and it corresponds to the *Minimal slice* in Example 1. As can be seen, nodes **break** and **if(Z)** are no longer part of the slice. The structure of this graph represents now a more realistic control dependence, where unconditional jumps to common destinations are not dependent on each other.

It is worth remarking the main difference between the solution presented in [11] and our approach: the amount of steps of the slicing process that are modified. Both approaches introduce a modification in the CDG generation process. While the amount of arcs generated by Kumar and Horwitz may be lower or greater than the amount of arcs generated in the initial proposal by Ball and Horwtiz [3], the amount of arcs generated in our approach is always equal or lower than in the initial proposal. In addition, the approach by Kumar and Horwitz needs to change the standard SDG-traversal algorithm, introducing an overhead when calculating slices. On the contrary, in our approach the SDG-traversal algorithm remains untouched, keeping the slicing process as a graph

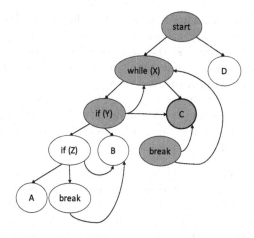

Fig. 5. CDG obtained by applying Algorithm 1 to the code in Example 1.

reachability problem and ensuring the slicing cost proposed by Ottenstein and Ottenstein in [14].

4   The Representation of switch Statements

Another frequent structure where this problem appears is the switch statement. It is considered good practice to terminate each case with an unconditional jump, such as return or break. This creates an environment where there are multiple unconditional jumps with the same target, a perfect example of the situation where our technique applies.

In comparison with Kumar and Horwitz's approach, ours behaves in the same way, with one caveat: it includes the appropriate case statements, while theirs ignores them.

switch statements can be represented in many ways. Regarding its control-flow representation for program slicing, the following patterns are applied (where s is the switch statement):

- The selector or argument of s (e.g. switch (a)) is connected to each case statement. Additionally, if s has no default case, it is connected to the first instruction after s. Otherwise, it is connected to the first instruction after s via a non-executable arc.
- Each case c is connected to the first instruction that will be executed if the selector matches it, which is typically the first instruction in its body.[2] Furthermore, c is connected via a non-executable arc to the default case, if present, or otherwise to the first instruction after s.

---

[2] Multiple languages allow chaining case statements.

– Statements within a `case` are represented as they would be in any other part of the program. The only caveat is: let s be the last statement of a `case` (c) statement's body, and s' the first statement in the following `case` (c') statement's body; if s does not jump, the following instruction would not be c', but s'. As an example; in the sequence of statements `a = 10; case 1; b = 1;`, the first will only be connected to the third, and not to the `case` statement. Thus, any unconditional jump at the end of a `case`, which is a common construct, will have a non-executable arc connected to the first instruction of the following `case` statement.

All these rules follow two maxims: (1) executable control-flow arcs connect instructions that may be executed sequentially and (2) non-executable control-flow arcs connect i to j, where i is any instruction and j is the instruction that would be executed in the case that i was a no-operation (a blank instruction that affects nor control, neither data). Regarding the control dependence graph, each part of the `switch` statement has sensible control dependencies:

– The selector is the source of data dependencies towards all instructions in its body, and this is the desired outcome: the selector is included if any `case` is; or in other words, the selector affects the execution of each `case`.
– Each case is the source of data dependencies towards the instructions in its body, and towards the default case (if present). The effect a `case` has on its body is clear, but the one on the default case may not be, though it is present. Consider a `switch` with n `case` statements and a default case. If any were removed, the default case would be affected, as the executions that previously passed through the deleted statement will now traverse the default case. Thus, the presence of each `case` statement affects the number of times the default case is run.
– Statements within a `case` c are control dependent on c, and possibly on unconditional jumps in previous `case` statements.

Example 4. Comparison of our technique against Kumar and Horwitz's in a simple `switch` statement.

Consider the code displayed in Fig. 6, where a simple `switch` statement is declared. On the right-hand side, its slice with respect to S3 (line 11). Only one of the `break` statements is necessary, as they perform an equivalent effect on the slicing criterion.

Figure 7 shows the augmented control-flow graph of this simple procedure, with non-executable arcs shown with dashed edges. Figure 8 shows the resulting SDG built using our technique, and the slice obtained matches the one in Fig. 6. Finally, Fig. 9 shows the result of applying Kumar and Horwitz's technique. Note how their approach, though it generates more arcs, traverses fewer of them, leading them to the same result as ours.

```
1   public class Switch {            1    public class Switch {
2       void f() {                    2        void f() {
3           switch (cond) {           3            switch (cond) {
4               case e1:              4
5                   S1;               5
6                   break;           6
7               case e2:             7
8                   S2;              8
9                   break;           9                    break;
10              case e3:            10                case e3:
11                  S3;             11                    S3;
12                  break;          12                    break;
13          }                       13            }
14      }                           14        }
15  }                               15    }
```

Fig. 6. A program with a simple `switch` statement and its slice with respect to S3.

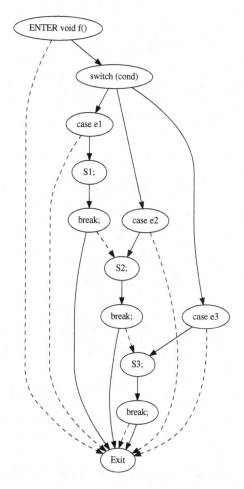

Fig. 7. The CFG obtained with our technique (common to both Kumar and Horwitz's and our technique).

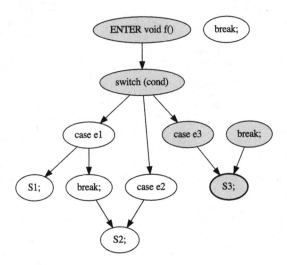

Fig. 8. The SDG and slice (gray nodes) w.r.t. to S3, obtained by applying our technique.

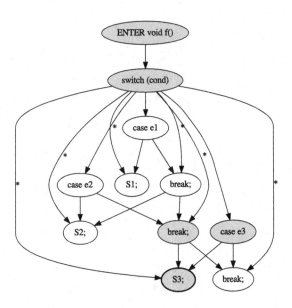

Fig. 9. The SDG and slice (gray nodes) w.r.t. to S3, obtained by applying Kumar and Horwitz's technique.

5   Implementation

Both our approach and Kumar and Horwitz's have been implemented in an open-source Java slicer, available at the URL https://github.com/mistupv/ JavaSDGSlicer. In the branch TAPAS-2020, one can generate graphs using our approach with the flag "-t TSDG", and using Kumar and Horwitz's with "PSDG".

The specific implementation can be seen in the following classes for our approach:

TapasPDG. Extends the implementation of the Augmented PDG (a PDG based on the ACFG), applying Algorithm 1 after generating the control dependency arcs.

TapasSDG. Extends the implementation of the Augmented SDG (a SDG based on the APDG), by basing it instead on the aforementioned TapasPDG.

CFGBuilder, ACFGBuilder. They implement the creation of the control-flow graph, specifically regarding the handling of the switch statement. The specific change can be seen in commit 3c771a29.

As for Kumar and Horwitz's approach, it is implemented in the following classes:

PPDG. Extends the implementation of the APDG, replacing the generation of control dependencies with their own.

PSDG. Extends the ASDG to use PPDGs instead of APDGs, and uses a compatible slicing algorithm instead of the classic one.

PseudoPredicateSlicingAlgorithm. Extends the classic slicing algorithm, with the additional restriction added in this approach.

6   Conclusions

Ball and Horwitz proposed the first program slicing technique with a specific treatment for unconditional jumps. Even though their technique produces complete slices in all cases, they were aware that accuracy could be improved, and they proposed a challenging example (analogous to Example 1) where the computed slice was bigger than needed. Some years later, Kumar and Horwitz solved this accuracy problem changing the definition of control dependencies and redefining the standard slicing algorithm.

In this paper, we propose an alternative approach that solves the problem performing fewer changes to the standard approach. Our approach only needs to change the CDG produced, and all the other phases of program slicing (including SDG traversal) remain unchanged. We have theoretically proven the correctness of our approach.

Acknowledgements. This work has been partially supported by the EU (FEDER) and the Spanish MCI/AEI under grants TIN2016-76843-C4-1-R and PID2019-104735RB-C41, by the *Generalitat Valenciana* under grant Prometeo/2019/098 (Deep-Trust), and by TAILOR, a project funded by EU Horizon 2020 research and innovation programme under GA No 952215.

References

1. Sun, C.A., Ran, Y., Zheng, C., Liu, H., Towey, D., Zhang, X.: Fault localisation for WS-BPEL programs based on predicate switching and program slicing. J. Syst. Softw. **135**, 191–204 (2018)
2. Aung, M., Horwitz, S., Joiner, R., Reps, T.: Specialization slicing. ACM Trans. Program. Lang. Syst. **36**(2), 5:1–5:67 (2014)
3. Ball, T., Horwitz, S.: Slicing programs with arbitrary control-flow. In: Fritzson, P.A. (ed.) AADEBUG 1993. LNCS, vol. 749, pp. 206–222. Springer, Heidelberg (1993). https://doi.org/10.1007/BFb0019410
4. Binkley, D.: Precise executable interprocedural slices. ACM Lett. Program. Lang. Syst. **2**(1–4), 31–45 (1993)
5. Chen, Z., Xu, B.: Slicing concurrent java programs. SIGPLAN Not. **36**(4), 41–47 (2001)
6. Ferrante, J., Ottenstein, K.J., Warren, J.D.: The program dependence graph and its use in optimization. ACM Trans. Program. Lang. Syst. **9**(3), 319–349 (1987)
7. Hajnal, A., Forgács, I.: A demand-driven approach to slicing legacy COBOL systems. J. Softw. Maint. **24**(1), 67–82 (2012)
8. Horwitz, S., Reps, T., Binkley, D.::: Interprocedural slicing using dependence graphs. In: Proceedings of the ACM SIGPLAN 1988 Conference on Programming Language Design and Implementation, PLDI 1988, pp. 35–46. ACM, New York (1988)
9. Horwitz, S., Reps, T., Binkley, D.: Interprocedural slicing using dependence graphs. ACM Trans. Program. Lang. Syst. **12**(1), 26–60 (1990)
10. Krinke, J.: Static slicing of threaded programs. SIGPLAN Not. **33**(7), 35–42 (1998)
11. Kumar, S., Horwitz, S.: Better slicing of programs with jumps and switches. In: Kutsche, R.-D., Weber, H. (eds.) FASE 2002. LNCS, vol. 2306, pp. 96–112. Springer, Heidelberg (2002). https://doi.org/10.1007/3-540-45923-5_7
12. Larsen, L., Harrold, M.J.: Slicing object-oriented software. In: Proceedings of the 18th International Conference on Software Engineering, ICSE 1996, pp. 495–505. IEEE Computer Society, Washington (1996)
13. Majumdar, A., Drape, S.J., Thomborson, C.D.: Slicing obfuscations: design, correctness, and evaluation. In: Proceedings of the 2007 ACM Workshop on Digital Rights Management, DRM 2007, pp. 70–81. ACM, New York (2007)
14. Ottenstein, K.J., Ottenstein, L.M.: The program dependence graph in a software development environment. SIGSOFT Softw. Eng. Notes **9**(3), 177–184 (1984)
15. Reps, T., Horwitz, S., Sagiv, M., Rosay, G.: Speeding up slicing. SIGSOFT Softw. Eng. Notes **19**(5), 11–20 (1994)
16. Reps, T., Rosay, G.: Precise interprocedural chopping. In: Proceedings of the 3rd ACM SIGSOFT Symposium on Foundations of Software Engineering, pp. 41–52. Association for Computing Machinery, New York (1995)
17. Sinha, S., Harrold, M.J., Rothermel, G.: System-dependence-graph-based slicing of programs with arbitrary interprocedural control flow. In: Proceedings of the 1999 International Conference on Software Engineering (IEEE Cat. No. 99CB37002), pp. 432–441. IEEE, May 1999
18. Tip, F.: A survey of program slicing techniques. J. Program. Lang. **3**(3), 121–189 (1995)
19. Towle, R.A.: Control and data dependence for program transformations. Ph.D. thesis, USA (1976). AAI7624191
20. Weiser, M.: Program slicing. In: Proceedings of the 5th International Conference on Software Engineering (ICSE 1981), pp. 439–449. IEEE Press, Piscataway (1981)

Logics

A Formal Model for a Linear Time Correctness Condition of Proof Nets of Multiplicative Linear Logic

Satoshi Matsuoka[✉] [ID]

National Institute of Advanced Industrial Science and Technology (AIST),
1-1-1 Umezono, Tsukuba, Ibaraki 305-8561, Japan
matsuoka@ni.aist.go.jp
https://staff.aist.go.jp/s-matsuoka

Abstract. In a previous paper, we have reported a new linear time correctness condition for proof nets of Multiplicative Linear Logic without units, where we gave a description of the algorithm in an informal way. In this paper, we give a formal model for the algorithm. Our formal model is based on a finite state transition system with queues as well as union-find trees as data structures. The model has been obtained by trial and error based on a concrete implementation of the algorithm. In addition, the algorithm has a subtle mechanism in order to avoid deadlock. We give an invariant property of the state transition system and it guarantees the deadlock-freedom.

1 Introduction

More than three decades ago, J.Y. Girard introduced the notion of proof nets of unit free Multiplicative Linear Logic (for short, MLL)[5]. It is a parallel syntax for MLL proofs, removing redundancy of sequent calculus proofs. In [5], he introduced MLL proof structures, which are graphs whose nodes are labeled by MLL formulas and then defined MLL proof nets as sequentializable MLL proof structures. Moreover he introduced a topological property called the *long trip condition* for MLL proof structures and showed that an MLL proof structure is an MLL proof net if and only if it satisfies the long trip condition. Such a characterization is called a *correctness condition* for MLL proof nets. Since then many other correctness conditions have been given for MLL and its variants or extensions by many researchers.

In [11], the author gives a new linear time correctness condition algorithm for MLL. This means that using the algorithm, we can check whether or not an MLL proof structure is an MLL proof net in linear time. The description of the algorithm in [11] is given in an informal way. Such an informal description is important because an algorithm supposed to be important should be understood by humans. In addition, an algorithm supposed to be important also should be understood by a machine and proved that it is correct easily: If an algorithm

M. Fernández (Ed.): LOPSTR 2020, LNCS 12561, pp. 311–328, 2021.
https://doi.org/10.1007/978-3-030-68446-4_16

turned out to be difficult to implement, then its interest would be limited to theoretical one.

In this paper, we give a formal model for the algorithm. The formal model, which is based on the implementation [12] of the algorithm, has been obtained by trial and error. Our model is presented as a finite state transition system. A notable point of the model is that a deadlock prevention mechanism in the algorithm is incorporated in order to guarantee the correctness of the algorithm and the deadlock-freedom is formalized as an invariant in the transition system.

Our implementation of the algorithm in [12] corresponding to the formal model is much faster than a naive quadratic algorithm, especially for bigger proof structures. It is an efficient implementation for a rewriting system and effectively exploits union-find data structures. Although so far several researchers have used union-find data structures in order to derive efficient algorithms in the context of logic-oriented computer science [6,8,13,15], union-find data structures have not been used for concrete implementations in the community in many cases. We believe that there are other places in this research area that can exploit union-find data structures effectively because they provide a method that implements various equivalence relations. One instance is given in [10]. We hope that our work is helpful for promoting the use of union-find data structures.

Our correctness condition has an application to "proof search as problem solving" paradigm potentially. In this paradigm a given computational problem is specified by a logical formula and in order to find a solution for the problem, search for a proof of the formula is tried. A found proof is then a solution to the problem. It is well-known that many computational problems can be specified by Linear Logic formulas in a direct way. In particular provability of MLL is NP-complete [7] and many NP-complete problems can be specified using MLL formulas [9]. Our efficient correctness condition may be a key component in a proof search engine for MLL in the following scenario: Construct an MLL proof structure (that is a candidate of a legitimate proof) of a given MLL formula, and then check whether it is an MLL proof net (that is a legitimate proof) using our linear time correctness condition.

2   Multiplicative Linear Logic, Proof Structures and Proof Nets

2.1   Multiplicative Linear Logic

We introduce the system of Multiplicative Linear Logic (for short MLL). We define *MLL formulas*, which are denoted by $F, G, H, \ldots$, by the following grammar:

$$F ::= p \mid p^\perp \mid F \otimes G \mid F \mathbin{\mathscr{B}} G$$

The negation of F, which is denoted by $F^\perp$ is defined as follows:

$$
\begin{aligned}
(p)^\perp &= p^\perp \\
(p^\perp)^\perp &= p \\
(F \otimes G)^\perp &= G^\perp \,\mathfrak{F}\, F^\perp \\
(F \mathfrak{F} G)^\perp &= G^\perp \otimes F^\perp
\end{aligned}
$$

The formula p is called an *atomic* formula. In this paper, we only consider the logical system with only one atomic formula: We can reduce the correctness condition with many atomic formulas to this simplified case by forgetting the information. We denote *multisets of MLL formulas* by $\Lambda, \Lambda_1, \Lambda_2, \ldots$. An MLL sequent is a multiset of MLL formulas Λ. We write an MLL sequent Λ as $\vdash \Lambda$. The inference rules of MLL are as follows:

$$
\text{ID} \;\frac{}{\vdash p^\perp, p}
$$

$$
\otimes \;\frac{\vdash \Lambda_1, F \qquad \vdash \Lambda_2, G}{\vdash \Lambda_1, \Lambda_2, F \otimes G} \;\mathfrak{F}\,\frac{\vdash \Lambda, F, G}{\vdash \Lambda, F \mathfrak{F} G}
$$

We note that we restrict the ID-axiom to that with only atomic formula p and its negation $p^\perp$. We omit the *cut* rule that has the form

$$
\text{Cut} \;\frac{\vdash \Lambda_1, F \qquad \vdash \Lambda_2, F^\perp}{\vdash \Lambda_1, \Lambda_2}
$$

because it can be identified with the $\otimes$-rule for our purpose.

2.2 MLL Proof Nets

Next we introduce MLL proof nets. Figure 1 shows the *MLL links* we use. Each MLL link has a few MLL formulas. Such an MLL formula is a conclusion or a premise of the MLL link, which is specified as follows:

1. In an ID-link, each of p and $p^\perp$ is called a conclusion of the link.
2. In a $\otimes$-link, each of F and G is called a premise of the link and $F \otimes G$ is called a conclusion of the link.
3. In a $\mathfrak{F}$-link, each of F and G is called a premise of the link and $F \mathfrak{F} G$ is called a conclusion of the link.

In the definition above F is called left premise and G right premise. An MLL *proof structure* Θ is a set of MLL links that satisfies the following conditions:

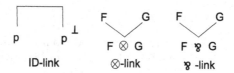

Fig. 1. MLL Links

1. For each link L in Θ, each conclusion of L is a premise of at most one link other than L in Θ.
2. For each link L in Θ, each premise of L must be a conclusion of exactly one link other than L in Θ.

A formula occurrence F in an MLL proof structure Θ is a conclusion of Θ if F is not a premise of any link in Θ.

An MLL *proof net* is an MLL proof structure that is constructed by the rules in Figure 2. Note that each rule in Figure 2 has the corresponding inference rule in the MLL sequent calculus. All MLL proof structures are not necessarily an MLL proof net.

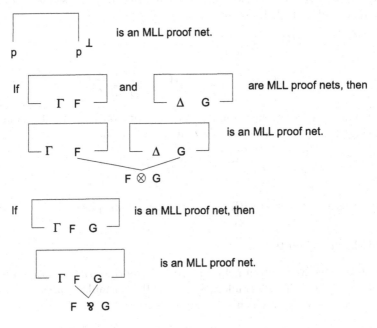

Fig. 2. Definition of MLL proof nets

3   The Rewriting System over deNM-Trees

In this section we introduce our rewriting system. Then we give our correctness condition based on the system.

3.1   deNM-Trees

First we define deNM-trees, which are inspired from de Naurois and Mogbil's correctness condition [14]. In the following we fix an MLL proof structure Θ.

Definition 1 (deNM-trees). *A deNM-tree is a finite tree consisting of labeled nodes and $\mathscr{B}$-nodes:*

- *A labeled node is labeled by a switch-label set S that is a subset of $S_{full} = \{l_{L_1}, r_{L_1}, \ldots, l_{L_\ell}, r_{L_\ell}\}$, where each L_j $(1 \leq j \leq \ell)$ is a $\mathscr{B}$-link. The degree t of a labeled node is at most the number of nodes of the deNM-tree. See Figure 3.*
- *A $\mathscr{B}$-node is a labeled by a $\mathscr{B}$-link L. The degree of a $\mathscr{B}$-node is 1 or 2. See Figure 3. As shown symbolically, we distinguish the port above of a $\mathscr{B}$-node from the port below.*

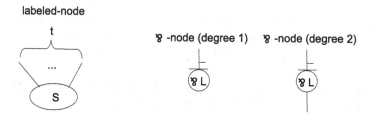

Fig. 3. Labeled and $\mathscr{B}$-nodes

Next we give a translation from Θ to a deNM-tree. The translation is slightly different from that given in [11]: it is suitable for a mechanical implementation. For that purpose, we have to make some preparations. We note that each formula occurrence in Θ is (1) a literal p or $p^\perp$, (2) a $\otimes$-formula $A \otimes B$, or (3) a $\mathscr{B}$-formula $A \mathscr{B} B$. We identify a $\mathscr{B}$-formula with the $\mathscr{B}$-node generated from it. Moreover, for each $\mathscr{B}$-link L, two labeled nodes n_L^l and n_L^r are generated, corresponding to left and right premises respectively. In addition if such a premise is a conclusion of an ID-link or the conclusion of a $\otimes$-link, then the labeled node associated with the conclusion is also generated other than n_L^l or n_L^r. When we say that a labeled node is associated with a literal or a $\otimes$-formula, we mean that it is a labeled node with the latter type. Moreover when a formula is a $\otimes$-formula or a literal, we conveniently identify the formula with the associated labeled node.

Let m be the total number of the $\otimes$-formulas and the literals, and ℓ be that of the $\mathscr{B}$-formulas in Θ. If $T(\Theta)$ is well-defined, then the number of labeled nodes is $m + 2\ell$ and that of $\mathscr{B}$-nodes is ℓ in $T(\Theta)$. Each labeled node n in $T(\Theta)$ has the following the associated data:

1. a queue $Q_{labeled}^n$ that includes the labeled nodes connecting to n,
2. a queue Q_{up}^n that includes the $\mathscr{B}$-nodes connecting to n from the port above,
3. a queue Q_{down}^n that includes the $\mathscr{B}$-nodes connecting to n from the port below, and
4. the switch-label set Lab^n on n that is a subset of the switch-labels $S_{full} = \{l_1, r_1, \ldots, l_\ell, r_\ell\}$.

Each $\bar{\otimes}$-node p in $T(\Theta)$ has the following associated data:

1. a labeled node up_p, which initially corresponds to the left premise of p,
2. a labeled node right_p, which initially corresponds to the right premise of p, and
3. the labeled node down_p connecting to p from the port below if p is not a conclusion in Θ. Otherwise, down_p is undefined.

We define a queue $\text{Below}(n)$ of labeled nodes for each labeled node n: If n is n_L^l or n_L^r where L is a $\bar{\otimes}$-link or n is a conclusion of Θ, then $\text{Below}(n) = \text{empty}$. Otherwise, n must be a literal or a $\otimes$-formula:

$$\text{Below}(n) = \begin{cases} A \otimes B & \text{(if } n \text{ is a premise of a } \otimes\text{-link with conclusion } A \otimes B) \\ n_L^l & \text{(if } n \text{ is a left premise of a } \bar{\otimes}\text{-link } L) \\ n_L^r & \text{(if } n \text{ is a right premise of a } \bar{\otimes}\text{-link } L) \end{cases}$$

According to the type of each link L in Θ, the associated data for the labeled nodes and the $\bar{\otimes}$-nodes for $T(\Theta)$ are defined as follows:

1. In the case where L is an ID-link, let $c_0 = p$ and $c_1 = p^\perp$ be the conclusion formulas of L. For each $i \in \{0, 1\}$,
   (a) $Q_{\text{labeled}}^{c_i} = c_{i+1 \bmod 2} \, \text{Below}(c_i)$.
   (b) $Q_{\text{up}}^{c_i}$, $Q_{\text{down}}^{c_i}$, and Lab^n are empty.
2. In the case where L is a $\otimes$-link, let $c = A \otimes B$ be the conclusion and $p_0 = A$ and $p_1 = B$ be the left premise and the right premise respectively.
   (a) $Q_{\text{labeled}}^{c} = \text{Above}(c) \, \text{Below}(c)$, where

$$\text{Above}(c) = \begin{cases} \text{empty} & \text{(if both } p_0 \text{ and } p_1 \text{ are } \bar{\otimes}\text{-formulas)} \\ p_i & \text{(if } p_i \text{ is a } \otimes\text{-formula or a literal and} \\ & \quad p_{i+1 \bmod 2} \text{ is a } \bar{\otimes}\text{-formula)} \\ p_0, p_1 & \text{(if both } p_0 \text{ and } p_1 \text{ are a } \otimes\text{-formula or a literal)} \end{cases}$$

   (b) Q_{up}^{c} and Lab^c is empty.

   (c) $Q_{\text{down}}^{c} = \begin{cases} p_0, p_1 & \text{(if both } p_0 \text{ and } p_1 \text{ are } \bar{\otimes}\text{-formulas)} \\ p_i & \text{(if } p_i \text{ is a } \bar{\otimes}\text{-formula or} \\ & \quad p_{i+1 \bmod 2} \text{ is a } \otimes\text{-formula or a literal)} \\ \text{empty} & \text{(if both } p_0 \text{ and } p_1 \text{ are a } \otimes\text{-formula or a literal)} \end{cases}$

3. In the case where L is a $\bar{\otimes}$-link, let $c = A \bar{\otimes} B$ be the conclusion and $p_0 = A$ and $p_1 = B$ be the left premise and the right premise respectively. Then we have the following labeled nodes $n_0 = n_L^l$ and $n_1 = n_L^r$ for L. For each $i \in \{0, 1\}$
   (a) $Q_{\text{labeled}}^{n_i} = p_i$ if p_i is not a $\bar{\otimes}$-formula. Otherwise, $Q_{\text{labeled}}^{n_i}$ is empty.
   (b) If $i = 0$ then $Q_{\text{up}}^{n_i} = c$. Otherwise, i must be 1. Then $Q_{\text{up}}^{n_i}$ is empty.
   (c) $Q_{\text{down}}^{n_i} = p_i$ if p_i is a $\bar{\otimes}$-formula. Otherwise $Q_{\text{down}}^{n_i}$ is empty.
   (d) If $i = 0$ then $\text{Lab}^{n_0} = \{l_L\}$. Otherwise, i must be 1. Then $\text{Lab}^{n_1} = \{r_L\}$.
   Moreover we have a $\bar{\otimes}$-node p for the $\bar{\otimes}$-link L.

(a) up_p is $n_0 = n_L^l$

(b) right_p is $n_1 = n_L^r$

(c) $\text{down}_p = \begin{cases} A' \otimes B' & \text{(if } c \text{ is a premise of a } \otimes\text{-link with conclusion } A' \otimes B'\text{)} \\ n_{L'}^l & \text{(if } c \text{ is a left premise of a } \text{⅋-link } L'\text{)} \\ n_{L'}^r & \text{(if } c \text{ is a right premise of a } \text{⅋-link } L'\text{)} \\ \text{undefined} & \text{(Otherwise)} \end{cases}$

Then we define the undirected graph $G_{\forall\text{left}}(\Theta)$ as follows:

1. The set of nodes consists of the $m + 2\ell$ labeled nodes and the ℓ ⅋-nodes as described above.
2. As to the incidence relation, each labeled node n connects to each labeled node in Q_{labeled}^n. Each ⅋-node in Q_{up}^n connects to n from the port above and each ⅋-node in Q_{down}^n connects to n from the port below.
3. Each labeled node n has the switch-label set Lab^n on n.
4. Each ⅋-node p for L has the label L on p.

If $G_{\forall\text{left}}(\Theta)$ is a tree, then the deNM-tree $T(\Theta)$ is $G_{\forall\text{left}}(\Theta)$. Otherwise it is undefined. If $T(\Theta)$ is defined, then we can easily see that $T(\Theta)$ is a deNM-tree.

As an example, let us consider the MLL proof net Θ_1 shown in Fig. 4, where the symbol ⊚ means a ⅋-link occurrence. Then Θ_1 is translated to the deNM-tree $T(\Theta_1)$ shown in Fig. 5.

pn-deadlock-1.txt

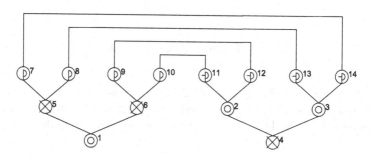

Fig. 4. An MLL proof net Θ_1

3.2   The Rewriting System over deNM-Trees

Next we introduce our rewriting system over deNM-trees. In the rewriting system we must specify exactly one node in a deNM-tree that is about to be rewritten, which we call the *active* node in the deNM-tree. The active node must be a labeled node. Our rewriting system has only three rewrite rules.

– The rewrite rule of Fig. 6 is called *⅋-elimination*: If the active node n is connected to a ⅋-node p_L labeled by L through the port above and the switch-label set S of n contains switch-labels l_L and r_L, then p_L is eliminated.

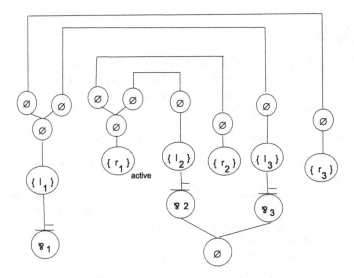

Fig. 5. The deNM-tree $T(\Theta_1)$ obtained from Θ_1

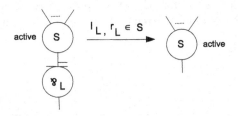

Fig. 6. ⅋-elimination rule

– The rewrite rule of Fig. 7 is called *union*: If the active node is connected to a labeled node, then these two nodes are merged. The switch-label set of the resulting node is the union of them of the merged two nodes.

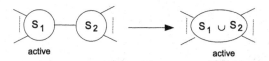

Fig. 7. Union rule

– The rewrite rule called *local jump* of Fig. 8 does not change any nodes: It just changes which labeled node is active. Note that in this rewrite rule, the precondition is that the active node is connected to a ⅋-node p_L through the port below and the postcondition is that the active node is the labeled node whose switch-label set contains r_L.

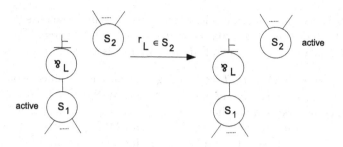

Fig. 8. Local jump rule

We denote the rewriting system consisting of these three rewrite rules above by $\mathcal{R}$.

Definition 2. *Algorithm A is defined as follows:*

> Input: *an MLL proof structure* Θ
> Output: **yes** *or* **no**.
> 1. *If the deNM-tree* $T(\Theta)$ *is not defined, then the output is* **no**.
> *Otherwise go to 2.*
> 2. *A labeled node* n *in* $T(\Theta)$ *is selected arbitrarily.*
> 3. *Rewriting is started with* $T(\Theta)$ *and the active node* n *using three rewrite rules above.*
> 4. *If the local jump rule is applied to a* ⅋*-link to which the local jump rule has been applied already, then the output is* **no**.
> 5. *When any of three rewrite rules cannot be applied to the current deNM-tree* T', *if* T' *consists of exactly one node labeled by* S_{full} *with degree 0, then the output is* **yes**.
> *Otherwise, the output is* **no**.

Theorem 1 *[11].*

1. *Algorithm A always terminates.*
2. *Let* Θ *be an MLL proof structure. Then* Θ *is an MLL proof net if and only if Algorithm A with input* Θ *outputs* **yes**.

Proof. (Sketch)

1. Algorithm A cannot be applied the local jump rule to a ⅋-link more than once. Both of the other two rules reduce the number of nodes in a deNM-tree.
2. – Only-if-part: Since Algorithm A terminates, we can suppose that Θ is an MLL proof net and Algorithm A with input Θ outputs **no**. If the deNM-tree $T(\Theta)$ is not well-defined in Step 1, then it means contradiction to the characterization theorem in [3]. Moreover application of the local jump rule to a ⅋-link twice in Step 4 also means contradiction to the characterization theorem in [3]. So Algorithm A reaches Step 5. In this case the deNM-tree at the termination is not one node tree. But it contradicts the characterization theorem in [14].

– If-part: We suppose that Algorithm A with input Θ outputs **yes**. It means that Algorithm A terminates with one node deNM-tree. Then the characterization theorem in [14] implies that Θ is an MLL proof net.   □

For example, the deNM-tree $T(\Theta_1)$ in Fig. 5, which is obtained from the MLL proof net Θ_1 in Fig. 4, can be reduced to one node deNM-tree by Algorithm A no matter which labeled node is chosen as active initially. On the other hand, while the MLL proof structure Θ_2 in Fig. 9 is not an MLL proof net, its translation deNM-tree $T(\Theta_2)$ in Fig. 10 can not be reduced to one node deNM-tree no matter which labeled node is chosen as active initially.

nonPN-cycle—1.txt

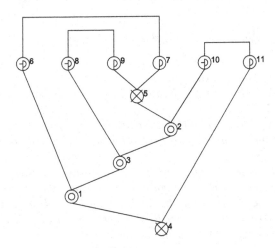

Fig. 9. An MLL proof structure, but not an MLL proof net Θ_2

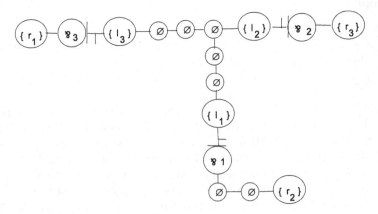

Fig. 10. The deNM-tree $T(\Theta_2)$ obtained from Θ_2

4   Linear Time Correctness Condition: A Formal Approach

Although our rewriting system $\mathcal{R}$ is surprisingly simple, it cannot establish linear time termination: Nodes in a deNM-tree T may have degrees depending on the number of nodes of T and then it may take linear time for each rewrite step in the case of a naive implementation. As a result, it may take quadratic total time for termination. Such an example can be seen in [11].

In order to establish linear time termination based on our rewriting system, we must restrict a way of application of rewrite rules using more sophisticated data structures. In [11] we gave such data structures and the linear time algorithm based on them in an informal way. In this section we give a formal specification of our algorithm. The formal specification is extracted from the implementation in [12], which performed tests on dozens of instances successfully. In particular, we have compared decision results of the new implementation with them of a naive implementation of the correctness condition by de Naurois and Mogbil [14]. As a result, we found that except for MLL proof nets to which the old implementation was not able to give an answer within a reasonable time, both implementations give the same decision results for all MLL proof structures that we provided. Moreover, the new linear time implementation is remarkably faster than the old quadratic time one.

4.1   Union-Find Data Structures

In this section we give a brief overview of union-find data structures. For a more detailed treatment, the reader can consult [2].

A union-find data structure S represents a partition of a finite set $\{1, \ldots, k\}$ but not statically: After operations defined below have been executed over S, the resulting partition can be different from the initial partition. An element S in S has the representative element of the subset of $\{1, \ldots, k\}$ to which S belongs. Initially each element S in S represents a singleton set $\{S\}$. The union-find data structure S has two kinds of operations:

1. union(S, S'): When S and S' represents disjoint subsets $\{u_1, \ldots, u_{k_S}\}$ and $\{v_1, \ldots, v_{k_{S'}}\}$ of $\{1, \ldots, k\}$ respectively, after the operation union(S, S') is executed, either S or S' becomes the representative element of the union $\{u_1, \ldots, u_{k_S}, v_1, \ldots, v_{k_{S'}}\}$ (both S and S' become elements of the union).
2. find(S): It is an element of $\{1, \ldots, k\}$ that is also the representative of a subset of $\{1, \ldots, k\}$ to which S belongs.

Note that after the execution of an operation union(S_1, S_2), the element returned by find(S) may be a different element from an previously returned element by find(S).

Let π be a finite execution sequence of operations of a union-find data structure S. Without any assumptions, the execution of π is beyond linear time. But if the base set $\{1, \ldots, k\}$ of S has an additional structure as a finite tree T and each union operation in π respects the structure, that is, each subset S in π is a subtree of T, then the time complexity of π is $O(|\pi|)$ in amortized cost [4]. This means that each operation in π can be regarded as a constant time operation. Our formal model exploits this fact: Each transition step can be executed in constant time since each union-find data structure in the formal model satisfies the above condition. That is the reason why our correctness condition is linear.

4.2 Data Specification

We suppose $T(\Theta)$ has k labeled nodes and ℓ $\aleph$-nodes. Our refined rewriting system will consist of rewrite rules that manipulate tuples having the form

$$\langle\langle S_{\text{labeled}}, S_{\text{up}}, S_{\text{right}}, S_{\text{Uup}}, S_{\text{Uright}}, S_{\text{elim}}\rangle,$$
$$\langle a, N, n, P, S_{\text{elim}}, \text{num}_{\text{labeled}}, \text{num}_{\aleph}\rangle\rangle,$$

where

- S_{labeled} is a union-find data structure representing a partition of the set $\{1, \ldots, k\}$. It maintains the information of indices of united labeled nodes.
- each of S_{up}, S_{right}, S_{Uup}, and S_{Uright} is a union-find data structure representing a partition of the set $\{1, \ldots, \ell\}$.
  - S_{up} and S_{Uup} maintain indices of $\aleph$-links that has been applied to $\aleph$-elimination regardless of its success.
  - S_{right} and S_{Uright} maintain indices of right premises of $\aleph$-links that has been applied to $\aleph$-elimination regardless of its success.
- the component S_{elim} is a union-find data structure representing a partition of the set
$$\{-1, 1, \ldots, \ell\}.$$
It maintains the information of indices of $\aleph$-links eliminated.
- the component a points to the current active labeled node index i. This means that a is an element of S_{labeled}.
- each labeled node i ($1 \le i \le k$) is represented by the following 8-tuple:

$$N_i = \langle Q^i_{\text{labeled}}, Q^i_{\text{down}}, Q^i_{\text{up}}, S^i_{\text{up}}, Q^i_{\text{right}}, S^i_{\text{right}}, S^i_{\text{Uup}}, S^i_{\text{Uright}}\rangle$$

where
  - Q^i_{labeled} is a queue data structure and includes a subset of $\{1, \ldots, k\}$.
  - Q^i_{down}, Q^i_{up}, and Q^i_{right} are a queue data structure and include a subset of $\{1, \ldots, \ell\}$.
  - S^i_{up}, S^i_{right}, S^i_{Uup}, and S^i_{Uright} are an element of S_{up}, S_{right}, S_{Uup}, and S_{Uright} respectively or undefined.
- Initially
$$S^i_{\text{up}} = S^i_{\text{right}} = S^i_{\text{Uup}} = S^i_{\text{Uright}} = \text{undefined},$$

where when S is undefined, it is identified with $\emptyset$ in the union operation. In addition we have defined the initial values of $Q^i_{\text{labeled}}, Q^i_{\text{down}}, Q^i_{\text{up}}$ already in Subsect. 3.1. The initial value of Q_{right}^i is j if $\text{Lab}^i = \{r_j\}$ $(1 \leq j \leq \ell)$ Otherwise, it is empty. Then we have the properties

$$\bigcup_{1 \leq i \leq k} Q_{\text{labeled}}^i = \{1, \ldots, k\}$$

$$\bigcup_{1 \leq i \leq k} Q_{\text{down}}^i = \bigcup_{1 \leq i \leq k} Q_{\text{up}}^i = \bigcup_{1 \leq i \leq k} Q_{\text{right}}^i = \{1, \ldots, \ell\}.$$

- For each $i\,(1 \leq i \leq k)$, n_i is an element of $\mathcal{S}_{\text{labeled}}$. Informally, n_i is the representative element of the subset of $\{1, \ldots, k\}$ to which i belongs. Initially n_i is i.
- Initially $S_{\text{elim}} = -1$
- Initially

$$\text{num}_{\text{labeled}} = k - 1, \quad \text{num}_{\mathcal{R}} = \ell$$

- Each $\mathcal{R}$-node p_j $(1 \leq j \leq \ell)$ has a triple

$$P_j = \langle \text{up}_j, \text{right}_j, \text{down}_j \rangle$$

where $\text{up}_j, \text{right}_j, \text{down}_j$ are an element of $\mathcal{S}_\cup$ and we have defined the initial values of $\text{up}_j, \text{right}_j, \text{down}_j$ already in Subsect. 3.1.

4.3 Operational Semantics

We suppose that the component a points to

$$N_i = \langle Q_{\text{labeled}}^i, Q_{\text{down}}^i, Q_{\text{up}}^i, S_{\text{up}}^i, Q_{\text{right}}^i, S_{\text{right}}^i, S_{\cup\text{up}}^i, S_{\cup\text{right}}^i \rangle .$$

This means that $\text{find}(a) = i$. Then when given a state

$$\langle a, N, n, P, S_{\text{elim}}, \text{num}_{\text{labeled}}, \text{num}_{\mathcal{R}} \rangle$$

we specify the next state. In the following definition, we only describe the components to be changed by applying the $\text{next}(-)$ operator to them. We do not describe the other components that are not changed.

1. **Union rule** is applied in the case where $Q_{\text{labeled}}^i = i_0 Q'_{\text{labeled}}$:
   (a) The case where $i = \text{find}(i_0)$:

$$\text{next}(Q_{\text{labeled}}^i) = Q'_{\text{labeled}}$$

   This case simply discards the index i_0, ignoring the redundant information.
   (b) The case where $i \neq \text{find}(i_0)$: Let i' be $\text{find}(i_0)$. Then,

$$\text{next}(a) = \text{next}(n_i) = \text{next}(n_{i'}) = \text{find}(\text{union}(n_i, n_{i'}))$$
$$\text{next}(N_{\text{next}(a)}) =$$
$$\langle \text{union}(S^i, S^{i'}), Q'_{\text{labeled}} +\!\!+ Q_{\text{labeled}}^{i'},$$
$$Q_{\text{down}}^i +\!\!+ Q_{\text{down}}^{i'},$$
$$Q_{\text{up}}^i +\!\!+ Q_{\text{up}}^{i'}, \text{union}(S_{\text{up}}^i, S_{\text{up}}^{i'}),$$
$$Q_{\text{right}}^i +\!\!+ Q_{\text{right}}^{i'}, \text{union}(S_{\text{right}}^i, S_{\text{right}}^{i'}),$$
$$\text{union}(S_{\cup\text{up}}^i, S_{\cup\text{up}}^{i'}), \text{union}(S_{\cup\text{right}}^i, S_{\cup\text{right}}^{i'}) \rangle$$
$$\text{next}(\text{num}_{\text{labeled}}) = \text{num}_{\text{labeled}} - 1,$$

where $+\!\!+$ is the concatenation operation for queues. The labeled node with index i is united to that with index i'.

2. **Local jump rule** is applied in the case where $Q^i_{\text{labeled}} = \emptyset$ and $Q^i_{\text{down}} = jQ'_{\text{down}}$:

(a) The case where $j \in S_{\text{elim}}$:

$$\text{next}(Q^i_{\text{down}}) = Q'_{\text{down}}$$

This case simply discards the index j. The $\wp$-link with index j had been already eliminated.

(b) The case where $j \notin S_{\text{elim}}$:

$$
\begin{aligned}
\text{next}(Q^i_{\text{down}}) &= Q'_{\text{down}} \\
i' &= \text{find}(\text{right}_j) \\
\text{next}(a) &= i' \\
\text{next}(S^{i'}_{\cup \text{up}}) &= \text{union}(S^i_{\cup \text{up}}, S^{i'}_{\cup \text{up}}) \\
\text{next}(S^{i'}_{\cup \text{right}}) &= \text{union}(S^i_{\cup \text{right}}, S^{i'}_{\cup \text{right}}).
\end{aligned}
$$

The active node has become the labeled node with index $\text{find}(\text{right}_j)$.

3. **$\wp$-elimination rule 1** is applied in the case where $Q^i_{\text{labeled}} = \emptyset$, $Q^i_{\text{down}} = \emptyset$, and $Q^i_{\text{up}} = jQ'_{\text{up}}$:

(a) The case where $\text{find}(j) = \text{find}(S^i_{\text{right}})$:

$$
\begin{aligned}
\text{next}(Q^i_{\text{up}}) &= Q'_{\text{up}} \\
\text{next}(Q^i_{\text{labeled}}) &= \begin{cases} Q^i_{\text{labeled}}\text{down}_j & (\text{if down}_j \neq \text{undefined}) \\ Q^i_{\text{labeled}} & (\text{otherwise}) \end{cases} \\
\text{next}(\text{num}_\wp) &= \text{num}_\wp - 1 \\
\text{next}(S_{\text{elim}}) &= \text{union}(j, S_{\text{elim}})
\end{aligned}
$$

The $\wp$-link with index j is eliminated successfully.

(b) The case where $\text{find}(j) \neq \text{find}(S^i_{\text{right}})$ and $\text{find}(j) = \text{find}(S^i_{\cup \text{right}})$:

$$
\begin{aligned}
\text{next}(Q^i_{\text{up}}) &= Q'_{\text{up}} \\
\text{next}(S^i_{\text{up}}) &= \text{union}(j, S^i_{\text{up}}) \\
\text{next}(Q^{\text{find}(\text{right}_j)}_{\text{right}}) &= Q^{\text{find}(\text{right}_j)}_{\text{right}} j
\end{aligned}
$$

The $\wp$-link with index j cannot be eliminated at this moment. But in order to eliminate it later, j is put in another queue $Q^{i'}_{\text{right}}$ for some i' $(1 \leq i' \leq k)$.

(c) The case where $\text{find}(j) \neq \text{find}(S^i_{\text{right}})$ and $\text{find}(j) \neq \text{find}(S^i_{\cup \text{right}})$:

$$
\begin{aligned}
\text{next}(Q^i_{\text{up}}) &= Q'_{\text{up}} \\
\text{next}(S^i_{\text{up}}) &= \text{union}(j, S^i_{\text{up}}) \\
\text{next}(S^i_{\text{up}}) &= \text{union}(j, S^i_{\cup \text{up}})
\end{aligned}
$$

The $\wp$-link with index j cannot be eliminated at this moment. The next trial to eliminate the $\wp$-link will be done with j in $Q^{i'}_{\text{right}}$ for some i' $(1 \leq i' \leq k)$ in $\wp$-elimination rule 2 below.

4. **$\b`⅋`$-elimination rule 2** is applied in the case where $Q^i_{\text{labeled}} = \emptyset$, $Q^i_{\text{down}} = \emptyset$, $Q^i_{\text{up}} = \emptyset$, and $Q^i_{\text{right}} = jQ'_{\text{right}}$ (this case is completely symmetrical to the immediately above case):

(a) The case where $\text{find}(j) = \text{find}(S^i_{\text{up}})$:

$$\begin{aligned}
\text{next}(Q^i_{\text{right}}) &= Q'_{\text{right}} \\
\text{next}(Q^i_{\text{labeled}}) &= \begin{cases} Q^i_{\text{labeled}}\text{down}_j & \text{(if down}_j \neq \text{undefined)} \\ Q^i_{\text{labeled}} & \text{(otherwise)} \end{cases} \\
\text{next}(\text{num}_{⅋}) &= \text{num}_{⅋} - 1 \\
\text{next}(S_{\text{elim}}) &= \text{union}(j, S_{\text{elim}})
\end{aligned}$$

The $⅋$-link with index j is eliminated successfully.

(b) The case where $\text{find}(j) \neq \text{find}(S^i_{\text{up}})$ and $\text{find}(j) = \text{find}(S^i_{\cup\text{up}})$:

$$\begin{aligned}
\text{next}(Q^i_{\text{right}}) &= Q'_{\text{right}} \\
\text{next}(S^i_{\text{right}}) &= \text{union}(j, S^i_{\text{right}}) \\
\text{next}(Q^{\text{find}(\text{up}_j)}_{\text{up}}) &= Q^{\text{find}(\text{up}_j)}_{\text{up}} j
\end{aligned}$$

The $⅋$-link with index j cannot be eliminated at this moment. But in order to eliminate it later, j is put in another queue $Q^{i'}_{\text{up}}$ for some i' ($1 \leq i' \leq k$).

(c) The case where $\text{find}(j) \neq \text{find}(S^i_{\text{up}})$ and $\text{find}(j) \neq \text{find}(S^i_{\cup\text{up}})$:

$$\begin{aligned}
\text{next}(Q^i_{\text{right}}) &= Q'_{\text{right}} \\
\text{next}(S^i_{\text{right}}) &= \text{union}(j, S^i_{\text{right}}) \\
\text{next}(S^i_{\text{right}}) &= \text{union}(j, S^i_{\cup\text{right}})
\end{aligned}$$

The $⅋$-link with index j cannot be eliminated at this moment. The next trial to eliminate the $⅋$-link will be done with j in $Q^{i'}_{\text{up}}$ for some i' ($1 \leq i' \leq k$) in $⅋$-elimination rule 1 above.

5. Otherwise, i.e., the case where $Q^i_{\text{labeled}} = \emptyset$, $Q^i_{\text{down}} = \emptyset$, $Q^i_{\text{up}} = \emptyset$, and $Q^i_{\text{right}} = \emptyset$: It terminates. If $\text{num}_{\text{labeled}} = 0$ and $\text{num}_{⅋} = 0$ then the output is **yes**. Otherwise, the output is **no**.

Remark 1. – In order to establish the correctness of the algorithm, we need the case 3.(b): without the case, the algorithm would lead to a deadlock state and it would judge that correct proof nets are not. Figs. 4 and 5 shows such an example: Θ is correct but it would not be able to eliminate $⅋_1$.

– Similarly, we need the case 4. (b): without the case, the algorithm would lead to a deadlock state and it would judge that correct proof nets are not. Figs. 11 and 12 shows such an example: Θ_3 is correct but it also would not be able to eliminate $⅋_1$.

pn-deadlock-2.txt

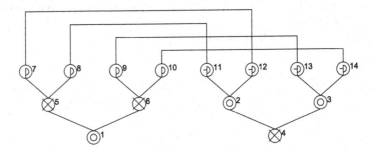

Fig. 11. An MLL proof net Θ_3

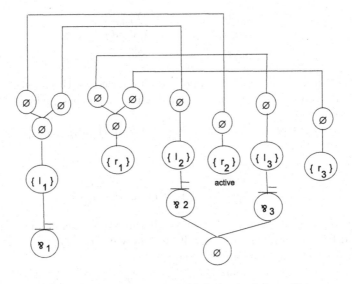

Fig. 12. The deNM-tree $T(\Theta_3)$ obtained from Θ_3

Theorem 2. *[11]. Let Θ be an MLL proof structure such that the deNM-tree $T(\Theta)$ is well-defined. We suppose that the initial state for $T(\Theta)$ is*

$$\langle a, N, p, P, S_{\text{elim}}, k, \ell \rangle$$

Then

1. *The rewriting system described above terminates in linear time.*
2. *Θ is an MLL proof net if and only if it terminates in*

$$\langle a', N', p', P', S'_{\text{elim}}, 0, 0 \rangle$$

for some a', N', p', P', S'_{elim}.

Proof. (Sketch)

1. The termination is by the first part of Theorem 1 and Remark 1 since our formal model implements a specific strategy of the rewriting system $\mathcal{R}$. The linear time termination is by the reason described in Subsection 4.1.
2. The proof is given by the second part of Theorem 1, Remark 1, and the following remark. □

Remark 2. In the proof of the only-if part of the second part, the following invariant, which claims deadlock-freedom, is essential: In each state of a transition process, for each j $(1 \leq j \leq \ell)$, if the $\wp$-link with index j is not eliminated at this moment, then for some i $(1 \leq i \leq k)$, Q^i_{up} or Q^i_{right} includes j.

5 Concluding Remarks

In this paper we have established a formal model of our linear time correctness algorithm for MLL proof nets based on a rewriting system over trees called deNM-trees, where in order to guarantee the correctness of the algorithm, we have introduced a deadlock prevention mechanism. Moreover we showed that the deadlock-freedom property can be formalized as an invariant of the formal model.

In the introduction section, we mentioned a potential application of our correctness condition to proof search. In order to realize it in a practical way, we have to incorporate an efficient backtracking mechanism to the proof search engine. But a naive approach would lead to an messy and inefficient implementation. Semi-persistent data structures [1] may give an elegant solution to this obstacle, although it is not clear at this moment.

References

1. Conchon, Sylvain, Filliâtre, Jean-Christophe: Semi-persistent data structures. In: Drossopoulou, Sophia (ed.) ESOP 2008. LNCS, vol. 4960, pp. 322–336. Springer, Heidelberg (2008). https://doi.org/10.1007/978-3-540-78739-6_25
2. Cormen, T.H., Leiserson, C.E., Rivest, R.L., Stein, C.: Introduction to Algorithms, Third Edition. The MIT Press, Cambridge (2009)
3. Danos, V., Regnier, R.: The structure of multiplicatives. Arch. Math. Logic **28**, 181–203 (1989). https://doi.org/10.1007/BF01622878
4. Gabow, H.N., Tarjan, R.E.: A linear-time algorithm for a special case of disjoint set union. J. Comput. Syst. Sci. **30**(2), 209–221 (1985). https://doi.org/10.1016/0022-0000(85)90014-5
5. Girard, J.Y.: Linear logic. Theoret. Comput. Sci. **50**, 1–102 (1987). https://doi.org/10.1016/0304-3975(87)90045-4
6. Guerrini, S.: A linear algorithm for MLL proof net correctness and sequentialization. Theoret. Comput. Sci. **412**(20), 1958–1978 (2011). https://doi.org/10.1016/j.tcs.2010.12.021, girard's Festschrift
7. Kanovich, M.I.: Horn programming in linear logic is NP-complete. In: Proceedings of the Seventh Annual IEEE Symposium on Logic in Computer Science, pp. 200–210 (1992). https://doi.org/10.1109/LICS.1992.185533

8. Martelli, A., Montanari, U.: An efficient unification algorithm. ACM Trans. Program. Lang. Syst. 4(2), 258–282 (1982). https://doi.org/10.1145/357162.357169

9. Matsuoka, Satoshi: Direct encodings of NP-complete problems into horn sequents of multiplicative linear logic. In: Gallagher, John P., Sulzmann, Martin (eds.) FLOPS 2018. LNCS, vol. 10818, pp. 17–32. Springer, Cham (2018). https://doi.org/10.1007/978-3-319-90686-7_2

10. Matsuoka, S.: A linear time algorithm for automatic generation of multiplicative planar proof nets (2019). https://akihisayamada.github.io/tpp2019/. The 15th Theorem Proving and Provers meeting (TPP 2019)

11. Matsuoka, S.: A new linear time correctness condition for multiplicative linear logic. CoRR abs/1902.09693 (2019). http://arxiv.org/abs/1902.09693

12. Matsuoka, S.: Proof Net Calculator. https://staff.aist.go.jp/s-matsuoka/PNCalculator/index.html (2019)

13. Murawski, A.M., Ong, C.H.L.: Fast verification of MLL proof nets via IMLL. ACM Trans. Comput. Logic 7, 473–498 (2006). https://doi.org/10.1145/1149114.1149116

14. de Naurois, P.J., Mogbil, V.: Correctness of linear logic proof structures is NL-complete. Theoret. Comput. Sci. 412, 1941–1957 (2011). https://doi.org/10.1016/j.tcs.2010.12.020

15. Paterson, M.S., Wegman, M.N.: Linear unification. In: Proceedings of the Eighth Annual ACM Symposium on Theory of Computing, pp. 181–186. STOC 1976. Association for Computing Machinery, New York (1976). https://doi.org/10.1145/800113.803646

Synthesis of Modality Definitions and a Theorem Prover for Epistemic Intuitionistic Logic

Paul Tarau[(⊠)]

Department of Computer Science and Engineering, University of North Texas, Denton, USA
paul.tarau@unt.edu

Abstract. We propose a mechanism for automating discovery of definitions, that, when added to a logic system for which we have a theorem prover, extends it to support an embedding of a new logic system into it. As a result, the synthesized definitions, when added to the prover, implement a prover for the new logic.

As an instance of the proposed mechanism, we derive a Prolog theorem prover for an interesting but unconventional epistemic Logic by starting from the sequent calculus **G4IP** that we extend with operator definitions to obtain an embedding in intuitionistic propositional logic (**IPC**). With help of a candidate definition formula generator, we discover epistemic operators for which axioms and theorems of Artemov and Protopopescu's *Intuitionistic Epistemic Logic* (**IEL**) hold and formulas expected to be non-theorems fail.

We compare the embedding of **IEL** in **IPC** with a similarly discovered successful embedding of Dosen's double negation modality, judged inadequate as an epistemic operator. Finally, we discuss the failure of the *necessitation rule* for an otherwise successful **S4** embedding and share our thoughts about the intuitions explaining these differences between epistemic and alethic modalities in the context of the Brouwer-Heyting-Kolmogorov semantics of intuitionistic reasoning and knowledge acquisition.

Keywords: Automatic synthesis of logic systems · Deriving new theorem provers via program synthesis · Epistemic intuitionistic logic · Propositional intuitionistic logic · Prolog-based theorem provers · Embedding of modal logics into intuitionistic logic

1 Introduction

Deriving new logic systems and discovering relationships between them not only requires a knowledge-intensive understanding of the intricate connections between their axioms and inference rules but it is also a time-intensive trial and error process for the human logician. This is especially the case for logic systems that depart from the usual expectations coming from the prevalent use of classical logic in today's computational tools and methodologies, as well as from our familiarity with more commonly used forms of modal logic (e.g., alethic, temporal).

This motivates our effort to explore ways to automate this process, resulting not only in discovering some salient relationships between new and well-established logic

© Springer Nature Switzerland AG 2021
M. Fernández (Ed.): LOPSTR 2020, LNCS 12561, pp. 329–344, 2021.
https://doi.org/10.1007/978-3-030-68446-4_17

systems, but also in software artifacts (e.g., automated theorem provers) facilitating reasoning in these less explored new logics.

Epistemic Logic systems have been derived often in parallel and sometime as afterthoughts of alethic Modal Logic systems, in which modalities are defined by axioms and additional inference rules extending classical logic.

In the context of Answer Set Programming (**ASP**) epistemic logics hosted in this framework like e.g., [1–3] show that *intermediate logics*[1] (e.g., equilibrium logic, [4]) can be extended with definitions of epistemic operators. Steps[2], further below classical logic or **ASP**, are taken in recent work [5], based on the Brouwer-Heyting-Kolmogorov (**BHK**) view of intuitionistic logic that takes into account the constructive nature of knowledge, modeling more accurately the connection between proof systems and the related mental processes. Along these lines, our inquiry into epistemic logic will focus on knowledge vs. truth seen as intuitionistic provability. Like in the case of embedding epistemic operators into **ASP** systems, but with automation in mind, we will design a synthesis mechanism for epistemic operators via embedding in **IPC**. For this purpose we will generate *candidate formulas* that verify axioms, theorems and rules and fail on expected non-theorems. For this purpose, we will use a lightweight **IPC** *theorem prover* and we will also show that this view generalizes to a mechanism for discovering, when possible, a simple embedding of a given logic into **IPC** and derivation of a theorem prover for it.

Our starting point is Artemov and Protopopescu's *Intuitionistic Epistemic Logic* (**IEL**) [5] that will provide the axioms, theorems and non-theorems stating the requirements that must hold for the definitions extending **IPC**. The discovery mechanism will also bring up Dosen's interpretation of double negation [6] as a potential epistemic operator and we will look into applying the same discovery mechanisms to find an embedding of modal logic **S4** in **IPC**, with special focus on the impact of the *necessitation rule*, which requires that all theorems of the logic are necessarily true.

To summarize, the novel contributions of the paper are:

1. a general program synthesis technique for discovering an embedding of a logic system into another
2. finding an actual embedding of **IEL** in **IPC**
3. synthesizing a theorem prover for **IEL**, for which no theorem prover exists

The Rest of the Paper Is Organized as Follows. Section 2 overviews Artemov and Protopopescu's *Intuitionistic Epistemic Logic* (**IEL**). Section 3 overviews the **G4IP** sequent calculus prover for Intuitionistic Propositional Logic (**IPC**). Section 4 describes the generator for candidate formulas extending **IPC** with modal operator definitions. Section 5 explains the discovering of the definitions that ensure the embedding of **IEL** into **IPC** and the embedding of Dosen's double negation as a modality operator. It also discusses the intuitions behind the embedding of **IEL**, including the epistemic equivalent of the necessity rule, in **IPC** and the adequacy of this embedding as a constructive

---

[1] Logics stronger than intuitionistic but weaker than classical.

[2] Actually infinitely many, as there's an infinite lattice of intermediate logics between classical and intuitionistic logic.

mechanism for reasoning about knowledge. Section 6 studies the case of the **S4** modal logic and the failure of the necessity rule, indicating the difficulty of embedding it in **IPC** by contrast to **IEL**. Section 7 overviews some related work and section 8 concludes the paper.

The paper is written as a *literate SWI-Prolog* program with its extracted code at https://raw.githubusercontent.com/ptarau/TypesAndProofs/master/ieltp.pro.

2 Overview of Artemov and Protopopescu's IEL logic

In [5] a system for Intuitionistic Epistemic Logic is introduced that

> "maintains the original Brouwer-Heyting-Kolmogorov semantics for intuitionism and is consistent with the well-known approach that intuitionistic knowledge be regarded as the result of verification".

Instead of the classic, alethic-modalities inspired **K** operator for which

$$\mathbf{K}A \rightarrow A$$

Artemov and Protopopescu argue that *co-reflection* expresses better the idea of *constructivity of truth*

$$A \rightarrow \mathbf{K}A$$

They also argue that this applies to both belief and knowledge i.e., that

> "The verification-based approach allows that justifications more general than proof can be adequate for belief and knowledge".

On the other hand, they consider *intuitionistic reflection* acceptable, expressing the fact that "known propositions cannot be false":

$$\mathbf{K}A \rightarrow \neg\neg A$$

Thus, they position intuitionistic knowledge of A between A and $\neg\neg A$ and given that (via Glivenko's transformation [7]) applying double negation to a formula embeds classical propositional calculus into **IPC**, they express this view as:

$$IntuitionisticTruth \;\Rightarrow\; IntuitionisticKnowledge \;\Rightarrow\; ClassicalTruth.$$

They axiomatize the system **IEL** as follows.

1. Axioms of propositional intuitionistic logic;
2. $\mathbf{K}(A \rightarrow B) \rightarrow (\mathbf{K}A \rightarrow \mathbf{K}B)$;   (distribution)
3. $A \rightarrow \mathbf{K}A$.   (co-reflection)
4. $\mathbf{K}A \rightarrow \neg\neg A$ (intuitionistic reflection)

Rule *Modus Ponens*.
They also argue that a weaker logic of belief (**IEL⁻**) is expressed by considering only axioms **1,2,3**.

3 The G4ip Prover for IPC

We will describe next our lightweight propositional intuitionistic theorem prover, that will be used to discover an embedding of **IEL** into **IPC**.

3.1 The LJT/G4ip Calculus, (Restricted Here to the Implicational Fragment)

Motivated by problems related to loop avoidance in implementing Gentzen's **LJ** calculus, Roy Dyckhoff [8] introduces the following rules for the **G4ip** calculus[3].

$$LJT_1 : \quad \frac{}{A,\Gamma \vdash A}$$

$$LJT_2 : \quad \frac{A,\Gamma \vdash B}{\Gamma \vdash A \to B}$$

$$LJT_3 : \quad \frac{B,A,\Gamma \vdash G}{A \to B,A,\Gamma \vdash G}$$

$$LJT_4 : \quad \frac{D \to B,\Gamma \vdash C \to D \quad B,\Gamma \vdash G}{(C \to D) \to B,\Gamma \vdash G}$$

Note that LJT_4 ensures termination as formulas in the sequent become smaller in a multiset The rules work with the context Γ being either a multiset or a set, and the calculus is *sound and complete* for IPC.

For supporting negation, one also needs to add LJT_5 that deals with the special term *false*. Then negation of A is defined as $A \to false$.

$$LJT_5 : \quad \frac{}{false,\Gamma \vdash G}$$

Rules for conjunction, disjunction and bi-conditional (not shown here) are also part of the calculus.

As it is not unusual with logic formalisms, the same calculus had been discovered independently in the 1950's by Vorob'ev and in the 80's–90's by Hudelmaier [9, 10].

---

[3] Originally called the LJT calculus in [8]. Restricted here to its key implicational fragment.

3.2 A Lightweight Theorem Prover for Intuitionistic Propositional Logic

Starting from the sequent calculus for the intuitionistic propositional logic in G4ip [8], to which we have also added rules for the "<->" relation, we obtain the following lightweight **IPC** prover.

```
:- op(525,  fy,  ~ ).
:- op(550,  xfy,  & ).        % right associative
:- op(575,  xfy,  v ).        % right associative
:- op(600,  xfx,  <-> ).      % non associative

prove_in_ipc(T):- prove_in_ipc(T,[]).
```

The predicate `prove_in_ipc` starts with an empty list of assumptions Vs corresponding to the context Γ in Dyckhoff's sequent calculus [8]. Its rules generate and reduce assumptions in this context.

```
prove_in_ipc(A,Vs):-memberchk(A,Vs),!.
prove_in_ipc(_,Vs):-memberchk(false,Vs),!.
prove_in_ipc(A<->B,Vs):-!,prove_in_ipc(B,[A|Vs]),prove_in_ipc(A,[B|Vs]).
prove_in_ipc((A->B),Vs):-!,prove_in_ipc(B,[A|Vs]).
prove_in_ipc(A & B,Vs):-!,prove_in_ipc(A,Vs),prove_in_ipc(B,Vs).
prove_in_ipc(G,Vs1):- % atomic or disj or false
    select(Red,Vs1,Vs2), % nondeterministic selection of reducible terms
    prove_in_ipc_reduce(Red,G,Vs2,Vs3),
    !,
    prove_in_ipc(G,Vs3). % further reductions, recursively
prove_in_ipc(A v B, Vs):-(prove_in_ipc(A,Vs);prove_in_ipc(B,Vs)),!.
```

Reductions in `prove_in_ipc_reduce` are performed by case analysis on different operators, among which the most important one is the reduction of the implication "->", as it ensures termination without requiring loop checking - the main novelty of the calculus described in [8].

```
prove_in_ipc_reduce((A->B),_,Vs1,Vs2):-!,prove_in_ipc_imp(A,B,Vs1,Vs2).
prove_in_ipc_reduce((A & B),_,Vs,[A,B|Vs]):-!.
prove_in_ipc_reduce((A<->B),_,Vs,[(A->B),(B->A)|Vs]):-!.
prove_in_ipc_reduce((A v B),G,Vs,[B|Vs]):-prove_in_ipc(G,[A|Vs]).
```

The predicate `prove_in_ipc_imp`, besides reducing implication, rewrites the other operators in terms of it, thus benefiting from the loop-free multi-set rewriting termination argument described in [8].

```
prove_in_ipc_imp((C->D),B,Vs,[B|Vs]):-!,prove_in_ipc((C->D),[(D->B)|Vs]).
prove_in_ipc_imp((C & D),B,Vs,[(C->(D->B))|Vs]):-!.
prove_in_ipc_imp((C v D),B,Vs,[(C->B),(D->B)|Vs]):-!.
prove_in_ipc_imp((C<->D),B,Vs,[((C->D)->((D->C)->B))|Vs]):-!.
prove_in_ipc_imp(A,B,Vs,[B|Vs]):-memberchk(A,Vs).
```

Note that, with the exception of the `!/0` and `memberchk/2` built-ins, used only as performance enhancers, the code is actually a set of Horn-clauses as `select/3` is a library predicate with a pure Horn clause definition.

We validate the prover by testing it on the implicational subset, derived via the Curry-Howard isomorphism [11], then against Roy Dyckhoff's Prolog implementation[4], working on formulas up to size 12. Finally we run it on human-made tests[5], on which we get no errors, solving correctly 161 problems, with a 60 s timeout, compared with the 175 problems solved by Roy Dyckhoff's more refined, heuristics-based 400 lines prover, with the same timeout[6]. We refer to [11] for the derivation steps of variants of this prover working on the implicational and nested Horn clause fragments of **IPC**. While more sophisticated tableau-based provers are available for **IPC** among which we mention the excellent Prolog-based fCube [12], our prover's compact size and adequate performance will suffice[7] for the tasks ahead.

4   The Definition Formula Generator

We start with a candidate formula generator that we will constrain further to be used for generating candidate definitions of our modal operators.

4.1   Generating Operator Trees

We generate all formulas of a given size by decreasing the available size parameter at each step when nodes are added to a tree representation of a formula. Prolog's **DCG** mechanism is used to collect the leaves of the tree.

```
genOperatorTree(N,Ops,Tree,Leaves):-
  genOperatorTree(Ops,Tree,N,0,Leaves,[]).

genOperatorTree(_,V,N,N)-->[V].
genOperatorTree(Ops,OpAB,SN1,N3)-->
  { SN1>0,N1 is SN1-1,
    member(Op,Ops),make_oper2(Op,A,B,OpAB)
  },
  genOperatorTree(Ops,A,N1,N2),
  genOperatorTree(Ops,B,N2,N3).

make_oper2(Op,A,B,OpAB):-functor(OpAB,Op,2),arg(1,OpAB,A),arg(2,OpAB,B).
```

4.2   Synthesizing the Definitions of Modal Operators

As we design a generic definition discovery mechanism, we will denote our modal operators as follows, generically.

---

[4] https://github.com/ptarau/TypesAndProofs/blob/master/third_party/dyckhoff_orig.pro.

[5] At http://iltp.de.

[6] https://github.com/ptarau/TypesAndProofs/blob/master/tester.pro.

[7] In fact, our prover is faster than both fCube and Dyckhoff's prover on the set of formulas of small size on which our definition induction algorithm will run.

- "#" for "□"=necessary and "**K**"=known
- "*" for "◊"=possible and "**M**"=knowable

After the operator definitions

```
:- op( 500, fy, #).
:- op( 500, fy, *).
```

we specify our generator as covering the usual binary operators and we constrain it to have at least one of the leaves of its generated trees to be a variable. Besides the `false` constant used in the definition of negation, we introduce also a new constant symbol "?" assumed not to occur in the language. Its role will be left unspecified until the possible synthesized definitions will be filtered. We will constrain candidate definitions to ensure that axioms and selected theorems hold and selected non-theorems fail.

```
genDef(M,Def):-genDef(M,[(->),(&),(v)],[false,?],Def).

genDef(M,Ops,Cs,(#(X):-T)):-
  between(0,M,N),
  genOperatorTree(N,Ops,T,Vs),
  pick_leaves(Vs,[X|Cs]),
  term_variables(Vs,[X]).
```

Iteration over integers N between 0 and M is provided by the built-in `between/3`. Variables are extracted from a term using the built-in `term_variables`. Next, leaves of the generated trees will be picked from a given set.

```
pick_leaves([],_).
pick_leaves([V|Vs],Ls):-member(V,Ls),pick_leaves(Vs,Ls).
```

We first expand our operator definitions for the "~" negation and "*" modal operator while keeping atomic variables and the special constant `false` untouched.

```
expand_defs(_,false,R) :-!,R=false.
expand_defs(_,A,R) :-atomic(A),!,R= A.
expand_defs(D,~(A),(B->false)) :-!,expand_defs(D,A,B).
expand_defs(D,*(A),R):-!,expand_defs(D,~ (# (~(A))),R).
```

The special case for expanding a candidate operator definition D requires a fresh variable for each instance, ensured by Prolog's built-in `copy_term`.

```
expand_defs(D,#(X),R) :-!,copy_term(D,(#(X):-T)),expand_defs(D,T,R).
```

Other operators are traversed generically by using Prolog's "=.." built-in and by recursing with `expand_def_list` on their arguments.

```
expand_defs(D,A,B) :-
  A=..[F|Xs],
  expand_def_list(D,Xs,Ys),
  B=..[F|Ys].

expand_def_list(_,[],[]).
expand_def_list(D,[X|Xs],[Y|Ys]) :-
  expand_defs(D,X,Y),
  expand_def_list(D,Xs,Ys).
```

The predicate `prove_with_def` refines our **G4ip** prover by first expanding the definitions extending **IPC** with a given candidate modality.

```
prove_with_def(Def,T0) :-expand_defs(Def,T0,T1),prove_in_ipc(T1,[]).
```

The definition synthesizer will filter the candidate definitions provided by `genDef` such that the predicate `prove_with_def` succeeds on all theorems and fails on all non-theorems, provided as names of the facts of arity 1 containing them. It iterates over theorems and non-theorems using the built-in `forall`. The negation-as-failure built-in `\+` is used to preempt success on non-theorems.

```
def_synth(M,D):-def_synth(M,iel_th,iel_nth,D).

def_synth(M,Th,NTh,D):-
  genDef(M,D),
  forall(call(Th,T),prove_with_def(D,T)),
  forall(call(NTh,NT), \+prove_with_def(D,NT)).
```

Note that the generator first builds smaller formulas and then larger ones up the specified maximum size.

Example 1. Candidate definitions up to size 2

```
?- forall(genDef(2,Def),println(Def)).
#A :- A
#A :- A -> A
#A :- A -> false
#A :- A -> ?
#A :- false -> A
#A :- ? -> A
#A :- A & A
#A :- A & false
#A :- A & ?
...
#A :- (A -> ?) -> A
...
#A :- (? v A) v ?
#A :- (? v false) v A
#A :- (? v ?) v A
```

5   Discovering the Embedding of IEL and Dosen's Double Negation Modality in IPC

We specify a given logic (e.g., **IEL** or **S4**) by stating theorems on which the prover extended with the synthetic definition should succeed and non-theorems on which it should fail.

5.1   The Discovery Mechanism for IEL

We start with the axioms of Artemov and Protopopescu's **IEL** system:

```
iel_th(a -> # a).
iel_th(# (a->b)->(# a-> # b)).
iel_th(# a -> ~ ~ a).
```

Note that the axioms would be enough to specify the logic, but we also add some theorems when intuitively relevant and/or mentioned in [5], as an empirical check of their consistency with the axioms. Our Prolog code, running in less than a second, is not slowed down by this in any significant way.

```
iel_th(#    (a & b) <-> (# a & # b)).
iel_th(~ # false).
iel_th(~ (# a & ~ a)).
iel_th(~a -> ~ # a).
iel_th( ~ ~ (# a -> a)).
iel_th(# a & # (a->b) -> # b).
iel_th(* (a & b) <-> (* a & * b)).
iel_th(# a -> * a).
iel_th(# a v # b -> # (a v b) ).
iel_th(# p <-> # # p).
iel_th(* a <-> * * a).
iel_th(a -> *a).
```

Again, following [5], we add our non-theorems. They act as a filtering mechanism rejecting candidate definitions that would contradict the system's intended semantics.

```
iel_nth(# a -> a).
iel_nth(# (a v b) -> # a v # b).
iel_nth(# a).
iel_nth(~ (# a)).
iel_nth(# false).
iel_nth(# a).
iel_nth(~ (# a)).
iel_nth(* false).
```

The *necessitation rule* in a modal logic requires that if T is a theorem than #T is also a theorem. This expresses the fact that the theorems of the logic are *necessarily* true, or in an epistemic context, that if T is an (intuitionistically proven) theorem, then the agent *knows* T. Thus, we define (implicit) facts via a Prolog rule that states that the (generic) necessity operator "#" applied to proven theorems or axioms generates new theorems.

```
iel_nec_th(T):-iel_th(T).
iel_nec_th(# T):-iel_th(T).
```

Finally, we obtain the discovery algorithm for **IEL** formula definitions and for **IEL** extended with the necessitation rule.

```
iel_discover:-
  backtrack_over((def_synth(2,iel_th,iel_nth,D),println(D))).

iel_nec_discover:-
  backtrack_over((def_synth(2,iel_nec_th,iel_nth,D),println(D))).
```

```
backtrack_over(Goal):-call(Goal),fail;true.
```

```
println(T):-numbervars(T,0,_),writeln(T).
```

Note the use of `backtrack_over/1` to backtrack over all answers to a given goal. We run `iel_discover`, ready to see the surviving definition candidates.

Example 2. Definition discovery without the necessitation rule.

```
?- iel_discover.
#A:-(A->false)->A
#A:-(A->false)->false
#A:-(A-> ?)->A
true.
```

Example 3. Definition discovery with the necessitation rule.

```
?- iel_nec_discover.
#A:-(A->false)->A
#A:-(A->false)->false
#A:-(A-> ?)->A
true.
```

Unsurprisingly, the results are the same, as a consequence of axiom A -> #A. This final list of candidates will need to be evaluated based on their relevance to the intended semantics of **IEL**.

Clearly, the formula `#A:-(A->false)->A` is not interesting as it would define knowing something as a contradiction that implies itself.

This brings us to the second definition formula candidate.

5.2   Eliminating Dosen's Double Negation Modality

In [2] double negation in IPC is interpreted as a "□" modality. This corresponds our second synthetic definition, `#A :- (A->false)->false`, that is equivalent in **IPC** to `#A :- ~~A`. It is argued in [5] that it does not make sense as an epistemic modality, mostly because it would entail that all classical theorems are known intuitionistically.

We eliminate it by requiring the collapsing of "*" into "#" to be a non-theorem:

```
iel_nth(* a <-> # a).
```

In fact, while *known* (#) implies *knowable* (`~#~` = *), it is reasonable to think, as in most modal logics, that the inverse implication does not hold.

After that, we have:

Example 4. The double negation modality is eliminated, as it collapses # and *.

```
?- iel_discover.
#A:-(A -> ?)->A
true.
```

```
?- iel_nec_discover.
#A:-(A -> ?)->A
true.
```

5.3   Knowledge as Awareness?

This leaves us with the #A :- (A -> ?) -> A.

Among the consequences of the fact that intuitionistic provability strictly implies classical, is that there's plenty of room left between p and ~~p, where both # and * find their place, given that the following implication chain holds.

p -> #p -> *p -> ~~p

Let us now find an (arguably) intuitive meaning for the "?" constant in the definition. The interpretation of knowledge as awareness about truth goes back to [13]. Our final definition of intuitionistic epistemic modality as "#A :- (A -> ?) -> A" suggests interpreting "?" as awareness of an agent entailed by (a proof of) A. With this in mind, one obtains an embedding of **IEL** in **IPC** via the extension

$$KA \equiv (A \rightarrow \textbf{eureka}) \rightarrow A$$

where **eureka** is a new symbol not occurring in the language[8].

In line with the Brouwer-Heyting-Kolmogorov (**BHK**) interpretation of intuitionistic proof, we may say that an agent *knows* A *if and only if* A *is validated by a proof of* A *that induces awareness of the agent about it.*

Thus knowledge of an agent, in this sense, collects facts that are proven constructively in a way that is "understood" by the agent. The consequence

$$KA \rightarrow \neg\neg A$$

would then simply say that intuitionistic truths, that the agent is aware of, are also classically valid.

5.4   The Theorem Prover for IEL

Thus, we can define our *newly synthesized* prover for **IEL** as follows.

```
iel_prove(P):-prove_with_def((#A :- (A -> eureka) -> A),P).
```

Interestingly, if one allows eureka to occur in the formulas of the language given as input to the prover, then it becomes (the unique) value for which we have equivalence between being known and having a proof.

```
?- iel_prove(#eureka <-> eureka).
true .
```

Similarly, it would also follow that

```
?- iel_prove(*eureka <-> ~ ~ eureka).
true.
```

Thus, one would need to forbid accepting it as part of the prover's language to closely follow the intended semantics of **IEL**.

---

[8] Not totally accidentally named, given the way Archimedes expressed his sudden *awareness* about the volume of water displaced by his immersed body.

5.5 Discussion

The most significant consequence of the successful embedding of **IEL** *into* **IPC** *via the epistemic modality definition* #A :- (A -> eureka) -> A) *is that we have actually derived a theorem prover for* **IEL**. The theorem prover is implemented by the predicate iel_prove/1 by extending a theorem prover for **IPC** with the induced definition.

As the **IPC** fragment with two variables, implication and negation has exactly **518** equivalence classes of formulas [14, 15], one would expect the construction deriving "∗" from "#" to reach a fixpoint. We can use our prover to find out when that happens.

```
?- iel_prove(#p <-> ~ # (~p)).
false.
iel_prove(*p <-> ~(*(~p))).
true.
```

Thus the fixpoint of the construction is "∗", that we have interpreted as meaning that a proposition is *knowable*. Therefore, the equivalence reads reasonably as "something is knowable if and only if its negation is not knowable". Note also that

```
?- iel_prove(~(*(~p)) -> #p).
false.
```

fails, by contrast to the equivalence $\Box p \equiv \neg \Diamond \neg p$ usual in classical modal logics.

6 Discovering an Embedding of S4 Without the Necessitation Rule

The fact that both **IPC** and **S4** are known to be PSPACE-complete [16] means that polynomial-time translations exist between them.

In fact, Gödel's translation from **IPC** to **S4** (by prefixing each subformula with the $\Box$ operator) shows that the embedding of **IPC** into **S4** can be achieved quite easily, by using purely syntactic means. However, the (very) few papers attempting the inverse translation [17, 18] rely on methods often involving intricate semantic constructions.

We will use our definition generator to identify the problem that precludes a simple embedding of **S4** into **IPC**.

We start with the axioms of **S4**.

```
s4_th(# a -> a).
s4_th(# (a->b) -> (# a -> # b)).
s4_th(# a -> # # a).
```

We add a few theorems.

```
s4_th(* * a <-> * a).
s4_th(a -> * a).
s4_th(# a -> * a).
s4_th(# a v # b -> # (a v b)).
s4_th(# (a v b) -> # a v # b).
```

We add some non-theorems that ensure additional filtering.

```
s4_nth(# a).
s4_nth(~ (# a)).
s4_nth(# false).
s4_nth(* false).
s4_nth(* a -> # * a). % true only in S5
s4_nth(a -> # a).
s4_nth(* a -> a).
s4_nth(# a <-> ?).
s4_nth(* a <-> ?).
```

Like in the case of **IEL** we define implicit facts stating that the necessitation rule holds.

```
s4_nec_th(T):-s4_th(T).
s4_nec_th(# T):-s4_th(T).
```

Finally we implement the definition discovery predicates and run them.

```
s4_discover:-
  backtrack_over((def_synth(2,s4_th,s4_nth,D),println(D))).

s4_nec_discover:-
  backtrack_over((def_synth(2,s4_nec_th,s4_nth,D),println(D))).
```

Example 5. The necessitation rule eliminates all simple embeddings of **S4** into **IPC**, while a lot of definition formulas pass without it.

```
?- s4_discover.
#A :- A & ?
#A :- ? & A
#A :- A & (A-> ?)
#A :- A & (? -> false)
...
true.

?- s4_nec_discover.
true.
```

Among the definitions succeeding without passing the necessity rule test, one might want to pick #A :- ? & A as an approximation of the **S4** "□" operator. In this case "?" would simply state that "the IPC prover is sound and complete". Still, given the failure of the necessitation rule, the resulting logic is missing a key aspect of the intended meaning of **S4**-provability.

7   Related Work

Program synthesis techniques have been around in logic programming with the advent of Inductive Logic Programming [19], but the idea of learning Prolog programs from positive and negative examples goes back to [20]. Our definition synthesizer fits in this paradigm, with focus on the use of a theorem prover of a decidable logic (**IPC**) filtering formulas provided by a definition generator through theorems as positive examples and non-theorems as negative examples. The means we use for our definition synthesis are in fact as simple as those described in [20]. The strength of our approach comes from the use of a theorem prover that efficiently validates or rejects definition candidates. The idea to use the new constant "?" in our synthesizer is inspired by proofs that some fragments of **IPC** reduced to two variables have a (small) finite number of equivalence classes [14, 15] as well as by the introduction of new variables, in work on polynomial embeddings of **S4** into **IPC** [17, 18].

We refer to [5] for a thorough discussion of the merits of **IEL** compared to epistemic logics following closely classical modal logic, but the central idea about using intuitionistic logic is that of *belief and knowledge as the product of verification*. Our embedding of **IEL** in **IPC** can be seen as a simplified view of this process through a generic "awareness of an agent" concept in line with [13].

In [1] the concept of *epistemic specifications* is introduced that support expressing knowledge and belief in an Answer Set Programming framework. Interestingly, refinements of this work like [21] and [3] discuss difficulties related to expressing an assumption like $p \rightarrow \mathbf{K}p$ in terms of **ASP-based** epistemic operators.

Equilibrium logic [4] gives a semantics to Answer Set programs by extending the 3-valued intermediate logic of here-and-there **HT** with Nelson's constructive strong negation. In [22] a 5-valued truth-table semantics for equilibrium logic is given. In [23] (and several other papers) epistemic extensions of equilibrium logic [4] are proposed, in which $\mathbf{K}p \rightarrow p$. By contrast to "alethic inspired" epistemic logics postulating $\mathbf{K}p \rightarrow p$ we closely follow the $p \rightarrow \mathbf{K}p$ view on which [5] is centered.

While we have eliminated Dosen's double negation modality [6] as an epistemic operator $\mathbf{K}p \equiv \neg\neg p$, it is significant that it came out as the only other meaningful candidate produced by our definition synthesizer.

This suggests that it might be worth investigating further how a similar definition discovery mechanism as the one we have used for **IEL** and **S4** would work for logics with multiple negation operators like equilibrium logic.

Besides the $\mathbf{K}p \rightarrow p$ vs. $p \rightarrow \mathbf{K}p$ problem a more general question is the choice of the logic supporting the epistemic operators, among logics with finite truth-value models (e.g., classical logic or equilibrium logic) or, at the limit, intuitionistic logic itself, with no such models. Arguably, this could be application dependent, as epistemic operators built on top of IPC are likely to fit better the landscape with intricate nuances of a richer set of epistemic and doxastic operators, while such operators built on top of finite-valued intermediate logics would benefit from simpler decision procedures and faster evaluation mechanisms.

8   Conclusions

We have devised a general mechanism for synthesizing definitions that extend a given logic system endowed with a theorem prover. The set of theorems on which the extended prover should succeed and the set of non-theorems on which it should fail can be seen as a declarative specification of the extended system. Success of the approach on embedding the **IEL** system in **IPC** and failure on trying to embed **S4** has revealed the individual role of the axioms, theorems and rules that specify a given logic system and their interaction with the necessitation rule.

Given its generality, our definition generation technique can be applied also to epistemic or modal logic axiom systems to find out if they have interesting embeddings in **ASP** and superintuitionistic logics for which high quality solvers or theorem provers exist. Our program synthesis process, when the embedding succeeds, provides a way to automate the exploration of a new logic system with help of its derived theorem prover and facilitates the work of the human logician to validate or invalidate the intuitions behind it.

Acknowledgement. We thank the participants to the **EELP'2019** workshop (A forum with no formal proceedings but insightful presentations and lively discussions on epistemic extensions of logic programming systems) and the anonymous reviewers of **LOPSTR'2020** for their constructive comments and suggestions.

References

1. Gelfond, M.: Strong introspection. In: Proceedings of the Ninth National Conference on Artificial Intelligence - Volume 1. AAAI 1991, pp. 386–391. AAAI Press (1991)
2. Baral, C., Gelfond, G., Son, T.C., Pontelli, E.: Using answer set programming to model multiagent scenarios involving agents' knowledge about other's knowledge. In: Proceedings of the 9th International Conference on Autonomous Agents and Multiagent Systems: Volume 1 - Volume 1. AAMAS 2010, Richland, SC, International Foundation for Autonomous Agents and Multiagent Systems, pp. 259–266 (2010)
3. Shen, Y.D., Eiter, T.: Evaluating epistemic negation in answer set programming. Artif. Intell. **237**(C), 115–135 (2016)
4. Pearce, David: A new logical characterisation of stable models and answer sets. In: Dix, Jürgen, Pereira, Luís Moniz, Przymusinski, Teodor C. (eds.) NMELP 1996. LNCS, vol. 1216, pp. 57–70. Springer, Heidelberg (1997). https://doi.org/10.1007/BFb0023801
5. Artemov, S.N., Protopopescu, T.: Intuitionistic epistemic logic. Rew. Symb. Logic **9**(2), 266–298 (2016)
6. Dosen, K.: Intuitionistic double negation as a necessity operator. Publications de l'Institut Mathématique, Nouvelle série **35**(49), 15–20 (1984)
7. Glivenko, V.: Sur la logique de M. Brouwer. Bulletin de la Classe des Sciences **14**, 225–228 (1928)
8. Dyckhoff, R.: Contraction-free sequent calculi for intuitionistic logic. J. Symbol. Logic **57**(3), 795–807 (1992)
9. Hudelmaier, J.: A PROLOG Program for Intuitionistic Logic. Universität Tübingen, SNS-Bericht (1988)
10. Hudelmaier, J.: An O(n log n)-Space Decision Procedure for Intuitionistic Propositional Logic. J. Logic Comput. **3**(1), 63–75 (1993)
11. Tarau, Paul: A combinatorial testing framework for intuitionistic propositional theorem provers. In: Alferes, José Júlio, Johansson, Moa (eds.) PADL 2019. LNCS, vol. 11372, pp. 115–132. Springer, Cham (2019). https://doi.org/10.1007/978-3-030-05998-9_8
12. Ferrari, Mauro., Fiorentini, Camillo, Fiorino, Guido: FCUBE: an efficient prover for intuitionistic propositional logic. In: Fermüller, Christian G., Voronkov, Andrei (eds.) LPAR 2010. LNCS, vol. 6397, pp. 294–301. Springer, Heidelberg (2010). https://doi.org/10.1007/978-3-642-16242-8_21
13. Fagin, R., Halpern, J.Y.: Belief, awareness, and limited reasoning: preliminary report. In: Proceedings of the 9th International Joint Conference on Artificial Intelligence - Volume 1. IJCAI 1985, San Francisco, CA, USA, pp. 491–501. Morgan Kaufmann Publishers Inc. (1985)

14. de Bruijn, N.G.: Exact finite models for minimal propositional calculus over a finite alphabet. Technical report 75?WSK?02, Technological University Eindhoven, November 1975

15. Jongh, D.D., Hendriks, L., de Lavalette, G.R.R.: Computations in fragments of intuitionistic propositional logic. J. Autom. Reasoning 7(4), 537–561 (1991). https://doi.org/10.1007/BF01880328

16. Statman, R.: Intuitionistic propositional logic is polynomial-space complete. Theor. Comput. Sci. 9, 67–72 (1979)

17. Egly, U.: A Polynomial translation of propositional S4 into propositional intuitionistic logic (2007)

18. Goré, R., Thomson, J.: A correct polynomial translation of S4 into intuitionistic logic. J. Symbol. Logic 84(2), 439–451 (2019)

19. Muggleton, S.: Inductive logic programming. New Gen. Comput. 8(4), 295–318 (1991)

20. Shapiro, E.Y.: An algorithm that infers theories from facts. In: Proceedings of the 7th International Joint Conference on Artificial Intelligence - Volume 1. IJCAI 1981, San Francisco, CA, USA, pp. 446–451. Morgan Kaufmann Publishers Inc. (1981)

21. Gelfond, Michael: New semantics for epistemic specifications. In: Delgrande, James P., Faber, Wolfgang (eds.) LPNMR 2011. LNCS (LNAI), vol. 6645, pp. 260–265. Springer, Heidelberg (2011). https://doi.org/10.1007/978-3-642-20895-9_29

22. Kracht, M.: On extensions of intermediate logics by strong negation. J. Philos. Logic 27(1), 49–73 (1998). https://doi.org/10.1023/A:1004222213212

23. del Cerro, L.F., Herzig, A., Su, E.I.: Epistemic equilibrium logic. In: Yang, Q., Wooldridge, M.J., (eds.) Proceedings of the Twenty-Fourth International Joint Conference on Artificial Intelligence, IJCAI 2015, Buenos Aires, Argentina, 25–31 July 2015, pp. 2964–2970. AAAI Press (2015)

Author Index

Printed in the United States
By Bookmasters